Praise for *The Soundtrack of My Life*

"The Midas touch. Until now, no one has written a book that reveals as much about the industry as Mr. Davis' book does. It is hard to imagine a better survey of popular music during its 50 year commercial peak than this one."

— *The Wall Street Journal*

"The pages of *The Soundtrack of My Life* are filled with fantastic scenes and revelations."

—*Los Angeles Times*

"His enormous success comes from luck and a phenomenal gift for recognizing, nurturing and selling talent. His drive helped make him one of the most visionary music men. In his memoir, *The Soundtrack of My Life*, the man who guided stars from Springsteen to Houston shares the secrets of his success."

—*People*

"Who put the bomp, Barry Mann asked in his 1961 single, in the bomp bah bomp bah bomp? Mr. Mann wanted to shake that person's hand. For much of the 1960's, 70's, 80's 90's and 00's, a pretty good answer to that existential question was *Clive Davis*. As the head of Columbia Records and then Arista, the label he founded, Mr. Davis had a knack for introducing good singers to good material. The results tended to be explosive, as if he were dropping packages of Mentos into two-liter bottles of Diet Coke."

—*The New York Times*

"There are so many incredible stories; this book is literally a walk through musical history."

—Ryan Seacrest

"In his new autobiography, the record biz legend reveals all about the music icons he's discovered and nurtured. It is easier to list the artists (legendary music business executive) Clive Davis hasn't worked with than the ones he has."

—*Entertainment Weekly*

"Clive Davis is a force of nature. His musical enthusiasms are legendary . . . and those 'golden ears.' Now comes his autobiography, *The Soundtrack of My Life,* filled with the often juicy behind-the-scenes stories of some of the best known artists of our time."

—Cynthia McFadden, *Nightline*

"Davis tells all in his sensational and engrossing memoir, *The Soundtrack of My Life.* There are tons of great stories. There are numerous jewels here about everyone: Whitney, Aretha, Dionne, Carly, The Grateful Dead, you name it. I couldn't put it down."

—Roger Friedman, Showbizz411

ALSO BY CLIVE DAVIS

Clive: Inside the Record Business (with James Willwerth)

The
Soundtrack
of
My Life

Clive Davis

with Anthony DeCurtis

SIMON & SCHUSTER PAPERBACKS

New York   London   Toronto   Sydney   New Delhi

Simon & Schuster Paperbacks
A Division of Simon & Schuster, Inc.
1230 Avenue of the Americas
New York, NY 10020

First Simon & Schuster trade paperback edition November 2013

SIMON & SCHUSTER PAPERBACKS and colophon are registered
trademarks of Simon & Schuster, Inc.

Insert, jacket, and endpaper photo credits appear on page 585.

For information about special discounts for bulk purchases,
please contact Simon & Schuster Special Sales at 1-866-506-1949
or business@simonandschuster.com.

The Simon & Schuster Speakers Bureau can bring authors to your
live event. For more information or to book an event contact the
Simon & Schuster Speakers Bureau at 1-866-248-3049 or visit our
website at www.simonspeakers.com.

Designed by Joy O'Meara

Manufactured in the United States of America

10 9 8 7 6 5 4 3 2

Library of Congress Cataloging-in-Publication Data is available.

ISBN 978-1-4767-1478-3
ISBN 978-1-4767-1479-0 (pbk)
ISBN 978-1-4767-1480-6 (ebook)

Contents

Introduction:
Welcome to the Party

Perhaps my favorite time of the year is the period at the beginning of February leading up to my pre-Grammy party. For that entire time I'm holed up in the bungalow at the Beverly Hills Hotel that is my second home and, during this time, the Grammy Party War Room. My son Doug, who is a music industry lawyer, is at my side, and we're intermittently surrounded by other family members and party-planning strategists. We have the layout of the ballroom at the Beverly Hilton Hotel on a large easel in front of us, with the names of the guests at the ninety or more tables each appended by magnetic tiles. I move those tiles from table to table as new inspiration strikes and news about cancellations and new RSVPs comes in. Along with the people who have already responded, we have to deal with the hundreds angling for last-minute invitations. It's the hardest thing in the world to say no, but the ballroom is only so big. What I value most about the party is how eclectic the guest list is, so it's not necessarily a question of how important a person is but what he or she can add to the mix. Guests of the artists who are performing for free obviously need to be accommodated to as great a degree as possible, but other than that it's simply a question of creating an unforgettable night. If people see the same folks that they see at every other music event, we've failed.

My first Grammy party took place in 1976 as a way to honor Barry Manilow's nomination for Record of the Year for "Mandy," a milestone for Arista Records, the label I launched in 1974. For years now the party has taken place the evening before the Grammy Awards in Los Angeles, but that year it was a brunch on the day after the event. That year I experienced the anxiety that everyone throwing a party goes through:

Is anybody going to come? Happily, when Stevie Wonder walked into the room, I knew that we were onto something. Stevie, an artist whom I've always loved and, unfortunately, only occasionally worked with, would become a regular at the parties, often taking the stage during the finale and seeming as if he would never stop playing to say good night, because he was having such a great time. Back then, I had no idea that the party would grow into the event that it's become. It soon symbolized a celebration of music and the music industry, a night for once-in-a-lifetime performances capable of stirring a crowd that, for the most part, thinks they've seen it all. Watching the likes of Gwen Stefani and Donald Trump leap to their feet as Aretha Franklin, backed by Whitney Houston and Toni Braxton, tears into "Respect" is just one such unforgettable moment. That the event is not televised only makes it more private and personal for the attendees.

Each year I try to seat people at tables where they'll be with people they ordinarily wouldn't meet socially. A couple like Jane Fonda and the producer Richard Perry provides an excellent opportunity to intermingle musicians and actors. Someone like Al Gore wouldn't be seated among politicos, but artists and executives who admire his brand of activism. Someone like Paul McCartney might be placed alongside acclaimed young R&B or hip-hop artists. Every celebrity is also a fan, so I look for opportunities for people to meet their heroes, or perhaps to discover new heroes and learn a bit about the history that preceded them. It restores everyone's sense of why they got into show business, and especially music, in the first place. Suddenly they're as wide-eyed as the people waiting outside the hotel for autographs.

The Grammys are almost always in Los Angeles and the timing of the party takes advantage of the fact that, along with the many musicians who live there, many artists will be in town for the ceremony. As mentioned, no one gets paid to perform, so we totally rely on the desire of artists to play for their peers. It's important that the show keep moving so, with rare exceptions, every artist is limited to two songs. The opening spot is often reserved for a rock band, like Mumford & Sons recently, because once the show has started, it's harder to change the set and pop artists can more easily take the stage and perform with the house band. And regardless of genre, the musical director, Rickey

Minor, ensures a level of quality that no one could match. Between sets, I like to speak to the crowd as if they're in my living room. I relate anecdotes from my own experiences with the performers and introduce various people in the audience, both to pay respect to industry titans like Quincy Jones, Mo Ostin, Berry Gordy, and the late Ahmet Ertegun, or to let people know that a reclusive superstar like Prince or the legendary Sly Stone is on the scene. I love for younger artists to meet veteran Hall of Famers, who in turn are moved to hear from the newcomers how important an influence they've been.

When I was starting out in the music industry, I was impressed by the shows Bill Graham used to stage at his Fillmore venues in San Francisco and New York. He wasn't afraid to challenge people's tastes and expose them to styles of music they might never have otherwise heard. He went for the highest common denominator, not the lowest. I have tried to do that with the labels I've run, and at the party I ignore all considerations of demographics and genre distinctions. And through the years everyone has loved it! What a treat to see Lou Reed backed up by Slash or dueting with Rod Stewart, or to hear Pink, sitting on a stool at the front of the stage and accompanied only by a guitar, deliver a beautiful and haunting rendition of "Me and Bobby McGee." And sometimes it's just so exciting to see artists rock the hottest song of the moment, as when Busta Rhymes and Puffy Combs lit up the room by opening the show with "Pass the Courvoisier." I never announce the performers in advance of the party so that the audience gets genuinely excited by the introduction of each new act.

As I've said, the hardest part is saying no, even to people I socialize with regularly. I had a good friend of many years write to me asking that I provide an invitation for her son, who had just gotten his first job in the music industry. His father was a prominent music business executive, so he was very well connected. Because she was a friend, I wrote her a long letter explaining that I believed it was important for her son to earn his way into such events, that it would diminish him in people's eyes if they felt that he was getting access and other perks simply because of who his father was, not what he had done. I pointed out that many accomplished, longtime colleagues request invitations, and how would it look if I turned them down but then admitted her son?

I ended by saying how much affection I held for her and her son, and hoped she wouldn't take this personally. The result? She didn't speak to me for three years!

Of course, like all parties, things occasionally go awry. The most devastating tragedy, needless to say, was Whitney Houston's death on the afternoon of the party in 2012. I could barely think straight, I was so distraught, but I ultimately made the decision that it was important for the party to proceed. Whitney was a guest every year, had often performed, and would have been the first to insist that the show must go on. The evening transformed into an unforgettable tribute to her and the music that she loved so well. And then there was the year that the fiery music business attorney Brian Rohan, infuriated by something David Geffen had done in the recent past, kicked the chair out from under David, sending him to the floor, prompting Paul Simon to exclaim, "You can't do that—that's David Geffen!" The famous agent Sue Mengers, sitting at the same table, shrieked, the press stampeded out of the room, and I sat there mortified at this sneak attack on my dear friend. I must say David is one cool cat. He kept his dignity and aplomb intact and clearly won the admiration of the crowd.

And smaller, vexing problems arise until the very last minute. Fire marshals interrupted me as I took the stage to start one evening, announcing that the show couldn't begin until several tables were dismantled in order to bring the ballroom in compliance with the fire code. A potentially awkward thirty-minute delay was turned into a not-to-be-forgotten memory when Robin Williams spontaneously quieted the crowd and launched into a hilarious stand-up comedy improvisation that made everyone there forget all the hustle and bustle going on around them to satisfy the fire chief. Artists scheduled to perform get ill, and last-minute substitutions have to be made, affecting the entire order of the show. Inevitably, Branden Chapman of the National Academy of Recording Arts and Sciences, which now co-sponsors the party, and I begin urgently to make calls, and somehow everything always works out in the end. Hopefully we're the only ones who realize there even was a problem. Meanwhile, as the big night approaches, I'm constantly checking the enormous board on the easel in my bungalow to make sure that the seating arrangements will make for lively conversations and interactions.

In a few years my party will mark its fortieth anniversary. My own time in the music business extends back even further than that, to 1965, when I began to run Columbia Records. It's been quite a ride, and all the stories—from signing Janis Joplin to discovering Whitney Houston, from helping to make Santana a star in 1969 to overseeing his dramatic comeback thirty years later—will be told in this book. My Grammy party will come up often because its spirit of celebration is what has animated my entire career. As you'll discover, I started out my professional life as a lawyer and grew a little disillusioned with that profession. I never had any aspirations or thought I had any particular talent that would enable me to be part of the music industry, and I didn't know what I could do that would really provide fulfillment and satisfaction. Discovering my love for music and my ability to find and develop artists has been the greatest gift of my life. It's filled even hard days with moments of excitement, and made it possible for me to have thrilling experiences that I never could have imagined. Hosting the night before the Grammys epitomizes the elements of surprise and delight that the best music always delivers. Over the course of nearly five decades amid plenty of hard work, I have never grown the least bit jaded about the powerful effect that music can have, how it can make all distinctions among people disappear and unite them in energy and pleasure.

Like the difficulties of staging this complex party, there are events in this story that were profoundly painful for me, and I talk about them in depth. But the overall journey has been an ongoing joy, and I welcome this opportunity to share all of it with you.

The Soundtrack of My Life

Straight Out of Brooklyn

I'm a Brooklyn boy. I was born on April 4, 1932, and grew up in Crown Heights, in an apartment at 1321 Union Street, one block south of Eastern Parkway, a wide, two-way thoroughfare with benches and greenery down the middle. We moved there when I was about five. This was the first apartment in which we had a refrigerator, not an icebox. Before that, I remember the iceman coming every week. That was typical in those days.

Both my mother and father were born in the United States, a significant fact given the waves of Jewish immigration to New York in the early decades of the twentieth century. My father's parents were born in Russia. My mother, however, jokingly referred to herself as a "Yankee," meaning that her parents were also born in this country. Both her parents died before I was born, so I never met them. My mother's family lived in Williamsburg, another Brooklyn neighborhood, and worked primarily in the fruit wholesaling business. Part of her family also were connected to the Russeks, who had established a prominent women's clothing store bearing that name in Brooklyn, as well as on Fifth Avenue in Manhattan. Perhaps for that reason, my mother, a lovely brunette, had a wonderful sense of style. She had a regal air, and was considered a great beauty. When she walked out wearing a fashionable hat or a suit, everybody on the block looked at her, which always gave me a rush. Her family—she had three brothers and three sisters—believed, correctly, it turned out, that in choosing to marry my father, who was an electrician and later a traveling tie salesman, my mother relinquished the opportunity to take up with wealthier suitors, many of whom pursued her because of how attractive she was.

My father's parents lived in Brighton Beach and they spoke only Yiddish, no English at all, so I never really was able to converse with them. Very often on Sundays about a dozen of us would gather at their apartment for a family feast. My father's rule was that I had to greet my grandparents first whenever I entered their home. Zadie and Bubby, who came to the United States from Minsk and Pinsk, respectively, always greeted me warmly in return, but, because of the language barrier, I had very little communication with them beyond that. I never knew how we got the name Davis. It was my grandfather's name when he arrived here.

Because Brighton Beach sits right next to Coney Island, every two or three weeks I would romp on the boardwalk there. I'd ride the scarifying Cyclone roller coaster, and the legendary mechanical "flying horses" that wound their way through Steeplechase Park as if you were in a horse race. In the summer, when we'd arrive at the beach, my father would put his fingers in his mouth and blast a high-pitched, highly distinctive whistle that would announce to the rest of the family who might already be there to come find us.

Our Sunday-night dinners were another ritual that framed my childhood. On those evenings I would accompany my parents to meet their friends, Anne and Bob Antis, and their two boys for Chinese food. Perhaps once a month we'd go to a restaurant in Chinatown in lower Manhattan that was simply called 48 Mott Street. More typically we stayed in our neighborhood and went to Mee Wah on Eastern Parkway and Nostrand Avenue. We didn't have Chinese food at any other time. To this day it's strange to me not to have Chinese food on a Sunday night, and equally strange to have Chinese food on any other day of the week.

On Sunday mornings we would have bagels and "appetizing," a Jewish term that essentially means the food you eat with bagels, like lox or sturgeon. We rarely had the money to afford more than an eighth of a pound of lox, which we had to share. Each of us would spot our bagels with just one or two dots of salmon. Even now, whenever I see people lift off whole slices of Nova Scotia to put on their bagels, it seems very extravagant. You never forget your childhood.

Neither of my parents went to college, and my sister, Seena, my only sibling, didn't, either. None of my mother's six siblings had gone to college, and, other than a nephew on my father's side who became a doctor, our family was not at all academically inclined. Perhaps because she was seven years older than me, Seena and I were not terribly close when I was growing up. She got married during the war and moved out when I was about twelve, so we never spent very much time together, except at family events.

Both of my parents were highly sociable, however, with engaging sparkles in their eyes. They were jovial, genial, likable, warm, and loving. My mother's name was Florence, and my father's name was Herman, but everyone called him Joe—"Good Old Joe." I never even knew his name was Herman until the first time he signed the back of my report card. Together they were Flo and Joe.

My father, who was nine years older than my mother, had a salesman's knack for making friends wherever he went. He was always ready with a joke, a glad hand, a slap on the back, and a smile. He was also a tireless practical joker. Once, for example, when my great-aunt fell asleep at a movie with him, she woke up with an unlit cigar in her mouth. Still, while we were never poor, we always had to struggle to make ends meet. I think that strain accounted for an element of sadness that seemed to underlie my father's characteristic good cheer.

As you can no doubt tell from Seena's name and mine, my parents clearly believed in odd names. Believe me, there were not many kids named Clive in Crown Heights. My mother, whose maiden name was Brooks, loved the movies and was particularly fond of a distinguished English actor of the period named Clive Brook. In accord with Jewish religious practice, the first letter of a child's name had to mirror that of a deceased family member, and her mother's name was Celia. Respect for tradition conspired with the fantasy world of the movies, and that's how I became Clive.

The youngest male child in a Jewish family, I felt very much cared for, and I loved my home life and neighborhood. I always liked school as well. I attended P.S. 161 on Crown Street between Nostrand and New York Avenues, so I'd walk to school every day. From the very start I fell in love with learning and became a straight-A student. Although we were not religious, I did go to Hebrew school to prepare for my bar mitzvah. The Yeshiva, as it was called, was right next to P.S. 161, and I went there after school for two or three years before I turned thirteen. My bar mitzvah was held at the Twin Cantors, which was something like a local nightclub setting. There must have been close to a hundred people there. That was a momentous day.

Although higher education was not part of my family background, it turned out that I was academically inclined. I enjoyed reading and what we now call public speaking. My school had an annual elocution contest, in which you would recite either poetry or a story, and I vividly remember winning that competition. I also developed an ability to sight-add numbers with lightning speed—a talent that not only impressed my teachers but came in handy over the ensuing decades. I attribute that skill to Miss Campbell, a teacher I had in the third and fourth grades. She would make a game out of her tests, putting columns of numbers on the blackboard and awarding stars to whoever got the most right answers the quickest. The challenge appealed to my competitive instincts, and I was a consistent winner. I would play that same game with my own kids in later life.

While I was deeply drawn to my studies, my parents' practicality exerted a decisive impact on me as well. I could have disappeared into my reading and assignments every afternoon, but my parents, and particularly my mother, were concerned that I be well rounded. My mother would also always say, "You know, book knowledge is good, but it can be dangerously narrowing. You've got to get out among people, and find ways to apply your knowledge. Common sense and people skills are vitally important." I took that advice to heart, and every year I was elected mayor of my class. My mother's views were typical of the striving ethnic communities in New York at that time. Education was viewed as the path to a better life, and that meant a profession, becoming a doctor or a lawyer. Abstract learning was fine, as far as it went, but that wasn't far enough. You needed to make your education count in the world.

Life in Brooklyn was very self-contained, and I felt completely at home there. Our neighborhood was about 80 percent Jewish, but there were enough Irish and Italians to make it somewhat of a melting pot, and we were all in the same economic bracket—working class, or lower-middle class. Your neighborhood was your block. Mine, like almost all of Brooklyn, was lined with four-story brownstones or low apartment buildings. The neighborhood teemed with so many children that if a kid was a couple of years older or younger, they were part of a different group from you. Because there was no air-conditioning, whole families would sit out on the stoops when evening came. The men would crowd outside the candy store waiting for the early editions of the next day's newspapers to arrive, and the women would chat with one another and watch the children play. Every night you'd solve neighborhood, local, personal, and world problems sitting on the stoop.

My father was often away, doing electrical jobs outside the city, and, later, working as a traveling tie salesman, so, along with wanting me to be well rounded, I think my mother also wanted to ensure that I engage in some typically athletic activities after school. That was fine with me. Every day, after getting my homework done, I would go out. I enjoyed hanging out with my friends and playing all the street games of Brooklyn—punchball, stickball, stoopball, touch football, and the like. Everything we did was competitive. Whether you played box ball, hit the penny, or whatever, somebody would win and somebody would lose. It wasn't mean-spirited, but everybody kept score and knew who had come out on top.

When my father was around, I would go with him to Prospect Park on Sundays to watch local and regional football games. More important, since we lived just a short walk from Ebbets Field, the immortal home of the Brooklyn Dodgers, I became an avid Dodgers fan. Back then, the city hosted three major-league baseball teams—the Dodgers (lovingly known, in true Brooklynese, as "dem Bums"), the Giants, and the Yankees. Loyalties ran deep as blood. (After the Dodgers' owner Walter O'Malley moved the team to Los Angeles in 1957, a joke in Brooklyn ran: "Q: What would you do if you were in a room with Hitler, Stalin, and Walter O'Malley, and you had a gun with only two bullets? A: Easy. I would shoot Walter O'Malley twice.")

I would go to Ebbets Field with my father when I was younger and then, when he was away more often as I got older, I'd go with my friends. Television didn't exist, of course, so if you wanted to see a game you had to go to the ballpark. On the radio, the Dodgers' announcer Red Barber re-created games from telegraph reports, evoking the sights, smells, and sounds of the game with extraordinary color, warmth, and insight. But going to the stadium itself was a magical experience, and I fell completely under its spell.

Teams played seventy-seven home games in those years, and I saw the Dodgers about twenty-five times a season. We always sat in the bleachers, which cost something like a quarter or fifty cents, though my father would often tip an usher and get us into the grandstands. In the bleachers, Hilda Chester, the Dodgers' biggest fan, led the cheers with her resounding cowbell, and we would all respond. Duke Snider and Dixie Walker were my Dodger heroes, but Dolph Camilli, Cookie Lavagetto, Joe "Ducky" Medwick, Pee Wee Reese, Carl Furillo, and Jackie Robinson also inhabited my pantheon. I tracked the team's statistics with enthusiasm and rigor.

Beyond the Dodgers, a big event would be going to downtown Brooklyn—not Manhattan, which seemed like another universe. My father did electrical work for one of the grander theaters downtown called the Albee, so we would sometimes go there.

More typically, we'd go to local movie houses like the Kameo Theater on the corner of Nostrand Avenue and Eastern Parkway or the Savoy on Bedford Avenue. I went to the movies on Saturday afternoon because there was always a double feature. Two movies for the price of one: It seemed like an incredible boon. Why didn't everybody take advantage of that? I was perplexed. It never occurred to me, of course, that adults might not want to watch movies in a theater packed with hundreds of kids.

I'd sometimes go to the movies with my mother, who dragged me to a never-ending series of films starring her favorite actress, Bette Davis. As a result, even as a kid, I was familiar with the complete Bette Davis oeuvre, along with Abbott and Costello comedies, horror flicks like *The Wolf Man,* and the rest of kids' matinee fare.

Every summer, our family would go to the Catskill Mountains in upstate New York, just a couple of hours outside the city. We could never afford one of the fancy hotels like Grossinger's or the Concord, but we'd go to a modest one in Kiamesha Lake called the Fairmount. When money was particularly tight, we'd rent rooms in what was called a *kuchaleyn,* a boardinghouse in which you would share the kitchen with other visitors and cook for your own family to save money.

The Catskills became known as the Borscht Belt, and not just because of the favorite soup among the Russian and Eastern European Jewish immigrants who vacationed there. Life at the hotels was about food, food, and more food. At mealtime in the dining room, there was no limit on what you could order. The food was delicious, the courses endless, and the clientele of connoisseur eaters satisfied far beyond reason. Three bagels and lox for breakfast? You got it. Two steaks for dinner? No problem.

I so much looked forward to those two-week vacations. To a city kid like me, the Catskills were wondrously rural, a marvelous world unto itself. There were pools, lots of kids and loads of athletics during the day, and wonderful shows at night. You always heard about Brown's Country Club or the Concord Hotel, where well-known entertainers would appear. The Borscht Belt earned a deserved reputation as the proving ground for such comics as Milton Berle, Henny Youngman, Jack E. Leonard, and Red Buttons. The Fairmount would get the scaled-down versions of shows like those, but still with credible singers and comedians.

I had a wide range of interests, but no single overwhelming passion. Unlike some of my friends, I did not collect records or comic books, but I enjoyed them both. I collected stamps, but I was not obsessed. I did love listening to music on the radio. The favorite program in our house was *The Make Believe Ballroom* on WNEW, which was hosted by Martin Block, a preeminent DJ in those days. Block would play records while pretending to be broadcasting from a dance hall in which the singers were actually appearing; hence, the title of his enormously popular show. (It was not that different, in a way, from the audio recreations of baseball games on the radio.) He played the likes of Frank Sinatra, Kay Starr, Dinah Shore, Bing Crosby, Dick Haymes, and Perry Como in his dance palace of the imagination.

When I was eleven or twelve, friends of mine began celebrating birthdays in Manhattan, and I would be excited to go to Radio City

Music Hall, the Roxy, the Capitol Theatre, or the Paramount. They all featured stage shows as well as films. It's amazing to think about today, but performers like Sinatra or Ethel Waters would do five or six shows a day. You could see a movie and then a performance by a prominent singer.

Because Sinatra was so adored by his audience of female bobby-soxers, I remember quixotically supporting Bing Crosby against him in the musical debates of the day. It seemed as if you had to take a side, and apart from his considerable talent, I liked Crosby because he was the underdog. Of course, as my ear grew more sophisticated, I came to realize how truly incredible a singer Sinatra was, deservedly honored as the master pop vocalist of his age. Whether working with big bands or in smaller settings, his effortless blending of jazz and pop, his innate musicality, and his natural gift for phrasing were spellbinding.

Until television came along, our family evenings would be spent sitting around the radio and listening to the prominent shows featuring comedians like Jack Benny, Fred Allen, Edgar Bergen and Charlie McCarthy, Groucho Marx, George Burns and Gracie Allen, and Bob Hope. In their insight, wit, quips, and repartee, they defined *funny*. To this day, I can laugh out loud remembering the notoriously tightfisted character Jack Benny used to play. In one of his famous routines, he got held up at gunpoint, and the robber demanded, "Your money or your life!" The radio would be silent for a long time, and the thief would grow agitated and insist, "I *said*, your money or your *life!*" With perfect deadpan timing, Benny would respond, "I'm *thinking*, I'm *thinking!*"

When I was thirteen I saw my first Broadway musical with a classmate of mine to celebrate his birthday. It was an operetta called *The New Moon*, with music by Sigmund Romberg and book and lyrics by Oscar Hammerstein, Frank Mandel, and Laurence Schwab. That was the beginning of my love affair with musical theater. I often couldn't afford to buy tickets myself, but my generous friends and their families quickly identified me as a most appreciative and enthusiastic guest.

When I saw *Follow the Girls* with Jackie Gleason and Gertrude Niesen, the audience demanded that Niesen come out for something like ten curtain calls after she sang "I Wanna Get Married." She added new bawdy verses with each succeeding call. It was intoxicating. The show-stopping numbers in Broadway musicals completely exhilarated me, and I came to love original-cast albums, stunned that so many classic songs could come out of one play. Such shows as *Oklahoma!*, *Carousel*, and *The King and I*, all written by Richard Rodgers and Oscar Hammerstein, were crammed with so many great songs, each one more compelling than the next. They were instantly memorable, and a lesson in the immediate and enduring value of aesthetic quality.

Within our family, I grew particularly close to two of my aunts: Jeanette, who lived with us for a while before she got married, and Dorothy, both of whom were younger sisters of my mother. I was at my aunt Jeanette's apartment on Lefferts Avenue on a Sunday in December 1941, having slept over, when we got word that Pearl Harbor had been bombed. I was only nine at the time, but I clearly remember it. As the war unfolded, I followed the daily progress. We underwent air-raid drills, and talk of the war was everywhere. One night I was kept awake by the continual, inconsolable cries and whines of our next-door neighbor's dog. The following morning our neighbors learned that their son had been killed in action.

I was transfixed and greatly inspired by the speeches of Churchill, and by the bravery of our allies in Britain as they endured ravaging bombing raids. It was so hard to imagine having to live through that. My hero was our president, Franklin Delano Roosevelt. To me, and pretty much everyone I knew, he was a benevolent father figure. It was an article of faith that he had guided us out of the Depression by ushering in the visionary and humane programs of the New Deal, and now he was commanding us to victory in war. Our faith in him was total. Then one day, as I was walking along Nostrand Avenue after school, I heard that he had suffered a cerebral hemorrhage and died. It was shattering.

After the war ended in 1945, we began to become aware of the horrifying magnitude of the Holocaust. It just seemed too staggering to comprehend. With the publication of books like Anne Frank's diaries, we learned more of the gruesome details. It was disorienting because

I personally had never experienced anti-Semitism. It would be spoken about, but all the rich textures of Jewish life were so intrinsic to my sheltered existence in Brooklyn that it seemed like an abstraction.

When it came time for high school, I enrolled at Erasmus Hall in Flatbush, a beautifully ornate campus school where I got a first-rate education. I commuted every day by subway. Barbra Streisand, Neil Diamond, Mickey Spillane, and Bernard Malamud are among its many notable graduates. Erasmus was demanding academically, which enlivened me and made me thrive. I was grilled and drilled in spelling and grammar, and to this day I diagram sentences in my head, and I'm innately distracted by grammatical errors. Watch those flying apostrophes! Does no one know the difference between *its* and *it's* anymore? (Once in a while I'd slip, and this occasional inability to resist correcting an egregious mistake in grammar in my executives' reports would later become a staple among the "Clive stories" that circulated in the music business. Fair enough.)

I did very well at Erasmus, and was active socially. As I did in elementary school, I ran for office and was elected lieutenant governor. I graduated in three and a half years, when I was seventeen. Beyond that, my life during high school remained much the same as before. We still lived in the same apartment, and I stayed friendly with the kids I grew up with on my block. Our family still enjoyed our two-week summer vacations in the Catskills.

I got my first summer job at sixteen, through a friend of Seena's. I was hired to work at the switchboard of the complaint department of Sears Roebuck. That entire summer, I listened to housewives lament that their Kenmore washing machine or dryer or refrigerator had broken down, and I dutifully scheduled the service calls. I also worked as a soda jerk for a while, at a candy store on the corner of Nostrand Avenue and Union Street. It was a dream job, because I loved ice cream.

There was an ice cream parlor in our neighborhood known as Schaffer's that made its own ice cream, and people from all over Brooklyn would go there. They used to serve quarter pints, which they called "gills." My mother's favorite was coffee ice cream, and that became my favorite, too. It would be a great night when either she or my father would bring home a gill of coffee ice cream. To this day, ice cream remains my favorite dessert. You can put pies, brownies, and cakes in front of me, and I'm perfectly content to leave them alone. But I do love ice cream.

It was almost subliminal, but at some point I became aware that people in my mother's family tended to die young. High blood pressure ran in her family, and that was deadly in those days. Both her parents died before I was born, and she lost her sister Esther at thirty-eight. Her two older brothers, Willie and Abe, both died at around fifty. Her brother Lou had a congenital heart problem, and died when he was forty-one. My father, meanwhile, had one brother who died in his fifties, though his parents lived into their late eighties, and his three sisters lived nearly that long as well.

In my mid teens, I became aware that my mother had high blood pressure. She was hospitalized for it at least twice that I recall, and I learned about the numbers and what they meant: If they rose above 200, it was threatening. They lacked effective treatments for hypertension, so she was put on a strict rice diet. Occasionally her pressure came down to 170 or 180 over 100, but it was never eradicated. I didn't completely understand the seriousness of it, but I was frightened by her condition, knowing the family history.

My father, meanwhile, continued to travel a great deal. His comings and goings weren't disruptive, exactly, but they made for a strange rhythm in our family dynamic. For the most part, he would just reenter the domestic flow whenever he returned. When I was about sixteen, however, it became apparent that a strain had developed in my parents' relationship. It was unspoken, but palpable. There was concern that my father had developed a relationship with another woman.

It was profoundly unsettling for me, even traumatic. I'd hear whispers. I'd walk in on arguments. Much against my own wishes, I began to believe it might possibly be true. Then one of my mother's sisters became suspicious of the widow of her brother—of *their* brother. She believed that my father was having an affair with their sister-in-law Ruth, who lived in the building next door to us.

One night, while I was playing punchball on our block, I saw Ruth walk out of her building, and I followed her. With my heart racing, I trailed her the two and a half long blocks to Bedford Avenue, and then watched, devastated, as she climbed into my father's car. I went back to her building and waited for her to come home. When she did, I confronted her. She couldn't deny that she had gotten into my father's car, but she denied that there was a relationship between them.

I couldn't bring myself to speak directly to my father about it, so I wrote a letter, confronting him with what I saw. My father loved me, there's no question about that. He was proud of me. I was the light of his life. But this situation came between us. I was furious with him for betraying my mother, and I was angry with my aunt as well. It was unheard of. This was Aunt Ruth, the wife of Uncle Lou, who had died at forty-one. We had gone on vacations with them. I was so close to her two daughters, my first cousins.

After my father read my letter, he came to speak to me. He, too, denied everything. "You jumped to hasty conclusions, and it's just not true," he said. "On certain trips, when I was away, yes, I might have been with other women. But it was never meaningful. My relationship is with your mother. When you grow older, you'll understand. For now, you're being too judgmental. The best thing for you to do is to forget about this."

To this day, I don't know what the full nature of their affair was. But I have never forgotten it. My father continued to live at home, but the underlying tension that had developed between us never abated. I did always feel protected and loved by him but there was a permanent rift.

Recovering from Shattering Losses

Despite the strain that my father's affair had introduced into our family, on the surface our lives continued as they always had, in part because he continued to travel a great deal. Most significantly, I graduated from Erasmus and, on the strength of my academic performance there, was awarded a full-tuition scholarship to Washington Square College, as the downtown undergraduate campus of New York University was then known. I was ecstatic, and my parents were extremely proud. I could never have afforded to attend a school like NYU without a scholarship, so the achievement had importance well beyond its prestige. I still had to live at home, because my scholarship didn't cover room and board, but that was fine with me.

My parents took great personal pleasure in my successes, but I was hardly spoiled. I always did my share of household chores. I cleaned the windows, waxed the floors, and helped around the house in general. It was hard work, but it was made clear to me that it was important and, indeed, necessary that I pitch in. That said, my mother, by nature, was openhearted, giving, loving, and selfless. I probably was indulged by her to some degree. As a kid, you don't even realize it. But my primary responsibility was to be a good student. That and that alone was regarded as the key to rising above one's station. Consequently, my doing well in that arena made everyone happy.

College entailed a certain amount of pressure, since I had to maintain a B average to keep my scholarship, but, fortunately, that didn't prove difficult. As for choosing a professional course for my studies, that wasn't too hard to figure out, either. My father the electrician was extremely handy, but his talents totally skipped my generation. My fix-it skills were nonexistent, so anything technical was out. Nor did I have a scientific bent, which I would have needed to study premed—plus I was a little squeamish about blood.

My parents had instilled in me the notion that the goal of education was to prepare for a profession. I just seemed to have a self-starting drive from birth. Because I enjoyed public speaking and had been elected to student council positions in both elementary and high school, I chose political science as my major, with the goal of eventually going to law school. Not that I had any particular idea about what that meant, or what lawyers actually do. I didn't know any lawyers. But I had to choose a profession, and law made the most sense.

Eager to participate in the social and political life of NYU, I ran for president of the freshman class. One day as I was campaigning in a motorcade around the Greenwich Village campus, my father, in another of his characteristic pranks, drove by in his car and loudly honked his horn. I was embarrassed and pretended not to hear him, though I can see now that it was his way of supporting me and expressing his pride. I did win the election.

My mother, meanwhile, had taken a job as a saleslady in a women's clothing store on Avenue J in Flatbush to help out with money at home. Then, in November 1950, when I was eighteen and in my sophomore year, I got a call that my mother had suffered a cerebral hemorrhage and was being taken to Kings County Hospital in Brooklyn. It was late afternoon, and I was home alone; my father was traveling for work. There was no one I could ask to take me to the hospital. Eventually, I managed to get there, and I saw her lying on a mobile bed. She turned, saw me, and waved me away as if she didn't want me to see her so ill. And then she died.

Needless to say, that was a devastating, life-altering loss. I had been so close to her, and, despite the warning signs about her health, her death at forty-seven seemed sudden and irrevocable. I was in shock. She was my emotional support system, my ultimate closeness. For the longest time, I couldn't even think of my mother without feeling myself go numb; the pain of losing her was too much to bear. It was the most profound loss of my life, no question. Over the decades that followed,

I made a point of keeping in touch with her two closest friends, just to maintain whatever tie with her I could.

Beyond its emotional impact, my mother's death raised important practical concerns. The primary one was where was I going to live? Would I stay in our apartment with my father, who was away so much? I was still a teenager, just a sophomore in college. Should he stop traveling to stay there more often and take care of me? How would he make a living? Even more to the point, the nature of his relationship with Aunt Ruth had never been resolved, and that remained a source of unspoken tension between us. Then, stunningly, just three months after my mother's death, my father suffered a heart attack. He survived, but now high blood pressure and potentially fatal heart problems clouded his life as well.

We decided that the best solution was for me to move in with my sister, Seena, her husband, Jerry, and their infant daughter, Honey. They had bought a small, semidetached, three-bedroom house in Bayside, Queens, for perhaps ten or fifteen thousand dollars, and I was able to take the third bedroom.

As I mentioned, Seena and I had never been especially close, primarily because she was seven years older than me and had moved out of our family's apartment when I was just twelve. But I became extremely grateful to her for sharing her home with me at this critical time, and it substantially deepened our relationship. People joke that family consists of the people who have to take you in when you have no place else to go, but it's a far more serious story when you really need help like that. That's when you know what "blood is thicker than water" actually means. When adversity hits, that family ethic establishes itself. Seena's automatic assumption of responsibility for me, her reaching out for me when I needed her most, is something that has stayed with me all my life, and profoundly impressed on me the true significance of family.

Eleven months after my mother passed away, my father had a second heart attack and died. He was fifty-six. It was another crushing loss. That there was so much unfinished business between my father and me only made it more difficult. Regardless, I had loved both my parents very much, and felt deeply loved by them. Losing them so close together at such a young age was like a violent entry into adulthood. It made me feel that anything, however cherished and secure, might be taken from me at any time.

Again, there were also practical matters to address. My sister didn't have much money, and I had none, beyond the little I could save from summer jobs. I knew that my father had a life insurance policy for ten thousand dollars, and I assumed that Seena and I would be the beneficiaries. Instead, I got a call from my cousin, a daughter of my father's sister. She said, "Clive, I know you're expecting ten thousand dollars, but over the last year or two, your father borrowed money from my mother against his life insurance policy. So there's only four thousand dollars coming to you and your sister."

It may have been naïve of me, but I was shocked that my aunt, who was quite well-to-do, would have repaid herself before giving the money to us. Obviously there are two sides to that story. I can see it now, but at the time, I couldn't believe it. Seena, with characteristic grace, gave her share to me. That was all the money I had in the world, and there was much of college and all of law school looming.

After those jolts to my world, my life went on, though with a tremendous hole in my heart. Bayside was a pleasant community, something of a placid, leafy suburb in those days, and I commuted to NYU every day from there. My sister lived on 214th Street near Horace Harding Boulevard, which is now the Long Island Expressway. I would take the bus from there to the 179th Street subway stop in Jamaica, Queens, where I would then catch the F train to NYU. The journey was somewhere between an hour and ninety minutes each way, which gave me plenty of time to read and study—and to shoot the breeze with my new best friend, Harold Lubell, who was in my year at school, and made the trip with me each day.

I grew closer with my sister as I lived with her, and luckily, Aunt Jeanette and Aunt Dorothy and their families had also moved to Bayside and lived just a few blocks away. I would have dinner at Aunt Jeanette's a couple of nights a week, which made for a nurturing, ongoing family life, however fragmented. It also eased the pressure on my sister of having me in such close quarters with her husband and a baby.

Jeanette had two children: Carol, who was eight years younger than I, and Jo Sue, who was five years younger than Carol. I often babysat for Carol on weekends. I'd bring friends over to Jeanette's house, and we'd play cards or other games while looking after Carol and, eventually, Jo. I grew so close with Jeanette that she became like a substitute mother. To this day, her daughter Jo is like a sister to me, and my closest friend.

I also developed a strong nucleus of friends at college. I joined a house plan, which was like a fraternity but didn't require living in a communal house or indulging in the excesses and biases of many frats. The house plan involved a good deal of socializing, which was great for me, and some of the friends I made then remain close to me today. Two school friends lived nearby in Bayside. One was Harold, who was in my house plan, and the other was a girl named Lola Fiur, whom everybody called Rusti because of her fiery red hair. I dated Rusti for a while, and she and I and Harold and his wife, Ruth, remained bonded over the years and continued to have dinner together every few months until Harold died just this past summer.

To make my travels a bit easier, I bought a very used car, a Chevrolet, for about a hundred dollars, so I could get around on weekends. The car also helped with one of my summer jobs—as a Scripto pen-and-pencil salesman. I would sell to stationery stores, candy stores, and the like, and I made good commissions.

Mostly, though, I threw myself energetically into life at NYU, in part to distract myself from my grief. Somewhere in the back of my mind I was always aware that I was an orphan, and I needed to find ways to fill that feeling of emptiness. As close as I became with my sister, her home was not my home.

Academically, I worked hard and maintained an A− average, keeping my scholarship safe. From being president of the freshman class, I went on to become secretary of the student council, vice president, and then president. And I kept my social life busy. The house plan always had events on weekends, and I actively dated.

Campus politics enlivened me as well. It gave me causes and a purpose, along with a kind of home. I felt imbued with the issues of the time, and it felt important to participate, to govern and have an impact, to help shape events rather than merely be governed by others. It provided the opportunity to deal with the most interesting and intelligent doers on campus. I felt that it lifted me out of the pack. Back to the advice of my parents again, it appealed to the part of me that was people-oriented, rather than just academic.

I was a political science major after all, and was genuinely fascinated by government and politics. I joined the Young Democratic Club of New York. I was a Roosevelt Democrat, and, like so many young progressives in the Fifties, a huge supporter of Adlai Stevenson, the liberal Democrat from Illinois who ran against Dwight Eisenhower for the presidency in 1952 and 1956, unfortunately losing both times. I thought that Stevenson, who was so witty, articulate, and principled, was the second coming, embodying everything a politician should be. He looked back to Roosevelt, but he also foreshadowed the farsighted domestic policies of Presidents Kennedy and Johnson in the Sixties.

Ever practical, I also was aware that all of my prominent activities were enhancing my résumé. As with college, I would need a scholarship to be able to go to law school, and everyone knew that you couldn't just rely on a stellar academic record. I needed to distinguish myself; these were my extracurricular activities, and I wanted them to be as strong as possible. So I was simultaneously bolstering myself against the losses I had suffered, working hard and enjoying myself as much as I could, and setting the stage for the next major adventure of my life.

A Harvard Man

With studying, student politics, and socializing, my remaining years at NYU passed happily and successfully. I did extremely well academically, and graduated Phi Beta Kappa. I was president of the student council, and was elected president of my alumni class as well. Best of all, I had a choice of first-rate law schools to attend. NYU Law School offered me a prestigious Root-Tilden-Kern Public Interest Scholarship, but I felt that it was time for me to explore life outside New York. Other than my family's vacations in the Catskills and a car trip I had made with some NYU friends to Miami Beach, I had hardly spent any time at all outside the city.

Also, Seena was pregnant with her second child, my nephew Fred, so it really would not have been easy for me to continue to live with her family in Bayside. Even if I had stayed in New York, I would have had to live in a dorm, which made the idea of leaving more enticing. Besides, as close as I had grown to be with my sister and my aunt, they were not my mother. I still felt that huge loss, and very much needed something to fill the void. Perhaps a change of scenery would provide it.

The idea of leaving New York took on vivid life when I was offered a full-tuition scholarship to Harvard Law School. So much lore surrounded Harvard that I felt it was a crowning achievement just to be accepted. To win a scholarship to go there was over the top, the epitome of everything I had worked for to that point in my life. Turning it down was inconceivable.

My accomplishments at NYU, capped by the scholarship to Harvard, had masked my characteristic insecurity, my subconscious expectation that something bad could happen at any moment. Harvard delivered on that expectation, and made those insecurities a reality. Suddenly I was in a world where it seemed that all my classmates had graduated at the top of their class, where everyone was Phi Beta Kappa. Every student, let alone the faculty, seemed polished and well spoken. At the same time, everyone felt the potential judgment of that classic line that incoming students would hear about Harvard Law: "Look at the person on your right, and look at the person on your left. One of you won't be here next year."

Similar to when I started at NYU, I was very conscious of my vulnerable scholarship status at Harvard. I needed to maintain a B average to keep my funding, and no wealthy relative was waiting in the wings to foot the bill if I fell short. I still had four thousand dollars to my name. I was not getting an allowance from anyone. The stakes were very clear and very high: If I didn't make the grade, I was out. I literally couldn't afford to slip up.

While I had consistently been an A student, I always ran scared and never took that level of performance for granted. I was all too aware that each grade had to be earned each time, and Harvard was going to be a crucial test in that regard. You had no formal exams until the end of your first year, so you never really knew where you stood. I had a wonderful professor named Warren A. Seavey, and we learned by the Socratic method, in which every question is answered by another question. It was intellectually exhilarating, a true stretching of the mind, but also very unsettling. Nothing was definitive, and it felt as if you could never be certain of what you knew or didn't know. It was excruciating, the most anxiety-ridden year I've ever spent.

Everyone around me at school was tense for the same reasons, but there were other reasons why I was tense. NYU had been an important step in my development, but Harvard really made me aware of the degree to which I had grown up on the block in Brooklyn and how small and narrow that upbringing was. Even in college, I'd had very little exposure to anything outside the cultural frame provided by my Brooklyn years, which revolved around school, street sports, family, and the Dodgers—and not necessarily in that order! My environment was lower-middle class at best, and overwhelmingly Jewish. A background like that was far more common at NYU than at Harvard, and I felt the difference acutely. It was a growing-up experience for me, a tremendous opening-up of my eyes. Leaving my hometown. Leaving the womb.

To this point in my life, my friends, my family, my activism, and my attainments had all shaped and shored up my identity, and all of them were either unavailable or didn't seem quite so special at Harvard. This was the first time that I was living outside New York, and, in a kind of delayed reaction, I was no longer able to insulate myself from the crushing loss of my parents. I was used to going home to my sister's house, with my beloved aunt just a few blocks away. Now I knew maybe three or four people in my entering class. When I'd go back to my room and close the door, I felt alone. The normal loneliness that you feel when you leave your family and home and go off to school was intensified by coming to grips with the death of my parents. I felt the enormity of the loss from the day I began Harvard Law School. I felt alone in the world.

I lived on campus that first year, in Hastings Hall, the law school's oldest residence. My roommate was from Wisconsin. He was bright and charming. We got along fine until we took our practice exams at the end of the first semester. I got Bs and Cs, which was terrifying, the lowest grades I'd ever received. Even worse, he got Ds and Fs. After that I never saw him. He would get up at six, go to his classes, and then hit the library until two in the morning. It was like living alone. On the rare occasions when I did see him, he looked stricken with panic.

The scuttlebutt at school was that you could expect to score a grade or two higher on your actual exams than on the practice ones, but there was no guarantee of that. I never assumed anything anyway, so I just bore down harder. It was horrendous. Everyone was worried. As the spring semester progressed, I grew increasingly anxious, the issues at school intensified by my inner feelings of loneliness.

Then, for the first and only time in my life, I began to experience anxiety attacks. Unlike now, very few people talked about this sort of thing in the early Fifties, and I felt as if I were completely losing control. I was studying hard and, as exams approached, I felt nervous and experienced an irrational, overarching sense of dread. I wasn't sleeping well, and I had difficulty concentrating. I began to be afraid that I was going to pass out, as if I might faint while taking my exams and would consequently fail. I was deeply frightened.

Things got serious enough that I made an appointment to see a psychologist at the health services center on campus. He was empathetic and reassuring, emphasizing the circumstantial nature of my complaints and the degree to which nearly everyone at Harvard Law was going through some version of what I was experiencing. There was no way to make the situation less of a strain, he admitted, so there was no magic fix. He simply encouraged me that if I hung in there and got through my exams, things would settle down and I would feel better.

I saw him once a week for eight or ten weeks as I was preparing for my exams, and he turned out to be right. I did very well, and got outstanding grades. I qualified for Law Review, but I was given another option, which I decided to accept. I was offered a spot on the Board of Student Advisors, which ran the school's moot court competition. What made the difference to me was that if you joined the Board of Student Advisors, you were considered a faculty member and you got paid five hundred dollars. That sounded good to me. I needed the five hundred bucks, so that decision was made.

No one's life is one-dimensional, so at the same time I was undergoing all that emotional turmoil, I actually also loved being at Harvard. I felt a certain exhilaration just walking around the university's main campus, which was separate from the law school, and Cambridge was a total delight. Hastings Hall, where I was living, was beautiful and evocative, the classic vision of what life at college might look like.

Though Jews were a distinct minority in the law school, they were still better-represented than in the general population—we're talking lawyers, after all! But Harvard was much more of a gentile society than I had ever encountered, with the eating clubs and those kinds of social organizations, and it definitely took some getting used to. It was very preppy. Everybody wore khaki pants and a tweed jacket. I liked that look, though, and had no problem adapting it to my own tastes. Boston is a great town. Radcliffe and Wellesley were nearby in the suburbs, and there were other schools close by as well. There were lots of young people around, and affordable places to eat and socialize, whenever I could spare a minute to do so.

I moved off campus for my second and third years, which lowered the heat on the law-school pressure cooker. Happily, my traumatized first-year roommate ended up passing, so he moved on as well. I was feeling much more comfortable and secure, having survived the first-year gauntlet and gotten a little used to life away from home. In the course of the year, I had made some like-minded friends at school, most of them New Yorkers, and four of us moved into a house at 54 Wendell Street, just a short walk from the law school.

We had a great house, and we all got along well. It was a really valuable learning experience. We took turns cooking, and shared responsibilities for the house, which I'd never done before outside a family or institutional setting. I began dating a woman named Leah Epstein, who was going to Boston University, and we saw each other for a year or so.

I also remained close to my family. I called my sister Seena and my aunt Jeanette every week, and saw them when I went home for breaks. Jeanette's younger daughter, Jo, became like a sister to me. I still kept in touch with my college friends, principally Harold Lubell and Rusti Fiur, my Bayside commuting partners. Whenever I came back to Queens, we would all get together with our other NYU friends, many of whom had also gone on to law or medical school. All of that kept me grounded and connected to my roots.

Finally, however, Harvard made me begin to wonder whether I was cut out for the law. A lot of the course work was dull, in my view, and the grind seemed implacable. Interestingly, though, I took a copyright course that required us to subscribe to *Variety*, the bible of the entertainment business. The paper had its own jargon and perhaps it was never going to win any literary prizes, but the writing in it was very lively, and I found myself drawn to all the statistics about hit movies and TV shows. I'd loved numbers ever since my days tracking the daily ups and downs of the Dodgers, and this seemed similarly enjoyable and precise—a measurable way to determine the impact of something that might otherwise seem ephemeral. At the very least, my devoted reading of *Variety* provided welcome relief from my law books—and an intriguing harbinger of things to come.

As I had at NYU, I continued to work over summer vacations and during semester breaks in law school in order to make money. After manning the complaint line for Sears Roebuck and doing sales for Scripto, I worked as a day-camp counselor one summer and as a busboy at the Avon Lodge in the Catskills. Then, after I finished my first year at law school, I took a job as head waiter at Camp Equinunk in the Pocono Mountains in northeastern Pennsylvania. The job paid well, and I got good tips, so I took the job again the following summer. Camp Blue Ridge was Equinunk's sister camp for girls, and it was there that I met my first wife, Helen Cohen, who was a counselor there.

Helen was eighteen at the time, and I was twenty-three. She was a student at the University of Michigan, and totally different from any girl I had ever dated before—pure, idealistic, innocent—and we fell in love. She was five feet seven inches tall with light brown hair, twinkling hazel eyes, a fair complexion, and a very appealing collegiate look, evocative of the girls I would see at Radcliffe and Wellesley. It was especially fun, because one of Helen's sorority sisters, Diane Intriligator, was working with her at Blue Ridge, and she fell in love with my housemate Steve Jacobson, whom I had convinced to come work at Equinunk with me. We all spent the following year, my third and final year at Harvard, traveling back and forth between Boston and Ann Arbor, and being in touch nearly every day.

Helen's family lived in a lovely home at 25 Grymes Hill Road on Staten Island, and they were quite well-to-do. I liked her father, Julius, although he was an archconservative Republican, and it was hard to take his political pronouncements, given my own decidedly opposite views. Her mother, Cherie, was a beautiful, gracious person whom I genuinely loved. Missing my own parents, I found Helen's family's obvious closeness very comforting and appealing.

Clearly, Helen and I were going to move back to New York after I graduated, so I spent my third year applying for jobs and interviewing with law firms. I decided that I wanted to go with a smaller firm, thinking that I would learn more, rather than simply doing the basic work that a larger firm would give to their regiments of first-year hires. Plus, after the upheavals in my personal life and the intense competitiveness of Harvard, I was in no hurry to plunge into the Manhattan legal rat race. I thought a smaller firm might be a bit easier-going in that regard. Coming out of Harvard, I had strong academic credentials, and assumed that I would end up with a range of attractive options.

It was during this job search that I experienced my first personal encounter with anti-Semitism. I had an interview with a prestigious Manhattan law firm. The conversation seemed to have gone well, and my interviewer was writing some notes when he got a call from a partner and had to leave the room. He left his notepad on his desk, and I couldn't help but peer over to see what he had written. Essentially, he noted that I had an outstanding record and that my interview had been good, but he wasn't sure I was—and these are his words and his quotation marks—" 'right' for the firm."

Maybe I'm doing him an injustice, but those quotation marks seemed damning. To me it meant that this was a white-shoe firm and perhaps as a Jew I wouldn't fit in. I can't imagine what else it could have signified. In any event, I accepted a job with Hale, Kay & Brennan, a small downtown firm where I would be doing nonlitigation work. Despite their size, they were willing to pay the going rate for top law school graduates, which in 1956 was, hard as it is to believe today, $4,500 a year. We had a deal.

Helen and I got married on September 2, 1956, shortly after I graduated. Her parents arranged a beautiful wedding at the Savoy Plaza, which was located in Manhattan at Fifty-ninth Street and Fifth Avenue, where the General Motors building is today. We couldn't have been happier, though one problem remained. I had been drafted, and without a student deferment there was a good chance that I would be called for service.

Given that uncertainty, we stayed with Helen's parents on Staten Island as we waited to see what would develop. I could easily commute to work from there because Hale, Kay & Brennan was located on Wall Street. Also not far from Wall Street, coincidentally, was 39 Whitehall Street, the Army Building later made famous by Arlo Guthrie as the place where new draftees go to get "injected, inspected, detected, infected, neglected, and selected" in his classic song "Alice's Restaurant." I said good-bye to Helen, her parents, my sister, and my aunts, and showed up at Whitehall Street for my physical.

My only hope for deferment was that I had bad allergies to certain foods, cats, feathers, and dust. My doctor wrote a letter describing my condition, and I brought it with me, not really giving it much thought. I went through the hours-long process Guthrie described, and finally was at the stage where I was about to be "selected." The man there looked at me, looked at my various forms and papers, and simply said, "Okay, you can leave." I said, "Leave? Where do I go?" He said, "You go home." I had gotten rejected based on my doctor's letter.

When I came home, Helen burst into tears, but we were euphoric. We immediately started looking for an apartment that we could afford.

A New Life Back in New York

The formula for figuring out an affordable rent at the time was one week's salary after taxes. Since my weekly salary was less than one hundred dollars, we were somewhat limited, to say the least, in terms of the type of place we could get. We certainly couldn't afford anything decent in Manhattan. I was familiar with Queens, of course, from living with my sister, and I knew that Jamaica Estates was a beautiful area with lovely apartment houses. So we rented a place at 182–25 Wexford Terrace for $125 a month. Its prize feature was a flexible dining room that could be made into a bedroom if necessary.

Understandably, that $125 outlay was much discussed between Helen and me, and among our families. "Don't take on more than you can afford" was the economic watchword, and I was so used to watching every penny that the last thing I wanted was to have to worry about my monthly rent. I knew that there would be a bonus at the end of the year, and I was confident that things would work out. But, absurd as it might sound now, it was a real issue. Once it was decided, we arranged to move, and settled in. Helen transferred to NYU from Michigan and set out to complete her BA. I commuted to Wall Street to work at Hale, Kay & Brennan. Our social lives revolved primarily around our families and friends from college and law school.

Things were a bit dull at work, but I was learning a great deal. Hale, Kay & Brennan handled estates and did corporate and tax work, and that's where my efforts were concentrated. I hadn't examined their client list closely enough to realize that a large percentage of their business came from one company, a firm called Cary Chemicals, for which I did no work. One day I learned through the grapevine that Cary was going to merge with another company, and Hale, Kay & Brennan was going to lose the account. The firm had started up in 1952, and had only three or four partners, and maybe three or four associates. I was the most recent associate to be hired, and therefore the most vulnerable.

As it happens, the firm lost Cary and another account, and did let two associates go, but kept me on. I was relieved, but rudely awakened to how precarious my situation was at such a small firm. I made up my mind that I had to protect myself. I consulted the Martindale-Hubbell law directory and wrote to twenty of the larger firms that had interviewed at Harvard in my last year there. One of the firms I applied to was Rosenman, Colin, Kaye, Petschek and Freund, which was among the most prominent so-called Jewish law firms in New York at the time, with about forty lawyers. Sam Rosenman had been a lawyer and speechwriter for both FDR and Harry Truman, and was a powerful figure in Democratic politics. His son Robert had been my classmate at Harvard. I met with Murray Cohen, one of Rosenman's nonlitigation partners, we hit it off, and I got hired.

Going to work at Rosenman was the first real lucky break of my career, not so much for the job itself but for the firm's client list and the particular work I was able to do. I'm not a fatalist. I believe that hard work makes things happen and helps you be prepared to take advantage when luck comes your way. But sometimes life just drops good things in your lap with no effort at all on your part, and without your even realizing it. This was one of those times.

Among Ralph Colin's clients were prominent painters and artists, but his biggest and the firm's most significant client was the broadcasting giant CBS and its pioneering founder, William Paley. I was doing some estate planning and tax work, but I was primarily handling the contractual work for Columbia Artists Management, Inc. (CAMI), which had been a part of CBS until antitrust laws forced a dissolution. CAMI mainly represented classical artists from overseas. I was doing immigration law to get temporary visas for the Russian Ballet or the Russian State Symphony Orchestra, and for renowned figures like Rudolf Nureyev or Mikhail Baryshnikov, if they were going to perform in the United States.

CAMI also had a subsidiary for which I did contracts, called the Broadway Theater Alliance, which ran the bus-and-truck troupe tours of Broadway shows that would perform around the country. It was far more interesting work than I had been doing, and, however unaware I was of it at the time, it was a significant step along the road that I would eventually travel.

In a truly life-changing moment, Helen gave birth to our son Fred in 1959, and, thrilled as we were, his arrival made things a bit crowded in our Wexford Terrace apartment, flexible dining room or no. By this time, I might have been making $9,500 a year, so we had a little breathing room. We looked around and bought a lovely home in Roslyn, Long Island. It even had a backyard, a basic amenity for most homeowners, but a much-appreciated luxury if you've lived in apartments most of your life. Helen loved to read, and we formed a book club with some of my colleagues and their wives, including a fellow associate at Rosenman, Walter Yetnikoff, who would eventually go on to a tumultuous career in the music industry. We'd all get together once a month to socialize and discuss the book we had chosen to read.

My boss, Murray Cohen, was a very special man, and I was getting invaluable, intense training under his aegis. I remember his coming into my office once after reading a will I was preparing, and saying, astonished, "You know, you missed two semicolons. How did you miss *two* semicolons?" I'll never forget it, and to this day I don't have a satisfactory answer for him! I know he thought a lot of me, and his perfectionism and attention to detail reminded me of what I enjoyed about my grade school grammar drills. It was a lesson I would apply throughout my career. Sure, vision and big ideas are important, but the smallest details matter, too. If someone is careless in that regard, they're likely to overlook big problems as well.

I liked the work at Rosenman, and it's a good thing, because I had to bill fifty hours a week, which meant working very long hours. The commute to Long Island didn't make matters easier. An additional complication was that, before too long, the ceiling of possibilities at Rosenman came into view. For a variety of reasons, the firm discouraged associates from bringing in new business. The name partners moved in a world where they were attracting multimillionaires and major corporations, and nothing else was needed beyond their efforts. As I was learning the rules of the game, that was fine. I wasn't moving in those social circles, so it's not as if I had a line on potential clients on that level anyway. But eventually I began to think, What will my life be like if I stay here? I really can only be a service partner; that is, I would be made partner, but my work would consist of supporting the business Sam Rosenman, Ralph Colin, and the other name partners brought in. My job would be secure, but not especially exciting, distinguished, or lucrative.

And I did still have to think about money. While my economic position had steadily improved, I had not been able to save very much, and now I had a family. Helen, by this point, had graduated from NYU, but she had a son to take care of, and some of the necessary constraints on her own life began to weigh on her. It wasn't easy for her. She had been a literature major, and was very interested in philosophy and poetry. To put it mildly, those pursuits weren't widely shared by our Long Island neighbors, and she felt isolated. We would socialize in Manhattan with our friends, but moving there was still out of the question. Helen was nineteen when we married and twenty-two when Fred was born. Though she had the responsibility of a family, she was still finding her way in her own life.

And then one morning I felt an overpowering sadness as I was walking to work along Madison Avenue, nearly enough to bring me to tears. The doubts I'd had about being a lawyer when I was at Harvard reemerged, exacerbated by the shrinking horizons of my job at Rosenman. I still hadn't found my niche. Something had to change.

Fortunately, my trend of lucky breaks continued. The chief lawyer for Columbia Records was a man named Harvey Schein, who had previously worked at Rosenman. The president of Columbia at the time, Goddard Lieberson, was planning to establish overseas subsidiaries of the company for the first time, specifically in the U.K. and France. Previously, they had only worked with licensees. Schein was working closely with Lieberson on the project. They were traveling together, and doing the planning for what a more international Columbia Records might look like.

Believe it or not, Columbia had a two-man law department at the time, Schein and an assistant. With the new plans for expansion taking shape, Schein wanted a stronger person in his assistant's slot, and he asked his contacts at Rosenman for a recommendation. Specifically he asked, "Who handles the CAMI account?" because that was the closest work Rosenman did to what he would need his assistant to do at Columbia.

The answer, of course, was me, and so, out of the blue, Schein came to see me. He asked if I enjoyed the CAMI work, which I did. I'd done a good job with the account, and Ron Wilford, who is still the head of CAMI today, and I got along very well. I knew he would vouch for me. Then Schein got to the heart of what he was thinking about. He said, "I've got a great opportunity for you. We're getting closer to doing this deal in the U.K. and France, and when it goes through, I know that Goddard is going to make me the head of International for Columbia Records. When I get that job, my assistant will take over my position, and the person I have now isn't capable of that. If you come in and replace him, I'll teach you everything about how the department works. If it all works out, I guarantee you that within a year you will be the chief lawyer for Columbia Records."

It was now 1960, and he offered me $11,000 to start. "I also guarantee you," Schein continued, "that when you become chief counsel, you'll make twenty-five thousand dollars a year." That had always seemed like a fortune to me, and it was only a year away. It triggered the memory of a real experience of mine. When we were first married, Helen and I were out with Steve Jacobson and his wife, Diane. We were all in a car one night speculating about the future, and Steve asked me what eventual permanent salary would satisfy me as a career goal. I was then earning $4,500 a year and I thought long and hard about it and remember my answer to this day: $25,000 a year! See, Harvard doesn't teach you everything.

Unfortunately, I knew nothing about music to speak of, not that it was a requirement of the job. When I was a teenager, I liked music, and had even studied it a bit in college, but it was never a hobby of mine or a craving. I enjoyed singing, and was a member of the glee club at NYU.

I still listened to the radio, but my tastes remained the conventional adult tastes of that era: Bing Crosby, Frank Sinatra, Dinah Shore, Kay Starr, Broadway theater albums—nothing out of the ordinary that would predict a career in the music industry, even as a fantasy or an "if only" desire.

As for early rock 'n' roll, I had little interest in it. Today, rock musicians tour and record into their sixties and seventies, and fans in their forties, fifties, and sixties seek out new music, even if only the latest releases by the artists they grew up with and love. In the Fifties, though, rock 'n' roll was for teenagers. It was inconceivable that an ambitious, married New York lawyer in his late twenties would seriously discuss the latest records by Elvis Presley, Little Richard, or Buddy Holly, let alone adopt their fashions or hairstyles. That would all come later. Unlike many people my age and older, I didn't see rock 'n' roll as the end of civilization. It just wasn't for me, any more than Hula-Hoops or coonskin Davy Crockett hats were. That music was for kids, and I was a grown-up with grown-up things on my mind.

Nonetheless, the prospect of working in the entertainment business was intriguing—particularly at the salary Harvey Schein had mentioned! But I wanted to make sure that going to Columbia Records would be the right move for me, so I talked it over with Ralph Colin, one of the two major partners in the firm, who handled CBS and oversaw CAMI, so he knew my work. He discouraged me. He viewed the New York showbiz world of popular music as tacky, filled with loud Broadway players who were gaudy and possibly even unsavory. I wouldn't fit in.

To some degree, I'm sure, his advice was premised on his perception of me. I came to work every day still wearing those khaki pants and tweed jackets I had developed a taste for during my sojourn in the Ivy League. He understandably viewed me as a Harvard Law grad who wanted to better my position in the world, not mingle with dubious characters who could only reflect badly on me. He assured me that I would be considered for partner at Rosenman in five years.

I appreciated his advice, and certainly weighed what he said carefully. No question, he had my best interests at heart. But I finally thought, He doesn't really know me. I knew that I came from Brooklyn, and that I could get along with all kinds of different people. Running for political office at NYU taught me how to balance the varied interests of a large, complex, and outspoken student body. The "people skills" my mother encouraged and my father's salesmanship and gregariousness, after all, were as much a part of me as the more refined world of the Board of Student Advisors at Harvard. Ralph Colin would not necessarily have any way of knowing that, but it was something essential for me to remember, something that was true and that remains true.

The decision ultimately turned out to be pretty simple. I could either stay at Rosenman and accept my likely future as a service partner, or I could leave to become the chief counsel for Columbia Records. I took the job.

The Offer That Changed My Life

As soon as I started at Columbia, I jumped in with both feet. True to his word, Harvey Schein began grooming me to take over his position and involved me in everything he was doing. I suddenly found myself flying to London and Paris with Harvey and Goddard Lieberson to set up Columbia subsidiaries. Harvey was traveling so much that, back at the office, I often functioned as Columbia's general counsel in his absence. I was formally offered the title in 1961. All in all, the entire process was exhilarating, but so intense and rushed that I felt a little insecure. There was no time for settling in, no learning curve, no lingering on the runway. As soon as I strapped myself in my seat, we were in the sky. But I was flying.

Apart from all the work on the European subsidiaries, the Columbia Record Club, a monthly subscription service that made new releases from a variety of labels available to consumers at discounted rates, was being sued by the Federal Trade Commission as a monopoly. The club had started in 1955, and now controlled 60 to 70 percent of mail-order record sales in the country. At the time, mail order was often the most convenient way for suburban and rural music fans to buy records, as it would remain for another decade or so.

Columbia had been so successful that RCA and Capitol Records had started mail-order clubs of their own in 1958. They were eager to get a piece of Columbia's huge market share, and the FTC had sided with their claim that Columbia was acting in restraint of trade by selling the products of other labels. The reasoning, however feeble, was that artists would be tempted to leave their labels for Columbia if the record club demonstrated that Columbia could sell their music more effectively. The FTC, therefore, was trying to force Columbia to divest itself of the club, which had become a major source of revenue for the company. Rosenman, my former employer, was representing Columbia in the suit, so I was working with the litigation team there and familiarizing myself with the various contracts involved. It was a highly prominent suit that got a good deal of media coverage, and I was right in the middle of it.

While working on that case, I realized how little I actually knew about unfair competition and antitrust law, and I hated that feeling of not being at the top of my game. I believe in completely immersing yourself in whatever you're doing and preparing with absolute thoroughness, so I took night courses at NYU Law School in copyright, patent, trademark, and unfair-competition law in order to be more firmly grounded in this aspect of my work. As a result, I was working long hours in the office every day, going to school two or three nights a week, and occasionally traveling to Europe for a week or ten days at a time. In the meantime, Helen was back home in Roslyn. Our daughter Lauren was born in 1961, so now we had two very young children. We had a car, but I parked it at the train station in Roslyn and commuted on the Long Island Rail Road to Manhattan. As my own horizons were expanding, Helen was feeling trapped.

The schedule was intense, but, because of the FTC suit, I was not merely supervising contracts, I was learning everything I could about every facet of the record business and thoroughly enjoying it. It was a unique opportunity and I took full advantage. I attended all the interviews with retailers and distributors involved in the case. I started going to the annual meeting of the National Association of Record Merchandisers, an extremely important music industry gathering, because I had met so many of the key players in that domain.

I was also meeting with artists who were called to testify in the case. Through that, and through my work on artists' contracts, I became friendly with Mitch Miller, who was the head of A&R at Columbia. A&R stands for "artists and repertoire," the part of the business that deals directly with the artists signed to the label and helps select the material they record if they don't write for themselves. It's the very heart of the music industry: If you can't find great performers and songs, you have nothing. Miller eventually became an artist in his own right with the hugely successful *Sing Along with Mitch* series, which led to a highly rated television show that made him a major national celebrity. Ordinarily, a lawyer would never have the opportunity to learn those sides of the business or move in those circles, especially back then. If you want to rise in a business setting, it's important to understand that every aspect of the business is important, not just the parts that inherently interest you. I was getting an essential three-dimensional view of how music was conveyed to its audience, and it would prove invaluable.

The FTC suit was dismissed, a major victory that preserved an important profit center for Columbia and boosted my standing there. None of the company's rivals ever made much of a dent in Columbia's dominance of the mail-order market, though more comprehensive changes in the business and in the culture at large eventually made that segment far less significant than it had been. But that wouldn't happen for quite some time.

Along with winning the antitrust case, we successfully established the Columbia subsidiaries in the U.K. and France. I was now solidly entrenched at Columbia, and I needed to find a number-two man myself. As Harvey Schein had done, I went back to Rosenman to find a suitable candidate, and recruited my old friend Walter Yetnikoff. Like me, Walter was no music expert, but he worked in litigation and had experience in antitrust law and other specialties that would be useful at Columbia. He had gone to Columbia Law School, and was extremely bright. Even in the early Sixties, he was a radical thinker—outspoken and rebellious, a nice counterbalance to my own analytic pragmatism. I told him how much I was enjoying Columbia and was delighted when he agreed to come on board.

Interestingly, my legal work at Columbia brought me into contact for the first time with Bob Dylan, with whom I would eventually develop a very good relationship. He was just a promising artist starting out at the time, nothing like the icon he would become. Regardless, we certainly got off to a bumpy start.

Dylan had been signed to Columbia by the legendary A&R man

and producer John Hammond, who, among other accomplishments, had discovered Billie Holiday and Aretha Franklin and worked with the likes of Benny Goodman and Count Basie. Dylan's first album, simply titled *Bob Dylan,* came out in 1962 and had not sold particularly well. His determinedly untrained voice and irreverent attitude had won him few fans among the more conservative elements at the label. Yet Dylan had received rave reviews in *The New York Times* and elsewhere, and his reputation as a songwriter had already made him an esteemed figure in the folk music world. So when Hammond came to my office in a panic because Dylan was threatening to leave Columbia, we knew we needed to find a way to keep him. It turned out that Dylan was a minor when he signed his contract with the label, and he had written a letter to Hammond disavowing the agreement on that basis.

Hammond was upset for both personal and professional reasons. Not only did he deeply believe in Dylan as an artist, he regarded him as a friend. He assumed—correctly, I believe—that Dylan had been persuaded to send the letter by his legal and business advisors, on the assumption that if they shopped him around they'd be able to land him a better contract than the standard deal he had with Columbia.

Legally, Dylan had the right to walk away from the agreement, but only if he did so before he turned twenty-one. That birthday had already passed. I asked John if Dylan had recorded in Columbia's studios, as all the label's artists were required to do, since he had turned twenty-one, and John said that he had at least half a dozen times. As far as I was concerned, that, along with his age, had confirmed his acceptance of his status as a Columbia artist. But John was still worried. And it's true that when dealing with artists, it's often best not to rely on strictly legal arguments if you can help it.

I asked John to be objective about how strong his relationship with Dylan really was, and he insisted that they were on excellent terms. I then suggested that he get Dylan to come to his office to discuss the matter, and that John strongly reaffirm Columbia's support for Dylan, in the present and in the future. I drafted a statement, essentially disavowing the disavowal, and told Hammond to ask Dylan to sign it when they were done. I believed, and John agreed, that if we went through Dylan's handlers, things would only get more difficult. I wasn't sure by any means that this more personal strategy would work. But John's meeting with Dylan went smoothly, and by the end of it, Dylan signed the statement. I can't imagine that the real authors of his original letter were pleased.

My other early run-in with Dylan was even more uncomfortable, in part because it involved a tense meeting with him—our first, an unfortunate way to get to know anyone, let alone an artist. It was 1963, and Dylan wanted to include a song called "Talkin' John Birch Society Blues" on his second album, *The Freewheelin' Bob Dylan*. The song was a satiric attack on the John Birch Society, the ultra-right-wing anti-Communist organization that had been much in the news since its founding in 1958.

In the song, which is sometimes titled "Talkin' John Birch Paranoid Blues," Dylan humorously imagines being someone joining the group and searching for Communists "under my bed," "in the sink," and even "deep down inside my toilet bowl." In the end, after nosing into the backgrounds of everyone else, including former president Eisenhower, for Communist sympathies, the singer is left with only himself to investigate. "Hope I don't find out anything," he muses hopefully at the end of the song.

All of that was fine, well within the scope of humorous political commentary, but two lines in the song were clearly libelous in my view. In them Dylan says that all John Birchers hold "Hitler's views," despite the fact that he annihilated "six million Jews." Technically, in legal terms, Columbia could have been sued by any member of the John Birch Society who felt slandered by Dylan's accusation. I couldn't allow the company to run that degree of risk, so I had to rule that Dylan could not include the song on his album.

I was in a terrible bind. As an avowed liberal, someone who had worked for Adlai Stevenson in the Fifties, I certainly was no admirer of the John Birch Society. I also was a free-speech advocate and a fan of Dylan's. But I had to take the legally responsible position for Columbia. Dylan was infuriated and asked to meet with me. He was just twenty-two at the time, and I was only nine years older. John Hammond accompanied him to my office, but for the most part left it to Dylan and me to argue the matter out—or, more accurately, for Dylan to argue, and me to apologize but hold firm.

"What *is* this?" Dylan exclaimed. "What do you *mean* I can't come out with this song? You can't edit or censor me!" I stayed calm. I emphasized the clarity of the legal issue as much as I could. I explained, "I hate to do this. I feel awful. It has nothing to do with my being conservative, or the company being conservative." For whatever it was worth, I outlined my liberal background and views.

None of it settled Dylan down. He clearly saw me and Columbia as toeing the Establishment line, the same way he viewed the CBS network executives who refused to allow him to perform the song on *The Ed Sullivan Show* around the same time. In later years, when we had occasion to work together very cordially, I don't think Dylan remembered that I was the lawyer who delivered this bad news to him. If he did, he never brought it up, for which I'm forever grateful.

More personally, in 1964, I was grieved to learn that my wife Helen's unhappiness was deeper than I had previously believed. She told me, first of all, that she couldn't live in Roslyn anymore. That wasn't much of a surprise, but then she explained that the life we had been building together was not really what she wanted. She said she loved me, and, of course, loved our children, and she knew how much I was enjoying the dynamism of my life at Columbia and all the new opportunities I had. But she felt that being the wife of a corporate mover and shaker was not how she saw herself or who she wanted to be. She didn't like living in a big city; she would prefer to live a more agrarian life. She was restless and wanted to travel, to see the world as I had been doing, but on her own terms.

She was clearly undergoing major emotional upset. And yet, apart from the separate directions our lives had taken, there was no discord between us. We weren't fighting. Quite the opposite, we were getting along very well. But she kept repeating that she didn't want to be a drag on my career, and she was in deep turmoil between her desire to travel and her devotion to our children. Difficult as it was, I felt her dilemma, and it was searing to watch her go through it. I really didn't know what I could do to help. That said, I had been happy, and to me it seemed that our idyllic world was collapsing, and I feared that its demise couldn't be prevented. I never pictured myself divorced, and I couldn't at all picture myself living without my children.

After many long discussions, I said, "Let's see if a therapist might be able to bring some clarity." She did see a therapist and she worked on this nightmarish conflict between being a wife and mother and her need to travel and discover herself. We tried to live through it for about a year. We both held on as she veered pretty wildly from one emotion to another. We loved each other, but her unrest was deep. Attempting to resolve all this was excruciating. Usually I don't love solitude, but I remember taking our car and driving by myself for a weekend at Lake George. I'll never forget my loneliness and my tears flowed endlessly. I finally had my own family and I didn't want to disrupt it, but I could feel the inevitability of change. When I got back, with great pain we agreed to divorce. Loving my kids, who were then three and five, very much, this was intense for me. Helen's parents were also distraught. We had all been one family. In those days it was virtually impossible for a father to get custody of the kids, so our separation agreement granted custody to her, but she could not take the children more than fifty miles from Manhattan. We also agreed to sell our house in Roslyn, and we moved separately into Manhattan.

Among her prospective travels, Helen, who was now twenty-seven, wanted to spend time in Israel, which really scared me because of the kids. It seemed dangerous, and having lost my own parents when I was young, just the thought of it petrified me. She explained to me that she wanted to go there for six months. It was a bit odd because, although her parents were Jewish, she had no particular religious leanings. It was more about the utopian dream of what Israel might be like, a desire to leave city life behind and live on a collective farm.

As she was formulating her plans, I bought a flexible three-bedroom apartment at the Pavilion, an apartment building at 500 East Seventy-seventh Street, between East End Avenue and the East River. I enlisted my mother-in-law to help me hire a live-in nanny from England, Mrs. Woolley, and I made the dining area into a bedroom for her. I enrolled both kids in the Town School, a private school right around the corner on Seventy-sixth Street. Helen got a small apartment a block or so away.

I came home every night to have dinner with the kids, even if I had work commitments afterward. For about six months, Helen was at our apartment all the time, because she was torn and couldn't bring herself to leave the kids and take her trip. Actually, for a while that was okay with me. This wasn't a war, we were still getting along fine, the kids enjoyed having her there, and she obviously was in tremendous conflict.

Eventually, though, this daily domestic scene, a kind of shadow play of what had been our very real marriage, became just too tough for me. I needed to get on with my life, and it was obviously going to be impossible with her constantly being around. I finally said to her, "Look, we're separated, but you're here all the time. There's got to be some boundaries. There's got to be visitations at certain times. I've got to start dating." Deep down she understood. She could see that the kids were settled and in school, and she decided that it was finally time for her to leave on her journey. She was gone for about nine months, the divorce went through, and during that time I met the woman who would become my second wife, Janet Adelberg.

In the meantime at CBS, things continued to change rapidly. Goddard Lieberson and William Paley embarked on an ambitious reorganization and diversification program in 1965, and anything involving music was fair game on the most spurious grounds. *Synergy* became the byword, and somehow, because CBS was involved in the record industry through Columbia, it was thought that the acquisition of musical instrument and equipment manufacturers like Fender Guitars, Leslie Speakers, Rogers Drums, Steinway Pianos, and Creative Playthings, which made musical toys, was a superb idea. How there could be synergy between records and musical instruments was beyond me, but suddenly, there I was doing all the contract work for those deals. Fender was located in Santa Ana, California, and I traveled a great deal between there and New York to get the deal done.

So Columbia Records was now about to have a musical instruments division, and diversification was taking place in other parts of the company as well. I remember working with some other lawyers to prepare William Paley for the annual CBS stockholders meetings at which cranky investors could be expected to ask tough questions about the diversification program. Theoretically, it all sounded great. CBS looked as if it was expanding and growing. But economically, it was not doing that well, so Paley needed ammunition to defend himself and the company. That involved a little sleight of hand.

CBS had bought Columbia Records in 1938 for $750,000, a bargain price, to say the least. The label had long ago earned that investment back, and there were years in which it did quite well. But since CBS was primarily in the broadcast business, and Columbia was a record company, it was counted as part of the company's ongoing diversification. Its profits counterbalanced the relatively poor performance of other acquisitions. It was a shell game, to be sure, but it got Paley through his interrogations.

One day in June 1965, Goddard called me into his office and announced that, because Columbia was expanding so rapidly, he was going to be made a group president, and he wanted me to head up the new musical instruments division. He knew I'd handled all the deals for those acquisitions, and had good relations with all the executives on that end of our business. It would involve a raise to $40,000, not a dramatic increase, but welcome nonetheless.

It was an attractive offer, needless to say, but it had a couple of drawbacks from my perspective, and I didn't leap to accept it, awkward as this was. For one thing, the wonders of synergy aside, all I really knew about the musical instruments business was that it didn't seem nearly as much fun as the entertainment industry. Traveling to Europe, meeting artists and the people who worked closely with them, attending Broadway openings when I'd handled the contracts for the shows—I loved all those aspects of my work. I knew I would miss them.

Even more important, the new job might entail my moving to California, because Fender was the central piece in our musical instruments business, and I would need to work closely with the executive team there. Goddard assured me that I wouldn't have to move, but I had the sense that, regardless of what he said, it might become inevitable. If that happened, my agreement with Helen stipulated that I would lose my share of custody of our children, and that was unacceptable. Even if I didn't move, I'd be in California a good deal of the time, and away from the kids, and that wasn't acceptable to me, either. Still, I felt that I couldn't simply turn down the job on the spot. So I thanked Goddard, but requested a little time to think about it.

And then pure luck once again entered the picture, making the issue moot. Lieberson had kept busy moving his own pieces around the political chessboard at Columbia, and less than an hour after our meeting, he called to retract his offer. He was apologetic, but Columbia's executive vice president Norman Adler, who had previously been general counsel there and who had also headed the record club, was eager for the opportunities he envisioned in the musical instruments division, and also he wanted to move to California. Boy, was I relieved! It had been hard for me to find a handle on how to turn that position down. And then, stoking my curiosity, Goddard went out of his way to assure me that he would be coming up with something good for me.

A week or so later, Goddard called me at about nine thirty in the morning, and asked me to come see him. After I sat down, he explained again why he had given the musical instruments job to Adler, and then concluded, "So I'm going to give you Columbia Records." I sat there in shock.

Running Columbia Records

The position that Goddard Lieberson offered me carried the title of administrative vice president, but it essentially meant that I would be overseeing all of Columbia Records, including A&R, the driving engine of any record label. It was a daring move on his part that rested, somewhat paradoxically, on what he perceived as my judicious temperament.

Partly because of the reorganization that he had set in motion, Columbia was a hotbed of political maneuvering. Goddard understood that, despite—or perhaps even because of—my lack of musical background and training, I was unlikely to make rash or unnecessarily provocative moves simply because I now had the power to do so. He had liked my work in helping to establish the Columbia subsidiaries in France and Britain and in leading the successful fight to get the FTC lawsuit against the Columbia Record Club dismissed. And while we had never discussed music, he had seen me at Broadway openings and other events whenever I had a legitimate business reason to be there. He was certainly observant enough to surmise that, while I wasn't a music expert, I obviously enjoyed music and got along well with both creative people and executives.

Goddard was in a unique position to be able to trust his judgment in that regard. By the time I joined Columbia in 1960, he was already a legend in the music business, a man who had raised the label to the very pinnacle of the industry. Born in England, he had studied classical music at the University of Washington and the Eastman School of Music in Rochester, and had been a composer himself. He took a $50-a-week job at Columbia in the late Thirties only after concluding that serious composers "could not make a living in the United States." He had been far-seeing in his ability to lead Columbia to preeminence in the worlds of classical music and Broadway show recordings, and, as a result, he was a towering figure in New York's cultural life. He and his stunning wife, Vera Zorina, a ballerina and actress who had previously been married to George Balanchine, were a glamorous power couple well before the term was invented.

In his manner and interests, Goddard epitomized the precise opposite of the jivey, finger-snapping music-biz types that Ralph Colin at Rosenman had warned me about when I was first offered a job at Columbia. Goddard was elegant, informed, incredibly witty, and very articulate, as attractive a figure to the high-end media as many of the artists on the label. He was always very handsomely turned out. Matching his pocket handkerchief with his English-made shirts was a signature element of his style, a touch I have adopted to this day.

He greatly appreciated and admired talents like Leonard Bernstein and Richard Rodgers, and moved comfortably in their circles. Without being pretentious or arrogant about it, however, he carried himself as if he were their peer, not simply the man who ran the label that put out their work. Indeed, he was as accomplished and well known a producer as he was an executive. His stature reflected on the entire company, and when he spoke at Columbia's annual conventions, he was invariably eloquent and always hilarious, and we were rapt. Everyone at Columbia was devoted to him, proud to have him as our standard-bearer. I felt that as keenly as anyone; none of it was lost on me.

What impressed me most about Goddard, though, is that, although he was a thorough product of Columbia Records, having joined the company in the late Thirties and worked his way up to the presidency in 1956, he never relinquished his identity to the corporation. He was his own person, exactly who he was at all times. In 1965, the nation was still coming out of the Fifties in many ways, and the notion of the faceless "man in the gray flannel suit" who loses his soul to the business world was still current. Goddard's charm, individuality, and personal command rendered him a superb counterexample of that stereotype of anonymity. If you walked into Goddard's office, he might be studying Japanese because his travels had begun to take him to Japan. If anything he remade Columbia Records in his own image, rather than the other way around.

But Goddard was far from a dilettante, and he took his corporate role extremely seriously. All of his interests, however erudite, produced concrete, and often groundbreaking, results. By urging Columbia to be an early and ardent adopter, he is widely credited with introducing the LP format—the vinyl, 33⅓ "long player" that replaced 78s, which held far less music—to the American public. Not coincidentally, the more expansive LP was ideally suited to the classical music and original-cast recordings that Goddard loved.

Eventually Columbia could boast of having the New York Philharmonic with Leonard Bernstein, as well as the Philadelphia Orchestra with Eugene Ormandy and the Cleveland Orchestra with George Szell, on its roster. The 1949 LP release of the original-cast recording of *South Pacific,* featuring songs by Rodgers and Hammerstein, was an industry milestone, as was the 1957 release of the classic *West Side Story* original-cast album on which Leonard Bernstein and Stephen Sondheim collaborated, and the 1959 release of the original-cast album of the landmark Rodgers and Hammerstein musical *The Sound of Music.* He produced the original-cast album of *I Can Get It for You Wholesale,* in which Barbra Streisand made her debut in 1962, and then signed Streisand to Columbia.

Important as those innovations were, they were hardly the whole story. The success of Columbia's original-cast recordings led Goddard to think about finding a way to record musicals that had been hits but that had never been recorded. These studio-cast recordings, in which leading performers sang the songs of popular musicals, became equally successful. In Goddard's hands as producer, those albums were sequenced and presented in such a way as to not merely compile great songs, but to evoke the musical's narrative and story lines. Columbia's release of the studio-cast recording of *Pal Joey* in 1951 is widely credited with sparking a successful Broadway revival the following year.

But perhaps Goddard's greatest triumph was persuading CBS to invest $400,000 to become the sole backer of the stage production of *My Fair Lady,* which premiered on Broadway in 1956. Let's momentarily set aside the show's extraordinary quality as, in my view, the best musical ever made. Not only did *My Fair Lady* set records for the longevity of its run, but the cast album, filled with Lerner and Loewe classics, sold millions of copies—and earned tens of millions of dollars—for Columbia. Indeed, in the first three years of his presidency, Goddard doubled Columbia's sales to $50 million.

Finally, Goddard was inspiring because he saw Columbia in three-dimensional terms. He was the founder of the Columbia Record Club, which had more than a million members when I joined the label. He responded to historical events with projects like the *I Can Hear It Now* series, which combined speeches, news reports, and narration by such CBS broadcast titans as Edward R. Murrow and Fred Friendly to summon the drama of, for example, the decisive developments of World War II. After President Kennedy was assassinated in 1963, Goddard oversaw the publication of *John Fitzgerald Kennedy: As We Remember Him,* a dignified and beautifully designed book that had the full cooperation of the Kennedy family. If he believed that something was important—like, for example, recording everything that Igor Stravinsky had written—he found a way to do it.

As I went on to work closely with Goddard, my respect for him only grew. Along with, in my experience, John Hammond at Columbia and Ahmet Ertegun and Jerry Wexler at Atlantic, Goddard was one of the very rare people who responded to music with a completely unalloyed passion. When he was listening to something he loved, all distinctions of age, class, race, and background evaporated. If you happened to be there with him, you could not help but feel the connection. Suddenly he was no longer the eminent Goddard Lieberson, but just a person being moved by what he heard and wanting to share it. It evinced an almost childlike openness, and I believe it's an important part of what made him relate so well to artists. Experiencing that with him was an important lesson for me.

We would have our differences later, but I owe Goddard a tremendous debt. I'm sure he didn't offer me Columbia Records because he believed I had some special musical talent. Hell, *I* didn't realize I had any special musical talent back then. I looked up to him and, in ways

I didn't understand at the time, he was close to a model for what I would go on to do. And, before I saw it myself, he sensed a unique ability in me, and for that I'm deeply grateful.

For all that, my new title of administrative vice president would lead to some problems. I was all of thirty-three years old, and, given the scale of the opportunity I was being offered, I certainly wasn't going to make an issue of my title. But it did clearly suggest that the job was administrative, rather than creative, and it contributed to an impression that Goddard wanted to hold on to the real power himself—at least until I had demonstrated what I might be able to do with my position. At the start he was most likely hoping that my business and legal acumen would enable me to keep the political struggles at Columbia under control while he defined his own new role as group president.

In any event, I wasn't about to make any dramatic moves when I began the new job. I certainly hadn't been given any mandate to do so, and I'm not sure what I would have done if I had. I wanted to get a clear sense of the state of the company, determine what we were doing well and where we needed to make changes, formulate plans on the basis of what I learned, and then systematically put those plans into practice. I also needed to settle the waters that had been stirred when the label's veteran executives, many of them men with significant reputations, learned that they would now be reporting to a young lawyer with no musical background. A lot of executives feel that they need to kick the applecart over as soon as they take their job, but I think it's essential to take some time and diagnose the situation thoroughly. Even in circumstances that have gone bad, not everything or everyone is a problem. You want to make the right moves, not just make moves for their own sake. So at first my approach was simple: listen, watch, observe.

Columbia was a storied name in the music industry, but the styles of music that had raised the label to that prominence were no longer in ascendance. That much was clear. Consequently, one of the first things I learned was that the company was flirting with serious financial problems. Classical music and Broadway cast albums had been mainstays of Columbia's success, but by the mid-Sixties sales in those categories had begun to stall. Mitch Miller's *Sing Along with Mitch* series, a block-buster success in the Fifties and early Sixties, had completely bottomed out. The weekly NBC television show of that name, which Miller had hosted beginning in 1961, got canceled in 1964, and Miller left Columbia in 1965.

His departure was timely. Goddard had first met Miller when they were both at the Eastman School of Music, and he brought him in to head Columbia's A&R department in 1950. Miller had an excellent run in that slot, and such artists as Tony Bennett, Ray Conniff, Percy Faith, and Johnny Mathis came to the label under his aegis, and all of them sold well. He produced hits for Doris Day and Rosemary Clooney, each in her own way a definitive female voice of the Fifties. It was a commercial golden age for pop music, and Miller took that gold straight to the bank.

Miller's taste for mainstream pop music, however, blinded him to the appeal of rock 'n' roll, and, with the notable exception of Johnny Cash, Columbia was entirely out of the running as the first generation of rockers made their mark in the Fifties. More problematically, Miller became an outspoken voice in opposition to rock 'n' roll. He famously described it as "musical baby food" characterized by "the worship of mediocrity." He declared that "much of the juvenile stuff pumped over the air waves these days hardly qualifies as music." As a result, Columbia came to be perceived as not merely indifferent but hostile to the music that was increasingly defining young America. Nobody at Columbia was looking at what the label didn't have, because the party line was that it was not significant and it was not going to have a long life.

Miller's views were hardly isolated opinions in 1958, and as long as pop music, Broadway show tunes, and classical music were rivaling or exceeding rock 'n' roll in sales, they didn't even make a meaningful business problem. It's the rare record company that generates hits in every style of music. More often you're performing well in some areas, lagging a bit in others. It's a continual process of evaluation and adjustment, and as long as your strengths consistently outweigh your weaknesses in sufficient measure, you can ride through the inevitable shifts in the public's tastes.

By 1965, however, the situation had become something of a crisis.

Despite its stellar reputation, Columbia's pretax profits were about $3 million dollars, roughly 3 percent of sales. That's pretty precarious, and didn't leave the label much room for any bold new moves at a time when it was seeming that some might soon be necessary. In addition, it was becoming undeniable that rock 'n' roll was not going the way of other teenage fads, but was in fact becoming the soundtrack of the age.

The Beatles, who were signed to Capitol Records, had arrived in the United States in 1964, and their impact had been cataclysmic. Not only had their music dominated the charts, but they were influencing every aspect of culture, from books to film to fashion. For the first time, even adults were beginning to take their style cues from this youthquake. Men began wearing their hair a little longer, women began wearing their skirts a little shorter, and Beatle boots and collarless jackets became trendy. A wave of English bands, most notably the Rolling Stones, followed the Beatles to this country, and suddenly America's unquestioned preeminence in popular music was no longer a foregone conclusion. Everything was changing, and lines were being drawn.

Where was Columbia Records in this rock revolution? Not entirely absent, but nowhere near where it should have been, either in terms of sales or significance. The most important exception in that second category, of course, was Bob Dylan, who in a few short years had become the most influential songwriter in the world. His sales had not risen to the level of his stature—they still haven't for that matter—but he nonetheless was a prize that any label would envy. In addition, Columbia had also signed the Byrds, whose electric cover of Dylan's "Mr. Tambourine Man" had just risen to number one, a fateful moment in the burgeoning history of folk-rock.

Simon and Garfunkel were also on Columbia. After their first album, *Wednesday Morning, 3 AM,* had not made much of an impact when it was released in 1964, the duo split up. To everyone's surprise, however, a track from that album, "The Sound of Silence," began to garner radio play, and inspired by the success of the Byrds, the Columbia producer Tom Wilson then overdubbed the song with electric instruments and drums. It became a massive hit, and Simon and Garfunkel, of course, went on to take their deserved place among America's foremost musical artists.

Interestingly, though, Columbia's best-selling rock act during this period was Paul Revere and the Raiders, whose outlandish Revolutionary War garb came to symbolize America's resistance to the British Invasion that the Beatles had unleashed, even though the Raiders had formed before the Beatles landed on our shores. They were mainstays on an afternoon music show produced by Dick Clark called *Where the Action Is,* and their raw, instantly accessible garage rock found a ready home on AM radio.

Epic, Columbia's sister label, was also part of my brief and boasted the Dave Clark Five, who came to the States right on the heels of the Beatles, and scored a run of Top 10 hits in 1964 and 1965 that would eventually earn them election to the Rock and Roll Hall of Fame. Another Hall of Fame group, the Yardbirds, a hard-hitting English blues band that featured on guitar Eric Clapton, then Jeff Beck and Jimmy Page, were also on Epic.

So that's what Columbia had going for it, but we needed much more. And we needed more not simply for aesthetic reasons. Nobody outside the company, and very few people within it, really knew what kind of financial shape Columbia was in. When a company's pretax profit is marginal, you keep it quiet. It's true for all industries, but the music business, in particular, is a business of talking hits, not precarious P&Ls. It is a business of creating the illusion of records bulleting up the charts, not enumerating the problems inherent in the company that have to be fixed, and fast.

So after a while I knew what the problems were, but I didn't yet know how to fix them. It's not as if I had taken the job because I was chomping at the bit to make Columbia Records over. I just knew that change had to take place at some point. I wanted to keep the best of what existed, but to be able to be much more competitive in areas that looked more vital for the future. We were very thin in the music of tomorrow.

It was an important lesson. When the music scene changes, you can't be content with just doing more of what you've been doing all along, however good you may be at it. You can't just relive your former glory. That's the hardest thing for executives, even very creative executives, to understand. For that matter, it's the hardest thing for artists to understand. You've got to know when you've got to build for the future. You can't just look in the mirror and see the embodiment of all the chart success and positive reviews you've gotten. You have to see yourself and the market as objectively as possible, as hard as that can be in a field as subjective as music. It's essential for a long, productive career.

It's become a cliché to say that change is good, but it is. However, it's also incredibly difficult and typically requires very hard work. It was during this early period that I began my lifelong habit of bringing home and listening to all the major records on the charts every week, just to develop a clear sense of what's going on. I do that to this day. You can never take your understanding of the market for granted. The market changes, and you need to absorb and comprehend the nature of those changes. You don't necessarily need to conform to them. If you believe in something strongly enough, you can defy them. But you can't act in ignorance of them. To break the rules creatively you have to know what the rules are. Your own taste is not the issue. At every moment you have to ask yourself, Is music changing? Is radio changing? Is the change coming, or is it here already? What was a hit five years ago might no longer be a hit today. Music is always evolving, and it's essential to understand how and when it does, and what you need to do about it.

Making A&R Moves

Before I could even begin asking those questions, however, I needed to solidify my position, which was the second most powerful spot at the company, with Goddard at the top. Goddard's extensive reorganizing had been enacted in accordance with the recommendations of a Harvard Business School study of Columbia that the company had commissioned. In a move that really surprised me, given that he had always regarded A&R as sacrosanct, the creative heart of the company, Goddard had given direct control of A&R at Columbia and Epic to two men who had previously been running their marketing departments: Bill Gallagher at Columbia and Len Levy at Epic. Neither man was especially equipped to handle A&R, though they were both determined to do so. And neither was particularly happy that they would now be reporting to me. Gallagher angrily went to Goddard with his complaints, but stopped short of issuing an ultimatum. Goddard, in turn, tried to placate him, but held firm in support of me.

Then there were the A&R men themselves. Like creative people in all businesses, A&R executives in the music industry understand that there is a reporting structure at their company, but in their own minds they regard it as a mere technicality. For the most part, they try to function as if they have to answer only to themselves. If they're good, they soon develop their own reputations for having the magic touch, for having ears, for making hits. Inside the company smart bosses give them as much leeway as possible in order to get the best out of them. Outside the company they're often treated like stars themselves. They get close to the artists they work with, come to identify with them, and often begin to regard the artists' perquisites as their own. For those reasons, as well as the veneer of glamour they offer, people vie aggressively for those jobs, whether they're qualified for them or not. That was certainly the case with Gallagher and Levy.

Columbia had its share of powerhouse A&R talents, none of whom were wild about their department being merged with marketing. Beyond that, having a lawyer with no music experience in charge of the company, as opposed to the exalted Goddard Lieberson, was a real blow. Musical tastes may have been changing, but that took nothing away from the work those men had done, and they were fiercely proud of it.

The A&R lineup at Columbia was truly a murderers' row. At the top, of course, was John Hammond, who had brought Billie Holiday, Bob Dylan, and Aretha Franklin to the label. Teo Macero, a jazz innovator in his own right as a musician and composer, had produced classic albums by Miles Davis and had brought Charles Mingus, Thelonious Monk, and Charlie Byrd to Columbia. Bob Mersey had enjoyed great success with Andy Williams, one of Columbia's biggest-selling artists. Ernie Altschuler had worked with Tony Bennett, Jerry Vale, and Ray Conniff. And, while still in his twenties, Mike Berniker had in a one-year span produced Barbra Streisand's first three albums, one of which, *The Barbra Streisand Album,* won the Grammy for Album of the Year. Clearly, regardless of new musical trends or Harvard Business School studies, these were not people who were used to being told what to do.

Len Levy at Epic was really not a problem. He was talented, hardworking, and cooperative, and, perhaps because it had less of a history to live up to, Epic seemed more willing to take risks and try new things than Columbia. Eventually, though, with so much at stake, I explained to Levy that I thought marketing was unquestionably his real strength. To run A&R at Epic I appointed Dave Kapralik, who used to work at Columbia (where, among other credits, he had made a spoken-word album called *I Am the Greatest* with Cassius Clay, soon to be Muhammad Ali). Kapralik had just discovered a band in San Francisco called Sly and the Family Stone that he was very excited about, an enthusiasm I shared. Levy left to become the president of Metromedia Records.

Gallagher was a different story. Running sales at Columbia was an extremely important and influential job, and Gallagher had used it to build a loyal following not only within the label but throughout the company's wholly owned, nationwide branch distribution system. He was a bright, street-smart, charismatic executive who had earned a substantial reputation in the industry. He was a power player, and he knew how to parcel out favors and motivate people—people, that is, in sales and marketing. Around Columbia he was known as "The Pope," and he was certainly capable of Vatican-scale intrigue as far as office politics were concerned. He also was earning a higher salary than I was—$45,000 to my $40,000—which encouraged his thinking that I was performing an administrative function for Goddard, not stepping into a true leadership spot.

Gallagher was probably the industry's best head of sales. What he lacked, however, was the creative gift that makes for a great head of A&R, as well as the ability to recognize and accept his own true talents and limitations, a must for real long-term success. It's one thing to push yourself out of your comfort zone, quite another to let ambition take over and drive you to become someone you're not. In a dead giveaway of the superficiality of his notions about the job, he began turning up at A&R meetings wearing neither a tie nor a jacket—this, from a man who had never previously been seen not wearing a suit. The eye-rolling in the room was practically audible. For my part, I continued dressing as I always had, and devoted my time to learning as much as I could.

Meanwhile, members of Gallagher's A&R staff were coming to me complaining about having to report to a salesperson, even as he was complaining to Goddard about having to report to a lawyer. To turn the screw one more tightening notch, Goddard was concerned, given his storied history, with maintaining his own A&R prerogatives. When Goddard spoke to me, he would say, "Now look, I'm giving Gallagher a shot at A and R, but he's reporting to you. In effect, everyone is re- porting to you." When he spoke to Gallagher, he would downplay my authority in order to avoid a direct confrontation. It was a delicate situ- ation, to say the least.

I laid back for a while as the office rumor mill churned, but finally I had no choice but to face the issue head-on. I met with Gallagher and told him that I wanted him to hire a head of A&R who would report to him, but who would inject fresh energy into the label. Predictably,

Gallagher wanted to keep that title—and its attendant prestige and power—for himself. Presiding over it simply wasn't enough. He tried at first to convince me that such a hire wasn't necessary. When I didn't budge, he dragged his feet.

His first recommendation for the job was one of his loyalists from sales, which I flatly rejected. Nine months had now gone by. I told him I would give him three more months to find somebody acceptable, a first-rate talent. He then asked if he could keep A&R and instead hire a head of marketing to take over that portion of his duties. He made that hire, but I made it clear that I still wanted a new head of A&R.

As all this wrangling was going on, Goddard changed my title to vice president and general manager, which brought no new responsibilities (or money) but at least got rid of the word *administrative* and finally made it clearer that I was running the show. On the A&R front, rebellion among the staff continued, and I finally told Gallagher that he had to hire a major figure to run the department or, very reluctantly, I would have to let him go. Finally, in the fall of 1967, he announced that he had received an offer from MCA to head their Decca and Kapp labels and he was going to accept it. I breathed a tremendous sigh of relief.

As I began to develop a firmer grasp of the situation at Columbia, I started to make some creative moves myself. Listening to Top 40 radio more consistently, primarily WABC and WMCA in New York, AM stations that were dominant forces in the market, had further convinced me that Columbia and Epic needed to get more in tune with the changes taking shape in music. (FM stations had not yet begun to make their decisive impact, though they would soon.)

My first signing, in 1966, was the Scottish folksinger Donovan. He wasn't especially well known in America, but I can't claim to have discovered him. He already had a Top 40 hit in the States with a beautiful ballad called "Catch the Wind," and in Britain he was being touted, however controversially, as a rival to Bob Dylan. He was signed to Pye Records there, and a small label called Hickory handled his distribution in this country. His contract was coming up, and I believed he had great potential, both artistically and commercially. Furthermore, he seemed exactly the sort of contemporary signing we needed to make. I asked John Hammond to approach Donovan and his manager, Ashley Kozak, at the Newport Folk Festival, and they were interested.

It might seem counterintuitive that we would be pursuing Donovan since we already had Dylan, but I've never liked to think that way. Complete originality only goes so far, and is rarer than people think. It's even rarer that it has commercial potential. Every artist, however groundbreaking, is similar to some other artist. One of the jobs of a record company is to identify the unique qualities in each of their artists, encourage those aspects in the music they make, and market them on that basis. And there were plenty of original qualities about Donovan. I thought the Dylan comparisons were unfair and superficial, based largely on a cap and a harmonica rack, Dylan touches that Donovan had affected. By 1966 every folk artist could be seen as influenced by Dylan, but Donovan was sweeter and more melodic, more drawn to the mystical elements in the Anglo-Celtic folk tradition. If he wasn't the revolutionary talent that Dylan was, he was more accessible and uplifting. I believed that he could have an important career.

When I met Donovan in New York, he seemed much like his music—gentle, smart, and engaging. He was filled with enthusiasm and ideas—about how the artwork for his albums should be handled, about creating music for children, about getting involved with theatrical projects. All of that was fine with me. I had always loved musicals, and told him about Columbia's long history with the theater. The label had also just added a line of children's books and records.

He then mentioned an interest in working with the English producer Mickie Most, who had created hits with the Animals and Herman's Hermits. Columbia had just arranged a production deal with him, so that was fortuitous as well. I felt that a producer like Most could play an important role in bringing Donovan's music to a larger audience, which turned out to be true. We ended up signing Donovan to Epic Records for $100,000 up front, with a guarantee of $20,000 a year for the next five years. Going with Epic rather than Columbia, which was Dylan's label, was our one concession to the Dylan issue. Putting that bit of distance between them seemed to make sense.

It wasn't an overly expensive deal, and Donovan quickly began to generate hits that made it look like a bargain. "Sunshine Superman" went to number one in the summer of 1966, and "Mellow Yellow" rose to number two that fall. "There Is a Mountain," "Hurdy Gurdy Man," and "Atlantis" all cracked the Top 20 in the next few years. Moreover, the albums *Sunshine Superman* and *Mellow Yellow* were both commercially successful and hugely influential. To this day, many young singer-songwriters reference Donovan's albums from this period as an inspiration.

In asking for control of the artwork for his albums, Donovan displayed an intuitive understanding of where his interests might take him. In the spring of 1967 the Beatles' *Sgt. Pepper's Lonely Hearts Club Band* made indelibly clear how far the possibilities of album art could extend, and Donovan proved similarly ambitious. For what would become his double album, *A Gift from a Flower to a Garden,* he conceived of an elaborate, colorful box set, with lyric sheets and lithographs enclosed. I initially demurred. Donovan's conception was characteristically beautiful, but would be prohibitively expensive. However, Sydney Maurer, one of Epic's designers, helped convince me that we could create the set without undue financial damage, so I went along with it. To his credit, Donovan agreed to assume some of the costs, and he also acceded to my request that we release each of the albums (titled *Wear Your Love Like Heaven* and *For Little Ones*) separately as well as combining them in the box. *A Gift from a Flower to a Garden,* as the box set was titled, ended up earning a gold record for sales, and is now a collector's item.

Around this time I also began looking for other ways to improve Columbia's bottom line. As albums, rather than singles, began to be the dominant format in the marketplace, it occurred to me that they were incredibly underpriced at about $3.79 retail. When albums consisted mostly of an artist's latest hit single and whatever additional songs—or "filler"—could be quickly pulled together, such pricing might have been justified. But now, because of Bob Dylan, the Beatles, and other visionary rock performers, artists and their audiences expected albums to be statements, to be events. Albums had become important, more desirable and more expensive to produce. Pricing had to reflect that new reality.

I knew that record retailers would require some convincing of the wisdom of this new approach, so I chose the NARM (National Association of Record Merchandisers) convention in March 1967 to make my case. In a speech at that meeting, I introduced the concept of "variable pricing," and put it into effect three months later with greatest hits packages by Bob Dylan and Paul Revere and the Raiders. I charged $5.98 for these sets, and included posters (the Dylan one, designed by Milton Glaser, is now a classic image) to sweeten the deal. Each album sold extremely well, and variable pricing was established as an industry standard.

There was another area where I felt the industry could make a necessary change. At the time, almost all albums were being produced in both monaural, or mono, and stereo versions, which was both expensive and wasteful. On the most basic level, two types of albums had to be created, two types of sales had to be tracked, and two types of albums had to be stored in warehouses. Once again, as listeners grew more serious and turned toward albums as their preferred listening experience, they also expected higher production values. As a result, mono was dying out. Psychedelia had made sonic effects more common on records, and consumers increasingly were purchasing stereo albums, which typically cost about a dollar more than the mono version.

I decided to price both mono and stereo albums at the higher level, thinking that this would eventually lead to the elimination of monaural recordings. I realize that some people continue to debate the relative merits of stereo and monaural sound, but this was a business decision and an extremely effective one. This time, the record retailers were immediately on my side. Displaying, storing, and tracking the sales of two versions of the same album were just as problematic for them as for the record companies. The industry again fell in line, profit margins grew, and monaural records were a thing of the past.

My personal life was undergoing positive new changes as well. In 1966, I married Janet Adelberg, whom I had met while my former wife, Helen, was on her travels through Europe and Israel. We met at a party in East Hampton. She was five feet seven, with dark hair and deep-set eyes that I found very striking. Janet was twenty-eight, and quite beautiful, a microbiologist who was also a graduate of the Metropolitan Opera Studio. I was impressed and really very surprised that she was still single. She, too, loved the theater and very patiently helped introduce me to the world of classical music and opera. Here I was, a divorced father with two young children, ages six and four, and I really felt very lucky. My children Fred and Lauren were living with me during our courtship, so it was a convenient time for them to come to know Janet a bit and for her to begin to feel comfortable with them. It was highly unorthodox for a father to have physical custody of his children in those days (as, for the most part, it continues to be), and, to be honest, as a bachelor I couldn't help but feel a little handicapped by it, as if it might somehow be seen as a drawback. It was just so unusual. But Janet and the children took to one another very well, which only made me feel closer to her.

Janet was from Baltimore, and we got married there. We regularly went there to visit her parents and her sister and brother. Her father, her brother, and her brother-in-law were all lawyers, so we had that in common. Both her brother and sister were married, and I liked it that Fred and Lauren would have cousins to play with and get to know. It felt good to be part of an extended family again.

When Helen returned from Israel and resumed living in New York, I would have the kids during the week, and she would pick them up on Friday at 5:00 and return them at noon on Sunday. It was the reverse of the stereotypical custody arrangement, and I can't say that it didn't create problems. Because we had the kids during the week, Janet became their de facto mother, caring for them when they were sick, managing their daily lives at school, and all the myriad things that role entails. For her part, Helen deeply loved Fred and Lauren, and took her role in their lives very seriously, despite her need for independence. The emotional dynamics of the situation were fraught at times.

Those problems are no different from the ones that arise after any divorce involving children, really, and Janet and I developed a rich life together. We had plenty of friends with whom we'd socialize on weekends. We went out often, and made the most of our shared love for the theater and music, and of the opportunities that my professional life was increasingly bringing our way. We eventually had two boys of our own, Mitchell and Douglas. It had become apparent early on that we would need a larger space to live in, and while I wasn't wealthy by any means, I was in a financial position to make that possible.

Around the time we got married, I found a wonderful apartment for us at a real bargain rate. It was a five-bedroom co-op at 88 Central Park West, near Sixty-ninth Street, which, because it was in disrepair, I was able to purchase for $55,000. It was spacious, and offered a number of terrific features. The elevator opened directly into the apartment, which had a large vestibule and dining room, and a huge living room overlooking the park, which became the site of many wonderful parties. The building is a classic New York address, and over the years many well-known figures in the world of arts and entertainment would take apartments there. I spent an additional $10,000 to fix the place up, and it was in tip-top shape when we moved in, an ideal home for the next phase of my life.

Success breeds confidence, so as my decisions produced recognition and results, I felt capable of making additional moves. One particularly fateful one was a label deal I set up with Ode Records, which was owned and run by Lou Adler, who had made his mark as the head of Dunhill Records and the brilliant producer of the Mamas and the Papas, Johnny Rivers, and Jan and Dean. Adler had sold Dunhill to ABC for several million dollars, and Ode was his new project. His lawyer, Abe Somer, and I had done business together many times and were very good friends. (Among other acts, Abe represented the English folk-pop duo Chad & Jeremy, who were signed to Columbia.) When Abe suggested that Lou and I might make a deal for Ode, I was immediately interested. And once I met Lou, I was in.

Adler was one of the most successful producers in the history of the music business. He was very stylish and understated in that L.A. way. He was married to, but separated from, the actress and singer Shelley Fabares, who had the number-one hit "Johnny Angel" in 1962. When I was around him he most often was with the actress Peggy Lipton of

The Mod Squad, one of the hip TV shows of the time. Like the deal I set up with Mickie Most, the arrangement with Ode was a way to modernize Columbia's music profile as I continued to work on sorting out the issues with the label's own A&R department.

I learned a great deal working with Lou. He combined creativity and business acumen in ways that were both natural and effective, and he knew how to work with artists. He could discover great talent, produce records with them, and market them successfully. He paid attention to every detail, making sure that every aspect of an artist's presentation—from the single to the album cover to the advertising— was entirely in tune. I had great hopes for our partnership.

The first song Lou brought to Columbia as part of our deal was Scott McKenzie's "San Francisco (Be Sure to Wear Flowers in Your Hair)." It was, in many ways, a perfect Lou Adler production. As part of the massive social changes taking place at the time, young people, many of them runaways, were flocking to the Haight-Ashbury district of San Francisco in search of a new, more communal society. It was, in some sense, a political movement, a rejection of the mainstream American values of success and competition in favor of peace and love. It seemed new and hopeful, but, particularly if you considered the role that psychedelic drugs were playing in it, it had an edge.

"San Francisco," which was written by John Phillips of the Mamas and the Papas, smoothed that edge, putting a soft, idealistic focus on the phenomenon. The earnest vocal by Scott McKenzie (born Philip Blondheim) brought that emotion home, and his lush, wavy hair and eyes perennially gazing into the distance didn't hurt, either. The song captured a cultural moment in a way that was made for AM radio, and it became a Top 5 hit. Our deal seemed off to a roaring start.

In another perfect Lou Adler touch, "San Francisco" wasn't simply a sensational song written for the first artist to record for his new label. It was a three-minute advertisement for a current venture of his. Both Adler and Phillips were among the producers of the Monterey International Pop Festival, which was set to take place in California on June 16–18, 1967. Monterey was the site of established jazz and folk festivals, and Adler and Phillips believed that, with all the new developments taking place, pop music deserved the same sort of showcase. The

Mamas and the Papas would be performing, along with, needless to say, Scott McKenzie. "San Francisco," then, was not only a great song but a brilliant marketing and promotion move.

Adler and Abe Somer encouraged me to come out West for the festival. I thought about it, and it made some sense. Columbia acts like Simon and Garfunkel and the Byrds were on the bill, and if nothing else, it would be a beautiful weekend in California with plenty of great music. So I decided to go.

I would never be the same again.

Monterey Pop

So here's what I wore to the revolution: a V-neck tennis sweater in the traditional white, maroon, and black, over white pants. In a reverse-hip sense, that outfit likely made me the most far-out person on the fairgrounds of the Monterey Pop Festival, since everyone else, both men and women, was wearing flowing robes, head scarves, beads, capes, bells, face paint, long hair, no shoes, and, in a few notable instances, absolutely nothing. Visiting musicians like Brian Jones of the Rolling Stones strolled amiably among the crowd, as did many of the performers when they weren't onstage. If Scott McKenzie's "San Francisco (Be Sure to Wear Flowers in Your Hair)" was, in part, a promotion piece for the festival, it provided a pure example of truth in advertising. Flowers, beauty, and innocent, angelic expressions were everywhere.

As my fashion statement would suggest, I was totally unprepared for what was happening in Haight-Ashbury, which seemed to have transported itself in toto to Monterey for the weekend as easily as I had flown in from New York. In that regard and so many others, Monterey proved to be an eye-opener that was stunning in its impact. It's funny, as sophisticated as New York is, you can also lead a pretty sheltered life there, particularly if you grew up the way I did. Going to Monterey was an incredibly broadening, maturing experience. If I'd had a hunch that music and culture were changing, here was vivid, colorful, undeniable proof. I had gone to the festival with my wife, Janet, figuring that we would spend some time with Lou Adler and Abe Somer, hear some music, enjoy California, and head home refreshed. I wasn't the slightest bit aware that this was the moment that would change my life forever.

That may sound melodramatic, but let me explain what I mean. Until Monterey, I was essentially an anonymous person attempting to find his way professionally. I had set out to be a lawyer, moved into the music industry, and struggled to establish myself. I'd had some luck and enjoyed a few nice wins. I was beginning to become known both within the CBS corporate structure and the larger music business.

But I was also thirty-five years old, and had not yet made my mark. I certainly hadn't become a public figure to any degree. To this point I didn't realize at all that I possessed skills that might ultimately distinguish me: the ability to recognize and nurture new artists; to help those artists create their best work; to bring that work to the marketplace and have it make a powerful impact. If you're lucky, there are moments in your life when you step into the outline of the person you might always have wanted to become, perhaps without even knowing it. You then feel truly comfortable for the first time. That process began for me at Monterey.

The event had all the more effect on me because I was simply there as a spectator, and I didn't really know what I was doing or what to expect. There was no coterie of Columbia people accompanying me, and while I later learned that Jerry Wexler from Atlantic was on the scene with Otis Redding, I didn't see him or any other record company executives. I thought that the performances would take place at night, but in fact bands were playing all day long. And, as it turned out, the daytime performances were where the action was. High-quality though they were, the headliners who performed in the evening—Simon and Garfunkel, the Mamas and the Papas, the Animals, Otis Redding— were all established acts whom everyone already knew were great. The epiphanies—certainly my epiphanies—occurred in the daytime, when the new acts took the stage, and I was in the audience simply because there was nowhere else to go.

One group that made a powerful impression on me was the Electric Flag, which featured the guitarist Mike Bloomfield and the drummer Buddy Miles. Bloomfield had actually been signed to Columbia a few years earlier by John Hammond, and did a few sessions for the label in 1964 that never went anywhere. He earned a sterling reputation as the lead guitarist with the Paul Butterfield Blues Band, and for his playing behind Bob Dylan, both during the sessions for *Highway 61 Revisited,* including on the number-two single "Like a Rolling Stone," and during Dylan's historic performance at the 1965 Newport Folk Festival. He was a musician that everyone in the know was watching, and the Electric Flag, a tough, hard-hitting blues band powered by a torrid horn section, was his latest move. Miles was an intense, highly respected R&B drummer who had played with Wilson Pickett. The Electric Flag hit with gale force, and I determined to sign them that day.

But my most startling and decisive revelation occurred on the afternoon of Saturday, June 17, when the second band of the day, Big Brother and the Holding Company, took the stage. They were a San Francisco group and did not have a record out yet. In the rigorously democratic spirit of that time and place, the band's singer, the electrifying Janis Joplin, received no special introduction or billing. But as everyone now realizes, she was unquestionably the star of the band, and her performance was incendiary.

Janis was not conventionally beautiful, but her face, framed by her long, unruly hair, had an elastic quality that made it exactly expressive of the raw emotions her singing conveyed with such fury. Her body seemed to vibrate with the modulations of her voice, which struck with equal impact whether she was wailing at the top of her lungs or delivering an intimate whisper. In the afternoon sun, she radiated a desperate sexual heat. Like all the other daytime acts, Big Brother played a short set, five songs, and were onstage for perhaps thirty minutes. But they took the crowd on an emotional journey that made it seem as if they had performed for hours.

Big Brother played a kind of blues-based acid rock. They were noisy and undisciplined, not virtuosos like Bloomfield by any means, but they seemed very much in tune with Janis. She, of course, was hypnotic. Mesmerizing. She had a voice like no other—raspy, pleading, dominating, aggressive, vulnerable, the most expressive white female soul singer anybody could ever have seen. She exerted full command of the stage, with a power that just took your breath away. Big Brother's closing number, a cataclysmic version of Big Mama Thornton's "Ball and Chain," is now regarded not merely as one of Janis's greatest moments onstage, but as one of the classic performances in rock history. It was simply overwhelming.

Happily, the essence of the band's jaw-dropping performance is captured in D. A. Pennebaker's landmark documentary *Monterey Pop*. Because Big Brother's manager at the time had refused to allow the group to be filmed on Saturday, they were offered a second spot on the bill on Sunday, the closing day of the festival, to ensure that they would be in Pennebaker's movie. They agreed, and, once again, brought the house down. In reaction to the Saturday performance, you can see Cass Elliot of the Mamas and the Papas, no slouch as a singer herself, shake her head and simply say, "Wow," after Janis brought "Ball and Chain" to an orgasmic close. Really, nothing more needed to be said.

Janis's performance somehow brought the entire meaning of the festival itself home to me. The impact of seeing an artist that raw, earthy, and fiery just floored me. This is a social and musical revolution, I thought, how could it be that none of us in the East knew that this was taking place? It was literally spine-tingling, and along with the larger insights that came to me about what was going on in the culture, I experienced a personal epiphany as well. This has got to be my moment, I thought. I've got to sign this band.

That was a defining realization. Although I had begun to make some creative decisions at Columbia, I had no idea that I would really be in the business of signing artists. I was still very conscious of my lack of a musical background. But opportunity conspired with necessity for me at Monterey. Yes, seeing Janis Joplin perform provided one of the greatest musical experiences of my life. But that occurred within the context of my continual, unspoken awareness that I was running a company that was virtually on the brink. Notwithstanding the grandeur of its past, Columbia was barely breaking even. I had to do something soon, or all my promotions and important titles would amount to nothing. I'd been relatively cautious for more than a year, but now I had to take some risks and put myself on the line. Time was of the essence.

Landing the Electric Flag was easy enough, even though Atlantic's Jerry Wexler was also interested in signing them. Albert Grossman managed the band, and he and I had a good relationship because he also managed Bob Dylan, who had recently re-signed with Columbia. I spoke with Grossman after the festival, and he initially proposed that, along with the Electric Flag, Columbia sign two other San Francisco groups that had played at Monterey, the Steve Miller Band and Quicksilver Messenger Service, for $100,000 total. That sounded good to me, but Grossman ultimately couldn't get managerial rights to Miller or Quicksilver, so I signed the Electric Flag for $50,000, which was quite a bit of money in those days. It was a risk, but it felt necessary.

The situation with Big Brother and the Holding Company was much more complicated. Not long after their performance, I found their manager, Julius Karpen, backstage and told him how the band had blown me away and how much I wanted them for Columbia. He suggested that I get in touch with the group's attorney, Bob Gordon, which I did after returning to New York. To my dismay, Gordon informed me that Big Brother had signed a deal in 1966 with Mainstream Records, whose owner, Bob Shad, had produced some demo sessions with the band over a three-day period in Chicago.

Shad was primarily a jazz producer and the band was unhappy with the results. Encouraged by the response to the band at Monterey and the subsequent media attention, however, Mainstream was determined to release the material as an album. Shad refused to allow the band any more studio time to improve the very rough recordings that had been done, and, on that basis, Gordon believed the band might have grounds to get out of their contract and then be free to sign with Columbia. Whether or not that was true, I thought it might be possible for the band to buy its way out of the Mainstream contract, with my help, so I continued to negotiate with Karpen and Gordon.

To give them a sense of what Columbia was about, I invited the two men to the label's annual meeting in Miami. They stayed for three days, and were impressed by the direction we were moving in. I made them an offer of $25,000 to sign with us, and $50,000 upon delivery of the first album. It was generous—a new band in those days would more typically get just $5,000 or $10,000 to sign, and perhaps $25,000 for the first album. But I wanted to demonstrate how important it was for me to sign the band to Columbia, and I also wanted to provide a financial cushion in case they needed to buy their way out of the

Mainstream deal. In the meantime, Mainstream impatiently released its demo recordings as an album, titled simply *Big Brother & the Holding Company*. It heated up interest in Janis and the band, but was regarded as very poorly produced and vastly inferior to what they were capable of. It made negotiations tougher, which Shad meant it to do, of course. But it didn't detract, in my view, from the definitive statement that their first album for Columbia could be.

Other labels began getting interested in Big Brother, and Mainstream refused an offer from Columbia of around $30,000 to cut the band loose. Finally, Albert Grossman came into the picture as Big Brother's manager after the group had a falling-out with Julius Karpen. In fact, Gordon had called me about Grossman, and I had recommended him highly. Grossman taking on the band was good news for me, since he and I got along well. But he was a famously tough negotiator, and the deal for Big Brother quickly got even more expensive.

Here's what happened. Likely because he knew I was waiting in the wings, Grossman arranged to buy Big Brother out of its contract with Mainstream for $200,000, which Columbia was expected to provide. Half of that would be recoupable against the band's future royalties; the other half would simply amount to the label's investment in what it hoped would be the band's lucrative future. Columbia would also advance the band $50,000 to record its first album for the label, money that, again, would be recouped if the album sold well enough. Mainstream also got a 2 percent override on the band's first two Columbia albums. Columbia, then, was putting up a quarter of a million dollars—a fortune back then—with 40 percent of that money a straight expense. I clearly knew this was an aggressive move, and possibly unprecedented in the talent marketplace, but on that rare occasion when you're dealing with an extraordinary—if not historic—artist, then you have to be bold.

Nearly a year after I first saw Big Brother and the Holding Company at the Monterey Pop Festival, the deal was finally done. It was easily one of the best investments I ever made.

Interestingly, however, I still had not met Janis. Then one day I got a call in my office from Grossman. The contracts were being prepared, and he said Janis and the band were in the CBS building, visiting the art department on the tenth floor, the floor below me. He asked if I wanted to meet them. I thought he might be checking with me on the etiquette of such a meeting: Should he bring the band up to my office, or would I come down?

The CBS building was an imposing skyscraper in midtown Manhattan that was routinely referred to as Black Rock. It would be hard to imagine a more forbidding structure. Given the changes taking place in society at the time—and as part of the changes I was trying to make at Columbia—the last thing I wanted was for the label to seem overly formal or coldly corporate. Small gestures matter, so I immediately said that I would come down to meet the band on the tenth floor. When dealing with artists or creative people generally, it's wise to make sure that you put them at ease. They tend to be wary of business people, even as they also want to be absolutely sure that you know how to take care of them professionally and don't want to be around them just because it's cool. Keeping boundaries clear while being as warm and friendly as possible always works best for me. I have always been available to artists from 9:30 a.m. to 8:00 p.m. every working day. I rarely do social dinners with artists. But up until the evening meal—usually around 8:30—I always take their calls and I'm ready with the best advice or information my expertise can offer.

As seemed to be true so often back then, my notions about what Grossman, or the band for that matter, had in mind were woefully naïve. "You know what Janis would really prefer to do?" Grossman asked. "She's talked about meeting you, and she thinks it only fitting and proper that she ball you to cement the deal. That would be her way of showing this is a more meaningful relationship—not in lieu of signing, but in addition, a way to make the signing different from what it normally would be in the business world."

Talk about boundaries! You don't learn how to deal with a proposition like that in school. I smiled to myself, and declined the offer as politely as I could, but assured Grossman I'd come to meet the band as soon as I could get free. Later that afternoon I went looking for the group and found them in a conference room. We all said hello and shook hands, and then started to chat. It was awkward at first. Unlike now, assumptions about business were largely negative in the Sixties, at least among the subculture that Janis and the band not only represented, but epitomized. There I was in my suit in a building that was about as potent a symbol of the Establishment as you could find. And I'd just turned down Janis's offer to have sex with me!

I decided to address the issue as directly as possible. I talked about the new direction at Columbia, how much I believed in the band, and how important they were in my plans. I told them that, whatever our offices might look like, I was determined to make Columbia the most artist-friendly label in the world. I assured them that, while a high level of organization was necessary for us to do the best possible work for our artists, at heart we really were informal people.

I don't know if I convinced them, but they all seemed to appreciate my effort. We ended up talking for about an hour, and it was fun. Then one of the guys said, "Wow, we've got a press meeting at six—we're going to be late!" A band member said that he had to get dressed, and another casually threw some clothes to him across the table. He'd been sitting there without a shirt on during our meeting—not typical, but not exactly shocking back then. When he stood up to put his clothes on, however, I could see that he had been sitting there nude the entire time.

Janis saw how taken aback I was, and laughed. My remarks about how informal Columbia was hung ludicrously in the air. "Well," she said with a twinkle, "this is how informal *we* are!"

Columbia Gets Hot

Not long after Monterey, Goddard appointed me president of Columbia Records, which was deeply gratifying. The title carried with it a salary of $75,000, as well as such perks as a car and chauffeur. I'd made some strides in what I wanted to accomplish with the label, and this promotion not only acknowledged that, but lent important momentum to my efforts. Columbia was definitely on the move—into the future and in virtually every style of music.

The appointment was also a reward for some deft negotiating that enabled Columbia to retain Bob Dylan, whose contract had expired and who had risen to unforeseen heights of influence and stature. After "going electric" and moving beyond the enclosed world of folk music, Dylan had blasted open the possibilities for artistic expression in rock 'n' roll. "Like a Rolling Stone" proved that he could even have hits. The two most recent albums he had made, *Highway 61 Revisited* and *Blonde on Blonde,* are now regarded as among the greatest in rock history. No artist, including the Beatles, was untouched by him. He had achieved a standing that no one in rock 'n' roll had even approached before.

All of that meant that Dylan was no longer the scruffy young man that John Hammond and I could conspire to have sign an agreement with Columbia on the basis of a friendly conversation. He was, quite simply, one of the most important artists in the world, and I believed that it was essential that we keep him on Columbia—for his own value, for the label's prestige, and for the artists whom he would potentially attract to Columbia merely by virtue of his presence there. He was now represented by the ubiquitous Albert Grossman, a manager known for being fiercely protective of his clients and aggressive in his demands on their behalf.

The Dylan negotiations were complicated by the fact that the contracts of Barbra Streisand and Andy Williams had also run out, and it was essential for Columbia to retain them as well. It might seem absurd to think about these very different artists in the same terms, but of the three Dylan was by far the least significant in commercial terms. Streisand was selling close to a million albums with each new release. Williams's sales were even bigger. He was not only one of the best-selling artists in the label's history, but he had a hugely successful network television show that bore his name. This was in the days when television largely consisted of the three major networks. His weekly, prime-time presence in millions of American living rooms provided incalculable promotional value both to him and, by extension, to Columbia.

Balancing the demands of wildly divergent artists is a critical part of running a label. In the surprisingly small world of the entertainment business, artists learn what other artists are being offered—and if they don't, their managers and lawyers certainly do. A sense of being slighted in relation to someone else builds resentments that can make even the simplest negotiations difficult. If Grossman was a tiger, Marty Erlichman, who managed Streisand (and continues to, to this day), and Alan Bernard, who represented Williams, were also as tough as they come.

Back then, an established label like Columbia had a carefully defined set of parameters regarding the kinds of contracts it could offer. There was little flexibility in how you could negotiate with artists whose concerns were as individual as, say, those of Bob Dylan and Andy Williams. The age of superstar artists who could more or less write their own ticket had not yet arrived (though it was right around the corner), so labels weren't used to having to be nimble in their approach to contracts. When you also consider that its scanty profit margin meant that Columbia was not exactly awash in spare cash, you can begin to understand the tight spot I found myself in.

Artists were expected to be prolific back then, and in 1965 Columbia had never paid more than half a million dollars for a five-year, ten-album contract—that was to Doris Day, then "America's Sweetheart." The label's standard royalty rate was 5 percent. Based on the success they had already demonstrated, Williams and Streisand were both ask-ing for more than a million dollars. Williams claimed that he'd gotten this kind of competitive offer from Warner Bros. I ended up getting him to stay by offering him $1.5 million for a five-year deal—a small amount these days, but a number that struck terror in my heart at the time. For that sum, however, Williams agreed to record fifteen albums. Three a year! Three is a decade's output for many artists these days.

I made the same kind of deal with Streisand, but, because she lacked Williams's track record, she agreed to do fifteen albums for a million-dollar guarantee. In the course of our discussions, Erlichman screamed, banged on my desk, stormed out of my office, and avoided my calls for weeks at a time. As I was learning, that was all part of the theater of negotiations, designed to intimidate or pressure me into making concessions. I can't say I was never rattled, and I remained as composed as possible, but I privately vented to and strategized with Walter Dean, who was Columbia's extremely capable head of business affairs. At the end of it, Barbra, Marty, and I were all happy.

With Dylan, however, things got tricky—very tricky. Grossman in-formed me that Dylan, in fact, was on the verge of signing a deal with the Records Division of MGM that guaranteed him a million and a half dollars and a 12 percent royalty rate for five years. Columbia was prepared to offer him a half-million-dollar guarantee and a 5 percent royalty. I pointed out to Grossman that, because of some differences in the way that royalties were computed at other companies, MGM's rate was really going to be something like 10 percent. Of course, that didn't matter much since 10 percent was still twice what Columbia was put-ting on the table. Now I was really nervous.

Goddard Lieberson and Harvey Schein still were not big believers in Dylan. All things being equal, they wanted to keep him on Colum-bia, but if his demands shattered all previous Columbia precedents, that overrode the value of holding on to him in their view. Finally, in a truly strange turn of events, Dylan had retreated to upstate New York in Woodstock, and in July 1966 had gotten into a motorcycle accident. Nobody knew how serious it was. Wild rumors of all kinds flew about it. Some people said the accident had been faked, that it was simply an excuse to give Dylan a much-needed break. Others insisted that Dylan had been injured so badly that he might never sing or play guitar again. For his part, Grossman said nothing at all. He simply made it clear that Dylan had an excellent offer from MGM, and was essentially prepared to sign it.

Negotiations are like poker games. People can bluff about rival offers, and unless you're willing to call their bluff—and potentially lose the deal—you really have no way of checking their veracity. But I could tell that Grossman was not bluffing. He spoke to me in a completely matter-of-fact way, with a minimum of drama. His tone suggested he completely understood that Columbia might not be able to match the MGM offer, and that I, in turn, would have to understand that he would have no choice but to take it for Dylan's best interests.

I, however, was simply unwilling to let Dylan go that easily. I felt that I had to find a way to keep him. I kept coming back to Grossman, sweetening Columbia's offer in whatever ways I could. But I just couldn't turn the situation around, and Dylan finally got to the point of actually signing the MGM deal. Now all that remained was for MGM to put its signature on the contract, and Dylan would be theirs.

Just at this moment, however, MGM's board of directors, which had to approve the deal, got into a proxy fight, and the Dylan contract got swept up into it. MGM was primarily a movie company, and while its Records Division was enthusiastic about bringing Dylan on board, others at the company didn't know much about him and wondered how spending that much money on a pop star could possibly be worth it.

When Allen Klein, the outspoken, controversial manager who was a major stockholder in MGM, came to me to ask my opinion of the deal, I knew I had found my opening. Klein managed the producer Mickie Most, who, in turn, brought him the Animals, Herman's Hermits, and Donovan as clients, and he and I had become friendly after I signed Donovan to Epic. Klein, of course, would go on to manage the Rolling Stones and the Beatles (except for Paul McCartney), and, whatever anyone might think of how he handled the affairs of those bands, he had some of the sharpest instincts in the music industry. I knew that the MGM deal was potentially in trouble if he was seeking my advice when he knew that Columbia had a stake in what happened with Dylan.

So on a Sunday, Janet and I traveled up to Klein's beautiful home in Riverdale, overlooking the Hudson River, and I brought Dylan's sales figures with me. I explained to him, first, that I had personally been negotiating to keep Dylan at Columbia. As for the MGM deal, I said that, while we all knew of Dylan's importance, the label should be aware that Dylan's sales figures were not what they likely believed them to be. I had the numbers with me, and I gave Klein a precise picture of how Dylan had performed commercially. Then I waited to see if our conversation would have any impact on MGM's decision.

It did. In addition to his experience in the music business, Klein had also produced films. As a result, he was in a uniquely powerful position with the MGM board. Both the music and movie factions valued his opinion, and, because he could be a tough, difficult businessman, nobody wanted to offend him. As it happens, Klein went to the board and argued in no uncertain terms that MGM would be making a huge mistake in signing Dylan.

Mort Nasatir, the head of MGM Records, went through the roof when he began getting pressure to drop the Dylan deal, which would have been a major coup for his label. He even threatened to sue Klein and me for conspiring to keep Dylan on Columbia. That was ridiculous, of course. I had no deal with Dylan; he was still free to go wherever he wanted to go. Right or wrong in his recommendation, Klein had no interest in Dylan one way or the other. Beyond that, the figures I had given Klein were true, the sort of information that a label would typically kill to get. And, most important of all, since Dylan had already signed the MGM agreement, all Nasatir had to do was convince his board to let him sign it as well, and nothing that I did or said would matter at all: Dylan would be an MGM artist.

Happily, that was not to be. As the MGM board waged its internal—and interminable—battles, Dylan took offense at the label's foot-dragging, a perfect example of how ignoring an artist's sensitivities can lead to catastrophic problems. Out of the blue, Grossman called and asked to meet with me, and he brought along Dylan's attorney, David Braun. At the meeting they made a counterproposal. Dylan was at a point in his career where he did not want to be locked into having to produce a specified number of albums within a specified period of time. As a result, he would be willing to re-sign with Columbia for five years with no money in advance if we, for our part, would not require him to make a minimum number of albums. In return, he wanted a 10 percent retail royalty. In short, if he wanted to make an album, he would be rewarded with what at the time was a very high royalty rate. If he didn't want to make an album, we had no ability to pressure him to do so. He was buying freedom in exchange for no financial guarantees.

I was ecstatic. Because my old boss Harvey Schein, who now ran Columbia International, had issues with how the deal would affect precedent regarding foreign royalties, it took longer to get the contract approved than it should have. I persisted, though, and it finally worked out. David Braun and I arranged to have lunch in the dining room of the Dorset Hotel to iron out the final details. We chose that location precisely because, although it was near Columbia, it was not a music business hangout, and we could talk and work in privacy. Consequently, we were stunned when the entire executive staff of MGM Records walked into the dining room just as we were starting our dessert. Fortunately, they were seated across the room and did not notice us. We finished our meal and walked out as discreetly as we could. The next day Braun informed MGM that Dylan had rescinded his agreement.

Beyond my joy and relief that this round of the Dylan saga was completed, I felt that I'd learned another valuable lesson about life in the entertainment world. Most artists work hard to stay in the public eye, and that's important. I believe in it. But the way that Dylan and Grossman handled the rumors about Dylan's motorcycle accident was very instructive. They felt no need to explain what was going on with Dylan, who, as it happens, was quietly recording the songs that would become known as *The Basement Tapes*. Even as he was negotiating million-dollar deals, Grossman issued no statement, and Dylan made no public appearances. He was just ninety miles north of New York City, and it was as if he had fallen off the face of the earth.

But he was not forgotten. Far from it. Interest in him just grew and grew. The mystery surrounding him made his every gesture a major event. Dick Asher, who was vice president of business affairs at Columbia, traveled to Woodstock to have Dylan sign the final version of the contract. He had a perfectly pleasant time chatting with him in the refurbished barn where they met. For Dick, who, like me, had been trained as a lawyer and had no background in music, it was a relaxed business meeting in a lovely rural setting, entirely uneventful. Imagine his surprise, then, when he returned to New York and was besieged with questions by everyone he talked to both inside and outside the company. *You met with Dylan?* What did he look like? Is he in good shape? Could he speak? What did he say? What was he wearing? How did he sound? Is he making music? Is he writing songs? No detail was too small; the curiosity was bottomless. And when Dylan released his next album, *John Wesley Harding,* at the end of 1967, the media treated it as if Moses had just delivered the Ten Commandments. It was a quiet, enigmatic record, something of a return to folk music, and it wasn't a huge commercial hit. Nevertheless, it did ascend to number two on the charts, and fans still hold it in high regard. The album didn't really include strong candidates for singles, though we did release two, neither of which charted. Needless to say, Dylan did virtually nothing to support it in terms of interviews and performances. That didn't help sales.

Regardless, I learned that, even in the showbiz world of hype and hustle, sometimes less is more, and the best PR move is to do and say nothing. Let people's imaginations fill the void. All strategies work, if they're applied at the right time and with the right artist. I never forgot that, and would have occasion to apply it in later years.

As all that behind-the-scenes drama was taking place, however, Columbia was having hits and, more important, was earning a reputation as an exciting place for artists to be. As we continued to make hot new signings and the artists who had been on the label produced important work that sold well, the notion that Columbia was inhospitable to contemporary sounds began to fade.

Simon and Garfunkel were a big reason for the positive turn in our fortunes. With their albums *Sounds of Silence* and *Parsley, Sage, Rosemary and Thyme,* they had begun to make some of the most beautiful and evocative music of the era. They were so successful that I was pleased that I had never approached them with my brilliant idea that they should change their name. "Simon and Garfunkel" sounded like a law firm to me, not a folk-rock duo, but it certainly didn't seem to bother their fans. Mores were changing in music, and it was part of my education to realize that, as with Dylan's refusal to engage in standard PR strategies, the very fact that "Garfunkel" was such a nonshowbiz name was part of its appeal. It sounded real and authentic in ways perfectly suited to the honesty and intimacy of their songs.

The Byrds continued to experiment, and, while helping to solidify Columbia's standing in the folk-rock genre that the band had pioneered, they also dramatically moved into the groundbreaking area of country-rock with their 1968 album *Sweetheart of the Rodeo*. Following up on "Mr. Tambourine Man," their single "Turn, Turn, Turn" had also gone to number one, while "Eight Miles High," "So You Want to Be a Rock 'n' Roll Star," and "My Back Pages" all cracked the Top 40.

Even as the emergence of folk-rock suggested that folk music itself was dead, Columbia released an album on the same day as Dylan's *John Wesley Harding* that, like Dylan's record, suggested otherwise. *Songs of Leonard Cohen* did not sell especially well at the time, but it made a significant impact nonetheless. The folksinger Judy Collins had already recorded "Suzanne," "Sisters of Mercy," and "Hey, That's No Way to Say Goodbye" on her own hit albums, and that paved the way for *Songs,* on which they all appeared in Cohen's own versions.

John Hammond brought Cohen to Columbia, and saw promise in him even though the singer was already in his thirties. He had a significant reputation as a poet and novelist, and his songs had reached the audience we were pursuing through Judy Collins's wonderful interpretations. So when Hammond made the case for him, I gave the go-ahead. The album became something of a talisman among the music cognoscenti and, of course, Cohen went on to a distinguished career, almost all of it at Columbia, and is now in the Rock and Roll Hall of Fame.

Not long after the Monterey Pop Festival, I signed Laura Nyro, who had performed there. She was managed by David Geffen, who was just beginning his fabled career and who was passionately loyal to her. Her set at Monterey, unfortunately, had been underwhelming. She attempted a style-conscious, New-York-white-girl R&B in the heart of hippiedom, and it was a poor match. Still, I believed she had something special. Although it didn't sell well, her 1967 debut album on Verve, aptly titled *More Than a New Discovery,* included the songs "Wedding Bell Blues," "And When I Die," and "Stoney End," which demonstrated very impressive songwriting prowess. Each of those songs became big hits for other artists.

When Laura auditioned for me on her home turf in New York, her magic came through loud and clear. She was extremely sensitive about the setting for her audition, and understandably so. Auditions are awkward under the best of circumstances, and the small room on the eleventh floor of Black Rock containing a piano, a television, and little else could hardly have been a less conducive spot for her. Upon entering, she immediately complained about the brightness of the lights, so we shut them off and she played by the glow of the TV screen. She performed songs that would appear on her first Columbia album, *Eli and the Thirteenth Confession,* and the impact of hearing them in that tiny space was overpowering. I decided right then to sign her.

Laura was a brilliant singer and songwriter, but she was not always easy to work with. She immediately won over a relatively small but fervent following and, once again, helped position Columbia as a vibrant, forward-looking label. Certainly, she could be quirky in her requests. She wanted *Eli and the Thirteenth Confession* to smell a certain way, so I arranged for a perfumed lyric folder to be enclosed in it. Her fans loved it.

Other artists had massive hits with Laura's songs, and I always felt that she, too, could make a strong commercial showing. In her whispery voice she would talk to me about wanting to be a star, about how she could be as big as Streisand. I yearned to make that happen. But, while most people who talk that way are prepared to do whatever they need to get to the top, Laura never was willing to compromise. It was as if believing you should be a star conferred on you the prerogatives of stardom. Streisand herself, for example, later recorded three of Laura's songs on her album *Stoney End,* including the title track, and enjoyed one of the biggest hits of her career. She didn't want to do those songs at first, because the music was so different from the kind she had grown up singing, but the brilliant Richard Perry, whom I had brought in to produce the album, and I convinced her that it would be a smart, modernizing move. She was willing to try it, and the result speaks for itself.

That's the sort of thing Laura would never do. Edit a song for a single? Absolutely not. She was extremely uncomfortable with the idea of doing anything for strictly commercial reasons, and left it to Geffen, as talented a manager as the music industry has ever produced, to handle all these issues. For his part, David was so taken with her, one of his first real clients, that if she didn't want to do something, that was the end of it.

As a result, her albums were ripe for providing demos that other artists could listen to and cull for hits. And Three Dog Night, the 5th Dimension, Blood, Sweat & Tears, and Barbra Streisand did indeed have huge hits with her songs. Laura was destined to play for and sell mostly to a devoted cult audience. I always respected her unique talent and her idiosyncrasies. I personally liked her enormously, and eventually accepted the situation for what it was. As far as the public was concerned, Laura's unwillingness to cash in just made her cooler, and for what I was trying to accomplish at Columbia, that was just fine, too.

Not long after I had signed the Electric Flag on the strength of their performance at Monterey, I learned that Al Kooper and Steve Katz of the Blues Project were forming a new group that, like the Flag, also incorporated a horn section. Eddie Mathews, a hard-charging Columbia A&R man, brought me down to hear the band rehearse at the Café Au Go Go on Bleecker Street in Greenwich Village, and I was immediately impressed. If anything, Blood, Sweat & Tears were even more adventurous than the Electric Flag. The group's songs drew on blues, R&B, jazz, folk, and rock, and I knew immediately that I wanted them for Columbia. As with Dylan and Donovan, I was not concerned that we already had one group with a horn section. If a band's music is strong enough, I believed a record company has to be confident that it will find effective ways to bring it to the public. We signed Blood, Sweat & Tears.

In the case of this band, I have to say that I did make known my concerns about the name they chose. As a Churchill admirer, I was well aware that he had popularized the phrase "blood, toil, tears, and sweat" in a dramatic 1940 speech, and I wondered about the appropriateness of using this variation on it for the name of a rock group. As typically happens in such cases, I was overruled by the band, and was resigned to let them call themselves what they wanted. I had better luck in that regard with the third horn group I signed, Chicago. The band released its first album, a two-record set, under the name Chicago Transit Authority. After its release, the group went along with my desire for a shorter name when the actual Chicago Transit Authority threatened a lawsuit. That change was very much for the better. For the most part, however, after that I was content to let artists call themselves whatever they wanted. I felt that it was part of my job to let them know if I genuinely believed their choice would hinder their career, or detract from their music, but artists generally know what's best for them, and if they're comfortable with the name, they'll find a way to make it credible to their audience.

The first Blood, Sweat & Tears album, *Child Is Father to the Man*, took its title from a line by the poet William Wordsworth and is now regarded as a classic of the period. *Rolling Stone* hailed the group as "the best thing to happen in rock and roll so far in 1968," and the band got a lot of media attention and drew strong, encouraging reviews. The album didn't generate a hit single and, consequently, didn't sell in big numbers, though it has accrued a significant reputation. Unfortunately, conflicts emerged within the group, and they couldn't agree about the type of music they should be doing. That culminated in Kooper coming to me and telling me that they were splitting up. I was dumbfounded and upset; it seemed much too soon. But there was nothing I could do.

The split worked out to Columbia's advantage on both ends, at least in commercial terms. The newly reconstituted Blood, Sweat & Tears with David Clayton-Thomas on lead vocals included Katz, the drummer Bobby Colomby, and other members of the original group. They became a hit-making machine in the late Sixties with such singles as "You've Made Me So Very Happy," "And When I Die" (a Laura Nyro song), and "Spinning Wheel." The second album, *Blood, Sweat & Tears*, rose to number one, won a Grammy for Album of the Year, and sold close to 4 million copies worldwide.

The ingenious Kooper, meanwhile, teamed up with Mike Bloomfield, formerly of the Electric Flag (that group had broken up, too!), and the guitarist Stephen Stills, who had just left Buffalo Springfield, to make an album called *Super Session* for Columbia. Interestingly, that album was partly inspired by Moby Grape, another hip Columbia signing at the time, brought in by the talented A&R man David Rubinson. To accompany their second album, *Wow,* Moby Grape had recorded an additional album called *Grape Jam,* which consisted of the band members and other musicians, including Kooper and Bloomfield, improvising in the studio together. As a not entirely successful experiment, we packaged both albums together, and sold them for the price of one.

Kooper believed that he could bring a more disciplined approach to the jamming-in-the-studio concept, and that was the premise of *Super Session*. The album anticipated the supergroup phenomenon that would soon produce such bands as Crosby, Stills and Nash and Blind Faith, and it earned a gold record for sales. Kooper also joined the A&R staff at Columbia, and in that capacity championed the Zombies' album *Odessey and Oracle,* which had been released in Britain but which I was reluctant to put out in the States since the band had broken up. Kooper insisted that it had potential, so I went along with him, and the single "Time of the Season" became a Top 5 hit and an enduring marker of the era.

On the country front, Columbia had always been a strong presence in Nashville, with its own label there run by Don Law, and an Epic label run by Billy Sherrill, the songwriter and producer who defined the so-called countrypolitan sound, a sophisticated mix of classic country and contemporary pop. Columbia artists were instrumental in breaking down the barriers between rock 'n' roll and country on both sides of that divide. Dylan had recorded both *Blonde and Blonde* and *John Wesley Harding* in Nashville, a daring move considering that he was probably the most potent symbol of the counterculture and Nashville was a bastion of conservatism. In his wake, innumerable rock and pop artists flocked to Nashville to record. Very influentially, Chris Hillman and Gram Parsons of the Byrds had pushed that band into the realm of country-rock.

But movement was also occurring on the other side of the cultural divide. Johnny Cash, signed as a Columbia country artist, had been outspoken in his admiration of Dylan, whom he regarded from the start as a country singer. Cash's outlaw image made him attractive to rock audiences. When he released his *Johnny Cash at Folsom Prison* album in 1968, that appeal deepened, and I made sure Columbia did everything possible to encourage it. The album drew rave reviews in hip outlets like *The Village Voice,* bearing out the declaration by *Rolling Stone*'s editor, Jann Wenner, that Cash "more than any other country performer is meaningful in a rock & roll context."

The next year, Cash's novelty single "A Boy Named Sue" propelled his follow-up prison album, *Johnny Cash at San Quentin,* to number one. If Cash's darker aspect was winning over the underground rock crowd, this lighter side of him attracted mainstream pop listeners. Cash sold 6.5 million albums in 1969, a staggering figure at the time and a testament to his ability to reach across disparate audiences. That reach only expanded when he was given a weekly network show that year, which provided an extraordinary platform for him. In person Cash radiated charisma without seeming even to try. Whenever he was in the room it was impossible not to feel his presence. Despite his rough edges and the hard life he had lived, even that early on he carried him-self almost formally. He always called me "Mr. Davis" despite repeated appeals that "Clive" would be just fine, and in conversation his words were always thoughtful, carefully chosen and considered. Still, you felt the personal force behind everything he said, and you just knew that it would not be any fun to get on his wrong side. Characteristically, he dressed all in black, but the severity of his look only made his frequent smile blast like a burst of sunshine. Stereotypes attached to country art-ists in those days, but Cash defied all of them. He was an artist of the highest order, of course, but also a hugely impressive man.

If the lines between rock and country were blurring, so were the bor-ders between rock and R&B. In 1968 Columbia enjoyed a breakout hit with the Chambers Brothers' rousing, psychedelic soul anthem "Time Has Come Today," another song that has come to be a reference point in subsequent movies and TV shows for the spirit of that era. But at the very forefront of that rock-soul merging were Sly and the Family Stone, the group that David Kapralik, my new head of A&R at Epic, had brought to that label. Sly was leaping over boundaries on so many fronts—the band was interracial and included both men and women. Singles like "Dance to the Music," "Everyday People," "Stand," and "Hot Fun in the Summertime" were hits that seemed to catch every positive vibration and hopeful possibility of that time.

Different as we are, Sly and I got along great. He seemed so vibrant and alive, the hardest-working artist I'd ever seen. I first met him when I asked David to bring him up to the office so the three of us could have lunch in my private dining room. We had a terrific time, but at the lunch Sly was also the good-natured recipient of one of my ill-fated suggestions. Much as I loved Sly's music, I thought that aspects of the band's dress and presentation—the glittery outfits, the coordinated stage moves, the platinum hair—might seem too Vegas-like to the rock audience that was beginning to respond to him and that I knew he could reach in a big way. I asked if those elements were important to what he was doing, and if he would consider changing them. Gently, even with a bit of amusement, he assured me that, yes, they were important, and, no, he would not consider changing them. That was enough for me!

Sly and I used to talk regularly, and he would visit me from time to time just to hang out. He loved to use the Columbia studios at all hours, often on the weekends when no one was there to admit him. Whenever that happened, he would call me at home at whatever hour and ask if I could have the studio opened up for him. I always tried to accommodate him. Occasionally, he would also ask for a cash "advance" of some sort, and, within reason, I tried to accommodate him in that regard as well.

One of the Columbia artists who paid close attention to what Sly and other label signings like Blood, Sweat & Tears and Chicago were doing was Miles Davis. Miles, of course, had long been one of the gems in Columbia's crown, a man who had blazed new directions in jazz many times. In Sly, as well as other contemporary black artists like Jimi Hendrix and James Brown, he sensed a boldness, energy, and willingness to take risks that felt similar in spirit, if not in style, to his own music.

In Blood, Sweat & Tears and Chicago, however, he heard something else, fairly or not—the sound of himself being ripped off. Miles was a notoriously cantankerous guy, and he would speak to me in blistering, racially charged terms about what he felt was going on with those bands. As the rock era took shape, Miles's record sales declined, though neither his personal tastes nor his sense of the kind of money he deserved took a corresponding dip. That young white bands with horn sections and elements of jazz in their music were selling millions of records while his sales could no longer crack six figures infuriated him. He would call me frequently and in his foreboding rasp sprinkle those complaints amid his angry requests for money.

For all that, Miles and I got along well, and I might even go so far as to say we liked each other. Touchingly, in his autobiography he called me a "great man" and said I "think like an artist," and he wasn't exactly the sort of person who would sling compliments. He knew I held him in the highest regard as an artist, and whenever he asked for money, I was as generous with him as I could be. In one of the more humorous aspects of our relationship, he would often send his girlfriends up to "interview" with me. I think he thought it would impress them that he could arrange such a meeting.

One of the things I was trying to do at Columbia was get some of the artists who had been on the label for a while to address the new rock audience, which was quite open-minded. In the case of Tony Bennett, unfortunately, it didn't really connect. I encouraged him to record the songs of writers like John Lennon and Paul McCartney, whose work, in my view, rivaled that of the great Tin Pan Alley songwriters whom Bennett revered. He did one album of such material, and it sold well. But abandoning the music he loved literally made him physically ill, so eventually we stopped even discussing it. It's ironic that decades later this wonderful, iconic artist would deservedly have a tremendous commercial resurgence dueting with the likes of k. d. lang, Elvis Costello, Amy Winehouse, and Lady Gaga. Of course, that came about because they embraced the traditional music that he loved. Sometimes, timing is everything.

I certainly wasn't going to tell Miles Davis what kind of music to record. But when he would insist to me that he wasn't selling because Columbia kept describing his music as "jazz," I felt that he had a point.

The young people who were going to the Fillmore in San Francisco and the Fillmore East in New York were up for anything they thought was powerful and authentic. Bill Graham delighted in putting together bills that challenged and expanded the rock tastes of his audiences.

So I told Miles that I agreed with him, which was about the last thing he expected to hear. He had to break out of the jazz world and play his music for new audiences. I went so far as to suggest that being in new environments with new listeners on bills that featured artists who admired him but who were not jazz musicians might even affect the music he himself would make. Whether it did or not, I was confident that it would increase his sales.

He went nuts. He told me he had no interest in playing for "those fucking long-haired white kids." Graham would only rip him off. In fact, if I thought this was a good idea, he wanted off the "fucking label." I later got a telegram stating that Miles would no longer record for Columbia.

Miles's manager called the next day to ask what was going on. He'd never seen Miles so angry. I figured a measured response was best. I told him about our conversation, and explained that I thought we all had the same goal. I still thought it would be a good idea for Miles to play the Fillmore, and I would be happy to help make that happen. I also explained that there wasn't the slightest possibility that I was going to let Miles out of his Columbia contract. I had made every effort in his behalf, and I had nothing to apologize for. A few months later Miles called, explaining that he realized he'd gotten a bit out of line. If I could work out the logistics—the right money, the right billing—he'd be happy to play the Fillmore.

I got to work. Miles found his first dates opening for Neil Young & Crazy Horse and the Steve Miller Band at the Fillmore East extremely unsatisfying, to say the least. But Graham then booked him for four nights with the Grateful Dead at the Fillmore West the following month, and that went a good deal better. I knew that Laura Nyro idolized Miles, so I contacted David Geffen, who worked out a run of Fillmore East dates for them as well. Four nights, equal billing, Miles and his band going on first, and Laura closing the show.

A week before the first Fillmore East show with Laura, I was in California for business when a package arrived at my hotel. It contained a pair of black-and-gray flared trousers, a black-and-gray striped vest, and a long-sleeved black silk shirt. Attached was a note from Miles asking if I would wear this to the opening night's performance. "I want you to look special," he wrote.

Beyond slipping on some beads at the Monterey Pop Festival and sporting an ill-considered Nehru jacket at some unspecified later date, I'd generally made a point of avoiding trends and simply wearing the clothes that I felt best in. This, however, seemed a very personal request, and I was actually kind of touched by it. I had the clothes properly fitted, and, along with playing a terrific set that night, Miles was knocked out that I wore the outfit. We posed for pictures together, one of which ended up on the cover of the music industry trade magazine *Cashbox*. *Bitches Brew,* the rock-jazz fusion album Miles released around the time of his Fillmore dates, once again redirected contemporary music. It also sold 400,000 copies, and brought Miles a new audience that sustained him until the end of his life.

Not that Miles and I ever stopped battling. He'd take shots at Columbia in the press, but when I'd call him about it, he'd simply say, "Don't pay attention to that. Sometimes you've got to say what people expect of you." On the other hand, he'd call and play his new music for me over the phone, as excited as a kid about whatever new direction he was moving in. He appeared at charity events for me, even if it was inconvenient for him and not the sort of thing he enjoyed. I can more than return the compliment he paid me: Miles was both a great man and one of the most extraordinary artists I've ever had the privilege to work with. It wasn't all fun, but it was all well worth it.

Pearl

An extraordinary encounter occurred while Columbia was waiting to release *Cheap Thrills,* the first album for the label by Big Brother and the Holding Company. Because I'd signed the band, the album had a tremendous amount of significance for me, both personally and professionally. But I was also eager to bring Janis Joplin to a much larger audience than the underground hipsters who were already converted.

In many ways, Janis created the model for the type of artist I would continually search for and try to sign. Every label executive understands the economic pressures of the music business, and no one's going to turn up his nose at a one-off hit. But, beginning with Janis, I found myself wanting to concentrate on artists who would be in it for the long haul, who had both the talent and the tenacity to achieve and sustain success on a large scale. That doesn't mean that every release has to be bigger than the last. Every career has its rhythms, its ups and downs, and in the case of true artists, periods of experimentation that might appeal only to the cognoscenti. But, generally speaking, I believe in artists who have star power, who want to play on the big stage. Janis epitomized those qualities, and I believed in her to the very core of my being. It was inconceivable to me that anyone who heard her wouldn't have the same ecstatic response that I had.

Now I realize that no artist, however worthy, generates that type of universal appeal, but one early hint of that truth occurred when I enthusiastically played Janis's version of George Gershwin's "Summertime" for the master Broadway composer Richard Rodgers. I ran into him at Columbia one day in 1968 as he was waiting to have lunch with

Goddard Lieberson. I introduced myself, and explained that I was a huge fan of his. After all, he'd co-written songs for some of the greatest musicals in history—*Oklahoma!, Carousel, South Pacific,* and *The Sound of Music* among them. He really had no greater admirer than me.

As we chatted, I got the idea to play "Summertime" for him. Brilliant in its own right, I was excited by the performance because it suggested Janis's early willingness to move beyond what was expected of her. Recording a Gershwin tune from *Porgy and Bess* was an unpredictable choice for an acid-rock soul singer from Haight-Ashbury, and it knocked me out. It seemed to me both true to the cultural moment and true to the spirit of the song. I hoped that Rodgers would be able to feel that, too.

He was open to hearing it. I told him a little bit about Janis, and he politely took a seat in my office. I put on the tape, and he listened without expression. When the song ended, he didn't say anything, which unnerved me. I thought that maybe "Summertime," ironically, might be too much a part of his world to be meaningful to him in this treatment. Other, more familiar renditions had likely made an imprint on him, and it might be too much to ask him to respond to Janis's rawer interpretation. I decided to play "Piece of My Heart" for him. Now that was a mistake. After about ninety seconds, he asked me to stop the tape. He told me that not only did he not understand what he was hearing, but he could not understand why anyone would like it—though he believed me when I told him that young people would respond to it. As for Janis's singing, it was impossible for him to imagine why anyone would think she was talented.

It got worse after that. "If this means I have to change my writing, or that the only way to write a Broadway musical is to write rock songs, then my career is over," he said, punctuating his remarks with emphatic gestures. "In no way could I possibly do this!" I meant to suggest no such thing, of course, and I was upset to have one of my idols respond this way. But a cultural reality lay behind his response, I think. Rodgers and I both knew that Broadway was losing luster, and that rock was becoming the dominant form of popular music. We didn't discuss anything like that, but it was in the air. I would never dream of asking someone like Richard Rodgers to write rock songs. What would be the point of that? Mostly, I was just curious to hear what he thought of Janis. Would it be possible for him to get it? Would he like it? Might there be something there that he could use? At the very least, he might tell his friends that he had heard this great new artist.

Such culture clashes were common at the time, and their results were mixed. Classical music was in a position similar to Broadway's; it had a distinguished history at Columbia but its sway was diminishing. Even the most renowned names on the label's classical roster struggled with the shift in musical priorities, and what it might mean for them. But sometimes the new music touched them regardless. One evening in 1967, Janet and I took Vladimir Horowitz, one of the greatest classical pianists of the twentieth century, and his wife, Wanda, who was the daughter of the famed conductor Arturo Toscanini, out to a discotheque in the East Village. The club blasted Motown hits all night, and they loved it. And Leonard Bernstein and I had many conversations about shifting musical tastes and their impact on the budgets for his recordings. Some of our talks were friendly, others were quite charged. Still, he not only hosted a television special titled *Inside Pop: The Rock Revolution* on CBS in 1967, but later incorporated aspects of the new music in his celebrated *Mass*. And the music he wrote for *West Side Story* provided a prime example of how Broadway could engage the contemporary world and, particularly in the movie version of the show, reach out to a new, younger audience. Rodgers, however, simply couldn't hear the new sounds. While that made for an uncomfortable few minutes for me, it detracts not one whit from his genius.

I was determined to acclimate Columbia and the music industry in general to the new music that was about to rise up from the underground, with Janis Joplin leading the charge. I brought the Electric Flag to the National Association of Record Merchandisers' convention in February 1968. It was not remotely the sort of music they were accustomed to hearing at that event, but the retailer group was responsible for 80 percent of record sales in the United States, and it was essential that they become familiar with it. I also took every opportunity to make it clear that Columbia was now in the vanguard of music's new direction.

Later in the year I took the same approach to Columbia's own company convention in Puerto Rico. The artists I showcased were Spirit, an adventurous California band that came to the label by way of our production deal with Lou Adler; the Chambers Brothers; Blood, Sweat & Tears; and Big Brother and the Holding Company. Although these conventions had previously featured more middle-of-the-road fare, these groups tore the house down. As the ovations grew louder, Janis hung with me backstage, sipped from her bottle of Southern Comfort, and grew increasingly insecure. "Jesus, how can I follow that?" she asked. Characteristically, her performance was sensational, but by the time Big Brother went on, the audience had already been rocked hard and couldn't rise any higher. She was disappointed.

Despite that, her disarming Texas charm was much in evidence during the convention as she easily mingled with the sales staff. It's the sort of thing that many artists, particularly the hipper ones, have a difficult time doing, but Janis enjoyed it. She veered from extreme vulnerability to being one of the boys, sometimes within the same conversation. Both those aspects of her touched a chord in the people she talked to. "Oh, you're going to be selling my album? I hope you like it," she'd say to one salesman with a girlish sweetness. To another, she'd declare, "I hope you can sell the shit out of my album, man!" She was quick to laugh in her enthusiastic, melodic cackle, and came across as utterly down-to-earth.

Beyond Janis's charm offensive with the Columbia staff, I needed to make sure that *Cheap Thrills* made a big commercial impact. At stake was my ability to continue operating aggressively at the label, to keep on making the signings I felt were necessary and bringing them to the marketplace with the flair I believed they deserved. When I listened to *Cheap Thrills,* I loved it, but it was apparent that the band would need a hit single for it to really do well. FM radio was beginning to reach a new audience with underground bands, and word of mouth, as always, was important. But they would carry the band only so far. They needed a Top 40 AM radio single to penetrate beyond the true believers.

"Piece of My Heart" was the likeliest candidate to get that job done. Written by Bert Berns and Jerry Ragovoy, the song was a soulful burner that Janis delivered with devastating power. The song had been released as a single in 1967 by Erma Franklin, Aretha's older sister, and had not performed well commercially. That meant nothing to me. In later years, one of my tests for hiring A&R staff would be for them to find five songs that had been recorded and failed to reach the charts that they believed could be hits for other artists. I felt that Janis and Big Brother had passed that test with flying colors with "Piece of My Heart."

Just one problem. The album version ran longer than four minutes, and simply did not repeat the chorus often enough to drive it home. The song would need an edit to become a hit. Conversations like these were not easy to have in the Sixties. As the album became the coin of the realm, releasing singles at all was anathema to some artists, a throwback to the days when rock 'n' roll singers were only as viable as their last hit. Editing an album track to have a commercial hit on Top 40 radio? That was going to be a tough sell to Big Brother.

The fact was, however, that without a hit single, the album was not going to sell the way I wanted it to, and perhaps needed it to. Moreover, I had a hunch that Janis very much wanted the album to sell well. True, the backslapping and flirting at the Columbia convention came naturally to her, but she also knew those guys would be selling her record and she wanted them to work their asses off. Big Brother's friendly San Francisco rivals, Jefferson Airplane, had a Top 10 hit in 1967 with "Somebody to Love." That band was also fronted by a female singer, Grace Slick, and though they were wildly different, the media often compared Janis and Grace. None of that would have been lost on Janis. It's also just common sense. If you've worked long and hard on a record, you want as many people as possible to hear it. That was definitely Janis's belief.

I thought the best way to proceed was to do the edit first, and then let Janis hear it and make a decision. That way she could feel its impact, hear it for herself, and understand from that emotional perspective why I wanted to do it. There was no point in debating in the abstract the propriety of doing an edit. That was a losing fight. So I called a tape editor into my office and explained what I was trying to do with the track. I didn't explain it in technical language; I couldn't even if I had wanted to. I simply told him that I wanted the chorus, the song's hook, to come in one more time, and we shortened the instrumental passage.

I liked the way it turned out: It was tight, hit hard, and made an indelible impression.

Now I needed to present it to Janis. I called her up, and asked if she would come by my office, because I had something I wanted to play for her. I had never done anything like this before, and when she arrived, I was nervous. "I'm not going to come out with this if you don't like it," I said. "But it's extremely important for you to have a hit single. Without a hit, your album might sell two to three hundred thousand copies. With a hit, you could double that, and you might even sell a million. The album is already out, and the album will remain exactly as it is. But I've edited one of the cuts in a way that will work for radio, and I hope doesn't offend you."

Finally, I played the tape. She listened, and didn't say anything. Then she shrugged, and simply said that if I thought it had to be done, it was okay with her. She clearly wasn't happy about it, and she knew that the fans she already had wouldn't care if Top 40 radio played a Big Brother song or not. But she understood it as a business decision, and agreed to let it happen. All in all, the meeting went much better than I had feared. And the results proved as good as I hoped. "Piece of My Heart" went to number twelve on the charts, and helped drive *Cheap Thrills* to number one, with more than a million copies sold.

By the end of 1968, though, Janis had left Big Brother and the Holding Company. Typically, I'm the voice encouraging artists to stay with their bands. I very strongly believe that, except in the rarest instances, the institution is bigger than the individual artist. I encouraged Al Kooper to stay with Blood, Sweat & Tears as long as he could, though the situation proved untenable. Janis was one of those rare instances, however, when I thought it might make sense for her to leave. She was clearly the star of the band, and critics and even other musicians were openly critical of Big Brother's musical limitations. When Columbia was getting ready to release *Cheap Thrills,* I called Albert Grossman and asked if we could credit the album to "Janis Joplin and Big Brother and the Holding Company." Her reputation had grown sufficiently that I thought it would help sales and also reflect the reality of the situation more honestly. I was turned down, and abided by that decision.

I was careful to stay out of the deliberations about Janis's leaving the band, beyond discussing it with Grossman when he brought it up. Then Janis called me personally to discuss it. When you're running a record company, you obviously have a stake in such matters, but it's a bit like trying to advise friends who may be splitting up. If you use a heavy hand—or even speak with too much honesty—you can end up alienating everyone. The best course is to listen sympathetically, and help the person get clear on their ideas and feelings. Then let them make whatever decision they're going to make. Emotions were complicated and understandably charged.

Talking to Janis, I got the impression that she had made her decision already, and was simply looking for my support. Her desire to work with more accomplished and versatile musicians seemed right to me. But she and the band had come through many hard times, and achieved great success. I kept the other members of Big Brother under contract, and we made two more albums together that sold reasonably well. But the band could never fully establish an identity independent of Janis, and there was only so far we could go with them.

As for Janis, as often happens in such situations, the breakup seemed to both fill her with a renewed sense of possibility and deepen her insecurities. She began to work with stellar musicians and producers, and she became one of the biggest rock stars in the world. But while she very much wanted it, none of that seemed to satisfy her.

You never knew quite what you were going to get with Janis. One night I ran into her backstage at the Fillmore East, where I'd gone to hear a group I thought I might want to sign. She was very drunk, and while I needed to meet with the band, I didn't want her to feel neglected. There was an awkward moment when we spotted each other, and then she simply said, "I understand you're on a gig, so go upstairs and do your thing. I know you didn't know I was here." It was a very generous gesture, particularly from someone as sensitive to slights as she was.

But she was not always so understanding. At one of Big Brother's early shows in New York, I brought Laura Nyro backstage to meet Janis. The performance had been a triumph. Janis was a rising star at that point, while Laura was barely known, and Laura just wanted to tell her how much she loved the show. Janis ignored her, while taking belts straight from her bottle of Southern Comfort and chatting up a boy she was interested in. When Laura became something of a star herself a little bit later, things got worse. "I can see I'm not the number-one female in your eyes anymore," Janis told me one day on the phone. "You're turned on to Laura now."

That idea was ridiculous, of course. Beyond the usual juggling act that all record company presidents have to do, I was not paying more attention to Laura than to Janis. Laura was active at the time, a new artist with a new album, and Janis was organizing her next move after leaving Big Brother. Consequently, Laura was more in the media spotlight at that moment. But she was still struggling to gain a foothold in the industry. Well beyond my personal affection for her, Janis was in the pantheon of Columbia artists due to both her stature and her sales. She never stopped being a major priority, either for me or for the company.

That said, Janis's raucous behavior was leading to bad publicity and tarnishing her reputation. She got arrested for disorderly conduct in Tampa in November 1969 after screaming obscenities from the stage at the police on the scene during her concert there. The charges were eventually dropped, but the event contributed to the perception that she was out of control. She seemed inseparable from her bottles of Southern Comfort, and, on a personal level, she was often capable of rude and coarse behavior. I would be speaking with her at a public event, when she'd spot a guy across the room and take off. "Wow, I'd like to fuck him!" would be her parting line.

How harshly would a male rock star be judged for such behavior? Probably not as harshly. And, as I said, Janis often took it as a point of pride to conduct herself like one of the boys. But carrying on like that ultimately doesn't win people over regardless of who's doing it, and even at the height of the sexual revolution, it was pushing boundaries beyond the edge for a woman to behave that way. Rightly or wrongly, Janis's image began to suffer. I thought a touch of high style might help turn things around for her. Janis was headlining a Madison Square Garden show in December 1969, and I told her that Janet and I would love to host a party for her afterward, a sort of midnight supper. She was thrilled by the idea. The party would take place in our apartment on Central Park West, which had a living room with a floor-length view of the park. It would be a magical night.

At Madison Square Garden, I stopped by to see Janis as she was getting ready to go onstage, and she already was anticipating the party, telling me I would be knocked out by the outfit she planned to wear. I had never seen this feminine side of her. Later, as she was wrapping up her encores, she told the crowd that she finally had to leave because "I've got to go get dressed. A friend is throwing this wonderful party for me." It was perfect Janis—treating an arena full of fans as if they were her intimate friends.

Parties like the one for Janis were to become natural for me, but this one had a larger purpose. I believed that Janis could have a long, productive career, and I wanted to demonstrate both the quality of people who would be interested in attending a party for her and the level of artistry that she could aspire to achieve. Along with Janis's friends and peers in the rock world, I invited the likes of Miles Davis and Tony Bennett, artists who had risen to the very top of their musical fields. I would also have some prominent members of the media there so the word would get out. I wanted to make it a truly extraordinary night for her.

Janis arrived at around 1:00, and though she was clearly high, she was in good cheer and made a vibrant entrance. She wore black satin pants and a sheer, low-cut black chiffon blouse. She seemed thrilled by all the attention from such a glittering array of guests. Bob Dylan came and didn't leave until 3:30, though he never took off his coat and hat. Other notable guests included Albert Grossman, Ahmet Ertegun, Neil Bogart, Lou Adler, Jac Holzman, Paul Butterfield, and Johnny and Edgar Winter. Dylan found Laura Nyro hiding in one of the bedrooms, and, to her astonishment, talked to her at length about how much he admired her albums and songwriting.

By the end of the night, Janis had tears in her eyes as she thanked Janet and me for creating this evening for her. All of us were deeply moved by how well it had gone.

Less than a year after that spectacular night, I was at home, still asleep, on the morning of October 5, 1970, when my son Fred rushed into my bedroom to tell me that he had just heard on WABC radio that Janis had died. Her body had been found the night before in her room at the Landmark Motor Hotel in Los Angeles, where she was staying while she worked on her new album. The cause of death, we later learned, was an accidental overdose of heroin. She was twenty-seven years old. Jimi Hendrix had died just a few weeks before, and Jim Morrison would die less than a year later, both at the same age. This was the grim establishment of the so-called 27 Club that would later claim Kurt Cobain and Amy Winehouse among its unfortunate members.

When what Fred had told me sunk in, it was like a huge void opening up inside me. Maybe that's what shock really feels like. Janis had meant a great deal to me personally. We had gone on a journey together. Seeing her perform at Monterey was a crucial moment of self-revelation for me: When she walked onstage that day I was one person; by the time she walked off I was someone else. How many people affect your life that profoundly?

It shook me to the core to think that the dreams I nurtured for her career as an artist, the dreams she nurtured for herself, would never come to pass. The last time I spoke with Janis on the phone, she was totally coherent and clear. She seemed so thrilled about the record she was making. She was so upbeat, so positive about her beautiful version of Kris Kristofferson's "Me and Bobby McGee." She just loved it. She called and played me a few of her new songs on the telephone, and she couldn't have seemed happier.

She had already achieved a great deal. I had no doubt that her music and her reputation would last, and, needless to say, that conviction remains. She's in the Rock and Roll Hall of Fame, and in a pantheon of her own. She continues to reach new generations of listeners. To date, *Cheap Thrills* has sold more than 2 million copies. A posthumous *Greatest Hits* collection has sold more than 7 million. And *Pearl,* the album she was working on when she died, has sold more than 4 million.

But Janis could have accomplished so much more. As I've learned since then, when you discover an artist, the real thrill of that discovery is in seeing how long that career can last. The relationship deepens and grows over time. You know that you didn't sign a one-hit wonder, that you signed someone that you're working with five years, ten years, decades down the line. So sobering. So tragic.

When the producer Paul Rothchild, who was working with Janis at the time of her death, sent me an early version of *Pearl*, I played it and I couldn't help but break down. This was an artist at the very top of her game. I listened to "Me and Bobby McGee" over and over. It was an instant classic. For better or worse, Janis lived by the carpe diem mandate: "Live for today and let tomorrow take care of itself." Or, as she sang, "Get It While You Can."

Janis's death also raised issues for me about the drug culture, and about the responsibility that any of us around her might have had for what happened. It made me wonder about how I should confront this issue with my artists. This was long before the age of interventions and recovery, and I was so new to my responsibilities. I knew Janis drank, obviously, but I was unaware of her drug use. I was too green. Overly naïve. Totally distant from recognizing that this could be a life-threatening situation. Nothing in my background had prepared me for it. Could I have been hipper and figured it out? Should I have known? Was I blind to it? In denial? Most important, was there anything I could have done?

Finally, I think that's fruitless speculation. I would be in a far more influential position with artists later in my life, and I discovered that unless someone truly wants to change, they don't. I never had reason to believe Janis's situation was so dangerous. All I know is that, when she spoke to me the week before her death, she was loving the album she was working on. And with good reason. It's now regarded as one of the greatest albums in rock history. She was exhilarated, and looking forward to the future. I didn't have a clue that her situation was as perilous as it turned out to be. And I was devastated to lose her.

Simon and Garfunkel

I was always—and, of course, I remain—a tremen-
dous admirer of Paul Simon's songwriting, and, musically, I truly treasure Simon and Garfunkel's albums. They were signed to Columbia by
the producer Tom Wilson in 1964, and after breaking up for a time the
following year, they not only became one of the label's signature groups
but eventually its most successful. Their melodic sophistication and accessibility; the transcendent vocal harmonies; the stunning literacy of
the lyrics—those elements combined to make their music both memorable and profound, satisfying on every level. You could come back to it
time and time again, with deepening rewards.

Fans responded emotionally and enthusiastically to Simon and Garfunkel and found in their music a way to make sense of and come to
terms with all the cultural disruptions of the Sixties. But I do believe
the beauty of their songs caused critics to undervalue them during that
decade. I personally felt that as a songwriter Paul Simon was in a class
with Dylan and Lennon/McCartney, and that Simon and Garfunkel
were qualitatively the equivalent of the Beatles. To me, rock critics
sometimes seem to value edge above all other qualities, and they're
drawn to artists whom they see as embattled or as underdogs. Simon
and Garfunkel's commercial success and easy way with melodies, their
desire to comfort as well as challenge, did them no favors in this regard.
While they were actively making records, their work, and particularly
Paul's songs, rarely got the serious consideration they deserved.

As I took on increasing creative responsibilities at Columbia, Paul,
Artie, and I began to interact more regularly, and you'd think that we
would have had a natural rapport. They were Jewish kids who had grown

up and gone to public school in Queens, as I had in Brooklyn, and we shared a kind of outer-borough feistiness, ambition, and desire for upward mobility that was very distinctive in those days. Artie was something of a loner, but, as time went on, Paul and I became friends in a way that has been rare in my professional experience. Once, after I'd left Columbia, I was doing some speaking engagements and was scheduled to appear at a small college in Pittsburgh. I dreaded going there by myself. Paul hated attending music industry events. So we made a deal. I would accompany him to the Grammys in Los Angeles if he would make a surprise appearance at my talk in Pittsburgh. We had a great time at both events, and the college kids were thrilled by Paul's appearance.

Friendship with artists is tricky, however, when you are in any way involved in their career. It's a joke—but only half a joke—among executives in the music industry that any conversation you have with an artist is invariably about that artist. That intense focus is necessary for their art—it helps give them the confidence to run the risks that great creativity requires. But it doesn't easily make for the mutuality that true friendship requires. Still, Paul and I had sons the same age and we became neighbors on Central Park West. My high regard for his songwriting didn't hurt, of course, but we shared interests outside the music business and eventually grew close.

None of that made working with Simon and Garfunkel any easier. A notable example of how difficult it was occurred after the director Mike Nichols asked Paul if he would write new songs for his 1967 film *The Graduate*. With some obvious exceptions, soundtrack albums at the time essentially amounted to souvenirs for people who had enjoyed the movie. Their commercial success depended less on the quality of the music than the box-office success of the film. However, I thought this project had real possibilities. Nichols had become one of the most important directors in the country after being nominated for an Academy Award for *Who's Afraid of Virginia Woolf?* His talent combined with Paul's songwriting seemed like a stellar match to me, so when Embassy Motion Pictures offered Columbia the soundtrack rights, I snapped them up.

The problems began when Nichols decided not to use the few new songs Paul had written for the film—a significant exception being a snippet of "Mrs. Robinson," named for the sultry character played by Anne Bancroft. He chose instead to use songs from previous Simon and Garfunkel albums, including versions of "The Sound of Silence" and "Scarborough Fair/Canticle." Paul wasn't happy about the whole experience of writing for the film, and when I asked him if there was enough music in it for an album, he said in no uncertain terms that there wasn't. Then, when the film opened and it was clear that it was going to be a blockbuster hit, I again asked Paul if we could somehow assemble a soundtrack album. Again he said no. Determined, I then went to the Columbia A&R man in charge of soundtracks and asked what he thought. He agreed with Paul.

This was disappointing to me for a number of reasons. Purely from a business standpoint, I felt Columbia was losing a major opportunity at a time when a big hit album could have really helped the company— not to mention help me continue to move things in the progressive direction I wanted. With relatively little effort we could have a soundtrack that was virtually guaranteed to be a major success. But I also firmly believed that the soundtrack could help propel Simon and Garfunkel to a new level of stardom, and also bring Paul some of the exceptional songwriting recognition he deserved. Their albums *Sounds of Silence* and *Parsley, Sage, Rosemary and Thyme* had done very well, but as *The Graduate* was being hailed as a definitive document of the era, finding a credible way to emphasize their association with it would be highly desirable. I just couldn't let that opportunity slip.

Finally, one day, in the middle of my work, I left the office and went to see *The Graduate* myself. As I sat in the theater and watched, it became obvious that the movie was terrific and was going to be enormously successful. What also became apparent to me was the potential solution to my problem. When Paul and my A&R man Ed Kleban told me that there wasn't enough music to put together a soundtrack album, they were thinking only of the Simon and Garfunkel songs in the film. But the composer Dave Grusin had written an instrumental soundtrack that was prominently used in the film. Vinyl albums typically contained somewhere between thirty-five and forty minutes of music. We could very legitimately assemble a soundtrack for *The Graduate* that combined Grusin's score and the Simon and Garfunkel songs.

The only remaining problem—and it was far from insignificant—was convincing Paul and Artie that it was a good idea. I called Mort Lewis, who managed Simon and Garfunkel, and made my case. He was blunt: Paul did not want a soundtrack album to come out, and Artie completely agreed with him. Justifiably, they believed that Simon and Garfunkel fans deserved a new album filled with new songs. Moreover, they were in the process of completing the *Bookends* album, and they didn't want a potential soundtrack either to delay the release of *Bookends* or confuse fans by cluttering the marketplace. I responded that the potential audience for the soundtrack was significantly larger than their own following, and would bring their music to new fans. In addition, many people who bought soundtracks simply wanted to reexperience the emotions they felt while watching the film. In large part, they were not really avid Simon and Garfunkel fans who would be expecting a new statement from the duo. The desires of that audience were no less valid than those of hard-core music fans, and the soundtrack as I envisaged it would totally satisfy them.

To seal the deal I spoke to Paul directly. I assured him that, in its marketing, Columbia would make it clear that this was not a Simon and Garfunkel album. They would not appear on the cover—which instead used the iconic seduction shot of a mesmerized Dustin Hoffman staring at the upraised, stocking-clad leg of Anne Bancroft. The large title on the cover would indicate that this was the official soundtrack album of *The Graduate,* and smaller type would read something like "Songs by Paul Simon" and "Performed by Simon and Garfunkel." Finally, I insisted that I had no intention of holding up the release of *Bookends*. In fact, if everything went as I hoped it would, *The Graduate* film and soundtrack would whet the appetite for a new Simon and Garfunkel album both in the duo's devoted fan base and the far more sizable movie audience to which they would have become familiar. That *Bookends* would include the complete version of "Mrs. Robinson," not just the snippet in the film and on the soundtrack, would only lend the new album increased momentum.

Paul was adamant. "We've been working on *Bookends* a long time," he said. "We are totally into it, and we think it's a major creative breakthrough. We don't want to wait six months to put it out." He needn't have worried. Not only did I think it made good commercial sense to release the albums back-to-back, but, in order to keep Columbia fresh, I was experimenting with release strategies, and this unlikely move fit perfectly with that approach. I was convinced that once the two albums were out, Simon and Garfunkel would be superstars.

However reluctantly, Paul and Artie agreed to let me release the soundtrack to *The Graduate,* which I did in January 1968. Predictably, it proved tremendously popular, hitting the top of the charts and eventually reaching more than 2 million in sales. That beautifully set the table for the April release of *Bookends* and its classic first single, "Mrs. Robinson." Both the single and the album shot to number one, and the album also went on to sell more than 2 million copies. Indeed, Simon and Garfunkel were now superstars. They had become household names all over the world. More important, with his evocative line "Where have you gone, Joe DiMaggio?" in "Mrs. Robinson," Paul had indelibly articulated the yearning for undeniable, uncomplicated heroism that all the tumult of the Sixties had engendered. It really should have been a great moment for all of us to celebrate and enjoy.

No good deed goes unpunished, alas, so relations between Simon and Garfunkel and Columbia, as well as with me personally, still grew tense at times. Despite the extraordinary career and financial benefits *The Graduate* soundtrack brought to them, Paul and Artie nursed a lingering resentment over its release. That puzzled me not only because it had worked out so well, but because I never would have done it without their agreement. There are definitely times when artists and executives don't see eye to eye. Perspectives just don't coincide. In this case, Paul and Artie were also upset because, in my ongoing effort to make variable pricing an accepted industry strategy, I had charged a dollar more than usual for *Bookends.* The anticipation for the album, which included a large poster, was so considerable that I figured it was a perfect moment to try it. That clearly didn't impede the album's sales, but in that countercultural heyday, it struck them as a hard-nosed business, Establishment-style decision, which I suppose it was.

I understood their concern, but as the president of a major record label, I did have concerns of my own. I needed blockbuster sales to offset the major decline in the sales of Mitch Miller and Broadway show albums, and I felt the decision was profitable for the artists as well as for Columbia. I really didn't feel any particular need to apologize for it. Inevitably, their contract came up for renegotiation and, while I didn't detect any gratitude for my efforts to make Paul and Artie superstars, it immediately was made extremely clear to me that they expected to be paid in a way commensurate with that status. Fair enough. But the strong feelings on both sides didn't create an ideal environment for negotiations. Eventually I gave them a royalty appropriate to their importance, and they extended their contract with Columbia.

It's ironic that all these tensions and difficulties were occurring while we were having nothing but success. Making it even harder, I personally liked Paul and Artie a great deal both as people and as artists, and felt that I had much in common with them. During my years at Columbia there were probably no other artists I listened to more often purely for pleasure than Simon and Garfunkel. For all those reasons I began to try to repair whatever damage had been done to our relationship. Paul and I began to have lunch together, and as we grew more comfortable, he confided in me about some of the problems he was having with Artie. In particular, Artie had agreed to a role in Mike Nichols's movie *Catch-22,* which was being filmed in Mexico. Shooting was taking much longer than anticipated, and Paul was eager to complete work on the *Bridge over Troubled Water* album. If you listen to Paul's song "The Only Living Boy in New York" on *Bridge,* you can get the feel for some of the emotions he was experiencing.

Finally the album was completed and, though it took a terrible toll on Paul and Artie's relationship, everyone was happy that it was done. I was invited to the studio to listen to the completed tracks with them and Paul's parents and brother. It was an incredible experience to hear that album for the first time with Paul and Artie present. Those situations can sometimes be awkward; the artists are so deeply invested in what they just played for you that if you feel any reservations at all, it's nearly impossible to express them. That was not the case in this instance. I was moved by the beauty and power of what I heard, and it was a pleasure to tell them so. I felt privileged to be in the room.

Knowing my conviction about the importance of hit singles, the conversation quickly turned to what the first single should be. We had released "The Boxer" as a single months before the album's release, and it had cracked the Top 10. Now we were talking about the single that would announce the album and, hopefully, drive its sales. When Paul and Artie asked me what I thought, I said, "It just has to be 'Bridge over Troubled Water.' " They were bowled over. It was not at all a standard move to choose a big ballad as an album's first single. They were convinced I would choose "Cecelia," a more rollicking track that would become a Top 5 hit a few months later.

"We love 'Bridge,' " Artie said, "and we planned to make it the album's title song. But do you really think it could be the album's first single?"

Because music was getting louder and heavier—Led Zeppelin and Jimi Hendrix, for example—releasing a ballad seemed like a counterintuitive strategy. And partly for that reason, it also seemed like the smartest strategy: ignore the trend and let Simon and Garfunkel do what they do best—create beauty, touch people's hearts, and define the cultural moment. And, most important of all, we had a stellar song that could accomplish all that. When you've truly got a great song, a potential all-timer, that trumps all the rules. "I can't be absolutely positive," I said. "But this is one time to go for a home run. It is the age of rock and this is a ballad—and a long one at that—but if it hits, it will become a classic." To this day, whenever I run into Artie on the street or at an event, he never fails to say, "Remember when you picked 'Bridge over Troubled Water' to be the single? I still can't believe that!"

Released in January 1970 on the same day as the album to prevent any other song on the record from jumping out ahead of it to radio, "Bridge over Troubled Water" won Grammys for Song of the Year and Record of the Year, and the album won for Album of the Year. The album spent ten weeks at number one, and to date has sold more than 8 million copies in the United States alone. The album and song have also become markers for the end of the Sixties and its great hopes, a consolation for all that was lost. They also became a marker for the end of the ongoing collaboration between Simon and Garfunkel.

By this time my relations were easy with both Paul and Artie. I saw Paul more often, as much due to proximity as anything else. At one lunch, Paul said to me, "I think our lives are going to be interwoven at some point. I may not always be a recording artist. I just know we will be more closely involved in some way." That has not proven to be the case, but I felt similarly, and Paul's sentiments speak eloquently for the connection that existed between us at the time.

Relations between Paul and Artie had become frayed beyond repair, unfortunately. As much as anything else, it was a case of two young artists whose ambitions and egos got in the way of the brilliance of their collaboration. Artie was seeking a film career in part because of feeling overshadowed by Paul's talents as a songwriter. Artie made about $75,000 for his role in *Catch-22*, while he made more than $1 million at the time from *Bridge over Troubled Water*, so he clearly wasn't acting for the money. Paul, on the other hand, grew jealous of the attention that Artie got as the group's main vocalist and "front man." Unlike those in the know, casual fans might not realize that Paul wrote all the songs, and might view Paul merely as Artie's accompanist. Paul has said in interviews that when audiences erupted in applause after Artie completed the bravura close to "Bridge over Troubled Water," he would be onstage thinking, yes, thank you, I wrote that song. That's not the way successful partners should be thinking.

So one day Paul called and said he wanted to meet with me at my office. When he arrived, he got straight to the point. "Before others find out, I want you to know that I've decided to split with Artie," he said. "I don't think we'll be recording together again." For all that I was aware of the difficulties they were having, I was still shocked. I was also torn in how I should respond. From a business standpoint, this was devastating news for Columbia. Simon and Garfunkel were standing in the highest tier of the most successful artists in the world at that point. They had become what I think of as an institution—a combination that is much larger and more significant than the sum of its parts. Even if the parts are not equal, together they mean more than any individual member. Rarely do solo artists, however successful they become, enjoy a success equivalent to institutional groups they leave. More personally,

I understood Paul's frustrations, and his desire to have more control over his music. I simply believed there were ways to satisfy those concerns without breaking up the duo. I also knew how competitive Paul was and how much he valued success. It would be extremely difficult for him to achieve alone anything like the stratosphere he had reached with Simon and Garfunkel. I believed he was underestimating the challenge of what he was setting out to do, and that it was my job to be honest with him and make clear the risk he was taking.

To a degree that I didn't fully understand at the time, Paul was not at all happy to hear this. Maybe my ideas just seemed so obvious to me that I didn't think sufficiently about how they might affect him. I read later in an interview that Paul wanted unqualified support from me, something that for both personal and professional reasons it was impossible for me to provide. It was simple: I did not want Simon and Garfunkel to break up.

Of course, Paul has gone on to an extremely successful solo career, and there's no doubt that he has personally lived with more fulfillment and less anguish by being able to proceed individually. I'm pleased, however, that he has also made room for occasional reunion tours with Artie. It's an arrangement not unlike what I originally hoped he might do, though in my fantasy scenario, he and Artie would have continued to record new material. That would have been the best of both worlds. Even *Graceland*, Paul's groundbreaking 1986 album, which was a commercial blockbuster, has not exceeded the staggering 14 million–plus sales of *Simon and Garfunkel's Greatest Hits*. There was a magic about that duo that would be tough for anyone to beat.

And speaking of institutions and solo artists, I had a memorable encounter with the definitive example of that contrast, and it was occasioned by my going to a studio in New York in 1973 to hear an early version of Paul's album *There Goes Rhymin' Simon*. He was extremely eager to play it for me, and I was knocked out by it. "Kodachrome," "American Tune," "Loves Me Like a Rock," and "Something So Right"—it seemed that one song after another was simultaneously thought-provoking and appealing. I was confident that he would do very well with it. Paul stayed in the studio to continue working on the album with the producer Roy Halee, and I left in an extremely good mood to go home.

I was still living at 88 Central Park West, and, as often happens with Jews, I got hungry for coffee and cake. So I met a friend and we went to a little coffee shop on Columbus Avenue and Seventy-second Street. We ordered, and as we were sitting there, my friend said, "My God, you'll never guess who's sitting behind us over there." It was John Lennon and Yoko Ono. No matter how many famous people you've met, a Beatle sighting is definitely a big deal, particularly then and particularly with Lennon, who so often seemed to go off the radar.

We had never met, but when I turned around to look at him, he saw me and gestured with his finger for me to come over to their booth. "Oh my God," I said. "What brings you here?" And Lennon said, "You know, we're going to move to the Dakota," the legendary New York building at the corner of Seventy-second Street and Central Park West, just a block from the café. I said, "I wish I had known you were in the neighborhood. I just came from the studio, where I heard Paul Simon's new album. I would have loved to have heard it with you, as someone from an iconic group who's also gone solo."

We discussed those issues a bit, and I told him how much I liked Paul's album. Then I asked him, "Do you listen to the radio a lot in order to keep current? Do you keep current?" I wanted to know if he kept track of what was happening when he was away from the music scene. He said, "I don't listen to the radio at all." I was flabbergasted. "Not at all?" I said, "When you're not recording, you really have no interest in knowing what else is happening? Not to copy, not to be imitative, just to hear what's going on? To see what else is out there?"

"No," he said. "I haven't listened to any new music at all." Then I said to him, "You know, I'm really shocked." He gave me one of those patented Lennon looks, half smiling, half well aware of who he was, and he said, "Clive, let me ask you a question. Do you think Picasso went to the galleries to see what was being painted before he put a brush to canvas?" It was an unforgettable rejoinder, and a telling comment on the nature of true, unique creativity.

Dylan

Bob Dylan's first live performances since his motor-cycle accident in 1966 occurred at two memorial concerts for Woody Guthrie at Carnegie Hall on January 20, 1968. Guthrie was Dylan's idol, of course, and it's hard to imagine what else at that point could have drawn him back to the stage from his tranquil, secluded life in Woodstock. In fact, Dylan had called Guthrie's manager, Harold Leventhal, shortly after Woody's death in October 1967 and suggested that they "do something" to honor the great folksinger and American icon. The seeds for the tribute concerts were planted in that conversation, a telling example of how a mere expression of interest on Dylan's part could make big things happen. A few small print ads appeared for the concerts and Dylan received no special billing amid the array of folk music all-stars slated to perform, but his name alone ensured that the two shows were instant sellouts. Curiosity gripped his fans once again. How would he look? What would he play? How would he sound?

I personally hadn't seen Dylan since we tangled over the lyrics to "Talkin' John Birch Society Blues" years before, and, since I was now the president of his label, I very much hoped that he either didn't remember or no longer cared about that contretemps. We'd negotiated a highly satisfactory deal for him in the interim, and, in the way that time seemed to elongate in the Sixties because so much was happening so fast, his protest days seemed a long way in the past. In any case, Dylan didn't bring the issue up when I went to visit him at the Park Sheraton Hotel before the Carnegie Hall shows to present him with his first gold records. Not only had the *Greatest Hits* collection we put out in 1967 gone gold, denoting sales of 500,000 copies, but it had triggered interest in his earlier albums, some of which had now gone gold as well.

Dylan's wife, Sara, was with him, as was his manager, Albert Grossman, when I dropped by his suite, and he seemed extremely pleased to get the gold records. He asked if I thought all his previous albums might now earn gold records, and I had to admit that, while I wanted nothing more, we had a way to go in a few cases. He seemed relaxed, even chatty, not at all the forbidding character I'd heard so much about. We exchanged some other pleasantries, and then I left to get ready to go to the concert.

It might seem odd that Dylan, who seemed so remote from all business considerations during that period, should care that much about his sales, but, as with Janis, it's just an indication of how seriously he took his music. It's not that sales were all he cared about, or that he was especially willing to do the standard things an artist can do to boost sales—releasing singles, touring, doing interviews, and the like. But sales were one measure of how effectively he was reaching people—and, in a world in which he could easily move to another label, an indication of how effectively Columbia was doing its job. On another occasion, for example, he asked why I thought *John Wesley Harding* had not sold better, and I told him that it was because we didn't have a strong single that we could release from it. As he often did in such conversations, he took that point in and didn't say much in reply. But with Dylan you could always be sure that he had absorbed everything you said, and you could never know when he might bring it up again.

The Carnegie Hall performances were a triumph. Backed by the musicians who would soon become the Band, Dylan played three lesser-known Guthrie songs—"Grand Coulee Dam," "Dear Mrs. Roosevelt," and "I Ain't Got No Home"—in rock versions that demonstrated once again his unwillingness to do what was expected of him. Still, he respected the communal nature of the event, mingling amiably with Pete Seeger, Judy Collins, Odetta, Richie Havens, Woody's son Arlo Guthrie, and the other artists on the bill, and participating with them on the group sing-alongs. The only drawback to the event was that, both at the shows and in the media coverage, Dylan's presence nearly overwhelmed the focus of the Guthrie tribute. It was another example of Dylan's extraordinary star power. The more he did to dim its glow, the more brightly it burned.

My meeting with Dylan at his hotel, brief as it was, helped establish a strong positive connection between us. After that, he would send me the tapes of each new album when it was completed and we'd discuss such issues as the release schedule, artwork, and possible singles. The conversations about singles were always the trickiest. I emphasized to him that, if he was concerned about sales, an AM radio single was essential to carrying his music beyond an audience of his devotees. In one talk we had he told me that none of his friends listened to AM radio, so how important could it be? To me that was exactly the point. His friends were typical of the audience we already had and would keep. If we wanted to move beyond them, however, AM radio was key. It was never an argument, always a discussion, but it was never definitively resolved. It was as if every time the issue came up we had to go over every point as if we'd never talked about it before.

After *John Wesley Harding* came out, Dylan's relationship with Albert Grossman began to deteriorate. I don't know all the reasons; my own working relationship with Albert had always been good. It eventually became clear, however, that the situation between them was not going to turn around, that the tie between them was severed. It was not the sort of thing Dylan would discuss with me; I'm not sure how much he really discussed it with anyone. Dylan, however, was not looking for another manager, and I began to be concerned that, by not having a manager, his tendency to privacy and life in Woodstock might make him grow too isolated.

In my view, Dylan was at his best when he was getting a lot of input—talking to other artists, going to see them play, discussing issues with the people around him whom he trusted. But he didn't really trust very many people, or maybe he did, just not for very long. Even if you felt that he trusted you, something would occur later that made you realize how wary and suspicious he remained. He liked to test the advice you gave him with other people, and, in turn, I could tell when he was running someone else's advice by me to see what I thought. The wheel of these various conversations would spin, and you wouldn't know when it would stop and he would reach his decision, let alone what that decision would be. It was his way of keeping everybody around him on their toes, and a big part of why he always seemed so mysterious and unpredictable. In his defense, though, few artists in any field have ever had so many expectations and desires projected on them as Dylan had in those days. He had understandable reasons for wondering about the motivations of everyone around him. Everybody seemed to want something from him.

I tried to handle Dylan the way I would any other artist I cared about and admired. While he clearly understood who he was, he hated sycophants. I simply attempted to be as straightforward and honest with him as I could. I even invited him to attend the Columbia sales conventions, figuring why not? He might enjoy making the rounds, meeting other artists and managers, and finding out a little bit about how the company worked. He had attended the 1963 Columbia convention in Puerto Rico with Suze Rotolo, his girlfriend at the time (who was also on the cover of his 1963 album, *The Freewheelin' Bob Dylan*), though that hadn't gone so well. Characteristically, Dylan could barely manage to be polite, or responsive at all, to the salesmen he met, and Goddard Lieberson had to convince the restaurant at the convention hotel to admit Dylan, who refused to wear a tie. He never brought any of that up, however. He'd just say, "That might be fun. It might be nice. When is it?" But he never came.

Consistently, though, I made a concerted effort, without being overbearing, to stay in touch with him and let him know I was there if he needed me. I didn't try to be his best friend. I was the president of his label and I kept our communications cordial, but businesslike, which I think he appreciated. I'd leave messages with his secretary and occasionally he would call back. I let him know, if only by implication, that I would be willing to help him if he ever thought my perspective might be useful. If there were any managers, producers, or business advisors he wanted to meet, I could certainly help arrange that. He would always listen politely, and would sometimes follow up on one matter or another.

When I heard the songs for *Nashville Skyline* I liked it immediately and got genuinely excited about its potential. The album reflected the quieter, more domestic life Dylan had been leading, and his writing was much more straightforward. I thought those factors might make the album easier for the public to relate to than some of his more esoteric work. He had also smoothed the edges of his voice, which had lost some of its rawness and acerbic tone. He said it was because he had stopped smoking. Who knows? In my view, it was just another plus as far as his commercial prospects were concerned.

I did want him to change the album's title, however, and we had several discussions about that. He had recorded the album in Nashville, but he'd done that before, so there was no particular need to highlight it. While there certainly were country elements to some of the songs, it was not in any literal sense a country album, and I felt the title might be misleading in that regard. More significantly, I believed the title might be a turnoff to rock fans. While rock and country musicians had moved closer together, their audiences were still poles apart. I doubted that Dylan would pick up many country fans, but he might alienate elements of his most natural audience in the rock and singer-songwriter realms. Dylan's invariable response in such conversations was "I'll get back to you." Most often that simply meant "I don't want to say no to you directly," but sometimes he would call later and say he had changed his mind. My strategy, such as it was, was simply to give him the most honest advice I could and then see what came back.

In this case, on the day the album covers were being shipped, a month after our last conversation on the subject, Dylan called to say that he'd been thinking about it and maybe I was right, maybe the album's title should be changed. I had to tell him it was too late; we couldn't change it. Now he grew concerned. Did I really think the title would impact his sales? I explained that a lot of factors went into which records sold and which didn't, that Columbia was going to promote the album as strongly as it could, and that if reviews were favorable we would do well. And, I added, if we had a hit single, we could do very well.

I don't know if that conversation did the trick, but when it came time to discuss the possibility of releasing a single from the album,

Dylan was open to suggestions. He called one day and said that he was going to be in the neighborhood. Could he drop by to talk about the album? When he came to my office, he had a lot of ideas, and a lot of questions. What song did I think would make the best single? Without hesitation, I said "Lay Lady Lay." He was taken aback. I think he was so used to getting into trouble over his lyrics that he thought the song's sexual suggestiveness would prevent it from getting played. I understood that, but I thought we might be able to have it both ways. By 1969 the sexual revolution was in full swing, so the erotic feel of the song suited the times. However, it was a warm, delicate, melodic ballad, a seduction, not a coarse come-on. It showed a side of Dylan that had never been heard before, one to which everyday music fans, not just hip insiders, could respond. Dylan admitted that he never really understood what would be a hit and what wouldn't, so he would defer to me. I should do what I thought best.

That was all the encouragement I needed. The first single we released from *Nashville Skyline* was "I Threw It All Away," another ballad that announced the shift to a gentler tone in Dylan's work, and it cracked the Top 100. Then we came out with "Lay Lady Lay," which broke into the Top 10 and helped propel *Nashville Skyline* to more than a million sales.

Another element that helped the album commercially was a duet with Johnny Cash on Dylan's beautiful folk ballad "Girl from the North Country." Cash had been one of Dylan's earliest supporters, and the two men had been friends for years. In the course of that time, Cash had become one of the biggest stars in music, shattering the boundaries between country and rock. His appearance on *Nashville Skyline* and his writing the liner notes for it lent Dylan a unique form of mainstream credibility that did not at all detract from his outsider status. No one but Cash could have done that for him.

When Cash invited Dylan to perform on the premiere of his prime-time network television show in June 1969, it was a major media event. Dylan had shied away from any type of exposure on that scale since his negative experience with *The Ed Sullivan Show*. Again, it's doubtful anyone but Cash could have coaxed him into such a high-profile setting. Dylan's appearance on *The Johnny Cash Show* brought him and his music to viewers who would previously have been wary of both. Cash, of course, benefited from the enormous prestige of attracting Dylan to network television. That both Cash and Dylan were Columbia artists made it all the sweeter for me.

The success of *Nashville Skyline,* coupled with everything else that was going well at Columbia, led me to believe that I had cracked the Dylan code. We seemed to understand each other, and we were communicating well. He was extremely pleased that *Nashville Skyline* had sold in such large numbers and that "Lay Lady Lay" was a Top 10 hit. I felt that we had figured out a way to build his audience without compromising his integrity or lowering his standards. I was poised to build on what we had already accomplished.

What followed was one of the most controversial few months in Dylan's career, which, given the number of controversies that have centered on him, is saying something. In June 1970 Columbia released Dylan's double album *Self Portrait,* which consisted of a few new Dylan songs, some live performances, and versions of traditional folk songs, Tin Pan Alley standards, and even recent popular tunes by other singer-songwriters, such as Gordon Lightfoot's "Early Mornin' Rain" and Paul Simon's "The Boxer." It was something like a musical scrapbook, a further retreat from the relentless demands of Dylan's most ardent fans that everything he release be a major statement of some sort. Calling this radical departure *Self Portrait*—and painting an actual self-portrait for the cover, a last-minute decision that delayed the album's release by a month—seemed a characteristic Dylan feint: I have no interest in being whoever you think I have to be. This gathering of unlikely fragments is my self-portrait.

The reviews were brutal. The eminent critic Greil Marcus began *Rolling Stone*'s lengthy discussion of the album with the question "What is this shit?" That pretty much summed up the tone of the reviews overall. Dylan was stung by many of the comments that were made. At first he was defensive, but in succeeding years he has gone to some length to distance himself from the album. In a 1984 *Rolling Stone* interview he even referred to *Self Portrait* as "a joke," prompting an excellent follow-up question by Kurt Loder: "But why did you make it a double-album joke?"

Personally, I wasn't shocked by the response the album generated. Artists of Dylan's stature inspire strong feelings, pro and con. He's a particularly restless artist, the kind that is going to win over new fans, while losing others, each time out. While as the head of his label I would have loved every Dylan album to be a huge hit, you can't hold him to anything like those expectations. Dylan is going to make his detours, and you simply have to allow for that. If you want to work with an artist like him over time, you have to learn to ride with those expansions and contractions. That's become a credo for me, and I learned it dealing with Dylan.

That said, Dylan had discussed his concept for *Self Portrait* with me as he was working on the album, and at no point was he as ironic about it as he would suggest in later years. I had even tried to arrange some sessions with the Byrds backing him up, but the band left town the day they were supposed to go into the studio, and Dylan was infuriated, as was I. I knew that he was having trouble coming up with new, original songs, and when he brought up the possibility of recording other people's material, I was not only fine with it, I encouraged it. I think it's fascinating when great songwriters choose to record other writers' work. In fact, Dylan has done it many times since then. We can argue about how successful he was in doing that on *Self Portrait*. That's a separate issue. I actually enjoyed the album, and it did enter the Top 5 and earn a gold record. And while I understood what people were complaining about, I thought the criticism was a bit excessive.

As if to quiet his detractors, Dylan came back four months later with *New Morning,* an album that conformed much more closely to what his followers might have expected after *Nashville Skyline.* The two albums are really something like companion pieces, though Dylan had changed his vocal style yet again, abandoning his croon and restoring some of the bite to his delivery. It was generally an upbeat record, as its title suggested. Critics nearly wept with relief. This time the *Rolling Stone* review began, "Well, friends, Bob Dylan is back with us again."

I believed that *New Morning* could be as big a record as *Nashville Skyline,* and encouraged Dylan to release a single. After our previous success, I figured he'd absolutely be for it. But for his usual ambiguous reasons, he hemmed and hawed about it, claiming that he hadn't thought about singles at all while making the album. The catchy "If Not for You" seemed the most logical choice, but it proved to be a bit too popular. George Harrison covered the song on his hugely successful album *All Things Must Pass,* which came out a month after *New Morning.* Olivia Newton-John, of all people, enjoyed an international hit with it, and used it as the title track of her debut album. We were slow getting to the party, and Dylan's version, when we did release it, failed to chart. *New Morning* earned a gold record, but ended up selling about half as well as *Nashville Skyline.* It was a missed opportunity.

In November 1971, Dylan wrote a song that allowed me to make up for my having to tell him nearly a decade earlier that Columbia would not release "Talkin' John Birch Society Blues." He had viewed the issue at the time as free speech, while, as Columbia's general counsel, I needed to protect the company from potential libel suits. This time the issue *was* free speech, and I was delighted to be able to speak out strongly on Dylan's behalf.

Dylan had written a song called "George Jackson" about a Black Panther who was killed during an attempted escape from San Quentin Prison. The event, one among many violent political confrontations at the time, had drawn enormous publicity, and Dylan weighed in with a hard-hitting ballad that recalled the protest songs that had established his reputation in the early Sixties. He wanted it released immediately and didn't care if it sold at all. I agreed, and Columbia put the single out the week after it had been recorded.

Critics were rhapsodic that Dylan had returned to political commentary, and the single entered the Top 40. Beyond its subject matter, the song became controversial because Dylan sang that Jackson "wouldn't take shit from no one." The label received a considerable number of complaints about the swearword in the song, and some radio stations refused to play it or bleeped out "shit," which was their prerogative. It gave me great pleasure, though, both to release the song and to defend in public the right of one of the country's most important songwriters to use whatever language he saw fit to get his message across.

Interestingly, Dylan wrote "George Jackson" during another of his songwriting dry spells. He returned to the type of song he had written in the past in an attempt to get his creative juices flowing again. Since he was not being especially productive, I thought it might be a good time to assemble another collection of his greatest hits, particularly since the first one had done so well. Because Dylan was such a significant figure, the set needed to be strong and distinctive, a coherent listening experience in its own right, not simply a random grouping of popular songs. I also wanted it to be a two-disc collection to give it more heft, and Dylan agreed.

I sent him a list of songs that I thought were candidates for inclusion, and then Dylan said that he also wanted to include some unreleased material on the collection. This is standard practice now, of course—another example of Dylan's farsightedness. At the time, however, it was not a typical move, and I was concerned that it would counter the idea that this set consisted of greatest hits; that is, his best and most popular work. Some of the performances he wanted to include also had not been well recorded, which bothered me but which, characteristically, didn't worry him at all.

Going back into the studio to work on them was out of the question, needless to say. He liked to work fast in the studio, and almost to a fault never belabored anything. The notion of going back to songs he had recorded years before in order to "improve" them was nothing he was interested in. He was the furthest thing from an audiophile, and he liked the performances the way they were. If the feel was right, that was enough for him. Also, Dylan bootlegs were beginning to make the rounds, and I think he felt that if people were interested in hearing that material, he might as well be the one to put it out.

I was concerned that, rather than being excited that they were getting previously unheard Dylan material, fans might think we were padding the set to fill out the two discs. But Dylan wanted to include the tracks, and if he wasn't going to be persuaded by the logic of my arguments, I then just wanted to keep him happy. Still, for all the back-and-forth about what to include, he hadn't finally agreed to release the set at all. I met with him one evening at a David Bromberg show at Folk City—he was there with George Harrison—to discuss some other ideas I had for the collection. He listened and said he would make a decision after hearing the entire double album in sequence.

Later that night, I went to the Greenwich Village apartment of Columbia product manager Don DeVito, who would go on to a long career working on Dylan projects, and, along with Mark Spector and Michael Klenfner, two former employees of Bill Graham's whom I had hired at Columbia, we combed through all of Dylan's catalog to come up with a definitive set list and sequence. The next day I sent a tape of it to Dylan, and he gave us permission to release it. To date that set has sold more than 2.5 million copies, which for a double album is the equivalent of 5 million sales, making it one of the most popular titles in Dylan's long career.

It seemed much too soon, but by 1972 Dylan's five-year contract was up, and we needed to negotiate a new deal. Was there no end to this? So much had happened in the intervening years and Dylan and I had developed a sufficiently good relationship that I was confident we would be successful. However, even though he was relatively inactive, Dylan had become one of the most revered and prestigious artists in the world of music, and I knew that he would be getting lavish offers from other labels. The process, inevitably, proved complicated.

Things initially looked bright when I negotiated with Dylan's attorney, David Braun, a new five-year deal with which everyone seemed satisfied. It took six months to reach that agreement. One of the issues that had come up was Dylan's desire for what would become known in the industry as a "key man" clause—that is, if I left the label for any reason, he would be free to leave as well. He was not the first artist to ask for that, and, of course, I was flattered. We had been working closely together for five or six years, and it was clear that he appreciated my efforts on his behalf. Since he's so hard to read I had sometimes wondered if he knew how much I valued him, so his desire to recognize our relationship that way was very gratifying. However, as a matter of label policy, I couldn't agree to such a clause. It would be a bad precedent, and potentially would lead to complications with other artists. It would also cloud my motives in the negotiation, or at least allow them to be misread, and put me in an uncomfortable position with the CBS brass. So I took that off the table.

Nonetheless, we came to terms. Then Dylan refused to sign the contract. He was uncomfortable committing to Columbia, or any other label for that matter, for five years, he said. It was his old issue of wanting to have as few commitments as possible. So back we went to the drawing board. We eventually struck a deal in early 1973 for two new albums, plus the *Pat Garrett and Billy the Kid* soundtrack, which I had encouraged him not to release after the film (in which he also appeared as an actor) got negative reviews. The soundtrack ended up including "Knockin' on Heaven's Door," which became a Top 20 single, and as a result the album sold pretty well. Dylan was right again.

Beyond that, the contract included no specified amount of time, so Dylan would be under no external pressure to record. Typically, freedom was his primary concern. His royalty rate would increase substantially, and he was promised a guarantee of $400,000 per album. Dylan also wanted the rights to his back catalog, something only an artist of his stature could even request. Ordinarily it would be out of the question. Catalog material is both valuable to a record company in commercial terms and useful leverage in preventing an artist from leaving to sign somewhere else. But this was Bob Dylan, so we had to find a way to meet this demand without giving up too much.

To do that we agreed that in five years, that is, in 1978, Dylan would get the rights to his 1961 debut album, *Bob Dylan*. After that, every time he turned in a new album to Columbia, the rights to another of his earlier albums would revert to him, with the exception of *Greatest Hits* collections. It was a nicely balanced arrangement that provided an incentive for Dylan to record, as well as to stay with Columbia. The better his new work, the more valuable his catalog would be. It was a win for everyone.

Unfortunately, after my stint at Columbia ended in 1973, the label pulled out of the deal. The simple fact is that after all those years, Goddard Lieberson, back in charge after I left, still was not convinced that Dylan deserved unprecedented terms, and was unwilling to go to the extra lengths to keep him at Columbia. The deal that had been negotiated was a good one all around—if you believed that it was essential to keep Dylan and that he was an artist whose importance would continue to grow. Given how traditional and precedent-obsessed Columbia was, the deal had pushed the label pretty far, however necessarily. Goddard would certainly have been happy to keep Dylan on more modest terms—that is, terms Dylan never would have agreed to and that every label in the country would have eagerly exceeded. Once I had left, no one of sufficient power remained at Columbia to fight for Dylan. Irwin Segelstein, who was put in charge of Columbia's Domestic Operations, had come to the label from television and couldn't be expected to find his footing so quickly in a situation this complicated and highly charged. So Dylan became free to go elsewhere.

The *Pat Garrett and Billy the Kid* film had just come out, and an infuriated David Braun demanded that Columbia stand by its commitment to put out the soundtrack, since it would be impossible for him to line up another label deal in a reasonable amount of time. Columbia agreed to issue the album at the royalty rate I had negotiated. In one more turn of the screw, when "Knockin' on Heaven's Door" began to move up the charts, once again demonstrating Dylan's ongoing significance, Goddard attempted to reopen negotiations. Again, however, there were limits to how far Columbia would reach, and, in what had immediately become a wildly competitive environment, that proved fatal.

In a move that was loudly trumpeted in the music business press, Dylan signed with David Geffen's label, Elektra/Asylum. It was a triumph for Geffen, and he played it for all it was worth. In those same stories in the press, Columbia desperately tried to spin its loss of Dylan, defensively claiming that the label refused to make a "no profit" deal to keep him. The waters were poisoned. Then Dylan dramatically announced that not only had he signed with a new label, but he would be going on tour again, backed by the Band, for the first time since 1966. The tour was a major media event that, again, made Columbia look bad. In response, Columbia rush-released a shoddy album of outtakes, titled *Dylan,* to capitalize on the tour and blunt the impact of *Planet Waves,* Dylan's first album for Geffen, which came out a couple of months later. It was an ugly situation that could easily have been avoided by honoring the deal we had struck.

Given the extensive publicity that accompanied Geffen's signing of Dylan, I was stunned to get a call from David Braun in March 1974, when I was not affiliated with any label, explaining that Dylan was thinking about not giving his next album to Elektra/Asylum. Braun told me that Dylan regretted the absence of my guidance and suggestions on the *Planet Waves* project, which he felt should have sold better. Geffen had made extravagant promises about how well the album was going to perform commercially, and even though it went to number one, it fell well short of the million sales Geffen had all but guaranteed.

It turned out that, true to his nature, Dylan had insisted on signing just a one-album deal with Geffen, despite extensive publicity that made it appear otherwise. Dylan and the Band's two-month tour had just ended, and it had been a roaring success. Five million fans had requested tickets for the shows through the highly touted mail-order process that Geffen had set up. It had been left unresolved whether the live album from the tour—Dylan's first live album, a two-record set eventually titled *Before the Flood*—would go to Elektra/Asylum. Since he had helped organize the tour and had signed Dylan to his label, Geffen believed he deserved it and that Dylan had agreed to it, at least informally. Dylan and the Band were weighing their options, and that's why Braun had called me.

One idea Dylan had was to sell the album exclusively through a massive television sales campaign. To his credit he was thinking outside the box, but I didn't like the idea at all. Dylan, to me, was as important an artist as America had ever produced, and to have his album hustled constantly on television was undignified and beneath him. It would also outrage the retail distributors and outlets that had helped build the music business, which would not only be bad for Dylan in the long term, but for the industry as a whole.

I came up with another idea, however, and Dylan flew me to Los Angeles to discuss it with him and Robbie Robertson of the Band at the Beverly Hills Hotel. I proposed that the album be sold directly to distributors and rack jobbers, an arrangement that would keep the retail network happy and that would earn Dylan and the Band a dollar more per album. The approach itself would generate considerable publicity for the album, and also allow room for a powerful national advertising campaign. Dylan and Robertson loved the idea, and Dylan immediately called Geffen and told him that he now planned to put out the live album himself. Geffen went through the roof.

That was hardly the end of the matter. Though the label didn't realize that I was working with Dylan, Columbia found out that the live album was up for grabs and jumped energetically into the game. Columbia had been stung by the publicity that resulted from losing Dylan, and ardently wanted him back. The label offered sixty cents more in royalties per album, which was less than the plan I had come up with, but far more than the Asylum bid.

Now the bidding war was on, and I watched from the sidelines with amusement. As original and potentially lucrative as my proposal was, it's ultimately a good deal easier to let a major label like Columbia or Elektra/Asylum manufacture and distribute your album than to do it yourself. As the money gap between my approach and going with a label closed, I got a kick out of the way Dylan and David Braun worked the situation to Dylan's advantage. One label was desperate to keep Dylan; the other was desperate to get him back. And it was my new marketing approach that had helped set the wheels in motion.

Eventually, Geffen matched Columbia's offer, and *Before the Flood* came out on Asylum and racked up platinum sales. After that Dylan returned to Columbia in another highly remunerative deal. The times had changed, indeed, and with a little help behind the scenes from a friend, Dylan proved as gifted in the rough-and-tumble world of business as in the loftier realms of his songwriting art.

What Kind of Career Do I Want?

As the Sixties approached their end and a new decade loomed, many of the changes I'd set out to accomplish at Columbia were fully in motion, and they were producing big results. When I had assumed the presidency of the label in 1967, Columbia, RCA, and Capitol could claim roughly equal shares of the market at 12 or 13 percent. By 1970 our market share was 22 percent. Our after-tax profits had risen to $6.7 million in 1968, then to $10 million in 1969, and, incredibly, to more than $15 million in 1970. The record division had jumped from a tiny fraction of CBS's overall profits to about one-third of its bottom line. It was a sensationally good period.

Columbia's success both reflected and caused significant changes in the perception of the label. Columbia had famously been determined to ignore the seismic changes taking place in the world of contemporary music and beyond. Now it was seen as embracing rock 'n' roll and all the energy, innovation, and new thinking that it represented. From lagging substantially behind, it was now leading the charge. We had hit-makers and prestige artists, and some who were both. We were firing on all cylinders.

Let me pause here for a moment to say that although everything was going so well, there was always something coming up that either caused worry or made me stop and think and question. On a personal note, I had always kept up my friendship and professional relationship with the lawyer Abe Somer. We knew each other when I was chief counsel for Columbia Records and he was the fastest-rising music attorney in the business. I went to Monterey because of Abe, made the Lou Adler deal because of Abe, and became friends with the Mamas and the Papas because of Abe. When I graduated to the presidency of Columbia he'd meet me at the airport in L.A. on every one of my West Coast trips with his close producer friends Richard Perry and David Anderle, and they'd help me develop my ears as we hit the Whisky A Go Go, the Troubadour, and later the Roxy in search of new artists and new music.

Through our friendship I knew that despite Abe's representing almost every new cutting-edge artist, he was a devoted son and grandson to his Orthodox Jewish mother and grandmother. He always wanted his mother and me to meet, and he arranged a dinner just for the three of us at his Doheny Drive estate in 1970. When I arrived, Abe and his mother came to the door to give me warm hugs. Abe turned to his mother and said, "Well, Mom, this is Clive, and you know I've been telling you about him for years. He was a lawyer but now he's president of Columbia Records and he's signed Janis Joplin and Blood, Sweat and Tears," and this artist and that artist, proceeding to list all my credentials. His mother, a short woman with a classic Semitic face, took it all in without a change of expression. She didn't say a word, and seemed lost in thought. Finally, she looked up at me, squinting a little, and asked, "You were a lawyer, right?" I immediately answered, "Yes." "And now you're signing all these musical artists?" Again I said, "Yes," this time a little proudly. And then she looked me squarely in the eyes and firmly inquired with a familiar ethnic shrug of the shoulders: "For this you gave up your profession?" She had me. I got it. I put my arms around her. There's nothing like maternal family!

Because of our successes, the energy level at the label was thrillingly high, and I wanted to keep it that way. Whenever the opportunity presented itself I hired young people who were genuine music fans and who would not be constrained by the traditions of Columbia's past. I informed the sales staff that, if they weren't already, they had to begin reading *Rolling Stone,* which had launched in late 1967 and become an increasingly important guide to music and the counterculture. As irritating as it could sometimes be in its offhand, assumed hipness, the music business needed it, and I personally found it invaluable. I did everything I could to support it, including paying for ads a year in advance and, for a time, letting members of its advertising staff work out of Columbia's offices so they could learn about our mail-order procedures. To say the least, this was hardly traditional journalistic practice, but *Rolling Stone* seemed to make up its own rules as it went along, and that's part of what made it so vital. The magazine's survival was essential as far as I was concerned, so I was happy to help. For better or worse, such cooperation never guaranteed the coverage I would have liked. But I enjoyed reading *Rolling Stone* with the same eagerness that I had read *Variety* in law school. I read every issue to this day.

I could not change the intimidating colossus that was Black Rock, the imposing building that housed CBS, but I did everything I could to ensure that the floors that housed the creative departments—the areas that visiting artists were most likely to wander through—looked alive and fresh, not staid and uptight. I tried as much as possible to protect Columbia from corporate incursions by CBS, and it sometimes felt as if we had carved out our own special domain within the company, one that channeled all the bumptious developments in the world outside and then generated music that both documented and provided a soundtrack for them. The rule at CBS was that the office of Frank Stanton, the company's very eminent, long-standing president, had to approve all the artwork that was put up on the walls, but let's just say that we went as far as we could to work around that restriction. It was the age of great poster art, after all, and it's not as if Stanton or William Paley were particularly eager to wander the corridors of the record division. That said, I got along well with both Stanton and Paley. Stanton may not have cared much about popular music but he certainly enjoyed the dramatic increases in our profits and market share. As for Paley, in addition to my helping to prepare him for stockholder meetings, I had lunch with him alone in his private dining room three times. He had a masterful charm and an effortless sense of power. You couldn't be around him and not be aware that he was an icon, a giant television pioneer. He, too, didn't know much about the record industry but he appreciated how well we were doing. In the record division we were trying to do something very new in the context of a company that had a long, distinguished history. I like to think that we still were businesslike, but in a way that recognized the undeniable pleasures of contemporary music. When you earn your living doing what other people do for fun, it seems like the only honest way to be.

To build esprit de corps at Columbia, I began holding meetings every Wednesday morning for the promotion, publicity, and A&R staffs, and whoever else might have a contribution to make on a specific project. The point of those meetings was to review the important releases for that week, track developments on projects that were already in motion, and prepare for upcoming releases. Everyone was expected to be fully prepared to discuss the strategies they had designed, and to detail both the challenges they faced and the prospects for their success. The atmosphere could sometimes be competitive, but it was meant to be cooperative, to give each relevant person a discernible stake in reaching our goals. The meetings were also meant to take full advantage of the intelligence and experience of Columbia's executive team. Everyone was encouraged to contribute ideas, and once a plan of action was agreed on, each person in the room knew exactly what he or she had to do to achieve our desired results. I've held such meetings throughout my career, and often invited artists, managers, and even the media when appropriate. These meetings provide a convincing look at how the label works, both pragmatic and dramatic, and force people out of their silos to understand the bigger picture of the label's overall mission.

Personally, along with the satisfactions of my creative work, I did have to deal with the corporate world of CBS in order to do my job. It might be too much of a stretch to say that I was living a double life, but it could sometimes feel that way. My education and experience at law firms made the formalities of the business world very recognizable to me, even, at their best, comfortable in a way. But it was certainly more invigorating to move in a world in which style was a personal statement, not something you suppressed in order to don the uniform you put on for work. My sideburns and hair grew longer. I had a Nehru jacket and, much to the amusement of my old friends from NYU, at least one velvet suit. There was a kind of Edwardian romance and elegance to the Sixties at their peak. That suited me, and I was happy to indulge in it occasionally.

What wasn't very much fun was fighting with CBS about my compensation. After three years as president of Columbia and dramatically improving the label's performance, I was earning $100,000 plus a $40,000 bonus. No one needed to organize a benefit for me, clearly, but CBS was notoriously tightfisted. It irked me, to cite just one example, that I was making far less money than the president of Capitol Records while delivering far more impressive numbers. I was regularly putting in fifteen-to-eighteen-hour days five or six days a week. Worse yet, a substantial amount of that time was devoted to aspects of the domestic operation that had nothing to do with the parts of my job that I loved best: signing artists, making it possible for them to do the absolute best work they could, and bringing that work to the marketplace with imagination, flair, and effectiveness. My job entailed being responsible for record-pressing factories in California, Indiana, and New Jersey; tape production and duplication facilities in Connecticut and Indiana; a research and engineering lab in New Milford, Connecticut; sales and promotion offices throughout the country; and our music publishing operations. All that was a far cry from editing "Piece of My Heart" so that Janis Joplin could have an all-important radio hit, or choosing a single for Simon and Garfunkel that would become one of the great classics of the period.

Columbia's dramatic transformation led to my receiving a number of job offers around this time, and I was tempted by two of them. In the spring of 1970 Mo Ostin of Warner Bros. called and offered me a position at Warner Communications (WCI) that paid $200,000, along with valuable stock options that could potentially have raised the offer up to a million dollars. The position would have involved overseeing the various labels under the WCI corporate umbrella, along with their dynamic leaders: Mo Ostin and Joe Smith of Warner-Reprise; Jac Holzman of Elektra; and Ahmet Ertegun and Jerry Wexler of Atlantic. Steve Ross, the brilliant chairman of WCI who was well known for treating his top executives like artists, asked me to lunch one day in his beautiful and spacious personal dining room. He explained that not one of his music executives would agree to report to any of the others. The only one all of them would agree to report to was me. I was flattered, but at the same time the offer was oddly off-putting. It was definitely a big job and the money was attractive, but I felt as if it would remove me from the front lines of artist acquisition and development, the action that had become my lifeblood. Those company heads that I would supposedly be supervising—all of whom I respected and some of whom I regarded as good friends—were not likely to be receptive to my involvement in their creative decisions. And, to be fair, I completely understood that—in their position it would have bothered me, too. But I was far too young and having much too good a time to get kicked upstairs at whatever salary.

I was also suspicious about WCI's motivations. WCI was on the move, and was now Columbia's principal music business rival. It was expanding rapidly, and I was hardly the only Columbia executive approached. And since I was also not the only Columbia executive having trouble getting paid in a competitive manner, I constantly had to fight to protect my staff from Warners' raids. It got so pervasive that one day I sent a telegram to Mo Ostin and Joe Smith that read along these lines: "Dear Mo and Joe: You've got to help me out. There is a young secretary on the seventh floor of our building who is in a deep depression because she's the only person at Black Rock who has not been offered a job by Warner Bros. I'm sure it's simply an oversight. Would you please do me the favor of offering her a position so that we can lift her spirits? With much appreciation, your friend, Clive." In such an environment, paying a million bucks to remove me from the front lines at Columbia into a corporate spot at WCI would be money well invested.

Before the WCI offer, Jac Holzman, an extremely bright, sharp, and impressive executive, had offered me a significant partnership in Elektra Records, before he sold it to WCI. But even more alluring, David Geffen had wanted me to join him as a full partner when he was launching Asylum Records, an opportunity I passed on and which I joke about regretting to this day. It was a characteristically incisive move on David's part. Here I was, the president of what had arguably become the most successful record company in the world, but he knew I was vulnerable and feeling underpaid. He threw all his interests as a manager and agent into the pie to invite me to join him as co-CEO of an independent start-up. David always had immense confidence, and it was infectious. There was 50 percent equity involved, which was a considerable upside, and I shared his strong optimism that together we would do extremely well. I obviously took his proposal very seriously. We sat by the pool at the Beverly Hills Hotel one day and discussed it at length. "You're building an asset worth millions and millions of dollars on the strength of the artists you've signed and developed," David said about my work at Columbia. "And what are you getting paid? With our own company you'll earn what you're really worth."

No one is more persuasive than David, but our discussions ultimately broke down because our visions of what the new company should be diverged. For all my problems with Columbia, I still saw it as the model of the kind of company I wanted to run—large, diverse, competitive in every area of music. David, meanwhile, viewed the future Asylum as an exclusive boutique label. At the time he wanted to limit it to ten artists. To me that notion much more reflected the vision of a manager, someone used to dealing with the very specific requirements of a small roster of clients, rather than a record executive. And it certainly doesn't represent what David's record companies eventually became. But at the time he was specific and adamant about what he wanted, and so I couldn't join him.

While I took David's offer seriously, I turned it down without ever discussing it with the CBS brass. The WCI offer, however, seemed another order of business. I did make them aware of it, along with the fact that I had just a week and a half to respond to it. I told them, "I don't expect you to match Warners' offer, but I do expect you to make a substantial change in my compensation. And I need your answer within ten days."

They ended up offering me an additional $25,000, along with an option of 10,000 additional shares of CBS stock. It didn't approach the Warner Bros. deal, but it was something—and it did mean something to me. Difficult as it was for me to admit, and as frustrating as it could be for me there, I deeply valued being at Columbia. Its storied history held a great deal of significance for me, and I took pride in having extended that legacy into the present. By this point, many of the people working at the label had either been hired by me or had demonstrated that they were very much in synch with my goals. I had signed or played an important role in the careers of many of the artists currently on the label, and I felt personally connected to them. WCI was owned by Kinney, a car-parking company. Columbia was owned by CBS, one of the most distinguished names in the media world. All of that felt good to me, regardless of whatever might not be perfect about my job.

At the end of 1970, CBS offered me a promotion. Goddard Lieberson would be retiring soon, I was told, and when that happened, I would be offered his position as head of the CBS-Columbia Group. For now, Goddard would be staying on, and I would be reporting to him as the group's executive vice president. I would be adding the international record division to my portfolio (along with the domestic division, which I already ran), but I would now also be assuming responsibility for Columbia's mail-order operation, musical instruments division, and Cinema Center Films, CBS's first film-production division.

Once again, however, this was a job that would remove me from the hands-on, day-to-day work of running Columbia Records. I would likely need to appoint a new president of Columbia, and I didn't want to do that. Turning down the promotion was a highly unorthodox decision, and Goddard suggested that I speak with Frank Stanton to explain my reasoning. Stanton might not easily understand why someone would turn down a major corporate post at CBS for the pleasure of running a record label. While he was perfectly polite, I felt that the primary conclusion he drew from our conversation was that I was no longer a candidate for his job, which he would be leaving in the near future. That was fine with me. I really had no interest in leaving the music business.

Finally, they divided the job up, making me a group president and putting me in charge of the domestic and international record divisions. That made sense, though I still did not want to appoint anyone else president of the Columbia Records division. My own preferences aside, it simply would not have been a good decision for our business. I'd achieved a lot, but the momentum was behind me now and there was plenty more for me to do. I simply was not done with that job yet. So I put Walter Yetnikoff, whom I had brought over from the Rosenman law firm, in charge of the international division. And I kept the domestic division for myself, a decision to which I finally got the CBS higher-ups to agree. Of course, my fancy new title, broader set of responsibilities, and seat on the CBS board of directors brought no increase in salary. Finally, after more battles, I got a $10,000 raise. Everything was going well. But they sure didn't make it easy.

From Santana to Springsteen

As all this action was taking place behind the scenes, I was also attempting to do my actual job of preparing Columbia for the years ahead. Maybe it's always true, but at the time the world of music seemed to be changing in dramatic ways, and I wanted the label to be ready for anything that might come. For whatever reason—my ethnic background, the early death of my parents, needing to maintain certain grades to keep my scholarships—I'm a worrier. No matter how well things are going, I not only don't take it for granted—I *can't* take it for granted. I'm simply incapable of it. Perhaps because I've always enjoyed my work so much, I feel that worrying is what I actually get paid to do. That's how I earn my money. Everything else is fun.

Even though Columbia was doing well, there were plenty of things to worry about. Janis Joplin had died. Simon and Garfunkel were breaking up. After the enormous multiplatinum success of their second album, Blood, Sweat & Tears had lost their mojo and were teetering on the brink of dissolution. Johnny Cash, Andy Williams, and Jim Nabors (a Columbia artist who played Gomer Pyle on *The Andy Griffith Show* and who had a run of successful albums in the late Sixties) all lost their TV shows in 1971. Sly's drug problems and erratic behavior had damaged Sly and the Family Stone.

Fortunately, I had made some signings that were more than counterbalancing our setbacks. The growth and momentum Columbia had shown made it possible to be aggressive both in bringing in new artists and in luring established stars from other labels where they were unhappy. One very notable signing came by way of a recommendation from Bill Graham. San Francisco was a musical hotbed in the late Sixties, and Bill called to tell me about a band that he was excited about. From his days working at the same Catskills resorts that were my old stomping grounds, Bill had always loved Latin music, and this band combined blues and psychedelic rock with relentless Afro-Cuban rhythms. The lead guitarist was a charismatic Mexican American, and the band bore his last name: Santana.

I was in Los Angeles when Bill called, and he invited me to come see the band at the Fillmore West. The group's performance was spine-tingling and transfixing—at once instantly accessible and completely fresh. I immediately expressed interest in signing the band, and we locked down both Santana and another San Francisco group called It's a Beautiful Day, who made terrific music but who, unfortunately, never were to make it big. I didn't realize at the time that Graham had also invited Ahmet Ertegun to hear Santana, but Brian Rohan, Graham's irrepressible lawyer, told me he'd passed. Frankly, I'm not sure what difference his interest would have made. Carlos Santana was thrilled to be on the same label as Bob Dylan and Miles Davis, yet another indicator of how artists can be important to a label in ways well beyond their sales.

The band's debut album, *Santana,* came out in August 1969, the same month as the group's unforgettable performance at the Woodstock festival. Word of mouth from that set, plus the Top 10 single "Evil Ways," propelled the album to more than 2 million sales. Santana was a genuine sensation. I would have loved to see the band's Woodstock set, along with Janis's and those of any number of the other Columbia artists who played that weekend. Unfortunately, however, I have to admit I never made it to Woodstock. I was on my way there with my old friend Abe Somer, who had invited me to the Monterey Pop Festival a couple of years before, and Jerry Moss, who owned A&M Records with Herb Alpert. Our plan was to spend a night beforehand at either the Concord or Grossinger's, two of the classic Catskills hotels, for some old-school food and entertainment, before heading up to Woodstock. While we were at the hotel, however, heavy rain started to pour. We heard all the news reports of the mud, the overcrowding, and the New York State Thruway being shut down. Finally came reports about possible outbreaks of scarlet fever! That did it. I ended up spending the entire Woodstock weekend at the Concord! Not very rock 'n' roll, but I had a great time nonetheless.

The real Santana explosion took place in 1970 when the movie *Woodstock* hit the screens and exponentially expanded awareness of the band. Millions of people viewed the group's now legendary performance, which drove further sales of the debut album. Then we released *Abraxas* later in the year, and the band achieved superstar status. Two irresistible singles, "Black Magic Woman/Gypsy Queen" and "Oye Como Va," drove the album's success. They also demonstrated Santana's distinctive musical reach. "Black Magic Woman" had been a minor hit for Fleetwood Mac, and "Gypsy Queen" was a tune by the jazz guitarist Gabor Szabo. Santana blended the two, made them his own, and the single rocketed into the Top 5. "Oye Como Va," meanwhile, was written by the mambo king, Tito Puente. Santana's ability to pull from such a range of sources to create music that everyone could respond to helped make his sound among the most personal and identifiable of that era. *Abraxas* rose to number one, and has sold more than 5 million copies in the United States alone. *Santana III* came out in 1971 and also hit number one, selling more than 2 million copies.

After that, Santana succumbed to the problems that afflict all too many bands at the height of their success. Personnel and drug issues stalled the group's momentum, and a falling-out occurred with Bill Graham, who had managed the group for a time. Spirituality became an essential focus in Carlos's life, and, while his music remained compelling, it also grew more esoteric and featured fewer of the sinuous rhythms and indelible riffs that had made his songs so commercially viable. I didn't have a close relationship with Carlos in those days. I would visit him backstage at his shows, and he was always polite and gracious, but we never communicated with the depth you can sometimes achieve with an artist whose work you feel as strongly about as I felt about his. None of our encounters suggested the extraordinary ride that would be ours nearly three decades later.

In the late Sixties, rock 'n' roll had become rock, and audiences had become more sophisticated. Albums had replaced singles as the music's definitive format, both artistically and commercially. A music press had risen up to document and critique the music with a seriousness that would have seemed unthinkable a decade earlier. Fans demanded that venues provide sound systems that enabled them to hear and truly appreciate the music their heroes were playing. One key aspect of those developments was that audiences became interested in virtuoso players, not just hit-makers. Carlos Santana was one of the beneficiaries of this new interest, but it was also one of the reasons for the harsh criticism of the musicians in Janis Joplin's band, Big Brother and the Holding Company.

Johnny Winter was another player who seemed just right for the time. A fiery, hugely gifted guitarist, he seemed to rise up out of nowhere and immediately generate an enormous amount of attention. That he was a tall, slender, delicate-looking albino with long, flowing white hair—the very physical antithesis of the raw, roaring blues he liked to play—only made him more intriguing. He had garnered a reputation as a teenager in his native Texas, but by the time he moved to New York and began turning up at venues to jam with other musicians, the buzz grew into a din. A friend called me after he had seen Winter sit in unannounced with Al Kooper and Mike Bloomfield at the Fillmore East. He'd been blown away, and advised me to check him out. He didn't need to say it twice.

Winter's manager was Steve Paul, who ran a club in New York called the Scene that more than lived up to its name. It was a popular after-hours hangout for musicians, who would frequently jam together on its tiny stage after their shows at other venues. Steve worked the press, and he relentlessly hyped Winter. He told me that Johnny was interested in three labels: Atlantic, Elektra, and Columbia. I met with Johnny and we had a terrific conversation that focused exclusively on artistic issues. Money never came up. Of course, that's one thing you never really have to worry about in these situations. Believe me, if anything's going to happen, or is even being seriously considered, money will become a topic soon enough.

Sure enough, Steve called three days later to tell me that RCA had offered Winter a $600,000 guarantee. RCA, mind you, was not one of the three companies Winter had courted. I figured that was it for me. There was no way I could go that high, nor did I want to. However, Steve assured me that Johnny was sticking to his plan of signing with one of the three labels he had mentioned. Atlantic had come in at around $400,000, and Steve told me that if we matched that offer Johnny would come to Columbia.

Columbia's terrific business-affairs negotiators Dick Asher and Elliot Goldman handled the back-and-forth on deals like this, and they had their work cut out for them this time. This would be the most Columbia had paid for a new artist, once again breaking precedent. I very much wanted Winter, so we set out to try to make the deal work. Our offer guaranteed $50,000 an album for six albums over a three-year period, with an option to renew for four additional albums. Steve immediately accepted, and Johnny Winter became a Columbia artist.

Then the problems started. Steve launched a barrage of publicity, and the numbers seemed to inflate with each new story. Suddenly, the word was that I had signed Winter for somewhere between half a million and a million dollars. The stories weren't true, but they created an environment in which no one was talking any longer about Johnny's sensational playing, only whether Columbia would be able to earn back its insanely extravagant "advance." It was publicity of the sort that did none of us any good.

As it turned out, we did fine on the Johnny Winter deal. He sold close to 400,000 copies of each new album, far more than we needed to break even. Signing Johnny also gave us the inside track on landing his keyboardist brother, Edgar, whose 1972 Epic album, *They Only Come Out at Night*, has sold more than 2 million copies. And Johnny is still out there playing, having built a long, well-respected, enduring career.

I first learned about Chicago through David Geffen, who had heard good things about the band (first known, as I've mentioned, as the Chicago Transit Authority) and thought I might be interested in signing them. It made sense for a number of reasons. I had already signed the Electric Flag and Blood, Sweat & Tears, groups that, like Chicago, employed horn sections in the course of blending elements of jazz, pop, and rock music. It was a groundbreaking approach at the time, and we had already begun to have considerable success with it.

Also, Chicago was working with a producer named Jimmy Guercio, who had signed a right-of-first-refusal deal with Columbia. Guercio had produced the second Blood, Sweat & Tears album, which would go on to sell more than three million copies, so he had a strong track record. I assumed Jimmy would bring Chicago to me as a matter of course, but for whatever reason he held back, not realizing that I had already heard about them from Geffen. I finally instructed Dick Asher to tell Guercio that we would not consider any of his other acts until he brought us Chicago. Finally, after a long, tense wait, he did. I signed them, and we went on to enjoy tremendous success. The band fired off a string of hits that included "Make Me Smile," "25 or 6 to 4," "Does Anybody Really Know What Time It Is?," "Colour My World," "Questions 67 and 68," and "Saturday in the Park." They would go on to be one of the best-selling bands of the Seventies, and they've been successful in every succeeding decade, selling millions of albums along the way. They're still active, and every year their fans lobby relentlessly for them to be nominated for induction into the Rock and Roll Hall of Fame, an honor the band very much deserves. So far, however, those efforts have been unsuccessful.

I had a close, if somewhat contentious, relationship with the group. In support of the third album, Chicago did a week of shows at Carnegie Hall in April 1971, and I hosted a party for them at Tavern on the Green. They were thrilled that I introduced them to Stevie Wonder and Miles Davis at that event—of course, without sharing Miles's bitter complaints that they had ripped off his sound. In return, they presented to me a beautiful, six-feet-tall antique music box from Germany, a very touching, distinctive, and generous gesture.

But our business dealings could be tough. As happened with Simon and Garfunkel for a while, the huge sales we were enjoying did little to make relations any easier, something that never failed to confound me. In fact, to a certain extent, those sales seemed to make things more difficult. For example, as I had done with Janis's "Piece of My Heart," I often proposed edits of Chicago's lengthy songs so the group could have hit singles. The full-length versions of those songs would still be available on the group's albums, but AM radio would never play songs that long, so there really weren't any options. No AM radio play meant no hits. No hits meant fewer album sales, and the band definitely wanted album sales. From my vantage, I was ultimately helping Chicago get its music into the hands of many more people. As I did with "Piece of My Heart," I would first do a rough edit in my office with an engineer. Then I'd pass it along to Jimmy Guercio, who completely understood my good intentions. He would put together a more polished version of the edited track in the studio and present it to the band. Invariably they would be resistant, and then eventually they'd go along. You'd think everyone would be happy when, one after another, the songs became gigantic hits, but the group at times seemed to resent their own success.

Then there was the question of packaging. From their debut, which was a two-record set, Chicago always wanted their releases to consist of more than one album, with posters, pictures, lyric sheets, and, in one instance, voter registration forms included. All of that ate into profits—the band never wanted to reduce its royalty rate, needless to say—and also helped contribute to the criticism that Chicago routinely took for over-the-top self-indulgence. It was a difficult situation. After Janis died, Simon and Garfunkel split up, and Blood, Sweat & Tears went cold, Chicago was the biggest band Columbia had, and it was my job to try to keep them happy. They said as much to me during a heated phone conversation in 1971, causing me to hang up in anger. Bruce Lundvall, my very talented and able vice president of marketing, tried his best to handle many of these issues, and Jimmy Guercio always attempted to be reasonable. But the band in almost every instance pushed back hard. It seemed a shame that we were unable to share all the joys of everything we were achieving together.

I don't know how the surviving members of Chicago feel about it, but from my perspective today all of the squabbles seem unimportant. What's clear is that Chicago released great music during that era, and their body of work really stacks up to quite an accomplishment.

Musicians, like all creative people, will surprise you. By nature they're hard to pin down and prone to following their own inclinations, which may or may not make sense to anyone else. So perhaps I shouldn't have been as startled as I was that day in 1970 when Jim Messina told me that he wanted to quit the country-rock band Poco, which he had founded with Richie Furay, to come to work at Columbia Records. Furay and Messina had been in Buffalo Springfield, and when that group imploded in 1968, Poco was born amid the wreckage. The group had been signed to Atlantic but came to me during the complex negotiations that led to David Crosby and Graham Nash being released from, respectively, the Byrds and the Hollies, so that they could form Crosby, Stills and Nash. I'd been trying to sign CSN myself, but when their manager, David Geffen, suddenly seemed determined to take them to Atlantic, which was Stills's label, I could fight him for only so long. I saw no point in forcing Nash to stay in a band that he wanted to leave or stopping Crosby, who had already been fired by the Byrds, from doing something he obviously wanted to do. People sometimes say that Hollywood is like high school with money. In the case of these negotiations, the music business was like kids swapping baseball cards that just happened to be worth millions of dollars. It just didn't quite work out the way I would have preferred.

Would I have liked to get CSN, and a short time later Crosby, Stills, Nash and Young? Of course I would have. Whenever I see Steven Stills to this day, I joke with him about how much he owes me. But back then supergroups were forming and breaking up at a dizzying clip, and there was no guarantee CSN was going to stay together for any significant length of time. Ahmet Ertegun of Atlantic and I even went back and forth on a potential deal involving one of us getting the first album from the band and the other getting "all the rest," as Ahmet put it—an indication that each of us quite legitimately feared that there might be only one album and no "all the rest." It didn't happen that way, of course, but no one had a crystal ball in 1969. Besides, the Hollies continued having hits after Nash left, including "He Ain't Heavy, He's My Brother" and "Long Cool Woman (in a Black Dress)." The Byrds kept making albums, including *The Ballad of Easy Rider,* which features the title song from that groundbreaking film. And Poco was a band whose bright melodic harmonies had a great deal of commercial promise, even though their first two albums, including the well-regarded *Pickin' Up the Pieces,* hadn't sold especially well.

But now, evidently, Poco was losing one of its founding members—

yet another split-up. Jim Messina had engineered and produced for Buffalo Springfield, and he wanted to come on staff at Columbia as an A&R man. I was used to A&R men who believed they should be treated like artists, but this was a reversal, though Al Kooper had also come on staff for a time after he left Blood, Sweat & Tears. Jim and I were discussing all this on the phone, so I suggested that he accompany me that afternoon on a short business trip during which we could talk in person. Perhaps I thought that a train ride to Philadelphia would cure him of whatever glamorous notions he might be entertaining about a life in the music business. I hoped that I could convince him to stick it out with Poco for a while and try to keep the group together. As usual, it didn't work.

Jim explained that the road had burned him out. I inwardly smiled at that, given that he was all of twenty-three, but to be fair he'd been in bands for a long time. He was married, and he wanted to spend more time with his wife, who was studying acting in Los Angeles. He and Richie Furay weren't getting along. He felt that signing and producing artists was the long-term direction he wanted to move in. I asked him to hold off for a month or so just to make sure he was making the right decision, but by the time we got to Philadelphia it was clear what was going to happen. Sure enough, not long after our fateful train ride, Jim sent me a detailed budget indicating what he would need in his new position, including transportation, rent, and salary requirements to the penny. I still wasn't sure he was making the right choice, but if he was that serious about it, I figured why not give it a try?

I had a demo of some songs that had been passed along to me by Don Ellis, who had been a manager of one of Columbia's Discount Records stores and later became head of Epic's A&R department. Ellis had gotten the tape from Dan Loggins, who also managed one of the stores for the Discount chain, and who wanted to help out his brother Kenny. I liked the songs and thought Jim would be a perfect fit as producer. Jim agreed to work with Kenny and see what might happen. I didn't hear anything for a while, which can be worrying. It turns out, of course, that the two men hit it off really well. I loved what I heard and suggested that they form a duo, but Jim was resistant to formally becoming Kenny's partner. Consequently, the first album, to my dismay, ended up being awkwardly titled, *Kenny Loggins with Jim Messina Sittin' In.* Of course, fans knew best, and the album was, and continues to be, commonly referred to as *Sittin' In,* which suits its engaging mood just fine.

Kenny and Jim toured together and began to build a sizable audience. Then Jim called one day and said that he and Kenny were finishing up a second album, but he still wanted to keep his options open and describe himself as just "sittin' in." This time I drew the line. He was writing songs, playing and singing on the album, and co-producing. "You're getting second billing, and you are not an added attraction," I said. "Make a commitment." Happily, the second album was simply called *Loggins and Messina,* and one of the most successful duos of the Seventies was born. Until they broke up in 1976, they were consistent million-sellers. They still occasionally reunite for live dates. True, they may not be Crosby, Stills, Nash and Young, but when you take into account the continuing strength of the Byrds and the Hollies and the major career of Loggins and Messina, I didn't really make out as badly on that deal as is sometimes thought.

As I've previously mentioned, my relationship with Miles Davis could sometimes be rocky, but it paid off for me in so many ways beyond even the extraordinary—and commercially successful—work he produced at Columbia. Santana, Chicago, and Laura Nyro were just three of the artists thrilled to be on the same label as Miles. Partly due to the breakthroughs that Miles's fusion albums had made, some people thought that jazz was going to be as big as rock 'n' roll in the Seventies. The rock audience was growing up and, as we've seen, growing more sophisticated in its tastes. The development of heavy metal seemed more geared to teenagers than grown-ups, so jazz seemed like a viable option for the generation that had come of age with rock 'n' roll and was still looking for something new and exciting. While jazz never rose to those commercial heights, it exerted a force in the marketplace that it has not done since.

One of the more meaningful signings at Columbia was the Mahavishnu Orchestra. The guitarist John McLaughlin, of course, had played with Miles on the groundbreaking sessions for *In a Silent Way* and *Bitches Brew,* so when he wanted to launch his own progressive jazz fusion band, it made sense for him to talk to me about it. I was struck by the beauty and ambition of the music he was making. We both knew the drummer Billy Cobham, who also worked with Miles and was in a band called Dreams on Columbia. I endorsed Billy as a hot choice. Additionally, I recommended that John check out the violinist Jerry Goodman, who was in another Columbia band called the Flock. McLaughlin signed him up, and the Mahavishnu Orchestra was born. The albums *The Inner Mounting Flame* and *Birds of Fire,* and the band's electrifying collaboration with Santana on *Love Devotion Surrender,* reached large audiences while expanding the boundaries of what popular music and jazz fusion could be.

Weather Report was another of my progressive music signings at Columbia. This outstanding group featured the keyboardist Joe Zawinul and the saxophonist Wayne Shorter, both of whom were veterans of Miles's fusion sessions, as well as the brilliant bassist Miroslav Vitous. Weather Report greatly benefited from the new audience's desire for music that was at once challenging and accessible. The group's first two albums, *Weather Report* and *I Sing the Body Electric,* now regarded as classics of the fusion genre, consisted of smart, stylish jazz that even novices could appreciate and enjoy. It was exactly the sort of music that I wanted Columbia to epitomize.

The keyboardist Herbie Hancock was still another Miles alumnus signed in the early Seventies. Herbie made one avant-garde album for Columbia called *Sextant,* but followed it up with *Head Hunters,* a jazz-funk fusion set that *Rolling Stone* has listed as one of the 500 Greatest Albums of All Time. Herbie would go on to have a fifteen-year run at the label, bringing jazz into the age of hip-hop and remaining truly progressive and vital to younger audiences in ways that few of his peers have been able to match.

One of the toughest things about the music business is signing artists that you thoroughly believe in but with whom you don't get to work for a truly satisfying period of time. As I've said, no record executive, if they're honest with themselves, is above signing a one-hit wonder now and then to help the bottom line. Ephemera can be profitable, and it's part of what popular music has always been about. That said, I really had very few one-hit wonders. Obviously I've signed artists who did not break through after the promise of a first hit and did not sustain lengthy careers, but that's different. The real joy comes from discovering artists whose work you know is absolutely first-rate and who you know you can bring to a large, appreciative audience. Such relationships thrive on mutual respect and deepen over time. When you have all that, you have every gratification that working in the music industry can bring.

There's no way around the breakages, though, if you have a long career. Artists move on for one reason or another, or you do. Some relationships just run their course. But when you know deep in your heart what's possible and you're not able to realize it, that's hard. I signed three stellar artists at Columbia that I never was able to work with as fully as I would have liked. All three are in the Rock and Roll Hall of Fame. They remain among the artists I most cherish and admire.

I first saw Aerosmith at Max's Kansas City in 1972, and I fell in love with the band immediately. I wasn't aware at the time that, knowing through their management that I was going to be there that night to hear another group, Aerosmith had paid to get on the bill. It turned out to be money well spent. I signed the group for $125,000, and I doubt the club demanded that much money from them to play! Signing Aerosmith was pretty much a no-brainer. Steven Tyler had undeniable star quality from the very start. I will admit to wondering if he didn't look and act too much like Mick Jagger, but I finally thought that a band could do far worse than be the American Rolling Stones. And something told me that both Tyler and the band would eventually overcome their influences, and that certainly has proven to be the case. Aerosmith's first album went platinum, and that was just the beginning of tens of millions of sales. And I will confess to being delighted when Steven Tyler sang "And then old Clive Davis said . . . I'm gonna make you a star / Just the way you are" in "No Surprize." I did tell him that at Max's. It's amazing how much Aerosmith has overcome in its career, and how much the band has gone on to achieve.

Billy Joel came to my attention through a Columbia promotion man named Herb "The Babe" Gordon, who had heard a live version

Al Hirschfeld

3

With my mother, Flo

2

On the day of the high school graduation of my
sister, Seena (*carrying flowers*). Others, from left:
Aunt Jeanette; my mother, Flo; my father, Joe; my
cousin Agnes; Agnes's daughter Eleanor, and my
Aunt Dorothy

4

My sister, Seena, and her husband,
Jerry. They took me in after my
parents died.

5

My wife Helen and I (right)
at the wedding of my best
college friend, Harold
Lubell, to Ruth,1957

Johnny Cash signs his Columbia
Records contract
in 1960

Signing Donovan to Epic Records
in 1966

7

6

With Janis Joplin at the party
celebrating the signing of
Big Brother and the Holding
Company to Columbia,
1968

8

9

Backstage with Angela Lansbury and, from left, Goddard Lieberson and composer/lyricist Jerry Herman in 1967, presenting a gold record for the original cast album of the Broadway musical *Mame*

10

Being declared an Honorary Citizen of Nashville, 1967

11

With Laura Nyro at Black Rock, 1968

With attorney Brian Rohan, the never-to-be-forgotten Bill Graham and A&R man David Rubinson, 1969

13

12

With Janis Joplin at the Columbia Records convention in Los Angeles, 1969

With Miles Davis in the clothes he bought for me to wear for his Fillmore East shows in 1969: "I want you to look special"

RIGHT: Lou Adler at the launch of his label, Ode Records, in a joint venture with Columbia, 1967

BELOW: Invitation to the post-concert dinner party my wife Janet and I hosted for Janis Joplin the night she performed at Madison Square Garden

Mr. & Mrs. Clive Davis

Janet and I would like to invite you to have a midnight supper with Janis Joplin after her Madison Square Garden concert on Friday, December 19.

We will be gathering about 11:00 p.m. at our home, 88 Central Park West, Apartment 5 South Kindly respond. 245-2642

Clive Davis

17

Gold record presentation for the first Santana album, 1970

18

Three boys from the outer boroughs by the pool at the Columbia Records convention, 1970

19

With Chicago, 1970

20

Alongside Goddard Lieberson, my early mentor, at the Columbia convention in 1971

21

With the great Kenny Gamble and Leon Huff, and also the Queen of Country Music, Tammy Wynette, at the Columbia Records convention, 1971

22

LEFT: With David Geffen, who tried to lure me away from Columbia Records, 1972

BELOW: At my summer home, 1972

23

24

The legendary Sly Stone at my summer house in Los Angeles, 1972

With George Harrison and Richard Perry in May 1973, during "A Week to Remember," a week of shows I organized at the Ahmanson Theater in Los Angeles

25

Garland Jeffreys, Gil Scott-Heron and Stevie Wonder at the Bottom Line in New York, as Arista exec Michael Klenfner sneaks in a word, 1975

26

Conferring with Bruce Springsteen after an explosive show at the Bottom Line, 1974

27

28

LEFT: With Barry Manilow, 1975

RIGHT: Patti Smith in a playful mood at my office, April 1975

BELOW: Patti Smith flexing with Arista executives Michael Klenfner (*left*) and Bob Feiden, 1976

29

31

ABOVE: With the *Saturday Night Live* cast in 1975. Arista released the show's only comedy album. Michael O'Donoghue (*seated on ground*) with Dan Aykroyd, Jane Curtin and Garrett Morris behind him. On the stairs, from top: Gilda Radner, Lorne Michaels, John Belushi, Laraine Newman

TOP RIGHT: Arista Salutes New York, 1975

RIGHT: Celebrating the signing of the Kinks to Arista with Ray Davies at the Dorchester Hotel in London, 1976

THE NEW YORK TIMES, SUNDAY, SEPTEMBER 7, 1975

ARISTA RECORDS SALUTES NEW YORK WITH A FESTIVAL OF GREAT MUSIC!

A unique star-studded day/night music festival
of Arista stars celebrating our first year
and the unique vitality of New York music!

A power-packed afternoon concert featuring these exciting contemporary artists:
12:00 Noon
★ GIL SCOTT-HERON & THE MIDNIGHT BAND ★
★ LARRY CORYELL & THE ELEVENTH HOUSE ★
★ ANTHONY BRAXTON ★
★ URSZULA DUDZIAK ★

An incredible evening show bristling with great talent:
7:00 PM
★ BARRY MANILOW ★
★ MELISSA MANCHESTER ★
★ LOUDON WAINWRIGHT ★
★ PATTI SMITH ★
★ ERIC CARMEN ★
★ LINDA LEWIS ★

Sunday, September 21, at The New York City Center—West 55th Street
Tickets: $6.50-$5.50 per performance
Available at all Ticketron Outlets and at the City Center Box Office

ALL PROFITS WILL BE DONATED TO THE CITY OF NEW YORK

32

33

At Feathers Ballroom with Andy Warhol, Lou Reed and promoter Ron Delsener, 1976

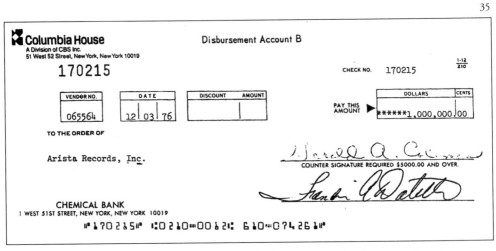

CBS's Columbia Record Club check for $1,000,000 for future mail order rights to Arista artists—better late than never, it was very emotionally satisfying to receive

Arriving with my wife
Janet at the premiere of
*Close Encounters of the
Third Kind,* 1977

36

With the Grateful Dead, 1977

37

Paul Simon and Miles Davis at the Anti-Defamation League Luncheon, 1970

Joe Smith, Mo Ostin and Berry Gordy, Jr., in February 1980 at the Martell Foundation luncheon at Le Bistro in Los Angeles

of "Captain Jack" on the radio in Philadelphia. Joel was essentially unknown at the time, but the track had become one of the station's most requested songs and Herb rightly thought that we should look into it. At the time Billy was signed to a company run by Artie Ripp, an extremely colorful record industry personality with whom Billy would dramatically fall out. At the time, however, Ripp was tireless in his promotion of Billy in ways that suggested the stereotypical music biz character. I knew he was capable of cranking the hype machine to eleven, but I always got a kick out of him. Artie insisted that I go see Billy perform in a club, and needless to say, he tore the place apart. He had already released one album, *Cold Spring Harbor,* but he was playing the songs that would eventually be on *Piano Man,* his first Columbia release. That was enough for me. He was clearly a triple threat—a gifted singer-songwriter, a torrid piano player, and a sensational live performer. I had to sign him.

Billy, too, very much wanted to be on Columbia, the home of his hero, Bob Dylan. *Piano Man* was an immediate smash, and has sold more than 4 million copies. Again, as with Aerosmith, that was just the beginning of a long, spectacular, and varied career. My only wish is that Billy would record another pop album, something he has refused to do since 1993. Just a couple of years ago, after I became chief creative officer at Sony, I called Billy and we met in my office. We had bonded all those years ago and I felt perfectly comfortable saying to him, "Look, if you've got a writing block, that's a reality and we have to live with it. But you're such a peerless entertainer as well. Why not return to the studio and do some recording so that your vast public can hear you again? Why not pick your favorite rock 'n' roll records of all time and do your own arrangements of them? I think it could be fascinating." He didn't yell. He didn't flee. He did say he'd have to think long and hard about it. Then one day, about five months later, I got a call from Lee Eastman, Jr., his lawyer, who said that Billy loved the meeting but just couldn't muster the desire to go back into the studio again. That's a shame. But even if he doesn't ever do so, Billy's created enough great music to conduct his artistic life however he likes.

And, finally, there's Bruce Springsteen. Bruce's first manager, Mike Appel, famously finagled a hearing for Bruce in John Hammond's office in May 1972, the result of Bruce's admiration of Hammond's seminal role in Bob Dylan's career. At his office, John got irritated when Appel insisted that Bruce, who had not played a note yet, was "better than Dylan." Bruce had ridden the bus into Manhattan from Asbury Park and didn't even have a case for the acoustic guitar he was carrying. But after Bruce played for John for two hours, John was hugely impressed—so much so that he wanted to hear Bruce play in front of an audience in a true performance setting. John made a call and arranged for Bruce to play a small Greenwich Village club that night, and, predictably, Bruce more than delivered on the promise he had shown in John's office. The following day John cut a fourteen-song acoustic demo with Bruce during a couple of hours in a small Columbia studio, and he sent the tape to me, along with a memo describing his enthusiastic response to Bruce and his songs. I listened to the demo and was no less impressed by it. I wrote back to John, saying, "I love Bruce Springsteen! He's an original in every respect. I'd like to meet him if you can arrange it." John set up the meeting, and Bruce once again took the bus into Manhattan from Asbury Park and auditioned for John and me in my office. We were both knocked out. The glow that emanated from John when he talked about an artist he truly loved was palpable, and everything he had told me about Bruce was fully borne out. We immediately signed Bruce to Columbia.

The "new Dylan" curse descended on Bruce, unfortunately, often at the hands of his greatest admirers. But in trying to compliment Bruce they were limiting him, setting him up to fail. I think perhaps even John viewed Bruce as a younger version of Dylan—but Dylan as he was in the past, not as he was in the early Seventies. John viewed Bruce as essentially an acoustic artist, whereas I felt that if Bruce went that route, his audience might be extremely limited. Even though Bruce has indeed made folk records from time to time, he is a rock artist by both taste and inclination. I believed it was essential to emphasize that element in his sound.

When I initially heard the songs for what would become *Greetings from Asbury Park, N.J.,* Bruce's debut, I told Appel that Bruce needed a couple more songs that might potentially bring him some radio play. To his credit, Bruce took that advice with the best possible attitude and wrote "Blinded by the Light" and "Spirit in the Night," two of the strongest tracks on that excellent first album. I was so taken by *Greetings* that I taped a presentation about Bruce to be broadcast throughout Columbia's broad distribution network on closed-circuit television. On it, I read from his lyrics and talked about how original and distinctive his imagery was and how important a songwriter and unique an artist I believed him to be. Bruce saw it, and while he has teased me about doing it, I know he was flattered. I was surely saying things that he wanted to believe about himself. Ironically, the fact is that Bruce really was a new Dylan. But he wasn't merely an imitation. He was a new Dylan for a new time and a new generation of fans. And over the years he's created an incredible body of work that rivals Dylan's own. In my view each of them has become an American poet laureate.

Greetings from Asbury Park sold only about 30,000 copies in its first few years, and its follow-up, *The Wild, the Innocent & the E Street Shuffle,* which came out only nine months later, sold fewer than twice that many. They were wonderful records, and Bruce was building something. But it was frustrating, especially for him, that he hadn't broken through the way we all hoped he would.

One of my last interactions with Bruce while I was still at Columbia occurred in May 1973 when I booked him to play during a climactic week of performances by Columbia artists at the Ahmanson Theatre in Los Angeles. He was opening up for Dr. Hook & the Medicine Show and the New Riders of the Purple Sage. I watched Bruce rehearse, and it seemed to me that he was very daunted by the enormous size of the stage, which was much larger than any he'd played on at that point. I was concerned that he would be dwarfed by it, and wouldn't deliver the galvanic performance needed to create a stir. So I walked onto the stage to speak to him. I told him, "Look, you know I love your music, but you have to take advantage of a stage this size. You can't let yourself be overwhelmed by it. Don't be daunted by it—use it!" I actually took him by the hand and walked him all the way from one side of the stage to the other, demonstrating how I believed he needed to move in order to put his incredible songs across in a setting like that.

A couple of years later, after I was no longer at Columbia, I got a call from Jon Landau, the very respected *Rolling Stone* writer who had helped produce *Born to Run,* which was just about to be released. Jon said, "Bruce is doing a run of shows at the Bottom Line, and he'd love to see you if you'd like to come out." Of course I went down to the Greenwich Village club, and Bruce, needless to say, was unbelievable. He had totally transformed himself into an electrifying rock 'n' roll performer. The club was small and jammed, but Bruce ran and jumped along the tabletops and used every inch of the available space. The shows are now enshrined in legend, and the one I attended is easily among the best live performances I've ever seen.

Afterward, I went to the tiny dressing room backstage to congratulate Bruce, who was dripping sweat and surrounded by friends and bandmates. The instant he saw me walk through the doorway, he burst into a huge smile. "So, Clive," he said, laughing, "did I move around enough for you tonight?" I could do nothing but laugh and tell him that, yes, he had bowled me over, shockingly doing everything I could ever have wanted him to do, and much, much more.

Talent Raids and
Finding the Company's Soul

It's always been clear to me that the most important job in a record company is discovering new talent. It provides the greatest satisfaction, as well as the most irrefutable proof that you're doing your job well. Regardless of what anyone says, there's never an absolute guarantee that someone you discover is going to become a star and go on to a long, successful career. That requires hard, intelligent work—and some luck never hurts, either. So when you identify new talent and help create the artistic and business environment in which they can both make great music and have an impact, that's what it's all about. You've done your job as well as it can be done.

But there is definitely another valuable talent for a record executive, and that is recognizing when artists are underperforming at other labels and might be ripe for poaching. That might sound a bit dodgy, and it's a tricky business at best. That type of artist raiding doesn't typically win you many friends, although people move around often enough in the music business that your competitor this year may well be your right-hand man the next. The fact is that artists are always after the most advantageous deals they can get, so your best guarantee of loyalty is to pay them as well as you can and do unassailable work on their behalf. After that, you let the chips fall where they may.

There are risks involved in raiding, the biggest one being overspending. No artist jumps labels to make less money. You have to be as sure as you can possibly be that the artist you're pursuing is capable of selling well enough to justify the money you had to spend to acquire him or her. Typically, enough money is involved in such deals that you can't afford to miss very often. My need to keep the momentum charging forward at the company meant that I had to bring in some established acts who I believed could have big success at Columbia. So I started to scan the horizon for worthy prospects.

Neil Diamond was an artist who I firmly believed could be much bigger than he was in 1971, when I began negotiations to bring him to Columbia. He had already had hits, but he was just beginning to earn a reputation as a performer. He was handsome, he moved well onstage, and he had a sense of drama. It was all there—real star quality. He had considerable experience as a songwriter and had written hits for other artists as well as himself, so he had that invaluable skill in his arsenal as well.

I had been made aware that Neil might be interested in leaving MCA by his attorney, the wise and ever-present David Braun. Neil still had two years to go on his MCA contract, and it was certainly not standard procedure back then to begin conversations with an artist who had that much time left on his existing deal. But this was right around the time when artists and their managers, agents, and lawyers were just beginning to understand the kinds of financial demands they could make. I had tried to sign Neil to Columbia a couple of years earlier when he was leaving Bang Records. The deal was all but signed and I even had sent Neil a telegram expressing how eager I was to have him on the label. The next thing I knew, he'd signed to MCA for a quarter of a million dollars. I was crushed, but there was nothing I could do. So this time I wasn't going to stand on any formalities. I told Braun I was very interested in signing Neil and that he should get in touch with Elliot Goldman, my vice president of business affairs, to make a deal. The year before, Neil had performed at a music industry event that Elliot and I attended. We were both incredibly impressed by the show he put on, which only made us more determined to make the deal work out this time. I visited Neil backstage that night, and it was evident that whatever awkwardness or bad feelings had existed over the MCA deal had disappeared. We were on very good terms again, and I wanted to capitalize on that.

So I vividly remember the day that Elliot came to my office and said he had talked with David Braun, and that Braun had asked for $400,000 an album for ten albums, and a royalty rate above 30 percent of wholesale. I must admit that my first response was that Braun was way out of line. There was no way we could make that money work. But Elliot had done an analysis and he assured me that if we could sell 250,000 albums each time out with Neil, we would break even. If we sold more, we'd start making money. I couldn't imagine Neil not being able to hit those marks. Our strategy was not to negotiate anything but to immediately agree to the terms, much to Braun's surprise. Evidently, Warner Bros., which had become Columbia's biggest competitor, had offered the same deal, but Neil knew that I had wanted him on our label for a long time and he wanted the opportunity for us to work together. I couldn't have been happier.

Neil was recording an album in Los Angeles for MCA when we were ready to sign the contracts, and Braun said that Neil wanted Elliot and me to come by the studio to sign the documents there. All the negotiations had been done in secret, of course, because Neil was still on MCA. On the night we were going to sign our deal, Elliot and I had dinner at Dan Tana's, a well-known restaurant and music industry hangout in L.A. That was probably a mistake, because as we were eating, in walked Mike Maitland, the president of MCA. He saw us, came over to our table, and chatted for a while. I was beyond nervous.

When he walked away, I said to Elliot, "He knows. He knows we're signing Neil. I can tell by the way he acted." Elliot tried to calm me down. "Look, Clive," he said, "everybody goes to Dan Tana's. There's nothing to worry about." But then later, after we left and had gotten in our car, I noticed that Mike was right behind us. I was beside myself. We made a turn. He made a turn. We made another turn. He made that turn, too. Finally we continued straight, and he turned off, probably to go home. Was I relieved!

When we arrived at the studio, Neil played us some tracks from his new album as we sat in the control room, and they sounded great. Then he invited us into the studio itself for the signing. When we entered, the room was completely dark. When the lights came on, it was as if we had been transported back in time. Neil had set up an antique desk and lamps, along with quill pens. Tapestries, shields, a suit of armor, and other heraldry decorated the room. It was like the signing of a major historical treaty in the days of old. It was so clever and witty, but also an indication of how seriously Neil took the event. It was very characteristic of him in all those regards.

When word about the deal began to spread, there was plenty of skepticism, to put it mildly, about the amount of money Columbia had spent. I was confident that Columbia would do well with Neil, so the substance of the criticism didn't bother me. But, as with the Johnny Winter deal, it did rankle to be portrayed as someone who threw money around in a profligate way. Because of my upbringing, I was always careful with money, both my own and the company's. I never spent what we didn't have. In Neil's case, Elliot Goldman, whom I trusted implicitly and who was hardly a spendthrift himself, had crunched the numbers and assured me that we were on extremely solid footing. And, what's more, Mo Ostin at Warner Bros. had offered Neil the same deal. It's a simple truth that you can't be in the entertainment business and be afraid to spend money. I'd passed on many artists whose demands I believed to be too extravagant. I never made the so-called banking deals, advancing a million dollars or more per album to entice the currently hot artist. But part of identifying talent is trusting your instincts. By the time of the Neil Diamond deal my instincts had been honed, so I was ready to forge ahead regardless of what anybody thought.

As time passed Neil and I became good friends, and often socialized when I was in Los Angeles. We're both Jewish, both from Brooklyn, so we shared similar backgrounds and cultural perspectives. Neil had broken into the music business at a young age and he understood every aspect of it thoroughly. I often thought that he could have been just as successful a music executive as an artist. I remember one time sitting with him in his car outside one of his favorite health food restaurants in L.A., eating sandwiches and talking about music literally for hours. He was full of opinions, loved expressing them, and wanted you to come back as forcefully as he put his ideas out there. This was the way my friends and I used to talk on the stoops of Union Street in Brooklyn, but this was Neil Diamond holding forth. I always relished those opportunities to hear his insights and enjoy his take on things.

Neil played benefits for George McGovern when he ran for presi-

dent in 1972, and because McGovern's running mate was Sargent
Shriver, the husband of Eunice Kennedy, he became friendly with the
Kennedy family. (In fact, he had written "Sweet Caroline" after seeing a photograph of the young Caroline Kennedy.) He invited me to
a McGovern-Shriver benefit in Washington, and we flew down from
New York on a private plane provided by Ethel Kennedy. I'm not an
easy flyer on such planes and it was an unnervingly bumpy ride, so if
staring mortality in the eye can bring you closer to an artist, Neil and
I grew even closer on that short trip. After we arrived, Eunice took us
on a personal tour of the Kennedy memorabilia in their home, and we
had a private lunch with her and other members of the family. It was a
fantastic day.

But my confidence about Neil's future success and the friendship
that had developed between us doesn't mean that I wasn't taken aback
when Neil told me that he wanted his first Columbia album to be the
soundtrack to the forthcoming film *Jonathan Livingston Seagull*. The
book on which the film was based, a fable about a seagull who embarks
on a journey of self-discovery, had been a major best-seller, but I immediately got worried. I was confident that Columbia could sell a Neil
Diamond album, but as with all soundtracks, this one would be dependent on the quality and success of the film, and I had no control over
any of that. Neil arranged for me to meet the director, Hall Bartlett,
who screened twenty minutes of the film for me. It was beautiful, but
I still felt queasy. After all the publicity about the cost of signing Neil,
I felt that my reputation was on the line. But Neil was determined and
once I had made my reservations clear, there was really nothing more
I could do.

Of course, what happened after that was unbelievable. The film
got very negative reviews, and Richard Bach, the author of the book,
even filed a lawsuit against the film's creators. Despite all that, Neil's
soundtrack immediately sold a million copies and rose to number two
on the charts. It turned out that his music spoke more directly to the
people who loved the book than the film did. Essentially, Columbia
made all its money back on that one album alone, and Neil Diamond
went on to a long, tremendously successful career at the label.

Neil Diamond was far from the only artist I signed from other labels. After the *Woodstock* movie came out in 1970, the English blues band Ten Years After began to garner attention on the strength of its guitarist Alvin Lee's torrid playing and showmanship. The band was unhappy at London Records and the very successful entrepreneurs Chris Wright and Terry Ellis (Chrysalis Records) brought them to us for a successful run of albums in the Seventies. I also signed Mott the Hoople, another distinctively talented English band, and their first Columbia album, *All the Young Dudes,* produced by David Bowie, is now regarded as a landmark glam-rock statement. Of course, not every raid was a success. I signed the Rascals and Delaney and Bonnie to lucrative deals, confident that the extraordinary musical talent the groups had already shown would lead to long commercial runs. The Rascals, in particular, had enjoyed a string of big hits. But in each instance feuds erupted between key band members and the magic got lost. Those were big disappointments for me, but while you should always try to learn from failures, you can never let them stop you from doing what you know you can do well. So I just kept on moving.

One signing that worked out incredibly well was Pink Floyd. The group had risen up during the late-Sixties heyday of the progressive, psychedelic blues scene in London, and had earned a significant cult following. The band's live shows were bold and experimental, and, partly because they were not widely known, the group had a seductive air of mystery about it. Syd Barrett, the group's main songwriter and lead singer and guitarist, had left the band after its first two albums due to emotional problems. He was a true visionary, but the group had reorganized itself with the guitarist David Gilmour joining and doing most of the singing, and the bassist, Roger Waters, handling the bulk of the songwriting. They were steadily becoming better known, but they clearly were capable of reaching a much bigger audience.

Kip Cohen at Columbia arranged for us to meet with Steve O'Rourke, Pink Floyd's manager. Steve explained that the group, which was signed to Capitol, believed that it was overdue for a breakthrough. The band's live shows routinely sold out, reviews of their albums were excellent, but sales lagged behind. Kip and I met with Steve a few times to make sure we fully understood his concerns. Then, to give him a sense of what Columbia was prepared to do for a band like Pink Floyd, I invited Steve to sit in on one of our weekly singles meetings. He saw how I tried to make sure that every relevant branch of the company was in step with an overall strategy for each active band that we carefully defined and were determined to execute fully. Heads of national promotion Ron Alexenburg and Steve Popovich always electrified the room with their zeal and their carefully thought-out strategic moves. Those meetings were filled with top-notch executives bursting with fresh ideas, and everyone was encouraged to speak up. O'Rourke was captivated by what he saw and heard, and decided that Pink Floyd needed to be on Columbia.

A couple of problems had to be overcome. First, as with Neil Diamond, Pink Floyd still had a couple of years to go on their contract with Capitol, so we had to move quickly before Capitol figured out what the band was up to and made a counteroffer. Second, O'Rourke asked for a $250,000 advance, which was quite a bit for a commercially unproven band. We had serious discussions about it at the label, and my business team had doubts about the wisdom of such a large outlay. Finally, a decision had to be made and I decided to take the leap. Even if the band didn't end up selling as well as I believed it could, it seemed unlikely to me that we wouldn't earn back that advance over time. So we agreed to the deal.

As it happens, Pink Floyd's next album for Capitol turned out to be *Dark Side of the Moon*. Now a definitive rite of passage for every young fan interested in rock 'n' roll, the album quickly sold 2 million copies and made the band superstars. After the group's deal with Capitol ended in 1974, the albums Pink Floyd released on Columbia included *Wish You Were Here*, *Animals*, and *The Wall*. Needless to say, that $250,000 became an incredible investment.

Even as Columbia was having hits in virtually every category of popular music, one genre in which it had failed to distinguish itself was soul music. Motown and Stax had created a popular version of R&B that appealed to black and white audiences alike. It had become, in Berry Gordy's immortal phrase, "the sound of young America," but Columbia had little representation in it. Even though it had occurred when I was a lawyer, it pained me that after John Hammond had the foresight to bring Aretha Franklin to Columbia, no one at the label, including John, was able to make hit records with her. When she went to Atlantic, Jerry Wexler immediately knew how to record her and what material she needed. He took her to church and helped make her the Queen of Soul. Obviously, considering the magnitude of her talent, Columbia should have been able to make the most of her great gifts and enjoy that success.

When I asked about our problems in this area at the label, the A&R team blamed promotion, insisting that potential hits had been lost because the promotion team couldn't get them played on the radio. The promotion team blamed A&R, claiming that they weren't getting the kind of music that radio stations wanted to play. It became clear to me that the real problem was in A&R. No one could bring me a track that credibly could have been a hit but on which the promotion team dropped the ball. We simply weren't signing the right artists and getting the best material from them.

To try to make things happen faster I decided to look outside the label to see if we could line up a suitable production deal. Then out of the blue I got a call from Kenny Gamble and Leon Huff, and the bells went off in my head. Gamble and Huff had been writing and producing hits from their base in Philadelphia, and they were ready to step onto the main stage. Seeing the direction the industry had recently taken, they wanted to sell albums as well as singles and to work with a company that could help promote and distribute their music across the entire world. They really wanted to be Philadelphia International, the now famous name of their new company. They had first approached Atlantic Records, but had gotten turned down. They were smart, serious music business professionals, and I knew that working with them would be mutually beneficial. They could bring Columbia the top-quality R&B we needed, and we could drive them to the top of the charts and then make real money for us both with album sales.

Gamble and Huff had been under contract with another label, and they moved quickly to bring that arrangement to a close. I then made a deal with Philadelphia International for fifteen singles for $75,000, and

$25,000 per album. It was not a huge deal by any measure—except the measure of its impact on the marketplace. Energized by the prospect of reaching a larger audience, Kenny and Leon began bringing us a red-hot series of hits by Billy Paul ("Me and Mrs. Jones"), Harold Melvin and the Blue Notes featuring Teddy Pendergrass ("If You Don't Know Me By Now"), and the O'Jays ("Back Stabbers," "Love Train"). Within nine months they sold 10 million singles, and realized significant album sales as well. Moreover, Gamble and Huff's Philly Soul sound reinvented soul music for the Seventies by blending sweetness and impeccable song structure with orchestral arrangements that added texture and depth. The music they released was satisfying in every aspect and immediately brought Columbia to the forefront of contemporary soul music.

I was working on multiple fronts to ensure that we maintained that status. I had conversations with Al Bell, who co-owned Stax Records, about purchasing a 50 percent interest in the company. I decided against that, but did arrange to distribute Stax's releases, which deepened our black music offerings. Most dramatically, though, I learned through Joe Wissert, their producer, that a promising new group called Earth, Wind & Fire was unhappy at Warner Bros. and potentially looking for another label. I went to see them in concert opening for John Sebastian, and I was knocked out. I met with the group's managers, Bob Cavallo and Joe Ruffalo, to learn more about what they were looking for. It was clear that Maurice White, the band's singer and founder, had recently reorganized the group and was taking it in a new, funkier direction. He had a strong jazz background, but he was interested in all kinds of music and had gotten the impression that Warner Bros. simply didn't understand what he was trying to do. Because EWF was still signed to Warners, we arranged a secret audition at a small studio in Los Angeles so I could hear some of the new music the group was working on.

Being able to listen to a powerhouse band like EWF in a situation like that is one of the great privileges of my job. The room was steaming, but after a while it was impossible to tell if that was because of the weather or simply the heat the band was generating. They were just sensational. Talk about star power! The level of musicianship was very high, and if they played that hard and put on a show that compelling for one person, I could only imagine what they were capable of in a packed hall. We went to great lengths to keep my interest in the band a secret. If Warner Bros. had learned that I wanted to sign the band, they either would have balked at letting the band out of its contract or the price would have skyrocketed. It ended up that we signed the group, and got their first album as well, both for about $100,000.

In 1972, for the first time, the annual Columbia sales convention was going to be held overseas, in London. I debated whether to spend the money and showcase Earth, Wind & Fire there. It would be expensive, but I was eager to demonstrate that the Gamble and Huff hits were a prelude to our building a powerhouse roster in all aspects of black music. Because of the range of styles incorporated into their sound, EWF could dramatize the links between Miles Davis's and Herbie Hancock's jazz-fusion breakthroughs and Philadelphia International's major crossover R&B hits. There could be no better way to herald the group as a major new signing and instantly bring them to the attention of the company worldwide. I was nervous. The group was different and unique. Would the Columbia field force get how special they were? Well, their performance was a triumph. Seeing Columbia executives from all over the world enthuse over how fantastic EWF's show was gave me the shivers and remains an all-time thrill. It never surprised me that the band became such an international phenomenon after that. Earth, Wind & Fire went on to sell well over 15 million albums for Columbia during their years with the label, and created music that eventually led to their induction into the Rock and Roll Hall of Fame.

Along with bringing great artists to Columbia either through new signings or raiding other labels, I always gave a great deal of thought to discovering the best ways to get our music to audiences who would genuinely respond to it. In the late Sixties and early Seventies, the cultural landscape was changing in dramatic ways, and the dynamism of the environment required new thinking. It's not as if the old ways had entirely become vestigial. Radio was still crucially important, as were advertising, promotion, and marketing. But television was now a significant factor. FM radio, which was critical, for example, to Pink Floyd's success, had to be taken into account. The music press had become a force. Media was proliferating, and publicity in general had become a valuable means of getting attention for your artists.

In the same way that I had faced potshots for being a Big Spender with the signings of Johnny Winter, Neil Diamond, and Pink Floyd, I was called to task for courting personal publicity during my time at Columbia. Guilty as charged. It was becoming apparent to me that, not just in music, but in the world of entertainment in general, people were becoming aware of figures who had previously been behind the scenes: producers, managers, directors, and record company executives among them. It was not uncommon at all to see Ahmet Ertegun, for example, profiled in a major magazine or newspaper—and deservedly so.

I knew it might prove controversial, but if I was presenting the Electric Flag or Blood, Sweat & Tears at the all-important NARM music retailers' convention, I made a point of introducing them myself. I knew exactly what I wanted to say and how I wanted them to be perceived by that audience. From my elocution contests at P.S. 161 to my political activism at NYU, I had lost any fears I may have had about public speaking, and maybe even developed some skills at it. I believed that I could tell the story of the artists and the music well, so when opportunities to speak out publicly or to the press presented themselves, I took full and enthusiastic advantage of them. I was invited to give the keynote address at NARM three separate times, and I made the most of it. Was it flattering and gratifying? You bet. But that wasn't the point. I believed that I could be an effective spokesman for Columbia, and I'm convinced my efforts in that regard helped the label become as successful as it was. I took some good-natured ribbing about it from my friends, and endured some cutting comments from competitors. When you put yourself out there, you have no choice but to accept whatever comes back. But I have no doubt it helped shine a light on everything Columbia was doing to set a new standard in the world of contemporary music. It was attracting new and established artists in a major way. I would never have continued it if it wasn't working. But it was.

Along those lines, I also believed in creating events that could call attention to the music, particularly music that might not be grabbing headlines on its own. The media will always chase the hottest, most current story, but that doesn't mean that's the only story worth telling. Even after a particular style of music falls out of fashion, it may still have millions of fans who don't care that it's not the music of the moment. It's often very difficult to get any coverage or exposure for music like that.

At Columbia I had gradually made a name for myself by signing and working with contemporary artists—mainly in rock. But the label was still home to a number of artists who had reached their peaks in the Fifties or early Sixties and who had been shunted aside by rock 'n' roll. They may not have been as big as they used to be, but they still had a sizable audience. What could be done for them? I decided to find out.

In December 1971 I spent about $100,000 for Johnny Mathis, Vikki Carr, Peter Nero, and Percy Faith, all backed by a sixty-piece orchestra, to leave their swank supper clubs behind for a night and perform together at Madison Square Garden. The artists, all on Columbia, performed for free, and the idea was to make middle-of-the-road music feel exciting again. We put up posters all over New York, and took out ads on MOR radio stations. I did an interview with the legendary New York disc jockey William B. Williams, which turned into an hour-long special about the artists who would be at the Garden. We sold out the house, and created a wonderfully memorable evening.

Then, in early 1973, I thought it might be noteworthy to take classical music out of the storied, and somewhat forbidding, concert halls that were its natural home, and stage it somewhere that younger audiences might be likely to frequent. So I booked the organist E. Power Biggs and the harpsichordist/conductor Anthony Newman to perform a midnight concert at Radio City Music Hall. We also had ten grand pianos onstage, which we dubbed the Monster Pianos; during the finale they would whirl around on stage platforms as they were being played. Such late-night shows had become fashionable in the rock world, so why not see if putting classical music in a new context—and providing a little showmanship—could win it some new fans? As I did with the MOR concert, I emceed the show that night, though this time the audience was more restless—and far more attuned to any perceived cultural slight. A reference, for example, to bringing "serious music to the masses" did not go over well! All in all, however, both the concert and the concept were very well received. We had offers to bring it to other venues in New York, Los Angeles, and Miami, but, unfortunately, it never could be arranged.

Finally, my most ambitious event-planning gambit was a week of concerts, beginning on April 29, 1973, at the Ahmanson Theatre in Los Angeles. I had grown frustrated with the seemingly endless run of stories around this time declaring that rock was dead, that somehow music itself was dying or had at least lost its luster. The closing of the Fillmore East and West in 1971 contributed to some of that gloom, but for the most part I couldn't understand it. I tend to be an optimist, but, setting that general proclivity aside, I saw nothing to be depressed about on the music scene. And for what I called "A Week to Remember," I planned to assemble a diverse lineup of Columbia artists to demonstrate how vital contemporary music remained.

Bill Graham, the brilliant promoter who had run the Fillmores, was my inspiration. I loved how he would book jazz greats and rock bands, blues giants and folksingers, all on the same bill. He did not assume that people's tastes were narrow, or that you had to pander to them if they were. He believed that if people heard great music of any kind they would respond to it. So that was my plan at the Ahmanson: to host a week of shows with that kind of breadth, and make them as compelling as possible. I already mentioned the evening that Bruce Springsteen shared with the New Riders of the Purple Sage and Dr. Hook & the Medicine Show. Anthony Newman performed on a bill with Loudon Wainwright III and the Mahavishnu Orchestra. Miles Davis; Earth, Wind & Fire; Johnny Cash; Loggins and Messina; Ramsey Lewis; and the Staple Singers are just a few of the twenty-one acts that performed that week.

Those shows were definitely one of the high points of my years at Columbia. They were not only a great success in showing the diversity and vigor of the music of the day, but they dramatically demonstrated how far we had come at Columbia and what had been accomplished at the label. I continually had to pinch myself. Never could I have imagined what the last eight years would be like, and this seemed like a breathtaking culmination. I couldn't read music. I had no musical training. But somehow I was not only surviving right in the midst of turbulent and revolutionary musical times, I was thriving, bristling with energy, and overjoyed at finding a passion that eclipsed anything I had ever felt before. And right in the thick of the competitive jungle that was the frenetic, fast-paced, and electrifying record business, we were outdistancing everyone! We had some failures, too, of course. But overall, the body of work, the range of artists across the full spectrum of music, well, that's what "A Week to Remember" at the Ahmanson Theatre was all about. From a company that had earned $5 million in profits in 1967, the year I became president, Columbia hauled in $50 million in profits in 1972. Fantasy and reality blurred into each other. Undoubtedly, new challenges lay ahead, and I was eager to embrace them.

The End of One Fantasy

New challenges came all right, but in a form I never could have envisioned. On Tuesday, May 29, 1973, right after Memorial Day weekend, I was called to a meeting with Arthur Taylor, who had become president of CBS less than a year before, replacing the esteemed Dr. Frank Stanton. When I arrived at his office on the thirty-fifth floor, Taylor was there with two lawyers. Our meeting lasted perhaps two minutes. I remember very little about it, beyond its purpose: Arthur told me that I was fired. There was no discussion. I could go to my office, take what I needed, and leave the building immediately afterward.

To say I was shocked would be a huge understatement. I felt paralyzed, said nothing, and turned to leave and head back to my office. At the door of Taylor's office I was met by two CBS security men, who served me with a civil complaint that CBS had filed against me, claiming that I had defrauded the company of $94,000 in expense-account violations during my six years as president of Columbia Records. The security men then escorted me to my office on the eleventh floor. It's funny, but revealing, how your mind works. As we rode the elevator I found my thoughts drifting to my thirteen-year-old cousin, Stephan John, who had died of cancer the previous week. He was the grandson of my aunt Jeanette, who had been like a mother to me after my parents died. We had watched Stephan's heartbreaking decline for months, and the family had visited with him every night during the final week of his life.

Why did Stephan come to mind precisely at that moment? My intense sorrow and depression over his loss were still fresh and immediate, of course; he was never far from my thoughts at that time. But it also offered a valuable bigger picture. Losing such a young relative whom everyone in the family loved—that was true devastation. Losing a job I loved, even under these horrible circumstances, that was something I had to bear. Thinking of Stephan helped me keep my emotions under control. As isolated and wronged as I felt at that moment, I kept things in perspective and held on.

That said, beneath the numbing effect of my shock, what happened to me did feel like a kind of death. My discovery of music had delivered me from a life that had seemed stultifying. My work and accomplishments at Columbia had brought me a level of satisfaction that I had never dreamed possible. I had devoted around-the-clock time, effort, and personal commitment to my work. I was living a passion and to an extent I perhaps had not even realized, my sense of identity was bound up in my job, the thrilling position that I had managed to attain. Could it possibly all be ending like this? What was happening to me seemed mind-boggling.

When I arrived at my office I packed my checkbook and some personal papers into my briefcase. I was too stunned to do anything beyond explaining what had happened and saying good-bye to my secretary, Octavia Bennett. Then I left, still accompanied by the security guards. I had been told that I could have my driver take me home in the company car that had been mine to use. When I arrived at my apartment, I learned that Janet was at my son and daughter's school. I asked my driver if he would mind going to find her and then bring her back to the apartment. Thirty minutes later someone from CBS called me saying that the driver had been gone too long and needed to return. Cold reality hit me even more sharply.

Bad news travels fast, but I had no idea how fast. The telephone never stopped ringing that day. My housekeeper took messages; I didn't feel up to speaking to anyone. Janet came home an hour or so after I arrived, and we discussed what had happened over and over again. No matter how much we talked about it, it didn't come any nearer to making sense. Close friends and family members came by. It was as if we were sitting shiva, mourning a loss that we couldn't even begin to comprehend.

I was able to keep my emotions in check until I watched the evening news. For better or worse, the distance provided by seeing the images on television freed my feelings, and I began to cry. Little did I know that that was just the beginning of a media avalanche, much of it driven by baseless speculation, that would consume much of my life for the next three years. Not all of it was negative. Some reports attributed my firing to corporate infighting and jealousy. Others pointed out the relatively insignificant amount of my alleged fraudulence, given the millions of dollars that I had made for CBS and the amount of money I could have earned had I taken any of the various offers that had been made to me by other companies.

But because of its glamour and excitement, the music industry has always been a target for people who believe that, beneath its shimmering surface, it must be a hotbed of corruption. So many stories clearly implied, if they didn't state outright, that CBS never would have fired such a successful president over some expense-account problems. Something deeper and darker must have been the real reason. That was the angle the coverage took, and a tidal wave of speculation began.

The month before my firing, Arthur Taylor had informed me that CBS had launched an internal investigation of its record division because federal prosecutors had been looking into the activities of Columbia's head of artist relations, Dave Wynshaw. As a result of that investigation I was told I had to fire Wynshaw because of a pervasive fraudulent invoice scheme he had been running, and I did. After that, the investigation expanded to include all of Columbia's executive roster, including me. Still, after in-depth conversations with Taylor and CBS's attorneys, I had not been given any indication that I had anything to worry about. I was assured that if any financial discrepancies emerged as a result of the investigation, we would certainly have an opportunity to discuss them. Since I knew I had done nothing wrong, I was not concerned. That April, in fact, after a full investigation of every matter pertaining to me, I had been reelected to the CBS board of directors at the annual meeting of the company's stockholders.

The task of firing Wynshaw was not a pleasant one. He was an extremely likable guy, as everyone who works in artist relations tends to be. He was not someone that I had hired, and he did not report directly to me. He had joined Columbia in 1960, the same year I came to the company, as a sales representative on the West Coast. When I moved out of the legal department to begin taking over Columbia Records, he was already established in the record division as an affable person who knew how to get things done quickly and efficiently—the very point of artist relations. If Barbra Streisand was performing somewhere, Dave could get flowers to her dressing room at the last minute. If an important manager was in town and wanted tickets to a sold-out Broadway show, Dave knew whom to call.

Tasks like that might sound trivial, but they are never-ending at a record company, and you don't want to be on the other end of the phone line when such niceties are botched or overlooked. But even more important, Wynshaw was adept at arranging for hotel rooms and flights and putting together the logistics for all the special business events and showcases that the record division staged at industry conventions and elsewhere. Increasingly, as the demands of my job at Columbia grew exponentially, I made the mistake of delegating more and more of such responsibilities, both professional and personal, to Wynshaw. That made my life much more manageable, and it freed me to concentrate on the creative work I thrived on. But, although I didn't at all realize it at the time, it turned out to be a very unfortunate mistake, and I was to pay dearly for it.

Wynshaw, it turns out, had been in cahoots with a second-tier New Jersey mobster named Patsy Falcone, who, among his other activities, worked on the fringe of the music business. Wynshaw had forged signatures, falsified invoices, and arranged kickbacks, a few of them involving aspects of my personal business. In 1972, for example, I received a $75,000 bill for a kitchen renovation in my Central Park West apartment, the large, spacious, five-bedroom dwelling that I had purchased six years earlier for $55,000, with another $10,000 kicked in for standard painting, floor scraping, and electrical wiring upgrades. I was flabbergasted. I had been expecting a bill of something like eight or ten thousand dollars for the refrigerator and dishwasher replacements and modernization of the same eat-in kitchen space. I went to Wynshaw, who knew the contractors had done previous work for CBS and who had volunteered to deal with them for me, and asked him what the problem was. He said it was obviously an error, and he would take care of it. Also in October 1972, I held a bar mitzvah for my son Fred at the Plaza Hotel. Because Columbia Records did so much business with the Plaza at the Persian Room banquet and cabaret space, Dave had also volunteered to deal with the Plaza about the arrangements so that I would get a favorable rate. In November and December, I asked him when I would receive the bill for the October event, and he kept telling me that there was still one issue or another that needed to be resolved before the bill could be issued.

Both of those projects were included in the civil suit that CBS brought against me. I had never intended to have CBS pay for my apartment renovation or, heaven knows, for my son's bar mitzvah, even though to this day it's often stated as fact that I had billed the event to the company. I never did that, and it never occurred to me to do so. These were just two of the fraudulent invoices involving many more people at CBS than just me that ended up sending Wynshaw to jail. In all of his media interviews and sworn testimony Wynshaw never directly or even remotely suggested that I knew about his activities regarding me or anybody else.

The problem was, when it became clear to Wynshaw and his attorneys that his joyride was over, he began making accusations about payola and drug use at Columbia and throughout the music industry in order to show active cooperation with the U.S. attorney's office and, thereby, lessen his eventual sentence. That threat of an ensuing scandal was ultimately to lead to my demise. The decision to fire me had nothing to do with the facts. As was eventually shown, I had neither participated in nor known about any drug use or payola at Columbia or anywhere else, and, other than Wynshaw, no other executive at Columbia ended up ever being charged with those crimes. Arthur Taylor had been president of CBS for less than a year when the investigation of wrongdoing at the label got under way, and he was just thirty-seven years old. He had previously worked at International Paper and First Boston, and had no experience in the music business. When a grand jury was convened as a result of Wynshaw's claims, the prospect that the Federal Communications Commission could strip CBS of its radio and television broadcast licenses came into view. I was told that their lawyers advised that CBS had to establish as much distance as it could from its record division, and Taylor had to be seen as taking decisive action. As a result, no individual, no matter what he had achieved or contributed to CBS, could be spared. So I was fired. I can think of no other way to explain the cruelty and unfairness of Columbia's actions.

Unfortunately, the firing was just the beginning. Once the charges of payola and drugola, as it came to be called, began to be hurled, the media spun out of control. It hadn't been that long since the original payola investigations had tainted the music business, and the industry, which had subsequently grown in seismic proportions, had been under suspicion ever since. Even at CBS, where under my supervision the record division was to account for one-third of the corporation's profits, music never rose to the level of prestige assumed by the broadcast division. Music was also at the forefront of cultural changes in the Sixties and early Seventies that made many people uncomfortable. The prospect of exacting some sort of revenge for what were seen as wildly indulgent excesses proved too enticing. It was a sexy story, just one step removed from artists whose own extravagant lifestyles were well known and had sometimes produced lurid consequences. The deaths of Janis Joplin, Jimi Hendrix, and Jim Morrison were all relatively recent events. Beyond that, the Watergate scandal was in full swing, and the investigative media were feeling their oats. Corruption in the Establishment was assumed, and the media, heady with the prospect of crafting their own legend, were heroes capable of exposing crimes and speaking truth to power. In such an environment, no one was going to score points by speaking up in defense of the music industry.

I'm not naïve. I heard the same stories everyone else did about colorful figures like Morris Levy of Roulette Records and his alleged questionable business practices. But I could never understand why the entire industry became tainted by those stories. The giants of the music industry—men like Goddard Lieberson, Ahmet and Nesuhi Ertegun, Jerry Wexler, Herb Alpert and Jerry Moss, Mo Ostin and Joe Smith, Doug Morris, Chris Blackwell, George Marek, Alan Livingston, Jac Holzman, Richard Branson, Seymour Stein, Chris Wright and Terry

Ellis, Berry Gordy, David Geffen, Charles Koppelman, Marty Bandier, Clarence Avant, Irving Azoff, Jimmy Iovine, Tommy Mottola, Donnie Ienner, Bruce Lundvall, Russell Simmons, Lyor Cohen, L.A. Reid, and Clive Calder among them—are upstanding, reputable, erudite, charity-minded, successful entrepreneurs. Why didn't their values represent the image of the music industry?

But the media had its own obsessions based on its poorly digested understanding of the music business and its own self-regard. The only problem with such cultural myths is that they do not apply in every instance, and they can damage and destroy lives when they are mistaken in their targets. The coverage of the music industry scandal was relentless, and the distinction between the most sensationalistic tabloids and the most respected newspapers, newsweeklies, and news programs not only began to blur, but essentially disappeared. Since no one had yet been charged with anything, almost all the reporting rested on innuendo, suggestion, implication, conjecture, and outright slander. The first shoe had fallen, and everyone believed the second one would inevitably drop. In their desperation not to be scooped and their desire to be seen as leading the righteous charge, no news organization was content to wait for the actual information to emerge. Since the results of the investigations were already certain in their eyes, what was the harm in suggesting in advance what those results would be?

The news division at CBS, perhaps in order to prove that it wouldn't pull punches when its own parent company was in the hot seat, was the worst of the lot. In August 1974, the network ran an hour-long special called *The Trouble with Rock* that focused in large part on my firing and the alleged involvement of the Mafia in the music industry. The special was, in part, a response to a completely uninformed column by William Safire in *The New York Times* claiming that my firing for expense-account fraud was "the second most massive cover-up of the past twelve months"—the first, presumably, was the one overseen by his former boss, Richard M. Nixon. With no evidence whatsoever, other than his cultural biases, Safire called for a CBS News investigation "of the new currency of the record industry, hard drugs" and the "penetration of the record industry by Mafia drug peddlers." The next day, CBS News formed a team of reporters to investigate the music industry. At the urging of James Buckley, the conservative senator from New York, the United States Senate launched an investigation of its own.

Like so much of the reporting about the scandal, *The Trouble with Rock* made no particular point but left the viewer with the impression that corruption was pervasive in the music business, and that my firing was a direct result of that fact. The expense-account issue was a cover-up for my assumed drug and payola crimes. It was the worst sort of damning by false association, which did not make it any easier to live with. Even *The New York Times* could run a news story with the following sentence: "The [music] business has been shaken by a scandal involving organized crime, payola and drugs following the dismissal of Clive J. Davis as president of Columbia Records." One event followed the other, hence, they must be linked, evidence be damned. It was like living in a Kafkaesque nightmare. I was apoplectically angry but I could never speak out. My lawyers were strict and unyielding. I could not comment on anything publicly. This was so uncharacteristic of me that I swear I swallowed my tongue more than once.

Once the initial shock passed, I had to devise a strategy to create a meaningful day-to-day life for myself, not to mention a conceivable future. My lawyers sternly advised me not to discuss any of the charges leveled against me in the press, and that was unbearably frustrating, but it was sound advice so I had no choice but to keep my feelings to myself. Reporters camped outside my building, attempting on at least one occasion to barge in as I tried to exit. My children had to be escorted out a side entrance when they left to go to school.

In many ways, it was worse for the people around me than it was for me. After all, I knew I was innocent, and I had some comprehension of the forces at play in this surreal drama. While my family trusted me implicitly and provided invaluable support, the situation came entirely out of the blue for them, and it was deeply disturbing. How could this possibly be happening? Also, needless to say, they were worried about me. I tried as much as I could to convey my confidence that ultimately everything would be all right. As grueling as this experience was, once

I got over the shock, I truly believed that. But I'm not sure I was always convincing.

One of the most difficult aspects of this experience was the degree to which Columbia attempted to write me out of its history—and, worse, actively sought to damage me and my ongoing career. I understand that the company needed to signal to its investors, Wall Street analysts, and the music industry itself that it was capable of moving ahead without me. And I know that CBS, due to fears of losing its broadcast license, needed to demonstrate to the FCC that it had taken decisive action regarding any possible problems with corruption in their record division. But did they really need to pretend that I had never worked for the company, let alone achieved the results that I had? After I left Columbia, my office was dismantled and any memorabilia, award, plaque, citation, or photograph in which my name was mentioned or my image appeared vanished from the premises. People used to joke that Black Rock was like the Kremlin, but I had never believed the metaphor to be that literal. My onetime mentor Goddard Lieberson came out of retirement after I was fired to oversee all of CBS Records. Within days of my leaving he announced in an interview with *The New York Times* that Columbia had been a force in rock 'n' roll long before I arrived there, and would continue to be now that I was gone. "The rock era began with me," he declared.

Goddard's response to my firing was painful and confuses me to this day. Perhaps his own feelings about it were confused. Some people speculated that in the course of my rise at CBS I didn't take sufficient care to acknowledge and maintain Goddard's eminence at the company. If that's true, it's certainly not anything I did consciously, nor is it anything that ever came up between us, though I understand that it would have been a difficult issue for him to raise. I can state unequivocally that Goddard not only gave me opportunities I never could have dreamed of, but he epitomized the type of creative executive that I hoped one day to become. I learned an immense amount from him, and feel only gratitude for all he did for me.

That said, Goddard seemed to want to have it both ways. While I was out of Columbia and on the sidelines he wrote to me saying that I should not believe everything I was reading in the press, that he would never say disparaging things about me. But then another story and another story would appear, all with quotes from him declaring that my departure would have no impact whatsoever on Columbia and that my contributions had not been as dramatic as people seemed to think. Even after I had gotten back on my feet and launched a success-ful new record label, Goddard confidentially wrote to an executive at *The New York Times,* which was planning to do a story about me, that I didn't really merit such coverage and the piece should be killed.

All of that was sad and painful, and it occurred within the larger context of Columbia's efforts to rewrite history—and write me out of it. Artists were told not to acknowledge me in liner notes or dedica-tions. When clips from the "A Week to Remember" concerts at the Ahmanson Theatre were used at the 1973 annual Columbia Records convention, I was completely edited out of the footage, which, given that I had organized and emceed the concerts, was shockingly inap-propriate. More darkly, it was understood at the label that it was not a good idea during the industry investigations to be seen as my friend, let alone a supporter. Even to be in touch with me was regarded as suspi-cious. In a subsequent *New York Times* story, journalists covering the music industry investigations told the paper that CBS's press office had planted negative information about me without providing a shred of evidence in support of it. That information was coming from the very same people who, when I was flying high at the label, were eager for me to appear prominently in the media, representing the company.

At one point in the course of the federal investigation, my lawyer advised that I get character references. I approached various artists and executives I believed could make convincing statements, including Dick Asher, whom I had hired to work in business affairs and whom I eventually tapped to run the CBS offices in the U.K. Walter Yetnikoff, a colleague and personal friend I had hired to work in the legal depart-ment at Columbia and who, after I was fired, was put in charge of CBS International, strongly advised Asher not to write the letter, warning him that he might get fired. Asher told him, "Walter, if anyone should write this letter, you should, because Clive did even more for you than he did for me. Regardless, I won't be able to live with myself if I don't write the letter, so I'm going to do it." Dick wrote the letter, and sent copies to Walter and to Arthur Taylor. I was and am extremely grateful for that. Years later, after he underwent rehab, Walter came to me to apologize. He said that as part of his program of rehabilitation he was asked to make a list of people of whom he most needed to ask forgiveness. We had lunch in the Edwardian Room at the Plaza and he touchingly said that I was number two on his list. (Number one was his late first wife, June.) He proceeded to ask for forgiveness for the things he did and said during the period of the investigation and afterward. I looked him in his eye and forgave him.

Another of my important hires, Elliot Goldman, also said that CBS executives warned him that his continuing friendship with me wasn't doing him "any good" at the company. Like Dick, Elliot, too, ignored that cynical advice and remained a trusted supporter during those trying times, as did my close friend, Charles Koppelman, a longtime major music player who had become head of A&R at Columbia, and his wife, Bunny. In fact, Elliot's family and mine spent the July Fourth holiday together at his home in Rye, New York, just a couple of months after my firing. Elliot and I took a walk together, and he shook me by saying that I might one day be glad I had been fired from CBS because he believed I would eventually go on to start my own label and would enjoy even greater success than I had at Columbia. At that time it was hard for me to see much beyond the very tough struggles I was going through, so all I could do was smile and say, "Well, you better be right, because what's going on now is very difficult to take." But I was grateful for his confidence and, while I could never say I was glad I was fired, he was right about everything else.

Another reason sometimes cited for my firing was that I was envious of Arthur Taylor because I supposedly wanted the job he got as president of CBS. I had been the boy wonder at CBS, this theory runs, and now Arthur, who was younger than I, had been made my boss. Plus, I supposedly resented that he knew nothing about the music business. None of that is true. Most certainly, I did not want his job. I was having too much fun in the music business to want to be that far removed from the action. As for Taylor himself, I had no problem with him, and he wasn't at CBS long enough before I left to have had any real effect, positive or negative, on what I was doing. It's true, as I mentioned earlier, that he had no experience in music, but as someone who had come to my own job without any musical background or training, I was hardly in a position to judge him harshly for that. I simply didn't have time to formulate much of an opinion about him one way or the other.

I did feel that by the time Taylor came on board in 1972, I had established a track record of success that earned me the right to do things as I professionally thought best. And, as before, I still felt the need, within reason, to keep the record division insulated from some of the more corporate aspects of CBS. Black Rock was still an imposing, monolithic environment, and it was essential to demonstrate to artists and their representatives that there was a creative heart beating within the company, and the record division throbbed with that pulse. Perhaps that protectiveness was resented at the corporate level, and, if so, it obviously didn't do me any good within the company. But from my perspective, at least, there was nothing new about that. It was the sort of corporate jostling typical of creative industries, and I had been dealing with it for years.

If Taylor believed that he deserved a greater degree of deference from me—and some of his public comments over the years suggest that he did—he never made that apparent to me, either through his words or his actions. There are many people who believe that if Frank Stanton, a seasoned veteran who had been through the ups and downs of the media wars, had still been president of CBS, the results would have been different. But without Stanton's presence, someone had to take the fall. Unfortunately, I was that person.

The investigation dragged on, and my name continued to be dragged along with it. The worst was yet to come. Because the federal investigators looking into corruption in the music industry could find no wrongdoing at all at CBS and absolutely nothing regarding me, they eventually got interested in the long-dormant civil suit that CBS had filed against me. Those allegations had nothing to do with drugs, and nothing to do with payola. My attorneys argued strenuously with the prosecutors that if they were going to pursue a case against me for tax evasion on the basis of my disputed expenses (the only possibility left for them), they should separate it from the indictments they were about to make against various low-level music industry figures. Needless to say, the prosecutors ignored that appeal. They clearly needed my name to make it seem as if their multimillion-dollar fishing expedition had landed at least one big fish. All the indictments were lumped together and announced on the same day in June 1975, and my name and photograph dominated the coverage. More than unfair, it was outrageous.

Characteristically, the media made no attempt to draw a distinction between the charges against me and the drug and payola charges leveled against the diverse low-level music industry figures in the indictments. Quite the opposite, in fact. As the prosecutors intended, I was once again judged guilty by association, and their findings were made to seem far more significant than they were. A prominent photo of me appeared in the *New York Post* under the headline "PAYOLA SCANDAL—Execs, Companies Indicted." The accompanying story, blurring all distinctions, announced "a massive series of indictments charging the recording, music and broadcasting industries with payola, bribery, income tax evasion, perjury and mail fraud." *The New York Times* quoted a U.S. attorney who insisted these indictments were "only the beginning" of a deeper inquiry into payola in the music business. "A nationwide investigation into the $2 billion music recording business— the so-called 'payola probe'—resulted in indictments yesterday against 19 industry officials, including Clive Davis, the former president of Columbia Records," the New York *Daily News* declared. Somehow the actual fact that I was completely exonerated of any charges related to payola or drugs went totally by the wayside. It just didn't make for compelling-enough copy.

Finally, in May 1976, three years after my firing, I received news that the government was dropping five of the six charges it had lodged against me. I was asked to plead guilty to failing to pay $2,700 in taxes on $8,800 of contested travel expenses. Four months later I was sentenced. I was placed on one day of unsupervised probation and fined $10,000. Inevitably, and forever depressing, this virtually complete exoneration received nothing like the coverage of all the baseless charges, rumors, and guilt-by-association whispers that I had lived with since leaving Columbia.

Judge Thomas P. Griesa, presiding at the sentencing, said it best in a highly unusual declaration from the bench. In his statement, he described "the really grievous suffering of this individual and his family because of the intolerable publicity he has been exposed to." In addition, he declared, "I have reviewed the press articles going back some three years and they are appalling in the innuendo and direct attempts to connect Mr. Davis with crimes with which he was never indicted and to say nothing of never having been convicted. . . . [O]n the face of it I see absolutely no excuse for the newspaper publicity that went on. But ultimately who was at fault for that, I really don't know but the results were there, the damages are documented. I have never had a case where . . . this situation has existed, at least in anything like the degree which it exists here."

I obviously found Judge Griesa's statement gratifying and, in general, felt vindicated by the outcome. The CBS civil suit was settled the following year. Beyond my case, it's important to note that despite years of investigation and the vast sums of money spent, not one person at CBS or anywhere else in the music industry went to prison on payola or drug charges. As Dave Marsh wrote in *Rolling Stone,* "In effect, what the prosecutor has done is vindicate the music business: given similar scrutiny, it's unlikely that any other $2 billion industry in America would have come away so clean. The corruption in the music business simply isn't the bottomless pit that the prosecutor and the columnists have claimed."

Soon after my case ended, I got a call that CBS wanted to show faith in me and my new company, Arista. They gave us a check for $1 million for future mail-order and record-club rights to Arista artists. A copy of that check is a prized possession of mine to this day. Four years later, in 1980, I was named Humanitarian of the Year by the T. J. Martell Foundation, a major music industry charity named after the son of the CBS Records executive Tony Martell. In presenting the award to me, Bruce Lundvall, then president of Columbia Records, said that the music industry was fortunate to have had a person of my dignity and ethics as its representative during that horrific investigation. That, too, was personally very satisfying.

To a troubling extent, however, an echo of the type of coverage vilified in Judge Griesa's decision persists whenever I am written about or profiled in the media to this day. Even well-meaning reporters mention, as if it were an established fact, that I wrote off my son Fred's bar mitzvah as a business expense, even though that is not true. Consequently, the case still follows me, and I sometimes wish that I had simply not pleaded guilty to anything and let it go to trial. I know that I would have been acquitted. At the time, my lawyers urged me to accept the terms the government offered. The prosecutors had caved on everything and simply wanted a conviction on one minor count in order to justify the millions of dollars they had foolishly spent on their investigation. The ordeal had dragged on for three and a half years at the time of my sentencing, and I, too, wanted to put it behind me. But, unfortunately, it never fully worked out that way. Perhaps even an acquittal at trial wouldn't have done it. At least, by any measure, the worst of it was over.

There is one additional footnote to this unfortunate episode. As a result of my conviction, my license to practice law could be affected. I had been assured by my lawyer that because my $2,700 tax conviction was a misdemeanor in New York State, my license would not be impacted. This was purely a theoretical concern. I was once again running a record label and, regardless, I didn't have the slightest interest in working as a lawyer. A subsequent federal court ruling, however, treated any tax violation on the part of an attorney as a felony. Consequently, my license to practice law was suspended, although I was free to apply for reinstatement to the bar.

I felt no particular need to do that, because I was so busy with my label. But, while I never discussed it with anyone, it did prey on my mind that I had never set this matter to rest. It was like a blight on my record. So eventually I did apply to be reinstated to the bar of New York State. As part of that process I needed to prepare for, take, and pass the bar exam, just as I had four decades earlier. That was no small requirement. I was running a record company and putting in my characteristically long days. It was one of the most successful periods of my life, in fact. In 1996, the year I applied for readmission to the bar, I earned more than $70 million, mostly from my phantom equity ownership interest in Arista Records, the label I launched after leaving Columbia.

But you don't pass the bar exam on the basis of your income or your stature, and I accepted—indeed, admired—that. So, late at night, after all my other work was completed, I made time to study for the exam between 10:00 p.m. and 1:00 a.m. I've always been a night owl, and there really was no other time that I could do it. I was determined. I got all the preparatory materials, and I studied for four or five months. It felt like being back in school again, but that was fine. I liked school. No one knew I was doing this but my family. When the time came, I registered for my seating ticket, went to the local school that served as a testing center, took the exam with hundreds of other applicants, and passed it very handily. I was to learn that I was in the top 3 or 4 percent. It felt really good. I hated feeling there were any limitations on my career options. Besides, my upbringing had come to the fore once again. A law degree was something to fall back on. After all, you never know what can happen and when you might need it.

Searching for a New Beginning

Once the dust settled from my firing and the various investigations were under way, I had to address the short-term issue of how I was going to make a living. Ultimately, regardless of the horrific publicity and whispered dire predictions about my future, I was always confident that I would work in the music industry again. Less than a month after Columbia let me go, *The Wall Street Journal* ran a story with a headline taken from a quote within it: "Everybody Hopes Clive Forms His Own Company." In it, a "prominent talent manager" says, "They'd all go with him. I hear every manager, artist, producer, agent in the street saying they hope he does it. There's no stigma at all. They all respect him and know what he can do."

That was encouraging, needless to say. However, I understood that companies might be hesitant to work with me until it was evident that I was going to be cleared of any significant wrongdoing, and given the glacial pace at which the prosecutors moved, who knew when that might be? In the meantime, while I had some savings and my family and I were not in any immediate financial danger, making some money seemed as if it might be a good idea. Among other things, my lawyer's fees were beginning to mount.

It turns out that all the publicity I was getting had at least one positive effect: There was widespread interest in my writing a book. Early on, I was introduced to a very talented editor named Jim Landis at William Morrow, and we hit it off really well. Despite all the media interest in alleged payola, drugs, and corruption in the music business, I was under strict orders from my attorney not to discuss any of that, and I made that clear to Jim. He believed that I could produce a strong book regardless. Before I was approached about it, it had never entered my mind to write a book. I didn't want to go into any potential scandals—I didn't know anything about them. But the more I thought about it, the more I realized that I did have enough experiences to warrant a book, and I had a story to tell. And now was the time to tell it.

I wasn't working, so I would have time to do the writing, editing, and revising that would provide the raw material for the book. I also needed to find a co-writer to work with me, so I arranged to meet with several whose work I admired. Of them, I got along particularly well with Jim Willwerth, who was on staff at *Time* and who had interviewed me for a long cover story he had done on the music industry. Although, or perhaps because, he wasn't strictly a music reporter—he had written a book about the Vietnam War, for example—he brought a discerning eye to both the artists and the executives he wrote about. I enjoyed his seriousness and his clear, distinctive voice as a writer. So we agreed to work together, and he took a leave from *Time* for the length of the project.

The process of doing the book turned out to be entirely satisfying. I rented a suite at the Hotel Ruxton on Seventy-second Street between Central Park West and Columbus Avenue, just a few blocks from my apartment. Willwerth and I would meet four or five days a week, beginning in the morning, and record an interview. We'd break in the late afternoon, and I'd work on the transcript from the previous day and return it to him with my revisions. It was very helpful, even therapeutic, for me to have the opportunity, amid all the madness that was going on, to recount all my challenges and experiences in the music industry. It was a bracing reminder that my life was not simply a chronicle of charges and countercharges, but an exciting journey alongside some of the most important artists of our time. Although I was under orders not to refute the false accusations that had been made against me, I could present an accurate picture of my life in music and the artistic milestones I had helped make possible. If Columbia was attempting to rewrite history and exclude me from it, I was reminded in the course of my interviews with Jim of everything that I had faced and accomplished there. I had no interest in settling scores, but I did want my life at Columbia and in the music business generally on the record. The process of writing the book gave me a needed chance to exhale before taking my next meaningful step forward.

The book, which we titled *Clive: Inside the Record Business,* appeared in the fall of 1974. I recall two quotes in particular from artists who wrote statements to help promote it. Elton John said, "When my recording contract was about to be renegotiated, Columbia Records was the only company I'd considered apart from MCA. Then Clive Davis left Columbia—I wasn't interested anymore. Clive was Columbia." And perhaps most relevant, Lou Reed wrote, "Never vindictive, this atypical man is a knowledgeable friend. I myself can only say that this succinct and concise prologue demands a sequel. I myself can't wait."

As I worked on the book, I did have some discussions regarding the next phase of my career. I previously described how I did some consulting for Bob Dylan when he was signed to David Geffen's Asylum label and was trying to figure out if he would release a second album there. He had left Columbia after I got fired, and the label failed to nail down the contract that I had already successfully negotiated with him. I got strong inquiries about whether I wanted to get into management, with Dylan, Neil Diamond, and Sly Stone brought up as potential clients. I was intrigued by the notion, and it made me feel good that there was interest if I decided to move in that direction.

But management is so highly personal that I ultimately didn't think it was the right move for me. One of the reasons, for example, that Marty Erlichman has been Barbra Streisand's manager for more than fifty years is that she has been without question the main focus of his efforts during that entire time. Usually the demands of a very visible major star are all-encompassing, and jealousies arise if managers take on clients of anything approaching equal stature. Finally, then, you're depending on the loyalty of one person who is constantly being approached by rivals determined to prove that they can produce better results than you have. Since I'd just received a jarring lesson at Columbia in how precarious loyalty can be in the entertainment industry, I didn't think I could comfortably put myself in a situation like that.

In a more promising development, I was approached by Chris Blackwell, the founder of Island Records, to enter into a joint venture with his group of labels, with me running the company. It was a terrific opportunity. Chris is not only an astute businessman, but a passionate and knowledgeable music lover who helped bring such artists as Bob Marley, Steve Winwood, and Jethro Tull to the world. He offered me 50 percent equity in the company, which very satisfactorily addressed what had been a major source of my discontent at Columbia. Our contract was fully agreed on and ready to be signed, when very significant tax issues arose. This was a period when tax laws in the U.K. were particularly onerous, and many British artists were becoming tax exiles. Because Island was based in Britain, forming an American label meant that any money leaving the U.K. would be taxed at an unacceptably high rate. Chris was extremely apologetic, but suddenly the deal was going to cost him something like 50 percent more than he had originally thought, which obviously wasn't acceptable. He pulled out and the deal fell apart at the last minute. I had been really pumped about it, so that was a totally unexpected blow for me.

Not long after that painful setback, however, Freddie Gershon, who held a very high-ranking position in the Robert Stigwood Organisation, contacted me and explained that Stigwood was keenly interested in my running the record division of his ever-expanding company. Again, this was a highly attractive prospect. Stigwood had been a partner of the Beatles' manager, Brian Epstein; had managed Cream and discovered the Bee Gees; had staged the musical *Hair* in London; and had produced the highly profitable film version of *Jesus Christ Superstar*. He saw early on how film, theater, soundtrack albums, and live performances could all work together. Just a few years after our conversations, the film *Saturday Night Fever,* a Stigwood production with a soundtrack on his RSO label, would stand the music industry on its head and become the most successful soundtrack in history until *The Bodyguard* topped it.

Stigwood and I met for two days in his tower suite at the Waldorf-Astoria Hotel in New York, discussing what each of us was looking for, where we saw the industry going, and how we could best work together. Our visions were extremely complementary, so much so that, when it came time to discuss a formal arrangement, I told him that I'd just spent months negotiating a deal with Chris Blackwell that had fallen through. Whatever else, the Island contract represented exactly what I was looking for. I offered to send it to him to see if he had a similar arrangement in mind. If so, it would essentially mean substituting the Robert Stigwood Organisation for Chris Blackwell in the contract's language, and then getting down to work. He agreed to have a look at the contract. Once he did, he quickly sent back word. Yes, this was exactly what he had in mind, and we could proceed on that understanding. I was thrilled.

Just one step remained: Stigwood was still bound by his contract with Atlantic Records, which was part of the Warner Elektra Atlantic (WEA) conglomerate. Atlantic was still run by Ahmet Ertegun, and Stigwood had told Ahmet that he was speaking to him in order to get a read on whether Ahmet was likely to approve it if we eventually were able to make a deal. Ahmet replied that he believed I had been treated terribly by Columbia, and he would be very sympathetic to letting Stigwood out of his contract if he and I were to reach a suitable agreement. Mo Ostin and Joe Smith at Warner Bros. and Jac Holzman at Elektra had already consented to let Stigwood out of his deal if he wanted to go into business with me. Everything looked good, and we arranged the closing of the deal for a Monday as we awaited final approvals.

On the Saturday before that Monday, I attended a party for James Taylor and Carly Simon, who were married at the time, at a restaurant called J.P. With the investigations going on and all the attendant publicity and speculation in the air, I had rigorously avoided all industry events. They would be awkward for me at best, and painful for a lot of reasons. The one thing I assumed people would want to talk to me about, I couldn't discuss. But with the Stigwood deal in the offing, I felt that it might be time for me to reemerge. When I walked into J.P. I was absolutely unprepared for the depth of emotion expressed toward me by all the artists and executives there. One after another they came over and embraced me with genuine fervor. Ahmet was sitting at the bar when I entered and was among the first people I saw. We embraced and greeted each other warmly. I walked home that night feeling so good, just floating on air. My standing in the music community was clearly undiminished. I could not have been greeted with more affirmation and warmth. And I was all set to get back in action.

That joy was to be short-lived, unfortunately. At 9:00 on Monday morning Freddie Gershon called me, and as soon as I heard his voice it sounded as if he were on the verge of tears. He told me that Ahmet had called Stigwood immediately after the party and gone to see him at the Waldorf. Ahmet told Stigwood that he just couldn't let him out of his WEA contract so that he could enter an agreement with me. Freddie told me that Stigwood was crushed and intended to try to turn the situation around, but he wasn't optimistic. In any event, for now the deal was off.

I was flabbergasted, and left to speculate what had happened between Ahmet's warm greeting of me when I entered the party on Saturday night and the time he made that fateful visit to Stigwood. The only interpretation I could come up with was that at the party Ahmet had witnessed firsthand the special relationships I had established with artists. He probably came to think that Stigwood and I would have been a very formidable team, an especially nerve-racking prospect given that he had the power to prevent it from happening. After what he saw at the party, he decided to exercise that power.

I don't at all believe that Ahmet's decision was personal, and I certainly don't think that he meant to do me any harm. He and I always had an intense but friendly competition. We would see each other wooing artists and managers by our cabanas around the pool at the Beverly Hills Hotel, and each of us would do the best he could to outmaneuver the other. Not much got by either of us; without rancor, we each noted the other's successes and failures. Our competitiveness, I believed, was always balanced by a mutual respect. Ahmet played hard, as I do, and to that extent I can rationalize why he made the decision to stop the Stigwood deal.

I must admit I was personally disappointed, but the professional esteem I held for him never diminished. I knew at my core that Ahmet was making a pure business decision, and for him business was business. I never discussed the matter with him. We always remained very friendly, and indeed over the ensuing years he was to go out of his way to show me great affection and respect. I invited him to the party I throw the night before the Grammys, and he came year after year. Whenever he was there I made a point of introducing him from the stage and acknowledging his stature and his incredible achievements.

Arista Means Excellence

In 1974 I was approached by Alan Hirschfield, who was president and CEO of Columbia Pictures, a long-established film and television company that also owned a record label, Bell Records. (Despite its name, Columbia Pictures had no relationship with Columbia Records.) Bell had enjoyed intermittent success with artists like Del Shannon, the Box Tops, Lee Dorsey, the Delfonics, the 5th Dimension, and Tony Orlando and Dawn. It was primarily known as a pop label, and its sales had largely been driven by hit singles, not albums, where real money could be made. It had just come off a very bad year. Alan impressed upon me that Columbia Pictures was eager to aggressively explore the prospect of not only turning Bell around, but making it an industry leader. That certainly got my attention. Personally, I had already successfully addressed the transition from singles to album sales both at Columbia Records itself and in Columbia's joint venture with Philadelphia International. I assured Alan that I could make it happen again. It was a question of identifying artists who were capable of making quality albums, and who could drive the sales of those albums with hit singles and dynamic live performances. Finding artists with those three-dimensional talents had driven my success at Columbia, and I felt I could repeat it in a new context. Indeed, I would welcome that challenge. It was exactly what I was looking for.

That Bell was experiencing difficulty obviously was not ideal, but it also presented an interesting opportunity. Ushering Columbia Records into the rock era had been a struggle precisely because the label had a long, distinguished prior history of which its executive team was justifiably proud. Many people at the label simply couldn't accept that that history had passed its peak, so I sometimes felt that I had to battle my own staff in order to get things done. Bell had no such history, and, hence, no emotional attachment to its past. It would be scary starting nearly from scratch, but it would also be exciting to line up a first-rate executive team, particularly in A&R, who understood what we needed to do and had the skills to make it happen.

My conversations with Hirschfield convinced me that he would help make such a transformation possible. We got along extremely well. He had come to Columbia Pictures in 1973 with the mandate to rescue the company, which was in serious financial difficulty. He was relatively young, and though his own background was in banking and film, he loved music and believed, as I did, that its significance and value were only going to grow. He had met with many key executives in the music industry about this position, and he came to me because he wanted someone with a proven track record who could make things happen fast. He was aware, of course, of the investigations that were under way. Columbia Pictures looked into the matter, and he and I discussed it in detail. He was confident of my innocence and more than willing to take a risk.

I accepted the offer in mid-1974. Initially, it was announced that I was consulting for Bell through an arrangement with Columbia Pictures, but all of my conversations and negotiations with Alan rested on the premise that I was going to be starting a completely new label. Columbia Pictures would invest $10 million in the company, and I would get a 20 percent equity stake. Depending on their contracts, I could keep or release any of the artists who were signed to Bell, and the same with the executive team at the label. Bell was an asset of Columbia Pictures, and the idea was for me to determine what was there of value that I might be able to use. It felt great to be back behind the wheel again.

Over the summer I began to work at Bell's offices, which were at 1776 Broadway, near Fifty-seventh Street. The primary advantage of the location was that it was about a block away from the Carnegie Delicatessen, which became something like our canteen. If the staff and I were working late or if we just wanted to get out of the office for a change of scene and some delicious, mountainous sandwiches, we often ended up at the Carnegie. I would go there at all hours. It was, and remains, a New York landmark.

Unfortunately, that wasn't enough of a reason to keep the label where it was, and among the first decisions I made was that we needed to relocate. However badly Columbia Records had treated me, the company still remained the standard that I wanted to aspire to in this new venture. With regard to location, that meant a prestigious address, one that would speak well for the label and inspire artists and their representatives who came to visit us there. Black Rock had its disadvantages, but no one who entered or even looked at that building could have any doubt that Columbia Records was playing on the world stage. In its own way, 1776 Broadway was a classic New York address, but with something like the faded, nostalgic feeling of Woody Allen's *Broadway Danny Rose*. The building is dark brick and located on the periphery of where the record industry was centered in midtown Manhattan. Everything about it suggested the tattered showbiz world that the modern music industry had risen up to replace. We badly needed a fresh start.

Elliot Goldman, who came over from Columbia to be my executive vice president, and I eventually found space in a handsome building at 6 West Fifty-seventh Street, just off Fifth Avenue. It was classy, dignified, and tasteful. We had offices built for us that conveyed the hominess and intimacy of a relatively small company that was just starting out, but it allowed us to make a distinctive impression on everyone who came to see us. We moved into those offices in July 1976, and remained there for nearly twenty-five years.

Right from the beginning I spent a lot of time coming up with an appropriate name for the new company. Without question, naming a record company is tough. You want something that is personally resonant for you, but isn't so individual that other people can't instantly relate to it. You want it to sound fresh, but not in a contrived way, as if you're trying too hard to be cool. And you don't want to be trendy. What's fresh today can turn very stale tomorrow. In the same way that Columbia competed in every area of music, I wanted the new label to be active in rock, pop, jazz, country, and R&B. That meant the name couldn't refer to just one style of music.

Finally I came up with what I believed to be the perfect name: Arista, pronounced 'Ar-is-ta, emphasizing the first syllable. It sounded unique, but somehow familiar as well, as if you'd heard it before but couldn't quite remember where. It didn't indicate any particular genre of music, but instead suggested a standard to which all the company's releases would be held. In truth, Arista was the name of the branch of the national honors society at my high school, Erasmus Hall. It derives from the same Greek stem that gives us the word *aristocracy*—in this case denoting a first-class status determined by talent, not luck of birth. In short, Arista means excellence. I was personally proud to be part of the honors society when I was a student and I wanted my new company to communicate that same sense of achievement. A beautiful logo that communicated both elegance and strength was internally designed, and suddenly the name was official. Now all we had to do is make sure that we lived up to the standard it conveyed. We would launch Arista in November 1974.

While I was consulting, I spent a great deal of time speaking with the executive staff at Bell to determine who needed to go and whom I would try to keep. I also met with people who were currently at other labels whom I wanted to recruit. Happily, there was a tremendous amount of interest on both fronts, and I was able to put together what I considered to be an exceptionally strong team. Among the people at Bell whom I kept on were David Carrico, as vice president of promotion, Gordon Bossin, as vice president of marketing and the unforgettable Milt Sincoff as vice president of production. As I mentioned, I recruited my loyal and astute friend Elliot Goldman to be executive vice president. Bob Feiden, a veritable encyclopedia of artist information whose wit and self-coined aphorisms were to become legendary, left RCA to become our first director of A&R. Aaron Levy, for years a major player in the industry, became chief financial officer. Rick Chertoff became my invaluable A&R song man. Bob Heimall joined us from Elektra to be director of creative services, and I poached the inimitable Michael Klenfner from Columbia to be our director of national promotion.

Those are just some of the bold-faced names, and they formed the foundation for a team that would evolve into a group of extremely gifted executives, a new generation of leaders who were eager to be part of this exciting new enterprise. Within the first one or two years of the label's existence, I brought in additional senior people of achievement and promise, many of whom went on to become heads of competing labels, or to make a significant mark in other areas of the entertainment industry. Dennis Fine, a well-known Solters and Roskin media executive, joined us to run Arista's publicity department. Richard Palmese came on board in 1975, and meteorically rose to head Arista's Promotion Department, spearheading many brilliant and successful radio campaigns for the label before leaving to join MCA Records, eventually becoming its president. Bob Buziak was hired as the all-encompassing head of our West Coast operation, was promoted to be our successful U.K. managing director, and went on to be president of RCA Records in subsequent years. Rick Dobbis became a tower of strength as Arista's senior vice president of marketing, and he also later had a stellar career, first as president of the PolyGram Label Group and then as president of Sony Music International. A terrific young Arista West Coast A&R executive, Roger Birnbaum, became a strong performer for us and then left the record industry for a major career as a film producer.

I can't emphasize enough the importance of having an absolutely first-rate management team. In our case, it clearly signaled this was no one-man show but a major label in formation with keen, farsighted, and contemporary executives who would demonstrate strong, in-depth leadership. I knew that whatever artists I might retain from the Bell roster, or I would sign to put Arista on the map, a major part of our success would be in the hands of these executives. Immediately, I had confidence that if the music had potential, this team would deliver.

Needless to say, a very key decision was determining which artists to keep and which to let go. It's fine to think of yourself as starting completely fresh and giving the label an entirely new identity, but I needed to retain some artists who could generate revenue immediately. I kept others because I saw possibilities in them that had not yet been realized. The $10 million Columbia Pictures put in was not a large investment, but I had enough goodwill in the industry that retailers and distributors would be as flexible as they could in order to help Arista succeed. And, as I mentioned, Columbia Records gave Arista a check for a million dollars as an advance on the rights to sell music by the label's artists in the Columbia Record Club, which personally meant a great deal to me.

Bell had perhaps fifty artists on its roster, and I listened to as much of their music as I could and went to see as many of them perform live as possible. Ultimately, I kept eight for Arista, including the 5th Dimension, Melissa Manchester, Peter Nero, Al Wilson, and Suzi Quatro. Tony Orlando and Dawn, who had a run of pop hits in the early Seventies, had left Bell to sign with David Geffen at Elektra/Asylum, but Bell retained the rights to enough of their material for us to release three additional albums by them in the next eighteen months. I signed quality artists in a range of genres whose work I looked forward to releasing in the coming year or two, including Gil Scott-Heron, Lou Rawls, Eric Andersen, Garland Jeffreys, Anthony Braxton, the Brecker Brothers, Melanie, and the Headhunters.

Most notably, I kept another Bell artist even though his first album for the label had not sold well. I saw him perform live, and I thought he had a very promising future as a great all-around entertainer. He had a terrific voice and an extremely engaging manner onstage. The audience loved him and, better still, you could tell they wanted to love him. He made them feel good. Once you get fans on your side that way, you can build a very loyal audience that can sustain you for years. The artist's name was Barry Manilow.

Manilow Mania

Barry Manilow's first album, simply titled *Barry Manilow,* had come out in 1973. The original version of the album might not have motivated me to take a deeper look to see if anything more promising lay beneath the surface, but because Barry was signed to Bell, I needed to evaluate him as one of the company's assets, just as I did all the other artists on the label. I knew that he had worked with Bette Midler, accompanying her on piano, co-producing her first two albums, and acting as musical director on her 1973 "Divine Miss M" Tour. Those credits vouched for his talents as a musician and arranger, but he was signed to Bell as an artist, and I needed to see if he had what it takes in that regard. So on June 24, 1974, I went to the Wollman Skating Rink in Central Park to see him open for Dionne Warwick. I was really taken by his performance. He was a terrific singer, and his manner was upbeat, funny, and self-deprecating. The audience loved him, which was impressive since he was essentially unknown and opening for a much more established artist, usually not an advantageous situation. Of course, he did his V.S.M. (very strange medley), which consisted of ubiquitous commercial jingles he had written or sung (or both) for McDonald's, Kentucky Fried Chicken, Pepsi-Cola, and Band-Aid. I realized that was not something that would endear him to critics—and, boy, was I right about that—but anybody who could create music that so many people positively responded to impressed me. I truly believed right from the start that he could be a star.

I went backstage, introduced myself to Barry, and told him how enthusiastic I was and that I looked forward to our working together. I later learned that he had been nervous about his future. He had been signed to Bell by Larry Uttal, the very talented former president of the label. Uttal, of course, was no longer there, and when artists are orphaned like that, they're often dropped. From my reputation at Columbia, Barry knew me as someone who had primarily signed rock artists, so he wasn't sure how he would fare with me. He was encouraged that I had responded so well to his set. He was already at work on his second album, and now he could proceed with confidence.

When he felt he was nearly done, he played the album for me. I listened carefully, as I knew Barry would be hanging on every word I said. What I spelled out was that I didn't think we had what I like to call a defining single—a song that not only could announce the album as a strong first single, but create enough momentum both to sell the album and to drive the singles that followed. The album would be Arista's first major release, and I really could not risk its not making noise. Beyond wanting to establish Arista in a dramatic way, the label, being a startup, needed to generate income quickly. I was feeling cautiously optimistic, however, because since I had seen him in Central Park, I had found a song that I thought Barry could do wonders with and that would deliver everything we needed from a first single. I explained all this to him. Barry politely heard me out, and then said, sure, he'd give it a listen and see what he could do with it. What I didn't understand at the time, though it would become a major issue in my relationship with Barry over the years, is that while I saw him as a charismatic entertainer, he viewed himself exclusively as a singer-songwriter. The singer-songwriter ideal was prevalent in the early Seventies, and for all the showbiz razzmatazz of his work with Bette Midler, Barry not only took himself very seriously as a musician and composer, it was his heart and soul. The notion of doing songs by someone else did not at all sit well with him, to say the least. He really did not see himself as a song interpreter, but as a songwriter. Fortunately, from my standpoint, Barry was still feeling insecure about his standing at the label, so he was willing to give my song a listen. If his first album had sold 500,000 copies rather than 10,000, we might have had a very different conversation and he might not have been so cooperative.

Beyond seeing Barry primarily as a singer and performer, I also had personally made up my mind to approach A&R in a much more robust way at Arista than I had at Columbia. Despite the singer-songwriter trend, I believed that there was still a sizable audience for pop singers who did not write their own material, and the key to their success would be finding the right songs for them to record. Many A&R executives believe that identifying talent is the essence of their job. That's obviously critically important, but it's not the whole story. If the artist isn't a songwriter, finding first-rate material for them is essential. People often say that a great singer can sing the phone book and people would buy it. To me, that's completely wrong. The better the singer, the more critical it is that the songs are challenging enough to showcase his or her talents at their absolute best. My A&R man, Rick Chertoff, was a great help to me in this regard at Arista. Along with being a gifted producer, he is a strong song man who helped me find appropriate hit songs for many of the artists at the label, including Barry Manilow.

In fact, while interviewing Rick for his position at Arista, I came up with the key procedure that became a test for virtually all of my subsequent A&R hires. I asked him to identify five previously released songs—overlooked gems—that had not been hits and that he believed could potentially, with different production or arrangement, be more successful in another singer's hands. It's really an excellent test of someone's ears. Artists occasionally bristle when you give them material that did not perform well for another artist, but that's ego entering the equation, and quite unnecessarily. If no one ended up hearing the song, what difference does it make if someone else recorded it first? A change in arrangement, a different approach to the vocal, or just the freshness of a new, more suitable voice can make all the difference between a song going nowhere and its being a smash hit.

The song I had in mind for Barry was called "Brandy," and it was unknown in the United States, though it had been a moderate hit in the U.K. for Scott English, who had co-written the song with Richard Kerr. Evidently, when I brought it to Barry, he thought it was a nice little ditty that might work as a track on his album, and he would work on it with his co-producer, Ron Dante, just to keep me happy. The first version he came up with was too upbeat, too peppy. I told him that I heard the song as more of a ballad, that a slower rendition would allow the emotion of the song to build and communicate more powerfully. I was also concerned that the title not be confused with "Brandy (You're a Fine Girl)," which had been a number-one hit in 1972 for a band called Looking Glass, which had been signed to Epic when I was overseeing that label. Consequently, I suggested that we rename the song "Mandy." Barry is an extraordinarily gifted arranger, and, when we were in the studio together, in about ten minutes he came up with a ballad rendition of "Mandy" that was everything I hoped for and more.

We released the album, titled *Barry Manilow II,* in October 1974, and put out "Mandy" as its first single. The public launch of Arista Records occurred at the same time, and the immediate commercial impact of "Mandy" made it clear that the new label was in the business of generating hits. The song soared to number one, and Barry instantly became a star. Just a year and a half earlier I had been fired from Columbia Records, and now the first release on my new label had hit the top of the charts. I also felt that there were some people in the industry who believed that my success at Columbia had been not so much a fluke, but no big deal—that anyone, even a lawyer with no musical background, who took over a label of such size and stature would inevitably make his mark. "Mandy" blew those doubts away. Barry Manilow was unknown when I decided to keep him for Arista, and I had found the song that rocketed to number one. This is to take nothing away from Barry. His arrangement and his performance of the song were absolutely stellar. But someone had to foresee that possibility, put the parts together, and make it happen. That was my role, and it's one that I've treasured ever since. It also began a professional relationship with Barry that would last more than thirty years, and a friendship that has lasted even longer.

The success of "Mandy" provided me with a strong platform from which to promote Arista, and, as I did at Columbia, I sought innovative ways to do that. Barry was always an enthusiastic participant in my efforts, and he and Arista grew together by leaps and bounds. In February 1973, NBC began broadcasting a weekly music show titled *Midnight Special,* which aired on Friday nights immediately after Johnny Carson's *Tonight Show.* If the late hour meant that only true music fans would tune in, following Carson ensured that the show would reach as many of those fans as possible. Just as the music industry began doing in the Sixties, television had to find ways to reach the new, younger, hipper audience of the baby-boom generation. *Midnight Special,* which enjoyed a successful run into the early Eighties, was one of those efforts, just as *Saturday Night Live* would be a few years later. In March 1975, I co-hosted *Midnight Special* with Mac Davis, a country singer-songwriter whom I had signed to Columbia. Along with Mac, the show featured artists I had signed at Columbia and Arista, including Loggins and Messina, Melissa Manchester, Martha Reeves, Gil Scott-Heron, and Blood, Sweat & Tears. I opened the show by introducing Barry as "the newest star for America," and to this day he plays that introduction, which leads into his performance of "Mandy," at the start of his concerts all over the world.

When Arista opened its L.A. office in February 1975, I threw a "welcome to the west" party in 1975 at the Hotel Bel-Air, and Barry performed once again, along with Melissa Manchester and Gil Scott-Heron. That September, in order to celebrate Arista's first anniversary and to lend momentum to the artistic revival that was helping to bring New York back from the brink of bankruptcy, I sponsored a two-show festival at City Center titled "Arista Records Salutes New York." I told *Billboard* magazine, "After a first year like we've had at Arista, I believe it's appropriate to make a festive celebration and share our feeling of excitement with the city of New York." Headlining the evening show, once again, was my fellow Brooklyn native Barry Manilow.

In late 1975 "Mandy" was nominated for a Grammy in the Record of the Year category, and I wanted to find an original way to celebrate that honor. It's hard to compete with the Grammys, of course, but I wanted to take advantage of the fact that so many important players in the music industry would be in Los Angeles for that event. I hit on the idea of having a party at the Beverly Hills Hotel the day after the Grammys. The Arista party in February 1976 was an enormous success, with Elton John, Paul Simon, Stevie Wonder, John Denver, and Carly Simon just a few of the celebrities who attended. The event would eventually become the pre-Grammy party, the equivalent of Swifty Lazar's famed Oscar party, and a music business institution to which invitations are highly coveted. It is one of my proudest achievements that it continues to this day.

As you can see, I was determined that Arista would succeed, and I was working as hard as possible to make that happen. Barry was ecstatic that his album was doing so well, and he, too, was tireless in his willingness to help promote it. *Barry Manilow II* cracked the Top 10 and would go on to be a million-seller. After "Mandy," we released "It's a Miracle," which Barry co-wrote, as a single, and it went to number twelve. We then remixed his 1973 debut album, retitled it *Barry Manilow I,* and re-released it in 1975. That album went gold, and the single from it, Barry's composition "Could It Be Magic," went to number six.

It finally got to the time for Barry to begin work on his true follow-up album to *Barry Manilow II*. Without my realizing it, our tremendous run of success had enabled Barry and me to avoid confronting the different perspectives we had about how we envisioned his career. He still very much saw himself as a singer-songwriter. He even debuted *Barry Manilow II* at the Troubadour club in Los Angeles, which was known for showcasing the likes of Jackson Browne and James Taylor rather than pop singers. He saw himself in the model of Elton John and Billy Joel. I, however, still viewed Barry primarily as a singer and an entertainer, and the success of "Mandy" demonstrated to me how huge he could become if he went down that road. I certainly respected Barry as a songwriter, and "It's a Miracle" and "Could It Be Magic" each showed that he was perfectly capable of composing hits. But I had to come back to the idea of a defining hit, and pop singers need hits on that scale to keep them in the public eye. As a compromise, Barry and I agreed that I could choose two songs for every album. He would write the rest himself. Once we came to that understanding, I stopped thinking about our differences and went back to enjoying our success and finding songs that I thought would work well for him.

We were still in the Bell offices at 1776 Broadway when Barry met with me to hear the songs I wanted to suggest for his next album. I had already identified "Tryin' to Get the Feeling Again," written by David Pomeranz, which would become the album's title track. Barry liked the song and had already begun performing it live, to great reaction. It would eventually be a Top 10 hit for him. Then I inadvertently put my finger right on the sore spot of our relationship. The next track I played for him was "I Write the Songs." Perhaps my enthusiasm over finding the song, which I was certain would be a massive hit for him, had blinded me to how he would respond to it. To say the absolute least, his response was not positive.

He bluntly told me that he couldn't possibly record that song. The suggestion truly offended him. Everything about it was a problem. He said that it made him sound as if he were on a monumental ego trip. "Here's a song that I didn't even write, and yet I'm declaring that I write the songs that make the whole world sing? It's out of the question," he said. I tried to reassure him. It's a great melody, with a powerhouse hook, I insisted. I could hear the arrangement in my head, and I knew that he could do a killer job with it. Once he put his stamp on the song, it wouldn't matter who wrote it. It would be his because he would be the one making the song believable for everyone who heard it. He wasn't having any of this. I believe Barry genuinely felt that I had insulted him. He stormed out of my office, and I didn't hear from him for two or three months.

We really had a big difference of opinion. To me, the song is not about any one person, but about music itself and how every singer is a conduit through whom music communicates to the world. It's a beautiful idea, really, and, underneath, one that Barry believes himself. But the simple fact is that, regardless of how beautiful or moving it was, it was painful for Barry to record a song called "I Write the Songs" when he hadn't written it himself. The very idea undermined how he conceived of himself. Beyond that, initially he took the song too literally. Most music fans listen to a song the way they watch a movie or a TV show: They respond to a performance. Critics, insiders, and more sophisticated listeners want to know the backstory, the behind-the-scenes information about songwriters, producers, session musicians, and the like. More casual fans just know how the song makes them feel when they hear it. That's the impact that I knew Barry could deliver.

As for the song itself, like "Mandy," it had a bit of history behind it that didn't bother me at all but may have troubled Barry. A very talented songwriter, Bruce Johnston of the Beach Boys, had written it, and it had been on an album by the Captain & Tennille. It had also been a moderate hit in the U.K. for David Cassidy. But for all intents and purposes, the song was unknown in the States and a perfect vehicle for Barry to realize all of its potential. I just had to hope that he would come to understand that. He didn't tell me, but privately he was playing the song to himself over and over again, trying to unlock its appeal and mystery. I had not dropped the issue. With a song I believed in less, I would have let it go. We'd had a lot of success already. Why anger an artist that had already played such an important role in putting Arista on the map? But in this case I would not be satisfied until he had at least tried it. Then one day I got the call from Barry. It was Barry the musician, the arranger, the producer who was calling. He had to see me. And when he played his demo of the song for me, it was magic, everything I had hoped for. To his complete credit, Barry came up with a brilliant arrangement. Deep down, he's always been a total pro. We released the album *Tryin' to Get the Feeling* in October 1975, one year after *Barry Manilow II,* and put out "I Write the Songs" as the first single. The single shot to number one, and the album rose to number five and went on to sell more than 2 million copies. The title track also entered the Top 10. Because of Barry's definitive performance of "I Write the Songs," Bruce Johnston was awarded a Grammy for Song of the Year, which goes to the songwriter. Barry had been nominated for Record of the Year, which goes to the performer and producer, but lost. "I Write the Songs," meanwhile, has gone on to become Barry's signature song, greeted with a standing ovation every time he performs it. Nobody worries whether he wrote it. His millions of fans are content to love it.

Barry maintained his extraordinary run of success through the Seventies and into the early Eighties, logging twenty-five Top 40 singles between 1974 and 1983. As I had seen with pop singers like Andy Williams when I was at Columbia, Barry was able to extend his commercial impact through television. Along with the Grammy he won in 1979 for his song "Copacabana," he also racked up a Special Tony Award for "Barry Manilow on Broadway," a ten-day run of shows he did at the Uris Theatre over the 1976–77 Christmas and New Year's holiday season. (*Barry Manilow Live,* the 1977 album we released from those performances, went to number one and sold well over 3 million copies.) In addition, his hour-long 1977 ABC show, *The Barry Manilow Special,* garnered an audience of 37 million people and won an Emmy. Then in 1978 we released his greatest hits album. It too was certified three times platinum in the U.S. When this kind of success happens, you know that hit records have graduated into major, long-lasting copyrights, assuring a charismatic live performer many years of headlining and touring success.

Beyond his domestic success, Barry became a superstar in the U.K., where the term "Manilow Mania" was coined by the tabloids to reflect the Beatles-level scale of his popularity. Even Frank Sinatra, when asked about Barry by the British press, declared, "He's next." In 1982 we released *Barry Live in Britain,* which was recorded at the Royal Albert Hall in London and debuted at number one in the U.K., making Barry the first American artist to achieve that milestone. In 1983 he filmed a documentary about his performance before a crowd of more than 40,000 fans on the grounds of Blenheim Palace in England.

Through all of that I do admit to feeling that I was playing a very key role in Barry's success. In the broadest sense, I was running his label and being very creatively involved in supporting him in all of Arista's promotional and advertising efforts. He was an absolute priority, and I made sure that everyone at the label understood that. But more personally and much more essential, I was making my two song choices count every time. Roger Birnbaum, at the time the head of West Coast A&R for Arista, brought me "Weekend in New England" and "Can't Smile Without You," both of which were big signature hits for Barry. Among the other songs I found for him were "Looks Like We Made It," "Somewhere in the Night," "Ready to Take a Chance Again," "Ships" (written by Ian Hunter of Mott the Hoople, whom I had signed to Columbia), "When I Wanted You," "I Don't Want to Walk Without You" (written by Jule Styne and Frank Loesser), "I Made It Through the Rain," "The Old Songs," "Somewhere Down the Road," and "Read 'Em and Weep."

Still, the tension that had begun over "I Write the Songs" persisted, if often in low-key, indirect ways. I knew that as much as Barry was enjoying his tremendous success, part of him resented that he was so well known for songs he hadn't written. That critics routinely pummeled him didn't help. Barry took every critical barb to heart, and that he was often being reviled for songs that were not his own only salted the wound. It got difficult. Barry's manager even asked me at one point if Arista was making the same promotional effort for the songs Barry wrote as for the ones that I picked. I was naturally hurt by that. I had absolutely no financial involvement in any of the songs I selected, and I wanted every one of Barry's songs to be a hit.

I respected Barry's songwriting—he had plenty of hits with his own material, such as "Could It Be Magic," "Copacabana," "Even Now," "New York City Rhythm," "This One's For You," and "One Voice," among others. In addition he had immense talent as a singer and arranger. Many of the songs I chose for Barry had been recorded by other artists and had not been successful. He really deserved full credit for everything he had achieved. But by the early Eighties Barry was getting advances of $1 million or $1.5 million per album, and to earn that money back Arista needed big sales—the kind of sales that only defining hits make possible.

Conversations with Barry about these issues were never easy, but when his sales inevitably began to slip in the early Eighties, things reached something of a boiling point. Musical tastes were changing, and the entire music industry was in a slump as the economy struggled and video games began to compete for the attention and purchasing power of young people. He was very upset. I finally told Barry that I felt that I had been an integral part of his success, that we had been great collaborators, but I personally wasn't able to enjoy it because he had such mixed feelings about the material I had given him. One day he said to me, "Look, I appreciate the songs you give me, but you're turning me into Andy Williams or Perry Como. I never thought of myself like that. I'm a musician, a composer!" I looked him straight in the eye, and with all the frustration that had been building up, said, "Well, if you were Irving Berlin, we would know it by now!" I realize that was harsh, but that was how Barry and I spoke to each other. We were two Jews from Brooklyn going at it, and no one was mincing words.

It certainly wasn't a result of that one conversation, but Barry left Arista and signed with RCA, where he released an album called *Manilow* in 1985, his first studio album in three years and an attempt to update his sound to make it more contemporary. It failed to enter the Top 40. Barry also released a soundtrack album on RCA for a made-for-TV movie he starred in, based on his song "Copacabana." The film was nominated for two Emmys, but, again, the album failed to chart. I was very sad that he had left Arista, but we were never on bad terms. Despite our differences, we never allowed our relationship to descend into anything hostile or adversarial. I don't know the economics of his RCA deal, but I can't imagine that he moved for less money, and it's tough to argue someone out of a higher offer than you're able to make. Plus, in Barry's case, it was something like a child leaving the house. If you've known only one environment, it's natural to be curious about how things might be better somewhere else.

Soon, however, I began to hear rumors that Barry was unhappy at RCA, and that he missed our relationship enormously. I felt the same way. One day our mutual friend Sandy Gallin, a very successful manager, said to me, "Barry really misses you." Then he posed a question. If he were interested in coming back to Arista, would I work with Barry again? I told him that nothing that had happened between Barry and me was personal as far as I was concerned, and, of course, I would be glad to work with him again. If he were interested in coming back, I'd be happy to continue. It's not as if I had showed him the door.

So Sandy arranged for Barry and me to have dinner together, and Barry could not have been more direct in stating that sometimes you have to leave home in order to truly understand what you had in the first place. Whatever his experience had been at RCA, it was entirely beneficial for us. He was a totally different person from that day on. Clearly he had gone through some kind of catharsis. He spoke very appreciatively, and with heartfelt emotion, of the songs I had selected over the years for him. He had fully come to terms with that issue, which had been so contentious between us. From the start at Arista, Barry had achieved a level of superstardom that can make it difficult for anyone to understand fully the contributions other people have made to what you've accomplished. You get so much adulation that it's easy to lose perspective. But I was struck—and delighted—by the level of maturity to which he had risen. So he signed to Arista and we were back together again!

Unfortunately, our positive new beginning didn't change anything about the challenges of bringing Barry's music to the market. It was 1987 now and the music scene had continued to shift dramatically away from Barry's style of music. Radio now considered Barry to be an adult contemporary artist, that is, a performer unlikely to appeal to the more youth-oriented Top 40 audience. Without the strong radio hits that drive album sales, adult contemporary artists are essentially a niche taste. That said, it's not an insignificant audience at all, and it's loyal. Barry still was able to do extremely well as a live performer and on television. He had hardly receded from the scene.

Consequently, I began to work with him on a series of concept albums organized around a specific theme. The trick with concept albums is that they have to be appropriate to the artist, and every track on the album must not only be related to the theme, but it must be immediately recognizable to listeners who are interested in that style of music. That Barry, who had restricted the number of outside songs included on his albums, would go along with this idea of recording entire albums of material he didn't write indicates how far he'd come emotionally. *Swing Street,* his first album after returning to Arista, featured jazz influences and contemporary arrangements, and included a number of duets. We also recorded a Christmas album, an album of Broadway show tunes, an album of Sinatra songs (which received two Grammy nominations), and a big-band album. All of them did well, kept Barry in the public eye, and provided strong material for his consistently popular live shows.

Eventually, however, Barry tired of the concept albums and once again wanted to explore his own writing in greater depth. I realized I was not going to be able to get him on contemporary radio, and, given what those albums were likely to sell—a few hundred thousand, at most—he went to the Concord label, a small, high-quality company, in order to be able to make the kind of records he wanted to make. I understood what he wanted to do, and supported his decision. We always remained in touch. In 2000, Barry performed on the NBC primetime special celebrating the twenty-fifth anniversary of Arista. Then, in 2002, Arista put out another greatest hits collection titled *Ultimate*

Manilow, a hugely successful album that soared to number three and sold more than 2 million copies. That very same year Barry was inducted into the Songwriters Hall of Fame. I threw a gala dinner party at my weekend home in Pound Ridge to celebrate this great honor, commemorating all that he had achieved as a composer. In a perfect follow-up the next year, the Society of Singers honored Barry with the prestigious Ella Award for his brilliance as an interpretive singer. He asked if I would present that award to him, and I took the occasion to warmly recall stories about our many collaborations. How appropriate for him to be honored in consecutive years for his spectacular achievements both as a songwriter and a singer! It was a perfect tribute to the extraordinary range and quality of his career.

When you have a relationship with an artist like the one I have with Barry, you never stop thinking about it, and whether or not it might be possible to work together again. Something within me said, I've got to keep trying because he's such a great performer. I regularly found myself exploring ideas that I thought might be right for him. Still, I think Barry was shocked when, in 2005, I turned up at a show during his Las Vegas residency. I had never seen him perform there and, as always, he was just terrific. I went backstage to see him, and the connection between us was palpable immediately. We hadn't worked together in a while, but we had shared so much over the years. As we chatted, I pulled him aside and said, "Listen, I'd like to do an album with you. I've come up with another concept that excites me, and I think you can do a sensational job with it. You know how much I enjoy showing how eternal great songs are. You should do the greatest songs of the Fifties, the music that you grew up with. Arista would energetically promote it on television, and it could provide a strong new section in your act and freshen it up." I was holding a little piece of paper in my hand with a list of the songs that I thought would be perfect for the record.

Barry took a look at it, and then fixed me with that blank look I knew so well. His head popped back. "The Fifties?" he asked. He was taken aback and a bit skeptical. "Let me think about it," he said. "I love that you're thinking about me, but let me study it." It didn't take him twenty-four hours to call me back and say, "Oh my God, this is gonna be great! I didn't sleep at all last night. I'm so moved and Garry's so moved by your endless faith in me." (Garry Kief is Barry's longtime devoted manager.) And so we were off and running again. We went over my list together, made some changes, and just had a lot of fun. We released *The Greatest Songs of the Fifties* in January 2006. It entered the charts at number one and sold more than a million copies! It is one of Barry's two number-one albums; the other is *Barry Manilow Live* (1977), nearly three decades earlier. Of course, Barry was right in the promotional center, appearing on the *Today Show, Dancing with the Stars,* and *American Idol,* and having a wonderful time.

A second rule for concept albums is, when the concept works, you come right back with it. Consequently, we released *The Greatest Songs of the Sixties* later that year. It went to number two, and earned a gold album. In 2007, *The Greatest Songs of the Seventies* cracked the Top 5 and also went gold, and later in the year we put out Barry's third seasonal album, *In the Swing of Christmas. The Greatest Songs of the Eighties* entered the Top 20 in 2008, and in 2010 Barry again rose into the Top 5 with *The Greatest Love Songs of All Time,* which also received a Grammy nomination.

By then, of course, this particular string had run out. Not that Barry's slowing down at all. He still is selling out arenas everywhere he plays, and he's releasing strong albums of his own songs. But the memories and the experiences sure do linger. The hits we made together are perennials, and guarantee his stature in the pantheon of pop artists. And what a thrill for me to enjoy success well into the twenty-first century with an artist and friend who helped launch Arista Records more than thirty years before.

Building a New Label

The enormous impact of Barry Manilow inevitably cast Arista as a pop-music label in its earliest days, though that was never my intention. Modeled on Columbia, I wanted Arista to be a complete major label, not a boutique devoted to any specific style. I wanted Arista to be competitive in every area of contemporary music, from pop to progressive and from R&B to rock. It was an ambitious notion, given that Arista was a new company and independently distributed, but I was determined that we could live up to it. We were aggressive in our signings across the board. From my perspective, Barry's success was just an opening shot across the bow.

Of course, quality pop music is nothing to be ashamed of, and Melissa Manchester, another artist who, like Barry, had been signed to Bell and whom I kept for Arista, was a singer for whom I nurtured great hopes. She was a friend of Barry's and had worked with him when he was Bette Midler's musical director and she sang background as one of the Divine Miss M's Harlettes. When I was evaluating all the artists signed to Bell, I went to see Melissa at the Shubert Theater in Philadelphia, where she was opening for the comedian Robert Klein. I thought she was a sensational singer with excellent and expressive range and real stage presence. I believed that she had the potential to fill a pop space somewhere between Barbra Streisand and Bette Midler. I decided on the spot to keep her.

Melissa had previously released two albums that hadn't made much of an impact. But in January 1975 she put out *Melissa,* which included the beautiful ballad "Midnight Blue," co-written with Carole Bayer Sager. It became a Top 10 hit. After that, however, her career plateaued, and she wasn't reaching her full potential. I encouraged her to consider recording outside material along with the songs she herself wrote. As it had with Barry, this proved to be a problem. Again, while I viewed Melissa's strength primarily as a singer and song interpreter, she very much saw herself as a songwriter. She worshipped Laura Nyro to the degree that, when she took a songwriting workshop with Paul Simon as she was starting out, he told her to stop listening to Laura in order to find her own voice. Ironically, just as Barry once accused me of trying to turn him into Andy Williams, Melissa accused me of trying to turn her into . . . Barry Manilow. "I want to go along the lines of Joni Mitchell or Bonnie Raitt," she would insist. "I don't see myself as a female version of Barry." It was nothing personal. She and Barry were and always remained great friends. She just didn't want his career.

Actually, Melissa's own songs were very pretty, middle-of-the-road fare. She wrote well. "Come In from the Rain," also co-written with Carole Bayer Sager, is a beautiful pop song. The problem was that she didn't write enough songs like that to sustain a major career. With additional hits coming from outside material, she could indeed have become a female Barry, at least in terms of her sales. Her perspective of being another Joni Mitchell or Bonnie Raitt was off the mark. She didn't have edge; she had vocal power and a wonderful pop voice. I simply wanted her to be the most successful version of herself. But you can only push someone so far. It makes me come back to the point that knowing who you are, both in terms of your strengths and your limitations, is an essential component of success, as much for an artist as an executive.

Though Melissa fought me tooth and nail, I eventually was able to give her two songs: "Don't Cry Out Loud" and "You Should Hear How She Talks About You." Both became Top 10 hits for her. "Don't Cry Out Loud" earned her a Grammy nomination and "You Should Hear How She Talks About You" won a Grammy in 1983. Frustratingly, Melissa hated both songs with a passion. In fact, Harry Maslin, whom I brought in to produce "Don't Cry Out Loud" with her, credits Melissa's anger at having to sing it for the strength of her performance. She was determined to live or die with her own songs, and when that kind of confrontation occurs, I defer. I know that ultimately an artist is the only person who can make that final decision. Did I feel bad? Was I frustrated? Yes. I just knew that Melissa could have had a much bigger career if she were willing to do a couple of outside songs per album, as Barry did. She could have written the majority of the songs on all her albums, and still enjoyed a level of recognition and commercial success that has eluded her.

On some level, I know she understands that now. Decades later, in 2004, when Diana DeGarmo was a contestant on the third season of *American Idol* and I was a mentor on the show, I chose "Don't Cry Out Loud" for Diana to sing. It got a great response, and became her signature song. She placed second in the competition, and I signed her to do an album for RCA, one of the labels I was overseeing at the time. Needless to say, one of the songs she recorded for the album, titled *Blue Skies,* was "Don't Cry Out Loud." As it happened, Melissa was recording in the same studio complex and dropped by the session in which Diana was cutting the song. She listened and, while chatting with some of the people in the control room, started reminiscing about the song. She said, "You know, I was so young when I had that difference of opinion with Clive. Thank God I recorded it, but I only did it because he pressured me to. I didn't realize the gift that was being given to me. I wish he had given me shock therapy or something to make me wake up and mature."

I don't say any of this for vindication. Melissa is truly a world-class singer, and she indeed had every right to determine the kind of career she wanted, but she was too young to make that kind of decision. Actresses take advice from agents or managers along the way. Melissa needed guidance here. She was perfectly capable of writing hits, and if she had delivered more songs with the power of "Midnight Blue" and "Come In from the Rain" none of this would have been an issue. But in the pop world, you simply can't go for long periods of time and not be on the radio or high on the charts. You're forgotten. It's a treacherous jungle, and the only way you can win is with the best material. So I felt bad when I heard what Melissa had said. Her awareness had come too late and it just underscored earlier frustrations.

I signed another artist early on at Arista who made a strong impact on the pop front, though he had first emerged as a rock artist with strong pop instincts. Eric Carmen had been the lead singer of the Raspberries, a power-pop band that had made a commercial impact in the early Seventies, particularly with their 1972 hit "Go All the Way." Certain one-dimensional critics dismissed the band because of its fondness for melody and big emotions, but smarter listeners, including many musicians, could hear the talent and genuineness in their beautifully structured songs. Bruce Springsteen, for one, has always been a big Raspberries fan.

When the Raspberries broke up, Carmen wanted a solo career, and his manager, Jimmy Ienner, whose brother Donnie would later work for me at Arista and go on to a major career in the music business, asked me if I'd like to hear the new music Eric was making. Of course I was interested, as were any number of other labels. So I flew to Cleveland, where Eric was living, and went to his apartment to meet him and hear his new songs. He wanted to meet people in his home in order to get a more personal sense of the executives who wanted to sign him, a smart strategy in my view. He sat at a piano in his living room and played "All by Myself," and I was floored both by the song and his performance. His ability to make me feel the emotional power of his song was something that I knew would communicate with a much larger audience. When Eric and I talked afterward we hit it off extremely well. I explained that I was launching a new label and that I had no agenda for him other than to get his music to as many people as possible. I certainly conveyed my excitement and enthusiasm for "All by Myself" and made it clear that if he kept writing songs like that he was going to be a very big star indeed.

Eric signed to Arista, and we brought out his first solo album, *Eric Carmen,* in 1975. It included "All by Myself," which rose to number two, and "Never Gonna Fall in Love Again," which went to number eleven. Again, Eric was one of the artists who made it clear from the very start that Arista was capable of delivering major hit records. Merv Griffin, who hosted a popular, nationally syndicated talk show, asked me to co-host with him a couple of times to showcase Arista and its artists for his national audience. I jumped at the chance to get that kind of exposure for the fledgling label. It was a major shot to promote Arista and its artists, and I took full advantage of it. It was a major platform, one particularly suited to pop artists, and both Melissa and Eric greatly benefited from their appearances there.

Eventually, however, Eric, like Melissa Manchester, hit a plateau. In his case, he strongly believed that he could still reach a sizable audience through rock radio, which had irretrievably lost interest in him after his huge pop hits. I, too, had initially thought of Eric as a rock artist on the basis of the Raspberries, but once I heard his new songs I knew there would be no turning back as far as radio and the industry at large were concerned. Arista's top-flight rock promotion team was bringing back that message. It was not only the scale of Eric's pop hits but their lyrics and their essential emotional core. He was now firmly categorized as a pop artist and, rightly or wrongly, was going to succeed or fail within that genre. In order to have the ascending career he envisioned for himself, he would have to write hits with the quality, consistency, and appeal of an Elton John, and Eric was not doing that.

Artists don't shower you with love and appreciation when you bring them news like that, and certainly Eric came to view me and the label as simply not understanding all the possibilities of his situation. While I didn't recommend that he record other people's material, I did suggest that he collaborate with co-writers, which he refused to do. The situation never got ugly, but it became clear after a while that we were at loggerheads. He eventually left Arista for another label, where his output continued along the same lines. Unfortunately, you can't have long-standing productive relationships with every artist you sign, even ones whom you respect as I do Eric.

Perhaps the most enjoyable pop breakthrough of Arista's early years were the Bay City Rollers, from Scotland. They were the first boy band to generate comparisons with the Beatles in terms of the hysteria they ignited among young girls. The comparison was absurd in that the Beatles, of course, were making music for the ages regardless of the mania they caused, while the Rollers were making frothy music for the pop moment. But there's nothing wrong with that, and in 1975 and 1976, the Rollers brought back an innocence to popular music that seemed to have disappeared, and helped establish Arista Records in the course of doing so.

The Rollers had been signed to the British branch of Bell Records, and they had a run of eight Top 10 singles in the U.K. between 1971 and 1975. I'm not sure if anyone had made an effort to break them in the States, but if they had, it had abjectly failed. As I was evaluating the Bell roster, I listened to all those singles, of course, and didn't hear much of anything that seemed suitable for an American audience. I did release in the United States a single of theirs titled "Bye Bye Baby." It had been a hit for the Four Seasons, and it was a massive U.K. hit for the Rollers, but did nothing in the States. Perhaps the Rollers were going to be just another in a long line of British bands that could never find a way to translate their popularity into American terms.

But I did hear a track on the band's 1974 album, *Rollin'*, that I thought might break the band here. It was called "Saturday Night," and was both anthemic in its spelled-out "S-A-T-U-R-D-A-Y" hook and melodic in its sweetly sung verses. We not only released the song as a single, but arranged for the band to perform it live by satellite on an ABC show called *Saturday Night Live with Howard Cosell*. The show was short-lived, but Cosell was a nationally known figure and it was on in prime time on Saturday night, a perfect tie-in for the song's title. After the band's appearance on September 20, 1975, the single exploded, and Rollermania was in effect. The Rollers were young and cute, and their fervent female fans dressed in tartan and went wild wherever the band appeared. "Saturday Night" became a number-one single, and "Money Honey," from their 1976 album, *Rock n' Roll Love Letter*, cracked the Top 10. I found the title track from that album for them, a Tim Moore song that proved to be a Top 40 single for the band. I also suggested that they cover "I Only Want to Be with You," which had been a hit for Dusty Springfield in 1964, and it shot to number twelve. The Rollers also enjoyed two Top 40 hits from their 1977 album *It's a Game,* and that was the end of their run.

But it was a good run. I remember seeing them perform in Philadelphia in 1976 and being shocked by the volume of their female fans' screams. I had never heard anything like that before in my life. But my

favorite memory of the Rollers involves Michael Klenfner, the passionate, highly colorful bear of a man with a distinctive mustache whom
I had hired at Columbia and then brought to Arista as head of rock
promotion. Michael had worked for Bill Graham at the Fillmore East
and, though he had a great sense of humor, he was dead serious in his
love of music. Despite his overwhelming passion for rock, Michael was
helping to promote the Rollers, and doing so with his characteristic
intensity. Wherever the group went, their fans ignited a riot of pubes-
cent ardor. To stir those passions further, Klenfner had the band ride
around in an open-top limousine, so that they could always be seen.
And sitting there with them, as the girls screamed and chased the car
and the band waved, would be Michael, with a huge smile on his face.
Mr. Rock 'n' Roll was having the time of his life. As were we all. Indeed, for two years no one at Arista was exempt from Rollermania.

The first rock band I signed for Arista was the Outlaws, a muscular,
guitar-centric Southern-rock group from Florida in the spirit of Lynyrd
Skynyrd. In fact, the Outlaws were opening for Skynyrd when Bob
Feiden, a key Arista A&R man, went to see them perform in Florida
in 1974, and he came back to me with a very strong report. So Bob
and I then flew down to see the band at the Civic Center in Columbus, Georgia, again opening for Skynyrd. During Skynyrd's set, the
singer, Ronnie Van Zant, called attention to my presence in the audience, much to my surprise. Addressing me from the stage, he said, "If
you don't sign the Outlaws, you're the dumbest music person I've ever
met—and I know you're not." That night I met with the band at their
hotel and told them I wanted to make them an offer.

I recommended Paul Rothchild, who had been so successful producing the Doors, to work with the Outlaws on their first Arista
album, simply titled *Outlaws*. While the band was rightly categorized as
Southern rock, they had excellent vocal harmonies and a true melodic
sense. The country element in their sound also recalled the Eagles, and
I hoped that with the right song, we might achieve a significant commercial breakthrough, even if not on the Eagles' scale. The closest we
came to that was "There Goes Another Love Song," which cracked
the Top 40 and helped earn a gold record for the band's debut. With

the nearly ten-minute "Green Grass and High Tides," a title cribbed from the Rolling Stones, the Outlaws even put in a bid on a Seventies epic, along the lines of "Free Bird," "Stairway to Heaven," and "Hotel California," on that album. If it didn't rise to those heights, it made a definite mark on rock radio, where it remained a staple for many years.

The Outlaws were to create another rock classic with "Hurry Sundown," and in 1981 they covered "(Ghost) Riders in the Sky," and cracked the Top 40 once again, though for the last time. Although they never broke into the highest pantheon of Southern-rock bands, they consistently made strong, credible albums, and Arista had a good seven-year run with them. They worked hard and toured constantly, and we released a live album and a greatest hits collection that were both successful. The Outlaws helped give Arista important standing as a welcome home to rock bands in its initial years.

They also were memorable participants in the unbelievable third-anniversary party I threw for Arista at Studio 54 in 1978. I'd become a regular there, and Arista had become so hot that Steve Rubell and Ian Schrager were happy to turn the club over to me for the celebration party. We had Latin Quarter chorus girls bathed in platinum, reflecting Barry Manilow's huge success, descend from the ceiling on poles to the floor. We had a roller-skating team come in to represent the Bay City Rollers. We had cowboys and Indians on horses there to represent the Outlaws. Every one of our artists was represented, as well as the "Arista-cracy," as *People* magazine put it, of the music industry. It was an amazing evening that more than lived up to the excessive spirit of that time. Not bad for a company that was only three years old.

On the other end of the rock spectrum from the Outlaws was the Alan Parsons Project, a progressive-rock act from the U.K. with which I was personally quite taken. To call the Alan Parsons Project a band would be something of a misnomer. It really consisted of Alan Parsons, an engineer, producer, and keyboardist, and Eric Woolfson, a pianist, singer-songwriter, and lyricist who also managed Alan. Together they composed haunting, highly atmospheric, literate songs that addressed ambitious, conceptual subjects such as the impact of mechanization on the human spirit.

While I might admire work like that, it rarely makes a commercial impact. And if the band itself is a conceptual unit that has no front person to promote and refuses to perform live, that typically would be something I would not even discuss. But the Alan Parsons Project seemed to capture something about the mid-Seventies that made me believe it could reach a large audience. Alan, after all, had worked as an engineer for the Beatles and Pink Floyd, and he retained the pop instincts and thematic ambition that characterize both bands. He had even been nominated for a Grammy for his engineering on *Dark Side of the Moon*. Eric's innate musicality found expression in his skills as an arranger, composer, and lyricist. When I met them, they had already made a very interesting album called *Tales of Mystery and Imagination*, based on the work of Edgar Allan Poe. I was intrigued. I approached them about signing with Arista, and they agreed to a three-album deal. They originally had conceived of their collaboration as a onetime event, and now they had plenty of room to explore their ideas more deeply. And that they did.

Their notion was to forge a career based on the auteur theory of cinema, which sees the director, not actors and certainly not movie stars, as the heart of the creative process in film. What that meant, in their view, was that music could become a producer's art, with singers and session musicians brought in as needed to complete the musical vision, which is exactly how the Alan Parsons Project made its albums. I grew up in the age of extraordinary, larger-than-life Hollywood icons, and if there's anything I believe in as much as sheer talent, it's star power. But there are exceptions to every rule. Pink Floyd had become a major musical force not on the strength of their looks or personalities but on their music's ability to transport its listeners to another world. I believed the Alan Parsons Project had that same ability. After all, I had signed Pink Floyd to Columbia before *Dark Side of the Moon* broke, and had sensed that part of the audience for popular music was moving in this more conceptual direction. This was also the era of *2001: A Space Odyssey, Star Wars,* and *Star Trek,* in which young people's vision of space was romantic and psychologically compelling. It seemed possible that the Alan Parsons Project could help create a soundtrack for that time.

Which is exactly what it did. While the single "Eye in the Sky" drove the success of the album for which it served as the title track, for the most part the Alan Parsons Project achieved huge success based on the conceptual ambition of its music. Beginning with *I Robot,* the group scored multiplatinum worldwide success, followed by consistent platinum and gold albums well into the Eighties. Some credit for that must go to Dennis Fine, who ran Arista's publicity department at the time. He had the extremely difficult task of promoting a duo who essentially did everything they could to remain anonymous, and his heroic efforts paid off. In keeping with how Alan and Eric viewed themselves, we would plot their album releases like Ingmar Bergman movie openings, emphasizing the scale of the new work and its cast of performers with extensive advertising and in-store displays to stir the imagination of fans. In the case of *I Robot,* which was based on stories by the science-fiction writer Isaac Asimov, we sent Alan and Eric on a ten-city press tour. They didn't perform, but like film directors, they did interviews about the album after it was played, or premiered, for major media outlets in advance of its release. We turned the problem of the duo's invisibility into the virtue of mystery, not even using their pictures on the album covers. It was complicated and occasionally frustrating as time went on, but it was also stimulating. When you can't employ the conventional promotional strategies, you're forced to think in fresh new ways, and that's always rewarding.

However, sometimes it's possible to get a bit overexcited, as I did, somewhat to my chagrin, when I heard that Columbia Pictures would be releasing Steven Spielberg's *Close Encounters of the Third Kind.* One of the advantages of being owned by Columbia Pictures was that Arista would be putting out the soundtrack for what was obviously going to be a hugely successful film. So, based on my sketchy knowledge of what the film was going to be, I asked for a meeting with Spielberg to discuss the music for the film. My objective was to see if I could arrange for the Alan Parsons Project to have a hand in the soundtrack. Spielberg agreed to get together, and I met with him and John Williams, who had composed the music for Spielberg's film *Jaws* and, by the way, had won an Academy Award for doing so. Even more significant, the two men had forged an unbreakable bond. Over the past forty years, Williams has composed the music for all but two of Spielberg's major feature films.

In my defense, I was unaware of that at the time, and I must confess I didn't think that Williams would be able to produce something that we could use as a single to promote the soundtrack on radio. What can I say? That's how I was thinking at the time. So I made the strongest case I could for the little-known new artist, the Alan Parsons Project. I played *I Robot* for Spielberg and Williams, set forth all of the group's credentials, and asked if there was any way we could incorporate their music into the film. Steven and John were very polite and respectful, but of course there was no way in the world it was going to happen. And while I still believe that Alan and Eric would have done a great job, I ultimately had nothing to worry about. Williams won two Grammys for his score and received another Academy Award nomination, though he lost to himself for the soundtrack to *Star Wars*. The *Close Encounters* soundtrack album was a Top 20 hit and sold more than half a million copies, earning a gold record. I may have been a little embarrassed, but I couldn't have been happier.

Of course, not every one of my early signings for Arista worked out. I was a big fan of a group called the Funky Kings, which included two excellent songwriters. Jack Tempchin wrote "Peaceful Easy Feeling" and co-wrote "Already Gone" for the Eagles, and Jules Shear would go on to write songs that became hits for Cyndi Lauper ("All Through the Night") and the Bangles ("If She Knew What She Wants"). They had enormous promise. I had the esteemed Paul Rothchild produce an album with them. But they just never wrote the kind of classics they gave to others for themselves, and consequently they never broke through. We later released a solo album by Jack, and Jules has gone on to a prolific solo career. But while they both have justly earned excellent reputations as songwriters, neither could definitively establish himself as an artist.

I showcased the Funky Kings and another group I loved, the Alpha Band, at the Arista convention in Camelback, Arizona, in 1976. The Alpha Band consisted of players who had backed Bob Dylan on his

"Rolling Thunder Revue," among them the now famous T-Bone Burnett and a young, handsome, charismatic rock violinist, David Mansfield. I really had great hopes for both bands, and had them perform at the convention in order to encourage the rest of the company to share my enthusiasm. Both bands brought the house down. But like the Funky Kings, the Alpha Band could never get traction on radio. They released three albums on Arista, and while they were all perfectly respectable efforts, none of them contained that signature song that can fully establish a group's identity with the public. Needless to say, T-Bone has nonetheless gone on to an extraordinary career as a producer, musician, and impresario.

Another artist I strongly believed in was Loudon Wainwright III. I had signed him to Columbia and then to Arista, making four albums with him between the two labels. Loudon is a hugely gifted songwriter, someone who can combine literacy, wit, and poignancy in ways that no one else can. He was good-looking and charming, and I was convinced that if he played with a rock band backing him up, he could have his own version of Bruce Springsteen's career. He tried it, but he never felt that it suited him. He was more comfortable playing in acoustic settings and performing in a more laid-back style. Finally, we had to part ways, though I never stopped enjoying his music and believing in its quality. Ultimately, you have no choice but to let artists be the final arbiters of the creative path they are going to take. And, as it turns out, Loudon has had exactly the sort of career he wanted. He has a devoted audience that supports him, and occasionally he has reached out beyond them with acting roles, by writing songs for films, and composing topical songs for National Public Radio and *Nightline*. Without question, he's one of the most distinguished and distinctive songwriters of our time.

A singer-songwriter whose work moved me was Eric Andersen. I signed him to Columbia, where he did have a hit album in 1972 with *Blue River*. He had written such songs as "Thirsty Boots," "Close the Door Lightly," and "Violets of Dawn," which are now part of the folk repertoire. Eric had been unfairly tagged a "new Dylan" when he started out, a label that has never done anybody any good. In fact, Eric's songs were sweeter and more optimistic than Dylan's. He seemed to have all the gifts you need. But he recorded two albums for Arista that, again, never produced the type of song that you could take to radio and build into sales.

The inability to break artists like the Funky Kings, the Alpha Band, Loudon Wainwright, and Eric Andersen underscores the importance of the hit single. There are so few album successes without the hit single being a key factor. To go gold or platinum, ninety-nine out of a hundred cases would show that if there was no breakthrough radio cut, the new artist was not likely to break 100,000 to 200,000 units. Even with good press and good critical reaction, history has shown that the overwhelming catalyst for a successful artist and album is the hit single. If you're an artist who writes, you must have hits of your own, your signature songs. Without them, almost invariably you can't make it. There have been exceptions to this but painfully few.

Finally, there's always the story of the one who got away. As Arista got more successful and began generating real buzz, I was approached by the English producer Denny Cordell about a joint venture with his label, Shelter Records. He had a deal with ABC Records that was about to end, and he had two artists I was particularly interested in: Tom Petty and the Heartbreakers and the Dwight Twilley Band. Dwight Twilley had a hit in 1975 with "I'm on Fire" and was thought to have great prospects. He was upbeat, great-looking, and had rock star written all over him. Petty, meanwhile, had recorded one album that hadn't yet made much noise, but his potential was clear. I met separately with Twilley and Petty and was very impressed by each of them. I thought both bands could really be big, and was very eager to conclude a deal with Cordell. But just before our arrangement was finalized, Denny called me and dropped the bombshell that he was having major legal problems with ABC and was not going to be able to bring both Twilley and Petty with him when he left. He could bring only one. Who would I pick?

I remember having a long conversation with Bob Feiden and Michael Klenfner to hash this out. I really liked both artists and sensed star power in each of them. I hated that we couldn't have both. Finally, though, we had to make a decision, and we decided to take Twilley. To be fair, Dwight already had a hit, and it seemed inconceivable that he wouldn't be able to follow that up. He radiated electricity and charisma, and worked hard. But we were never able to generate another hit with him, and we all know what Petty went on to do. You can't win them all, as they say. And, fortunately, you don't have to. We'd won more than our share in Arista's early years to propel the label well on its way to decades of success.

Patti Smith and Lou Reed

It was a long journey, geographically and emotionally, from the sunshine and flowers at Monterey to a narrow, grimy bar on the Bowery, but I was always prepared to let the music lead me, and in the first years at Arista most of the excitement was emanating from the streets of New York City. The second half of the decade erupted with new sounds around every corner. It was an opportune time to be launching a new Manhattan-based label, and I went all over town to check out artists. The music was everywhere, from bathhouses to Broadway cabarets like Reno Sweeney, which featured performers ranging from Diane Keaton to Meat Loaf to Tom Waits to a lanky, dark-haired female poet who performed there with her guitarist, taking her first tentative steps toward becoming a full-tilt rock 'n' roll visionary. The Bottom Line opened in 1974, and immediately became an important showcase venue that booked an adventurous mix of artists. Barry Manilow headlined a week of dates there in May 1974, and another string of dates in December. Earlier that year, a downtown bar called CBGB began booking bands such as Television. Max's Kansas City, after closing for a while, reopened in 1975 and became another place for the bands invading New York City to play.

Certainly Bob Feiden and I traveled extensively, and I set up private showcases in Los Angeles. There were a lot of air miles racked up to find signings, but I always thought it was perfect that we were in the center of the city, a few blocks from 30 Rock, where *Saturday Night Live* went on the air in October 1975, within sight of the new *Rolling Stone* offices that opened in 1977, the same year that Studio 54 opened its doors to anyone who could get past the velvet rope. It was a quick cab ride to anywhere: Trax, Hurrah, the Mudd Club. Arista was a label with a distinct New York City sensibility, encompassing jazz, disco, R&B, Broadway, and rock. We even released a "single" of Robert De Niro's voice-over narration from one of the quintessential Seventies New York City movies, *Taxi Driver,* with Bernard Herrmann's underscore. "Diary of a Taxi Driver," for some reason, didn't become a hit. "Are you talkin' to me?" may be a classic film line, but it isn't a lyrical hook.

Our first two breakthrough pop artists, Barry Manilow and Melissa Manchester, came from Brooklyn and the Bronx. And two of my first signings to the label defined what it meant to be a New York rock artist. Lou Reed came from Long Island, and Patti Smith from New Jersey, but the music they made is as identified with Manhattan as the Chrysler Building. They're two of the city's living landmarks.

My acquaintance with Lou Reed predates the formation of Arista, and for a period of time was mainly social. If you wanted to witness the flip side of New York City nightlife, the seamy underbrush of colorful and sexual goings-on, the transsexuals and transvestites, the whole real-life Rocky Horror Show, Lou was the quintessential guide during that period. One night, he took me on a fast-paced tour, not trying to shock me, just to point out this was part of the world he moved in, that these were some of the people he knew. But he also would come to my home to watch the Thanksgiving Parade float down Central Park West, and nosh on bagels and appetizers, just a Jewish guy who grew up in Freeport, except with dyed hair, incredibly long fingernails, and the palest skin, which was not surprising given his nocturnal ways. One weekend, I asked him to take a drive to Bob Feiden's summer cabana in Long Beach. "We'll listen to music, we'll relax, it's isolated and really fun," I said. He said he could never do that. "Clive," he told me, "if I ever get a tan, my career would be over."

I'd always respected Lou as a cutting-edge, influential rock figure, beginning with the Velvet Underground and into his years as a solo artist. He took rock music into dangerous, forbidden territory. When the Velvet Underground emerged in the Sixties, they were a stark contrast to the prevailing musical trends: Songs such as "Heroin," "Sister Ray," and "I'm Waiting for My Man" couldn't and wouldn't be played on even the most free-form FM rock stations, but their innovation and influence were seismic. And then with the albums *Transformer,* produced by David Bowie, and the dark and abrasive *Berlin,* he continued to take his music into previously unexplored corners. *Transformer* even had a hit on it, "Walk on the Wild Side." I was definitely a fan of his music and, as I said, enjoyed his company. He was unfailingly smart, witty, acerbic, highly articulate—and he had an excellent sense of humor.

One day, Lou called to tell me he was unhappy at RCA, was aware of what we were up to at Arista, and asked if I'd be interested in signing him. Of course I was, and that began an association that while it had its interesting moments and creative high points, such as the *Street Hassle* album, was frustrating as well. Because I always thought he was so talented, I wanted things to happen for him in a major way, but there were contentious issues starting from the first Arista album, *Rock and Roll Heart.* I thought the title track could be a radio record with some minor tweaking. It sounded a little sparse to me. I wouldn't and didn't give Lou any specific direction, only asked him to consider fleshing it out, and he refused. Not at all surprisingly, he didn't want to hear any suggestions, no matter how well intentioned.

Lou did get exceptional reviews for *Street Hassle,* especially for the title track, which I'd heard in its original, shorter form and thought might be expanded into more of a set piece. This time he did listen, and the revised cut, with a cameo spoken-word portion by Bruce Springsteen, got a lot of acclaim. (Interestingly, I had taken Lou to see Bruce at the Bottom Line three years earlier.) Yet the album failed to sell meaningfully. That's always difficult to explain to an artist. Good critical reviews often don't translate into sales. The artist, of course, gets disappointed, and in this case, Lou was crushed. By the time he launched a multinight stand at the Bottom Line in May 1978, he was in rare, venomous form. He used the stage like a Vegas insult comic, lashing out at his perceived enemies in the press and at anyone else in his path. The album that Lou assembled from that engagement was appropriately called *Take No Prisoners,* a double-album set that included only ten songs spread over its four sides. It was as if those songs were mere musical interruptions of a free-associative rant that *Rolling Stone* called "a barrage of invective, self-laceration, barbarity, and the all-out savaging of just about everybody who happened to pop into Reed's head."

After another album, *The Bells,* was released to disappointing sales, Lou again took to the mic and this time he saw me in the club, gave me the finger, and said, "Here, this is for you, Clive. Where's the money, Clive? How come I don't hear my album on the radio?" It was an embarrassing incident, and Lou quickly issued a press release apologizing: "I've always loved Clive and he happens to be one of my best friends. I just felt like having a business discussion from the stage. Sometimes, out of frustration, you yell at those you love the most. I have a mouth that never sleeps, and I suppose that's why I make rock 'n' roll records."

My professional relationship with Lou lasted a while longer, but never produced the success both he and I would have wanted. I have so much admiration for him that I really regret that it wasn't a more auspicious period of his career. You would think the timing couldn't have been better. Here were all these bands coming up, Television and Talking Heads and Blondie and Mink DeVille, all obviously creative offspring of Lou and the Velvet Underground. It was the moment when he could have stepped up to make rock music that showed everyone where the roots of the new music lay. It still feels like a missed opportunity, although when I think of Lou Reed, it's always with warmth. Underneath it all, he's totally genuine. And overall, it was good for the label for Lou to be an Arista artist. He was edgy, farsighted, independent, and hugely influential. He clearly showed there was not one kind of Arista artist. Yes, we entered the pop arena with a roar of success, but we were open to the daring artists who carved out their own creative territory. And I think it's particularly apt that the rock artist I became most associated with in the Seventies used to include compelling versions of the Velvet Underground's "Pale Blue Eyes" and "We're Gonna Have a Real Good Time Together" in her sets. In part, she began as another disciple of Lou Reed, but her originality soon became undeniable. There had never been anyone like her, and there has not been since.

Most stories that are told about my first encounter with Patti Smith set the scene at CBGB, the club on the Bowery where she was fast becoming an artist who was causing a commotion. Although I definitely spent any number of nights there, at a table close to the tiny stage, that wasn't where I saw her initially. There is a tendency to follow the adage from the film *The Man Who Shot Liberty Valance:* "When the legend becomes fact, print the legend." There is a seedy glamour to imagining a trip down to a club in a still scary part of town, but truthfully, I was afraid—not of the neighborhood, but that my presence in the club would tip off my interest, get other labels intrigued, and set off a bidding war. There was already enough buzz around Patti—the esteemed critic John Rockwell had raved about her in *The New York Times,* and she had already recorded demos for RCA. I preferred to stay under the radar.

For that reason, I set up a private showcase for me and Bob Feiden in a downtown studio through her manager, Jane Friedman. Patti and her band charged through a set that had us riveted from the moment they hit their first chords. Urgently and with a sense of purpose and firm theatrical command, she sang those songs that, without exaggeration, wound up changing the entire musical landscape. It was simply overwhelming. What she was doing really had no precedent. It had elements of garage rock and girl-group pop, and obviously the influences of Dylan and the Stones and the Beat poets and downtown performance artists, but she shaped it all in a totally unique way. In her club and concert performances to follow she would start out with a basic rock premise, such as "Land of a Thousand Dances" or "Hey Joe" or "Gloria," and she would just explode it into pieces that would ricochet everywhere. It was very dramatic. She'd read her poems about Edie Sedgwick or Marianne Faithfull in the most percussive, insistent way. She would prowl the stage, caught up in the music, squatting to pee if the need arose, always seemingly on the edge but always with a measure of control. Rather than only being interested in destroying the past, Patti revered the bold, subversive icons in rock 'n' roll, film, art, and literature, but was intent on extending their revolutionary power into the present. She was a rebel with a profound respect for the tradition of rebellion, a woman who wanted to create a new future while preserving the most inspirational elements of the past.

To me, it was the most original thing to happen in rock at that time, and I knew I wanted her on Arista. It would be a huge statement to sign her. As undisciplined as she was, she just gave me chills. When people ask me what are the most memorable performances I've ever seen, the ones that I'll never forget, definitely they would include Patti's. She has always been haunting, hypnotic, and riveting in concert.

We did bond instantly. She knew I trusted her. And I did venture down to see her at CBGB once it was decided that we would work together. Patti chose John Cale, formerly of the Velvet Underground, as the producer of her debut album, and its impact can't be overstated. How many albums exist where so many people, to this day, can quote the opening line? "Jesus died for somebody's sins, but not mine." That's simply indelible, and the album builds from there. Over the years, when I was to meet Bono, or Michael Stipe, or Courtney Love, they all expressed variations on the same emotion: "*Horses* had such a profound influence on me," or "*Horses* made me want to form a band." It was literally, for many musicians, a life-changing album. It's on every list of the most important rock albums of all time. Everything about the album, and about Patti as an artist, was brilliant conceptually.

Even the album cover, instantly iconic, was unlike any way a female rock artist had been presented before. Robert Mapplethorpe, her close friend from the time she first came to New York City, took a black-and-white photo that was direct and daring, with a hint of androgyny and an air of insolence. It really captured Patti. It exuded a rumpled confidence, the horse-pinned blazer flung over her shoulder Sinatra-style, the pale gray background, the look straight into the camera, daring you to open the album jacket and discover what's inside. I admit, at first I was conflicted about the image; I was aware of its power, but with my label-president concern, I thought it might confuse the uninitiated (who, outside of New York City and a few other major cities, was pretty much everybody). Who was she, and what was she projecting? Whatever reservations I had, I dismissed them quickly: If I was going to have faith in Patti and her music, I was going to trust her artistic instincts thoroughly. And obviously those instincts were, in this case, genius. That photograph is a work of art that absolutely conveys her point of view, and like the album itself, the cover of *Horses* is now regarded as an undisputed classic. There's a reason for that. Patti is obsessed with imagery, drawing on poetry, film, art, and fashion to enhance her music. She saw herself as a convergence of all these influences, the poets she devoured, filmmakers like Jean-Luc Godard, and all her rock heroes. She also demolished every cliché about what a woman playing rock music should sound, act, and look like. She's been a groundbreaking artist in every regard.

By her side on guitar was Lenny Kaye, a former rock writer, curator of the influential garage-rock compilation *Nuggets,* and someone with a vast knowledge of all strains of rock, from the primitive to the progressive. He was key to shaping her sound, along with her other band members, the pianist Richard Sohl, the bassist Ivan Kral, and the drummer Jay Dee Daugherty. Together with Cale, they made what I and many others believe is among the most impressive, original debut albums in rock history.

After releasing the less acclaimed album *Radio Ethiopia* (1976) rather quickly after *Horses,* Patti was performing in Tampa in January 1977 when she fell off the stage and broke several of her neck vertebrae, necessitating a long period of rest and rehabilitation. She was out of the picture musically, but we remained in touch, and I was content with her staying out of the public eye. I could wait. I remembered that after Dylan's motorcycle accident in 1966, his instinct was to lie low and not send out any signals about what he was up to. Let the clouds of mystery gather. That resonated with me and I learned from it. No one knew, at the time, that Dylan and the Band were making the surreal, visionary music that would ultimately be released as *The Basement Tapes.* They were sealed off in upstate New York. In a similar way, Patti was holed up in her apartment at One Fifth Avenue until she was out of traction. I would visit her from time to time and see the closeness of Patti and her family. Her mother was an intimate part of her life, ran her fan club, and passionately believed in Patti, her music, and her growing number of ardent fans. As different as we are, I recognized a kindred spirit in Patti, someone who wanted to make her mark in the big world outside, but who always remained grounded in the family that loved and in many ways defined her.

In typical fashion, when Patti was prepared to reenter the music world, she would call her artistic resurrection *Easter* (1978). Something one should know about Patti: She always wanted a hit. She came off as the ultimate rebel, a creature of the demimonde, without a commercial thought in her head, but she grew up in an era when all her heroes, from Dylan to the Stones, were on the radio, and she wanted to be on WABC-AM also. She wanted to sit on the sofa on *The Tonight Show* and trade quips with Johnny Carson. Those were goals she shared with me, and while I never would have taken the route of trying to find that hit song by an outside writer for her, or pushing her toward a more pop-friendly producer, I was ecstatic when I heard that one of the key songs on the new album would be a collaboration with Bruce Springsteen.

Bruce was working on the album that became *Darkness on the Edge of Town,* and as was his process, he demoed many, many songs before paring them down to the ten that would make the cut. One that he'd begun but hadn't finished was a dramatic, erotic rock ballad called "Because the Night." When Bruce found out from Patti's producer, Jimmy Iovine, that the album they were recording didn't have an obvious single, Bruce gave Jimmy a cassette of the unfinished track. Building on Springsteen's demo, with Patti adding personal lyrics of her own (she's said that the line "Love is a ring, the telephone" came from waiting at home for her new boyfriend, Fred Smith, formerly of the MC5, to call), the Springsteen-Smith composition became a track that instantly stood out. At one of Patti's comeback shows, before *Easter* was ready for release, Bruce joined her onstage to share vocals on the new collaboration, and the audience reaction made it clear that we had the elusive hit. The track was beautifully performed and produced, with a great hook, the ideal marriage of Patti's poetic language and Bruce's urgency and dynamics. It was thrilling. When it came out as a single, worked persistently by Arista's promotion team, it rose to number thirteen and Patti finally got the chance to hear herself on Top 40 radio.

I think that even without "Because the Night," *Easter* would have been a classic album, with "25th Floor," "Space Monkey," and "Till Victory." She characteristically courted controversy with the song "Rock 'n' Roll Nigger" and with the stark cover photograph of her unshaven underarms. Although we did have a conversation about how there might be commercial obstacles, she had her clear vision. That was the core of our relationship: She presented her work; I gave her a frank assessment of which elements might prove to be bumps in the road. She always listened with respect, took my concerns to heart, but as the artist she is, she ultimately followed her own heart, as she should. Driven by excellent reviews and searing shows (both Patti and Bruce hit peaks as live performers in 1978, with each of them delivering powerful readings of "Because the Night" in their sets), and an undeniable hit single, *Easter* became Patti's best-selling album, which it still is.

Patti's next album, *Wave*, produced by Todd Rundgren, had some standout songs, including "Dancing Barefoot," which a number of artists, most notably U2 and R.E.M., have covered, and it did fairly well for an album without a big single.

I was completely unprepared for what happened next. Unknown to me at the time, Patti felt as though her personal life was veering out of control, and that despite having achieved the recognition she had always sought, the life in rock music was activating certain demons that made her fearful. I really do believe that she thought her life might be in danger if she continued on that path. When Patti did something, she did it with all her soul, and just as it had been with her music, that's how it was with her choice to leave music behind. She'd fallen in love with Fred Smith and moved to Detroit to be with him and raise a family. And just like that, she disappeared. As the months of her hiatus extended into years, we would speak from time to time, every couple of years or so. I never asked for an album. She was immersed so deeply in her personal life that I just knew not to intrude on that privacy. She would record when she was ready.

Naturally, I was disappointed. Patti's potential seemed unlimited. I truly loved her shows, which were always inspiring. She made you feel and think at the same time, and lose yourself in the spirit of rock 'n' roll that she believed in as deeply as a religion. I sorely missed her. I also knew that momentum, once lost, is so hard to pick up again as time passes and new artists clamor for attention. But I loved Patti, trusted her, and knew instinctively that I should stay away, that her personal life at that point was more important to her than her career, a conclusion that I respected.

Then, as suddenly as she'd vanished, she reappeared years later, calling to tell me she was ready to record. She said she had to do it. The retreat had been her salvation, she told me. It was a whole new chapter, an entirely different life, and she deeply felt that she might not have survived if she hadn't separated herself from the pressures of the music industry. But she was reenergized, and together with Fred Smith and Jimmy Iovine, she made *Dream of Life* (1988). As soon as I started playing it, I felt as though we'd picked up without missing a beat. The urgency was still there. Maybe with more maturity, more reflection, but with the same impact. "People Have the Power" became a modern anthem, a collective rallying cry at the end of every "Vote for Change" show during the 2004 presidential election, and the album was filled with beauty and drama on cuts like "Paths That Cross" and "Up There Down There." I was so happy to have her back, but it was a brief return.

Another long hiatus followed, during which Patti was hit with a series of tragic, devastating personal losses. Her husband, Fred, her brother Todd, her longtime friend Robert Mapplethorpe, and her keyboard player, Richard Sohl, all passed away, and one can only imagine the severe emotional toll all those deaths took on her. But that's where resilience and the support of friends and family come into play. Patti moved back to New York with her children, and she was encouraged, by R.E.M.'s Michael Stipe among others, to get back on the road. In late 1995, Bob Dylan invited her to open for him on a short tour, and every night the two of them would duet on his "Dark Eyes." The next year, she went back into the studio to record the somber, affecting *Gone Again,* reviving interest in her as an artist and kicking off a more consistent string of albums for Arista. Both *Peace and Noise* (1997) and *Gung Ho* (2000) earned Patti Grammy nominations, and she ended her more than quarter-century tenure at Arista with the career-spanning anthology *Land.*

When I signed Patti Smith to Arista, back when the label and she were young and finding their footing, there was no Rock and Roll Hall of Fame. I knew she was an artist for the ages, someone whose importance and influence would last far beyond whatever was on the charts at that precise moment in time. There was, however, no "official" way to recognize that type of career achievement. Once the Hall of Fame did start inducting artists, I mentally started counting the years until Patti would become eligible (twenty-five years after her debut, per the Hall's requirements). That would be the class of 2000. I took it for granted that she would get in: A generation of musicians, both male and female, owes something to Patti's bold, groundbreaking approach to rock.

In 2000, I was inducted into the Rock and Roll Hall of Fame in the nonperformer category, an honor I deeply appreciated and accepted with pride. And Patti graciously and passionately gave the speech inducting me, making that night all the more special. I couldn't help thinking, however, that she should be getting, as well as bestowing, an award from that organization. As far as I and many of her peers were concerned, Patti had exemplary Hall of Fame credentials. But year after year we waited, until finally, in 2007, she made it in, and took the stage at the Waldorf-Astoria Hotel to rapturous applause. "When I came to Clive," she said, "I was really awkward, arrogant, couldn't really sing. I had pretty clumsy movements. I had a lot of guts, not a whole lot of talent, but he had faith in me and let me go out of the gate, just a colt, and stayed with me."

She's wrong, of course. She had the kind of talent you're lucky if you stumble upon once in a generation. A talent that was piercing right from the beginning. As I watch her to this day, winning the National Book Award for her beautiful and moving memoir *Just Kids,* continuing to give epic performances like the closing show at CBGB, I confess I get very emotional thinking about Patti. She's unquestionably a true visionary, and yet her humility is real and touching. I've been transfixed by her writing and her insight and truly mesmerized by her powerful performances. She can be dispassionate and coolly objective, but her heart is very big. Her love for her husband, her parents, her siblings, her band, and, of course, her children Jackson and Jesse, has always been so pure, so intense. I marvel at Patti's spirit and I can only say I'm one lucky guy to have been in her corner watching that spirit soar and letting her vision take her where she was destined to go.

Ready to Rock

There was never any question that Arista would have a major rock component. I had spearheaded the rebuilding of Columbia through an intense concentration on rock, and it was my mission with Arista to follow that blueprint. Having pop success was gratifying, and certainly jump-started the company in a visible and lucrative way, but I knew that rock careers were less ephemeral, and that rock was still the genre taken most seriously by the industry and the press, despite the irrefutable impact of Top 40, R&B, and what was still called "middle of the road" music. We had to look beyond AM radio and the singles charts. It was never my intention to just crank out pop music.

Getting a credible debut from the Outlaws was a beginning. But it was always difficult breaking a band from scratch, and I couldn't count on the first effort from every new signing, especially in rock, to find immediate acceptance. You can strategically work a pop single through the promotional system and, if you're lucky, run something all the way up the charts, but rock artists generally require more patience, and the early days of Arista were not a patient time. For one thing, we didn't have a catalog whose sales could sustain us. So we crafted a rock signing philosophy that was a mixture of new and established artists.

As I mentioned, we signed promising bands such as the Funky Kings and the Alpha Band, and there was also Baby Grand (some of their members eventually achieved success as the Hooters). At the same time, I looked around for artists who I thought were in transition, who had a record of achievement but who struck me as marking time or floundering. There were definitely candidates out there. I just had to identify them, and then convince them to take a chance with a record label that was still young and growing. There was a sense of urgency to this, and a spirit of adventure. We had to strike with the right artists at exactly the right time.

Well, the right artists did come along but, unfortunately in some cases, not at the right time. Fleetwood Mac were very unhappy at Warner Bros. Their album sales were stuck in the range of around 200,000, a less than respectable figure for a band of their stature. In 1975, I saw them at the Beacon Theatre, and was very impressed by the new lineup, which had only recently released an album, titled *Fleetwood Mac* as if to assert that while the band had the same name, it had a completely new identity. Joining the original rhythm section of Mick Fleetwood and John McVie and the exceptional singer, keyboard player, and songwriter Christine McVie were Lindsey Buckingham and Stevie Nicks. There was such depth in the band, such chemistry and charisma. Through the good offices of their attorney, Mickey Shapiro, I personally met with them, and did learn that they felt they weren't being given the attention they warranted at the label. They thought the infusion of new energy with the addition of Lindsey and Stevie was going unnoticed at Warners. The album was released in the summer with little fanfare, a single, "Over My Head," was just coming out, and at the time, it didn't seem to the band that the label was 100 percent behind them. We made a deal, and all went out to lunch at a great New York restaurant of the era, Maxwell's Plum, to celebrate. I still have the contract, ready for signatures, in my files.

A similar scenario played out with Jefferson Starship. I'd always been a fan of Jefferson Airplane, and thought there was a lot of life left in the spin-off band. They were feeling unloved at RCA Records, and we came to terms with them as well. Fleetwood Mac and Jefferson Starship: pretty impressive signing coups. Each of those bands still owed two albums to its label, and the albums that were released while we were in talks with them exploded. *Fleetwood Mac* took the refurbished group from a 1974 album that didn't even go gold to one that went five times platinum. The Starship's *Red Octopus*, propelled by the hit "Miracles," sold more than 2 million copies (up from gold on their 1974 album). Good news for the bands, but not for us. Needless to say, once those album sales racked up, Warners and RCA didn't want to lose them. They made offers that, in pure dollar terms, were equal to ours, but made those deals retroactive to the current smash albums. Based on what those albums sold, the bands were in a position to clear $2 million or more just from that aspect of their deals, and we couldn't possibly compete with that. We weren't the ones making the income (and dramatic profits) on those records. What bad timing for us, and how it stung when I saw the sales of the next Fleetwood Mac album, *Rumours*. If their albums hadn't broken wide open when they did, there's no question Arista would have had both of those bands. And I should add that we were also in talks with Electric Light Orchestra, and came close to signing them. All three of these major bands were on the verge of coming to Arista within a six-month period.

I had twice attempted to sign the Kinks when I was at Columbia. There has never been any doubt that the band's leader, Ray Davies, is a towering talent. Once, when I had just become head of the label, they decided to stay with Reprise. The second time, in the early Seventies, they accepted an offer from RCA. Although they are in the Rock and Roll Hall of Fame, to me the Kinks have been relatively underappreciated. Just look at the body of work the band has built, the number of Davies songs that are classic, the way the band could totally command an arena with highly charged rock and then do more pop-oriented songs that are wistful and lyrical like "Sunny Afternoon" and "Waterloo Sunset." It was obvious that Ray could write hits; he'd done so many times over the years, and he also wrote big, sweeping pieces like "Celluloid Heroes." In mid-decade, however, he got bogged down making concept albums. From 1973 through 1975, there were four in a row: *Preservation: Act 1, Preservation: Act 2, Soap Opera,* and *Schoolboys in Disgrace*. It had become a creative treadmill, and none of those albums did very well. Bob Feiden and I strongly believed they were due for a turnaround, but we didn't want another album-length conceptual extravaganza. We wanted the kind of songs that we knew Ray was capable of writing, the brilliantly concise radio hits that had drawn people's attention to him in the first place.

When I met with Ray, I was blunt with him. We knew each other fairly well, and he had an apartment close to mine on the Upper West Side, so we would get together for dinner from time to time. There was no upside to equivocating, or signing the band first and then having to deal with this big creative issue later. What if he wanted his next project to be *Preservation: Act 3*? I told him, "If the Kinks are going to continue with concept albums, I'm really not interested. It would be too tough a job to break you. But you're wonderful in person, and if you still feel the magic in songs, I just know the future of the band could be brighter than ever." After I gave this candid take on the state of the Kinks, Ray assured me that my input was welcome, and refreshing—no one at RCA had ever dealt him such straight talk—and we made a deal. In June 1976, in the Terrace Suite of the Dorchester Hotel in London, I finally signed the Kinks, a decade after I made my initial overtures to the band.

I then took a risk and sent Ray three songs by other songwriters. I certainly knew that writers of his stature could easily be offended. How do you submit material to the man who wrote "You Really Got Me," "Waterloo Sunset," "Lola," and "Celluloid Heroes"? I didn't at all care if he recorded the songs I gave him, and I made that clear. I just wanted him to think about them, be competitive enough to want to top them, and then come up with his own. Whether it spurred him on to write the material that ended up on their Arista debut, *Sleepwalker,* I can't say for certain. But in any event, when *Sleepwalker* came out in 1977, with highlights such as "Juke Box Music," "Life on the Road," and the title cut, both fans and the press enthusiastically greeted it as a return to form. It was also the Kinks' highest-charting album since Reprise's *Greatest Hits* set in 1966. From the initial wave of British groups that emerged in the Sixties, there were few bands—perhaps only the Stones and the Who—that not only survived but thrived in the second half of the Seventies, so for the Kinks to have an album do so well was a big achievement. Arista not only brought back the Kinks, but over the next few years, the band that had once been banned by the American Federation of Musicians from touring in the United States became an arena-filling act for the first time, supporting a consistent series of successful albums.

For a while, the Kinks kept coming up with records that solidified their credentials as a tough-rocking band anchored by the peerless Ray Davies. Everything I'd hoped for when I signed them was coming to fruition. 1978's *Misfits* featured the band's first Top 40 single since "Lola," a beautifully crafted and performed Davies song called "A Rock 'n' Roll Fantasy." The following year's *Low Budget*, although not a "concept album," included a group of songs that tapped the "malaise" of the tail end of the decade: "A Gallon of Gas," "Catch Me Now I'm Falling," "(Wish I Could Fly Like) Superman," and the title track. It became the highest-charting non–greatest hits album in the band's history, and after a live album capturing the electricity they were now generating on the road, two more albums also cracked the Top 20: *Give the People What They Want* and *State of Confusion*.

But when I heard the cut that was earmarked as the lead single from *State of Confusion*, I definitely had some concern. It had a swirling pop catchiness, a sweet nostalgic theme, and was an obvious single candidate. But "Come Dancing" was far more pop than rock, and the Kinks' string of gold albums was built on tracks that got heavy airplay on AOR radio. "Come Dancing" had some of the wistful charm of older Kinks songs from their *Village Green Preservation Society* days, and would appeal to those fans, but it lacked the aggressive punch that would allow it to be embraced on the rock side of the dial. That was an issue for us, and I lobbied to have the lead track from the album be something with more of an edge, like the title song, which kicked off with blistering staccato guitar. The whimsical keyboard hook of "Come Dancing" was undeniably appealing, but it was soft. In no way did I want to stifle Ray's artistry, but I felt we could save the song for later in the album's cycle, allowing it to establish its rock identity before we brought "Come Dancing" forward. Ray felt differently and went straight ahead to make a video for "Come Dancing." MTV loved it, and it became a big hit single. That was the good news. But the rock audience, the younger fans that had recently discovered the Kinks and didn't have a history with the band, didn't connect with Ray's more pop side. Despite the chart success of "Come Dancing" and to a lesser extent the follow-up, the lovely but also quite soft ballad "Don't Forget to Dance," *State of Confusion* proved to be an appropriate album title for the new generation of Kinks followers. The album did hit number twelve, but it was the first since *Misfits* not to go gold.

I know this might sound strangely contradictory. I have always championed the hit single, and believe that strategically the way to kick off an album is with an undeniable smash, like "Bridge over Troubled Water." The difference is that with Simon and Garfunkel, the audience expected the beautiful sheen, poetics, and vocal blend. To sell albums, a single should be, in a way, reassuring: There's a new album coming, and you love this artist, and here is a sample of what's in store. Audiences respond to stylistic consistency, and what's most effective is to make a fresh statement in a familiar way. I really believe that if there had been a big AOR cut out first, bringing in the core fans, followed by Top 40 singles, *State of Confusion* may well have become the biggest Kinks album of their Arista years. Instead, they got caught in a pop/rock divide for no good reason.

As it turned out, the Kinks would make only one more album for the label, 1984's *Word of Mouth*. No big track, pop or rock, came off the album, although one of its songs, "Living on a Thin Line," written and sung by the lead guitarist, Ray's brother Dave Davies, was given overdue exposure when it was used prominently in one of the first episodes of *The Sopranos*. When I met with Ray in 1976, I was a believer that there could be another significant chapter in the Kinks' story. I told him what I thought it would take to get this genuinely great band back on track, and then marveled as he delivered one album after another filled with some of his best songs. The Kinks did indeed enjoy a much-deserved second life.

To complete the picture, I do want to add that there were some artists that for one reason or another did slip away from us. I went to Boston to see the Cars, and was completely won over. It was an intense war, but we wound up being substantially outbid by Joe Smith at Elektra. Meat Loaf did a showcase for me, doing the Jim Steinman songs that would wind up on the album *Bat out of Hell,* but we, like nearly every label, passed. Perhaps I was being too practical. The songs were coming over as very theatrical, and Meat Loaf, despite a powerful voice, just didn't look like a star. We made the final four of the many American labels who were going after the Sex Pistols (it came down to Arista, Columbia, Casablanca, and the victor, Warners), and came away with the consolation prize of signing the band's publishing to our company Careers Music, run by the ever-resourceful Billy Meshel.

The rock scene in Britain was bristling with urgency in the late Seventies. It was one of those revitalizing periods that come along once in a while to shake things up, and candidly, I kept waiting for Arista's U.K. company to get into the game. I was eager to be a part of that rock renewal. Rather than depend on our London office to become more adventurous—they were much too stuck in the pre-Arista pop-single mentality of Bell U.K.—I decided to be more aggressive. Like everyone with an ear affixed to what was going on, I was aware of what was happening with the new, independent label Stiff Records, formed in 1976 and coming out of the gate with attitude in its signings and in its marketing. It launched with a record by Nick Lowe, who'd been in the band Brinsley Schwarz, continued with the Damned and the Pink Fairies, and then in 1977 introduced Ian Dury, Wreckless Eric, and Elvis Costello. I got Elvis instantly. *My Aim Is True,* which I heard as an import LP, showed a command of songwriting that doesn't come along often. His lyrics were blistering and defiant, but he also could write something as melodic and affecting as "Alison." This was someone bursting with talent, and his persona—the name, the glasses, the suits—was unusual and attention-grabbing. Stiff didn't have U.S. distribution yet, and I went after them very hard. If Arista U.K.'s A&R wasn't going to provide the company with cutting-edge British rock, then an association with Stiff would fill that gap. The label had already shown how smart and driven and in touch it was.

We made the deal, and then right before everything was signed and sealed, Jake Rivera and Dave Robinson, the label's founders, split up. Robinson kept Stiff; Rivera got Elvis and Nick. This was very disappointing news, and I could have backed out at that point, but I still felt the label had A&R smarts, even without those two key artists, who wound up at Columbia through a deal that Rivera made there. We moved ahead, and our initial two albums under the arrangement were a live album from a Stiff tour that included Costello and Lowe (so we did get a couple of tracks from them after all), and the debut by Ian Dury and the Blockheads, *New Boots and Panties!!* In keeping with the spirit of Stiff's promotional campaigns—one of their (in)famous slogans was "If It Ain't Stiff, It Ain't Worth a Fuck"—we announced the Stiff alliance in early 1978 with a provocative trade ad, pitched to me by a young copywriter who'd recently been hired. He'd sketched out a map of the United States, with Florida turned around and pointing northeast. The headline: "America Gets Stiff."

Dury's *New Boots and Panties!!,* now considered one of the defining albums of its era, should have been bigger in the States. It went platinum in the U.K., got raves in the press, and the songs Dury wrote with Chaz Jankel deserved to get radio exposure. I wanted to release the jaunty single "Sex & Drugs & Rock & Roll," but my promotion department informed me that no record promoting sex and drugs in its title was going to get airplay, so instead we went with track one on the album, "Wake Up and Make Love with Me," which also promoted sex, but at least kept drugs out of the equation. Despite its relatively milder content, it didn't become a hit, and neither, sorry to say, did the album. It's some small consolation that it turns up regularly on critics' lists like *Q* magazine's 100 Greatest British Albums and *Rolling Stone*'s 500 Greatest Albums of All Time. If only there were a more direct connection between critical acclaim and album sales.

Arista ran into that same critical/commercial divide with the Bus-Boys (who did get some recognition for a song from the Eddie Murphy film *48 Hrs.,* "The Boys Are Back in Town"), and especially with Graham Parker. I watched Parker from a distance as he put out one strong album after another on Mercury Records, albums that still hold up today. He had an exceptional band, the Rumour, drawn from the same London pub-rock world that generated Nick Lowe. In one year, 1976, Parker and the Rumour released a pair of game-changing albums, *Howlin' Wind,* produced by Lowe, and *Heat Treatment,* produced by Mutt Lange. It seemed inevitable that he would break: In addition to the quality of his writing and recorded work, I hadn't seen live reviews like his since early Springsteen. I caught a show at the Palladium in the fall of 1977, and Parker looked to me like the real thing. No artifice, no frills, just pure passion and adrenaline. By that point, his displeasure with Mercury was evident. His third album hadn't been received as well, he delivered a surprisingly unimpressive live album to finish off his Mercury contract, and, somewhat disconcertingly, he'd written and recorded a diatribe called "Mercury Poisoning," lashing out at the label for being ineffective. I thought, There but for the grace of God goes any one of us, being disparaged so publicly. Still, the feistiness was part of the package. That's who he was, high-strung, always a little nervous and defensive, but that all went into his performance and made him such a live wire onstage, as if he could snap at any moment.

It was a competitive situation. When someone as distinctive as Parker gets the kind of press he received and becomes available, a skirmish among interested labels invariably occurs. This time Arista prevailed, and Graham Parker joined our roster. He went into the studio with Jack Nitzsche, who'd worked with legendary figures like Phil Spector, Neil Young, and the Rolling Stones as an arranger, musician, and producer, and went on to compose soundtracks for films like *One Flew over the Cuckoo's Nest.* Every musical aspiration we had for Parker's Arista debut was fulfilled by *Squeezing Out Sparks,* released in March 1979 and instantly, wildly acclaimed. It's another Arista rock album that appears on *Rolling Stone*'s list of the five hundred greatest albums ever, and in 1979 it won the prestigious *Village Voice* national critics' poll as the best album of the year.

With attention like that, you would expect the public to take notice, but despite our intensive efforts—we even released a promo-only live version of the album, *Live Sparks,* recorded in San Francisco and Chicago—something didn't click. No matter how many times I live through it, it never fails to upset me when there's such a vast disconnect between the quality of an album and the public response. Although we did try harder than his prior label did to break him, and stuck with him for a few more albums, I can see why an artist who delivered so brilliantly would be motivated to write a "Mercury Poisoning." Who can explain why Graham Parker's one-two punch of *Howlin' Wind* and *Heat Treatment* didn't do for him what *My Aim Is True* and *This Year's Model* did for Elvis Costello? Or why his finest album, *Squeezing Out Sparks,* only squeaked into the Top 40 on the album chart? That was better than he'd fared at Mercury, where no album peaked higher than number 125, but not good enough. We did keep trying with him, and he did continue to make good music after he left Arista, for Elektra, RCA, and others, but the public's indifference toward him remains mystifying.

Looking back on that period in the label's early history, I really enjoy reflecting on the range of rock artists we signed. I only emphasize that because Arista's reputation for pop and urban music has in some circles eclipsed it. It's difficult to reframe people's perception of what a label does, but I like to think that any true rock fan would find plenty of pleasure in the music we helped bring into the world.

With Los Angeles Mayor Tom Bradley and
Dionne Warwick at the L.A. Street Scene
in 1981, commemorating Los Angeles's
Bicentennial and my role as Honorary
Entertainment Chairman of the Bicentennial

With Aretha Franklin at the piano at the
Beverly Hills Hotel after she signed with
Arista, 1980

From left: Mo and Evelyn Ostin and Quincy Jones, 1982

43   Signing Whitney Houston to Arista in 1983

44   Watching Whitney lift off in Los Angeles at her debut showcase at the Vine Street Bar and Grill, with Arista executive Roger Birnbaum (*in white shirt and tie*), 1985

From left: Gerry Griffith, Dionne Warwick, Whitney Houston, Jermaine Jackson and Arista executive Neil Portnow, 1985

Introducing Whitney to the world on *The Merv Griffin Show* in 1983

Checking in with the Eurythmics, who provided all the props and accessories for our signing photo shoot at the Hemingway Suite of the Ritz Hotel in Paris, 1989

With Alan Hirschfield, the Columbia Pictures executive who bankrolled Arista, and Michael Masser, who wrote several classic hits for Whitney, 1984

Dionne Warwick, Donna Summer and Whitney Houston at the Beverly Hills Hotel in 1985

Jamming with Ray Parker, Jr., in his dressing room, 1982

51

With my beloved cousin Jo Schuman in 1986, getting ready for my annual pre-Grammy party

52

Beating the drums with Carly Simon and her manager at the time, Tommy Mottola, 1978

53

The Grateful Dead celebrate the success of *In the Dark* with the Arista executive team, including Abbey Konowitch (*second from left*), Donnie Ienner (*back row, to Jerry Garcia's right*), Roy Lott (*over Garcia's left shoulder*), Rick Bisceglia (*behind Lott's left shoulder*), and, from right, Sean Coakley and (*back row*) Melani Rogers, 1987

With Kenny "Babyface" Edmonds and Antonio "L.A." Reid at the signing in Atlanta of the joint venture between Arista and their brand new label, LaFace Records, 1989

Presenting a $500,000 installment check for amfAR to Elizabeth Taylor on Dionne Warwick's television show *Solid Gold*. From left: Carole Bayer Sager, Burt Bacharach, Dionne, Stevie Wonder and Gladys Knight, 1989

Celebrating seven straight number one singles, a record that has yet to be broken, with Whitney Houston and, to her left, her mother, Cissy, 1989

Producer Narada Michael Walden, Aretha Franklin and Whitney Houston at the recording of Aretha and Whitney's 1989 duet single, "It Isn't, It Wasn't, It Ain't Never Gonna Be"

The CBS network television special celebrating the fifteenth anniversary of Arista on the stage of Radio City Music Hall in 1990. Joining the many musicians on hand for the finale were, from right: Michael Douglas, Melanie Griffith, Jane Curtin and Chevy Chase

With Patti Smith and her husband Fred Smith, 1990

Aretha Franklin in her amazing tutu performing with the City Center Ballet Company at the Friars Club event honoring me, 1992

```
The Friars Honor Clive Davis!

                "THERE'S NO DAVIS,LIKE THIS DAVIS!"

                                           Special Lyrics
                                           SAMMY CAHN

(Bb)  VERSE: (No tempo at direct cue!)

           THIS SONG IS BY BERLIN
           AND HE WAS THE BEST
           AND THE BEST TO DAVIS,WE MUST GIVE!

           IF PRAISES WE'RE HURLIN'
           THEN LET ME SUGGEST
           DAVIS IS A PURE SUPERLATIVE

           HE SIMPLY IS THE GREATEST YOU'LL AGREE
           SOMETIMES I THINK,--HE THINKS THAT HE,--IS ME! (to tempo not fast!)

(Db)  CHORUS: (With real style but slowly!)

           THERE'S NO DAVIS,LIKE THIS DAVIS
           LIKE NO DAVIS I KNOW

           SPEAK NOT OF THE DAVIS WHO WAS BETTE
           SAMMY WAS A FAMOUS DAVIS TOO
           BUT COMPARED TO CLIVE,THEY BOTH SEEM PETTY
           FORGETTING SAMMY BECAME A JEW

           THERE'S NO DAVIS,LIKE THIS DAVIS
           THE REST AT BEST,PLACE AND SHOW,---(go out of tempo!)

     *  YOU CAN'T COUNT THE TIMES THAT HE'S BEEN NUMBER ONE
        NO ONE HAS DONE WHAT THIS MAN HAS DONE
        HISTORY MAY THINK HE'S AHMET ERTE-GUN   (to tempo)

           THERE'S NO DAVIS,LIKE THIS DAVIS
           LIKE NO DAVIS I KNOW!!!

           (Play from asterisk * again) (again NO tempo!)

     *  MAY I ASK HIS FRIENDS WHO'VE GATHERED WALL TO WALL
        IF THEY WOULD ALL RAISE THEIR ALCOHOL
        HELP ME TOAST THE GREATEST DAVIS OF THEM ALL  (To tempo slower -add band!)

           THERE'S NO DAVIS LIKE THIS DAVIS,
           LIKE NO DAVIS I KNOW!!! (tag)
           THERE'S NO DAVIS LIKE THIS DAVIS,
           LIKE NO DAVIS I KNOW!!!

                                           New York,N.Y. 5/29/92.
```

The great Sammy Cahn wrote these special lyrics in 1992 to the tune of "There's No Business Like Show Business" for the Friars Club Testimonial Dinner that year

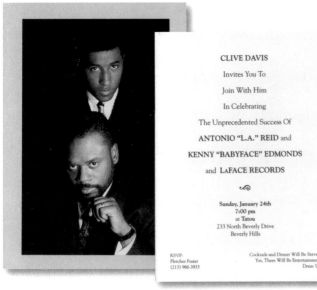

62

Party invitation
for LaFace Records
celebration, 1993

CLIVE DAVIS

Invites You To

Join With Him

In Celebrating

The Unprecedented Success Of

ANTONIO "L.A." REID and

KENNY "BABYFACE" EDMONDS

and LaFACE RECORDS

Sunday, January 24th
7:00 pm
at Tatou
233 North Beverly Drive
Beverly Hills

RSVP:
Fletcher Foster
(213) 966-3933

Cocktails and Dinner Will Be Served.
Yes, There Will Be Entertainment.
Dress: Up

Bonnie Raitt, Annie
Lennox, Carly Simon
and Sheryl Crow in
1995 for the pre-
Grammy party at
the House of Blues
celebrating the success
of the *Boys on the Side*
soundtrack album

63

Barry Manilow standing against a wall of platinum, 1995

LEFT: Tim DuBois, Alan Jackson, Kix Brooks and Ronnie Dunn in 1997 enjoying the success of Arista Nashville

BELOW: With one of America's top songwriters, Diane Warren, 1997

65

BELOW: Getting a star on the Hollywood Walk of Fame at Sunset and Vine on January 28, 1997. Seated or kneeling left to right: Dick Clark, Deborah Cox, Kenny G., Barry Manilow, Blood, Sweat & Tears' Bobby Colomby, L.A. Reid and Narada Michael Walden

66

67

Receiving in 1998 the amfAR Humanitarian of the Year Award along with Bar-
bara Walters and Tom Hanks from amfAR's Dr. Mathilde Krim. Sharon Stone
MC'd the evening. Left to right: Barbara Walters, Tom Hanks, Rita Wilson
(Mrs. Hanks), Sharon Stone and Dr. Mathilde Krim

With Puffy at my pre-Grammy gala, 2002

With Clive Calder, Thomas Middelhoff and Strauss Zelnick, 1999

Sammy and I relax in my Park Avenue apartment, 1997

Luther Vandross at my New York apartment, 2000

At a dinner in 2000 to introduce Luther Vandross to the J Records executive team at my New York apartment: (*from left*) Trevor Jerideau, Julie Swidler, Ron Gillyard, Luther's manager Carmen Romano, Luther, Charles Goldstuck, Tom Corson, Richard Palmese, Peter Edge, Larry Jackson and Hosh Gureli

With Busta Rhymes, 2000

Carlos Santana and I haul away the Grammys for *Supernatural*, 2000

The Grateful Dead

As early as the tail end of the Sixties, I wanted to be involved with the Grateful Dead's career. Even before they broke through with the more focused, song-oriented country-folk-flavored albums *Workingman's Dead* and *American Beauty,* I felt that they had something no other band, then or now, has ever been able to replicate. They thrived on spontaneity, improvisation, and inventiveness. They turned every show into an unpredictable journey, and what they lacked in terms of polish and discipline, they more than made up for in the unique bond they created with their audience, and their willingness to take musical risks. I was by no means a Deadhead, but I loved going to their concerts, seeing how the crowds would gather outside the venues' parking lots long before the shows would start, how everyone in their audience seemed to know one another. It was like a big family gathering. And the music was wonderful.

My first exposure to the Dead was at Monterey, but I have to admit, they didn't make the strongest impression on me at the time. Earlier that night, Big Brother and the Holding Company played the second of their two sets, the one filmed for *Monterey Pop,* and the Dead's slot was sandwiched between explosive sets by the Who and the Jimi Hendrix Experience. In the midst of all that performing firepower (literally in the case of Hendrix, who ignited his guitar at the end of his set), the Dead seemed relatively sedate. What I realized, seeing them at other shows, is that they really do need the freedom to stretch out musically, and that a relatively short performance on the bill of a festival isn't the ideal way to "get" the true Grateful Dead experience. Their long, improvised sets take so many twists and turns. You have to get fully on their wavelength for that musical journey to really make emotional sense. Once you do, a Dead show can be an almost mystical experience, and for many of their fans, the ritual of seeing the Dead became like a pilgrimage. There was nothing else like the community of Deadheads, traveling from city to city to see the band, comparing tales of different concerts as if each had its own beguiling narrative. No two shows were the same, and you could sometimes see the band huddled onstage together between songs, mapping out where to go next. Dead fans were a real underground network. The Dead built up their community show by show, by word of mouth. It was a true phenomenon. Even before they started selling albums to a significant extent—their first three hadn't done very well—it was apparent to me that any band with that ability to convert concertgoers into a mass of the devoted would put it all together and reach a large and faithful record-buying audience.

I first tried to sign them to Columbia in 1969, before their manager renegotiated an extension of their three-album deal with Warner Bros., and then, when that period ended in 1972, I made another serious attempt to bring them to the label. By that time, they had proven that they could broaden their loyal base with songs such as "Uncle John's Band," "Truckin'," and "Casey Jones," all of which became staples on album-oriented rock radio stations, and their album sales benefited as a result: They were now not only the most impressive live ambassadors of the San Francisco scene, they were a platinum recording act. I really wanted them for Columbia Records.

They, however, had other, more radical ideas. Once the band was free to leave Warners, Ron Rakow, a member of the band's management team, convinced them that the next visionary step was complete autonomy, not only creatively, but in every facet of business. They couldn't reconcile their incredible concert ticket sales upon announcement of the live dates with the much smaller album sales upon the release of a new record. They didn't think they needed an established record company, and thought they could do better on their own. Obviously, my team and I at Columbia, most vocally our head of rock promotion, Michael Klenfner, a big fan of the Dead, tried to convince them otherwise. I'd been asked by their lawyer, Hal Kant, if I would come out to San Francisco to meet with the band, and Klenfner and I made the trip in November 1972 to try to steer them in our direction.

That meeting is forever memorable. We gathered around a large conference table with all the members of the Dead, including Jerry Garcia, Bob Weir, Phil Lesh, Bill Kreutzmann, Mickey Hart, and their various advisors. The band grilled us methodically on topic after topic, including the grain of vinyl used in pressing their albums. (Klenfner assured them he personally would exercise quality control, since he wanted to hear them sound perfect.) Despite their success at Warners, and the fact that Jerry Garcia had already been, in effect, a Columbia artist as the pedal steel player in the New Riders of the Purple Sage, they had an innate distrust of record companies. I suppose they thought of us as the Establishment, a typical assumption at the time, and believed we were too stuck in traditional ways of selling records. One of their innovative solutions to getting around the record-label distribution system was to sell their albums directly to the consumers through a fleet of ice-cream trucks. Without insulting them, I tried to impress upon them just how impractical and inefficient that system would be. That was one notion they eventually abandoned.

I not only made an impassioned case for coming to Columbia, I was candid about their utopian plan to realign the record industry. "Listen," I told them. "I think you're making a big mistake. I understand what you're saying in theory, but you don't realize you're going to have enormous credit and collection problems. How do you get paid for your records? You're naïve about how distribution works, about how radio promotion works." I spoke at great length and with great conviction about how so many artists who are big live attractions can't translate that loyal following into record sales. I told them what they really needed was a better fit with a record label. I stressed that we would pay attention to whether they were writing material that would get played on the radio, that there would be more promotion and marketing and awareness of a new Grateful Dead album on Columbia. They listened respectfully to our pitch, and we systematically addressed all their questions and concerns, but in the end, they made the decision to start the autonomous Grateful Dead Records (and an affiliated label, Round Records), one of the first of the artist-owned independent labels. I didn't think the experiment would work, but the Dead had beaten the odds before, made many bold moves (playing free concerts, encouraging audience taping of their shows), and had come out all right. I was sorry not to have them on Columbia. I thought they were taking a crazy risk at a point where they were getting all the recognition and record sales they'd worked for since forming as the Warlocks in 1965. They were putting a lot on the line for no particularly good reason.

The Dead ended their association with Warners with a triple live album, *Europe '72,* and a contract-fulfilling single-disc compilation, and launched their noble venture—financed with some bank credit and an advance for foreign distribution—with 1973's *Wake of the Flood.* That was the start of a shaky few years for the Dead. *From the Mars Hotel* came out in June 1974, and fell short of gold. And starting in October of that year, they took a break from touring, playing only some local gigs for well over a year.

By that time they'd realized that, however idealistic, their goal of avoiding the traditional record-label system wasn't turning out as they'd hoped, and they made a deal with United Artists to distribute Grateful Dead Records. That arrangement didn't turn things around, and two more albums, and a number of solo projects, came and went without causing so much as a sales ripple. It was a steep tumble from where they'd been five years earlier.

Then I got a call from Hal Kant, asking if he could see me. I was in Los Angeles at the Beverly Hills Hotel, and he came over to my bungalow. He said that everything I'd predicted would happen to the Grateful Dead in those four or so intervening years since we'd met at their offices had come to pass. He also told me that the band admired my forthrightness, my honesty, and my expertise. "They want to be with you," he told me. "They very much like the fact that you started Arista from scratch. They know who you've signed and what you've done, and they know exactly how you've conducted operations there. They've met with a lot of people, a lot of labels, and they feel you're head and shoulders better." To me, that was so satisfying, so critical, to get that endorsement from a band with such huge credibility. I'll never forget that. Arista's doors had been open for only two years, and a band like the Grateful Dead, which despite its recent sales slump still could have signed with any of the majors based on their track record and reputation, wanted to be on Arista. That kind of faith definitely moved me.

But as gratifying as this news was, I still had to talk with the band. Five years in the music business is a long time, and they'd gotten off track, so we needed to have a frank conversation about where the band was heading, what the expectations were on both sides, and how I saw things unfolding. This time the meeting took place in my hotel rather than the Dead's headquarters, and it was a much smaller gathering, just me and the members of the band. I told them there were three vital issues for me: I wanted them to record away from San Francisco in order to get a fresh perspective, to use an outside producer, and to commit to touring extensively again to reconnect with their fans and get recharged as a band. From 1974 to 1976, while the band wasn't playing live much, there were too many side projects on Round Records that diluted the Grateful Dead brand: Garcia had solo albums and a bluegrass album with Old and in the Way; Weir had a Kingfish album; Mickey Hart recorded with the Diga Rhythm Band. They were in danger of losing their identity as the Grateful Dead. On each point, the band agreed.

I admired the crisp, vivid sound of the first Fleetwood Mac album with the new members Buckingham and Nicks, the way the production walked the line between rock and pop and framed the musical personalities in the group. I thought the album's producer, Keith Olsen, might be the right match for the Dead. In late 1976, I met with Keith, and although he was skeptical at first about shaping the band's music into an album that was accessible and commercial, he agreed to meet with them, and they hit it off. At that point, I stepped out of the picture and Keith and the band went into the studio that November to begin recording *Terrapin Station*.

Critical and fan opinions vary about what Olsen, and the string arranger Paul Buckmaster—orchestral arrangements on a Grateful Dead record!—brought to *Terrapin*, but I was very pleased. Side one of the album had five strong songs, including "Estimated Prophet" by Weir and John Barlow; a Motown cover, "Dancing in the Street"; and a very Dead-like transformation of the traditional "Samson and Delilah." Side two was devoted to the title piece, interweaving songs that meshed into one sixteen-minute suite. I felt so good about it, and the band was also upbeat. Garcia said, "It actually sounds like a record. People won't believe it's us." And Weir agreed. He told an interviewer, "It's the Dead without all those wrong notes."

As soon as the album was completed, even before it hit the streets, the Dead went on the road to premiere the material, on a tour that has taken on legendary status among the Dead faithful. It kicked off at Winterland in San Francisco for three nights in March, then came east for a series of dates that fans consider an absolute pinnacle in the band's illustrious touring career. A new album, and the resumption of being on the road after the break, clearly lit a fire under the band. A recent *New York Times* article said that among Deadheads, the shows introducing the *Terrapin* material on the east coast in May 1977—in particular the May 8 show at Cornell University and shows in Hartford and Buffalo—are generally regarded as the best Dead shows ever. The album came out in July, and it's safe to assume that word among the fans had circulated about the band's revitalization. Anticipation for the album was high, and it became their first studio album to achieve gold status since *American Beauty*. The band's and my faith in each other was validated, and I couldn't have been happier.

A second gold album followed, *Shakedown Street,* produced by Lowell George of Little Feat. It seemed like an inspired pairing, and the album has its strong moments ("I Need a Miracle" and "Fire on the Mountain" became live staples), but I do think it suffers from not having enough first-rate original songs by Garcia and Weir. After *Terrapin,* each of them had released a solo album—Bob's *Heaven Help the Fool,* and the Jerry Garcia Band's *Cats Under the Stars*—and if they'd held on to some of their best songs, like Weir's "Bombs Away" and Garcia's "Rubin and Cherise," until the next Dead album, those tracks would have improved *Shakedown Street.* I always worry when, between band projects, the individual members go off and do their own thing. I understand the impulse to work outside the format of the band and spread your creative wings, but with the rare exception, solo excursions don't do as well, and then the band has to scramble to come up with an album's worth of material. That's exactly what happened this time. Neither Weir's nor Garcia's album cracked the Top 50. I couldn't intervene, or tell the members how to allocate their songs. I just hoped they'd realize that the band had to be the creative priority.

The Dead began the Eighties with *Go to Heaven,* an album probably most famous for the photograph on its cover: the band in snazzy white suits. That image probably wouldn't have been more than amusing in any other period, but in the post–*Saturday Night Fever* world, it brought to mind John Travolta on the dance floor of 2001 Odyssey. Had the Dead gone disco? That would be the ultimate betrayal. After all, the Stones had released "Miss You" in 1978, the same year Rod Stewart scored with "Da Ya Think I'm Sexy?" The cover of *Go to Heaven* hinted that the Dead might be the latest rock artists to cross over to the dark side. That wasn't the case: songs like "Alabama Getaway" were, if anything, vintage Dead. But whether it was perception or simply that at the start of the new decade the rock audience was moving on, or that some collective spark was missing, *Go to Heaven* was the band's lowest-selling album on Arista.

It was also their last studio album for a long while. There was a Bob Weir Bobby and the Midnites album in 1981, and Garcia's *Run for the Roses* in 1982, but for years they didn't go into the studio as a band. To fill that gap, we released two double albums from a 1980 tour, *Reckoning* and *Dead Set,* but neither had breakout sales, and we waited and waited. It felt as though the Grateful Dead were going to remain strictly a touring band, playing to their tie-dye-hard followers year after year. I never considered giving up on them, but I also never pressured them to get back into the studio. As with Patti Smith, I could sense from a distance that the band was going through a time of adjustment. There were rumors that Jerry Garcia was struggling with a severe drug problem. I didn't see any point in making demands that the band begin recording. I had to be patient. What were my options? I suppose I could have gotten exasperated and let them out of their contract, but one thing I'd learned: You can never count true artists out. All you can do is wait.

Seven years went by, a lifetime in the music business. Since the last Dead album, the industry had undergone vast changes. In 1985, Dire Straits had become the first band to sell more than a million copies of an album on compact disc. MTV, launched one year after the Dead released *Go to Heaven,* had utterly transformed the industry. *Thriller, Born in the U.S.A., Purple Rain,* and *Like a Virgin* had all come out and defined the blockbuster Eighties album. In 1986, Garcia collapsed into a diabetic coma, and everyone connected with the band waited to see if he would live, and if he did, whether he would fully recover. Garcia had become not only a master musician, but a symbol of the sixties and everything hopeful that it represented. To lose him would have been devastating. When word began to spread that he would survive and was recovering well, the entire music world seemed to exhale and smile.

I personally had always gotten along well with him, as well as with the rest of the band. When he was ill I thought about how, after one of the Dead's run of shows at Radio City Music Hall in 1980, I had thrown a party for the band at the Rainbow Room atop Rockefeller Center. Arista's head of promotion, Richard Palmese, and I sat down with Garcia at a table. Garcia was friendly and extremely bright, but he would never want to discuss business in a setting like that. I could see Richard wondering how our conversation would go. Garcia and I were chatting, and I simply took out a pen, drew a tic-tac-toe board on the tablecloth, and we all sat there and played for the next hour or so. Only with Jerry Garcia would a surreal moment like that make perfect sense. Still, the fact was that by 1987, it had been two decades since I'd first seen the Dead at Monterey, where they and bands like them represented the future. In 1987, the Dead were hardly forgotten, but who knew what they were up to, whether they'd reemerge, how they'd fit into this new world.

In January 1987, the Dead set up on a stage in a theater in Marin County, with no audience, and played a collection of new songs. Then they took tapes of those performances into a studio, overdubbed what was needed, and as simply as that, there was a new, self-produced (by Garcia and John Cutler) album by the Grateful Dead: *In the Dark.* I remember the first time I heard it. Immediately, "Touch of Grey" jumped out. It was what I'd always hoped would happen one day in my relationship with them: Here was a song that had all the distinctive, unmistakable trademarks of the Dead sound, that quintessential spirit of the band, but at the same time had an irresistible hook and a lyric anyone could relate to. I felt it instantly. I brought it into one of my Arista staff meetings to share with all the label's top executives, and everybody just lit up (metaphorically, of course). It was really a very special moment, to hear the band sounding so fresh and spirited, and watch how the company responded. Many of them had never had the chance to work a Grateful Dead record before, to be a part of that experience. We all knew we had something unique. A potential anthem for the band, for the Deadheads, for the baby boomers, maybe even for the MTV generation. What great joy to see that happen!

We convinced the band to edit down the album version, which was almost six minutes, to a more radio-ready four and a half minutes. The track went to number one on the Mainstream Rock airplay chart, and Top 10 on the Hot 100, the first time any record by the Dead had achieved that. Gary Gutierrez directed the "Touch of Grey" video, featuring skeleton marionettes of the band segueing into a performance by the live band. And as we'd hoped, MTV raved over it. Seeing the Dead among all the younger rock bands on the channel was incongruous, as was hearing them on Top 40 radio, but it was an undeniable song, with a chorus that resonated with any audience: "I will get by / I will survive." For them to emerge with that song, seemingly out of the blue (they had, in fact, been playing it live for a while), was a revelation. That Garcia, who had been at death's door not long before, characteristically sang the song at the very top of his register, reaching for the notes as if they were life itself, only made the song more moving and resonant.

"Touch of Grey" was making its wildly unexpected journey up the charts, and *In the Dark* had been out for only a week when I went to see the Dead play to a sold-out Giants Stadium in July 1987. Around 75,000 people gathered on a summer Sunday to see the co-headliners, the Grateful Dead and Bob Dylan, and it was an incredible day; the Dead backed up Bob throughout his set, doing classic songs like "All Along the Watchtower" from *John Wesley Harding,* and for the encore, "Touch of Grey" led directly into "Knockin' on Heaven's Door," one of the last signature songs I'd shared with Dylan at Columbia. "Touch of Grey" was still a relatively new song, but the stadium erupted when the band started it, and sang along, and the transition into the Dylan song was a great moment. I went backstage and went from one dressing room to another, reconnecting with Bob, congratulating the Dead on their triumph. I treasure days like that.

Two other songs from *In the Dark,* Weir's "Hell in a Bucket" and "Throwing Stones," did well on rock radio, and when all was said and done, it became the first Top 10 album in the band's history, and only its second studio album, after *American Beauty,* to go double platinum. That was a peak for the band, a victory lap twenty years after their debut album, and definitely a milestone in their association with Arista and me. Every thing I'd promised them when they took the leap to sign with us had happened. There were two more Arista albums after that, both gold. After 1990's live *Without a Net,* the band continued to tour, but extremely sadly there were no more new Dead albums. Jerry Garcia passed away in 1995, a year after the band was inducted into the Rock and Roll Hall of Fame. In 2012, the Hall's museum presented a spectacular exhibition devoted to the band, called *Grateful Dead: The Long, Strange Trip.* Strange it was. Along with my role as president of their record label, I have another distinction in Dead history. There's a line in the Dead song "Jack Straw" that goes, "We used to play for silver / Now we play for life." At one point in the late Seventies, John Belushi, a big fan, came up with a variation: "We used to play for acid / Now we play for Clive." As I heard the story, Jerry Garcia passed this along to the rest of the band, and in various shows around 1979–80 that's how Bob sang it onstage. You can hear it in the numerous Dead shows that circulate on the Internet, such as one from Nassau Coliseum. It was quite a thrill to have been there with the Dead for much of their absolutely incredible ride.

Gil Scott-Heron and
Ghostbusters

When I started Arista my mission was to have the label be a home of excellence and innovation that was involved in virtually every musical genre. We never considered a classical division, and it was way too soon to plant our flag in Nashville to get into country music, but with those exceptions, it was anything goes. I always used Columbia as the template, and was determined to build the broadest, most inclusive and enviable artist roster in the industry. At Arista, the most mainstream pop artists imaginable could coexist with the daunting jazz of Anthony Braxton. Soul, fusion, classic jazz, and funk, and the boldest younger musicians from Larry Coryell and Pharoah Sanders to the Headhunters all were a part of our early years. Randy Brecker, whom I'd known from Blood, Sweat & Tears, formed a band with his brother Michael, and we signed the Brecker Brothers.

The executive I principally collaborated with during these years regarding progressive music was an intelligent and astute A&R man, Steve Backer. Steve knew his jazz and his input was always valuable. We acquired the catalog of Savoy Records, a treasure trove of classic jazz and early R&B, and embarked on an ambitious reissue program that brought such unexpected successes as selling more than 50,000 copies of a five-record set of the complete Charlie Parker Savoy masters. Through the labels Novus and Freedom, we released important albums by artists such as Air (Henry Threadgill, Fred Hopkins, and Steve McCall), Archie Shepp, Cecil Taylor, and Ornette Coleman. Of course, the financial rewards weren't nearly commensurate with the acclaim and cultural significance, but any label would have been proud to assemble a roster that eclectic and distinguished.

How would you describe Gil Scott-Heron? Where does he fit in? His music has elements of R&B, certainly, but there were also jazz influences. His songs could be terse and angry, with whip-smart political insight and command of language and rhythm. There are extended, mesmerizing instrumental passages, but at the center is his passionate voice and poetic sensibility. He was an original, and he was, if not the very first, among the first two or three artists I wanted to sign to Arista. Gil had started to generate rumbles of excitement with his albums on Flying Dutchman, where Bob Thiele had signed him. His debut on that label, 1971's *Pieces of a Man,* introduced the songs "The Revolution Will Not Be Televised" and "Lady Day and John Coltrane," and it was obvious that here was someone with a genuinely new voice, who had a fresh take. It was all these elements, the simmering rage of the Nixon years, the timing of the rise of blaxploitation films (Melvin Van Peebles's *Sweet Sweetback's Baadasssss Song* and the breakthrough smash *Shaft* both were released in 1971), and how Gil fused funk and jazz and spoken word. There was something really eye-opening about what he was up to, but his reputation was still very underground. Then he recorded *Winter in America* for the independent label Strata-East. That album, which came out in May 1974, included the track "The Bottle," and I could sense from the reaction to that single that his appeal could be much, much broader. Thankfully, the Strata-East deal was for only one album, and when Gil and his Midnight Band started recording their next project in the summer of 1974, they didn't have a label.

I went to see Gil Scott-Heron at the Beacon Theater, and was floored. Everything that was so impressive on his albums was right there onstage—and more. Gil was a striking, charismatic figure, young and compelling, very much of his moment in time. Sometimes you come across an artist like that, who embodies the cultural energy around him, synthesizes it, and presents his vision in a striking way. I hesitate to use terms like "spokesman for his generation" or "voice of his era," because they sound so grandiose, but when I was in the audience watching Gil, I thought, Here's someone whose impact can be profound, who's forceful without being didactic, and who's shaping his music in a direct and communicative way. He did "The Bottle," which dramatizes the impact of substance abuse on the African-American community, that night, and it was a total anthem, and he had other new songs that were comparably strong. I got word to him that I wanted to talk about my new venture, and making him a part of it. He would very much be a cornerstone of what I wanted Arista to represent.

The label was in its infancy; there was no staff yet. In an interview, Gil recalled that, at the time, it was only me and my assistant, Rose. So for him to believe in me and put his career in my hands was a big deal. He decided to call the album he was recording *The First Minute of a New Day,* because that's what it was for each of us: starting over, a beginning. Appropriately, the album was released in January 1975, the start of the first full year of Arista's existence. I thought it was great. The spoken track "Pardon Our Analysis (We Beg Your Pardon)" addressed the aftermath of Nixon's Watergate scandal, and cuts like "The Liberation" and "Winter in America" took Gil into more sophisticated musical territory. If you look at the album cover, you'll notice that the album is credited to the Midnight Band, with the names Gil Scott-Heron and Brian Jackson in smaller type down in the lower right corner of the jacket. This bothered me: I wanted the spotlight to be on Gil, to bring him as an artist to the wide audience I felt he deserved. But his picture isn't on the cover, and his name is given secondary placement to the overall band name.

I understood his democratic impulse, and I meant no disrespect to the contribution of Brian Jackson or the other players, but to me the star was Gil, in the way that Janis Joplin was the star of Big Brother and the Holding Company, and I wanted him to emerge in that manner. It did become a point of contention, and I know it angered Brian Jackson, who felt I wanted to diminish his role in the music. It was a tough situation, but with an artist like Gil, it has to come down to his decision; this is his work, and he has the creative power. I would have rather seen his name and likeness on the cover than "Midnight Band" and a drawing of a gorilla, but my misgivings didn't slow my mission to bring Gil Scott-Heron to the national stage. For an album by an artist whose commercial track record hadn't been that impressive, and who never reached a mainstream audience, *First Minute of a New Day* was released with considerable fanfare. I told *Rolling Stone,* "I'm very excited to be starting with Gil. I just couldn't be happier. There's an element of Dylan there. Also something of Miles, of Stevie Wonder and Sly [Stone]. But there's no borrowing, and you really can't make comparisons. Gil is unique. His statements are as sharp and penetrating as those of any social leader. Just think of the effect he could have."

When I was asked to host *Midnight Special* in March 1975, Gil was one of the exciting new Arista artists I brought on, exposing him to millions of people who never had heard of him. He performed "The Bottle," his best-known song at that point, and "Must Be Something" from the new album. Word continued to spread. He was personally invited by Richard Pryor to be on one of the first episodes of the new show *Saturday Night Live*. One of the conditions of Pryor's hosting the show was that Gil would be his musical guest. Then I featured him at a big Arista show I presented at City Center in New York City. I had Arista work the album beyond the jazz world that he had been relegated to at his previous labels. Our effort paid off: The album not only made it to number five on the jazz chart, but went Top 10 on the R&B chart, and even made it to number thirty on the overall *Billboard* album chart, the first time he'd ever reached that level. Gil followed up that album the next year with *From South Africa to South Carolina,* featuring a great track called "Johannesburg," one of the first songs to address the issue of apartheid. He was really a vital cornerstone artist for Arista, someone who gave depth and credibility to the label.

There was a great level of respect for Gil. I remember going with Stevie Wonder to his show at the Bottom Line; Stevie admired Gil so much, and years later asked Gil to open for him on the tour that doubled as a campaign to support the movement to have Martin Luther King's birthday declared a national holiday. Gil was also one of the few black artists invited to perform at the "No Nukes" concert at Madison Square Garden, alongside Bruce Springsteen, Tom Petty, Crosby, Stills and Nash, Jackson Browne, and other rock and pop legends. He performed his antinuke song "We Almost Lost Detroit." To me, Gil was one of those artists who was always on the verge. I knew that with the right record, his sales would explode and he would become a major star. That clearly was my mission. Yes, I wanted to document someone who had so much to say, to give him an outlet; it was like publishing an acclaimed author whose voice mattered in the national conversation. But you also have a commercial responsibility, you stay with him hoping for a best-seller. It almost happened with the song "Angel Dust" from the album *Secrets* in 1979, and that album did become his first since his Arista debut to make it into the *Billboard* Top 100.

I so wanted Gil to break through in a giant way, to have hits. We continued with a series of albums that were politically on target (he took on Ronald Reagan on "B Movie" and "Re Ron"), and he did stretch out musically when he began collaborating with the producer Malcolm Cecil. From time to time, I suggested other collaborators, other ways of getting commercial traction, but there was stubbornness and strength in his belief, and he always resisted my efforts. Boy, was he charismatic in person. Electricity was always in the air. And despite his resistance to making any concessions for a commercial breakthrough, he was always warm to me. He knew I cared. I believed in his future potential and he was grateful. But, to me, it always felt like a lost opportunity; it's not like the basic hooks weren't there, and with a little nudging in a more compact musical direction, he could have gotten that commercial base that can sustain an artist for a lifetime. Just a little more structure, a frame for his lyrical ideas, but he just wouldn't be moved. Eventually I backed off, and he was never to have that defining, chart-topping record, so in 1984, after putting out a compilation album of his best Arista work, we parted ways. I have to say that before it came to that, I had begun to see the way his drug use was affecting him: His face was getting more hollowed and drawn, his appearance was definitely changed. You could see the toll drugs were taking.

But what a force he was! It's some vindication of his vision and prescience that so many hip-hop artists point to him as an influence, from Chuck D of Public Enemy to Darryl McDaniels of Run-D.M.C. Gil's songs "The Revolution Will Not Be Televised," "Home Is Where the Hatred Is," and "We Almost Lost Detroit" have been sampled on records by artists such as Kanye West and Common. Almost four decades after I heard him for the first time and wanted him as one of Arista's founding artists, you can see his profound impact. Obviously, you always want the artists you work with to have success, to seize their chance to reach people, to leave a lasting impression. When I heard the tragic news in May 2011 that Gil Scott-Heron had passed away, after leaving behind one last well-received album, 2010's *I'm New Here,* I did have strong regret that he eventually fell short of his potential. But I also knew how much his music meant to so many, and how it's still filtering into our lives all these years later. In a way, Arista began with him, and in the hip-hop Arista released into the twenty-first century, he's still very much a presence.

Getting into the pocket in R&B and jazz fusion took some trial and error, but they were both areas I pursued from the outset. As I did at CBS with Gamble and Huff, I had to look outward to A&R sources to identify the creative people on the verge, and supplement what we were signing in-house. In 1978, I started associations with two labels, Buddah and GRP Records.

Buddah had been around since 1967, and had gained momentum at the end of the decade and into the Seventies with the Isley Brothers, Melanie, the Edwin Hawkins Singers, Bill Withers, Curtis Mayfield, and the incredible Gladys Knight and the Pips. By the time I made the Buddah distribution deal with Art Kass, the composer-arranger-producer Norman Connors was taking on a major creative role at the label, steering it in a more sophisticated R&B direction. That seemed like a solid fit with Arista, giving our R&B promo staff a flow of releases to take to urban radio. They added muscle to our efforts to build a homegrown R&B artist roster and enabled us to afford a full national R&B promotion team. I made the announcement at the 1978 Arista convention, showcasing Buddah's upcoming releases: Norman Connors's *This Is Your Life,* Michael Henderson's *Do It All,* Phyllis Hyman's *Somewhere in My Lifetime,* and a single by Gladys Knight and the Pips, "Sorry Doesn't Always Make It Right," co-written by Michael Masser and Pam Sawyer.

It was an encouraging start, and the relationships with Henderson, Connors, and Hyman continued over a string of albums. Some of the projects were commercially rewarding, but I always wished there were a better solution to the Phyllis Hyman situation. Phyllis did work with talented producers we suggested, like James Mtume and Reggie Lucas, and also with Narada Michael Walden, and she did have a big dance/

R&B hit in 1979 with "You Know How to Love Me," but basically she was unhappy with the material. Unfortunately, the songs she favored were not at all radio-friendly. Phyllis was strikingly attractive with a big, expressive voice, and all four of her albums did go Top 20 on the R&B chart, but it was never fulfilling for her or Buddah or us. She did have great potential but it was never reached to the real satisfaction of anyone. What a shame it was, but it always gets down to the songs, no matter how outstanding the voice.

What the Buddah distribution arrangement provided was a way for Arista to get on the R&B scoreboard, and that we did. We were being recognized and we were building an identity. During this same period, we were to generate some serious jazz-fusion heat through the newly formed GRP Records. The *G* and *R* stood for Dave Grusin and Larry Rosen, who had their own production company, Grusin/Rosen Productions, discovering a string of talented, significant artists: Lee Ritenour, Earl Klugh, Patti Austin, Noel Pointer. I was very impressed by their talent-spotting acumen in this area of jazz, or, more accurately maybe, pop-instrumental music. Identifying it as jazz can be tricky; true jazz enthusiasts rarely have nice things to say about "smooth jazz" or "jazz fusion" or "crossover jazz," and I can understand their point. By sticking the word *jazz* in the description, you inevitably run into the fact that very little about the genre connects to true jazz in a substantial way. It's shorthand that does the genre little favor. Still, there is a meaningful audience for this style, whatever you want to call it.

I had wanted to sign Jon Lucien, one of Grusin/Rosen Productions' artists, to Arista in 1975, and was disappointed when they took him to Columbia, but I'd continued to watch what they were up to. I bumped into Larry on a flight in 1977, congratulated him on everything that was happening at their company, and then we arranged a meeting to discuss the possibility of their setting up shop at Arista with a production deal. Dave, Larry, and I spent time together, and they were real bright and musically attuned, and whatever they played for me, I enjoyed. Over the course of our talks, they said that they were looking to start their own label. So we financed GRP Records. They'd already started working with the flautist Dave Valentin, and he became the label's first official artist, combining strains of Latin jazz and funk on the album *The Hawk*. He also led Grusin and Rosen to the singer Angela Bofill.

From track one of Angela Bofill's debut *Angie,* the self-written "Under the Moon and Over the Sky," it's clear that this is someone with a magical spark. There are touches of jazz, R&B, and Latin music, but it has a spirit of its own. She doesn't so much enter the song as float into it, guided by Valentin's flute, and her voice just shimmers. It's a captivating sound, and at the time it was groundbreaking. The Grusin-Rosen production has elegance and momentum. This was the kind of record I was counting on GRP to deliver, and Angela was a real discovery. She did a lovely version of the Gwen Guthrie and Patrick Grant song "This Time I'll Be Sweeter," and while her original songs weren't crafted like radio hits, they showed genuine melodic flair. I thought it was a strong debut, and the follow-up, *Angel of the Night,* did even better, hitting number two on the jazz side and crossing over to become a Top 10 R&B album.

In between Angela's second and third albums, she left GRP and signed directly to Arista. As you'd expect, this led to some tension between Dave and Larry and myself, but I didn't want to lose Angie and I believed she could be an even bigger crossover star. So I put her in the studio with Narada Michael Walden for her 1981 Arista debut, *Something About You,* a Top 5 jazz album, followed by another collaboration with Walden, *Too Tough,* with a title track that made her a bona fide R&B and dance music star.

GRP's streak continued with the trumpeter Tom Browne's 1979 debut, *Browne Sugar,* still another Top 10 jazz album for the label, and on 1980's *Love Approach* they came up with an instantly infectious and funky track, "Funkin' for Jamaica (N.Y.)." I didn't make the deal with Grusin and Rosen because I expected them to deliver hits for R&B radio and dance clubs, but however surprised I might have been, I did have the feeling that this could be more than a candidate for airplay on jazz radio. Arista's urban and dance promotion departments ran with it, and the track exploded, becoming GRP's first number-one R&B single, as well as a Top 10 dance track. And the album went to number one on both the jazz and R&B charts. It's always an event when a record breaks loose from its genre, and it's those left-field hits that remind you to stay alert, and listen to everything on every album. You never know what track will trigger a response and perform beyond everyone's expectations.

With Valentin, Bofill, and Browne, GRP gave Arista a foothold in the world of progressive pop-jazz, and we added our own artist that fit the genre when we signed a group called the Jeff Lorber Fusion in 1979. We released Lorber's *Water Sign* that year, and it did really well. The next year, the group's *Wizard Island* went to number one on the jazz charts. All the songs on those albums were written by Lorber, with one exception, "Fusion Juice" on *Wizard Island*. That track was composed by a new addition to the group, a young saxophone and flute player named Kenny Gorelick, who was to stay with the Lorber group for only one more album, *Galaxian*. That was also the final album made under the Jeff Lorber Fusion name, but Jeff continued to make his mark as a solo artist. So did his former sideman.

Arista wrapped up the decade by directly signing, and breaking, a major R&B artist: Raydio, built around the singer-songwriter-musician-producer Ray Parker, Jr., who would emerge as one of the most consistent R&B hit-makers—with considerable crossover success—of the late Seventies into the Eighties. It all began, as things so often do, with hearing one undeniable song, the very catchy and clever "Jack and Jill." At the time, Parker was an in-demand session guitarist. He'd played on numerous hits for Holland-Dozier-Holland's label after they left Motown, was part of Barry White's studio group, and toured as a sideman for Stevie Wonder. He also started to write songs that were attracting attention, including "You Got the Love," co-written with Chaka Khan for the group Rufus, a big crossover smash in 1974. So I was aware of him; I'd seen his name on album credits, and when a tape reached me with some of his demos, I was immediately impressed. I set up a meeting with him to go over his material, and although he wasn't presenting himself as an artist, I asked him to record "Jack and Jill" for Arista. He was very surprised by the offer and said he didn't consider himself a great singer. Maybe he wasn't technically an outstanding vocalist, but there was a charm about him that came through effortlessly in his singing, and he was good-looking. I saw him as someone who could develop into a real artist. I thought it made sense to work with him as a vehicle for his own material, to put him center stage.

Ray had some terms to propose. He didn't want the record to be under his name, and he created a group identity, Raydio, for the project. And he wanted to be his own producer. This was an unusual request for someone who'd never produced a hit for anyone before, and I was a bit hesitant to give him that type of control in the studio. But I liked the overall approach of what he'd done on his demos, and I finally agreed. I just had a feeling about him, and that's how he ended up singing, writing, producing, and playing guitar on his first album. Everyone mentions how Prince negotiated that kind of contract with Warner Bros., and how daring it was for a label to give an unknown artist all the keys to the store, but the fact is that we did just that with Ray almost a year before Prince came out with his first single, "Soft and Wet." I announced the Raydio signing at the 1977 Arista convention in San Diego, and played "Jack and Jill" for the national staff of the label, convinced that we had a big hit on the horizon.

It's rare when a debut single by an R&B artist is accepted out of the box by pop radio. Ray, however, had a pop sensibility, and the whole story of Jack and Jill was a familiar premise told in a fresh way. Pop radio jumped on it, and in early 1978, it was Top 10 in both formats. Over the next few years Ray kept making hits that defied the boundaries of R&B and pop: "You Can't Change That," "A Woman Needs Love (Just Like You Do)," and "The Other Woman" were all R&B and pop Top 10 singles. And his image evolved, step by step. On the second and third Raydio albums, Ray was prominently shown on the cover, and the other band members were clearly the supporting cast. Then, on *A Woman Needs Love,* the cover was a close-up of Ray seducing the camera and now the billing was "Ray Parker Jr. and Raydio." The album after that, no more Raydio. It took half a decade, but finally we had a Ray Parker, Jr., album.

For all his success, there were a few bumps. At the beginning of MTV, the channel didn't make much room for black artists. It's been well documented that black music wasn't as well represented as rock and pop, and it took a while for that nonexplicit but nonetheless quite real barrier to crumble. In 1982, for the title track from *The Other Woman,* Ray made a conceptual video with dancing corpses and vampires, well before "Thriller," and MTV wouldn't play it. Not because the song wasn't a hit—it was number four on the pop charts; we were told, off the record, that it was too controversial. The corpses weren't a problem, but Ray's white leading lady was. Musical crossover was one thing; implied interracial sexual crossover was another. So that video had to be replaced by one more palatable, a straight-ahead performance of the song. We like to pretend that in the music world there's more enlightenment, more color blindness, but there was definitely a conservative streak when it came to getting black artists on AOR radio and MTV.

In 1984, Parker made the record that no one, not even MTV, could ignore: "Ghostbusters," from the blockbuster film, was an enormous hit single, with a heavy-rotation video and from a hugely popular soundtrack album. I have to confess that when it was first played for me, I was a little worried that it was too much of a novelty record. Certainly there's nothing inherently commercial about the title, the lyrics are a little silly, and the production is extremely pop. However, it has that "Who ya gonna call?" hook, it's ridiculously catchy, and when I saw a screening of the film, there was no question that we should release it as a single and assemble a soundtrack album. The all-star video—Chevy Chase, Peter Falk, Danny DeVito, Carly Simon, and John Candy were among the celebrities shouting "Ghostbusters!"—didn't hurt, either. The single went to number one, the song earned Parker an Oscar nomination (he lost to his old employer Stevie Wonder), and the soundtrack went platinum.

To capitalize on *Ghostbusters,* Arista put together a career-spanning Ray Parker, Jr., *Chartbusters* album. It became his sixth and, as it turned out, final gold album for us. There was one final studio album, *Sex and the Single Man,* and then he left Arista to sign with Geffen Records. Unknown to me, David Geffen had begun pursuing Ray, and offered him a big seven-figure payment if Parker would agree to sign immediately, even though Ray still owed us one more album. The Geffen deal would commence right after he delivered that last album to us. It wasn't that we refused to match the offer, or that we didn't want to negotiate. We weren't told about it until after Ray had signed. I know it's a competitive business, and I've been on the other side of the table making that kind of proposal to artists who still owe product to their labels, but I couldn't help but be disappointed. When people talk about the big R&B artists of the late Seventies and Eighties, you hear about Michael Jackson, Prince, Rick James, and there's no denying that they're the pinnacle. They changed everything radically, made history. Still, for a long stretch of time, Ray Parker, Jr., was right there in the mix, consistently generating hits with independence and single-mindedness.

Before recording each album, Ray would meet me in my bungalow and he'd play me his new songs. Each song would always have a lyric that would trigger at the least a wide smile, but most usually an enthusiastic guffaw. He was clever and smart and had an innocence about him while being slyly wicked at the same time. I provided little creative input, maybe occasionally suggesting getting more edge in a particular lyric. Overall, it was a very strong run of songs from "Jack and Jill" through "Ghostbusters," and Ray was the first artist to plant Arista's feet solidly in the world of R&B.

Broadway, Soundtracks, and Comedy

Piece by piece, we were assembling a label that had the breadth and stature of a major, that could compete with any company in pursuing the most prestigious artists, and that could acquire projects that signaled my determination to be involved in almost every musical area, and some nonmusical as well. One thing that was clear to me from my years at Columbia was that diversity was key. While I was developing artists, or waiting for them to deliver new albums, I was always on the lookout for albums that came from other sources, from movies, television, Broadway, comedy. That kind of event album could be very meaningful if the stars aligned and the film, show, or comedian burst out of the gate to cause media excitement. The album became part of the experience, a souvenir, something you could listen to again and again to recapture the emotions you had experienced. The era of the blockbuster original-cast album was behind us in the Seventies. Broadway musicals simply weren't generating the kind of lasting songs and chart hits that they were even into the late Sixties with smashes like *Hair* and *Jesus Christ Superstar*. There also hadn't been a comedy-album phenomenon in a while. Nonetheless, I knew that these genres could still reach large audiences. One of the advantages that Columbia Pictures, Arista's parent company, had to offer me was access to its soundtrack albums to help fill out the mission in our early years.

One album I knew I wanted right off the bat was the soundtrack to *Funny Lady*, Barbra Streisand's long-awaited sequel to her starmaking vehicle *Funny Girl*, with new songs by John Kander and Fred Ebb. At the time, 1975, Barbra was as hot as she'd ever been. A year before, she'd had her biggest movie-album success with *The Way We Were*. Getting the rights to *Funny Lady* would be a real coup for a brand-new label. Imagine having the top female singer-actress in the world on a soundtrack album basically upon opening the doors for business. But even though the movie was going to be released by Columbia Pictures, that didn't mean we would automatically get the soundtrack. Historically, artists of substantial importance had always released the soundtrack albums of their films on the label to which they were contracted. No matter what studios the movies were made for, you never saw an Elvis Presley soundtrack album on any label except RCA. Certainly, years later, it would have been unthinkable for the soundtrack to *The Bodyguard* to come out on Warner Bros. Records, even though it was a Warners film, when Whitney Houston was the musical center of the project. But I had worked with Streisand at Columbia. I had introduced her to her producer Richard Perry and to the songs of Laura Nyro and other contemporary songwriters. *Stoney End* proved to be a signal album for her. As a result we had a very good relationship. After many discussions between me and her devoted manager, Marty Erlichman, he and Barbra agreed to let Arista have the album. In talking to Arista's independent distributors about our release schedule, it was really impressive that we were able to announce that we had *Funny Lady* coming up. It definitely put the industry on notice that a special new company was emerging unlike any new label that had begun in years, and it gave us immeasurable credibility in that first year of operation.

Funny Lady became the first Top 10 soundtrack album, and second gold album, in our short history. That same year Arista released the original-cast album from another Kander and Ebb project, the Broadway musical *Chicago*. Once again, I had some history to draw on. While at Goddard Lieberson's side at Columbia, I was involved in the cast album from Kander and Ebb's masterpiece *Cabaret,* which opened in late 1966. *Cabaret* had virtually swept the 1967 Tony Awards, winning eight, including Best Musical and Best Original Score. It seemed to me that *Chicago* had all the makings of a smash hit, including a cast headed by Gwen Verdon, Chita Rivera, and Jerry Orbach, and with first-rate songs: "All That Jazz," "Razzle Dazzle," "Class." With Bob Fosse directing and choreographing, it felt like a no-brainer. I knew one of the producers, Marty Richards, very well and approached him about the rights. This was another competitive situation, and although Arista was new in the game, we prevailed. The Broadway musical is a big part of my cultural DNA, and for me there really is nothing like the opening night of one of those shows. It was definitely a world I wanted Arista to be a part of, and starting out with *Chicago* was starting out with a bang.

When it came to motion picture soundtracks, I was very selective about what we released. Each one had to have some element that made it truly stand out: the film itself, the composer, the opportunity to incorporate and launch hit songs. We had our share of misfires—*1941* is hardly the most auspicious entry in the Steven Spielberg filmography—but we also released some of the most memorable soundtrack albums of the era, including John Williams's majestic score from Spielberg's *Close Encounters of the Third Kind,* and the final Bernard Herrmann score from Martin Scorsese's urban masterpiece *Taxi Driver.* In 1977, we released the soundtrack to *The Greatest,* a biopic about and starring Muhammad Ali. For that film, Michael Masser and Linda Creed wrote a stirring title song, to be sung by George Benson, called "The Greatest Love of All." My promotion staff and I felt that the record had a real shot, and it very nearly reached the top spot on the R&B chart. I can just imagine a certain fourteen-year-old girl in New Jersey hearing that record on the radio and being moved by it, maybe singing it in her room in a young and glorious voice.

The recording artists we were breaking on Arista began to be pursued by music supervisors looking for songs to enhance their films. I found the song "Ready to Take a Chance Again" for Barry Manilow to sing in the Chevy Chase and Goldie Hawn comedy *Foul Play*. Melissa Manchester had a hit with "Through the Eyes of Love" from *Ice Castles*. Each of those songs was nominated for an Oscar, and Arista had the albums from both films. It was ideal synergy. This type of creative interplay between Arista artists and films would deepen and achieve more success in the Eighties and Nineties, long after our connection with Columbia Pictures had ended. Carly Simon contributed to Mike Nichols's hit *Working Girl* and won an Academy Award for Best Original Song. As mentioned in the previous chapter, Ray Parker, Jr., had a smash with the theme from *Ghostbusters*. The rock guitarist Jeff Healey was at the musical center of *Road House,* and LaFace Records assembled a big soundtrack for Eddie Murphy's *Boomerang.* And, of course, Whitney Houston conquered the movie and music worlds with *The Bodyguard, Waiting to Exhale,* and *The Preacher's Wife.* I'll discuss them all as this story rolls on, but I do want to make particular mention of the soundtrack to the 1995 film *Boys on the Side.*

Reflecting the strong female sensibility of the film, we decided to put together an all-woman, all-star album, creating a listening experience that genuinely complemented and enhanced the movie. This wasn't about breaking a big single from the film; it was about an album that could be played from start to finish with a unified feeling, like a series of scenes from a film. Naturally, I wanted two of Arista's most prominent female artists—Annie Lennox and Sarah McLachlan—involved, but I looked outside our roster to put together a powerful lineup of iconic female and female-fronted artists: Bonnie Raitt, Stevie Nicks, Sheryl Crow, the Pretenders, Melissa Etheridge, the Indigo Girls, and Joan Armatrading among them. I remember playing the songs for the director, Herbert Ross, and he was completely blown away by how this music reflected the attitudes and themes of the film. The movie did okay, but our soundtrack companion piece proved to be so much more than that, going platinum and connecting musically regardless of whether people had seen the movie. It was a terrific project, the result of being inspired by the opportunity the movie provided to create something that stood proudly on its own.

Through the Seventies, we were also looking into television for significant opportunities. For example, we had a Grammy-winning soundtrack from *The Muppet Show.* I remember signing the contract for that album and posing for a trade photo shaking hands (well, hand to frog's leg) with Kermit. The album has such Muppet standards as "Mahna Mahna," "Bein' Green," and "The Muppet Show Theme."

Arista's television connection had begun almost immediately, with two teams of artists who used the medium to radically transform sketch comedy in the Seventies: Monty Python and the cast of *Saturday Night Live.* It's been said that comedy was the rock music of that decade. Richard Pryor, Lily Tomlin, Albert Brooks, Monty Python, *National*

Lampoon, the original cast of *SNL,* Andy Kaufman, George Carlin, Steve Martin—it was a golden era of groundbreaking comic art, and like everyone who cared about what was happening, I was aware that this was a renaissance period. I knew that it would be valuable to capture some of that work on record. At Columbia, we'd made albums with the innovative comedy group Firesign Theatre, one of the few nonmusical acts to get airplay on underground rock radio stations and establish a large cult following, and I saw in this wave of comic inspiration a chance to tap into something that was exciting and new. I started by approaching Monty Python.

By the time *Monty Python's Flying Circus* hit the States, it had already run on the BBC from 1969 to 1974. There had never been anything like it, the level of absurdity, the hilarious comic premises, the abrupt transitions and animated segments. The troupe—Graham Chapman, John Cleese, Terry Gilliam, Eric Idle, Terry Jones, and Michael Palin—took modern British humor to the next level. In the spirit of *The Goon Show* and *Beyond the Fringe,* they mixed the cerebral with the ludicrous, building sketches on Proust and Thomas Hardy one minute, doing "silly walks" and dressing in drag the next. It was completely unpredictable, and the collective inspiration of the group had some critics calling them the Beatles of comedy. Attention in the States had been slower in building, although a couple of albums and a 1971 movie of sketches called *And Now for Something Completely Different* had caused a stir in the comedy underground and on college campuses. In late 1973, *Rolling Stone* profiled the Pythons and they appeared on *The Tonight Show,* and the following year PBS stations across the country began airing the entire first series. After reading a rave in *The New York Times,* I first saw the show on Channel 13 in New York, where it became a ratings sensation. It was clear that something was happening, and I wanted Arista to be part of it.

Through their U.S. manager, Nancy Lewis, and their attorney, Ina Meibach, I began discussions about releasing Monty Python albums in America. Although the group was a little skeptical about their chances of breaking through in the States, they signed with Arista in early 1975. Luckily, Michael Palin kept and published diaries throughout the Pythons' career, reminding me as I read through them of what happened during that period. Palin's entries say that in March we threw a press party for the group at Sardi's, where around 150 people were assembled. I'll let him tell the rest of the story: "I had to pinch myself to believe it was all happening. Were we really in Sardi's, the renowned Broadway restaurant, with Clive Davis, the renowned record producer, surrounded by a crowd 'ooohing!' and 'aaahing' with uncertain delight as a not brilliant sketch about Thomas Hardy writing a novel was played over a hastily rigged-up record player system?"

The project we were premiering was *Matching Tie and Handkerchief,* a "three-sided" album: One side was mastered two different ways, so that depending on which groove the needle originally settled down on, one of two alternate "sides" played. This was one infrequently used benefit of the LP format. Since the album didn't have a track listing, this feature would come as a complete surprise to the listener, who might on a future listening hear totally unfamiliar material. In April, when the group came back to New York City for a six-week engagement at City Center, we all went to another party, at the Commodore Hotel. Palin remembers me introducing him to Andy Warhol. Members of Led Zeppelin were there, along with Jeff Beck and Dick Cavett. The Pythons had just finished shooting the film *Monty Python and the Holy Grail,* and were looking for a U.S. distributor.

We continued our association with Monty Python, releasing in 1975 and 1976 *The Album of the Soundtrack of the Trailer of the Film of Monty Python and the Holy Grail* and *Monty Python Live! At City Center.* For a while, the group concentrated on films and solo projects, but they still owed Arista one more album. They took the "owed" part literally, and called that final effort *Monty Python's Contractual Obligation Album.* Reflecting the state of the group at the time, Cleese isn't on the album very much, and Idle is carrying most of the creative weight. It's a consistently funny—and frequently filthy—album that earned them another Grammy nomination. The Pythons were brilliant and built an extraordinary body of work. With all that talent under one roof, they were a true comedic force.

The next shot fired in the comic revolution on TV came live from New York. *Saturday Night,* as the show was called at first, premiered in October 1975, airing from the NBC studios just a few blocks downtown from the new Arista offices on West Fifty-seventh Street. In terms of geography and sensibility it was a perfect fit. On the most obvious level, we were signing artists that got booked on the show, like Loudon Wainwright III, Gil Scott-Heron, and Patti Smith. More broadly, however, it felt as though *SNL* and Arista, along with the creative nightlife that was stretching from the Bowery to midtown to the Bronx, were all part of a revived spirit in a New York that seemed as if it were falling apart just a year or so before. I had met *SNL's* producer, Lorne Michaels, and we became friends. We would go to dinner with members of the *SNL* cast, often at Elaine's, on Second Avenue and Eighty-eighth Street. It was really fascinating for me to experience the repartee and the competitiveness, and to see firsthand the role that Lorne was playing in bringing this entire scene together.

Watching Dan Aykroyd, John Belushi, Chevy Chase, Jane Curtin, Garrett Morris, Laraine Newman, and Gilda Radner perform on the show was like seeing an all-star band play a nonstop set of exceptional material. Week after week, they delivered to a hip, young, live audience of millions. Lorne and I talked about putting together an album that would be like a "greatest hits" of *SNL,* with a monologue by Lily Tomlin; some of the show's most famous sketches with guests like Richard Pryor, Paul Simon, and Peter Boyle; popular characters like Gilda Radner's Emily Litella; and commercial parodies. It ran seamlessly, and in those days before home video, this album was the only way to have the *Saturday Night Live* experience outside of airings of the show. *Saturday Night Live* became the best-selling comedy album of 1976, and earned a Grammy nomination for Best Comedy Album.

Lily Tomlin was another trendsetting, cutting-edge comedic talent of that era. Her 1974 and 1976 ABC specials won Emmys for Outstanding Writing; she was nominated for an Oscar for her film debut in *Nashville;* and she had won the Grammy for Best Comedy Album in 1972. In April 1977 she opened on Broadway in *Appearing Nightly,* an ingenious collection of scenes that were not just comically inspired but insightful, with real dramatic depth. She was the first woman to appear solo in a Broadway show, and she was on the cover of *Time* as

"America's New Queen of Comedy." I adored *Appearing Nightly,* and jumped at the chance to do a combination original-cast/comedy album from the show. Lily has always been eager to stretch and experiment, and the album holds up as a unique document. It was nominated for Best Comedy Album in 1978.

After that run of comedy albums in the Seventies, during which Arista got four Grammy nominations for Best Comedy Album, I never again found the kind of rare, mold-shattering talent that drew me to Monty Python, *SNL,* and Lily Tomlin. I never want to be in the position of signing someone simply to fill a category. My criteria for getting into comedy are no different from looking at a rock band, or a jazz artist, or a pop singer: Is this truly out of the ordinary? Is this going to make a commercial or cultural impact? As much as I like being a part of the Broadway and comedy worlds, it's ultimately about identifying something special. In the decades since the Seventies, I rarely felt that drive to be involved in those areas. Nevertheless, my affection for Broadway is undiminished and I'm always looking for the right project to create a classic new musical. When it came to motion picture soundtracks, however, there were to be some dramatic events ahead.

Dionne Warwick

In the late Seventies it was really a thrill to help revive the career of Dionne Warwick, whom I consider to be one of the greatest pop singers of all time. Dionne, of course, initially made her mark in the Sixties with a spectacular run of hit singles, almost all of them composed by the legendary songwriting team of Burt Bacharach and Hal David. Those songs, including "Anyone Who Had a Heart," "Walk On By," "Alfie," "I Say a Little Prayer," and "Do You Know the Way to San Jose," are so melodically complex that Dionne's unique gift was to make them sound conversational and intimate. They are only bravura performances in their extraordinary subtlety. I don't know any other singer who could have floated through those lyrics the way that she did. If you weren't paying attention, you could easily miss how brilliant her renditions were. Only a world-class singer could make those songs sound so simple and true. The greatest gift songwriters can have is a singer who can bring across their material so effortlessly, and in providing Dionne with such winning songs, Bacharach and David clearly understood that.

However, by 1978 Dionne unbelievably was prepared to consider ending her career as a recording artist and just concentrate on performing live. When I met her around that time she was not signed to a label and she had given up on the record business. Her early signature hits had been on Scepter Records, and she had signed with Warner Bros. in 1972. Her deal there ended in 1977, and she just didn't see any prospects for herself. Disco was dominating radio and the charts, and she could not imagine getting airplay for the kind of quality pop songs that she loved to sing.

My situation and perspective were different. My success in finding hits for Barry Manilow and Melissa Manchester had made me a lightning rod for publishers and songwriters who were hungry for artists who could take their music to the top of the charts. With a member of my A&R staff, I would meet with music publishers who would play us their best available new songs. To this day I always insist that they also bring a lyric sheet for each song. While a lot of today's electronic dance music may not be dependent on lyrics, most hit song candidates are. Naturally you're listening for the musical hook, the chorus that is instantly familiar and irresistible and that literally compels you to sing along. But to me what is equally important is gauging the lyric's emotional payoff. Very often the hook can be there but the lyric is banal, dated, commonplace, or "so what." I would keep refining my criteria, and this process was working. I was building a proven track record, but the problem was that I had few opportunities for the songs that moved me. Barry had limited me to two outside songs per album, and Melissa, with rare exceptions, really only wanted to record her own songs. As a result, I had built up a backlog of great songs, and, out of respect for the songwriters, I could only hold on to them for so long without placing them with a major artist.

That's the dilemma I was facing when I heard "I'll Never Love This Way Again," written by Richard Kerr and Will Jennings. I knew it met every criterion and could be a big hit and that I had to find a home for it. It was intended for Manilow, but I already had more than enough songs on hold for him for a few years of albums. The song had been recorded before, including by Kerr himself, but had not made an impact. (Kerr, as you may recall, had co-written "Mandy," Barry's first hit.) That really didn't faze me, as I felt confident that with the right singer and with the right arrangement and production it could be a smash. So I was in a quandary. I yearned to find a classic, timeless artist whose talent could still explode up the charts. I loved the opportunity to show how long a career can last and I knew it could be as rewarding as identifying future stars. In this case I wanted to give it to a female singer so that it wouldn't compete with Barry. I asked myself, Who's not making records who should still be making records? Dionne Warwick was still in her thirties. How could it be possible that her career as a recording artist was finished?

When I first approached Dionne about signing with Arista, she was a little reluctant. She had given up on the music business, she told me. I understood why she might say something like that, but I told her that the music business had not given up on her. As far as I was concerned, she could still be a major star and I would do everything I could to make that happen. Dionne was thankful—she really wanted to hear just that. Once a singer has reached the heights that she had attained, they always secretly believe that it's possible to hit that peak again. But I wasn't simply telling Dionne what she wanted to hear. I not only knew it could be true, I had the song to make it happen.

When I played "I'll Never Love This Way Again" for Dionne, she immediately loved it. I knew that Barry Manilow was a major fan of Dionne's, so I asked him if he would be willing to produce the track for her. He jumped at the chance. In fact, Barry produced Dionne's entire first Arista album, which came out in 1979, titled simply *Dionne*. "I'll Never Love This Way Again," the first single from it, went to number five, selling more than a million copies. The second single from the album, "Déjà Vu," written by Isaac Hayes and Adrienne Anderson, entered the Top 20. The album itself achieved platinum sales, and Dionne achieved something no female artist had ever accomplished before: She won Grammys for Best Pop Vocal Performance, Female ("I'll Never Love This Way Again") and Best R&B Vocal Performance, Female ("Déjà Vu") in the same year. (Ironically, one of the artists Dionne beat out for Best Pop Vocal was Melissa Manchester, who had been nominated for "Don't Cry Out Loud.")

Maintaining that momentum was not automatic. Veteran artists always represent a challenge in that regard. Dionne's next album, *No Night So Long,* entered the Top 40, as did its title track. She scored another Top 40 hit in 1981 with "Friends in Love," a duet with the inimitable Johnny Mathis. Fortunately, a timeless pop singer with genuine mainstream appeal such as Dionne has additional opportunities to make a significant impact. In January 1980, Dionne co-hosted a two-hour television special called *Solid Gold '79,* which turned into a weekly hour-long music show that she co-hosted into 1981, and then again in 1985–86. That exposure kept her in the public eye and helped maintain her commercial appeal.

I continued to believe Dionne was capable of having big hit records, so I was constantly on the lookout for material for her. One of my best finds came to me in a most unlikely way. Three or four times a year I visited my aunt Jeanette, who, a few years after the death of her husband, Jerry, had married a close childhood friend of hers, Lenny Pines. As I've mentioned, my aunt had been a substitute mother to me after my own mother passed away, and our relationship was extremely close. She had moved into Lenny's Fort Lauderdale home, and their late-in-life romance was quite the fabled story. Lenny was the driving force that built his father's company, Hebrew National, into a nationally known brand. They lived in a beautiful home, and my family and I were always welcome to stay there. Barry Gibb of the Bee Gees lived with his family in Miami Beach and had heard of my frequent visits to his corner of the world. He called and invited me to lunch with him at his home.

At the time Barry's career was at its apex. Not only had the Bee Gees a few years earlier ignited their all-time success with *Saturday Night Fever,* but he, as a peerless songwriter and producer, had just enjoyed a towering triumph producing the Barbra Streisand album *Guilty.* I was bowled over to learn out of the blue that he wanted to work on a project with me and produce an album for me. I came to the lunch prepared with an alphabetized artist roster in my vest pocket. After a delightful meal with Barry and his wife, Linda, we turned to discuss which artist he would most like to work with. Out came the roster, and I anxiously awaited his response as he perused it. I had to bide my time and wait until he reached *W* and saw Dionne's name. He immediately broke into a wide grin and professed his love, respect, and admiration for her. That was it. He would immediately get to work and send me a demo of a song for her. I really couldn't believe it could be that simple, and when I heard that I'd get the demo in ten days, I stared at him in disbelief. Sure enough, well within the ten-day period came "Heartbreaker," written with his brothers Maurice and Robin. I totally flipped out. I loved the song, and the "demo" Barry sent me was as fully realized as any I've ever heard. It was perfectly arranged, and it truly sounded like a Bee Gees big hit single. It was so hard to believe that he was giving it to me on a silver platter for Dionne.

I immediately called Dionne and played it for her over the phone. In her memoir, Dionne claims that she didn't like the song and consented to do it only because she heard my passion loud and clear, she trusted me, and she was confident that the Bee Gees knew what a hit record was. Maybe she was only being polite on the phone, but I was totally taken in and vividly remember her fully sharing my enthusiasm. I was determined to have her record the song before Barry changed his mind, and she readily agreed. I want to mention here something that Barry Gibb did that touched me then, and the memory of it touches me now. When I called him back to say that Dionne would love to do the song, I asked him when Dionne should come to Miami to record it with him. After all, Barry was the hottest producer in the world, and he'd written a potential hit song that he clearly could have kept for the Bee Gees. He impressed me forever by saying, "Look, Clive, I'll go wherever Dionne wants to record. She's the artist and she's a woman. I'm at her service." If anything defines class, that surely does. Barry held all the cards here but chose to act with grace and thoughtfulness, and meant it. In the end, Dionne did record in Miami, but it was her choice only. Then, just as Barry Manilow had with the *Dionne* album, Barry Gibb wanted to be involved in the entire album, which ended up being titled *Heartbreaker*. He co-produced the album with Karl Richardson and Albhy Galuten, co-wrote six of its ten songs with his brothers, and co-wrote three others with Galuten, who had worked extensively with the Bee Gees. The title track was a big hit around the world, and the album went gold and was a bona fide worldwide hit as well.

When you're talking about a rare talent like Dionne, who influenced so many of the singers who came after her, there is no shortage of significant artists who want to work with her. Among her greatest admirers was Luther Vandross, and I arranged for him to produce her next album, *How Many Times Can We Say Goodbye*, which came out in 1983. Luther wrote or co-wrote half the songs on the album, including the title track, a Top 40 hit on which he sang with Dionne. For her next album, *Finder of Lost Loves*, I reunited her with Burt Bacharach, who was now married to and co-writing with Carole Bayer Sager. The couple wrote the album's title track, which was the theme for a short-lived Aaron Spelling TV show of the same name, and Stevie Wonder and Barry Manilow each performed duets with Dionne on the album.

The best, however, was yet to come. Dionne's next project would have an impact far beyond her own career, and far beyond the world of music. By 1985 the AIDS epidemic had hit with devastating force, and it was all the more terrifying for being so little understood. Thousands of people were sick or had died, and very little had been learned about where the disease had come from or how it had spread. Even worse, if that's possible, the fear and ignorance surrounding it had created an atmosphere in which even many progressive people refused to come forward to do benefits or make contributions. AIDS had leveled the creative industries, but even there, people were reluctant to take a stand. That hesitancy, unfortunately, had much to do with people's fears of being linked to a disease that at that point was associated almost exclusively with gay people, intravenous drug users, and minorities.

Something needed to be done. I spoke to Dionne and she was more than ready to get involved. She had already participated that year in the "We Are the World" project to fight hunger in Africa, and a renewed sense of social commitment was in the air. Now we needed a song that could not only raise money and awareness but would serve as a theme for the willingness of the music community to let its voice be heard on this critically important issue. "That's What Friends Are For," written by Bacharach and Sager, had been end-credit music for the 1982 film *Night Shift*. Rod Stewart had sung the song, but it came and went without consequence. It was ideal for our purposes, however. I knew that Dionne could do a beautiful job with the song, and if we coupled her with some other sympathetic superstars, we would have the makings of something very special.

Dionne contacted Stevie Wonder and Gladys Knight, and both immediately agreed to do it. I wrote a letter to Elton John explaining everything, and Dionne ran into him in a supermarket. He agreed to participate on the spot. What I love about the artists' performances on that song is that, for all the star power on hand, they are all working in service to the song's message. Elegance, restraint, genuine sincerity, and hopefulness shine through, all virtues perfectly suited to the cause that brought the group together. The single, credited to Dionne and Friends, went straight to number one, and all proceeds from it were donated to the American Foundation for AIDS Research (amfAR). When I say all proceeds I mean every penny—not only the artists, but the composers, the record company, the musicians, and everyone involved at every level worked for free. More than $3 million was raised. Stevie, Gladys, Elton, and Dionne won Grammys for Best Pop Performance by a Duo or Group with Vocal, and, as the songwriters, Bacharach and Sager won for Song of the Year. *Friends,* the album on which the song appeared, rose to number twelve and went gold. Most rewarding of all, Mathilde Krim, the founder of amfAR, told me that the vast majority of the organization's funding for its first two years of essential work came from the proceeds from "That's What Friends Are For." In response I can only say what I thought the first time I heard it: That title says it all.

Dionne continued to record for Arista through the mid-Nineties, but, as so often happens, even a run as good as ours eventually came to an end. I served as executive producer on her 1987 album *Reservations for Two,* and "Love Power," her duet with Jeffrey Osborne on that record, was a Top 20 hit, the last one she would have. She made a beautiful album, *Dionne Warwick Sings Cole Porter,* in 1990, that the great Arif Mardin produced. Though it wasn't as commercially successful as I would have hoped, it served as an inspiration for the *Great American Songbook* albums I would later make with Rod Stewart.

My relationship with Dionne continues both in its depth of affection and its mutual appreciation. "That's What Friends Are For" became the theme of Arista's star-studded fifteenth-anniversary celebration, which took place at Radio City Music Hall in 1990 and became a two-hour CBS television special. Dionne and her cousin Whitney Houston closed the show, and all the others who had appeared earlier joined them for the memorable finale. In 2011, I devoted the closing performance of my annual pre-Grammy party to celebrating Dionne's fifty incredible years in the music business. As I said when I first signed her, she may have given up on the music business all those years ago, but a singer of her talent and grace will always represent the very best of what the music industry can produce.

The Queen of Soul

One spectacular, if completely unintended, consequence of my working with Dionne Warwick is that it called me to the attention of Aretha Franklin. Aretha, of course, had altered the course of popular music with her monumental string of hits in the Sixties on Atlantic Records, masterpieces of soul music that included "Respect," "(You Make Me Feel Like) A Natural Woman," and "Chain of Fools." John Hammond had signed her to Columbia in 1960, but no one at the label knew what to do with her and her incredible voice. She was to spend six years there doing some jazz and pop-R&B, but far too much middle-of-the-road material, including songs like "You Made Me Love You," "Over the Rainbow," and "If Ever I Would Leave You." The records were beautiful, but no one led her to material that would take her to the cutting edge of contemporary music or translate to radio hits. Aretha left Columbia and, in 1967, signed with Atlantic, where Jerry Wexler found the key. He brilliantly produced her, helped her find first-rate material, and guided her to her immortal standing as the Queen of Soul. Their collaboration was a model of how a partnership between an artist and a creative record executive can work.

Wexler continued to produce Aretha through 1975, when he left Atlantic. Their hit-making magic had been diminishing for a few years at that point. Among the last successful singles they did together were "Rock Steady" in 1971 and "Day Dreaming" in 1972. Wexler also worked with her on two Top 10 live albums in the early Seventies: *Aretha Live at Fillmore West* (1971) and *Amazing Grace* (1972). They did have a Top 10 single in 1973 with "Until You Come Back to Me (That's What I'm Gonna Do)," but Jerry and Aretha came to feel that it might be good for her to work with another producer, and agreed that Quincy Jones would be a good choice. Aretha and Quincy made a jazz-oriented album titled *Hey Now Hey (The Other Side of the Sky)*. It was Aretha's first Atlantic album not to enter the Top 25. Aretha also worked with Curtis Mayfield on the *Sparkle* soundtrack album, which he wrote and produced. It generated the hit single "Something He Can Feel," but overall a decline had set in. Somehow Aretha's relevance was being challenged. She made another album with Mayfield, and one with the Motown hit-maker Lamont Dozier, but neither made much of an impact. In an attempt to ride the Seventies dance-music wave, Aretha then collaborated with the producer Van McCoy, composer of the disco classic "The Hustle," on *La Diva*. That album, which came out in 1979, turned out to be the least successful of Aretha's Atlantic years, and it marked the end of her relationship with the label.

To see Aretha's reversal of fortune and the waning of her dominance was dismaying to anyone who had been moved and uplifted by her truly landmark recordings during the Sixties and early Seventies. It seemed as though she were floundering in unknown waters, trying to find a place to fit in. What you hear on *La Diva* and on some of her records leading up to it is less creative confidence and a lack of solid guidance. It probably would not have occurred to me that I could step in to orchestrate a comeback, but in her search for revitalization, Aretha took notice of the revival that Dionne was then enjoying with "I'll Never Love This Way Again" and the *Dionne* album. She got in touch with me, explained her situation, told me that she loved what I had done with Dionne, and, most important of all, described how she once again wanted a collaborative relationship of the sort that she had experienced with Jerry Wexler. She wasn't simply looking for a new deal or a new label. She was looking for a creative partner, someone who would be involved in all aspects of her career—from selecting songs, choosing producers, and recommending duet partners to conceptualizing promotion, marketing, advertising, and publicity strategies. Would I be interested in discussing the possibility of playing that role for her?

Would I? This was the ultimate challenge for me. From day one I always knew that whatever Aretha did would be chronicled as history—the heights she had reached, the influence she had exerted on other artists and on music itself were unparalleled. People toss around a term like "national treasure," but when you're talking about an artist of Aretha's stature there's just no other language you can use. Her singing combines incomparable power and range with the spiritual fervor of gospel, the grit of the street, and the passion and technical facility of opera. For my money, she was quite simply the best singer in the world, an assessment that *Rolling Stone* trumpeted when it voted her the greatest singer of all time in 2008. I had to consider not only her unparalleled musical gifts and relative youth—she was still in her thirties when she left Atlantic—but the responsibility of being entrusted with her future. Could she ever rebound? Was there a place for her in the musical landscape of the Eighties? And if we failed, would it tarnish her legacy? I was nervous and expectant when we met at her home in Los Angeles. She cooked a meal for us, and we talked music nonstop for two hours. I was impressed with her awareness of the current music scene. She listened to the radio all the time and was up to date with her likes and dislikes. She was not at all tentative, and in fact she radiated confidence that she could get back on track. Equally significant to me was her clear desire to be back on top. This was no regal queen content to rest on past laurels. This was a working woman determined to give it her all. I relished the conversation and knew that everything was flowing naturally and smoothly. We had connected, and from that point on we were in business.

As it happens, Aretha experienced a resurgence of her own in 1980 after her explosive performance of "Think" in the *Blues Brothers* movie. It sometimes takes an out-of-context moment like that to remind audiences of how much they miss a beloved star. It renewed attention and generated enthusiasm for her, and served as a perfect setup for her first Arista album, *Aretha* (1980). The album was produced by Arif Mardin and Chuck Jackson, who had both worked with Aretha before. I joined them in looking for material, and while sales didn't go through the roof, the singles "United Together," "Come to Me," and "What a Fool Believes" did well on the R&B charts, reconnected Aretha to her core audience, and reinforced the momentum from *The Blues Brothers*. She also received a Grammy nomination for her absolutely torrid version of Otis Redding's "Can't Turn You Loose." We followed *Aretha* in 1981 with *Love All the Hurt Away,* which Arif Mardin also produced. Once again, the title track, a beautiful duet with George Benson, and a great version of "It's My Turn," written by Michael Masser and Carole Bayer Sager, became R&B hits. We were indeed turning the corner. Album sales were not erupting, but she was once again at the top of the R&B singles charts, and her sizzling cover of Sam and Dave's "Hold On, I'm Comin' " won a Grammy in the Best R&B Vocal Performance, Female category, her first since 1974.

I felt we were doing good work with Aretha, but I knew she and we could do better. For her next album I decided to try something new. I read a story about Luther Vandross in which he said that the three most important singers for him were his idols Dionne Warwick, Aretha Franklin, and Diana Ross. Since two of those women were Arista artists and Luther was emerging as one of the defining figures of soul music in the Eighties, I immediately reached out to him. Luther was a true multidimensional talent. A world-class singer, he also was a first-rate songwriter and producer. He was thrilled to hear from me and instantly seized the opportunity to work with Aretha.

The result was *Jump to It* (1982) the hit album we'd been waiting for. Luther co-produced the record with Aretha, and wrote four of its songs. The title track, which Luther co-wrote with Marcus Miller, was the perfect blend of old and new, striking the exact balance I thought possible when I signed her. It deftly combined the power and verve of Aretha's classic material with the more polished dance rhythms of the Eighties. It became Aretha's first Top 40 hit since 1976, went to number one on the R&B charts, and brought her another Grammy nomination. The album went gold and sat atop the R&B charts for seven weeks. This was the kind of success we needed. It felt so good, and Aretha was really enjoying it.

Luther then produced the 1983 follow-up album, *Get It Right.* It cracked the Top 40, and the title track was another number-one R&B hit. It didn't break into new territory for Aretha, but it did maintain momentum. After all, anytime you have a number-one hit, it's nothing to sneeze at. But we wanted more. Aretha and Luther had clashed as she was recording the vocal for "Get It Right." Aretha is not the sort of singer who likes to do multiple takes. She holds to the doctrine that you get the feeling right the first couple of times you sing the song. After that, you're simply trying to recapture what you had in the first place. Luther, on the other hand, was a modern-day studio perfectionist. He felt that he had helped restore Aretha to her former glory and had earned the right to direct how her vocal should go. Aretha pointed out that Luther had learned his own vocal style from her records, and that she had been an international star for years before anyone knew who Luther Vandross was. They strongly expressed these views to each other, and then Aretha walked out of the New York studio, threatening to fly home to Detroit. I intervened, not for the last time, and encouraged Luther to apologize, which he did, though Aretha initially insisted it was "halfhearted." But she, too, apologized, and the record finally got done. I go into this confrontation only to give a flavor of what happened. I must add that these fireworks were only temporary. Aretha and Luther loved and had enormous respect for each other, and when each was to look back at the experience, it was remembered with the warmth and nostalgia of a family fight that only led to a better end result. So where would we venture next?

I had worked well with the songwriter and producer Narada Michael Walden on albums by Angela Bofill and Phyllis Hyman, and I knew that he was dying to work with Aretha. I arranged for their collaboration, and the happy result was *Who's Zoomin' Who?* (1985), a Top 20 album and a million-seller. It was Aretha's first album ever to be certified platinum. The album's singles all performed brilliantly. "Freeway of Love," co-written by Walden and featuring Clarence Clemons of the E Street Band on saxophone, rose to number three and brought Aretha a Grammy for Best R&B Vocal Performance, Female. The title track, which Aretha co-wrote with Walden and his writing partner Preston Glass, cracked the Top 10. (Aretha had come up with the title phrase, inspired by a boyfriend who thought he was getting over on her, when perhaps the opposite was true.) *Who's Zoomin' Who?* was an undeniable smash. The album's third major hit came to me through Annie Lennox of the Eurythmics. She and Dave Stewart had written "Sisters Are Doin' It for Themselves," a feminist anthem that they dreamed they could record as a duet with Aretha. I always revered the Eurythmics, and I thought the song was perfect for Annie and Aretha. I was determined to make it happen. Despite the Eurythmics' prominence at the time, I doubt Aretha was familiar with them, and at first she said that scheduling problems would make it difficult for her to record the song. I persisted and told her that the song would undoubtedly be a hit, and she really had to find the time to do it. In matters like this Aretha trusted me, and when I stayed on an idea she would eventually come around, as she did in this case. Dave and Annie flew to Detroit to record the track with her. The song became a Top 20 hit and a video sensation. Aretha was making her biggest impact since her Sixties heyday.

Since Aretha and Narada had been so successful and got along so well, he returned to produce her next album, *Aretha* (1986). That album included "I Knew You Were Waiting (for Me)," a duet with George Michael and Aretha's first number-one single since "Respect" in 1967. George and Aretha were unlikely duet partners; she was more than twenty years older, among several other disparities. I had run into him at a major awards ceremony in London, and he told me that I had an artist he very much wanted to sing with. I assumed he was talking about Whitney Houston, who had just emerged as a worldwide sensation, but he quickly added, "It's not who you think. It's not Whitney. I love her. She's great. But I'm talking about Aretha Franklin." Initially, I was really taken aback. Then, as I pondered it, I thought, This guy is really smart. He's twenty-two years old, and he's trying to establish himself as a solo artist after being in Wham!, an extremely successful, but somewhat bubblegum pop group. Because Wham! were perceived in certain quarters as lightweight, many people didn't realize how terrific a singer George is. Their preconceptions colored what they heard, and they could only see him as a pretty boy. What better way, George must have thought, to make people take notice of his talent than to duet with an iconic singer with unimpeachable credibility? As a concept it was certainly ballsy and shrewd. Meanwhile, from the other perspective, it would be great for Aretha to reach a young audience all over the world that George would inevitably bring with him. I was sold. So I said, "Well, do you have the song?" He simply said, "No, I hear you do that, so perhaps you could come up with the song. Just know that I'll be there when you find something good." I immediately put the word out to the publishing community, and Tom Sturges, who was at

Chrysalis Music at the time, came up with "I Knew You Were Waiting (for Me)," written by Simon Climie and Dennis Morgan. George and Aretha both loved it, and he flew to Detroit to record it with her. It accomplished everything we hoped it would and more. The song won a Grammy for Best R&B Vocal Performance by a Duo or Group and the album won for Best R&B Vocal Performance, Female. The album went gold and sold close to a million copies.

Aretha's soulful version of the Rolling Stones' "Jumpin' Jack Flash" also appeared on *Aretha,* and it grazed the Top 20. The song served as the theme of the 1986 film *Jumpin' Jack Flash,* starring Whoopi Goldberg. Keith Richards and Ron Wood flew to Detroit to record the song with Aretha and appear in the video. Keith, who produced the song, insisted that Aretha play piano on the track, just as Jerry Wexler had her do on the classic songs they recorded together in the Sixties. Aretha didn't allow sitting at the keyboard to dampen her sense of style for the video shoot. "But how does a lady dress for a video with the Stones?" Aretha asked in her memoir. The answer? "How 'bout tiger-striped tights, superbad black leather jacket, and a purple punked-up hairdo with a funky ponytail hanging to the side?" She looked sensational, and the track rocked to the core.

Aretha had asked me if I thought Andy Warhol would do a portrait of her for the cover of *Aretha,* and I told her that I would ask him. Andy and I had become friendly around the time I signed Lou Reed and Patti Smith. We would run into each other at Studio 54 and would always chat—by chat, I mean I would speak and he would listen intently, nod, and occasionally mutter a word or two. It was a little enigmatic, but he always seemed pleased to see me and eager for me to talk.

I got a call one day from Andy's friend and colleague the writer Bob Colacello, who told me that Andy would love to have lunch with me. So I arranged to meet him one day at the Russian Tea Room, and Bob joined us. At the lunch, Bob and I spoke enthusiastically about the worlds of music and media, and, as usual, Andy listened intently, nodded, and occasionally contributed a word or two. In a crowded club where it was hard to hear, that behavior didn't seem so strange, but over lunch with just three people in a beautiful, well-lit restaurant, it was a little unsettling. I didn't know what to think. Afterward, I called Bob and said, "Okay, what's the verdict? Did we have a good time at lunch?" Without missing a beat, Bob replied, "Andy told me he had a fantastic time! He got such a kick out of the conversation, and all the gossip and information we shared. Anytime you want to have lunch with him, just say the word. He would love to see you again."

On the strength of that recommendation, I felt quite comfortable calling Andy and asking if he would do a portrait of Aretha for the album cover. He immediately agreed, and delivered an excellent piece. Both Aretha and I loved it. After the album had been out a few months, I called Andy to tell him how much I liked the cover and to ask about buying the original artwork. How much would it cost? He told me he wasn't sure and would get back to me. He called back the next day and told me that the price would be the same he was charging Deborah Harry of Blondie, for whom he had also done a cover portrait: $25,000. I obviously should have said that was fine, and arranged to purchase the piece. I don't know what came over me, but instead of doing that, I stupidly asked, "Would I get five thousand dollars' credit for the fee we paid to use it for the album cover?" He replied, "Oh, I don't really know. Let me look into it." I was never to hear back from him, since very shortly afterward Andy died. In addition to the real sadness I felt at his very unnecessary death, I felt really dumb for trying to save $5,000 on an artwork I would have loved to own. To drive home even more powerfully the lesson about being penny-wise and pound-foolish, I was recently in a first-class restaurant at Park Avenue and Fifty-third Street called Casa Lever. On the wall was the Warhol portrait of Aretha. Without going into the backstory, I inquired about it, and asked the restaurant's manager if he happened to know how much it was worth. His answer: $3.7 million. I lost my appetite and, good and hospitable as the restaurant is, I have difficulty going back there.

For her next release, Aretha decided that she wanted to do a live gospel double album, similar to the one she had done in 1972 titled *Amazing Grace*. That might seem like a counterintuitive move, given how successful *Who's Zoomin Who?* and *Aretha* had been, and it might not have been what I would have recommended if she had asked me. But gospel music lives deep within Aretha's soul, and this album was something that she felt she had to do. If you're going to work with an artist of her stature, it's essential that she believe that your understanding of her goes well beyond sales. Unless you're a fool, you don't tell Bruce Springsteen that he can't take a left turn and make an album like *Nebraska*. And you don't tell Aretha Franklin that she can't make a gospel album. Especially since *Amazing Grace* has sold more than 2 million copies, making it the most successful album of Aretha's career.

Despite its quality, *One Lord, One Faith, One Baptism* (1987) did not remotely approach that sales figure. One reason might be the title Aretha chose for it. "Amazing Grace" is a song that everyone knows, and even if someone isn't a Christian or even religious at all, the song's message of redemption is universal. I'm sure it wasn't Aretha's intent, but *One Lord, One Faith, One Baptism* draws a much harder line in the sand between believers and nonbelievers. If there is only "one faith," how are you supposed to feel if your beliefs don't conform to it? Still, Aretha did a beautiful job with the album, both as a performer and a producer. It brought her a Grammy for Best Female Soul Gospel Performance and earned another for Jesse Jackson, who delivers a fiery sermon on it.

In 1987 Aretha was inducted into the Rock and Roll Hall of Fame, the first woman to receive that honor. She had planned to attend the ceremony, but just a couple of days beforehand she called to ask me if I would accept the award on her behalf. In recent years she had developed a phobia about flying, and she didn't feel up to the long bus ride from Detroit to New York. I strongly encouraged her to deal with her fears and go accept the award herself, and also perform at the now legendary jam that takes place at the end of the night. She told me she just couldn't do it, much as she would have liked to be there. So of course I was proud to represent her on that illustrious night, and proud that she had received such a prestigious honor. To say that she earned it would be a vast understatement.

For *Through the Storm* (1989), Aretha's last album of the Eighties, we brought back Narada Michael Walden to produce, along with Arif Mardin. A host of guest stars graced the album, including James Brown, the Four Tops, and Kenny G. Elton John dueted with Aretha on the title track, a Diane Warren song, which became a Top 20 hit.

Diane also composed "It Isn't, It Wasn't, It Ain't Never Gonna Be," on which Whitney Houston, who had become a superstar by this point, performed with Aretha. Whitney's mother, Cissy Houston, had sung background for Aretha with the Sweet Inspirations, so their relationship went back a long way. In fact, Aretha was Whitney's godmother. Aretha was "Aunt Ree" to Whitney, and Whitney was known to Aretha by her childhood nickname, Nippy. Whitney had spoken of how prominent an influence Aretha had been on her singing, so their performing together was much anticipated. For whatever reason, the artistic chemistry between them never really ignited. There might have been too much difference in maturity and experience. To many, the record was certainly a good one, but magic just didn't happen. Aretha later wrote, "I think Nippy felt unappreciated, and nothing could have been further from the truth."

Aretha's 1992 album *What You See Is What You Sweat* underperformed, despite containing some strong material, including the beautiful "I Dreamed a Dream," from the musical *Les Miserables*. When the newly elected President Clinton invited Aretha to perform during his inauguration celebrations in January 1993, Aretha invited me to accompany her, and we discussed what she should sing. Given the great happiness we both felt that a Democrat was going to be in the White House for the first time in twelve years, "I Dreamed a Dream" seemed an ideal choice. Little did I realize how even my high expectations for what Aretha might do on a historic evening like that were going to be dwarfed by the brilliance of her actual performance. I vividly remember her standing on the stage in a floor-length yellow gown, masterfully building her performance, altering the lyric to "I Had a Dream," chillingly turning the song into a potent reminder of Rev. Martin Luther King, Jr.'s, inspiring message, and the responsibility of the new president to live up to those sacred ideals. It was something only an artist of Aretha's genius could do. Working the stage in the packed arena with total confidence, she electrified the crowd, which roared its approval when she finished. She looked beautiful and sounded amazing, and I got goosebumps watching her. It was easily one of the most magical and memorable performances I have ever seen. Of course, in January

2009, Aretha delivered a spellbinding performance of "My Country 'Tis of Thee" outdoors at the Lincoln Memorial to help celebrate the election of the first African-American president, Barack Obama.

In 1994 Aretha achieved another career milestone: a Grammy Lifetime Achievement Award. Even when such honors are fully merited and, in Aretha's case certainly, inevitable, they still deliver a great thrill when they arrive. To mark that event, we assembled a greatest hits collection drawn from her Arista years, 1980–94. One track we added to that compilation was "Willing to Forgive," a lovely ballad co-written and co-produced by Kenny "Babyface" Edmonds. The song became a Top 40 hit and helped drive the collection to more than a million sales. Aretha would work with Babyface again on "It Hurts Like Hell," a track on the brilliant *Waiting to Exhale* soundtrack, which he produced.

Let me reflect here that I'm under no illusion about my role in Aretha's career. I recognize that her legendary reputation primarily rests on the groundbreaking records she made with Jerry Wexler at Atlantic in the Sixties. Even the greatest artists most often achieve that kind of seismic cultural impact only once in a lifetime, and it would have been impossible to re-create it. Radio had forever changed and what the public wanted to hear was totally different. The extraordinary quality of the music she made then was just one factor of her uniqueness. The emergence of the civil rights movement and soul music's transition into the mainstream were elements as well, and you have no control over forces like that. You can't remake history.

But my major objective was to help extend the artistic life of a landmark artist, not only by having hit records with her but by making her relevant to contemporary audiences without pandering to trends. Fans who had grown up with Aretha could continue to enjoy the music she made on Arista, and new generations of younger listeners were able to discover her. She once again became a vital presence on radio and even MTV, a classic artist actively engaging current audiences. With the passage of time, many stellar artists come to be more admired than listened to. That was not the case with Aretha. It was an especially gratifying moment for me when Jerry Wexler wrote in his memoir, "And my hat is off to Clive Davis. Teaming Aretha with Arif Mardin, Luther Vandross

('Jump to It'), and Narada Michael Walden ('Freeway of Love'), Clive brought Lady Soul back to the charts; her pairing with George Michael ('I Knew You Were Waiting') was a smash." To know that Jerry appreciated the work Aretha and I did together means a lot.

Aretha and I were not done yet. She hadn't made a studio album in six years when we released *A Rose Is Still a Rose* in 1998. Music was continuing to evolve, and soul music had been profoundly affected by the beats and production techniques of hip-hop. The goal for this project was for Aretha to collaborate with some of the freshest, most innovative talents on the neo-soul scene. Among the artists, songwriters, and producers who contributed to the album were Lauryn Hill, Sean "Puffy" Combs, Dallas Austin, Kelly Price, Jermaine Dupri, and Darryl Simmons. The standout track is the title song, which Lauryn Hill wrote and produced. It brought Aretha back to the charts, nearly four decades after she'd had her first hit, and helped the album earn a gold record. The song was even a number-one hit on the dance charts!

It's a powerful testament to the range of Aretha's singular brilliance that shortly before the successful release of *A Rose Is Still a Rose* she transported the billion-plus worldwide audience for the Grammy Awards broadcast with a blinding performance of the classic Puccini aria "Nessun Dorma." And she did so on less than half an hour's notice. Luciano Pavarotti had received a Lifetime Achievement Award at the 1998 Grammys and had been set to sing the aria. When he canceled at the absolute last minute due to illness, Ken Ehrlich, the show's main producer, was frantic about what to do. As I'm sure other people also did, I suggested that he ask Aretha, who had, in a stunning coincidence, performed the aria at the MusiCares fund-raiser in her honor two nights before. Aretha had already sung "Respect" on the Grammys show to promote the *Blues Brothers 2000* film, in which she appeared. She immediately agreed to sing the aria, even though she had less than fifteen minutes to prepare. In addition, because there was no time for adjustments, she would have to sing in Pavarotti's key, not her own. She listened to the arrangement, a much lusher orchestration than the setting for her performance two days before, on a boom box. Then she came out and knocked the audience off its feet. Her singing was soaring and passionate, and the response was overwhelmingly positive. It's the rare singer who would have both the talent and the confidence to pull off such a performance. Aretha is that rare.

Happily for me, music has been only one aspect of my relationship with Aretha. She is a great friend, and as extraordinary as our professional partnership has been to me, we have shared just as many good times and wonderful laughs together on a personal level. She is funny and completely unpredictable. She loves to kid around and tease, and she laughs just as hard when she's the butt of the joke as when she's putting one over on you. She's simply a complete delight.

Among my most frequent topics of conversation with Aretha are food, fashion, and men, not necessarily in that order. As is widely known, Aretha has struggled with her weight over the years, but she has a good sense of humor about it. She keeps up with the latest diets, and will tell me over the phone which one she's following and how she's doing with it. She'd call and tell me, "Wait until you see me. I'm on that Jenny Craig diet, and I'm doing great with it." Then I would see her a few weeks later, and it wouldn't look to me as if she'd lost much weight. I'd take her aside and whisper, "You're not on the Jenny Craig diet, clearly. I think you must be on the Shirley Craig diet!" She'd laugh and laugh.

One time I turned my pre-Grammy gala into a tribute to Aretha. On this occasion it was at the Plaza Hotel in New York, and I kept the tribute aspect of the show a surprise. There were two opening performances before Kenny "Babyface" Edmonds took the stage to sing a song he had written especially for this night in tribute to Aretha. And then one star after another—Toni Braxton, Natalie Cole, Whitney Houston, Cissy Houston, Gladys Knight, and Kenny G—all performed in Aretha's honor. Finally, in a star-studded finale, they joined together for "(You Make Me Feel Like a) Natural Woman" and then "Respect." I have always emceed these shows, and as the performers began "Respect," I walked to the foot of the stage, leaned forward with the microphone in my outstretched right hand, and motioned for Aretha to take over. And did she ever take over! She stood up and literally kept soaring as she belted out the choruses. It was Gwen Stefani's first pre-Grammy gala, and I looked over to see her gasp in awe. Donald Trump and Martha Stewart began standing, and as the rest of the room stood up, Aretha kept singing. She was on fire and everybody knew this was a lifetime performance. When Aretha finished, pandemonium erupted and for fifteen minutes I was besieged with congratulatory hugs. Suddenly I realized I hadn't seen Aretha and we had not exulted together about the surprising, unforgettable tribute crowned by her genius. I looked around and there was no Aretha. She had left, so I disappointingly trudged out. Flash to the next night at the Grammys ceremony itself. I entered Radio City Music Hall and got to its center aisle about five minutes before showtime. Amazingly, there was Aretha in her gown arriving at the same time. We embraced, and I immediately blurted out, "Aretha, last night, last night!" I was ready for the big thank-you, but Aretha's mind was on something else: "Clive, last night, it was absolutely incredible. That lobster appetizer—I never tasted anything like it! And the chicken main course—in my life I never had chicken as good!" I don't think my mouth has closed to this day.

Famously, Aretha doesn't like to travel. She's afraid of flying and suffers from acrophobia, a fear of heights. I'll tell her I'm vacationing in St. Barts or St. Tropez, and we'll have many conversations about it, how she would enjoy it to the hilt. She'll want to know who was there, where we stayed, what everyone said and did, what they wore, who else was there, and all the good gossip that I heard. She'll devour every scrap of information and then say, "Oh, Clive, that sounds so great. Next time I'm definitely coming with you!" But acrophobia ensured there hasn't been a next time.

Of course, there have been times, unfortunately, when Aretha has extended invitations to me that I was unable to accept. I accompanied her to the White House on one occasion, but two other times she invited me and I just couldn't go, because I had to be elsewhere. One of those times she really pushed it because the event also involved a soiree hosted by Pamela Harriman, one of Aretha's heroes. She absolutely could not get over a woman who had attracted a son of Winston Churchill, Edward R. Murrow, Prince Aly Khan, and W. Averill Harriman, among many other lovers. Aretha said, "My goodness, I've got to meet that woman. I've got to find out what she has that allows her to dazzle the most attractive, intelligent men of our lifetime." As fate would have it, I just couldn't go with her, and consequently the meeting never took place.

My memory is replete with Aretha stories. One time I hosted a party in honor of Aretha at Top of the Sixes at 666 Fifth Avenue in New York after one of her shows at Radio City Music Hall. It was a great space for a party, a classic New York locaton with breathtaking views of the city. The problem was that I didn't yet know at the time about Aretha's fear of heights. Elevators to high floors are not her thing. It was a real dress-up affair with a glittering guest list. Everyone knew that Aretha would have to change after the show, and it would take her at least half an hour to arrive at the party. So we were waiting. And waiting. And waiting. Thirty minutes. Forty minutes. Fifty minutes. An hour. No Aretha.

Finally we got word over a walkie-talkie that she'd entered the building. We didn't take into account that in that building you have to switch elevators somewhere around the twentieth floor in order to get to the penthouse. Aretha had no idea where in the building the party was. She got into the elevator like a trooper, but when she arrived at the floor where she would have to change elevators it created such palpitations within her that she fainted. She never made it to the party.

It was a glorious party—great music, great food, great guests. Everybody was having a wonderful time. We never announced what had really happened. All that we said was that Aretha wasn't well. The next day the tabloids ran headlines about Aretha being a no-show at Clive Davis's swank party for her. But that was the first time I realized the extent of her acrophobia. I would never make the same mistake again.

Aretha's fear of heights was also a factor on another of those years when I had my pre-Grammy party at the Plaza Hotel. I held a cocktail party before the event for the artists and the non-music-industry celebrities to get to know one another at my penthouse apartment on Park Avenue, two floors, each with 360-degree views of the city. Unfortunately, Aretha obviously couldn't attend because she couldn't take the elevator to my top-floor apartment. I was prepared for that this time and most people understood, but some were a bit disappointed because, in my experience, Aretha is one of the few stars that even other celebrities genuinely want to meet. Just about every artist and every producer that she worked with would ask if they could bring their parents or their children or their spouses to the studio to meet her. I remember Ralph Lauren taking me aside at the major lifetime career retrospective celebration for the designer Valentino Garavani in New York and saying, "Clive, I'm sorry. I never do this, but would you please introduce me to Aretha Franklin?" Afterward both he and his wife, Ricky, said, "Wow, what a thrill. There's meeting some famous person and then there's meeting Aretha. It's a whole different thing."

At the pre-Grammy cocktail party at my apartment it was Donna Karan who was dying to meet Aretha. I explained to her that Aretha wouldn't be coming to the party, but that she was waiting for me downstairs in my limousine. I suggested that Donna ride with us, and she and Aretha could chat in the car. They really hit it off. Aretha was totally familiar with and loved Donna's clothes, and asked if Donna could design something for her. After a few minutes, we arrived at the Plaza. It was just Aretha, Donna, and me in the car, and we didn't want Aretha's elaborate gown to get wrinkled or crushed. So I did what I had to do: I carried Aretha's long train up those famous Plaza steps and into the lobby. Donna, meanwhile, was busily smoothing some of the creases in the gown as we walked. Andre Harrell, the founder of Uptown Records and later the CEO of Motown, got the biggest kick out of it. "Say what you will about Clive," he laughingly was quoted in the press, "he might take the limelight when he's promoting his company, but he truly knows the difference between an artist and a record executive. And if he's got to carry Aretha's train, he'll carry Aretha's train!" There's no doubt about it. When you go out in public, Aretha *is* the queen and you just know you have to treat her like one!

On another occasion, though I was not a member, the Friars Club came to me in 1992 and said they wanted to give me not a roast but a lifetime achievement dinner. The dais was packed with celebrities. Most of show business was there. Again, to make the evening even more memorable, I arranged for Barry Manilow, Dionne Warwick, and Kenny G to perform. And the closing act, of course, was going to be Aretha. Well, in one of our famous telephone conversations, Aretha started with a buildup like I'd never heard. "Clive," she said, "I know that all your major stars are going to be there. I'm not going to tell you what I'm going to do, but I will tell you it's going to knock your socks off. I can't even talk about it, but just know it's going to be amazing!" So the night finally came, and I was filled with sky-high anticipation. It was the night to end all nights for me. All of the performers were incredible. And everything was building to Aretha. No one except me even knew that she would be performing, so I was thinking, My God, what does she have in mind for this? It turned out to be something that I and everyone there never could have imagined and that absolutely no one will ever forget. It's such an indelible memory. The curtain went up, the orchestra started playing, and Aretha came on—in a tutu! I'm not kidding. A tutu. And right behind her were members of the City Center Ballet Company, with whom she had rehearsed for two months. This was the Friars Club and everyone had heard about their roasts, so the audience didn't know how to respond. Titters were heard. Other people were transfixed. Everyone's jaw was dropping. But Aretha with great seriousness and concentration started performing the ballet she had thoroughly prepared. She went through pirouettes and dancing with very impressive agility. This was the Queen of Soul in a tutu and ballet slippers delivering a hypnotic performance. She truly got a great ovation. And then she sang. It was probably the only time in history that Aretha's singing almost seemed like an afterthought.

I have a memorable story about Aretha's sense of stage drama. One of her favorite designers is Arnold Scaasi, who has made many gowns for her. One day she called me and said, "I hope you're coming to my opening-night concert at Radio City. I can't describe it, but I have an outfit by Scaasi that is just unbelievable!" Of course I was going, and I'm friendly with Scaasi so I called and asked if he would be there. I also told him what Aretha had said. "I'll absolutely be there," he said. "And, Clive, the outfit is sensational. I can't tell you, but you obviously have to see it." So I went to Radio City. I have to be honest: As much as I love Aretha, I'm always a little apprehensive at her concerts because she takes such liberties with her material. It's not that you only want to hear an artist's hits, but you do want to hear them. Aretha, however, will sing whatever song strikes her fancy—ballads by other artists, snippets or a medley of songs that everyone wants to hear in full. When she's on, she's magic; when she's unpredictably doing purely what she wants to do, it can be a little frustrating. Even in the studio, she has her own rules, her own traditions. She'd only do a couple of takes, and if a song was intended as a single the producer would often call me and say, "She just wouldn't sing the melody and she wouldn't do another take. What am I supposed to do?" I would always let it go if it was an album track. After all, Aretha is Aretha. But for a potential single I would call her and explain that we had to have a song that we could get on the radio, so she needed to go back in and nail the melody of the chorus to make sure the song registered as fully as it should. Eventually Aretha would cooperate because she's the ultimate pro.

This Radio City concert was a magical night. As I said, when Aretha is on, there's nobody better. Soon we came to the last song of the night, a ballad, and she walked out in a gorgeous Scaasi gown. I was sitting near Scaasi and watching him as the song kept building, and as it got to the climactic high point, he was transfixed. Something was going to happen. Then I noticed that Aretha was struggling with the bottom half of her gown. She was clearly attempting to remove it to reveal something underneath, but she couldn't get the hook to come loose! She was singing and clutching at her gown, and it was very apparent that something was amiss. She looked helpless, and Scaasi looked as though he were going to have a heart attack. There was obviously supposed to be a big revelation, but it wasn't happening. Scaasi got out of his seat and headed backstage. Aretha looked stricken. Finally, she left the stage, and when she came back out she was wearing glorious, spangly hot pants! The Queen sure has nerve, and Aretha in hot pants got a huge reaction from the crowd—perhaps not quite what it would have been had she been able to whip off the dress to reveal the hot pants underneath, but Aretha triumphs over everything, including wardrobe malfunctions!

There's a second Scaasi story that I could never forget. A couple of years after that incident, Scaasi called me and said, "I'm having a retrospective of my work. Everybody I've designed for has turned in the gowns I need to borrow except Aretha. She refuses to send her gown. You've got to help." I figured there had to be a reason, so I agreed to call her. I really shouldn't have, but I did. When I asked Aretha about it, she said, "I'm not going to send him the gown. I went for three fittings, and it still didn't come out right. I ended up taking it, but we never agreed about the last payment, so I know he's trying to get that gown back from me. This retrospective business is just a ploy. He's going to keep it." I said, "Oh, I don't think he'd do that. I'll call him and get this resolved." So now I was totally in the middle. I called Scaasi and told him what Aretha had said. He replied, "That's ridiculous. Of course I'm going to give it back. Please tell her. Clive, you have my word." I then called Aretha and said, "Listen, Aretha, you have to trust my judgment. He's going to send it back to you. As a matter of fact, I'm so convinced of it, if you don't get it back, I'm writing you a letter that says I will replace the gown." She said that if I wrote that letter to her, she would send Scaasi the gown. Then she added, "And you'd better write that letter, because he's going to keep that gown!" I wrote the letter. The retrospective took place. Everything was fine. Six months later, I got a call from Aretha: "Clive, he hasn't sent me the gown. The retrospective has been over for three months. I don't care if he sent it by donkey, it would have reached me by now. And remember, I do have your letter." I couldn't believe that I was still involved in this. I called Scaasi: "Arnold, what are you doing to me? The day after the retrospective ended, you should have sent it back. I'm telling you, I'm on the line here. I had to write a letter guaranteeing that you would send back the dress. I'm going to have to replace it if you don't." He said, "Clive, from New York, the retrospective went to Vancouver, and then to Toronto. I've got a series of showings lined up." I said, "Well, when is it going to be over, so I can give Aretha a date?" Finally, maybe three or four months later, I called him again and told him that I didn't care what he had lined up, he had to send the gown back to her immediately. So he sent it back, and finally we were done.

In November 2010 Aretha announced that she was canceling all the concert dates she had scheduled through the following May. Then in early December she underwent successful surgery for a condition she refused to specify. Rumors circulated about how serious her health problem was, and there was considerable speculation that she had incurable pancreatic cancer. Aretha repeatedly denied those reports, though they persisted. Once she emerged again in public and announced that she had lost eighty-five pounds, speculation turned to the possibility that she had undergone gastric bypass surgery and had subsequently suffered complications. Regardless of the cause, I was concerned. I didn't want to pry into her personal affairs, but I wrote to her expressing my sympathy as well as my willingness to help in any way I could. Aretha surprised me by publicly thanking me for my concern and my letter when she delivered a brief statement from her home after a musical tribute to her on the 2011 Grammys.

I met with Aretha for dinner in New York not long after that, and we began discussing the possibility of making a record together again. Aretha had released her last Arista album in 2003, and since then we had talked about collaborating, but I felt that her financial demands were unrealistic. The music industry had changed dramatically, and everyone, artists and executives alike, had had to adjust expectations. That was a difficult reality for Aretha to accept, but we continued talking, and at her seventieth-birthday party in March 2012, she announced that we would be making another album together. The plan is for her to record signature songs by a list of legendary divas, potentially including the likes of Billie Holiday, Dinah Washington, Sarah Vaughan, Whitney Houston, Alicia Keys, and Adele. It's thrilling beyond words to think of attempting to make history again with Aretha more than three decades after I signed her at Arista. Creating great music with a peerless icon has rarely been so eventful and so much fun.

New Wave, Heavy Metal, and Eurythmics

There was a fear, as the Seventies were drawing to an end, that the music industry was on the brink of a crash, or at least a recession. We continued to have more than our share of hits at Arista, but I looked around and could see that the big bang of the late Seventies—when soundtracks such as *Saturday Night Fever* and *Grease* were selling in the tens of millions, when disco helped establish new labels like Casablanca and RSO as powerhouse forces, when rock artists such as Fleetwood Mac, the Eagles, Boston, and Meat Loaf were generating huge sales—was about to fizzle. The problems were industry-wide, and spared no one. Disco had peaked, those soundtracks proved to be unrepeatable phenomena, and the newer, hit-driven labels, without any catalog to sustain them, were on the brink of collapse. People looked for scapegoats: Home-taping was a scourge; video games were distracting the kids and stealing their pocket money, cash that would otherwise have been spent on records. Columbia Pictures looked at the landscape, didn't like the view, and decided to get out of the music business. Part of this decision was, from their perspective, practical; they didn't want to bank on the music business reversing course.

I was always sure that we would thrive, not just as a company but as an industry. I became an outspoken voice for the continued viability of music as a cultural and commercial force. It seems strange, looking back, that anyone would have to step out and defend the role of music, argue that it mattered, and insist that it would survive. But I didn't really feel threatened by video games. They weren't true competition as I saw it. A lot of commentators thought we would be eclipsed by this more interactive form of entertainment, but I thought we eventually would coexist. I felt compelled to share my thoughts on the perceived "threat," and *Billboard* published my commentary with the attention-drawing headline "You Can't Hum a Video Game." It began, "As proclaimers of doom, record industry pundits have to rank with the most portentous Greek choruses. There always seems to be a cataclysm around the corner." I went on to say, "Record company presidents are quoted in the *Los Angeles Times* as heralding the coronation of Space Invaders and, once more, the end of recorded music as we know it." While I acknowledged the novelty and allure of gaming, and its appeal especially to the younger demographic, I pointed out that it was no match for the broad, durable impact of music. "Great songs," I wrote, "bring us closer to ourselves and to each other. They truly become the kind of experience that no man-against-machine contest can hope to equal. . . . These games make sounds, but they don't create melodies. They don't engage us in ideas, or go to the heart." I felt it was vital to speak out on behalf of music and the music business. I also knew that Arista would prove that Columbia Pictures was making a big mistake by abandoning the boat at the first sign of clouds. I couldn't have predicted the elements that would turn things around; all I could do was what I'd always done, look for music that spoke to its time and moved people.

In the summer of 1981, the brand-new channel MTV began airing on cable systems around the country, although not in New York City at first; it took a while for MTV to come to my hometown. But I could see the opportunity, especially for rock music. In the beginning, MTV was very much a rock channel, and it happened that the U.K. was ahead of the curve in terms of making music videos. It was much more common over there to invest in this medium, so a disproportionate number of videos airing on MTV were by new British bands, the post-punk bands of the New Wave. Soon the States would catch up, but for a while, bands that had a limited avenue of exposure on rock or pop radio had a vehicle to reach middle America. It changed—revolutionized, really—the process of breaking rock artists. With rock, that process had always been a grind, getting the bands on the road, chipping away at album-oriented radio, building a following market by market, letting word of mouth about live shows spread, crossing over a track from rock to pop. How did kids in smaller cities, in rural America, find out about new bands, other than through the music press or the songs that cracked tight radio playlists? Now there was MTV, enabling a whole new kind of artist who might not break through using traditional methods to reach people everywhere. And MTV was open to the unusual, to the visually compelling, to sounds and looks that lay outside the box—the neo-rockabilly of the Stray Cats, the gender-bending pop-soul of Culture Club, the spacy synth rock of A Flock of Seagulls.

Arista released A Flock of Seagulls through a label deal with Clive Calder's U.K.-based Jive Records. I had always believed in Calder and thought that Jive would substantially enhance our rock presence. I had met Clive earlier and was very impressed by him: He was highly knowl-edgeable, incredibly bright, and had made his mark representing the band City Boy and the producer Mutt Lange. Mutt was an exceptional rock producer, and I began using him on some Arista projects like the Outlaws and the Michael Stanley Band. So I very much wanted to be in business with both Mutt and Clive. I had even offered Clive a job heading Arista's West Coast operations, but he had other goals, and through his management and publishing company Zomba Music, he and his partner Ralph Simon started Jive Records. The first acts they brought us were a mixture of pop acts like Q-Feel and Tight Fit and rock bands like the Comsat Angels, Roman Holliday, and A Flock of Seagulls. Jive/Arista released the first Flock of Seagulls EP in 1981, and the following April, the band's debut album came out, featuring the truly infectious single "I Ran (So Far Away)." MTV put it on, and the combination of its modern synth-pop sound, a catchy guitar line, lyri-cal hook, and without question the elaborate winged haircut of the lead singer, Mike Score, made it a smash hit. Needless to say, I was confident this would be only the first of many rock acts that would come through the door courtesy of Clive Calder and Jive Records. But it didn't turn out that way. Arista did have many more hits with Jive, but not in the rock world.

We had often looked across the Atlantic for rock and pop-rock art-ists. Through Virgin Records in the U.K., we acquired the U.S. rights to another synth-rock band, Heaven 17, which made an impact with

"Temptation" and "Let Me Go." Our U.K. company signed the band Haircut One Hundred, and made a big splash in Britain, scoring four consecutive Top 10 singles and a platinum album there. I really enjoyed their contagious, upbeat sound, and thought their lead singer, Nick Heyward, had tremendous appeal. But while MTV did get behind tracks like "Favourite Shirts (Boy Meets Girl)" and "Love Plus One," the band surprisingly just didn't connect in the States. We had more success with a Liverpool band called the Icicle Works and their song "Birds Fly (Whisper to a Scream)," and most dramatically with another Arista U.K. signing, the Thompson Twins, who were not twins (or even related) and not named Thompson. They were a trio—Tom Bailey, Alannah Currie, and Joe Leeway—and they made some of the most exhilarating pop-rock records of the Eighties, starting with their first U.S. hit single, "In the Name of Love," produced by Steve Lillywhite. The track launched them in America and was followed by a series of hits, "Love on Your Side," "Lies," "Doctor! Doctor!," and "Hold Me Now." The last two songs were both on the platinum-selling album *Into the Gap,* released in 1984. By that time, they'd become a regular fixture on MTV, were playing arenas, and even shared the stage with Madonna at the massive "Live Aid" concert at JFK Stadium in 1985. After playing their hit "Hold Me Now," they were joined by Madonna and Nile Rodgers to perform the Beatles' "Revolution."

While Arista was staying competitive in this new wave of British rock, there was a definite gap in our rock roster. We were missing something: Arista never did come to grips with the resurgence of hard rock, primarily an L.A. and U.K. phenomenon. In addition to providing a home for the more adventurous side of rock on shows like *120 Minutes,* MTV was also greatly responsible, through regular programming and the popular show *Headbangers Ball,* for a rebirth of harder rock and metal, and that's where we came up short. We did make a very serious pitch to sign Aerosmith in the mid-Eighties; their sales clout had seriously declined, and many people in the industry counted them out (their notorious drug problems were no doubt a contributing factor). But I'd always believed in the band since I'd given them their first record deal at Columbia, and I thought a resurgence was possible. There are few bands with that type of star power and musicianship, and with artists like that, you're always only a couple of songs away from reclaiming your rightful place at the top. I wanted to work with them again, and we had negotiated and agreed to all of the points with their attorney, Brian Rohan. We went to contract, but at the last minute, they decided to go for the money and sign with Geffen Records for what we were told was a million dollars more than what we'd settled on with them.

Geffen Records, formed by David Geffen in 1980, became a dynamic force in rock during the decade. In rock, success begat success. When Nirvana started being chased by the major labels after causing some noise with *Bleach* on Sub Pop in 1989, they were brought to my attention by one of our A&R men, Ken Friedman, but we were told by their manager, Ron Stone, that no other label really had a shot: Kurt Cobain and the rest of the band wanted to be on Geffen, because that's where Sonic Youth was signed. And so Geffen signed this seminal rock band that really changed music.

Somehow, although our position in the industry had never been stronger—we were breaking all records in pop and R&B and racking up sales beyond any period we'd ever had—we weren't identifying the young and important hard rock bands. I was looking around, wondering why I hadn't gotten the calls from Arista's West Coast A&R staff to come check out the bands who were turning the Sunset Strip into a glam-metal mecca, why Arista in the U.K. wasn't developing bands like Def Leppard and Whitesnake. We were being outscouted by John Kalodner, Gary Gersh, and Tom Zutaut at Geffen, and the other A&R men scurrying around places like Club Lingerie. Bottom line: We missed the big West Coast rock migration to L.A. and Seattle. You want to be a part of everything that's causing a commotion, and we were out in the cold.

The closest we came was with a band from Switzerland, of all places. We had gotten Krokus through Ariola, and in 1980, we released their album *Metal Rendez-vous,* followed by *Hardware* a year later. We finally had our breakthrough with *One Vice at a Time,* then back-to-back gold albums with *Headhunter* and *The Blitz.* The band wasn't subtle—one of their biggest tracks was "Long Stick Goes Boom"—but, with songs like "Midnite Maniac" and "Screaming in the Night," they did connect with the audience for aggressive rock.

We did get some traction with an Australian band, the Church, who scored a big rock track with the song "Under the Milky Way"—one of the rare "alternative" tracks that crossed over to the pop chart—and a gold album for *Starfish*. And we signed a young blues guitarist from Toronto, Jeff Healey. When he was brought to me, he was described as a new-generation guitar hero in the tradition of Johnny Winter, Carlos Santana, and Mike Bloomfield, all of whom I had signed to Columbia. Healey's band was merely functional, and he had very little going on in the way of original material, but he had an unorthodox way of playing the guitar—he stayed seated for much of his set, his instrument spread across his lap—and despite his blindness, he demonstrated a flair for showmanship. We flew the trio down from Toronto, engaged in something of a war with Elektra Records to sign them, and set about shaping the debut album. That was the beginning of a typical creative tug-of-war: Jeff and his band thought they were writing material that was strong enough to make an impact on rock radio, and we felt differently, so there were many discussions, some heated, about what would go on the album. Healey's A&R person, Mitchell Cohen, who also had brought the Church to the label, took a trip to Nashville to look for suitable hit material and came back with a few songs that I favored, two of them by the songwriter John Hiatt: "Confidence Man" and "Angel Eyes." The first went on to become a big AOR track, and the second, with some postproduction overdubs and remixing, was a Top 5 pop single. Then the Jeff Healey Band were cast in the film *Road House*, resulting in more exposure and a successful soundtrack album. Along with Stevie Ray Vaughan and Robert Cray, Jeff Healey was one of the young blues-influenced guitarists creating a stir in the second half of the decade.

The problem that continued to arise was the writing of Jeff and his band. Their songs were mediocre at best. Ideally, a rock band should be self-contained; I rarely signed a rock artist who did not have material of his or her own. That was part of their identity. Yet it would be foolhardy not to be aware of the exceptions. What did it matter that Eric Clapton didn't write "After Midnight" or "Cocaine" or "I Shot the Sheriff"? When he performed them, they became his signature songs, and no one in the audience keeps score regarding which songs he wrote and which ones he didn't: They're all Clapton songs. The same with Santana and "Evil Ways," "Black Magic Woman," and "Oye Como Va." The smart artists recognize the power of a breakthrough song, no matter where it comes from. They know such songs generate album sales and become centerpieces of their live shows, and they accept that there's a trade-off in not getting publishing money. In the end, they win. But some artists dig in their heels, and that was the case with Jeff Healey, to the point of diminishing returns. He didn't write the hits on his platinum album debut, *See the Light,* or on the *Road House* soundtrack, but when it came to doing the all-important second album, he demonstrated stronger resistance to outside material, even from Hiatt, who'd provided the songs that broke down the door. The band wanted to write more, and in the end, they gave in only slightly, accepting a song submitted to them by Dire Straits' Mark Knopfler and doing a cover of the Beatles' "While My Guitar Gently Weeps" that George Harrison agreed to appear on. Those tracks did well on rock radio, but without a crossover hit, the sophomore Healey album only went gold. The bottom line was that we had considerable success with Jeff Healey, but there were a number of missed opportunities as well. He was a very gifted musician, with an encyclopedic knowledge of jazz and blues, and when he prematurely passed away in 2008, I wistfully remembered those early shows, so charged with possibility.

One of the outstanding bands launched in the MTV era was Eurythmics, and I was always in awe of Annie Lennox, her artistry, her hypnotic power, her just being a quintessential visual rock star. She has a presence on camera almost like the screen goddesses of earlier eras, Garbo or Dietrich. Simply transfixing. And Dave Stewart gave her such excellent material: "Sweet Dreams (Are Made of This)," "Here Comes the Rain Again," "Would I Lie to You," "Who's That Girl." I followed their career closely, and always with the highest level of admiration, so I was really excited when they became available. Their streak of hit singles had slowed a bit since their peak in the mid-Eighties, but I had no hesitation. Some artists are simply important, and that's rare. I didn't think of them in terms of pop hits, although they had so many. They were, to me, more in the category of David Bowie, a creative entity.

I didn't ask to hear new material, and it never dawned on me to submit songs to them. When I signed Eurythmics in 1989, I saw them as being larger than the sum of their hits, and I felt there was much more life in the group.

I remember that I was at the Ritz Hotel in Paris when I got a call that Annie and Dave wanted to do something fun to celebrate their signing to Arista. They were coming to Paris, and they arrived at the Hemingway Suite, where I was staying, wearing sunglasses, and they brought pairs of sunglasses for me to wear in the signing photos. It all felt good and I just let myself be directed by them, whether it was on the couch or the three of us on the bed, anywhere and everywhere all over the suite. I let them run with it and the photos reflect that playfulness, that wit and intelligence. I wanted to let them know that I understood them and believed in them. When their first, and only, Arista album came out in September 1989, we threw them an outdoor celebration in Los Angeles on a huge back lawn, invited the press, and set up speakers so the two of them, without the band, could perform. It was just so vivid, watching them, because it never mattered where they were, what the circumstances were, when Annie was singing she created her own mystique, her own magic, and drew you in. It's always inspiring to hear her. She's the kind of artist who, if you're with a young singer just starting out, you want to point to her and say, "That's how you should communicate, not only with your voice and movements, but with expressiveness and commitment. That's what makes a true star."

Eurythmics' Arista album, *We Too Are One,* produced by Dave Stewart and Jimmy Iovine, didn't do quite as well as we'd all hoped, although it did go Top 10 in many countries outside of the United States. The single "Don't Ask Me Why" didn't go all the way. That turned out to be the last Eurythmics album for quite a long time, although I continued to work with Dave and Annie separately. Dave and I got an out-of-the-blue hit together when a film track he did with a sax player named Candy Dulfer, "Lily Was Here," was released as a single and, unusual for an instrumental, exploded everywhere from its radio play. Then, in 1992, we released the first solo album of Annie Lennox's career, the unadulterated critical and commercial triumph *Diva,* produced by Stephen Lipson. Worldwide, the album sold more than 8 million copies, and there was a companion "video album" of seven songs from *Diva,* including the indelible, mesmerizing video for "Why," in which Annie begins with her bare, un-made-up face and gradually applies makeup. It's very striking; there are so few videos where you can remember every single shot, each raising of an eyebrow, her haunting stare as she sings the lyrics of the song. Who else can command attention like that? Annie had always been known for her shifting personae, her different hairstyles and costumes, but this was a major breakthrough in terms of a solo artistic identity, a coming out from behind the image of the Eurythmics into a sphere all her own. She was already a star, but "Why" and the other videos from *Diva* created a different aura around her. There was something defining about it, and even casual observers of the pop scene, who might not have even known her from Eurythmics, were enraptured. From that point on, I think, Annie was one of the very few examples of a true album artist, and probably the most important female artist to emerge from the U.K. scene in the decade.

I was always in awe of and really thrilled by what Annie had accomplished on *Diva,* and she definitely became one of Arista's premier artists. Of course, she performed at my annual pre-Grammy party. And when I was honored for a second time by the Martell Foundation in 1995, I invited her to perform, alongside Aretha and Patti Smith. That night was a career highlight, and a singular memory, for me to be at this prestigious industry event in the company of artists of that stature, to see Annie and Aretha perform "Sisters Are Doin' It for Themselves." When it came time to follow up *Diva,* Annie decided to do an album of covers, titled *Medusa,* all chosen by her, songs by composers such as Paul Simon, Bob Marley, and Neil Young. The lead track, "No More 'I Love You's,'" won her a Grammy, and the album was nominated for Best Pop Vocal Album. *Medusa's* success, without a hit single, proved that Annie had indeed become, as a solo performer, the type of star artist I'd thought Eurythmics had the potential to be: someone whose audience would follow her down all her idiosyncratic paths, regardless of where a song was on the charts.

Annie continued to follow her own muse, to make albums on her own terms and her own timetable, and whenever she'd perform it became a major event. Over the years, I must admit that I would have loved to submit material to her. She was the quintessential artist to me. I wished we had the kind of intimacy where we might have had a private dinner and I could say, "Hey, I've got this great song that I'd like you to hear," but the circumstances never seemed right, and there was never a request forthcoming from Simon Fuller, her manager, on her behalf. I just couldn't simply pop a song in the mail to her, or play it for her over the phone. I would listen, and realizing how transcendent she is, think about what the right outside hit song might bring her. I mean, there are so few artists in her league, artists like Sting or Eric Clapton, who could leave a successful group and become a giant solo artist without connecting with a series of hit singles. That she resides in such rare company is a credit to her electrifying personality and the depth of her artistry. It always seemed intrusive for me to try to wedge a song into her finely crafted albums. I knew she wanted commercial success, but creatively she was to stay on the outer fringe of music. She didn't exactly try to keep up with what was current. There's no question that Annie did soar and we did share hits, success, and major impact together, but it was eventually coupled with a certain amount of frustration that some collaboration might have been very beneficial. Although the subject never came up, if it's anyone's fault it's my own for not summoning up the courage to air the issue. I just know with more contemporary in-the-pocket material, Annie could be dominating pop music for years.

Whitney

Without question this is the most difficult chapter for me to write. I met Whitney Houston when she was nineteen, and for many years we enjoyed one of the most extraordinary rides in the history of the music business. For a long time, Whitney could do no wrong, and the only problem we had was how we could keep topping ourselves. When drugs and her marriage to Bobby Brown affected Whitney's career, I never ceased believing that it was possible for her to right herself and to achieve once again the artistry and historic success that had come so effortlessly to her when she was young. I believed that until the day she died. When you have the rare opportunity to collaborate with an all-timer like her, you just never give up. Her death was an absolutely crushing blow to me.

My creative partnership with Whitney had a storybook beginning. I first heard about her in 1983 from Gerry Griffith, who was an A&R man at Arista and who had kept his eye on her for a year or so. She was singing backup for her mother, Cissy Houston, who, as a member of the Sweet Inspirations, had sung backup for Aretha Franklin and many other artists. Whitney was also doing session work and occasional modeling around town. At Gerry's urging, I went to see her at one of Cissy's shows at Sweetwater's, a club at Sixty-eighth Street and Amsterdam Avenue, not far from where I lived at the time. Cissy was showcasing Whitney during her set, and would bring her forward to sing two songs. Whitney performed "Home," a song from *The Wiz,* and, ironically enough, "The Greatest Love of All," a song written by Michael Masser and Linda Creed that I had commissioned for George Benson when I oversaw the soundtrack to the 1977 Muhammad Ali biopic, *The Greatest.*

Needless to say, Whitney blew the roof off Sweetwater's with those two songs, and I immediately determined to sign her. I could not believe that a teenager could bring such overwhelming passion to "The Greatest Love of All." I sat there awestruck. That she was also incredibly beautiful only made her performance more magical. Michael Masser and I had become great friends, and when the show was over I called him in Los Angeles and told him he had to jump on a red-eye and come to New York to hear Whitney with me the following night. He did just that, and was literally moved to tears by her performance. A buzz had already begun building about Whitney, and I knew the competition to sign her would be keen. Elektra and Epic, to cite just two labels, were already in the game. But I knew we had a couple of strong points in our favor. I was already successfully working with Whitney's cousin Dionne Warwick, as well as with Aretha Franklin, who was her godmother and a dear friend of Cissy's. I was assured they would both give me enthusiastic endorsements.

In addition I personally spoke to Whitney and confirmed to her that I was more than eager to play the same role in her musical life that I had for Dionne and Aretha. Cissy was on the case as well. Whitney later told *Rolling Stone,* "Let's say a company offers you a contract, and they're saying: 'Whitney, you can choose the songs. You can produce the songs. You can do whatever the hell you want to do.' As opposed to Arista, with Clive Davis saying: 'We'll give you this amount of money, and we'll sit down, and as far as the songs you want to do, I will help you. I will say: 'Whitney, this song has potential. This song doesn't.' So my mother was saying to me, 'You're eighteen years old. You need guidance.' Clive was the person who guided me." I'm not going to say that I knew immediately that Whitney would be as big as she eventually became—I'm a worrier and I run scared; I never take anything for granted, always picturing the obstacles in the way—but I was convinced from the outset that she would be a star and that we would make great records together.

My promise to her would turn out to have some unintended consequences. Whitney would sign with Arista only on the condition that she get a "key man" clause stipulating that she was to work only with me. If I left the company for any reason, she would be free to go as well.

I was flattered, of course, that she; her managers at the time, Gene Harvey and Seymour Flics; and her lawyer Paul Marshall demanded that guaranty. However, those kinds of arrangements always create problems at a record company. Most important, they open the door for other artists to make similar demands. In Whitney's case, however, I knew that my having worked successfully with artists whom she regarded as family was the most compelling reason in favor of her signing with the label. Arista was part of RCA Records at the time, and the RCA brass had to approve this precedent-setting arrangement. I had been asked several times but I had never granted a key-man clause before. I wanted this artist so badly that I supported breaking precedent, and RCA approved the deal. We immediately went to work.

As soon as I signed her in April 1983, I brought Whitney to *The Merv Griffin Show*. I had previously co-hosted two special versions of the show with Merv that were entirely devoted to Arista artists and that helped give our new and emerging label an identifiable national image. Rather than wait for a third, Merv gave me his word that as soon as I signed a new artist that I felt was going to be a superstar, he would make his show available to me. I took him up on that promise with Whitney. I introduced her on the show as the next major star for the new generation. Whitney performed "Home" to absolutely spellbinding effect. That instantly got the word out that a spectacular new artist was waiting in the wings and would eventually make her recording debut on Arista.

As for Whitney's first album, I was on the line and knew I had to embark on a campaign to get her the strongest possible material. To me she was a potential all-timer, and I had to pull out all the stops. To make that happen I arranged showcases for her in New York and Los Angeles so that the best songwriters in the business would come see her, understand how rare a talent she was, and give her their best songs. That's how we did it. The album would be two years in the making. My A&R staff and I listened to and evaluated literally hundreds of songs. The process was truly exhaustive, but you know it was worth every minute of that time and attention.

Michael Masser ended up producing and co-writing four songs on Whitney's debut, and each one became a classic. He co-wrote "The

Greatest Love of All," "Saving All My Love for You," "All at Once," and "Hold Me," which became a duet with Teddy Pendergrass. Teddy included the track on his 1984 album, *Love Language,* and released it as a single in May of that year. At the time that seemed fine, just another way to indicate that a hot new artist was coming onto the scene. (But it would have consequences that neither Whitney nor I ever could have foreseen.) Kashif was a very talented R&B artist I had signed to Arista, and he produced what would be the opening track on Whitney's first album, as well as its lead single, "You Give Good Love." "How Will I Know" was originally written by George Merrill and Shannon Rubicam for Janet Jackson, who had turned it down. They brought it to Gerry Griffith and me, and we gave it to Narada Michael Walden to produce. He transformed it into a perfect, sassy, Motown-style setting for Whitney.

When the Jacksons' "Victory" tour came to New York in August 1984, I threw a party at the Limelight for Jermaine Jackson, who had released *Dynamite,* his first album for Arista, earlier that year. I also used the occasion to provide exposure for Whitney, whom I had introduced to Jermaine. They had become lovers and had an intense relationship during a time when rumors were swirling that Whitney was gay. Jermaine was married, though I believe he was separated, so the relationship never became public even though everyone around her knew about it. As for the Jacksons, there couldn't possibly have been more heat surrounding them. Michael was still basking in the glow of *Thriller,* and the "Victory" tour was filling stadiums across the country. So I asked Jermaine if he would sing a duet with Whitney at the Limelight, which he agreed to do. Ultimately, Jermaine produced three tracks on Whitney's debut, and he sang with her on two of those: "Nobody Loves Me Like You Do" and "Take Good Care of My Heart," which also appeared on *Dynamite.*

We released *Whitney Houston* on Valentine's Day in 1985, and its impact would be cataclysmic. We marked the event by sending roses to radio programmers around the country along with a copy of "You Give Good Love," the first single. It took two years to make the album, and it took fifty weeks for it to reach number one, but it kept building the entire time, and ended up spending fourteen weeks at the top of the charts. One single after another made explosive impact. "You Give Good Love" rose to number three, and then "Saving All My Love for You," "How Will I Know," and "The Greatest Love of All" each went to number one. Beginning with *Thriller*, the Eighties began the era of the blockbuster album. Whitney joined the ranks of Michael Jackson, Madonna, Bruce Springsteen, and Prince, and *Whitney Houston* became one of the best-selling landmark albums of all time. Whitney was literally in shock, and I kept asking her, "Are you pinching yourself?" We both really couldn't believe this was happening, and we just kept pouring it on. She was absolutely tireless in her willingness to make sure the album reached its full potential. She did showcases, television appearances, interviews, photo shoots, and awards shows—whatever was necessary. She toured as an opening act for Luther Vandross and Jeffrey Osborne, and then finally launched her own headlining tour in 1986. The album's momentum was unstoppable, and its worldwide sales are estimated to be more than 23 million copies. Whitney became a juggernaut, a true phenomenon.

As Whitney began to do live performances, it was evident that, as with all young performers, she needed to get used to sustaining an entire set on her own, rather than simply doing a few songs as part of her mother's show or at a showcase or TV appearance. After seeing her perform on February 12, 1985, just as her album was about to come out, I sent her the following letter in an effort to help guide her in this area in which she would eventually excel. Whitney, of course, had her astonishing voice and great material, but other qualities come to bear in live performance, and that is what I tried to convey to her in this letter, which I include here in full:

> *Dear Whitney: You were terrific last night and even though the sequence of the set leaves something to be desired, your basic, wonderful, glorious natural talent triumphed over any of the kinks that need to be worked out. Your bearing is excellent and, even allowing for nervousness, your spontaneous charm wins out over everything.*
>
> *I thought it would be useful to make some constructive suggestions. Some of them are pretty important for the tough*

to please and others I'm sure will be corrected after opening night jitters go away. But I did want to make sure that everything is brought to your attention. To me, the artists that make it are constantly striving for improvement. Our goal should be for a few standing ovations during the set, not just one. We both must strive for the ultimate reaction, even when we're not surrounded by family, friends and sympathetic ears.

So here are the comments: 1) The opening of "The Greatest Love" will be fine for now but it should not lead into "Solid." I have two basic concerns about you doing "Solid." The first is that every Las Vegas lounge act is covering that tune. I do think that you should go into an up-tempo driving cover song but it's different if you were to do the Stevie Wonder song or any other up-tempo cover of something older. Covering the current number one song is what the synthetic imitators do and we should avoid this in building you as a unique and original talent. Although the average listener will respond to you doing that song because it is a current hit and it will get a decent response (as it does in every Vegas lounge act), we shouldn't be misled by that. Secondly, and candidly, when you do a cover, you should have a different interpretation and do it as well or better than the original. With almost all of your covers, you accomplish that. In this case, you don't. Both in person, and with a video, Ashford and Simpson's version is hotter than yours and introducing your gigantic talent at the beginning of your set you should not be coming off second best. So, in summary at this point, I would substitute for "Solid" any driving up-tempo number you have in your current repertoire. I really feel strongly about this point and I hope that you take it to heart in the constructive manner I intend it and that you are able to do it for tonight's performance.

2) Going to "Someone for Me," I think this is a good choice to keep the up-tempo mood. As we discussed, everything works regarding this song except the ending. It's certainly okay to improvise at the end of the song and to extend it and give it a soulful feeling but it can't go on and on just aimlessly. When you do extend the same phrase, it should build into some sort of climax resolution.

*Otherwise, it looks like you don't know how to end the song.
I would think carefully about this because the same problem arises
with "How Will I Know" and "All at Once." To keep repeating the
hook is fine and to keep giving it soulful variations is fine, but at
some decisive point it should rise to a dramatic resolution and be
over and out.*

*3) At this point, I think you're ready for a song that gets
a standing ovation and cheers. I would strongly suggest "I'm
Changing." Although you might have been doing this song for a
while, let's not lose patience before your career begins. With this
song, you emphatically say that "I'm Whitney Houston and I'm
going to make my mark!" No other song, including those in the
album, does it as effectively. This is a show stopper and by the
fourth song a new artist who is going to make her mark should
have a show stopper.*

*4) The medley here ["Nobody Loves Me Like You Do" and
"Take Good Care of My Heart"] would work beautifully. You and
your brother sing very well together and the impact on the audience
of your togetherness is strong. Since you give your brother all of
the Jermaine parts, and since Jermaine has really more to sing the
way that the records have been produced (he was the dominating
performer when they were recorded and it was natural that he was
given more of the lines), it makes sense for this to follow the show
stopper. Then, it does not matter for him to be featured somewhat
more than you in doing the duets because it looks very good for
you to showcase him even though it's your debut engagement. So,
the medley would work beautifully here following "I'm Changing"
and it would keep the momentum going.*

*5) From the duet medley, I would go into "How Will I Know"
and, to repeat, I would work out an appropriate strong ending at
the conclusion of the shortened improvisation and I would follow
with "All at Once."*

*6) I would then introduce the band. This extended introduction
of the band can only work if each of the brief solos is really hot.
Last night only the piano player really was hot. The band members
should be told that they have 20 to 30 seconds to heat up. If they*

*can't really create steam, then I would substantially cut short the
band introduction and not draw it out as long as it went.*

*7) I would then go into "Home" and "You Give Good Love"
in whatever order you prefer. You might try one first at one
performance and the other first at another performance and see
which works better. "Home" is clearly the stronger of the two in
person and it would get a standing ovation without question.
I don't mind then coming back with "The Greatest Love of All,"
which is another ballad, because it is the shortened version. It's
also difficult to have your new single follow "Home" because it
can't get quite as good an audience response since "Home" qualifies
as a show stopper.*

*So, there you have all my comments. It's only meant in the spirit
of you and I against the world that we have to conquer. I hope that
you're flexible enough to give this a shot and to compare it against
what went before. In any event, you are terrific and I could not be
prouder of you. This is an exciting stage for us all and as we work
to bring everything into shape, let's enjoy it too. Love, Clive.*

There was never any dialogue between us on the content of my letter, but I know that Whitney absorbed everything and she did indeed
make a number of changes in her act that responded substantively to
what I was suggesting.

When the time for Grammy nominations came around, Whitney
was obviously a strong contender. She was the odds-on favorite for
the Best New Artist prize. But as it turned out, she was disqualified
from that category because her duets with Teddy Pendergrass and Jermaine Jackson had been released during a previous awards period. We
were stunned, and naturally Whitney was very disappointed. I sent a
strong letter to the head of the National Academy of Recording Arts
and Sciences (NARAS), the organization that oversees the Grammys,
and I wrote a commentary in *Billboard* that began: "How is it that
a recording artist can be voted 'Favorite New Female Artist' by the
readers of *Rolling Stone,* named 'Newcomer of the Year' in music by
'Entertainment Tonight,' 'Top New Artist' (in both pop and R&B)
by *Billboard* . . . and not be considered a candidate for 'Best New Art-

ist'?" The NARAS rule on the matter reads as follows: "An artist is not eligible in the best new artist category if the artist had label credit or album credit, even if not as a featured artist, in a previous awards' year."

The rule seems clear enough, but in its history NARAS had applied it very arbitrarily. Crosby, Stills and Nash, Cyndi Lauper, and Luther Vandross had all been voted Best New Artist when they had extensive past credits. But my protests didn't change anything. *Whitney Houston* was nominated for Album of the Year, "The Greatest Love of All" for Record of the Year, and "You Give Good Love" for Best Rhythm & Blues Song. Whitney herself received nominations for Best Pop Vocal Performance, Female, and Best R&B Vocal Performance, Female, and she won in the pop category for "Saving All My Love for You."

Whitney Houston, the album, succeeded beyond my wildest hopes. History has also treated it well. *Rolling Stone* voted it among its 500 Greatest Albums of All Time and the Rock and Roll Hall of Fame listed it among the definitive two hundred albums that every music lover needs to own. Such accolades are deeply satisfying and of course I'm very proud of them. But as I write this I definitely feel the pain that Whitney's not here to relive this with me.

Now, the real challenge with success on the scale of *Whitney Houston* is following it up. Of course, we were in a much stronger position the second time around. We didn't need to showcase Whitney to get songwriters and publishers to submit material for her. Instead, we had first-rate songs left over, and we were inundated with other high-quality submissions. Neither Whitney nor I saw a need for a significant departure on her next album. The world was still clamoring for more, and she had plenty more to give. We called the second album *Whitney*—no last name required this time—and all the producers who worked on the first album returned, except for Jermaine Jackson. Narada Michael Walden produced seven of *Whitney*'s eleven tracks, including the number-one hits "I Wanna Dance with Somebody (Who Loves Me)," "So Emotional," and "Where Do Broken Hearts Go." Kashif produced "Where You Are," and Michael Masser produced and co-wrote "Didn't We Almost Have It All" and "You're Still My Man." Jellybean Benitez, the hot dance producer of that era, was at the board for "Love Will Save the Day."

A huge audience was eagerly awaiting the album's release in June 1987, and it entered the charts at number one, the first album by a female artist to do so. It stayed at number one for eleven weeks. The first single, "I Wanna Dance with Somebody," was written by George Merrill and Shannon Rubicam, the same team that had written "How Will I Know." As had happened with that song, Narada was to rework it considerably. When I heard the demo I knew it could have been recorded by anyone—it was done along the pop lines of Olivia Newton-John. I pictured the ultimate recording of it to be much, much funkier, and Narada totally agreed. He laid down a great track, and then Whitney really nailed it, bringing a sensuality to her vocal that makes it clear that dancing is a metaphor for more intimate physical contact. It went straight to number one. When the next single, "Didn't We Almost Have It All," also hit number one, we sensed that something really special was happening. Including the last three singles from her debut album, Whitney now had five consecutive number ones. She was just one away from tying the Beatles and the Bee Gees, who each had landed six consecutive number ones.

That clearly upped the stakes for the next single choice. "So Emotional," written by Billy Steinberg and Tom Kelly, came to me through the Arista A&R man Mitchell Cohen. Its original title was "Emotional," but Mitchell and I felt it was important for the song's title to emphasize its catchy chorus, so we called Billy and he agreed to change it. When "So Emotional" became the first number-one single of 1988, Whitney had tied a record set by two of the most successful bands in music history. Now the pressure was really on. For the next single, the potential record breaker, we had to decide between "Just the Lonely Talking Again," written by Sam Dees, or "Where Do Broken Hearts Go," written by Frank Wildhorn and Chuck Jackson. "Where Do Broken Hearts Go" had been one of my favorite songs on the album and I was strongly predisposed to it. Initially, Whitney was a bit skeptical of the song but together we listened and relistened to it and she gradually came around. When she recorded it, she was really into it and did a beautiful job. So "Where Do Broken Hearts Go" it was.

I had always said that as a label Arista wanted every song to be a hit and that our promotion staff should work all of them as hard as possible, playing no favorites. But what we had here was clearly a unique situation. In baseball, you can say that you don't play any harder in the seventh game of the World Series than you do in the middle of the season, but when there's so much at stake it does bring out all your competitive instincts. History was upon us and we all knew it. Everyone geared up to fight the fight. There was some anxiety at the outset as the song didn't immediately shoot to the top, but hard work paid off and the video sure helped. Whitney's beauty was astonishing and her ravishing good looks brought a movie-star charisma to her visual performance. The record gained momentum and soared to number one. Whitney and the entire Arista team were ecstatic.

If everyone in the music world had become blasé, getting used to Whitney's outsized success, this record-setting achievement of seven consecutive number ones refocused their attention on just how extraordinary her impact had been. The next release broke the string; it was "Love Will Save the Day," the Jellybean Benitez production. It's a very upbeat track and a little edgier than the rest of the album. It sounded hip, which was good for Whitney at the time, and it did make the Top 10. It just didn't go all the way. No apology is necessary for this strong, infectious record. At the Grammys, Whitney received three nominations, and, once again, won for Best Pop Vocal Performance, Female, this time for "I Wanna Dance with Somebody." In addition, the songwriters Michael Masser and Will Jennings were nominated for Song of the Year for "Didn't We Almost Have It All." Worldwide, *Whitney* has sold more than 22 million copies.

Through all this, Whitney and I honestly couldn't believe how well things were going. Whatever success I'd had before, nothing was comparable to this. Whenever we would see each other, she knew what was on my mind and she would volunteer, "I'm pinching myself!" And I knew she meant it. Even though we were at the center of the commercial storm and making the decisions that were driving it, sometimes it felt as if we were simply being swept along by the momentum, just like everybody else. Past a certain point with phenomena like this, events take on a life of their own and your control is limited. Of course you're taking care of every detail that you can, but when the numbers get as big as this, you just stand back in awe and wonder. Whitney and

I would take in those moments, enjoy them together, and then get back to work. She still was working incredibly hard. There was nothing that she wouldn't do. She was wide-eyed about her unparalleled success, and always expressed love and gratitude for it. I detected no attitude at all on her part.

Of course, it wasn't all sunshine and roses. Because of Whitney's close friendship with Robyn Crawford, who worked for her management company and whom she had known since high school, the rumors about her being gay persisted. She denied them, and I knew of various boyfriends that she had, but the rumors never abated, and I know Whitney found them disturbing. On the other end of the spectrum, Whitney was being perceived in certain quarters as being too squeaky-clean and too white-identified—"Whitey" Houston, as particularly nasty naysayers put it, or "The Prom Queen of Soul," as *Time* dubbed her. At the 1989 Soul Train Awards show, some in the audience booed her. Because her second album had not dramatically shifted styles, we were accused of sacrificing art in order to cash in and make a risk-free guaranteed follow-up success. That criticism was particularly irksome because there is no such thing as a guaranteed success. It's naïve to believe that you can simply follow a certain formula and then sit back and watch an album sell more than 20 million copies. I certainly never took Whitney's sales for granted. To my ears, the *Whitney* album holds up extremely well. If its legacy hasn't been as distinguished as the debut album's, that's largely because the debut, which seemingly came out of nowhere, is the record that announced Whitney Houston to the world and established her as a superstar. That's inherently dramatic, and any follow-up is inevitably going to be overshadowed, regardless of its quality and commercial success. But song for song, *Whitney* is a powerful collection, and a milestone in Whitney's career.

Another speculation that arose was that I was a Svengali pulling the strings and Whitney, regardless of her talent, was little more than my puppet. The notion was insulting, both to Whitney and to me. Whitney may have been young when I met her, but she was hardly naïve. She grew up with a mother who was a well-known, highly respected, and successful professional singer. How many aspiring teenage artists can just pick up the phone and call iconic figures like Aretha Franklin and Dionne Warwick for advice? I worked with Whitney exactly the way I did with Aretha and Dionne. With the help of my A&R team, I found the best songs I could, identified the most skillful and sympathetic studio producers, and presented the strongest options I could determine. You can have arguments and make the strongest case that you can, but if artists don't believe that they are in control of their career, you have a much bigger problem than missing out on a hit song. Even if you know you're right, you're better off acceding to their wishes and making the next-best choice. So if Whitney finally didn't want to do something, we didn't do it.

The fact is, however, that Whitney and I got along unbelievably well, and we agreed most of the time on almost everything. As Whitney explained in *Rolling Stone,* "I wouldn't be with anybody who didn't respect my opinion. Nobody makes me do anything I don't want to do. You can't make me sing something I don't want to sing. That's not what makes me and Clive click, because if it was, I'd have left Arista a long time ago. Clive and I work well together. We basically like the same things, which, thank God, allowed us to get along all these years."

One issue that Whitney brought up herself around this time was writing songs. She would come up to my office, order her characteristic hamburger and Coke, and we'd listen to music and discuss all these matters. Inevitably, after all of the commercial success, something of a critical backlash had set in. Whitney rightly felt that, despite Grammy nominations and awards, she wasn't getting the respect she deserved. She understood that rock critics dominate the media's music coverage, and they have much greater regard for artists who write their own material than for those who don't. In addition, Madonna and Janet Jackson had been writing songs, and Whitney wondered if she should do likewise. Of course, money was a factor as well. Songwriting can be extremely lucrative, and many singers whose records sell especially well often attempt to coerce writers into sharing songwriting credits and the resulting income. It speaks very well of Whitney that she never even considered taking that approach. But actually writing songs herself was a different matter.

When she raised the issue with me, I said, "Look, I'm not going to be the one to tell you not to write songs. I never want to sell you short. You should try it. But all I know is that we've had seven straight number-one singles, an all-time record. If you can write better songs than those, it's fine with me. It only makes my job easier. So many times managers shortsightedly convince artists to write in order to get a piece of the copyright so that they make more money. What they don't realize is that a bigger percentage of nothing does not amount to much. To me, you are in the tradition of Billie Holiday, Dinah Washington, Sarah Vaughan, Aretha, Sinatra, Streisand, Lena Horne. All of them are Olympian artists, and, for the most part, none of them wrote. With your exceptional, God-given voice, that's the tradition you're in." She never brought the issue up with me again.

For Whitney's third album, it was clear that we needed to shore up her base in the black community. This was not a response to what happened at the Soul Train Awards or to any of the other criticisms of her, which Whitney and I never discussed. It just seemed the next logical step in her growth and progression as an artist. Up until this time, our goal had purely and simply been to find the best songs for her. Frankly, I was color-blind, and perhaps a little naïve in that I didn't try to find pure R&B songs that only black-oriented stations could claim for their own. I had been receiving call after call from prominent and successful African-American artists who were suffering financial stress because the number of albums they were selling based exclusively on R&B play was not recouping their recording and video costs. They were dazzled that Whitney was selling tens of millions of albums worldwide with her first two albums, and they wanted that kind of success for themselves. That said, for a singer of Whitney's pedigree to be white-identified was unfortunate and wrong, and we set out to correct that impression. To do that, I approached the very successful songwriting and production team of L.A. Reid and Kenny "Babyface" Edmonds. They had had an amazing run of nineteen number-one R&B hits, but they had never had a number-one pop hit. With Whitney, we'd enjoyed an unprecedented degree of pop success, and now we wanted to enhance her R&B credibility. It was an ideal marriage, and it would soon lead to our founding together L.A. and Babyface's label, LaFace Records, as a joint venture with Arista.

L.A. and Babyface produced four songs for Whitney's third album,

I'm Your Baby Tonight (1990), including the title track, which they also co-wrote. That song was the album's lead single, and it achieved what everyone wanted: L.A. and Babyface's first number-one pop hit. They also produced the Top 20 hit "My Name Is Not Susan," and produced and co-wrote the Top 10 hit "Miracle." I contributed the album's other number-one hit, the great ballad "All the Man That I Need," written by Michael Gore and Dean Pitchford. Significantly, all four of those songs were Top 10 R&B hits, as was "I Belong to You," which Narada produced. The album sold more than 4 million copies in the United States, which is certainly a strong showing, though admittedly far fewer than *Whitney* had done before. It peaked at number three on the pop charts, but was a number-one R&B album, so it fulfilled our objective of meaningfully crossing Whitney over to a very sizable African-American audience.

One of the most transcendent moments in Whitney's career occurred in January 1991, when she sang "The Star-Spangled Banner" at the Super Bowl in Tampa. The United States was fighting in the Persian Gulf War at the time, and patriotic feelings were running high. Whitney was at the height of her vocal powers, and her performance of the song was electrifying. It was soulful, passionate, supremely confident, and rousing. Seconds after she finished, her fists raised in the air triumphantly, four fighter jets roared over the stadium. It was a moment of unforgettable drama and pride. I believe that if you took a poll about the greatest version of our national anthem ever performed, Whitney's would win hands-down. The performance generated such an enormous response that we released the song as a single and arranged for all proceeds from its sales to benefit the American Red Cross Gulf Crisis Fund to aid military families. Whitney's performance had become so acclaimed, such an indelible statement of American resolve, that Arista released it again after the 9/11 attacks, this time donating the proceeds to organizations benefiting first responders and victims' families.

When I learned through her agent, Nicole David, that Whitney was looking for movie roles, I can't say that I was thrilled. We had made only three albums, and as far as I was concerned, we still had plenty more work to do in order to build her career to a level worthy of her extraordinary talent. I was well aware that you can't stand in the way of an artist's desire to diversify, but there are potential pitfalls. Although a number of singers had successfully made the transition to acting, they were the exception, not the rule. It would be very easy to make a mistake, to negatively affect Whitney's image and damage everything that we had worked so hard to achieve. From standing at the very apex of the world of music, she would go to being a novice in the film world. If she took a small role, it could seem beneath her and make her seem smaller. If she took on a leading role, the possibility of an embarrassing failure loomed large. And if she was a great success? Well, she already was a huge star. Would she make another movie then, or record an album? Whitney had begun moving in circles where she was around some of the major actors of the time, and she was clearly struck by the level of stardom they enjoyed. She had even dated Eddie Murphy for a while. There is unquestionably still an aura to Hollywood, and Whitney felt it. She was determined to try, so I really had no choice but to go along and provide the best support and guidance that I could. I never advised her, "Don't do it." I definitely encouraged her to explore it. But I was as clear as I could be about the potential problems. I often say that I get paid to worry, and at this point I was earning my money.

From the very start, I had concerns about *The Bodyguard*. The original script I saw wasn't terribly exciting, and I knew that it had been knocking around for a while, and at one point was meant to be a vehicle for Steve McQueen and Diana Ross. But when I was sent the initial rushes of the movie, I got extremely concerned. Whitney was a natural beauty, but she was not a natural actress. She held her own, but you couldn't say her performance was inspiring. Even more disturbing, I felt that the film itself had serious problems, and now I had no choice but to let my views be known. I wrote a lengthy letter to Mick Jackson, the film's director, and Jim Wilson, one of its producers, and I sent a copy to Whitney as well. In the cover note to Whitney, I wrote: "Last night when I saw the film I was filled with happiness for you as well as pride for you. In a very demanding role, you sure give it your all and you were outstanding. Regarding the film, in the interest of constructive suggestions, I have the attached comments that I'm faxing today to Mick Jackson and Jim Wilson. I hope it doesn't come off badly as I'm sure that at this stage they would prefer total cheerleading. But you know it's the results that count."

In the letter to Jackson and Wilson, with a copy to Kevin Costner, I wrote:

I'm writing this in the spirit that this movie will be a big winner for everyone involved and that what is good can be even better. I think that music can obviously play a much stronger role than the temp score indicates, not just for the usual record company reasons, but for the essential strength of the film. Yes, the film is primarily a portrait of a bodyguard, but to make that work, two other elements must work also. (A) Whitney must be believable in the role as a star, and (B) the relationship and its conflicts must be understood. In this connection Whitney is never really allowed to show her stardom until the very end. She sings earlier, but never in any bravura way to indicate the magnitude of her stardom. You are therefore dependent on the trappings of stardom and it just flits back and forth between these trappings and glimpses of stardom. Because the audience isn't allowed to experience her singing as a star, when it comes time to see her vulnerability, it doesn't register the way it should. If you felt her singing stardom (like giving her a chance to really belt the chorus of "I Have Nothing"), it would make much more believable the entire conflicted relationship. To depend only on the artifacts of stardom hampers the impact of the eventual vulnerability. This is being said not to get Whitney more footage. Yes, the focus of the story is about a bodyguard, but a lot of time is devoted to their relationship, and so this must fit together from the beginning much more integrally. Costner defines The Bodyguard. *Whitney should be allowed to show her "stuff" earlier. It would help underline the movie, not weaken the Costner focus.*

I didn't hear anything back for three or four weeks. In part, I feared that my letter would be discounted as simply the sort of criticism a record company president would make—of course anyone in my position would want more music in the film and a greater emphasis on the performer's artistry. That's why I tried to embed my suggestions in a discussion of the film as a whole. If Whitney were playing an actress or a politician, it would be an entirely different matter. But she was playing a singer, and the audience needed to experience her extraordinary power in that role. As it happened, my letter had a far greater impact than I could have imagined. Kevin Costner completely agreed with my suggestions, and that contributed to his falling-out with Mick Jackson. Suddenly music was one of the film's prime points of emphasis.

From the very start, the soundtrack was going to be one of the most important aspects of the project, from both an artistic and a marketing standpoint. As always, finding the right songs was critically important. Gerry Griffith brought me "Run to You." I loved it. It had started out as a breakup song, so the lyric needed to be rewritten to make it a love song for the purposes of the film, and both versions were excellent. David Foster, the leading producer of the soundtrack, and his wife at the time, Linda Thompson, wrote the power ballad "I Have Nothing." We came up with the idea of Whitney doing a remake of the Chaka Khan smash "I'm Every Woman." Whitney helped arrange and co-produced the gospel standard "Jesus Loves Me" with the gospel singer BeBe Winans, and she shared a writing credit with Daryl Simmons and L.A. and Babyface on the highly rhythmic dance track "Queen of the Night."

But of course the song that defined both the movie and the soundtrack is "I Will Always Love You," which Dolly Parton wrote. Costner had originally wanted the main song for the movie to be a version of the Motown classic "What Becomes of the Brokenhearted," a 1966 hit for Jimmy Ruffin. Whitney and David Foster could never get a version they really liked, and when Foster and Costner learned that the British soul singer Paul Young had recorded the song for the soundtrack to the film *Fried Green Tomatoes,* it was dropped. Then Kevin Costner suggested "I Will Always Love You." When he sent it to me, I loved it, and both Whitney and Foster were extremely enthusiastic as well.

That's when the fun really began. David Foster and I have always had great mutual respect. He has had a truly wonderful career, and he deservedly comes with a very strong sense of what he wants to do. I, of

course, am not shy about expressing my own ideas. In this case Costner told Foster that he wanted Whitney to sing the first forty seconds
or so of "I Will Always Love You" a cappella. It was a bold idea, and
definitely not the sort of thing you would typically hear on the radio.
Foster recorded it that way, but he had a much more orchestral vision
for the song. Knowing that I have my own sense of how a song should
finally sound on a record, Foster deliberately sent me a version that he
regarded as outrageously underproduced, "substandard" in his own description of it. He says that he put it together in about twenty minutes,
though I didn't know that at the time. His idea was that I would give
him copious notes, he would revisit the song, address some of my ideas,
incorporate all the embellishments he wanted, and ultimately wind
up with a rendition of the song as he envisioned it. The only problem
that surfaced was that I absolutely loved the spare, underproduced version that he sent me. When I heard it, it reminded me of listening to
"Bridge over Troubled Water" for the first time. A lengthy, idiosyncratic
ballad, it violated all the rules for a lead single from an album. But in
the face of true greatness, the rulebook needs to be thrown away. Genius like that makes its own rules.

When I told Foster that, he was at a loss for words. He kept sending
me "tweaks" and sweetening "touch-ups" that amounted to major revisions that lost the very qualities that appealed to me about the original
version. That rendition combined extraordinary intimacy with overwhelming power, a rare and entirely compelling combination. Weeks
went by, and we were having yet another disagreement on the phone
about the song when he told me that the version I'd heard no longer
existed, that it was a rough mix he hadn't bothered to keep. Fortunately,
I'd kept the digital audiotape that he had given to me. By that point
the movie studio was haranguing me to release "I Will Always Love
You" as the first single. It needed the record out there to promote the
movie. Time passed and I kept waiting for David to send me the greatly
simplified new version I was requesting. It never came. Finally, the
deadline for the single had arrived. I had the toughest decision to make.
I literally held my breath and had my preferred version mastered and
released.

Without notice, David immediately heard it on the radio, and he called me up and laced me with every obscenity known to mankind. I had no desire to argue any longer. I thanked him for the fantastic job he had done with the song. After all, he had done every version, including the one I chose. Happily, David and I remain great friends, and we joke about this hair-raising situation to this day. He is gracious and generous with his praise that I stuck to my guns.

By now the commercial impact of *The Bodyguard* soundtrack is part of music history. It has sold more than 34 million copies worldwide, making it the best-selling soundtrack of all time and one of the best-selling albums of any kind. Because, as almost all soundtracks do, it includes songs by various artists, Whitney usually isn't credited, as Michael Jackson or the Eagles are, as personally having such a giant seller. But no one can doubt that Whitney's six songs are what made the soundtrack so successful. "I Will Always Love You" spent fourteen weeks at number one, a record at the time. To date, the film has grossed more than $450 million worldwide. The soundtrack earned Whitney three Grammys, including Album of the Year and Record of the Year. I still remember on Grammy night Whitney and David insisting that I join them onstage to accept the Album of the Year Grammy with them. It was a perfect ending for such a glorious project.

As unbelievably successful as *The Bodyguard* was, Whitney did not at all enjoy making the movie. She liked to work quickly in the studio, and moviemaking is an impossibly slow process, and it frustrated her. Consequently, I was more than surprised when she decided to do *Waiting to Exhale*. Admittedly, it was an attractive project, based on a novel by Terry McMillan, with Forest Whitaker directing and an ensemble cast that included Angela Bassett, Loretta Devine, and Lela Rochon. When I first saw the rushes for this film, I was very pleased by how much more relaxed Whitney seemed, how naturally she interacted with the other women in the cast. I was very concerned about the temporary music, however. Here was a contemporary film about African-American women finding their way through their lives, and the music I was given included the "Love Theme from *Romeo and Juliet*" by Henry Mancini and songs by Stephen Bishop and Johnny Mathis. There's clearly nothing wrong with those songs in the right context, but they're simply not what the women in this film would be listening to. I contacted the head of the studio and explained my concerns. I strongly suggested that he get in touch with Babyface and simply turn the soundtrack over to him. I had come to know Babyface very well by this point, and I knew he would do an extraordinary job.

Initially, Babyface wanted Whitney to record the entire soundtrack, but she rightly declined. Part of the point of the movie is to defy any stereotype of African-American women, to demonstrate the wide variety of their values and outlooks. Having a range of voices and musical styles represented on the soundtrack seemed like the best way to drive that point home. So Whitney had two solo tracks on the album, including "Exhale (Shoop Shoop)," a number-one hit, as well as a duet with CeCe Winans. Joining her were the likes of Mary J. Blige ("Not Gon' Cry"), Brandy ("Sittin' Up in My Room"), TLC, Toni Braxton, Aretha Franklin, and Chaka Khan. The album delivered hit after hit and sold more than 7 million copies in the United States alone, continuing Whitney's matchless commercial run. The film, meanwhile, broke ground for movies on African-American subjects, and has grossed close to $70 million. Then, in 1996, Whitney starred opposite Denzel Washington in *The Preacher's Wife*, which allowed her to record a gospel soundtrack and to achieve the best-selling gospel album of all time. Finally, in 1997, Whitney co-produced a multiethnic version of *Cinderella* in which she played the fairy godmother and Brandy played the title role. It was nominated for seven Emmys, and won one.

For all the successes through this period, one incident comes to mind. It didn't seem that significant at the time, but thinking back, it seems weighted with meaning. Babyface had once given me a ballad for Whitney titled "Why Does It Hurt So Bad." I kept trying to get her to record it, and atypically she always refused. The song is about a woman who leaves a man who had treated her badly, but finds that she still has feelings for him and can't get him off her mind. Whitney would sit there eating her burger and fries and tell me over and over that she couldn't relate to the emotions in the song. Why would a woman feel bad about leaving someone who had hurt her? She would never allow a man to treat her that way, she said, and she certainly wouldn't pine for such a relationship after she had ended it. How could she sing the song if she couldn't feel the emotions, or even think they were valid? There was no anger involved, but it was the only song we ever really reached an impasse over. I always tried to convince her that the emotions in it were universal, but she wasn't having it. Finally, when she was working on the *Waiting to Exhale* soundtrack, she called me out of the blue and told me she was ready to sing the song. "I know what that song's about now," she simply said. "I'm ready to sing it."

I'm not one of the people who blames Whitney's problems on Bobby Brown. People get involved with one another for all kinds of reasons, and certainly no one forced her to marry him. They passionately loved each other, but very early on they developed a co-dependent relationship that did neither of them any good. Whitney was always comfortable and loving around me, and Bobby was perfectly friendly. I want to emphasize that Bobby was never present when Whitney and I discussed her career or listened to songs together or anything like that. She may or may not have discussed all that with him later, but when we were working together it was always only the two of us. On a couple of occasions she asked me if I would listen to some tracks that Bobby was considering recording himself, and I did that. Again, on those occasions, I was just with Bobby alone. I really do try to keep those boundaries clear and in place. And in all those conversations both Whitney and Bobby were focused and disciplined.

As close as I get to the artists I work with, I try not to get involved in their personal lives. When we socialize, it's invariably on occasions related to our work, at performances or music industry events in which we're celebrating our professional lives. I don't vacation with artists, or mix my business and personal life. For the most part I think they appreciate those boundaries. But as the tabloid stories and rumors about Bobby and Whitney proliferated, it was getting harder and harder to imagine that they were all untrue or exaggerated. If your help isn't solicited, it's hard to know what you can or should do, so I tried to concentrate on the aspect of our lives that had always gone well: making great music together.

In August 1997 I sent a letter to Whitney that was not easy to write, but that was designed to get her focused and back on track.

Dearest Whitney, You know my love for you goes beyond the professional nature of our relationship, which in and of itself is almost as long as the age you were when I met you. To put it succinctly, I'm seriously concerned. I know that I have absolutely no right to reflect on anything but your professional recording career, so let me address that. You have not done a studio album in seven years. You have only recorded a total of seven pop songs during the last five years, and those were chosen to integrate into the characters of two motion pictures. So, insofar as your position as the number one contemporary recording artist in the world is concerned, you have been practically missing in action. Obviously, I know what you now get paid for a movie and when you perform before a sultan. [In 1996 the sultan of Brunei arranged for Whitney to perform in his country for a very lavish sum.] *I know what HBO will pay you and what a far eastern tour might throw off. But you are first and foremost a recording artist and in that regard I honestly and frankly believe you are now being reckless in your avoidance of your "job." You know that's what this is: it's your job. Now, everyone wants to take time off. Everyone wants to live life. Everyone wants to try something else once in a while. I know this. But everyone—even mogul billionaires—have a job unless they're going to become a dilettante playboy or playgirl. Whitney, the job you have is music—contemporary music. In this connection, we agreed that you would at last begin your studio album in August. . . . Well, the day of reckoning is now upon us. Your recording career—and its need for full concentration and participation on your part—must begin again. I'm reluctant to urge you any more strongly because I know of your fierce independence. But in your heart you know I care. I've been there from the beginning and my life doesn't depend on this. I'm involved because I do love you and have aspirations for you. So, stop putting this off. No more being tired. No more loss of voice. No more no time. I'm asking you to come to work. I love you, Clive.*

The letter did affect her. She called me up and was clearly in a playful mood. She was warm and affectionate and told me she was ready to record. So we began working on some tracks to invigorate a greatest hits collection we were putting together. However, we got so many good songs in and Whitney was singing so well that it led to *My Love Is Your Love* (1998), her first studio album in eight years. Soul music had moved much more aggressively in the direction of hip-hop, and the album reflected that. Rodney Jerkins, Wyclef Jean, Missy Elliott, and Lauryn Hill did productions for it, along with stalwarts like Babyface and David Foster. The trials and tribulations of Whitney's personal life had reached the tabloid press, and the skeptics had a field day. Could Whitney still have hits? Would she come back and dominate as she had in the past? Well, we ignored all that and concentrated on the songs. Wyclef and his close associate Jerry Wonder came up with the title cut, and it was a total multiformat winner. It all sounded fresh, and the video showed Whitney irresistibly vital. Rodney Jerkins played "It's Not Right but It's OK" for me the day I was to meet Whitney at the Beverly Hills Hotel to go over the material. She came to my bungalow at midnight in her pajamas, and when I played her Rodney's song, her face lit up. We kept playing the song over and over, dancing from room to room. Whitney amazed me before the night was over by singing the whole song with all the lyrics and already interpreting it in her own inimitable way. She was back big-time and would soon be dominating the airwaves and clubs all over the world.

The album sold 4 million copies in the United States and more than 10 million worldwide. It was a strong, contemporary look for Whitney, and likely because of its somewhat harder sound, the album elicited the most positive reviews of her career. One notable aspect of the album was the duet between Whitney and Mariah Carey on "When You Believe," a song from the animated film *The Prince of Egypt*. The two singers had been positioned as rivals by the media, and it was fascinating to see them perform the song together on television and at the Oscars, where it won for Best Original Song. While I never discussed Mariah with Whitney, I was always struck when I spoke with Mariah by the awe she felt for Whitney and Whitney's voice. She was extremely gracious and always deferential when speaking about her.

In 2000, shortly before I left Arista, we did release Whitney's *Greatest Hits* album, a two-disc set that included four new songs and a substantial number of remixes in order, once again, to address the shifting musical landscape and keep Whitney current. The collection has sold 3 million copies domestically, and topped the charts around the world, selling more than 6 million copies abroad. More about this later, but the sad news is that Whitney and I would not work together again for a couple of years. That didn't mean we would not interact. With the entire media world watching to see if she could perform at her characteristic peerless level, Whitney delivered a riveting performance at the twenty-fifth-anniversary celebration of Arista Records, which was broadcast as a prime-time special on NBC in 2000. And earlier that year I had decided that my pre-Grammy gala, which was particularly emotional since it would be my last one while solely with Arista, would showcase only two artists: Carlos Santana and Whitney. She was never in finer form. She knew the evening would be very significant to me and she didn't let me down. After Santana had performed a scorching set, she took the stage and electrified the star-studded audience who rose to salute her time and again. Then with the last two numbers she came to the foot of the stage and sang them solely to me. "I Believe in You and Me" from *The Preacher's Wife* took on new meaning. She was making clear to everyone that somehow, somewhere we would continue as a team. My spine tingled every time she got to the title phrase, and I was transfixed. I totally lost it with "I Will Always Love You," and I was joined in that emotion by everyone in the room. Whitney was spellbinding and unforgettable. When I said at her funeral that she was always there for me, this is a shining example.

But there did come a time when there was no longer any denying how erratic Whitney had become. She had been scheduled to perform at the Academy Awards in 2000 but was fired from the show after singing the wrong song during a rehearsal with the musical director, Burt Bacharach, and displaying a careless and "defiant" attitude toward the process of preparing for her performance. That her voice also was not in good shape only worsened matters. The producer, Lili Zanuck, later declared, "We didn't want to work for six months for this to be a show about how fucked-up Whitney Houston was." Also, Whitney had agreed to perform when I was inducted into the Rock and Roll Hall of Fame in 2000, but, highly uncharacteristically, she canceled. She personally showed up at the Waldorf-Astoria to show me the hoarseness in her voice, but I worried that its cause was more than a cold. I decided that I had to do something.

First I contacted her mother, Cissy, and her agent, Nicole David, to discuss my deep concerns, which, needless to say, they shared. I offered to participate in any intervention that would be organized, and I think one did take place, though I was not there. I spoke to addiction specialists about Whitney's situation. And I decided that I needed to speak with her directly. Bobby Brown would be in jail for a couple of months on a parole violation, which provided an opportunity. They obviously both needed to get clean, but it would be easier to get her to go to rehab if he was already out of the picture. And if he had been kept drug-free while in prison that would also help.

So I invited Whitney to spend a few days with me at my weekend home in Pound Ridge, New York. She came with her and Bobby's daughter, Bobbi Kristina, and three or four other family members. I didn't say anything about what I had in mind. After dinner, her relatives went to my guesthouse, and I gestured to Whitney that I wanted her to stay behind. When she and I were alone, I spoke to her with as much urgency, sincerity, sympathy, and love as I could muster. I said, "You and I really have never had occasion to speak about the dimension of your problem. Seeing all the trouble that your family is going through, seeing that Bobby is in prison, wouldn't this be the best time to go into rehab?" I told her that I didn't need to hear details, apologies, or confessions. I just wanted her to get her problem taken care of. I told her about other artists who had been deeply important to me, how Janis Joplin had lost her life to drugs, and Sly Stone had destroyed his career. I couldn't let this happen to her. Once Bobby was out of jail, we could get him into treatment as well.

Whitney was quiet the entire time I spoke. She didn't storm out of the room. She listened intently to every word I said. Then she told me point-blank—politely, but in no uncertain terms—that whatever was going on with her was a personal matter and she had it under control. There was absolutely no need for her to enter rehab. I had been as direct as I could be, and it was evident that she was in complete denial. I was depressed and frustrated, but at least for the moment, I felt that

I was out of options. I knew that if an addict does not want to get help, there ultimately is very little that anyone else can do.

After I left Arista, Whitney and I were not in regular contact. Arista, under L.A. Reid, who now ran the label, believed that it was essential to keep Whitney after I left, so she signed a $100 million deal with the label for six more albums. It was one of the largest deals in the history of the music industry. Just before the 9/11 attacks, Whitney appeared at Michael Jackson's thirtieth-anniversary concerts at Madison Square Garden. I was in the audience and I literally lost my breath at the sight of her. She looked skeletal. Her appearance triggered so much commentary that her publicist had to issue a statement explaining that Whitney had been "under stress due to family matters." The tribute in honor of Michael was spread over two nights, and though Whitney was slated to perform at both concerts, she canceled the second night's performance.

I wrote to her a week after her appearance at the Garden:

Dearest Whitney: When I saw you Friday night at the Michael Jackson concert I gasped. When I got home, I cried. My dear, dear Whitney, the time has come. Of course I know you don't want to hear this. Of course I know that you're saying that Clive is being foolishly dramatic. Of course I know that your power of denial is in overdrive dismissing everything I and everyone else is saying to you. But I know somewhere down deep there is the real you that knows that you are being confronted this time by everyone who loves you, who cares for you and who wants you well. You are now being begged by these same people who know that this problem is bigger than you can deal with alone. I join your mother in pleading with you to face up to the truth now, right now, and there is no more time or postponement. You must think not only of yourself but you must think of those who love you. Our anguish, our fear, our pain is just too much to bear. You must get help for yourself and for your close extended family.

Whitney, our lives intertwined almost twenty years ago. You learned to trust me even when you had doubt, and professionally you soared with your God given talent and genius to all time heights. Now, I reach out personally and I ask you to trust me.

I ask you to trust me in blind faith. You need help and it must
begin now. I will stand by you with love and caring to see you
through it to new found peace and happiness in every way as a
woman, as a mother, as a role model to inspire the rest of the world.
Love, Clive.

I verified that she received and read the letter, but I never got a response from her. Then, to help promote her first album under the new
contract with Arista, Whitney did her *Prime Time* interview with Diane
Sawyer. It was one of the most anticipated interviews in television
history, and, from the standpoint of anyone who cared about Whitney, it was an unmitigated disaster. Whitney was guarded, vague, and
defensive, and their conversation launched a thousand parodies. The
takeaway line was her status-conscious insistence that she didn't smoke
crack because it's "cheap" and "crack is wack." The appearance, which
was meant to reassure fans that Whitney was back and had finally gotten it together, did precisely the opposite. *Just Whitney,* her first album
without me at the helm, came out at the end of 2002. The public's curiosity was there, and the album sold 205,000 copies in its first week, but
none of its four singles even came close to cracking the Top 40.

What is it about certain artists who seem bent on self-destruction,
notwithstanding their secure position as the very brightest of stars? No
doubt, the risk of failure is omnipresent and one can never totally rest
easy. There is fragility always in the mix, along with the acute vulnerability that so often accompanies intense creativity. But I don't think
that's the total answer. Among the artists I have known, like Whitney
or Janis Joplin, there always was a false assumption of survival. They
had been affected by the adulation and had developed a bravado, a belief that nothing could topple them. Also, in each case, alcohol or drugs
fueled a feeling of omnipotence, a denial of the life-threatening risks
being undertaken. Yes, it may be obvious, but it bears repeating: Drugs
are devastating and often lethal, and they are an undeniable common
denominator in artistic self-destruction.

During this time, Whitney and I didn't see each other. We didn't
have a falling-out or anything as dramatic as that. I kept closely in
touch with Nicole David because I was still worried about Whitney's

condition, but we were not working together, so the most obvious reason for us to communicate was no longer present. Then, in 2004, I accepted the incredible BMG offer from Rolf Schmidt-Holtz to head the entire RCA Music Group, which included Arista, so, amazingly, I was once again overseeing the label I had founded. I was also set to be honored that year on a network television special by the Princess Grace Foundation as part of the World Music Awards. I used that occasion to contact Whitney, since once again we were to be reunited as a result of my new position. She was thrilled. I was thrilled. She sounded real good on the phone and assured me that she looked good, too. I told her of the upcoming honor and she immediately insisted that she come to Las Vegas for the occasion. There could be no lifetime achievement award for me without her participation. I held my breath because the last time I had seen her, which was at the Michael Jackson tribute, she wasn't Whitney. I called her sister-in-law Pat Houston, who was acting as her manager and who had become her personal confidante, and she assured me that, yes, Whitney was looking good and was making every effort to get back into vocal shape. Pat felt that it would be great for Whitney to have incentive, to meet with me and have the goal of her performance to shoot for.

I agreed to meet with Whitney in Las Vegas but we would keep everything secret until after we saw each other. I did believe that the more firmly she found her footing as an artist and shifted the perception of her away from drugs and domestic squabbles the better off she would be. I was apprehensive as I prepared to meet her when she arrived in Las Vegas. We met in my suite and, lo and behold, Whitney was Whitney once again. She looked great, and spoke well. She wanted to work and insisted that she would do us both proud. I went along with her, and invited her to a reception I was having for all the artists appearing on the awards show the next night. Alicia Keys was there, along with Usher and Avril Lavigne. Even my friend Andre Agassi was there for support. Whitney walked in unannounced and everyone was shocked. She clearly had lost none of her star quality. Every eye was fixed on her. And the next night at the MGM Arena, she was glowing. No one knew she was coming. I made the surprise introduction of her from the stage to the audience of fifteen thousand, who couldn't believe their eyes. She truly was a vision in a gorgeous gown and with a hairstyle that showed her classic beauty. Before she sang a note, a standing ovation for her lasted two full minutes. Every artist appearing that night, including Céline Dion and Patti LaBelle, came from backstage and all had tears running down their faces. Her performance was absolutely incandescent. She sounded like the Whitney of old. It was a memorable moment, and demonstrated what she was still capable of achieving.

Unfortunately, things did not exactly proceed without incident after that. In 2005 Bravo began airing the reality show *Being Bobby Brown,* which Whitney had foolishly agreed to be part of. She felt that as Bobby's wife she had to support him, and he wouldn't have gotten the deal if she didn't participate. Inevitably, the show became more about Whitney than Bobby, and it showed her most unfavorably. "Hell to the no!" became a catchphrase associated with her, a far cry from the days when we had to worry if she was perceived as being too much of a goody-goody. Happily, the show, despite its ratings success, ran for only one season, because Whitney finally refused to film any more episodes. In 2006 Whitney separated from Bobby, and filed for divorce. Again, I don't believe Bobby caused Whitney's problems, but the two of them brought out the worst in each other. They were "crazy in love," as Whitney put it, and nothing was going to change as long as they stayed together.

Finally, I called her one day and told her that it was time she got back to work. I assured her nothing would change. I would lead the search for material. My key A&R man, Larry Jackson, would be right there with me, putting out the word that Whitney was back. At first there was silence but I knew that Whitney would be glad to have her career back. She might have been scared, but she agreed that it was time. Calls went out to R. Kelly, Akon, Jermaine Dupri, and Diane Warren, among others, and the creative process began to bind us together again. One of the first artists to tell me that she wanted to be involved in Whitney's comeback was Alicia Keys. Whitney had been a huge influence on her, and, after hearing her perform at one of my pre-Grammy parties, she wanted nothing more than to play a positive role in her reemergence. Alicia and her husband-to-be, Swizz Beatz, co-wrote "Million Dollar Bill," which was to be the album's strong lead single. It took several months for Whitney to be in shape to record. She was often hoarse, and where she used to come into the studio and nail her parts right away, she now required much more preparation and many more takes. I did not discuss drug use with her. I didn't see any evidence of it, and figured that I had made my position about it clear. But I did know that she was smoking cigarettes—the equivalent of leaving a priceless Stradivarius out in the sun—and I relentlessly urged her to quit. We were changing arrangements to accommodate the limitations of her range. She insisted that I was being unrealistic. "Clive, you want me to sound like I'm still nineteen years old," she'd say. But I saw no reason why her voice couldn't recover if she took care of it. We wouldn't fight about it, but it was a persistent, tense topic of conversation between us.

It all went slowly, but gradually Whitney got stronger and the takes got better. I ended up being very pleased with how the album, titled *I Look to You,* turned out. To announce the album's release in 2009 we held listening parties in London, New York, and Los Angeles, one more glamorous than the other. We created a strong worldwide buzz about it, and in the States it sold 305,000 copies in its first week, the best opening week in Whitney's career. And then, very shortly after its release, Whitney did a long interview with Oprah Winfrey that ran as two hour-long specials. I accompanied her to the taping to show support, and this time Whitney came across as candid and forthright, providing harrowing details of what she'd been through. I was encouraged that she had put drugs behind her but I knew that cigarette smoking was something she couldn't quit. Knowing how fragile Whitney's voice was, I wasn't happy when I heard about her plans for a world tour. She never discussed it with me, because I'm sure she knew what I would say. I'd imagine that money played a big role in her decision, but however much she made, the tour clearly was a mistake. The publicity was horrendous. Once again the focus was back on how her voice wasn't what it used to be. I don't know if Whitney thought she could wing it and get by on showmanship, or if she thought her fans would love her anyway, even if she missed some notes. Regardless, all anyone heard about those shows were the bad reviews and the excuses.

Whitney and I stayed in touch after the tour ended in the middle of 2010 and spoke repeatedly about the prospects for recording again. This time I told her very directly I would not go into the studio with her until she had regained her voice. I told her that she needed to cut out cigarettes entirely—cutting back was not enough. And she would have to commit to a regimen of vocal exercises. She would tell me how hard it was and that I didn't understand. I told her that no one could do it for her. When we were in Los Angeles at the same time we would meet. Occasionally her brother Gary and his wife, Pat, were there. I was unyielding and they were supportive. Whitney was still headstrong and holding out, but we loved each other and we both knew it. She knew that she would always have all the help and support I could provide.

On February 11, 2012, I was deep into the preparations for my annual pre-Grammy party, which was scheduled to begin in just a few hours. When you're organizing an event in which virtually every guest is an A-list celebrity, in which many of those celebrities are performing, and the full national media is present, complications arise until the very last minute. I'm personally involved in every aspect of the event—from the song selection of the performers to the seating arrangement for the 950 guests. While exhilarating, even after more than thirty-five years, the crazy process never gets easier.

It was a Saturday afternoon, and the phone rang in my bungalow at the Beverly Hills Hotel, which was no big deal since the phone rang constantly that entire week. This call was different, however. It was from Stacy Carr, who administers the event for me every year. She was sobbing, telling me that Whitney had been found dead in her suite at the Beverly Hilton Hotel. There are moments when time stands still, and you feel as if you can't even begin to comprehend the words that are being spoken to you. That's how I felt right then. Fortunately, my children and my closest friends were there. I was overwhelmed by so many conflicting feelings. How could this have happened? Just a few days before, Whitney and I had sat together in this very suite, talking and listening to music. She played some songs from *Sparkle,* the upcoming film that she was producing and acting in, and I played her some new songs that I was working on. She assured me that she was committed through vocal exercise to get her high notes back, that she was swimming daily and getting into shape. She said with authority that she would seek help to cut out cigarettes entirely, not just cut back, and that she would be ready to go into the studio in August. Maybe I should have been more skeptical, but I've always been optimistic, and I felt hopeful. It felt like old times.

Now she was dead. So many memories and emotions were rushing through me, but there was no time to process any of them. I was desperate for more information about what had happened to her. The media worldwide were in an uproar, and every outlet, many of which were covering my party anyway, was trying to get hold of me. Pat Houston was at the Beverly Hilton and I needed to reach her, and I needed to call Whitney's mother, Cissy, too. And what about the party? Should we cancel it at the last minute or transform it into a tribute? So much had to be done and so many decisions had to be made very quickly. Maybe that was for the good. I'm not sure what I would have done otherwise. Our team spoke to Whitney's representatives and outlined the evening's tribute to Whitney and the minute of silence that would precede it. We, and the National Academy of Recording Arts and Sciences, which sponsors the event, decided to proceed with the party. My conversation with Whitney just a couple of days earlier confirmed what I always knew was true about her: that she was musical to her very soul. She loved this party and came to it every year. She was not scheduled to perform this time, but she wanted to be there anyway. I completely understood if some guests or performers decided that they couldn't be there, but on this night, in Whitney's honor, the decision was made that the show would go on.

Needless to say, it was quite an emotional night. I began the evening by explaining that I felt no need to conceal my feelings in front of the audience assembled. I was personally devastated. I called for the moment of silence in Whitney's memory, and then the performances began. Everyone who sang that night—from Tony Bennett and Diana Krall to Alicia Keys, from the Kinks' Ray Davies (with Jackson Browne and Elvis Costello) to Jamie Foxx and Diana Ross, from Wiz Khalifa to Pitbull—honored Whitney. Sean "Puffy" Combs put everything in perspective for everybody and spoke beautifully, as did Neil Portnow from NARAS. No one left. I believe that everyone who was there took a part of Whitney's spirit with them at the end of the night. At the Grammys on the next night, Jennifer Hudson sang "I Will Always Love You" in honor of Whitney, and that, too, was healing and profound.

The days that passed before Whitney's funeral were a surreal blur of overwhelming sadness and pragmatic decision-making. Finding a quiet moment to mourn my beloved Whitney was extremely difficult. Most important, I helped Pat and the family organize the memorial service. Many ideas, suggestions, and rumors were flying around, but I encouraged the family to make the event as private and personal as possible. Too much of Whitney's final years had been a media circus. I believed that a relatively small ceremony at the New Hope Baptist Church in her hometown of Newark, New Jersey, was the way to go. Anything that restored Whitney to the roots that represented her most enduring values would serve her best.

So many people at the service spoke movingly about her, and of course R. Kelly, Alicia Keys, Stevie Wonder, BeBe and CeCe Winans, and the gospel choirs all performed with powerful emotion. In my remarks, I tried to emphasize the passion for music in Whitney's life, the part of her that always seemed to get forgotten amid all the publicity about her problems. It was also the part of her that I knew best. I remembered, and still remember, our meetings in my hotel bungalow at one in the morning, sitting on the carpet listening to demos of "My Love Is Your Love" and "It's Not Right but It's Okay" and hearing her magical voice begin to transform those songs into her own indelible statements. Right to the very end, in such moments of exquisite intimacy it seemed as if we were back at the start of her extraordinary rise, a time of innocence when everything was possible and seemed as if it would last forever. Whitney's loss grieves me more than I can say.

Beyond the House
That Barry Built

In 1979 Columbia Pictures and I had sold Arista to Bertelsmann AG, an international media company based in Gütersloh, Germany. That sale for approximately $50 million brought to an end a complicated couple of years in Arista's relations with its parent company. I had an excellent rapport with Alan Hirschfield, the Columbia Pictures CEO who brought me in to establish Arista. He understood music, saw the great possibilities of what the music industry could become, and encouraged me to think big and be aggressive in my aspirations for Arista, all of which I deeply appreciated. We also got along personally, so it was an ideal professional relationship. However, a highly public scandal broke out at Columbia Pictures when David Begelman, the highest-ranking executive there, embezzled funds from the company, and the atmosphere became highly charged and intensely political. Justifiably shaken by what Begelman had done, Alan fired him. But the company's board of directors, which had close ties to the professionally extremely talented Begelman, rebelled and attempted to fire Alan.

Dan Melnick, the head of the company's motion picture division, and I helped rally company executives in Alan's defense. In my case, it was partly out of loyalty to Alan, partly because I remembered my own unfair treatment when I was fired at Columbia Records, but mostly because I believed he was doing a very good job. We managed to save Alan temporarily, but the handwriting was on the wall. He was eventually pushed out, and the new CEO, Herb Allen, Jr., an otherwise brilliant man with an illustrious career, was just not as interested in the future of music as Alan was. Given that I was on the wrong side of the political divide and was part of a company that now was just not optimistic about the music business, finding a new home for Arista was a priority.

Bertelsmann was primarily a publishing company, but in the late Seventies it was in expansion mode and very hot on music. It did own a label called Ariola, which had done well in Europe but had never found success in the United States. At one point Monti Lüftner, the head of Bertelsmann's music operation, had approached me about running Ariola in the States, but I wasn't interested. In the course of those conversations, however, I came to like Lüftner a great deal. He was passionate about and understood music, and was full of enthusiasm for, and sensitive to, artists. I could tell that if we ever did go into business together, he would be extremely supportive. As a result of our meetings I knew that he was eager for a bigger stake in the U.S. music market, so I alerted Herb Allen, Jr., aware that Herb was likely looking for a buyer for Arista. Both Herb and I agreed that Bertelsmann as represented by Monti Lüftner would be an outstanding prospect. So we approached Monti and the deal was completed in 1979. Later, in 1986, Bertelsmann also bought RCA Records, and Arista and RCA became part of a new entity called the Bertelsmann Music Group (BMG). Bertelsmann would be Arista's home for many years to come.

Such transitions often provide the setting for new beginnings, and that was certainly the case with Arista. There was no question that despite the depth of artistry on the label's roster, and all the diverse musical areas we were involved in, there were some observers who regarded it as the House That Barry Built. From late 1974 through the end of the decade, Barry Manilow's streak of hit singles—and, even more important, his very sizable album sales—generated a considerable amount of Arista's revenues. A run like his gave us a great deal of breathing room and time to sign and develop artists, all the while knowing that a new Manilow album would be in the wings to more than compensate for whatever investments we were making in new talent.

But what happens when, inevitably, that unbroken string of hits begins to fray? With artists who make their mark in the pop world, especially the softer, more adult-contemporary pop world, a time comes when their sound becomes overly familiar, when radio stations and their listeners feel like moving on. You try to extend the shelf life as long as possible, and you make adjustments that you hope will contemporize the sound. But the clock winds down, and with Barry, that happened as the Seventies were drawing to an end and the Eighties loomed on the horizon. He had his final Top 10 pop single in 1979, and although he continued to have big adult-contemporary singles into 1983, I knew that it would be difficult to continue to sell millions of albums based on singles. His music would mostly live on easy-listening radio stations, with songs like "The Old Songs," "Memory," "Somewhere Down the Road," and "Let's Hang On."

Consequently, Arista had a lot of financial ground to make up as the Eighties approached. Where would the hits come from? I had no desire for Arista's impressive early years to be perceived as a fluke. I knew that continuity was vital. It was a critical time, and the industry's eyes would be on us, especially after the Bertelsmann deal in 1979. Could we thrive when other Seventies start-up labels were struggling? Once more, in an unpredictable business that went through many more cycles than most, we had something to prove. What began as a period of uncertainty, a transitional phase in the life of the label, went on to become a decade of almost unprecedented dominance of the entire sphere of pop music, with records and artists coming from all directions. Luckily, one of the first artists I found to share what I suppose you'd have to call Barry Manilow's big slot in the lineup was a pop duo from Australia that had a very winning way with romantic ballads.

The moment I heard Air Supply's "Lost in Love," I thought it would be a hit. I was not aware of the group's background as a moderately well-known duo in their home country, that they'd released a 1977 album on Columbia in the States that had flopped, or that "Lost in Love" had been passed on by at least ten American record companies. Even if I had known all that, it wouldn't have mattered. I don't base my decisions on whether something has made the rounds and been rejected before finding its way to me. The only things I judge are material and performance. In that sense, I try as much as possible to be a blank slate: All I want to do is listen. The Australian single came to me from Billy Meshel, the head of Arista Music Publishing, and the A&R man Bud

Scoppa. I contacted Air Supply's producer, Robie Porter, without realizing that the duo, Russell Hitchcock and Graham Russell, were actually on the brink of breaking up. Porter had decided to take one last shot at finding a receptive ear in the States. I felt the song had true potential, that the vocal sound was unique, and that there is always a market for a well-crafted love song. I immediately made a deal to release it as a single, with an option to release an album, but first, I wanted to enhance the record. I didn't ask for one change in the song itself, in the melody, the lyric, or the lead vocal, but I felt that the production could be stronger. My A&R man Rick Chertoff, a young producer-engineer named William Wittman, and I did additional production on the track, not simply remixing it but adding background vocals and other overdubs to make the song more competitive on radio. Porter and the band, at first, thought we should leave the record alone, but I really envisioned something more sweeping, a fuller, more radio-ready approach. So at the end of 1979, we made the changes. "Lost in Love" was one of Arista's first single releases of the Eighties: We sent it to radio in January 1980, and since we didn't have any new material for the B side of the commercial single, we used a cut from a previous Australian Air Supply album. Things began happening very fast. The single took off, and was rapidly climbing the charts when we knew we had to exercise the option on the album and get that moving.

Here's where strategy really comes into play, and illustrates how a record company can maximize the potential of a given artist or album. I suppose we could have taken some tracks that had already been released in Australia, added the new mix of "Lost in Love," and slapped together an album to take advantage of the single's momentum. And that album would have done all right. But I knew that by recording at least a couple of new songs that had the potential to be hits, we would extend the life of Air Supply, identify them with more than the one song (thereby removing them from the ever-growing list of one-hit wonders), and sell many times what an album with only "Lost in Love" to drive it could. This game plan paid off big-time: The album ended up with two more Top 5 pop hits, and wound up going double platinum.

I have to add: I did play an unusual personal role in the album's second single. Graham had written a lovely song called "All Out of Love," which had already come out in Australia, and I thought it could work in America, but I knew the lyrics had to be changed. As I recall, one of the lines was "I'm all out of love, I want to arrest you." I explained that that line wouldn't work, and I pointed out other lines that needed to be rewritten. I then sat down and wrote the revisions myself. So for the first and only time, I took credit as a co-writer on a song. Thank goodness it became a huge hit, otherwise I never would have heard the end of it from artists and writers that the sole example of my songwriting skills resulted in a stiff. As it turned out, "All Out of Love" did even better on the charts than "Lost in Love." It peaked at number two. I came that close to co-writing a number-one hit!

The third Top 5 single was "Every Woman in the World," a song written by Dominic Bugatti, Frank Musker, and an American producer I brought into the project, Harry Maslin. And even with all this painstaking effort to upgrade the album, it did make the record stores by March. We almost hit a snag in the scheduling when we had to get Graham and Russell cleared to enter the United States to record, and we were really having a hard time getting them passports. Finally, we ended up flying them into Canada, where border clearance was easier. I asked Roy Lott, then in Business Affairs, to expedite this by any means necessary. "Every week you don't get them into the United States," I told him, "you're losing the company one million dollars." I might have been exaggerating a little, but we really were racing to chase a big single, and the album stakes were high.

So it truly became a joint effort working with Air Supply, taking the best songs written by Graham and finding others to be candidates for their hits. I made the same type of arrangement that I had with Manilow. In this case, I could choose three outside songs per album to give them, and I really wanted to make those songs count. So on their second album, which was mostly produced by Harry Maslin, Graham came up with the title track, "The One That You Love" (we hadn't run out of "love" songs yet), and another single, "Sweet Dreams," while I gave them "Here I Am (Just When I Thought I Was Over You)" by Norman Sallitt. Again, all three of those songs cracked the Top 5. The album went platinum, as did the next one, *Now and Forever*. The title track was by Graham, and I supplied another Top 5 single, "Even the

Nights Are Better," written by the team of Terry Skinner, J. L. Wallace, and Ken Ball. It was a smoothly running partnership, a true collaboration, and there was one more smash hit from the group. Although they'd had only three Arista albums, we thought by 1983 that there were enough giant singles to warrant a greatest hits collection. I did want to add one new exclusive single to the album, and I turned to the premier maker of grandiose song epics, Jim Steinman, who had created the Meat Loaf album *Bat out of Hell* and had most recently written and produced "Total Eclipse of the Heart" for Bonnie Tyler. I thought his flair for musical melodrama and the expressive voice of Russell Hitchcock would be an ideal match, and the result was one of the biggest singles of Air Supply's and Steinman's career, the number-two hit "Making Love out of Nothing at All."

That song, together with the other hits, showed we really had scored with major pop copyrights with Air Supply. They had truly registered with the public, and when banded together as Air Supply's *Greatest Hits,* the album soared over five million copies. That was the peak of the group's popularity. After one more gold album, *Hearts in Motion,* which didn't generate any major hits, it was obvious that, at least as measured by sales and radio play, Air Supply's time in the sun was waning. Tastes change so quickly, and as the Eighties moved along, even adult-contemporary radio wanted to shake things up. But I do believe that the songs of Air Supply are remembered, maybe as emblematic of a specific time, maybe as a guilty pleasure. They didn't simply have turntable hits: They had a distinctive sound and they were embraced by fans who genuinely cared about them. Russell Hitchcock's tenor voice came through on those records, and combined with the quality of the songs, the group moved people. You know, when you're working with artists such as Air Supply, that the music isn't groundbreaking and you're never going to get the press behind you. If you want to call Air Supply the Nicholas Sparks of Eighties soft-pop music, that's fine. People still go to hear them in concert, and still sing along to "All Out of Love," more than thirty years later.

Perhaps some labels would have been happy to pick up "Lost in Love" as a single master, celebrated when the song became a smash hit, taken shortcuts to exploit the single, and never mined the longer-term potential of Air Supply. At Arista, we just never had the luxury of being able to hit and run. We needed to maximize each and every release and build artists who could sell year after year. We relied on current product; we couldn't let up for a moment because we never had catalog sales to help pay the bills. As the Eighties progressed, we proved that we could take projects that seemed highly unlikely, or designed for immediate gratification, or geared to a narrow market, and mobilize all our energy and expertise to bring them to very successful levels.

Along those lines, Arista picked up twelve-inch single masters by the dance-pop trio Exposé from Miami and a former wedding singer from Long Island, Taylor Dayne, and helped turn those artists into hit-making machines. And we weren't content with marketing albums by a long-haired, Jewish saxophone player from Seattle just to the niche audience for smooth jazz, a musician whom no one could have predicted would become the most commercially successful pop instrumentalist of all time, selling more than 30 million albums over the course of two decades. Stories like that are improbable, but true.

Although there are never any guarantees, some artists just seem destined for stardom. The instant impression they make is so seismic that you can almost see the future unfolding as you watch them for the first time. For me, it was like that with Janis, Patti, Whitney, Alicia, and maybe a handful of others. Then there are the ones that have presence and talent, something out of the ordinary, but you can't really project how events might evolve. You take a chance, based on your instinct and sense of where they might fit in. That was the case with Kenny G. He was under my radar for a while as a member of Jeff Lorber's group. Lorber was doing well for Arista in the jazz-fusion world, but I admit I didn't look at the album credits so closely that I noticed the name of the sax player, who also was writing the occasional track. But as the Lorber group toured, I kept hearing about the young guy on sax who would step out from time to time to take a solo, and whose showmanship and musicianship invariably incited sustained ovations.

Curious, I went to the group's next gig in New York City at the Bottom Line, and saw for myself the reception Kenny Gorelick received. He would take long, spiraling solos on soprano sax, and was animated in the way he worked the stage. He was magnetic, and the crowd loved him. Soon after that show in 1982, I called him up and asked if he'd like to make an album as a solo artist for Arista. Naturally, he was delighted with the opportunity to step into the spotlight, and we began making his debut album. In the meantime, he continued to wow Lorber's fans, and by the time the group came back to New York for another series of Bottom Line dates, the group was being billed as "The Jeff Lorber Fusion featuring Kenny G." Kenny was already on the brink of becoming a star in that musical world.

I had little to do creatively with Kenny's first album, but seeing how well it did for an instrumental project, and how well he connected live, I encouraged him to expand his sound, to move away from the fusion influences and incorporate more contemporary R&B elements. I can't say that I was certain where this would lead, but I did feel strongly that he was placing limitations on how far he could go by sticking to the type of jazzy instrumental pop he'd been exploring. I saw what he was capable of, and how audiences—especially women—reacted to him, the way he'd step off the stage of the clubs and walk between the tables while playing his instrument. He got cheers, standing ovations. This was remarkable: When had this type of music last broken out a major personality, someone with sex appeal and charisma? I didn't want him to be relegated to the clubs. He could go beyond that. I could see him on a much bigger stage.

To help him with his transition, I recruited Kashif, an R&B writer-producer who was also signed to Arista as a recording artist, and the producer Wayne Braithwaite. Kashif contributed a couple of songs on the 1984 *G Force* album as a co-writer, and another track, "Hi, How Ya Doin'," written by Steve Horton, featured a vocal by Barry Johnson. The rest of the album was in line with what Kenny had been doing previously, so this was very much a case of carefully moving forward while keeping one foot in the familiar. It worked, and *G Force* became the first Kenny G album to hit both the jazz and R&B charts. Bringing those two genres together proved to be the winning formula for Kenny. *G Force* went platinum, which was extraordinary. Kenny had never attempted to enter the world of urban music before, and to the extent that his style of music could be considered jazz fusion, that's where his base was. Now here he was with this breakthrough. The challenge was to keep it going, which we did in 1985 with *Gravity,* another platinum album that Kenny produced with Wayne and Kashif. To have a primarily instrumental artist with back-to-back platinum albums was definitely unusual.

However, to give a fair account of what was going on with Kenny, I have to add that, to put it mildly, the critics were not treating him kindly. The more rock-leaning writers, of course, would always find the type of music he played inconsequential, but jazz writers were even more disparaging. Because Kenny came from the world of jazz-fusion, not the most respected genre among jazz purists to begin with, critics saw what he was doing as watered down. But I never thought Kenny aspired or pretended to be a jazz artist. Just because a musician plays instrumentals on a saxophone, that doesn't make him a jazz artist or mean that's what he wants to be. I personally never considered him a jazz artist, and that's meant neither as a compliment nor a criticism. I'd worked with Miles Davis, Herbie Hancock, Weather Report, and the Mahavishnu Orchestra at Columbia, and we signed Anthony Braxton to Arista. I knew what jazz was, and the degree to which it could adapt and expand while maintaining its integrity and credibility. I viewed Kenny as a pop musician with some jazz leanings, and now some R&B influences. If you compare him with John Coltrane or Stan Getz, he's never going to touch their genius. In terms of approach and impact, Kenny had more in common with Herb Alpert's phenomenally successful Tijuana Brass. Although he was a big jazz enthusiast who played trumpet, Herb knew he wasn't making jazz. Who would have ever thought to compare him with Miles Davis or Chet Baker? He made very distinctive and entertaining pop instrumental music that definitely tapped into something, and it's one of the signature sounds of the Sixties. To me, Kenny was doing exactly the same thing in the Eighties.

After the success of *G Force* and *Gravity,* I felt the chemistry of Kenny's music needed some shaking up, so for the next album, I asked him to work with Narada Michael Walden and Preston Glass. Again the album was a mixture of instrumentals and songs with guest vocals. The first two singles did very well on the R&B charts: "Don't Make Me Wait for Love," written by Narada and Preston with Walter Afanasieff, and a remake of the Motown hit by Junior Walker & the All Stars "What Does It Take (to Win Your Love)." It looked certain that we would have our third consecutive platinum album with Kenny, which would have been a major achievement. But then came the third single. We'd never before serviced a Kenny G instrumental to any radio format—pop, R&B, or adult contemporary. The odds against an instrumental gaining meaningful traction were so daunting that it just didn't seem worth the effort. But something about "Songbird," the first cut on the *Duotones* album, haunted me. It had a quality, a lilt and an old-fashioned sentimentality, like a love theme from a classic movie. Except there was no movie to help promote it, no unusual promotional angle. It was simply a very pretty five-minute instrumental, and how do you break that? I believed, however, that the song was an appeal to the listener's imagination, and it would be all the more powerful for that. There was one more vocal track on the album, called "You Make Me Believe," and it would have been a safer bet to go with that. But the more I and Arista's promotion chiefs Donnie Ienner and Rick Bisceglia listened to "Songbird," the more we were convinced it deserved a shot. What was the worst that could happen? Another "only platinum" album?

The first thing we did, with Kenny's permission, was edit a minute from the album version to bring the record down to a bit over four minutes. Then I took, for me, the unprecedented step of composing a letter to send to every single radio programmer. It was a personal plea. I asked them to put their preconceptions aside and, if they'd ever been moved by the music Arista had released over the years, to do me a favor and listen to "Songbird," put it on the air to test it, and see how their listeners responded. Meanwhile, the pop and adult-contemporary promotion departments went into action to persuade reluctant programmers to take a chance on this unorthodox single. It was like a military operation. A number of stations did take a chance, if only to get us off their backs, or as a good deed, or out of genuine belief the record could be a hit. In every market where it got played, the phones lit up with listeners wanting to hear it again, asking who the artist was. One radio story led to another, and soon this serene oasis of melody was a sensation everywhere: "Songbird" became a number-four pop single, a number-three adult-contemporary single, a hit video at VH-1, and a worldwide smash. *Duotones* wound up going five times platinum. Kenny was now in the sales stratosphere. There were people who thought that was the pinnacle, that an instrumental hit leading to blockbuster album sales wasn't a repeatable event. Surely, sales would drop off the next time and return to more normal levels. After all, there had occasionally been one-off instrumental hits over the years, Chuck Mangione's "Feels So Good," George Benson's "Breezin'," Dave Brubeck's "Take Five," and there was no reason to think that "Songbird" wasn't just the latest in that tradition.

Kenny debunked that theory quickly. The title song from his next album, "Silhouette," was another lovely instrumental, and another hit. And the album sold four times platinum in 1988. Kenny and Arista closed out the decade with a triple-platinum live album, but we were by no means finished. In fact, Kenny's *Breathless* album, his first of the Nineties, shattered all previous records, going twelve times platinum. I'm going to repeat that: twelve times platinum. It's difficult to convey how remarkable that is, what a milestone that represents, regardless of genre, but especially for an album that has only two vocal cuts on it. I've tried over the years to explain the phenomenon of Kenny G, to try to make sense of the arc of his career. It's best to just lay out the facts, which speak for themselves.

Kenny did have big hit singles, but there are artists whose track records of hits are longer but who never came close to being the type of consistent album seller that Kenny became. He's spanned genres, but he primarily resides at the crossroads of adult-contemporary and urban-contemporary music, and those formats have established only a handful of artists who have sold tens of millions of albums. He never received accolades from the press, or multiple industry awards, but his longevity for someone in his musical category is unique. I think it goes back to the impression I had the first time I saw him step out from his sideman role to seize his moment in the spotlight and own the stage: There is something that happens between Kenny and the audience. He reaches them in an intimate way, and they respond. He speaks a musical language that's accessible. His tone is his own. It takes only a couple of notes to know who's playing. If you enjoyed what you heard when he played, there was only one place you could find it: on his albums.

Arista's and my journey with Kenny continued well into the Nineties. *Miracles: The Holiday Album* became one of the best-selling Christmas albums of all time. But as with almost all artists, there comes a point where sales level off and then start to dip. No matter how remarkable the streak, it has to stop at some point, and I could see the signs that while there was still an audience for the Kenny G sound, he was no longer going to meaningfully connect with original material. It was time, I thought, to start having him record familiar songs, to stamp the classics with his signature approach. I had to work hard to convince him, because he'd had this incredible period of multiplatinum sales, and creatively and financially he wanted to continue in that vein of doing mostly original instrumentals with the occasional outside song that I and my A&R staff found for him. Eventually he and his manager, Dennis Turner, did agree, and we made *Classics in the Key of G,* which was produced by Kenny, David Foster, and Walter Afanasieff. It was a strong selection of songs, some from jazz (Thelonious Monk's " 'Round Midnight," Duke Ellington's "In a Sentimental Mood"), some bossa nova, some pop, and a "duet" with Louis Armstrong on "What a Wonderful World." Some commentators felt that posthumously mingling Louis Armstrong with Kenny was sacrilegious. I'll only say that the record was never intended to equate Armstrong and Kenny in any way. Kenny always felt it was his tribute to the great master.

In any case, *Classics* proved to be the last platinum album we shared together. After more holiday albums, an album of originals, a duets album, and a covers album of romantic melodies, my relationship with Kenny became a little contentious. From Kenny's viewpoint, I can understand why he tired of doing concept albums. He had an eagerness to return to the charts with his own material, but it was my job to tell him that could no longer happen. His sound had peaked on radio. They would no longer play his new material. No artist likes hearing that, but it was the truth. The concepts were a way to sustain the career of a major artist who could continue to sell albums. But I can see why Kenny thought they weren't rewarding or challenging enough. When you reach that point, you have to break apart professionally, which is very painful. You've been through so much and reached such heights. You try to keep it warm and cordial, try to focus on the really incredible shared experience you've had, but nearly all endings are sad endings. You've been like family for many years. I had been to Kenny and Lyndie's wedding, had shared their joy when their son Max was born. Kenny always performed for me whenever a special occasion arose. So I wanted to keep it going but just knew I couldn't. Without the opportunity of working on a new album with an artist, your lives do separate. But, at least for me, the bond is always there. For such a long time it had been Kenny and the label forging new territory, overcoming the knives of harsh critics, getting radio to be an unprecedented ally. I know that what we did together was exceptional, and from my perspective it always will be.

This last story has nothing to do with my musical relationship with Kenny, but I learned an important life lesson at his fortieth-birthday party in 1996. The party was held in the beautiful home that he and Lyndie had built in Seattle, his hometown, a few years before. There were some musicians there, but also a number of very successful technology entrepreneurs, including Craig McCaw, who had made a fortune in the cellular phone business. I was unaware of his background at the time, but we were seated next to each other, and he was very interested in music so we had a great conversation. Kenny came over and told Craig a little about my background, but didn't say much to me about Craig, so I was a bit in the dark about him.

While we were talking I asked about his summer plans, since Kenny's birthday is in early June. Craig mentioned that he wasn't sure. He was going through a divorce and had had a difficult couple of months. He said that he thought his wife would be using the boat they usually chartered outside Nice. The odd coincidence was that during this summer, for the first time, I felt that I would really splurge and charter a yacht, and it would be chartered in Nice as well. Given my upbringing, leasing the yacht was a wrenching decision. I never imagined that I would be able to afford something like that. It was a huge extravagance. If you went to a great hotel and took a big suite with a few bedrooms, you could expect to pay something like $3,000 a night, which is obviously $21,000 a week. That itself is certainly a lot of money. Well, when you charter a boat, it's more like $125,000 to $250,000 a week. I can well remember how my hands were shaking when I signed the contract.

Still, chartering this boat was a proud moment for me. It could house twelve people, and I could invite anybody I wanted to. So I was sitting there with this very nice guy, whom I don't know very much about, and told him that I was chartering a boat in Nice as well. We quickly figured out that his soon-to-be-ex-wife and I were going to be there at the same time. So he said to me very enthusiastically, "Listen, I'll call my wife, and you can spend a day on my boat. It will be great!" I was a little put off. I said to him, "With all due respect to your wife, as I mentioned, I have a boat myself. Why would I want to spend the day on your boat?" He paused for a beat. Then he said, "Well, does your boat have a helicopter? You can take the helicopter and go anywhere you want, and then come back."

I smiled to myself because it's a good lesson to learn in life: Just when you think you've really arrived, there's always something better. There's always something bigger. The moral: It's important to enjoy what you have. Measure yourself by your own standard and don't be concerned about what others have or don't have, do or don't do. I ran into Craig a few years later in St. Barts, and told him what I was thinking during our conversation that day. We had a good laugh over it, but I've still never forgotten it.

Arista Pop Explodes . . .
Into Milli Vanilli

The Eighties were a new era for Arista, the beginning of a second chapter that would remarkably go on to surpass everything we'd accomplished in our groundbreaking early years. In the beginning of 1983, I had brought in a very bright and aggressive head of promotion named Don Ienner, who'd been doing exceptional work for his brother Jimmy Ienner at Millennium Records, and he proceeded to strengthen and energize our efforts even more. Donnie, as everyone calls him, was to emerge as a leader and major player as Arista's executive vice president and general manager. He played a pivotal role in promoting and marketing all the artists we were releasing from 1983 until he left to become president of Columbia Records in 1989. Donnie is fierce in his competitive drive, impressive in his desire to win, intensely loyal if he respects you—and thank God I had his respect. He was colorful, with a direct, no-holds-barred manner of speaking, mixed with an infectious laugh that allowed him to charm those who might otherwise have been put off by his intensity.

In addition to Donnie, there was a new A&R staff and new press and marketing people. We'd safely navigated the rough patch of the late Seventies and early Eighties. We were breaking Air Supply and Kenny G and were invigorating Dionne Warwick and the Kinks. And behind the scenes, I was preparing Whitney's debut. Our offices hummed with excitement. Everything was happening at such an accelerated, exhilarating pace. At every one of my weekly staff luncheons, there was more news to report, more new music to share, more reports on sales and airplay. In those days before SoundScan and sophisticated means of measuring radio play, Arista's sales and promotion teams had to gather up information on the telephone, and get reports from retail and radio. They would come into the conference room with stacks and stacks of data, waiting for me to grill them on how each of our records was performing. Every detail mattered. Every market where a record was performing well, or slipping, every sign of progress or a problem was pored over and analyzed.

As I previously mentioned, Arista's association with Jive Records began with the thinking that Clive Calder's label would give us a boost in the rock world, and I didn't anticipate that the label would bring us one of our biggest pop artists of the Eighties. From 1984 through 1988, we had a tremendous run of hits with a U.K.-based pop-R&B singer named Billy Ocean, starting with the Grammy-winning smash "Caribbean Queen (No More Love on the Run)" and ending with the international number-one hit "Get Outta My Dreams, Get into My Car." In between, he alternated smoothly between tender ballads such as "Suddenly" and up-tempo hits like "When the Going Gets Tough, the Tough Get Going," and his three albums on Jive/Arista all went platinum or double platinum. Ocean, along with the dynamic rap duo Whodini, represented the high point of our relationship with Jive. Whodini's 1984 album *Escape* was one of the first hip-hop albums ever to be certified platinum. It contained the hits "Friends," "Five Minutes of Funk," and "Freaks Come Out at Night."

Over the years, it's been occasionally reported that Arista ended its association with Jive because I was disappointed that the label had decided to focus more on hip-hop than rock, but that's hardly the case. I was very pleased that Arista played a part in breaking Whodini and bringing rap further into the mainstream, and I certainly was very happy with everything we were accomplishing with Billy Ocean. But when the initial period of the deal was up, both sides felt that Jive would be a better fit within the BMG family at RCA. Arista was doing extremely well in urban music, and RCA was struggling in that area, so given Jive's strength in hip-hop, the change made sense. Would I have loved to have R. Kelly, the Backstreet Boys, Britney Spears, and 'N Sync on Jive/Arista? Do you really have to ask? But I always knew that Clive Calder's taste and foresight were exemplary, and that Jive would be a major industry force.

In the meantime, Arista itself was hitting in almost every genre. In one case, David Jurman, who headed dance promotion for Donnie Ienner, brought to my attention a single called "Point of No Return." It was a cut above most of the generic post-disco dance records. It had the required insistent beat, but there was something more to it, a pop freshness, a hook that stuck with you. I didn't know anything about the group, Exposé, or about the record's writer-producer, Lewis Martineé, but the single was making some noise in Miami, where they were based, and was starting to spread on Martineé's independent label, Pantera Records. I felt that this record had the potential to become an across-the-board hit. I asked to hear more of Martineé's songs, and I felt that he definitely had follow-ups if "Point of No Return" broke. Financially, it wasn't much of a gamble; it was a singles deal with the option to make an album. It was the rare occasion that I didn't arrange for a showcase, and I never even met the girls in the group before making the deal. In 1985, we picked up distribution of the "Point of No Return" twelve-inch single, and it reached number one on the national dance charts. But then a second dance single, "Exposed to Love," failed to reach the Top 10, and that might have been that. So many acts that released dance singles never crossed over to the pop arena, and that could easily have been the fate of Exposé, but I had the distinct feeling that there might be more life in the project. We decided to roll the dice and start recording an album. Talking with Martineé, I learned that he was going to replace the original singers on "Point of No Return" with three new girls, now that he knew the stakes were higher. They were on a major label now, and every element of the package had to be right. So he found Ann Curless, Jeanette Jurado, and Gioia Bruno, and they became Exposé.

We released "Come Go with Me," sung by the new lineup, and that was the beginning of an amazing run of seven consecutive Top 10 singles, all written and produced by Martineé. Not since the Supremes had a girl group scored so many Top 10 pop singles in a row. To follow up "Come Go with Me," Martineé rerecorded "Point of No Return" with the new singers, and the debut album also included "Let Me Be the One" and the change-of-pace ballad "Seasons Change," which became the group's only number-one pop and adult-contemporary single. The album went triple platinum.

We did go on to have more hits with Exposé, and three of the songs on the second album, *What You Don't Know,* did make it to the Top 10, but unfortunately none of those singles were what I would call "money songs" that would sell albums the way "Come Go with Me" or "Seasons Change" did. And although the three girls were attractive and each could sing lead, they didn't exude real star power. So we eventually lost momentum with them. Ultimately, they had one more big single, Diane Warren's "I'll Never Get Over You Getting Over Me," but it was evident that their moment had passed. They would always be the group from Miami with the dance hits, reflective of a pop moment that almost by its nature was fleeting and ephemeral.

You really never know where the next hit is going to come from, and in the mid-Eighties at Arista, it was a series of unexpected, left-field surprises. In 1986 MTV began airing episodes of the Monkees television series, reviving interest in the group and introducing them to a new audience. Since Arista owned the Monkees catalog, we decided to package a new "Best Of" album, adding three newly recorded songs by the members Micky Dolenz and Peter Tork, produced by Michael Lloyd. One of the new songs we gave them, "That Was Then, This Is Now," became a Top 20 hit, and combined with a "20th Anniversary" reunion tour, helped our compilation album sell more than a million copies. We never could have planned for a Monkees revival, but we leaped at the opportunity. Instead of simply slapping together a package to take advantage of the TV exposure and tour, we took the extra step of finding a new song—one that had been written and recorded by an unknown New York band, the Mosquitos—that could get airplay, and we included rare versions of older Monkees tracks for collectors. Details like those matter, and they can make the difference between a gold album and a platinum album. And that means millions of dollars for the company.

I'm including Exposé and the Monkees' compilation here to make the point that not every effort can be long-term inspired. Just as in television, where you primarily look for a series, if a onetime event takes place that can be dominant in the ratings, you go for it. The same is true for the blockbuster film that can't start a franchise or generate sequels. You still go for it. Just from the albums of Exposé and the Monkees compilation, Arista generated more than $50 million in sales, making Jim Cawley, Arista's head of national sales, and his hardworking team ecstatic. That sure helped the bottom line with no new massive Barry Manilow album forthcoming.

One of Arista's newer A&R people, Andy Fuhrman, played me a record called "Tell It to My Heart" by an artist named Taylor Dayne. It was brought to him by a young, Long Island–based producer, Ric Wake. As in the case of Exposé, this was a dance-pop record, not the most novel or inventive song in the world, but well crafted, and definitely well sung. Dayne—whose given name was Leslie Wunderman—was impressive; there was genuine passion and power in her voice. Most singers on dance records are simply vehicles for the production; they could be anyone, and no personality bursts through. The exceptions, like Donna Summer, are rare, and they're the ones who can emerge from the genre and go beyond the clubs. I thought Taylor had that quality. I could feel a presence when she sang. But once more, as with Exposé, she needed a hit to break the door down. Without that base, there would be no market whatsoever for an album.

So we made a deal to release "Tell It to My Heart," and it took off. Then we were faced with an enviable problem: getting an album recorded. All we had was the one song, and that one song was becoming a hit. There was a growing sense of urgency. It wasn't enough to find nine more songs. There had to be follow-up hits among them. Otherwise, when the single started dropping down the charts, the album would fall as well. We put the call out to every music publisher that we were looking for songs for Taylor Dayne. My A&R team—Andy Fuhrman, Mitchell Cohen, and Richard Sweret—and I listened to probably hundreds of demos, and we each found songs that had single potential, songs by writers such as David Lasley, Billy Steinberg and Tom Kelly, Shelley Peiken, and Seth Swirsky (who co-wrote "Tell It to My Heart"). We added a cover of the Honey Cone hit "Want Ads," and were determined to show, through the breadth of the material, that Taylor was more than this year's dance diva, that she could sing a power ballad, that she could handle a rock-flavored song. We were on the clock because we had the single to chase, but in the end, the *Tell It to My Heart* album became far more than just one hit plus a bunch of second-tier songs. When all was said and done, every other single on the album matched or surpassed the chart showing of the title track: "Prove Your Love" by Swirsky and Arnie Roman, "I'll Always Love You" by Jimmy George, and "Don't Rush Me" by Alex Forbes and Jeff Franzel each did better than the one before, with the final single from the album peaking at number two. And all, with the exception of "Tell It to My Heart," with material we gave her.

Tell It to My Heart went double platinum at the end of 1988, so we had a lot to live up to when it came time to make Taylor's second album. You never assume you'll duplicate that type of debut success, and you're always starting from scratch with an artist whose sales are predicated on how big the hit singles are. For Taylor, that meant starting the process of song selection all over again. By this time, I had forged a close relationship with Diane Warren, a songwriter whose career was really heating up. She would come to see me at the Beverly Hills Hotel, open up a big bag filled with cassettes, and play song after song for me, so intensely and with so much nervous energy that you would think her life literally depended on what I thought. Diane lives, breathes, is consumed by music. I'm not entirely certain if she ever sleeps. She's extremely prolific, and her percentage of exceptional songs is very high. I would listen to song after song, each one preceded and followed—and often interrupted—by her breathless questions. "Do you love it? Is this not the best song I've ever written?" She would practically be hyperventilating. Most of the time, she'd mention Whitney, which was understandable. No one was bigger, and getting a song placed on a Whitney album was a coveted achievement. But most of the songs Diane was writing then weren't right for Whitney. We were going for songs that could also get R&B play for Whitney, and Diane's songs tended to lean toward pop.

Insecurity, that need for confirmation that I felt so often in Diane, seems to be a universal quality of our very best songwriters. I'll never forget right after the first few years of Barry Manilow's hit-after-hit period, I got a phone call from one of America's greatest songwriters, Jule Styne. Jule had written "Don't Rain on My Parade," "Diamonds Are a Girl's Best Friend," "People," "Three Coins in the Fountain," "The

Party's Over," "Just in Time"—you get the idea. He said, "Clive, I understand you've got the newest and biggest male star, and I've written a brand-new song for him. Can I come right over and play it for you?" Naturally, I was a little startled but of course said yes. Jule, who had written his great standards mainly for Broadway, was coming to pitch a new song to me; I wasn't going to say no. Well, he arrived and was full of life and energy. There was a little small talk and then he went straight to the piano in the conference room, sat down, and immediately started playing the song. After the first verse and first chorus, he looked up and nervously asked, "Well, what do you think? Isn't it great?" What I thought was that I loved Jule's adrenaline pumping as he approached eighty. I loved his being hungry for his next hit. I loved his quick need for affirmation. I loved his insecurity. The song? Well, it was a theater song, a very good theater song but not a commercial song for pop recording. Of course I was honest with this master of song about that, but the experience—the experience would never be forgotten.

It's fascinating how that deep degree of insecurity somehow seems to fuel talent. Diane Warren came to my bungalow on one occasion and played me three hit demos, one after the other. I was beside myself. This was a banner day. First she played "I'll Be Your Shelter"—which I later found out she'd originally pitched to Tina Turner, who passed on it—and then she played "You Can't Fight Fate." After that, she sat down at the piano and played and sang "Love Will Lead You Back." I liked each and every song, but had to explain to her that these were not Whitney songs. They fit Taylor Dayne perfectly and I wanted to record all three with her. Even though Taylor was coming off a hit album, Diane was still a tough sell. I persisted, and to Diane's credit she agreed, so all three ended up on *Can't Fight Fate*. "Love Will Lead You Back" became Taylor's first number-one hit, and "I'll Be Your Shelter" went to number four. There were two other hits on the album: "With Every Beat of My Heart," by Tommy Faragher, Lotti Golden, and Arthur Baker; and "Heart of Stone," by Elliot Wolff and Gregg Tripp. Most impressive, the album sold as well as the debut. Taylor was now an established pop star, with seven straight Top 10 singles in a little over two and a half years. It was a dramatic rise, and it seemed as though nothing could stand in the way of her doing as well the third time. Unlike

Exposé, Taylor was able to transcend genre. She wasn't identified with a specific type of material, and as long as the songs were good, she could really deliver on their potential. I considered her a long-term artist.

So what happened? The short answer is that Taylor fell victim to her ambition to be a songwriter, but that would be an oversimplification. You could argue that after two double-platinum albums, she'd earned some creative leeway, and there was no reason she shouldn't try to co-write some songs. Singers who start selling albums get bombarded from all directions by writers trying to get on their albums, and by producers they're working with: "Hey, let's get together and co-write!" As if that's something that anybody can do, no matter what their experience or track record. How hard can it be? Well, even for professional, established songwriters, it's hard. It's not something to be treated casually, and it's truly condescending to the people who do it for a living to assume that you can put anyone in a room and have them come up with a worthwhile song. It's really nonsense, and it's exasperating to have that conversation time and time again, to come up against the claim that a true artist also needs to be a songwriter. That not only disrespects the songwriting craft, it disrespects artists who have never written. From her first hit, "Piece of My Heart," to her last, "Me and Bobby McGee," Janis Joplin relied almost entirely on material written by others. So did Streisand and Aretha and countless other pantheon artists in every single musical genre. What indication did Taylor Dayne ever show that she had songwriting ability? Hit song after hit song was given to her and her very capable producer, Ric Wake.

Nervously, I decided to let her try to explore her songwriting ability. If she was going to have blinders on regarding her career, it was my place to give her the benefit of my expertise and advise her, but I couldn't stand in her way. She at least could start the process, and we'd see where it took her. The process took years—years during which she wasn't on the radio, wasn't visible to the public. For a singles-based artist, that's a lifetime to be away, and you'd better come back with a blockbuster hit. You can't expect your fans to wait around, or radio programmers to jump on a new single just because it has your name on the label. It became an impossibly tough effort, culling the decent songs from the ones Taylor was co-writing, shoehorning in some outside songs, putting together a presentable album. When it finally came out in 1993, *Soul Dancing* was a nonevent. The best bet for a lead single was a Barry White cover, "Can't Get Enough of Your Love." It's a bad sign when you have to kick off an album with a remake. And instead of Ric Wake's consistently strong production, this one was a cluttered assemblage. In addition to Ric, the producers included Shep Pettibone, Humberto Gatica, Clivilles and Cole, Narada Michael Walden, and Taylor herself. The album lacked focus. More critically, it lacked hits. It marked the end of Taylor's time at Arista.

Many years later, I was shopping at Armani in Beverly Hills, and a salesman came up to me and said, "I have to confess to you, my girlfriend was one of your artists." It turned out to be Taylor, who had moved to Los Angeles, but never was able to meaningfully revive her recording career. He said she would absolutely love to be working with me again. Subsequently, she wrote me a long letter, saying how deeply she regretted not listening to me years ago, how young and inexperienced she was at the time, how she let herself get steered off her path. When I read that I mainly felt sad that Taylor had allowed her big chance to fall by the wayside. Too much time, too many years had elapsed for Top 40 to be a realistic goal. I always thought she was a terrific power singer. She had one of those rich, projecting voices, as well as a facility with all types of material. I look at the track listing of Taylor's *Greatest Hits* album and every single song stands up. I wish that circumstances would have been different, and that she and I could have worked together long enough for at least a *Greatest Hits: Volume Two*.

Carly Simon had been one of the biggest artists of the Seventies. With hits on Elektra Records like "Anticipation," "You're So Vain," "Mockingbird" (with her then husband James Taylor), "Haven't Got Time for the Pain," and "Nobody Does It Better," her career was at its zenith. Then her record sales started to slip late in the decade. She switched labels and signed to Warner Bros., and in the mid-Eighties she made one disappointing album for Epic. Professionally, she was at her lowest point since her auspicious 1971 debut. This frequently happens: Artists go through phases when everything they do is rapturously received, and then somehow they skid off the commercial track. I've seen it many times, and I've never allowed a recent—or even a sustained—slump to deter me if I felt an artist had a substantial and productive renaissance ahead: The Dead, the Kinks, Dionne Warwick, and Aretha were all in a similar situation when I signed them to Arista. Although the challenges are different with a singer-songwriter, I had a really good feeling about Carly. She was still strikingly attractive, with tremendous sex appeal, and her voice had lost none of its strength and luster. She was hungry and determined to prove that she still had it. Before signing to Epic, she had changed management and attorneys, and was now working with Tommy Mottola at Champion Entertainment and the top industry lawyer Allen Grubman. They told me Carly was free, and in 1986 I signed her to Arista.

It didn't take long for the perfect opportunity to come along. Mike Nichols asked her to contribute new music to his film *Heartburn*, a romantic comedy-drama about relationships, geared toward a female audience and starring Meryl Streep and Jack Nicholson. It was an absolutely ideal project for Carly, completely in synch with her sensibility. For the film, she did a fresh take on the children's song "Itsy Bitsy Spider," and wrote a terrific new song, "Coming Around Again," that became her first Top 20 pop single in years. The single earned her a Grammy nomination for Best Female Pop Vocal Performance. The album of the same name featured songs from the Nichols film and had three more Top 10 adult-contemporary hits, all of which she wrote or co-wrote. It's a lovely, varied album, one of the best of her career, and it was her first to go platinum in nearly a decade. It was a very sweet victory for Carly.

Carly's anxiety about performing live is well known, and she very rarely tours, but after *Coming Around Again*, we really wanted to document a live show. When Carly decides to go for it, when she leaves stage fright behind, she's an electrifying live performer. She works the stage, totally takes over, and has the audience in the palm of her hand. How could we persuade her to perform live for a nationwide TV special? Well, by making everything extracomforting, extrafamiliar, and very much like home. Carly spends most of her time on Martha's Vineyard, so we persuaded HBO to shoot the special there. We planned to do the show on a beautiful summer day in Gay Head, a picturesque part of the island with stunning clay cliffs. Carly was disarmed. She felt good. This was her hometown and she would know most of the people in the audience. Her performance was exhilarating and self-assured. Our reward was a second platinum album when we released selections from the concert as *Greatest Hits Live* in 1988. It was Carly's first live album and it paid big dividends.

Also in 1988, Carly reunited with Mike Nichols for the smash film *Working Girl,* and we released the soundtrack album. Carly's theme song, "Let the River Run," was still another triumph for her: It won her an Oscar, a Golden Globe, and a Grammy for Best Song from a Movie. Only one other solo artist/songwriter in history, Bruce Springsteen, has won all three awards for one movie song. There were two albums by Carly in 1990. The first, *My Romance,* was a lush and warmly performed album of standards, with arrangements by Marty Paich and participation by such excellent musicians as Michael Brecker, Jay Leonhart, and Steve Gadd. Once more, there was a related HBO special, *Carly In Concert: My Romance,* with Harry Connick, Jr., as Carly's guest. *My Romance* didn't do as well as the prior Arista albums, but it was a project very close to Carly's heart, and eventually she would have a hit album with material from this era when she and her longtime producer Richard Perry made *Moonlight Serenade* for Columbia. She does have an innate, natural feel for the great American songbook. Her second 1990 album for Arista was the entirely self-written *Have You Seen Me Lately,* which had a big adult-contemporary hit, "Better Not Tell Her," but no songs that crossed over. Although Carly went on to make high-quality albums—the personal *Letters Never Sent,* the haunting *Film Noir* with Jimmy Webb, and the deeply intimate *Bedroom Tapes*—none of them made a lasting commercial impact.

I do want to say that it was very meaningful having worked with Carly. We shared hit records and platinum albums, and it was a joy to be there when she conquered her fears and gave those memorable live performances. Undoubtedly, Carly had her vintage years before we got together, but to help her star continue to shine provided a great deal of personal satisfaction.

The Eighties were closing on an extremely high note. Arista was launching one hit after another, like Hall and Oates's "Everything Your Heart Desires" and Lisa Stansfield's "All Around the World," and we were ready to step into the new decade with an appropriately named hit by Snap!: "The Power." Arista had become the Power in the world of pop music. We were breaking every sales record in the label's history, and we were really pumped up by this continuing hot streak. What could possibly spoil the feeling?

In the Woody Allen film *The Purple Rose of Cairo,* Mia Farrow says, "I just met a wonderful new man. He's fictional, but you can't have everything." Well, as it turned out, Milli Vanilli was fictional. Not that Rob Pilatus and Fab Morvan didn't exist, for better or worse, but Milli Vanilli was a studio creation by the German überproducer Frank Farian. Everyone knows the basic story. It's music-business legend: the scandal, the stripping of the duo's Best New Artist Grammy, the lawsuits. Every time an artist is caught lip-synching at a live show or on television, you'll hear accusations of doing a Milli Vanilli. This was, I hardly have to say, a total embarrassment, made all the worse by the certitude—in the media, at least—that I and everyone at Arista were in on the plot as co-conspirators, with the intention of duping the public, that it all was hatched to sell millions of records and win awards, and that somehow, in the course of this deception, no one would ever discover that these two performers were not the vocalists on the recordings. Over the years, I've tried to comprehend how that might have played out, how the discussions with the producer might have gone: "Look, we all know that these aren't the singers on the tracks, but let's pretend we don't know, and pull off this musical fraud"—at which point I might have stroked a cat in my lap like Dr. Evil. Why in the world would Arista have gone along with this? It all could have been solved by placing Rob and Fab down in the mixes and adding one line on the album package, "Vocals by so-and-so and so-and-so and Rob and Fab," if that's how we wanted to play it. When people say, "You had to have known," I'm mystified. But I also realize that many might not know the real saga of Milli Vanilli, how they came to Arista's attention, and the extent of my involvement in the creative process. I know I have the reputation of being hands-on. In this case, however, I couldn't have been more distant.

At the time, Frank Farian was one of the hottest producers in Germany, held in the highest esteem by Bertelsmann, which gave him total creative autonomy in the acts he brought them. He'd had huge international success with a studio group called Boney M, had put together another act called Far Corporation, and had produced an album with Meat Loaf that had done well outside the United States. So he had established a strong track record, mostly in the area of manufactured pop, and his newest project was a group called Milli Vanilli. BMG signed them in Germany, made a licensing deal in the U.K. with the independent Chrysalis Records, and offered it to me purely as a master pickup for the States. Since they were already a BMG act, it was essentially a free record for Arista. I was in Berlin at the time, and a representative from BMG played the first single, "Girl You Know It's True," for me in a limo from the airport. I said that Arista would distribute the single in the States, and we'd then see what would happen after that. That was the extent of my commitment. Clearly, if the first single had stiffed, that would have been the end of our involvement. It was partly a favor to Arista's parent company, which had promised Farian U.S. distribution of the record, and partly it was a sense that the infectious song could possibly take off.

It was literally as casual as that: We'd put it out. So this was a no-risk singles deal for an urban-flavored pop dance act from Germany. With an act like that, you don't need to showcase the artist live, as you would a rock band, or a singer for whom you'd need to find material and a producer. It was self-contained pop. If Milli Vanilli had been a rock band, I would have either gone myself or sent an A&R person over to Germany to check them out in performance. I would have wanted to see the group to find out what they were all about. It's not that the visual component didn't matter; it was that the whole deal was predicated on whether this free single would make some noise, and we'd take it from there. It wasn't too different from the situation with Lewis Martineé and Exposé: The record was handed to me. I would have had no way of knowing for certain whether the three girls Lewis said were singing on "Point of No Return" were the same girls he was presenting as the faces of the group. Why would I have doubted him, or had any suspicions? And who can say for certain whether Exposé weren't augmented by other vocalists in the studio? You simply trust the credits given to you and that what you're being told is accurate. Also, since nearly every act, even rock bands, lip-synchs in videos, that wouldn't have tipped us off, either.

It wasn't as though Milli Vanilli were a top-priority Arista act. "Girl You Know It's True" was sent to radio programmers as the third track on a sampler CD that also featured new singles by Aretha with the Four Tops, the Gap Band, and Jermaine Stewart. We did work it, and it began to react strongly, so we started to put together an album to capitalize on the hit. There was an existing album in Germany, called *All or Nothing,* but neither I nor our promotion staff thought it had enough good songs for the U.S. market, and we set about looking for material. I sent Farian a few songs: Diane Warren's "Blame It on the Rain," "More Than You'll Ever Know" by Ernesto Phillips, and "Take It as It Comes" by Simon Climie, Rob Fisher, and Dennis Morgan. We also suggested a remake of the Isley Brothers' "It's Your Thing," and discussed adding an extended mix of the first single. Farian agreed to cut the new songs, but when I told him I wanted to send one of my A&R men, Richard Sweret, over to Germany to be on the sessions and relay my notes, to be my representative in the studio, he refused. Well, it was his group, and he would call the shots. He kept it all behind his walls, and I don't think it ever dawned on him that he was doing anything wrong: The use of session singers was his method. Rob and Fab were the public image of Milli Vanilli, and the creation of the music was a whole other matter. He submitted the credits to Chrysalis in the U.K. and to us in the States, and two male artists, Rob and Fab, were definitely listed as the vocalists.

I can't say whether anyone from BMG in Germany knew the extent of Farian's ruse, but my feeling is that they were as much in the dark as we were. Not one single person from Arista in the United States ever met Rob and Fab until August 1989, five months after the album had been released, by which time we were already celebrating its going double platinum. I and about six other top Arista executives took the group and their manager to Windows on the World in the World Trade

Center to toast the album's runaway success. Throughout this initial encounter, Rob and Fab kept up the charade of being the singers on the album. While suggestions were made that the duo—who spoke heavily accented English—could use some lessons to be more comfortable in media situations, no one ever questioned their legitimacy. There had been many other international acts who sang flawlessly in English despite having foreign accents and English not being their first language. ABBA is one example. Maybe we were being naïve or myopic, but we were certainly not being intentionally deceitful.

The following March, in fact, Milli Vanilli were one of the artists invited to participate in Arista's fifteenth-anniversary concert at Radio City Music Hall, an AIDS benefit entitled "That's What Friends Are For," after the giant Dionne and Friends single. They performed along with every major star on the label, including Whitney, Kenny G, Hall and Oates, Patti Smith, Dionne Warwick, and so many others. Certainly, if we felt we had anything to hide, or thought there was a potential scandal brewing, we wouldn't have put the spotlight on them at such a high-profile, significant label event being taped for national broadcast on CBS. Rob and Fab were tall and great-looking, although their bodies were almost too perfectly sculpted. It might seem ludicrous to say, but their miming interpreted their song with sensuality and a sense of humor as well as edge. They held their own with their performance at the concert. Around that same time, Farian was preparing what would have been the second Milli Vanilli album, which we were planning to release in late 1990.

What Arista was told was that there was a rift between Rob and Fab and Farian, which we interpreted as the usual friction that can come about after a success as gigantic as Milli Vanilli's. At that point, the act had sold more than 6 million albums in the States. Rob and Fab felt that they weren't being properly compensated on the worldwide record sales of the album. All the money was going to Farian, and they said they were getting only union scale as the project's "vocalists." So their attorney, John Branca, was earnestly trying to get a fairly rich separate deal in the area of $1 million per album for Rob and Fab as recording artists, and we were definitely considering this proposal. How could we not with those sales, and the potential to keep the hits coming, this time with A&R input from me and my staff? Also, this would be a direct Arista signing, so we would keep more of the income. Again, had we—or Branca, I assume—known what was going on behind the music, this would never have been an option to consider.

As much as we basked in the album sales, we at Arista would cringe when we'd see Rob and Fab's outrageous comments in the press (in one interview, they asserted that they were more talented than Bob Dylan), and no one was deluded enough to truly believe that they deserved their Grammy for Best New Artist. They were a pure pop concoction from Frank Farian that somehow caught on, and everyone was taken aback by the magnitude of their popularity. So when the rumors picked up momentum, based to some extent on Rob and Fab's suffering a backing-tape glitch while "singing" at a live MTV show, the knives came out. (Although this didn't cause much comment or commotion at the time, probably since most of the acts on that Club MTV tour were lip-synching, or singing along with a prerecorded track, to a greater or lesser degree.) I can't say they were unjustified. To anyone who thought that the records were unsubstantial fluff, or that Milli Vanilli's awards were unwarranted (they'd swept the American Music Awards, winning three trophies), this was proof of what went on behind the scenes. Rob and Fab, who gave those arrogant interviews, accepted those awards, and were asking for $1 million per album for a new contract, had nothing to do with the records that were being played on the radio and being bought by fans. The album credits were lies. The press and the public were outraged when the truth was revealed by Farian.

Along with everyone else, we learned that when it came to choosing the final takes on the records, Rob and Fab's vocal tracks were not among the ones that Farian used, even though the credits he submitted said they were. What particularly stung, and still does to this day when the subject comes up, is the assumption that we at Arista knew about the deception and were somehow complicit in it, or at the very least in covering it up. Nothing could be further from the truth. I was shocked to learn that because I was a well-known music executive, and I'd submitted songs for this notorious album, people thought I was in on this elaborate scheme. Actually, it never would have entered my mind to take Rob or Fab aside and say, "Honestly, between us, is that really you singing?" Or to grill Farian on the details of the recording sessions. Before the story broke, Arista was in talks to sign Rob and Fab! They really thought they could sing, that they had genuine talent, and that they could make records on their own.

Music history is filled with stories of artists who were essentially studio inventions, who had session musicians like the famous Los Angeles–based Wrecking Crew play on their records, whose vocals were heavily supplemented by other singers. It's part of the fabric of pop music. Maybe Frank Farian should have made Milli Vanilli an animated group like the Archies. In the end, whatever his intention was, it turned out to be a colossal blunder, and one that reached out and embroiled Arista. We were barraged by innuendo and direct accusation. Rob did send me a letter expressing regret for the deception and for the repercussions for Arista. It says in part, "I have gained some wisdom as it relates to my behavior and I want to personally apologize for my lack of appreciation for your efforts on Milli Vanilli's behalf, and the creating of a 'marketing sensation' that went far beyond our most reasonable expectations. I hope you will accept this apology on behalf of Fabrice and myself for the mistakes we have made as it relates to you and Arista's involvement with us."

It had all begun so innocently, with a song I listened to on a business trip, one that sounded as though it might catch on. Almost everyone at Arista believed that Milli Vanilli and Farian were making hit records, and they were. And that Rob and Fab had a fun, visually arresting image that enhanced the music, and they did. Unfortunately, the music and the image didn't add up. They were separate and distinct halves of a commercially successful whole. If the experience weren't so painful, I'm sure I'd go back and listen to those singles now, especially Diane's "Blame It on the Rain," and smile at the sheer gloss of the records, and reflect on how the music itself found such a huge audience for this improbable German pop act. After all the whole commotion died down, what was left behind was the music.

And it turned out that the consumer outrage wasn't nearly as pervasive as the press had reported. There were class-action lawsuits, but the main beneficiaries were the attorneys who brought the cases "representing fans" who were, allegedly, demanding justice. Lawyers, according to the *Los Angeles Times,* also filed suit against New Kids on the Block, C+C Music Factory, and Paula Abdul for vocal—or nonvocal—crimes. In the end, many of the suits were dropped or consolidated, and a settlement was reached: Arista and BMG agreed to donate money to charities, including the music industry's T. J. Martell Foundation, and offered fans cash refunds of varying amounts for Milli Vanilli albums, singles, and concert tickets. The judge who ruled on the case said, "The court hopes that this humble controversy will soon come to an end, and that the courts of this and other jurisdictions can devote their time to the resolution of controversies of a more significant social and economic nature." The attorneys made a fortune; the fans kept their Milli Vanilli records. Of the more than 6 million albums, plus millions more singles sold, considerably fewer than a fraction of 1 percent were returned for the rebate. Perhaps some people thought they were holding on to future collector's items. Many simply liked the music and wanted to keep it. They probably don't play them a lot—pop records are kept for sentimental value—but they remember hearing the songs on the radio, and even if they think, Those were the guys who didn't really sing on the records, they can't deny that the songs hooked them.

Arista Nashville
and New Country Music

During my years at Columbia, I always loved going to Nashville, and being involved in the careers of such artists as Johnny Cash, Tammy Wynette, Charlie Rich, Lynn Anderson, and George Jones. I visited frequently, met with producers Billy Sherrill and Bob Johnston to discuss upcoming releases, and used to go to Fan Fair in the early Seventies when it was still held at the Tennessee State Fairgrounds, a music gathering unlike any I'd ever seen, where the artists not only performed but met one-on-one with fans who stood on line for hours and hours in the summer heat to get autographs and have their pictures taken with the stars. The artists played at Fan Fair for free, and stayed in their tents long after their shows were over, forming a unique bond with the country audience. It was so personal, this artist-fan relationship, unlike anything in the pop, rock, or R&B worlds, the desire to bridge the gap and not create a distance. There was some professional expectation that the big country artists would show up for Fan Fair, but there was also genuine gratitude being expressed, the acknowledgment that the loyalty of the country audience was not something to be taken for granted. It was great to see that kind of respect and intimacy, and it was similar on the industry side, on Music Row. It was the purest form of A&R interaction I'd ever encountered. It was how I imagine the scene was in New York City in the early Sixties, when record companies turned to the songwriters in the Brill Building and at Aldon Music at 1650 Broadway to find hit material for their artists. That type of friendly interdependency still existed in Nashville, with its open-door policy for songs and the recognition that nonwriting artists were dependent on strong outside material. A publisher or a songwriter could easily get access to any A&R executive on the Row, because you never knew where the next hit was going to come from.

Experiencing that gave me inspiration when I founded Arista in 1974 to apply the Nashville model to pop, to sign more artists who had performing and vocal skills but just didn't write, to do A&R in the most fundamental meaning of the term: matching artists with repertoire, getting back to that nearly lost, but exciting and fulfilling, part of the record-making process. Nashville definitely encouraged me to add those other strings to my creative bow. And I also had, in the back of my mind, the intention to get back into country music when the time was right. I knew that it was something I couldn't do right away: I had to establish Arista as a force in other musical areas before making the leap to country. That wasn't something you simply started puttering around in. I couldn't open a Nashville branch and run it from New York City. I'd spent enough time in Nashville to know that the music industry there is a day-to-day way of life. Everything revolves around it. Events, dinners, showcases, golfing, long business lunches over big steaks or at the "meat-and-three" places where, as the name implies, you got three side dishes with your main course. You don't drop in, shake hands, and go home. You take it seriously. The people in the music business in Nashville are always extremely cordial, and always made me feel welcome when I came down to visit CBS Records or attend the country awards shows, and I made a conscious effort to show them my appreciation and commitment. Encouraged by Billy Sherrill and others, I would go there to do lectures, like one in a huge, packed hall at Vanderbilt University. The mayor gave me the keys to the city, and I was made an Honorary Citizen. I knew that there was a meaningful relationship between me and Nashville, and I was never going to go back and start a new enterprise there until I was absolutely certain that I was ready. It was never a case of hanging up a shingle at a house on Music Row that said "Open for Business." If I was going to expand Arista's musical landscape to include country, it had to be at the right time with the right people.

So I waited, and in early 1989, I made the decision. How would Arista keep growing? Where would a new group of artists come from, artists whose stature and success would derive from the combination of well-crafted, melodic songs and distinctive vocal presence? I knew that white pop artists were struggling commercially, that there were fewer and fewer slots for that type of music. Nashville, at its core, was a world that revolved around great songs. I felt we could make an impact there, and that's when I approached BMG and made my case to its CEO, Michael Dornemann: Arista Nashville was the next step in the development of the brand, a country label that reflected my musical values and what Arista had come to stand for in the worlds of pop, rock, and urban music. The next step was finding someone to run the company, since there was no way I was going to micromanage Arista Nashville from Fifth Avenue and Fifty-seventh Street in Manhattan. So I called Joel Katz, a very successful, well-known entertainment attorney who lived in Atlanta but had a number of Nashville-based clients and was very familiar with the Nashville scene, and I asked him to do me a favor and go through all the potential top executives, and set up meetings for me with six or seven different people. And I give Joel a lot of credit: He presented me with an exceptionally strong list of candidates, and I spent two days in Nashville having these meetings, each one lasting a few hours. One of those meetings was with Tim DuBois, who at the time was running the Nashville office of the very successful Fitzgerald Hartley management company, and was also a hit country songwriter, with big hits to his credit like Jerry Reed's "She Got the Gold Mine (I Got the Shaft)," Alabama's "Love in the First Degree," and Vince Gill's "When I Call Your Name." I liked Tim instantly. He had an unusual number of qualities that impressed me. He was good with people, savvy, businesslike, and disciplined, but also creatively sympathetic, and I valued and appreciated that he was also a songwriter. It's rare to find that combination: someone who could run the business side of a company who also had creative credentials. I was sold.

In actuality, Tim may not have been sold, at first. When we contacted him, he was considering opening up his own publishing company. He has said that he was more interested in meeting me than he was in the idea of running a record label. But my plan for the label definitely resonated with him, the Arista model of being extremely selective about signings, hiring the best people, and putting a tremendous amount of muscle behind each project. This was my most important appointment, because this man was going to build the company, and I had to be prepared to delegate, trust his musical instincts, and respect his firsthand knowledge of the country music business. Tim was someone I was confident could take charge, and I couldn't be more fortunate that he accepted the position, because what he accomplished was simply extraordinary, right from the beginning.

What neither I nor Tim could have fully anticipated was that the formation of Arista Nashville would coincide with the emergence of a new generation of country stars, a period that began exactly when the label did. The artists that made their debuts or broke in that year became known in country music circles as the Class of '89: Garth Brooks, Clint Black, Travis Tritt, Lorrie Morgan, Mary Chapin Carpenter, and the very first artist signed by Arista Nashville, a singer and songwriter from Newnan, Georgia, named Alan Jackson. Remarkably, Alan had been passed on by most of the major labels in Nashville. His demo tape, produced by Keith Stegall and financed by Glen Campbell's publishing company, made its way to Tim, who heard tremendous promise in the music and went to see Alan perform at a showcase. After seeing him live, Tim was convinced that Jackson should be our premiere signing. As Tim recalled, Alan came to a meeting with a brown paper bag filled with cassette tapes, took out one after another to play, and Tim was knocked out by the quality of the material. Although Alan was without a record deal, and without any solid prospects, he still had to be sold on being the first artist for a brand-new company. Any artist would have wanted to know what he was getting into, signing a contract with a completely untested label, so Tim arranged for me to fly down to Nashville and sell Alan on Arista. Before I met with Alan, Tim played me some of his songs, and they were very strong. He was a true artist, a really great singer-songwriter. When we had our meeting, Alan was impressive in every way. He had presence and natural quiet charisma. He said few words, but he was to the point and articulate, sincere, soulful, and exceptionally good-looking. He truly had everything, and I honestly couldn't believe that he was really available, that he could be our flagpole artist, the one who would stand for the artistic vision of the label right out of the gate. I remembered how I felt when I first heard Springsteen's songs, when I first experienced Patti Smith's poetry. It didn't matter that they're all so different. They are originals. I went into high gear and pitched him very hard, assuring him that I wasn't some East Coast carpetbagger, telling him about my involvement with the country artists on CBS. I impressed upon him that I came with roots and credentials and I understood where he was coming from musically, that I'd worked with giants he admired like George Jones and Johnny Cash and I saw him as being in that tradition. We hit it off immediately, and he saw how passionate and determined I was, so he signed with us. It created a real bond between us; I never forgot that he chose to go with me and Tim, and put his career entirely in the hands of an untested new venture, and as his career erupted, I presented him and touted him at any given opportunity as one of the unique, signature artists on Arista irrespective of genre.

Tim and his staff found office space on a quiet corner of Music Row, 29 Music Square East, and began preparing the label's inaugural releases. I flew down to the company's opening party at the Renaissance Hotel in May 1989, and could see instantly that Tim had assembled a team of driven, talented executives ready to take on the challenge of making a big noise in Music City. As one new Arista Nashville executive, Mike Dungan (now president of Universal Nashville), has said, "The country industry had been six major labels. Arista came in and immediately became the seventh. We were the new kids on the block, we were having fun, we had great music, and we worked hard." That spirit was obvious from the start. Tim was developing his first few acts: In addition to Alan, within Arista's first year he signed Pam Tillis (daughter of the Country Music Hall of Famer Mel Tillis), Lee Roy Parnell, Radney Foster (from the hit country duo Foster and Lloyd), and a new group called Diamond Rio that Tim saw open for George Jones (when they were known as the Tennessee River Boys). The inaugural roster was maybe seven or eight artists. He would send me demos when he was about to sign an artist, so I was very much in synch with what was going on, but I really left the creative matters in his hands, and he showed sharp A&R instincts. He also went out on the road with Alan, Lee Roy, and a Canadian country singer named Michelle Wright, personally taking them around to visit country stations, introducing them as the new label's first artists, and asking the program directors to give the new records a shot.

It was Alan who took off. His debut single was a catchy up-tempo song called "Blue Blooded Woman," which made a respectable showing on country radio and introduced him to that audience. Then came the songs that really broke through and showed what an all-timer he would be as a singer-songwriter. The first time I heard "Here in the Real World," I knew it was a career-maker, simply a beautiful, heartfelt country tearjerker that showed off Alan's softer side. It had a stunning lyrical hook, exactly what you look for in a great song in any genre. It was the first of *seventeen* consecutive Top 3 country singles for Alan. The debut album, *Here in the Real World,* also had Alan's first number-one country single, "I'd Love You All Over Again," and the trademark hit "Chasin' That Neon Rainbow," a semiautobiographical song about trying to make it and "livin' that honky-tonk dream." Well, by the time that single came out in 1990, he was living that dream. In June 1990, he headlined Arista's afternoon concert at Fan Fair and played to thousands of adoring fans. He was a genuine star. Some of us from Arista in New York watched from the wings of the stage and looked out at the sea of people singing along with "Chasin' That Neon Rainbow," and it was like a scene from a movie, just so exhilarating. Arista Nashville had been in operation for only one year, and to see the level of excitement its artists were generating onstage that afternoon, and the incredible response to Alan as country's newest star, was the fulfillment of everything I could have imagined. That year, Alan was named Top New Male Vocalist at the Country Music Awards, and Arista Nashville threw its first post-CMA party. It had to submit a budget for the party to the finance department in New York City for approval, and we were pretty astonished when the estimated cost for the whole celebration came to around $1,000. By New York or Los Angeles awards-party standards, that wouldn't cover the price of napkins, but that's how Arista Nashville did things: They celebrated their first CMAs, and their tremendous success, with chili and beer. And we all had a blast.

Alan's career continued to rocket. His second album, *Don't Rock the Jukebox,* had four number-one country hits, including the clever title cut. He really was able, as much as anyone else in Nashville at the time, to tie two generations of country together, to make a fresh, modern video of a song that was really contemporary honky-tonk, and incorporate George Jones as a bow to his influences. Alan was a new traditionalist, certainly a fan of country giants like Jones and Merle Haggard, whom he revered, but with a contemporary spin, and as the Nineties went on, not one single of his that Arista Nashville released fell short of the Top 10 until 1997. Every Jackson album in the decade went at least platinum. Two went four times platinum, and his biggest, *A Lot About Livin' (and a Little 'Bout Love)*, went six times platinum, extraordinary at that time for any country artist not named Garth.

In addition to Alan Jackson, Arista Nashville began having other breakthroughs. Pam Tillis had a gold album in 1991, driven by the hit single "Maybe It Was Memphis." Diamond Rio released its debut single, "Meet in the Middle," the same year, and it became the first time a debut single by a country music group ever went to number one.

Later on, there were double-platinum albums by the the Tractors, a country-rock band from Oklahoma and a personal favorite of Tim's, and by a group called BlackHawk. One of BlackHawk's members was the guitarist Henry Paul, from the Outlaws, so two decades after achieving success with his first band on Arista, he was back having hits for our country division. Arista Nashville became a key part of the Arista family, and at every company convention, attended by a strong Nashville contingent, I turned over an entire session of my upcoming-product presentation to Tim, who rattled off with great enthusiasm and humor the records that had broken, and he played the forthcoming key cuts from new artists and new albums.

One act he was particularly proud of, and with good reason, was the duo of Kix Brooks and Ronnie Dunn. Brooks and Dunn were a model of what a creative executive's vision can bring about. In 1990, Tim had met both Kix and Ronnie, each of whom was trying to make inroads in Nashville as a solo artist, and although Tim thought each of them had talent, particularly in their writing ability, he didn't think either was ready to be signed. But he did like their songs, and he suggested that the two get together and try to collaborate, just as writers.

That's such a part of the Nashville system, the constant collaborations among writers. Writing appointments are routinely made by publishers and writers, often a couple in a day, where two or more writers get in a room, toss ideas for songs around, and sketch out promising ideas in demos. It gets the motor running, and it's one of the reasons songwriting in Nashville is such a well-oiled machine. That was the idea behind Tim's matchmaking. But then he heard the demos that Kix and Ronnie had done, and he strongly urged them to team up as artists. There hadn't been a hit male duo in country in a long time, even though it's a long-standing tradition, going back to the Louvin Brothers, Johnnie & Jack, the Everly Brothers, and many others. If this teaming worked out, Kix and Ronnie would pretty much have the whole field to themselves. (And, as it turned out, they did: Brooks and Dunn won the CMA award for Vocal Duo of the Year every year but one between 1992 and 2006.) Although each harbored a desire to make it on his own, they took Tim's advice and joined forces, and released their debut album for Arista Nashville in the summer of 1991, when the label was already riding the charts with Alan Jackson's *Don't Rock the Jukebox,* Pam was on her way to gold, and Diamond Rio's debut was heading to platinum. The first four singles from *Brand New Man,* starting with the title track, all went to number one, and the fourth single made a kind of country music history in an unexpected way.

By the time Tim was ready to release the bouncy, almost novelty song "Boot Scootin' Boogie" as a single, there was a boom in line-dancing. Even before Brooks and Dunn cut the song, which was written by Ronnie, Tim had recorded it with the western-swing band Asleep at the Wheel on their album *Keepin' Me Up Nights.* And originally, it had been stuck on the B side of the number-one Brooks and Dunn single "My Next Broken Heart." But it began to catch on in the country dance clubs, with choreography that had been designed especially for the song. Brooks and Dunn's producer Scott Hendricks came up with the idea to do an extended dance remix, a commonplace-enough tactic for a pop-dance record, but unheard of in country. Although there was definitely some internal disagreement about whether to go forward with this—some thought it would never work, and would hurt the record's chances on country radio—it was novel and innovative. Eventually Kix and Ronnie approved it, Tim and I were on board, and the mixer Brian Tankersley took the original track, which had been produced by Don Cook and Scott Hendricks, and, Kix later said, "added a synthesizer and pumped this hillbilly record full of steroids." The remix broke all the country rules sonically, and at six and a half minutes was radically long, but it swept through the country club scene and became another number one. It was even the first Brooks and Dunn song to hit the pop Top 50. When the last boot had scooted, and one more single was released to wind up the album, *Brand New Man* had gone six times platinum (even though the notorious remix wouldn't appear on an album until their next one, *Hard Workin' Man*), an incredible achievement for any album, especially a debut, even during that era of the Nashville boom. Remarkably, the follow-up did nearly as well, going five times platinum and winning them their first Grammy award, for the title track.

Looking back, the sheer numbers alone were off the wall. To start from absolute zero, with no artists with any meaningful track record whatsoever, and get to a point where Alan and Kix and Ronnie were going multiplatinum on nearly every release, and almost half the artists on the label were at least going platinum, was a level of success that would be enviable for any well-established label. At its peak, the label was responsible for around 20 percent of all of Arista's revenues. I think back on that first decade at Arista Nashville as a period of great camaraderie and excitement, with people who went to work every day with a sense of purpose, dedication, and belief in what they were doing. As a start-up in Nashville, I really can't think of anything comparable. It's not as though Tim went out to sign two or three known acts, the way Atlantic Records did when it made its initial move to Nashville and signed Willie Nelson. I'm sure there were established artists who would have loved to have been on Arista Nashville and get that kind of personal attention, but the label did everything from scratch. Tim found artists who were not only performers and great singers, but who also had unique writing ability. Although I was apprised of each signing, was played singles, shown rough cuts of videos for my input, and formed relationships with the artists, it really is a tribute to Tim and his staff that they created an environment that was so attuned artistically and so unstoppable commercially. It was a golden decade for country music, with wildly popular artists such as Garth Brooks, Shania Twain, and Faith Hill who shattered all preconceptions of what a country artist could sell, and Arista Nashville was a shining example of new blood on Music Row, all through the Nineties.

Then, in a decision that to this day strikes me as inexplicable, in that dramatic year of 2000, BMG decided to fold Arista Nashville into RCA Nashville, keeping Arista Nashville as a brand, more or less just a logo, but losing its creative identity in the process. You can make arguments about centralization, or cost cutting, or efficiency, or however you want to characterize the reasons behind the move made by BMG and its president and CEO, Strauss Zelnick, but it still appears shortsighted and ultimately destructive to assume that the creative heart of a label can continue to beat after such a drastic operation. Not that Arista Nashville didn't continue to flourish. In the wake of 9/11, Alan Jackson wrote and sang "Where Were You When the World Stopped Turning," a poignant, measured response to that shattering event, and one that struck a chord not only with the country audience but with the nation as a whole. It was a simple embrace of American values, an expression of our confusion and our resolve, our ultimate strength. Sometimes, the right song by the right artist can encapsulate a historical moment and resonate, and that's what Alan's soft-spoken anthem did. He premiered the song on the CMAs, mere days after he wrote it, and radio stations began airing a tape of that television performance even before the single was officially released. Even some pop stations started to play it. It won Song of the Year and Single of the Year at the 2002 CMAs, and Alan also won awards that year for Album of the Year (for *Drive*), Male Vocalist of the Year, and Entertainer of the Year, the first time in his career that he'd won in those categories. "Where Were You When the World Stopped Turning" also won Alan his first Grammy, for Best Country Song. I think he should have won that award many times over for his catalog of classic songs throughout the Nineties, but there was no denying him it for this song that moved so many people during such trying times.

So Alan had this major resurgence, and Brooks and Dunn were

still on the label until they broke up as a team in 2009, but they were the last surviving artists from the years that Tim ran Arista. Recently, Alan Jackson left the label and signed with Capitol Nashville, which at that time was headed by the very talented and able former senior Arista executive Mike Dungan. In the post-Tim Arista Nashville era, the two artists that made the most impressive and lasting impact have been Brad Paisley and Carrie Underwood. Paisley was, in fact, one of Tim's last signings. As Brad told *Billboard,* "I wanted to be on Arista Nashville before I moved to Nashville. I look up to Tim DuBois as a friend and a man. To have gotten a chance to work with him has been a tremendous goal accomplished for me. He may not be head of my label anymore, but he will still be part of my career. I signed there because of the people. Tim DuBois created a company where people would work ten to twelve hours a day, then at the end of a long day, you'd see them hopping on an elevator together and going to dinner. At the end of the week, you'd see a couple of guys going camping. He put together a company that is totally a family." In fact, Brad's most consistent co-writer, and one of the partners in his publishing company, is Tim's son Chris DuBois, bringing everything full circle. I think it's poetically apt that the original team Tim and I put in place began by signing one of the most important male country stars of the Nineties and ended in 1999 by signing maybe the most important male country star of the twenty-first century. What Alan Jackson and Brad Paisley have in common, aside from each building a career that essentially started out with an emotional ballad (Brad's was the touching "He Didn't Have to Be") and was sustained with an amazing string of well-crafted and well-chosen songs, is that they were both signed and launched under the watch of Tim and Mike and the rest of the people who made Arista Nashville such a special place.

Brad Paisley is as good an artist as country music has produced in the last decade. He's just been a consistently on-his-game writer; his songs have sensitivity and humor, and a sharper edge than many of his contemporaries; and he's a great performer who, a dozen years after his debut, is at his peak. In 2010, he was named Entertainer of the Year at the CMAs (he won Album of the Year in 2006 for *Time Well Wasted* and Male Vocalist of the Year in 2008 and 2009). He's had sixteen number-one country singles, with a record ten consecutive singles hitting the top spot.

Arista Nashville's other major contemporary signing came in the door through *American Idol,* which I'll talk about in much greater detail later. Carrie Underwood was the one *Idol* winner who flourished outside the pop machinery, and who managed to have consecutive multiplatinum albums, and do it in a way completely different from her predecessors. Carrie, who won in the show's fourth season, is the real thing. Simon Cowell predicted on the show, before she had even made the Top 10, "Not only will you win this show, you will sell more records than any other previous *Idol* winner," and he was right.

I have to say that however fulfilling my subsequent years were at J Records, there was definitely a part of me that missed being a part of Nashville and the country music world, the warmth I always felt when I visited, the conviction and the commitment in the musical community, and the sheer depth of the singing, performing, and writing talent. I cherish the experience of working with Tim DuBois, Mike Dungan, and everyone at Arista Nashville, and remember that time with nothing but the warmest recollections of the spirit, the music, and the chili.

LaFace Rules!

When I called on L.A. Reid and Kenny "Babyface" Edmonds to produce some tracks for Whitney Houston on *I'm Your Baby Tonight,* I didn't realize that they were interested in starting up their own label. But as we worked together we grew closer, and I began to get a feel for their aspirations. As different as we were in terms of our musical backgrounds, we had very similar approaches to our work. They were musicians, writers, and producers, and what we shared is that all three of us ate, slept, and breathed music. In addition to his prodigious songwriting ability, Kenny was also an artist with true star potential. L.A. had serious ambitions and the talent to be a major executive, and was the more extroverted of the two. Their strengths both overlapped and complemented each other, and I soon came to believe that we could accomplish great things together.

I learned that they were done with the idea of producing a track for an artist and turning it over to a label that might or might not know what to do with it. They had already produced nineteen number-one R&B records and had accomplished as much as they could doing that sort of work. They now wanted to discover and groom artists, and then oversee how the music they created with them got to the marketplace. In other words, they wanted a label, and we had many in-depth conversations about the most effective strategies for establishing and breaking artists. Their long success in the R&B field was obviously well known, and their new worldwide success with Whitney was so high-profile that other companies were naturally eager to go into business with them. But the three of us had really connected and, luckily for us, Clarence Avant, their highly respected advisor (as he was to countless African-

American executives and artists), saw and felt this connection and was in our corner. I decided that Arista should actively put its hat in the ring to bankroll the label they decided to call LaFace Records, a name clearly derived from their two nicknames. I was thrilled that they chose us to be their home. They then decided to base the label in Atlanta, which was rapidly becoming a hot spot for contemporary African-American music. Bobby Brown and the producers Jermaine Dupri and Dallas Austin were among the music industry figures who lived there, and a label like LaFace would help pull the scene together.

My own hope was that L.A. and Babyface would operate the way Gamble and Huff did when I made the Philadelphia International deal at Columbia. As it was in the early Seventies, R&B was going through a transition in the late Eighties. The sound retained some of its traditional elements, but it was now being made and listened to by a younger generation that had grown up under the influence of hip-hop. They favored rap-inflected vocals and harder beats and lyrics, along with the more conventional love themes and song-oriented elements of R&B. Just as Gamble and Huff brought Columbia into the Seventies on the R&B front, I wanted L.A. and Babyface to help do that for Arista in the Nineties.

The first LaFace signing was the R&B duo Damian Dame, who spun off some urban radio hits but didn't break through in a big way. It was a classic example of the difference between hit-makers and stars. It's possible for a talented act to have hits, but the goal that L.A., Babyface, and I had defined was identifying and nurturing stars, artists who can fill large halls and go on to long, productive careers as headliners. Maybe that could have happened eventually with Damian Dame, but when one member died in an accident shortly before the duo was set to record its second album, their career was sadly cut short.

I had signed Jermaine Jackson to Arista and, like L.A. and Babyface, he had also worked with Whitney Houston. We had some success with his three albums for the label, but as we were getting started on his fourth, I thought he might be an ideal fit for LaFace. As Michael Jackson's older brother, Jermaine was now in his late thirties and, beginning with the Jackson 5, had been making records for more than two decades. I thought that working with L.A. and Babyface would give him a new sound, expose him to a younger audience, and bring him success on the scale that he so badly wanted. Jermaine loved the idea, and L.A. and Babyface, who had grown up with the family mystique of the Jacksons, were excited as well. It seemed like a well-made match.

As the three of them began working on Jermaine's first album for LaFace, which would be titled *You Said*, Jermaine was startled to learn that his brother Michael had approached L.A. and Babyface and offered them very substantial amounts of money to work on songs for his new album, and surprisingly they had agreed to do it. Everything they wrote during this immediate, well-defined period of a couple of weeks would be for Michael to use. Jermaine couldn't believe that Michael, his close brother, would hijack his producers' material this way. The tensions that existed within the Jackson family are no longer a mystery to anyone, and the sibling rivalry between Michael and Jermaine was certainly one element of them. Jermaine spent his professional life very much in his younger brother's shadow, and, as brothers will, he saw himself as every bit Michael's equal in terms of talent. That was not the case, of course. Really, it's hard to think of any artist who could be compared to Michael Jackson, but Jermaine could not accept that. Consequently, he regarded Michael's hiring L.A. and Babyface as a profound betrayal, and he was shaken to his core.

I had dinner with Jermaine in Paris around this time, and he was totally disconsolate throughout the entire meal. He was crying, indeed sobbing at times, so deeply hurt that his brother would do this to him. Unfortunately, that hurt turned to anger, and Jermaine recorded a song called "Word to the Badd" that was a bitter excoriation of Michael. It was leaked to radio and instantly created a sensation. In the song, Jermaine vilified Michael for lightening his skin; for being "a child," not "a man"; and for "takin' my pie," a seeming reference to the situation with L.A. and Babyface. The tabloid media covered the song intensely. Jermaine was accused of leaking the song himself to piggyback on the media attention Michael was getting for his album *Dangerous,* which had come out not long before, and to call attention to his own album *You Said.* I have no idea if Jermaine did that or not, but the publicity backfired. He came off as petty and desperate. Of course, no one knew about the dramatic situation that had triggered his anger and generated the song in the first place.

"Word to the Badd" was set to go on *You Said,* and there wasn't much I could do about that, even after Michael Jackson personally called me to complain. Michael and I had always been on good terms. We would often run into each other during the glory years of Studio 54. Both of us would be taking all of it in, and he always felt comfortable being next to me. He was a huge early fan of Whitney's, and loved her music. In later years I would regularly invite him to my pre-Grammy party. He never ended up coming; his legal problems had already started, and I'm sure his lawyers advised him that it would not be a good idea while litigation was ongoing. But in the week before the show, he would call me every day and insist that he would be there. His security and publicity people would visit the venue, and he would want to know what table he'd be seated at and with whom he'd be sitting. He'd also want to know who would be performing. I never reveal that in advance, but in his case I knew he wouldn't tell anyone. When the O'Jays were going to be there, he was so enthusiastic: "They've got to play 'Back Stabbers'!" he declaimed. "Tell them I insist they perform 'Back Stabbers'!" We would take turns singing songs together on the phone as we talked about the various artists who would be performing and his favorite hits of theirs.

It was in this spirit that Michael called me to pull "Word to the Badd" off Jermaine's forthcoming album. He said, "I know you have respect for me, and I have respect for you. How could you let my brother do this? I don't want you to release that record." I told him, "Look, Michael, Jermaine is an artist on a label in which I have an interest. I do have great respect for you, but this really is a problem between the two of you. You've got to deal with him directly." As uncomfortable as I was with what Jermaine had done, I felt it would be wrong for me to tell an artist to take a song off his album. This was a family and personal matter that they needed to resolve themselves. Michael said that Jermaine was avoiding him and he couldn't find him anywhere. I told him, "He's just gotten to your parents' house. I spoke to him ten minutes ago." A few hours later, Jermaine called me. "You'll never guess what happened," he said. "I'm at my parents' house, and Michael went around to the back, climbed up and went through a window, and came down the stairs and confronted me with the problem. We really had it out." Jermaine stuck to his guns and kept the song out there, but eventually he and Michael came to some sort of understanding. Jermaine softened the lyrics to the song and changed its focus. It stayed on *You Said*, but much of the sting had been taken out of it. Still, even recast as a lovers' quarrel, the song says a great deal about the hurt Jermaine felt about what Michael had done: "You never think about who you love / You only think about number one / You forgot about where we started from / You only think about what you want / You don't care about how it's done." Ultimately, the album didn't make much impact, so the song is most interesting for the personal story it tells.

The good news was that LaFace was about to catch fire and really explode with one hit after another and one distinctive artist after another. Toni Braxton, TLC, Outkast, Usher, and Pink—each soared to the top of the charts. For the most part L.A. and Babyface ran their label with little involvement from me, and that's the way it should be. Their dream was to be entrepreneurs and they deserved their shot. Yes, Arista provided invaluable promotion and sales support, and I know they valued my company's expertise. They were soaking everything up and additionally we were all benefiting. L.A. was building a hardworking and dedicated staff and was effectively running the label. And Babyface was writing up a storm. I wanted to maximize his talent and use his songs to best advantage. *Waiting to Exhale* is such a perfect example. He wrote songs exactly suited to both the artist and the essence of the film. The soundtrack sold more than 7 million copies, and helped elevate Babyface's stature to the top rung of contemporary music's most gifted songwriters. Even when LaFace made Atlanta its home, Kenny continued to live in Los Angeles, and I would see him whenever I went out there. He would come to my bungalow to play me his new songs, and it was very special to hear them. We would talk for hours about music. It might not have been a total pleasure for him, though, because he would come wearing a heavy jacket or several sweaters. I always keep my bungalow on the cold side so I would stay alert and not miss anything while hearing new songs, but Babyface always thought it was freezing.

From the outset, L.A. and Babyface and I tried to cooperate and help one another. Arista had signed a group of five sisters called the Braxtons, and I thought they might be a better fit for LaFace, so I asked L.A. and Babyface to audition them. When they did, they wisely isolated Toni Braxton as the true vocal talent of the group. They signed her, and showcased her on the million-selling soundtrack for the 1992 Eddie Murphy film *Boomerang*. The movie itself wasn't a massive hit, but the soundtrack, which came out on LaFace and which L.A. executive-produced, was a great success, selling more than 3 million copies in the United States. Toni sang with Babyface on "Give U My Love" and had her solo debut with "Love Shoulda Brought You Home," both of which were co-written by Babyface and were hit singles.

That triumph provided an ideal setup for Toni's 1993 debut album, *Toni Braxton,* which proved a monster hit, selling more than 8 million copies and earning Toni a Best New Artist Grammy. That album had a long run on the charts, so Toni's follow-up, *Secrets,* did not appear until 1996. For that album I provided a song that Diane Warren had brought to me called "Un-Break My Heart." Initially, Toni didn't want to record it. She had become known as a queen of heartbreak, and she didn't want to reinforce that image. I understood her concern, but generally believe that artists tend to overthink issues like that. Surefire hits are not so easy to come by, and "Un-Break My Heart" was obviously going to be major. Its lyric was moving and universal, and that melody—oh, that melody—was memorable and infectious on first listen. I vividly recall Diane playing it for me on the piano in Bungalow 8 of the Beverly Hills Hotel and when she assumed her classic burning and beseeching look after the first chorus, which meant only one thing— was this a surefire number one?—I just looked at her and nodded, and we both knew this was a rare moment. Eventually, Toni came around. We recorded both ballad and dance versions of the song, and both became all-time hits. "You're Makin' Me High" from *Secrets* became Toni's first number-one pop hit, and "Un-Break My Heart," which sat at the top spot for eleven weeks, was her second. The two songs earned Toni Grammy awards for Best Female R&B Vocal Performance and Best Female Pop Vocal Performance, respectively. Following up a success like Toni's debut album was a challenge, but LaFace managed it in textbook form with *Secrets,* which also sold more than 8 million copies.

After that astonishing success, Toni shockingly filed for bankruptcy and even sued to get out of her contract with LaFace and Arista. It was hard to know what had happened with the money she had earned, and since it was primarily LaFace's problem, I stayed out of it. The suits were eventually settled, and Toni recorded a third album for LaFace, titled *The Heat,* which came out in 2000. It was an attempt to move her away from ballad-oriented material and give her a harder sound, and Toni co-wrote seven of the twelve songs on the album, including two with her husband, Keri Lewis. The album sold more than 2 million copies, and the single "He Wasn't Man Enough," co-written and produced by Rodney Jerkins, earned a Grammy for Best Female R&B Vocal Performance. But *The Heat* didn't make nearly the impact, either culturally or commercially, of her first two releases. Her 2002 album, *More Than a Woman,* which she recorded on Arista, earned a gold album, but, again, left a relatively minor impression.

Overspending, grandiose productions and videos, ultraexpensive touring costs, and a desire to write her own material all contributed to Toni's failure to continue the stellar success of her first two albums. I went to see Toni perform in a co-headlining tour with Kenny G, and I was taken aback by how lavish the production was, far more than the venues she was playing could possibly sustain in terms of revenue. But the heights that Toni reached with the first two albums certainly were enough both to establish her as a significant star and to provide LaFace with a very impressive launch.

The trio TLC were another LaFace act that, like Toni Braxton, made a huge commercial impact but also ran into financial difficulties and generated headlines for reasons that had little to do with their music. The three girls—Lisa "Left Eye" Lopes, Tionne "T-Boz" Watkins, and Rozonda "Chilli" Thomas—each had a distinctive personality and an identifiable image, and their effortless fusion of hip-hop, R&B, and pop made them one of the edgiest and most successful acts of the Nineties. It had been L.A.'s recommendation that TLC replace one of its original members with Chilli, another example of his keen eye and ear.

TLC were smart, visually compelling, wrote many of their own songs, and, working with a dream team of producers, made music that defined their era. Their 1992 debut album, *Ooooooohhh . . . On the TLC Tip* sold more than 4 million copies and generated three Top 10 singles: "Ain't 2 Proud 2 Beg," "Baby-Baby-Baby," and "What About Your Friends."

After that TLC was all over the news because Lisa burned down the Atlanta mansion of her boyfriend, the NFL football star Andre Rison. Dangerous as it was, to TLC's young, hip-hop-oriented audience Lisa's action only lent the group a sharper edge, as TLC's appearance on the cover of *Vibe* in firefighter outfits attested. Rather than run from the controversy, they embraced it, and the strategy paid off. The group's next album, the aptly titled *CrazySexyCool,* not only summed up the girls' public image in one deft phrase, it also captured the fun, anarchic spirit of their music. That album, too, blew up. It sold more than 11 million copies, and sent two songs to number one ("Creep" and "Waterfalls") and two others ("Red Light Special" and "Diggin' on You") into the Top 5. The group was nominated for four Grammys and won two, for Best R&B Album and Best R&B Performance by a Duo or Group for "Creep." Without question, *CrazySexyCool* was one of the decade's milestone albums, and it didn't seem as if TLC could get any bigger or that LaFace could get any hotter.

Then, amazingly, in 1995, TLC declared bankruptcy. The girls were obviously upset about their financial situation, so much so that they burst into my office one day, grim and stone-faced, and demanded to know where their money was. I had been having a meeting with Sean "Puffy" Combs as we were planning the launch of a new artist on the Bad Boy label that we had founded together in 1993, but they said they had flown to New York from Atlanta, evidently at Lisa's urging, just to meet with me, so Puffy politely deferred to them and left the room. Apparently, they also posted a security man at the door of my office to make sure that no one else entered, though I was unaware of that at the time. Later, rumors circulated that they were armed, but I never saw any weapons, and T-Boz later laughingly denied that in an interview. They were definitely upset, however. Before they came to me they had gone into a conference room where there was a plaque or picture of the group and they had taken it down. Now they were in my office, and they claimed that L.A. had told them that Arista had their money, and they were here to get it. There was definitely tension in the room. They wanted to show that they meant business, and they wanted the facts. Privately, I had my doubts that L.A. would ever have said anything like that to them. I kept my cool, and certainly didn't talk down to them. As calmly as I could, I explained the nature of their deal with LaFace, and they listened carefully. I pointed out that Arista had paid the total amount of money due from their sales to LaFace, and it was LaFace's obligation to pay them. I had never seen their contract, and there really was nothing further I could do or say. When you have a label deal, you don't interfere in the label's relationships with its artists. You respect the label's autonomy. And that was it as far as my meeting was concerned. There was nothing ever in my personal relationship with TLC that was adversarial or hostile. But this was indeed a serious meeting. Ultimately, they left. L.A. obviously found out about the meeting and what had happened but he and I never personally talked about it.

Without question, TLC's situation was complicated. The group's manager, Perri Reid, who as a recording artist had been known as Pebbles, had been married to L.A. Reid, and they had gotten divorced. TLC's deal had gone through Pebbles's production company, so ending that management arrangement was probably expensive. This was an era in the music business where managing money and being efficient did not rule the day. Substantial sums were being generated but a tremendous amount was being spent in recording, in touring, in video production. All of that was charged to the artists and ate up what they would normally obtain from royalties based on sales of this magnitude. TLC spent a fortune on videos, which drove the sales of their records but still had to be paid for. So apart from the personal drama, these vexing financial problems were certainly not entirely LaFace's fault.

The members of TLC must have worked out their issues with LaFace, because in 1999 the group released *FanMail,* an album that sold more than 6 million copies and included the number-one singles "No Scrubs" and "Unpretty." TLC scored eight Grammy nominations and won three, for Best R&B Album, Best R&B Song, and Best R&B Vocal Performance for "No Scrubs." The trio, unfortunately, was still enmeshed in financial squabbles, this time with the producer Dallas Austin, whose demands the group found excessive, despite his being in a relationship with Chilli. They were also fighting among themselves. Left Eye called the author of a *Vibe* cover story on the band shortly before the magazine went to press, stating that, despite a more positive interview she had given for the story in the preceding days, she could not "stand one hundred percent behind this TLC project." While she never left TLC, she continued to express her discontent in the media and would go on to make a solo album, before dying so prematurely at the age of thirty in an automobile accident in 2002.

It's to TLC's credit that their financial, professional, and personal difficulties never detracted from the quality of the music they produced. Their three albums remain repositories of positive messages about young female empowerment, and *CrazySexyCool,* in particular, has earned its place on *Rolling Stone*'s list of the greatest albums of the Nineties. The trio epitomized exactly the sort of group and music that I hoped LaFace would be able to identify, and they absolutely made the label a leader in defining hip urban sounds.

That hipness factor was strongly reinforced by three of LaFace's other adventurous artists: Usher, Pink, and Outkast. Each defied genre expectations while rising to superstar-level success. They were also attention-getters, the sort of artists who, beyond merely generating hits, gather cultural heat around themselves and drive the music scene as well as thriving within it. I'm talking about that essential quality of star power, and L.A. and Babyface became masters of identifying artists who radiated that potent charisma. Pink and Outkast had successful debuts, while Usher, who was sixteen when his first album came out and who has gone on to become perhaps the biggest star of the three, got off to a mildly disappointing start. Interestingly, rather than produce his debut album themselves, L.A. and Babyface sent Usher to New York to work with Puffy in order for him to "learn how to be a bad boy." It was a bold move, and Usher did pick up some elements of style and swagger from Puffy. After that Usher always presented himself in a way that communicated that he was a star.

But Usher, Outkast, and Pink were all allowed to go on their individual aesthetic journeys, with Pink dramatically turning toward a harder rock sound and Outkast becoming increasingly experimental, essentially creating a style of high-impact, greatly commercial alternative rap. None of these artists was especially compliant; they all had very specific ideas about what they wanted to do at every point in their career. I certainly stayed out of LaFace's dealings with them, and it's to the label's credit that these artists were given the freedom to create groundbreaking work that LaFace managed to turn into millions of sales. It should be mentioned that LaFace also signed the influential Atlanta hip-hop act Goodie Mob, which first introduced the world to Cee-Lo Green, who would become a big star later.

Outkast was the first rap act that LaFace signed, and it was an inspired choice, another example of the label's seeming ability to foresee the future. Consisting of André "André 3000" Benjamin and Antwan "Big Boi" Patton, Outkast forged an exhilarating style that drew unpredictably on many genres of music, past and present, and that appealed to rock and pop audiences as well as to hip-hop devotees. Over the course of six studio albums and a greatest hits collection, all released between 1992 and 2006, the group has sold close to 25 million records in the United States alone. Outkast's most successful and most audacious release was the two-disc set *Speakerboxx/The Love Below,* which came out in 2003 and has sold more than 11 million copies. (The purchase of a double album counts as two sales.) Outkast has racked up six Grammy awards, and, most notably, *Speakerboxx/The Love Below* won for Album of the Year. That album and *ATLiens* (1996), *Aquemini* (1998), and *Stankonia* (2000) regularly turn up on all-time and decade-specific greatest lists. Both André and Big Boi have been extremely gracious to me over the years in expressing gratitude for Arista's role in promoting and marketing their records. They've been vocal in their shout-outs in interviews and on television when accepting their many awards. Their performance at my pre-Grammy party is vivid in my memory. Outkast went on hiatus in 2006, and everyone dearly misses them, but the good news is that they never formally called it quits. Both Big Boi and André 3000 remain active, and, in fact, while claiming that they have no plans to record, Outkast signed once again with L.A. Reid, who is now the CEO of Epic Records, in 2011.

In the case of Usher and Pink, I did eventually get involved with them when problems arose and it seemed that I could help. After I had left Arista and founded J Records, I gave Usher a label deal in 2002, though it never quite got off the ground with the force we both would have liked. As he got interested in running a label, he began spending more and more time with me. Whenever he was in New York he would come to my office and sit with me for a few hours, just watching me go through my day and learning. I'm sure he picked that up from L.A., who was always very generous in telling artists how much he had learned from me. Then, in 2004, when I became head of the RCA Music Group and merged the LaFace and Jive labels, Usher wanted to move onto J Records, but I told him he needed to stay where he was under Barry Weiss, who had worked closely with Clive Calder at Jive. Usher wasn't happy, and neither was his mother, Jonetta, who served as his manager at the time. Since he had started out as a teenager, Usher had pretty much grown up with me, and we had done that label deal together. Still, I didn't feel comfortable poaching him for J. I was overseeing the entire label group, and I assured him that I would personally always keep an eye on him, but he needed to deal with Barry. As it developed, his relationship with Barry and the Jive team was often stormy, and at points they weren't even speaking. From time to time Usher sort of went on strike and just withdrew. As he saw it, after selling tens of millions of records he was being "nickel-and-dimed." I never tried to get deeply enough into the issues to make a judgment. It was his problem to solve with Barry and Barry's team. Artists never think they're getting everything they need, and if you try to be prudent with them they can bristle. Partly it was just a different environment for him. LaFace's attitude about money had been that you never wanted to miss a really strong opportunity because you were afraid to spend. If you overspent, then you had to deal with the consequences of that. Barry came up in a company atmosphere that worried more about spending, which occasionally led to problems with artist relations. (A truly successful music executive should be cost-efficient on a day-to-day basis, but when you have an album that has million-selling potential you can't decide every expenditure divorced from the big picture. Yes, you have to be judicious, but boldness is also important and does separate the men from the boys.) Usher would come and tell me that he wasn't going to record for Jive, and I would simply respond, "You have to. You're going to have to come to an accommodation. This is how it works." I felt that I had to stand behind the label. Usher's career was exploding and the label was trying to be cost-efficient.

As for Pink, she had initially been signed to LaFace as part of a trio called Choice, and once again, L.A. Reid keenly identified her as the star and pulled her out of the group. Her 2001 album *M!ssundaztood* sold more than 5 million copies and really made her a superstar. But after her 2003 follow-up, *Try This,* fell considerably short of that commercial mark, I listened to the songs she had done for her next album, *I'm Not Dead,* and, other than "Stupid Girls," I didn't hear any candidates for hits on it. I felt that she needed to go back into the studio and record some more, something artists never want to hear when they think they're done. As it turned out, Barry agreed with me and had told her manager, Roger Davies, so, but Pink was refusing to take direction. Responding to Roger's request, I agreed to intervene and flew to Los Angeles to meet with her. At that meeting I explained that on her previous album she had presented herself as a rock artist and didn't factor in her need for Top 40 hits. Yes, her voice was great and, yes, she was cutting-edge, but she was cutting-edge as a pop artist. She wouldn't get meaningful acceptance in the United States as a rock artist, and she didn't. Her sales dropped precipitously. With her new album she needed hits or her career might be at risk. She wasn't ecstatic to hear that I personally didn't hear any breakthrough candidates on it, but I was there with her at the beginning of her career and she went along with my judgment. She was a thorough professional and she went back into the studio. Since then, Pink's continued to flourish, and she's done so with the flair, style, and individuality that have made her one of the twenty-first century's definitive artists.

Before leaving LaFace I want to tell the story of a related joint venture that didn't produce the strong results that LaFace did. Through L.A. Reid I had met the Atlanta-based songwriter and producer Dallas Austin, who was in his early twenties and had already had major hits with Boyz II Men, TLC, and other artists. He wanted to start a label of his own, and I went down to Atlanta to spend some time with him and get to know him. Dallas is smart and serious, and, along with the work he'd already done, he impressed me. I funded the label, which he called Rowdy Records. The first artist Dallas brought to me was Monica, who was barely a teenager at the time. Working with singers that young usually doesn't interest me, so I wasn't exactly jumping for joy. You just have to be so careful about the type of material you give very young teenagers. But Monica clearly was an exception. She was unusually mature for her age. I had her sing at one of my weekly singles meetings where forty or fifty executives gather in a conference room to discuss the music we're going to be working that week. A girl that young from Georgia could easily have been intimidated, but she strolled around the room and really registered with the poise of someone five or six years older. Now I was convinced that we had a new, very distinctive talent.

Each of Monica's first two albums, *Miss Thang* and *The Boy Is Mine,* sold more than 3 million copies. I worked closely and cooperatively with Dallas on *Miss Thang*. Monica moved to Arista after the first album, and I was very personally involved in *The Boy Is Mine* as executive producer. The title track, her duet with Brandy, became one of the biggest hit singles of all time. I brought in the top producers Jermaine Dupri and David Foster to work on the album, and lined her up with a couple of Diane Warren songs. Her singles "The First Night" and "Angel of Mine" both went to number one. Ultimately, though Monica has never dominated an era the way Whitney Houston or Mariah Carey has, she did make a big impact with her first two albums and she's still creating strong music and enjoying a meaningful career.

Despite my initial wariness because of her age, Monica was precisely the sort of artist I imagined Dallas Austin signing to Rowdy. Perhaps the name he chose for the label was a giveaway, but after that he began signing pure rock artists and left-of-center acts. As far as I was concerned, he had moved out of his sphere of expertise in R&B. I finally felt that I needed to discuss this with him, so I traveled to Atlanta for a meeting. I said, "Look, it's your label. You don't have to get my approval, but I think you might be falling prey to the syndrome of taking for granted the type of artists and hits that you can deliver. It came so easy for you at such a young age that you're not at all respectful of that track record. I want to make clear, however, that it's on the basis of that track record that I gave you this label deal." I like Dallas enormously, and we weren't arguing at all. His attitude was "I already know I can do that. I've done that." I emphasized again that that's what I was betting on—his ability to continue to do that. What I didn't take into account was his desire or willingness to do it. He somehow felt that he had to move on and prove himself in a different way, prove that he wasn't a one-trick pony. He seemed to lose sight of the fact that it's hard to do even one trick very well. I just said, "I hope you're right." But it turned out he wasn't right.

And that is the complicated issue with a label deal or a joint venture. You have to be extremely careful. You give someone as much freedom as you can, but you can never be entirely sure how they're going to handle it. I made such arrangements very sparingly. Every time a producer becomes successful with more than five or six hits, you usually get asked about a label deal. I almost always said no. What you are gauging is more than the ability to create hit records. You're evaluating whether the producer can find stars. Hit records don't necessarily mean hit albums, nor do they guarantee a long career as a headliner. When I explored the ambition of the producer to be an entrepreneur, rather than just a hit-maker, I always asked to see the talent they would sign if they had their own label. Often I was very disappointed. The auditioning artist might technically sing well, but he or she wouldn't have the charisma, the presence, the star power, to demonstrate that as a headliner they would be able to lift an audience out of their seats. Being a hit-maker is not at all synonymous with being a major developer of talent. Gamble and Huff changed the game in the late Sixties and the Seventies with Philadelphia International Records, and L.A. and Babyface did it in the late Eighties and the Nineties. As a result, LaFace more than made its mark. Babyface has continued as a successful artist, producer, and peerless songwriter, and L.A. Reid has become one of the music industry's most important and successful star executives. And now on to another label deal that was, if anything, just as spectacular.

76

RIGHT: With Whitney Houston, shooting the cover of her *Greatest Hits* album, 2000

BELOW: Backstage with the Foo Fighters at Irving Plaza, 2007. Back row: Chris Shiflett. Top row: Nate Mendel, Charles Goldstuck, Dave Grohl, Ashley Newton, Taylor Hawkins, actress Gina Gershon. Bottom row: Tom Corson, Richard Palmese and the Foo Fighters' manager, John Silva

On the way to my 2002 pre-Grammy gala with Alicia Keys, 2002

With Charles Goldstuck, Busta Rhymes and Alicia Keys, 2002

Ahmet Ertegun presents me with a Lifetime Achievement Award from the New York branch of the National Academy of Recording Arts and Sciences, 2002

Alicia Keys receives a plaque for selling ten million copies of her debut album, *Songs in A Minor,* 2003

With Kenny G and
Charles Goldstuck, 2004

With Annie Lennox, 2004

BELOW: Flanked by Jamie Foxx and Usher, 2006

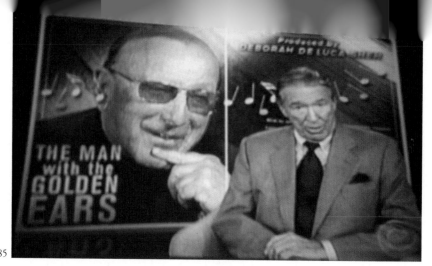

85

Mike Wallace introduces a *60 Minutes* segment about me in 2009

With Whitney, 2006

BELOW: With Charles
Goldstuck and Carrie
Underwood, 2005

86

Celebrating the enduring success of Randy Edelman's Barry Manilow song "Weekend In New England" thirty years later, with Randy, Roger Birnbaum and Stanley Buchthal

On the set of *American Idol* with Simon Cowell, Randy Jackson and Paula Abdul, 2007

RIGHT: With Whitney, Mary J. Blige and Barry Manilow at my 2007 pre-Grammy gala

BELOW: The *Bodyguard* musical team reunites in Phoenix as I'm honored in 2008 by the Celebrity Fight Night Foundation, Muhammad Ali's Parkinson's charity. From left: Kevin Costner, Whitney and producer David Foster

With Doug
Morris, chairman
of Sony Music
Entertainment, 2011

With Rod Stewart and his manager Arnold Stiefel

At the Clive Davis Theater at the Grammy Museum in Los Angeles, 2010

Speaking at Whitney's funeral service, 2012

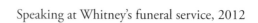

Accepting an honorary doctorate from NYU at Yankee Stadium in 2011

Alicia and her husband, producer Swizz Beatz, and Puffy at the club Espace, 2012

With Barbra Streisand at my 2010 pre-Grammy party, which included a tribute to her

With Jennifer Hudson, 2011

100 On vacation with friends at Ristorante Villa Verde in Capri, 2012. From left: Rosanna Krekel, Dr. Jennifer Mieres (*standing*), Greg Schriefer, Tig Krekel (*standing*), Lois Walden, Margot Harley, Randy Sturges, Thom Dugal, Mindy Whitehead, Glenn Whitehead and Lesley Glover

101

St. Tropez, June 2012. Left to right: Milene Koblasa, Patrice Ablack, Brian Cohen, Barbara Davis, Greg Schriefer, Nikki Haskell, Tim Bush, Xavier Boyaval and Lesley Glover

Left to right (*sitting*): Jim Budman, Mindy Whitehead, Rosanna Giacalone, Randy Sturges, Kathryn Kranhold, Dan Pallotta, Sebastian de Kleer and Rusti Fiur. Left to right (*standing*): Jeff Guthrie, Michael Palumbo, Glenn Whitehead, Jimmy Smith and Lisa Banes

RIGHT: With Barbara Davis at her Carousel of Hope Ball for Juvenile Diabetes in Beverly Hills, at which George Clooney was honored and Neil Diamond entertained, 2012

BELOW: Davis family portrait, 2012: From left: Clare, Harper, Mitchell, Douglas, Fred, Rona, Charles, Austin, Julius, Lauren, Matthew. In front: Hayley, Sloane

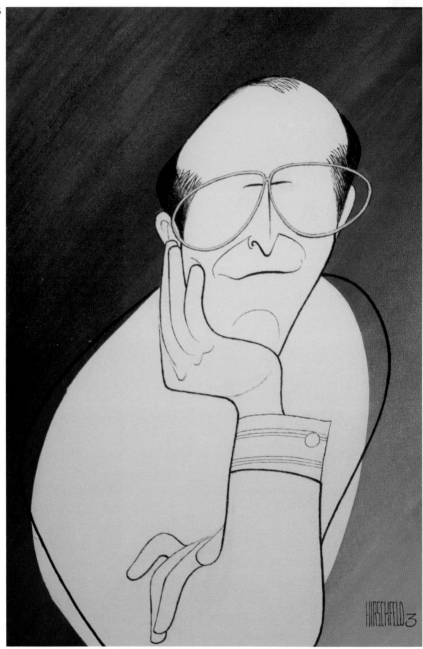

A second Hirschfeld portrait, this time in color

Bad Boy

When I was first asked to meet with Sean "Puffy" Combs in 1993, I didn't know much about who he was. While it's been reported differently in the media, I know that it was Puffy's accountant, Bert Padell, who first told me about him and set up our introduction. Before I met with Puffy, I discussed him with L.A. Reid. That was important because Puffy was seeking a label deal, and I wanted to be sure that what he wanted to do fit well within the overall Arista structure. L.A. was enthusiastic from the very beginning. He felt that such a deal would give both Arista and LaFace street credibility and access that would greatly benefit both labels.

At its best, a label deal should help you accomplish something that you couldn't do on your own. If LaFace had helped expand Arista's presence in the world of contemporary R&B, Puffy's label would provide us with a strong platform in modern-day hip-hop. That music had taken a darker, harder turn in the early Nineties, and its commercial impact was completely undeniable. Once the *Billboard* charts began relying in the early Nineties exclusively on sales information scanned at point of purchase, it became apparent how well rap records were selling. I was open to finding a promising young entrepreneur who would plant Arista's flag in that important area. Puffy proved to be just that person.

When I met with him Puffy was still in his early twenties, and he had just been fired from Uptown Records by the label's founder and CEO, Andre Harrell. In just a few years Puffy had gone from being an unpaid intern at the label to being on the A&R staff and actively involved in the careers of Jodeci and Mary J. Blige, among other artists. Though I'd never worked with Andre, I knew him and liked him a lot, and I'm not sure exactly what went wrong between him and Puffy. Puffy, young as he was, probably felt that he was ready to run his own shop and was overly aggressive within the structure of Uptown. Andre no doubt realized that it was time for Puffy to move on. They remained on good terms, however. In fact, it was Andre who suggested that Puffy contact me about backing the company he wanted to start.

When I met Puffy I found him to be very impressive, and we instantly hit it off. I was looking for him to provide Arista with a street presence that I didn't feel we could establish on our own. With an objective like that, you can't be sure what you're going to get in terms of poise and business savvy. Puffy delivered in every regard. He wore a sharp suit to our first meeting, and he was all business. He had high ambitions. For one thing, he was determined to redefine the nature of Top 40 and mainstream contemporary music. He was convinced that hip-hop could be much bigger than it had already become and could shape the music scene around itself. When he first said that to me I thought he was being a little naïve about the difficulty of penetrating Top 40. It was a tall order, but I nevertheless believed it was a healthy and ambitious dream to have. He wanted to be big. He believed that he and I would be an excellent match because of my track record in Top 40 music; what I had done with rock 'n' roll was of much less interest to him. "I want you to help me make the music that I do friendly to Top 40," he said to me, "because big money comes when that happens. Otherwise it's a limited pie." He saw that Whitney had sold more than 22 million copies of each of her first two albums, and he aspired to numbers like that for his artists. He genuinely had a vision. I asked L.A. Reid to attend our second meeting, and his support of Puffy continued to be strong and passionate. They had obviously had their own interactions and believed they could complement each other very well.

Puffy had already been working with a few new artists at Uptown when he got fired, so before I could consider any deal, I asked to hear some examples of the music he wanted to make. At that meeting, the first track he played me was "Flava in Ya Ear" by Craig Mack, and it instantly felt like a hit. In commercial terms, rap is no different from any other type of music: The same basic principles apply. Are your emotions affected? Is the hook infectious and memorable? "Flava in

Ya Ear" was undeniable. Then he played three or four songs from what would become *Ready to Die,* the now legendary debut album by the Notorious B.I.G. That was something unforgettable to this day. When he spoke about him, Puffy made Biggie's star power mythical and irresistible. What I heard was very powerful and I immediately became a full-fledged participant. I made the deal with Puffy to bankroll Bad Boy Records.

Frankly, I wasn't crazy about the name he chose for the label, and at first I tried to talk him out of it. Puffy was already a controversial figure. He had just gotten fired very publicly, but also, in 1991, he had produced a benefit concert at City College in New York and nine people died during a stampede after the event was oversold. He and the rapper Heavy D were declared responsible for the deaths by a court, but the finding brought with it no legal penalties. Still, Puffy would face lawsuits for the next decade because of that tragedy.

In our discussions, I questioned Puffy very directly about the wisdom of naming his label Bad Boy. Suppose he were to sign an artist like Bob Dylan or Bruce Springsteen or Prince, none of whom I suspect would want to be on a label with such clear associations with its founder. Certainly if he wanted to reshape Top 40 this was a question he had to think about. Puffy, however, was unyielding. He felt the label name suited him, and it suited all the artists he was planning to sign at the moment. In the end, since it was his company, Bad Boy became its name. Right after we made the deal I invited Puffy to one of my singles meetings to describe his vision for Bad Boy to the Arista executive team. That meeting was eye-opening for everyone there. All the executives had heard about Puffy's controversy. They knew I rarely committed to a label deal, and I'm sure they wanted to see what he was all about. Puffy had his share of detractors who had been very vocal, expressing skepticism about whether he was the real deal, whether he was all show and little substance. Puffy came to the meeting well prepared, and even at the young age of twenty-four, he was masterful in conveying his ideas, dreams, and specific goals. He won everyone over right then and there, and contagiously prepared them for the musical revolution that he saw just around the corner.

Craig Mack's "Flava in Ya Ear" came out in the summer of 1994, and became a Top 10 hit. It has subsequently become something of a hip-hop classic. We celebrated its release and the launch of Bad Boy with a party at the Plaza Hotel, a touch of the high style that I know Puffy appreciated and enjoyed. At that event I introduced Puffy, Biggie, and Craig to the crowd, and made my support of the label resoundingly clear. Bad Boy was to really make its impact with the release in September 1994 of *Ready to Die,* the Notorious B.I.G.'s debut album, which has gone on to sell more than 4 million copies. If the goal of making a deal with Puffy was to bring Arista hip-hop credibility, this album and this artist could not have done a more perfect job. Biggie, a Brooklynite whose birth name was Christopher Wallace, was larger than life in every conceivable sense. Physically, he stood six feet three and weighed well over three hundred pounds. With hits like "Juicy," "Big Poppa," and "One More Chance," the latter two of which cracked the Top 10, *Ready to Die* enraptured hard-core rap fans, critics, and more mainstream listeners. In fact, just as Puffy claimed it would, the album did help redefine and expand the mainstream.

Russell Simmons, one of the founders of Def Jam Records, credited me in the press with encouraging Puffy to give Big's tracks more radio appeal. Radio appeal is simple: Does a song have verses and choruses that include the elements for a potential breakthrough? Is it the type of song that radio stations that play the hits would play? What Russell said might be true, but I must say that I never offered Puffy specific creative suggestions along those lines. I'm sure, however, that he absorbed it when sitting in on my meetings with Arista's promotion and marketing departments, product managers, and A&R staff. He made it a point to come to my office every few weeks and hang out for hours, observing how the various components of Arista worked together. He used to call it going to school. At those meetings, I continually emphasized the value of hit singles, the essential fact that regardless of media coverage, great reviews, excellent songs, or anything else, it was the depth of hit singles that primarily drove sales into the stratosphere. Having taken all that in, Puffy didn't need me to tell him explicitly what *Ready to Die* required. Working closely with Biggie, he took the rapper's dark, hard-edged songs and sweetened them just enough to maximize their commercial—and ultimately their cultural—impact. As a result, *Ready to Die* is now regarded as one of the most important hip-hop albums ever made, and it routinely turns up on lists of the greatest albums in the history of contemporary music. It earned a place on *Rolling Stone's* list of the 500 Greatest Albums of All Time, and *Spin* listed it as number twenty-seven among the hundred best albums released between 1985, the year *Spin* was founded, and 2000.

Significantly, the album also helped restore New York to an eminent place in the rap world after a few years of domination by L.A.-focused West Coast hip-hop. That proved to be a mixed blessing at best, because Biggie, Puffy, and Biggie's wife, Faith Evans, who recorded three successful albums for Bad Boy, all became enmeshed in the violent, high-stakes drama of the rivalry between the East and West Coast rap scenes. Tupac Shakur, who had been friends with Biggie, somehow became his archrival, and when Tupac was shot and robbed in a New York studio in November 1994, he accused Biggie, Puffy, and Andre Harrell of setting him up for it. Biggie released a taunting song called "Who Shot Ya?" and Tupac responded with "Hit Em Up," in which he addressed Biggie directly and claimed that he'd had sex with Faith Evans: "You claim to be a playa, but I fucked your wife."

Similarly, Puffy had been friends with Marion "Suge" Knight, the head of Death Row Records in L.A., the home of Dr. Dre, Snoop Doggy Dogg, and Tupac. But as the atmosphere of the rap scene became increasingly poisonous, Puffy and Suge fell out in a big way. At the annual awards show sponsored by the rap magazine *The Source* in New York in 1995, Suge took the microphone onstage and said, "If you don't want the owner of your label on your album or in your video or on your tour, come to Death Row." It was an obvious slap at Puffy, who loved making such cameo appearances and had definite artistic aspirations for himself.

In 1996 Tupac was shot and killed in Las Vegas. Biggie was shot to death in Los Angeles the following year in what was widely seen as a retaliatory strike. With two major rappers murdered in cold blood within a year and no arrests made for the killings, the media was aflame with coverage. While in legal terms nothing remotely ever came of it, as far as the speculation, the rumors, the innuendos, and the conspiracy

406 The Soundtrack of My Life

theories went, Puffy was at the center of it all. Nor was that the end of Puffy's problems. Three years later, in 1999, Puffy was charged with assaulting the record executive Steve Stoute over issues related to a Nas video, and he was also arrested on gun charges, though he was acquitted after a trial. The same club fracas that led to the weapons charges against Puffy resulted in the rapper Shyne, who was signed to Bad Boy and being groomed by Puffy, being sentenced to ten years in prison, essentially derailing his music career.

Do you find it hard to believe that I never spoke with Puffy about any of this? I must say that I do, too. My meetings with him were always very businesslike, an aspect of him that had impressed me from the very beginning. He would occasionally complain about money or a difficult financial issue, but it was no different from the problems that would arise with any other artist or label executive with whom I or my invaluable executive vice president Roy Lott had to work while maintaining a close, cooperative relationship. Striking that balance was our goal. We were having a great deal of success, which always makes things easier. Puffy was growing up, and I knew that he knew that if he wanted to talk with me about any of the controversies that were flying around him, he could have brought it up. He always appeared confident that everything was under control, that he was blameless and would emerge unscathed. When your partner signals that, you don't conduct a separate investigation. He had my trust.

How different is it from an artist having personal problems of any other kind? At what point does it become imperative to intervene? Puffy knew that if he had ever asked me for help I would have done whatever I could for him, but he moved in a world that I honestly didn't fully understand. That was the point of my making a label deal with him in the first place. Wild stories of all kinds circulated about the major figures in hip-hop. How much of it was true, and how much of it was mythmaking? It was hard to tell from the outside. I rarely saw Puffy when he was on the street. I wasn't there with him when he was socializing in St. Tropez and giving champagne or vodka out to everyone in the club. But I was there watching him as an ever-maturing leader of executives. I saw an intense competitive streak. I saw an innate intuitive sense of who was up and coming and who could be employed to assure that he was staying ahead of the trends. I also saw someone who was very aware of the significance of black culture and the need to make sure that the youth of tomorrow knew that as well. And I saw someone who courageously put himself out there to test all of his talent and attempt to fulfill his dreams. He was not just a showman or a rapper. He was an actor, and serious roles on the Broadway stage and in film became part of his repertoire. No coward was he.

What does strike me as odd and is really hard to believe as I look back was my lack of concern for my own safety. When I went to artist showcases or parties Puffy threw for his label's stars in clubs around the city late at night, I never once brought a bodyguard. At some of these events it seemed like even the coat checks had security, but I would just walk in with whomever I'd had dinner with that night. And I have to say that I was always treated with the greatest deference and respect, and never felt as if I personally were in any danger. One time I was at a party and the next day I heard there was a shooting after I left. So I probably was like Mr. Magoo or just plain stupid. But nothing ever happened when I was there, and I never changed anything about myself when entering the hip-hop scene. I'm not espousing this or recommending it, but I think everyone in the scene appreciated that. I was myself, and I let them be themselves. I heard that other labels had armed undercover security teams on their premises in case violence ever broke out, but inexplicably it never occurred to me to do that at Arista.

People accurately talk about my being a strong, hands-on record company head, but I have to say I always tried to allow other personalities to emerge. And there never has been a larger personality than Puffy. In fact, once he was getting a major award at a ceremony in New York and he asked if I would get up and speak about him. It was a large hall filled with all the power players, both artists and executives, in the hip-hop community. I was concerned that I might not fit in or that I would be perceived as not fitting in, so I asked a friend how I should approach this event, and he said, "You should just go with your natural Clive loft." Well, I didn't want to be thought of as living in an ivory tower, totally above it all. I wanted to break any wall of artificiality, so right at the beginning, I said: "Let me just get one issue out of the way right here and now: Tonight you motherfuckers are gonna get the real Clive Davis!"

Well, that opening definitely broke the ice. People were laughing and clapping. I continued: "Puffy, I'm so grateful that you have now come into the industry. Like you, I've been very visible. I've been on TV shows. I've been a spokesman for the music business as well as a keynote speaker at major events. But you, Puffy, have taken all this to totally new heights. You've refined it to a level that dwarfs anything I've ever done. To see you so out front in the media. To see you in every artist's video. I can only picture what my life would have been like if you had come along well before me, and I mirrored your standard of exposure."

I then played a video that I'd had my creative services department put together. It opens with the scene from the video for "The Greatest Love of All," where Whitney Houston is singing on the stage at Carnegie Hall. When she runs off the stage, though, instead of running into the arms of her mother, I'm standing there and she runs into my arms. Then it moved to a scene from the video for "I Will Always Love You," and when Whitney is in the snow and turns to see Kevin Costner, I'm standing there in his place. In the video for the Tony Rich single "Nobody Knows," when he enters the bathroom, I'm the bathroom attendant handing out towels. And, finally, in the Toni Braxton video for "You're Makin' Me High," she and some girlfriends are watching these superfit guys come out of an elevator and they're rating them. I'm in the elevator making a muscleman pose and they rate me a 10. All this simply brought the house down.

My relationship with Puffy also highlighted certain elements of my lifestyle that played well in the hip-hop world. In the rock world, even if you're selling tens of millions of records the standard modus operandi is to insist that you really don't care about money or success. You present yourself in jeans and vintage shirts, as if to dress up would reveal a desperate conformity or eagerness to impress. I am passionate about music and my work to the bottom of my very soul, but I also very much enjoy good clothes and some of the finer things in life. Rappers do, too, and perhaps it's one of the reasons I've been welcomed so warmly into their world. Like so many hip-hop artists who came after him, Puffy established a fashion line and invested in restaurants, two cultural worlds I also enjoy. Different as we are in many ways, Puffy and I both grew up in New York and shared similar ambitions and goals.

Well beyond Puffy's scrapes with the law, Bad Boy was to score giant successes and make an enormous commercial and cultural impact. In 1997 the label released Biggie's second album, *Life After Death,* a two-disc set that more than lived up to its eerily predictive title. Big's death lent a grim, compelling authenticity to the album's chronicle of feuds and its depiction of hip-hop as a Mafia-style existence in which life is in the balance at every moment. The album more than met the high standard established by *Ready to Die* and ensured the Notorious B.I.G.'s place in hip-hop history. He is hailed by many as the greatest rapper of all time. The album also made painfully clear what a loss his death meant to contemporary music. It sold 5 million copies and was certified ten times platinum because it was a double album. In 1999 Bad Boy released *Born Again,* a posthumous album of Biggie material that consisted of unfinished songs, previously unreleased material completed by collaborations with other rappers, and the controversial and hugely influential song "Who Shot Ya?"

Just a few months after *Life After Death* came out, Puffy released his own album *No Way Out,* which was another tremendous success. As much as Puffy was chided for his taste for the limelight, he channeled that energy into his own performances and became a major star. The album was credited to Puff Daddy and the Family, and just as Puffy had appeared on so many of his artists' songs, virtually the entire Bad Boy roster performed on *No Way Out.* The album entered the charts at number one, sold more than 7 million copies, earned five Grammy nominations, and won the Grammy for Best Rap Album. The album's first single, "Can't Nobody Hold Me Down," went to number one, and "It's All About the Benjamins" rose to number two. But the album's tour de force was "I'll Be Missing You," Puffy's poignant tribute to the Notorious B.I.G. The song rides on a sample from the Police classic "Every Breath You Take," and Sting joined Puffy to perform it live at the 1997 MTV Video Music Awards. Also performing on the track were Biggie's wife, Faith Evans, and the R&B quartet 112, making the song something of a Bad Boy family farewell to Biggie. Puffy was criticized in some quarters for exploiting Biggie's death with the song in order to sell his own album, which seemed really unfair. I knew how shattered Puffy was over Biggie's murder, and a person like Puffy is not going to respond to an event like that in a small, private way. His instinctive response to his loss was to put Biggie out there in as significant a way as possible, both in Biggie's own work and in a salute to him like "I'll Be Missing You." I think that for Puffy, Biggie was more than an artist or even a friend. He seemed to represent everything that Puffy hoped he could achieve, a living embodiment of everything he believed that music could be. Biggie was the prime example of Puffy's vision for a new Top 40 shaped by hip-hop. For all those reasons, I thought Puffy's ongoing public celebration of Biggie's legacy was legitimate and deeply felt. As a result of the sales of "I'll Be Missing You," Puffy was able to establish a $3 million trust for Biggie's children.

In 1998 Puffy collaborated with Led Zeppelin's Jimmy Page and Rage Against the Machine's guitarist, Tom Morello, on "Come with Me," which sampled the Zeppelin classic "Kashmir" and appeared on the soundtrack for the film *Godzilla*. The film is now forgotten, but the single broke into the Top 5. As a result of all his success, Puffy asked Arista for a huge $100 million advance against Bad Boy's future royalties, and that request got into the press. In actuality, the label settled on a $28 million advance, not just against royalties but also against Puffy's share of accumulated profits, past and future. After all, in 1998, for twenty-two of the year's fifty-two weeks, a Bad Boy song had topped the singles charts. But this is a fast-changing world, and no one could ever have predicted all the events that would arise to make the finances of this ordinarily sensible deal somewhat problematic.

Partly because he became so ubiquitous with *No Way Out*, Puffy faced a backlash when he released his follow-up, *Forever*, in 1999. The single "Satisfy You," which featured R. Kelly, went to number two, and the album sold more than a million copies, normally a substantial achievement but here far less impressive than *No Way Out*'s success.

Similarly, Puffy had signed the New York rapper Mase, whose 1997 debut album *Harlem World* sold more than 4 million copies. Mase became Puffy's sidekick, filling a void that had been left by Biggie's death. However, shortly after his second album, *Double Up,* appeared in 1999, Mase announced that he had experienced a spiritual breakthrough and was leaving the world of music to become a minister. So he did little to support the album, which earned a gold record, again a success by standard measures, but disappointing given how well *Harlem World* had done. As always seems to happen in the world of hip-hop, rumors swirled about the "real" reasons for Mase's departure, but the fact is that he unexpectedly gave up on a spectacular musical career, and that hurt Bad Boy.

Other Bad Boy acts followed similar trajectories. The hard-core hip-hop group the Lox went platinum with its 1998 debut album, *Money, Power & Respect,* but the group had creative differences with Puffy and ended up taking their platinum follow-up, *We Are the Streets,* to another label. The first two albums by the R&B quartet 112 went double platinum, while the group's third album sold platinum. The female R&B trio Total registered platinum sales with their 1996 debut album, *Total,* but dropped to gold with their second album, *Kima, Keisha and Pam,* two years later. Faith Evans's career got entangled with the issues surrounding Big's death and she never quite took off. Bottom line, the continuing platinum and gold successes were good, but Bad Boy's sales were no longer in the higher stratosphere.

This is how things were going toward the end of Bad Boy's relationship with Arista. I'm not sure how much even Puffy understood the degree to which Biggie's death had unsettled him and the label. At first Puffy seemed energized by his effort to memorialize his friend, but there were plenty of rumors that Puffy's own life was in danger. It's difficult to concentrate on running a business and being a successful artist when so much is distracting you.

I deeply value the working relationship that Puffy and I had, as well as our friendship, which continues uninterrupted. When Whitney Houston died, Puffy had been scheduled to introduce me at my pre-Grammy party. He called me before the evening got under way to check up on me and helped soothe my paralyzed emotions. Then together we reviewed how we would make the night a very special tribute to Whitney. Right from the start, when he introduced me, he was on fire. He, more than anyone else, set the tone for the entire evening. He was calming, eloquent, and truly brilliant in riding that precarious thin line between doing justice to Whitney's unparalleled place in music and in people's hearts, and allowing the audience to feel and enjoy the wonderful artistry of all the performers to follow, performers that Whitney herself had cherished. It was a real tribute to his character and a heartfelt tour de force.

Beyond that, Puffy has remained a major force in the music industry, one of the most colorful, successful, and adventurous figures that hip-hop has produced. When we launched Bad Boy it immediately became a dominant label on the music scene, and it more than fulfilled Puffy's dream of altering the nature of mainstream music. As for Puffy himself, I have no doubt that he will remain a visible, dynamic cultural figure—an entrepreneur, a ringmaster, an impresario, an actor and performer—for many years to come.

Sarah McLachlan, Ace of Base, and the Freewheeling Nineties

It was big news in the music industry when Arista's executive vice president and general manager, Don Ienner, left in 1989 to become president of Columbia Records under Tommy Mottola. Certainly, Donnie made a major contribution to Arista during his tenure, and it wasn't surprising that he would be offered a top position with one of Arista's competitors. That had happened over the years as rivals saw what we were accomplishing. It was almost as though I were training a generation of industry leaders, which on the one hand does give me a sense of pride, but on the other gives me the drive and urgency to make my team strong enough to survive any one executive moving on.

Of course, we were beginning the new decade with Whitney Houston and Kenny G on the marquee, the brand-new LaFace Records getting off the ground, and a number of other artists whose winning streaks were continuing. And I had a great group of executives in place. Roy Lott stepped into the position of executive VP and GM with exceptional savvy and tenacity; our head of promotion, Rick Bisceglia, had come up under Donnie and shared his go-for-the-kill approach; and there were very skilled senior executives in place in marketing (Richard Sanders, Marty Diamond, and Tom Ennis), publicity (Melani Rogers), creative services (Ken Levy), international (Eliza Brownjohn), urban promotion (Tony Anderson), and really across the board. I had complete confidence that if A&R—which at the time was handled by the VPs Richard Sweret and Mitchell Cohen, along with Ken Friedman, and later Keith Naftaly and Hosh Gureli—continued to be aggressive and we kept our very high standards for what we signed and released, there would be no obstructions in our path. The music, obviously, was the top priority.

There are some people who persist in describing Arista Records as primarily a "pop label," and while it's true that pop music had always been a key element, I think there's a bit of confusion between pop music and pop success. From my perspective, those are often two very different things: The Grateful Dead and Patti Smith had pop success at Arista, but no one would ever say they made pop music. Aretha isn't a pop artist, but when there was pop potential in one of her records, we made sure that we delivered on that potential. The same principle applies whether you're talking about Annie Lennox, Usher, or the Notorious B.I.G. I always asked: What is the broadest audience for this music? I didn't ask: Is this music sufficiently pop? As we entered the Nineties, Arista had pop success with artists that came from so many different musical directions, with acts as left-field as the KLF and Crash Test Dummies. They were brought to my attention by the A&R men Richard Sweret and Ken Friedman, respectively, and neither act was in any way a likely candidate for pop radio. The KLF—the British producer-musicians Bill Drummond and Jimmy Cauty—were making inventive, some might say subversive, acid-house music, a genre more at home in the clubs than on the radio. But we saw the possibility of broader appeal, and were proven right when the anthemic "3 a.m. Eternal" became a Top 5 pop hit. And their next hit was even more unorthodox, one of the most incongruous duets imaginable, as they recruited the country legend Tammy Wynette to sing on their track "Justified and Ancient." It was completely out there as a concept, and yet it became Tammy's biggest single ever on the pop chart, and the first time she'd even been on that chart in well over a decade. Almost as unexpected was the acceptance on pop radio of Crash Test Dummies, a quirky folk-alternative band from Canada whose lead singer, Brad Roberts, had a deep, slow rumble of a voice, like a young Johnny Cash on quaaludes. First they hit with "Superman's Song" from *The Ghosts That Haunt Me,* and then from their following album, *God Shuffled His Feet,* came the defiantly odd "Mmm Mmm Mmm Mmm," one of the strangest Top 5 singles we ever promoted. The group ended up with three Grammy nominations, including for Best New Artist.

Arista had high hopes for a more mainstream artist, a "blue-eyed soul" singer named Curtis Stigers. My son Fred, at the time a very tapped-in music-business attorney, invited one of my A&R men, Mitchell Cohen, to see Curtis play in a venue called Wilson's on the Upper West Side of Manhattan. Intrigued by their enthusiasm, I went one Monday night to Wilson's to check out Curtis for myself, along with what seemed like half the A&R people in New York. Curtis's weekly residency was becoming the "in" place to be, and before long, there was interest from around ten different labels. There was such confidence in his performance; he was doing mostly standards, with one or two original songs, and he had a rich, believable voice, with elements of jazz as well as soul and pop. He was good-looking, with shoulder-length hair, and he also played saxophone. He had nearly everything except hit material, and at the time Mitchell and I thought we would be making calls to publishers to find songs. Once we had talked Curtis and his manager, Winston Simone, into signing with us, it became clear that Curtis saw himself as more of a singer-songwriter than an interpreter. In the end, Curtis co-wrote nine of the eleven songs on his debut album. The lead single, "I Wonder Why," written with Glen Ballard, was a Top 10 hit, and the album sold fairly well in the United States, and very well internationally (especially in the U.K. and Germany). But we'd spent a lot of money signing Curtis, as well as making and promoting the album, and by the end of the project's cycle, both Curtis and Arista were deep in the red. Coincidently, at that time we were looking for some songs to complete the soundtrack for *The Bodyguard*. Curtis had been doing a cover of Nick Lowe's song "(What's So Funny 'Bout) Peace, Love and Understanding," which had famously been covered by Elvis Costello, in his live set, and we decided to have him record a studio version and submit it for the film.

Curtis's studio version did indeed make the film. It was a windfall for Lowe, whose royalty check on *Bodyguard* sales reportedly amounted to around £1 million, and of course for Curtis. The worldwide sales of the *Bodyguard* soundtrack album were so extraordinary that that one track effectively wiped out Curtis's entire debt to the company with enough left over to buy him a new house.

I continued to believe in Curtis, and the international sales of his album showed that there was a definite market for his music. But when it came time to do a second album, the process kept dragging on over the typical creative battles, where the material was going to come from, what the musical point of view was. Curtis saw himself as a rootsy rock-soul artist, and I didn't have faith that he would be accepted by radio in that world. Plus, I just didn't think his writing was strong enough. In the end, the album, *Time Was,* came out, and it didn't register. By that time it was 1995, four years since his debut. Could he have hits and did he have charisma? The answer is a resounding yes. But he was resolute in his resistance to outside material and to the world of pop. He eventually decided he wanted to record a straight-ahead jazz album, and regrettably it was time to part company. Curtis has found his place singing jazz, playing clubs and festivals, and he's happy with the road he's taken. To me, he's at the top of the list of artists I would have banked on going all the way.

It's crazy. You can go through a grueling bidding war, sign a dream artist, spend time and energy and resources and have every weapon at hand, and then unexpectedly fall short. And then someone else can come in the door with music that's finished and available, and you decide to take a chance, putting aside any notion of format or singles. Sarah McLachlan was a moderately successful singer-songwriter who'd put out an album in Canada on the independent Nettwerk label that was available for the United States. *Touch* had some pretty songs on it, especially "Vox" and "Steaming," but no one could say it would break through here. Richard Sweret believed that Sarah could become the Joni Mitchell of the Nineties, and the more I listened to the album the more sense that made: There really wasn't anyone who filled that role, a female singer-songwriter with a pristine voice, a melodic gift, and an ethereal, mysterious air, an artist almost exclusively for women. (I had no idea, years before Lilith Fair, how prescient that would be.) There were hints of real drama, and her wordless aria on the title track was really gorgeous. So we made the deal with Terry McBride and Nett-werk, and remixed *Touch,* adding one track, and released it on Arista. Around the same time, I had the chance to see Sarah live, and she was absolutely hypnotic. She was creating her own musical space; it was almost post-hippie/New Age, intimate and hushed, with candles all around her, and she was lovely and vulnerable. There was something otherworldly and out-of-time about it all, and you couldn't help but be captivated. Even though *Touch* didn't take off, there was definitely something happening. You could see how she was connecting. She was doing it the old-fashioned way, market by market. If she played a hundred-seat club the first time in a city, on her next visit the audience would triple, and then by the third time go to a thousand. She was building a fan base without much airplay, certainly without hit singles.

When someone is working that hard on her own, methodically going from city to city, and you're seeing the results, you have to have patience. Because then if the money songs do come along, there's a built-in audience, so the artist isn't merely hit-driven. It's just building loyalty, and no one did that better than Sarah. Beginning in the early Nineties, her following built geometrically from album to album, each doing better than the previous one: *Solace,* and then *Fumbling Towards Ecstasy,* her most critically well-received album and one that had a re-markably long stay on the charts, very nearly two years. That's the sign of someone who is catching on in a way that is not propelled by radio, because few tracks can sustain airplay for that long. It was touring, word of mouth, and press. And then she had her first breakthrough song with "I Will Remember You" from the film *The Brothers McMul-len,* a song that took on a second life years later when it was used in memorials and newscasts around the 1999 Columbine shootings.

But before "I Will Remember You" reemerged, Sarah wrote and recorded new songs for the album *Surfacing,* released in early summer 1997. The album was her strongest collection yet, including "Angel," "Adia," "Building a Mystery," and "Sweet Surrender." For a certain audi-ence, it became one of those must-own albums, a life soundtrack. Sarah was more than a singer-songwriter, she wore the mantle of a cultural touchstone, and she built on that image by beginning Lilith Fair. She'd been frustrated by concert promoters who didn't want to book more than one female artist on a bill, and by radio programmers who wouldn't play female artists back-to-back. She thought this was a form of discrimi-nation, and she was right. It was incredibly narrow-minded and anachro-nistic. By that time Marty Diamond had left Arista's marketing division to start his own booking agency, Little Big Man, and as Sarah's agent, he shared her exasperation with the way touring female artists were com-partmentalized. Together, Sarah and Marty came up with the concept of Lilith Fair, a nearly all-female (there were some male musicians in the bands) coast-to-coast tour. The bill would change from city to city, but among the major headliners along with Sarah were such major stars as Jewel, Fiona Apple, Tracy Chapman, Suzanne Vega, and Emmylou Harris. It became an absolute sensation, and showed how right Sarah was to orchestrate this groundbreaking event. It was the summer's top-grossing music festival, and the success and publicity, combined with the songs breaking from *Surfacing,* just caused the album to explode, going triple platinum and winning her two Grammy awards. When the first Lilith Fair came to the New York area, we threw Sarah a wonderful party at the Boathouse in Central Park, a fitting setting on a beautiful night, nearly ten years after I heard her first album. What a remarkable time that was for her. I have to say, although we were supporting her at every step, the creative impetus was hers, the maturation of her songwriting, the dedication to touring, the cultivation of her audience. In a way she did what artists like Joni Mitchell and Carly Simon did before her, and Norah Jones and Adele did after her: She spoke to a mostly female audience, the sensitive young women in college, the professional young women who could relate to her, the housewives who gravitate toward music that touches them personally. When you can reach that audience, not all of whom purchase very much music, you do so by conveying sincerity and believability, by expressing basic emotions poetically. When you mention Sarah McLachlan, it conjures up an image beyond the individual songs, more of a musical presence. It all came together so perfectly, a combination of hard work, foresight . . . and a touch of magic.

With artists like Sarah, who wind up leaving a lasting imprint, the rewards unfold over time, from album to album, and that's enormously rewarding. And then there are the records that burst out of the gate with red-hot currency, the ones that almost have a date stamp on them, the essence of pure pop. We definitely had our share of those singles. In the early Nineties, Arista broke Haddaway's "What Is Love" (used to great comic effect in the classic Will Ferrell–Chris Kattan *Saturday Night Live* dance-club sketches), the Real McCoy's "Another Night" (and its follow-up, "Run Away"), and a run of big hit singles by the Swedish pop group Ace of Base.

As with one of my earlier pop signings, Air Supply, I discovered after hearing the music that Ace of Base's records had fallen on deaf ears here in the United States. They couldn't get an American distribution deal, despite having hits overseas with the singles "Happy Nation" and "All That She Wants." Polygram, who distributed Ace of Base in Europe, had the option to pick them up for the States, but passed, as did every other U.S. label until Richard Sweret brought them to my attention. I remember that he gave me the music to listen to, and I was on vacation on a yacht when I first heard it. Well, I loved it, and Richard had told me that the head of Mega Records, their Swedish label, wanted to hear from me directly. The problem was that there was no telephone reception on the boat, and this was before the Internet and e-mail, and I was literally at sea. I knew I had to find a spot where I could get a phone connection, and we had to reroute the yacht to get to land, so that I could call Mega and close the deal. I certainly wasn't swayed one way or another by the European success, because 95 percent of hit singles from overseas never make it in the States. I thought "All That She Wants" was a hit, pure and simple, and as with Air Supply, Exposé, and Milli Vanilli, I picked up the record without ever meeting the artists or seeing them live. I did see the original video for the song. It was very basic, inexpensive, with no frills, but I liked the look of the group, two guys, two girls, and we locked up the rights for North and South America and Japan.

All the songs on the group's *Happy Nation* album were written by the two guys in the group, Jonas Berggren and Ulf Ekberg. I thought it was a good album, but I didn't hear any obvious follow-up hits to "All That She Wants." You need several hits to sell a pop album. I knew from experience, from Air Supply and Manilow and so many others, that it's the depth of singles that makes the difference and sends sales through the roof. I encouraged the group to come up with new potential hits, and Jonas responded with "The Sign," a first-listen smash that wasn't on *Happy Nation*. In fact, I was so impressed by the new song that we changed the album title to *The Sign*. I personally sent them an Albert Hammond and Diane Warren song that had been a Tina Turner B side and a U.K. hit by the group Aswad. I felt that with the right arrangement, this could be a song that stamped them as a more international group. "All That She Wants," "The Sign," and "Don't Turn Around" all became huge hit singles, and our newly configured version of the album was a massive success, certified diamond by the Recording Industry Association of America for sales of more than 10 million. *The Sign* is the top-selling debut pop album of all time, and only Guns N' Roses and Linkin Park have had bigger first albums. With only "All That She Wants," the original sequence of the album might have done fine, but clearly many millions of sales were added by evaluating what was on the album, asking for more material, and finding an outside hit. Those factors are so critical, and what record label you're on can indeed make a difference.

You can imagine how eager I was to hear new Ace of Base songs. Although I did feel that their presentation needed upgrading—they came off live as very glitzy, very European, with an abundance of sparkliness that underlined all the pop elements in the music—I thought Jonas in particular showed a strong flair for writing pop hits, and there was so much riding on the next album. However, in the material coming from Jonas there were no real hits, and at the same time there was a shake-up in the group when one of the girls quit. I could sense the opportunity slipping away. I tried to perform creative triage by getting the very successful producer Max Martin to come in as a co-producer with Dennis Pop, who'd done the first album, and by imploring Jonas to do some co-writing with Billy Steinberg, who'd had a lot of hits (including Madonna's "Like a Virgin," Cyndi Lauper's "True Colors," and Whitney's "So Emotional"), but there was only so much I could do. Ace of Base lived in Sweden and they really weren't my group, even though I was behind the strategy for the U.S. album. Sometimes when a writer isn't thinking in English as his first language, and doesn't have a feel for words and colloquialisms, it's hard to come up with strong lyrics that flow naturally, and that was the major problem with Jonas's songs. When he came in with the song "Life Is a Flower," not exactly a hit title, I brought in the hit songwriter Mike Chapman to help rewrite, but it still didn't work.

In the end, the second album, *The Bridge,* was a disappointment. It felt insubstantial. Since the group lacked genuine star appeal and were reliant on radio play for sales, the album fell well short of the debut.

From a label standpoint, there's not much you can do; you can't schedule a charisma implant, and you can't adjust the lighting to make the group more dynamic onstage. It's either there or it isn't, and I think in the case of Ace of Base, there was something so fresh and appealing about the sound on *The Sign* that it almost seemed like a musical illusion. And then, as quickly as they appeared, they were gone. They just couldn't pull it off a second time. But, in fairness, that's true of a lot of artists who capture something on a debut that for some reason can't be repeated. That's what happened with Ace of Base, but that diamond designation will be affixed to *The Sign* forever.

Another signing from that period, a striking young urban-pop singer named Deborah Cox, had some record-breaking R&B and dance hits in the Nineties, but may have been burdened with too many expectations. From the very beginning she was in the shadow of Whitney, and the perception was that I was grooming her for that type of success. I can understand why that was, and it made for snappy industry shorthand, "Clive's new diva" or "Arista's heir apparent to Whitney," but what singer is going to live up to that? Whitney was a one-in-a-generation artist, and although I did see Deborah Cox as someone who could conceivably record some of the excellent material that was being sent to me with Whitney in mind, the comparison didn't help her any.

I met Deborah in Los Angeles in 1994, when she was out there to sing backup vocals for Céline Dion on Arsenio Hall's show. Her demos showcased the creamy power of her voice, and I signed her to Arista. We took our time making the album, and launched it with considerable fanfare in the fall of 1995. We made solid inroads on R&B radio with the singles "Sentimental" and "Who Do U Love," and the album went gold. Normally, a debut album going gold is a grand achievement, but those expectations I described affected how Deborah's success was perceived. Compared with Whitney, half a million sales didn't seem like very much.

Momentum began to increase when it became clear that Deborah was building a strong fan base in the dance market. From the first album, club mixes of the track "Who Do U Love" had broken out. And then Deborah scored a major number-one dance hit with "Things Just

Ain't the Same" from the *Money Talks* soundtrack in 1997. The Hex Hector remix of that track became a hit, and was included on Deborah's next album. Building on that track's success, the second album was launched with the single "Nobody's Supposed to Be Here," written by Montell Jordan and Anthony "Shep" Crawford and produced by Crawford. This track exploded and at the time set the record for most weeks at number one on the R&B chart (fourteen, only recently broken by a Mary J. Blige single), and spent eight weeks at number two on the pop chart. A remix of the record did hit number one on the dance chart. And so with this track, and a follow-up number-one R&B single, "We Can't Be Friends," featuring R.L. of the group Next, Deborah did become a big multiformat artist for the first time. The album went platinum, and with a constant stream of club mixes, Deborah became the queen of dance clubs everywhere. She was a prime example of how strategically using remixes could meaningfully enhance the profile of an artist and expand the life of a project. Later on, when we had her record a duet with Whitney, "Same Script, Different Cast," we did far better with the track in terms of dance club play than we did in any radio format. In this realm, our A&R man Hosh Gureli was a prime mover. He was tuned in to who the hottest remixers were at any given moment, what types of mixes were getting reaction at the clubs, and he knew all the go-to people, the pulse of that world, and made sure that all our remixes, for the spectrum of Arista artists, caught the right musical waves. In the case of Deborah, this was vital: She had number-one dance hits on tracks that weren't hits in any other area. It was great that Deborah was embraced by the club crowd, and it sustained her when the mainstream R&B hits stopped, but she just never had the long-term album-selling career envisioned from the beginning. Still, she definitely did have her shining moments. But did she become heir apparent to Whitney? No. I've always felt some guilt that perhaps our initial aggressive campaign to get her debut album attention unintentionally invited unfair comparisons. I never mentioned Whitney in my presentations, but the industry sure did. Deborah was and is really good, and she later was to receive acclaim on Broadway when she replaced Heather Headley in the starring role in *Aida*. But neither Deborah nor anyone else I've ever seen or heard could ever be "another Whitney."

Supernatural Santana

The bright red cherry topping the cake of Arista's skyrocketing success in the Nineties was Carlos Santana's 1999 album *Supernatural.* I, of course, went back many years with Carlos, having signed Santana to Columbia in 1968, and we went on a terrific run together at that time. He had major hits, delivered a now legendary performance at the Woodstock festival, and sold millions of albums. By the time I left the label in 1973, however, Carlos had already begun to drift away from the type of music that drove his success on the pop charts. While the music he made after that was often adventurous, the audience that had come to him through the irresistible appeal of songs like "Evil Ways," "Black Magic Woman," and "Oye Como Va" was confused by it, and eventually drifted away. For years his career swung unpredictably between progressive and spiritually inspired music on the one hand and, on the other, less than successful attempts to engage the trends of the times and reconnect with a larger audience.

Needless to say, regardless of whatever approach he was taking, Santana remained an iconic figure. As a guitarist he ranked in the supreme pantheon with the likes of Eric Clapton, Jimmy Page, and Jeff Beck, and in 1998 he had deservedly been inducted into the Rock and Roll Hall of Fame. I was proud of having signed Santana and always basked in the warm memory of our time together at Columbia. Though we had not been in touch for two decades at least, I still kept an eye on him and his career. Signing an artist, particularly when you do it early in both of your careers, is a little bit like having a child. Regardless of how independent they become and however far afield they travel, you're always aware of them and how they're doing. So even though Carlos and I didn't communicate directly, he stayed in my thoughts. And, as it turns out, I had stayed in his thoughts as well.

So even though in one sense it came out of the blue, I was not entirely surprised when one day in 1997 I got a call from his manager saying that Carlos would love to have me attend his forthcoming concert at Radio City Music Hall and to come by and say hello. I said yes immediately, and found myself really looking forward to the show and seeing him again. The concert itself was eye-opening. As a player, Carlos still had a magical touch, a sound that was beautifully lyrical, dazzlingly virtuosic, and instantly recognizable. The audience loved him, and he had lost none of his energy and passion. Something about the evening felt very contemporary to me. He was playing with young musicians. The diversity of the audience was impressive—young, old, white, black, and Hispanic, both men and women. The growing Latino population of the United States was a current topic, and the cultural impact of that community could be felt in the air as well as in Carlos's music. It was certainly palpable at the show. Gloria Estefan was already a star, and in the next couple of years, Jennifer Lopez, Enrique Iglesias, Ricky Martin, Shakira, and Marc Anthony would all make breakthroughs. Carlos, without question, was one of the artists laying the groundwork for them. Beyond that, our meeting backstage was enthusiastic and emotional. I genuinely complimented him on the show, and I was very affected by being in his presence again. He, in turn, responded extremely warmly to me. We couldn't really speak in any depth there, but it turned out that we were both going to be in Los Angeles the following week, so we arranged to meet.

Still, I wasn't quite sure what was on Carlos's mind. We certainly had a long-standing connection, but I did get the feeling that he might be interested in working with me again. Based on what I saw and heard at the show, I started thinking of ways in which our collaborating might make sense. I certainly didn't want to sign Carlos to Arista just for old times' sake, but there was something about the challenge of taking a fifty-year-old classic artist and making him relevant to a younger audience that definitely intrigued me. I love the idea of artistic longevity, and as much as I respect the shifting moods of popular taste, there's something about challenging the preconceptions underlying those shifts that I enjoy. Even more than enjoying it, I think it's important. So I came up with some thoughts and ideas before getting together with Carlos, and was very interested to hear what he was thinking about as well.

We met at my bungalow at the Beverly Hills Hotel, and, like the week before, the warmth between us was evident. It turns out that the invitation to the Radio City show had not simply been a prelude to a friendly stroll down memory lane. Carlos very specifically wanted to meet with me to see if we could work together again. He had not made a studio album since 1992, and he felt that the time was right for his re-emergence. For all the past recognition he had gotten, he did not want to become a museum piece. He intuited in the same way that I had that it might be possible for him to reach a younger, more contemporary audience. He told me that he had three children and it was hurtful to him that they had never heard him on the radio, except on oldies stations. He strongly believed that I was the person who could get him on the radio again.

All of that made sense to me, though given Carlos, it came within the context of far more mystical musings. For example, when I asked Carlos what he wanted to do with his music, he told me that his goal was to connect "the molecules with the light." Being on the radio would be his means of accomplishing that. As for what connecting the molecules with the light meant, that was a message he got from the angel Metatron, a figure who appears in a variety of religious and spiritual traditions and with whom Carlos believes he speaks regularly. Metatron also advised him to be "patient, gracious, and grateful." When he discussed with his spiritual advisor how he might implement those messages, he was asked who had helped him get on the radio in the first place. Carlos explained that I had done it. Then, as he later told *Rolling Stone,* before contacting me about attending his concert, "I chanted for Mr. Clive Davis twenty-seven times each day. I'd picture him coming out of a car or a limousine, and a cab passing by, playing my music. So wherever he goes, I want him to be connected with my music."

Whether or not you accept Carlos's cosmology, when I boiled down what he had to say into simpler terms it actually made a lot of sense. I had reconnected with Carlos's music at the Radio City show. By connecting the molecules with the light I assumed he meant bringing his uplifting spiritual message (the light) to a new, dynamic, receptive audience (the molecules). And while I hardly needed an angel to convince me of the value and importance of getting an artist played on the radio, Carlos was given excellent advice in suggesting that radio would be the means of communicating his vision. I, however, spoke to Carlos in much more direct terms about the potential ideas I had for his next studio album. I wanted him to understand fully what I had in mind, and I didn't want any miscommunication between us. I always try to be clear and up front, and in this instance I thought it was especially necessary. I asked Carlos, "Are you hungry for your career right now?" He answered, "I am. Without question, I am dedicated to doing whatever I have to do to come back in a major way." I then said, "What you do live is incredible, but getting on the radio is another matter entirely. Are you willing to work with contemporary artists, and have them perform with you on the album?" He didn't hesitate for a second. He said that he would open his heart to those artists and do absolutely the best work with them that he could.

So far, so good. Then I laid out my plan for him. I told him, "All right, then. Let me describe the blueprint I've come up with for the album I would like to make with you that I believe could be a winner. You would need to turn half the album over to me. I will come up with songs that I think are suitable candidates for singles and will do my best to make sure those songs are organic to the project and to you at this stage of your career. There will be nothing artificial and nothing that makes you uncomfortable. Ideally, they will be written by people that have been influenced by you, and whom you would enjoy having produce or perform on the track. In every instance you will always have the option of saying no. As for the other half of the album, you take control of it and come up with Santana-originated material that speaks for you and all your fans."

Carlos and his first wife, Deborah, were intently listening. Carlos immediately said, "I'm there one hundred percent." So that became the blueprint for *Supernatural*.

When the word got out that I had signed Carlos Santana to Arista the response within the music industry was definitely mixed, as you might expect. People who were aware of my helping to revive the careers of Dionne Warwick and Aretha Franklin were intrigued, curious about what I might be able to accomplish with an artist I had first signed three decades earlier. Others saw it as indulgent, as if I had signed Carlos for sentimental reasons, regardless of what his commercial prospects were. Finally, the more hard-nosed observers felt that I had overextended myself, that my belief in my abilities to fan the flames of a waning career had gotten the better of my common sense. The signing was known to those people as "Davis's Folly," a fool's bet that an artist who had not sold more than 150,000 copies of a record in years could suddenly have hits as if it were 1969 all over again. To be honest, I understand that position completely. But if you play the safe percentages all the time, you exclude the possibility of magic, the very reason the record business is so great. I knew how difficult it would be to bring Santana to Top 40 radio, but I also knew what Santana was capable of and how finding the right song for the right moment could shatter all the paradigms. Difficult does not mean impossible, and I was determined to make it happen.

One of the essentials of assembling *Supernatural,* the resulting album, was that somehow Carlos had to remain at the center of it, even though he is not a singer. His voice would have to be his guitar, which, fortunately, has such a recognizable sound that as soon as people hear it, they think, "Santana!" But hits have to have instantly memorable melodies and lyrics that people can relate to. Would different voices and styles dilute the album's cohesion? Still, I reasoned that Santana had always explored a variety of styles; that was a big part of his appeal. I felt confident that his brilliance as a player, the respect that other artists held for him, and his sheer presence would bind the songs together. So I got to work.

First, I began the process of calling in songs for the album, and given the reverence in which Santana is held, it was no problem finding quality artists and songwriters who wanted to participate. I was working with Lauryn Hill on "A Rose Is Still a Rose" for Aretha Franklin, and we really got along well. She came to my office one day and, as we were chatting, she asked what else I was working on. I told her I was beginning to pull material together for a Santana project. "You're kidding," she said. "I love Carlos Santana!" Lauryn was working on her debut solo album, *The Miseducation of Lauryn Hill,* which would go on to sell more than 8 million copies. Carlos agreed to play on the deeply personal track "To Zion," which Lauryn wrote about her young son. In return, Lauryn wrote and performed on "Do You Like the Way," on which Cee-Lo Green also appeared, for Santana's album. Lauryn was already a highly visible and respected artist with a superhip young following, so having Carlos work with her was a real coup.

I was also working with Wyclef Jean, who had just written and produced "My Love Is Your Love" for Whitney Houston. Like Lauryn, Wyclef was beside himself when I told him I was looking for songs for a new Santana album. "Let me write a song for that," he insisted, and within a week he came up with "Maria Maria," which he also co-produced and which featured the brand-new R&B duo the Product G&B. When Wyclef brought the demo to my office with his writing and production partner, Jerry "Wonder" Duplessis, I couldn't believe how great it sounded. I wanted Carlos to hear it on the spot, so I called him immediately and played it for him over the phone. He was instantly turned on. Carlos and Wyclef then stayed on the phone, and we had another first-rate track for the album.

I read a Dave Matthews story in *Rolling Stone* in which he mentioned that Carlos Santana was one of his musical heroes, so I called his manager, Coran Capshaw, and arranged for Dave and Carlos to meet and record together. Carlos came up with a melody line derived from a Brahms symphony, and Dave wrote the lyrics to "Love of My Life" on the spot. Everlast, a rapper and songwriter with a fondness for classic rock, wrote and performed on "Put Your Lights On." Eagle-Eye Cherry, whose father, the jazz artist Don Cherry, was much admired by Santana, co-wrote and delivered a vocal on "Wishing It Was," which the Dust Brothers co-produced. Eric Clapton was wrapped up in his own projects and initially was unable to commit to working with Carlos on *Supernatural,* but when he caught Carlos's spellbinding performance on the Grammys with Lauryn Hill in early 1999, he promptly raised his hand. "All I could think was, 'What am I thinking?' " Clapton told *Rolling Stone*. "I quickly sent him a message, 'I'm sorry I've been such a dick—is there still room for me?' " Clapton didn't have a song, so he and Carlos went into the studio together and jammed, an event Carlos described as "two Apaches with some sage at the Grand Canyon calling out the spirits." ("Ah, that's hilarious. That's Carlos," Clapton responded when he heard that description.) Santana and his band transformed the jam into a song titled "The Calling" that became *Supernatural*'s closing number.

Finally, I had a label deal with Matt Serletic, who had produced Matchbox Twenty, among other bands. He had mentioned to me that Matchbox Twenty's lead singer, Rob Thomas, was interested in doing some writing outside the band, and that if I ever had a project that I thought might be right for Rob, I should let him know. That conversation was in the back of my mind when Peter Ganbarg, the Arista A&R man who was working closely with me on *Supernatural*, brought me an insinuating track that the songwriter Itaal Shur had come up with. I liked it a lot and sent the track to Matt to see if Rob might like to do something with it. About a week later we received the demo for "Smooth," with Rob Thomas singing what he had written to the track. It was incredible. I sent it to Carlos and he was ecstatic. "I'm so indebted to you, this is fabulous!" he said. "I love it. Who is the singer? He's fantastic!" I explained to Carlos that Rob Thomas had co-written the song and had sung on the demo, but that he might not be able to sing on the version for *Supernatural*. Matchbox Twenty was huge and, because they were signed to Atlantic, there might be a permissions issue; there could also be political issues with the band.

As far as Carlos was concerned, it was as if I were speaking a foreign language. "Clive, we've got to get him to sing on the record," he said. "He's perfect. No one else can do it as well as he can. Can you make it happen?" This is the sort of situation in which you earn your money. Getting permission for Rob to sing on the track was anything but a slam dunk. I know from my own experience that if you have any question about the wisdom of what an artist on your label might be doing, the easiest thing is to say no. If the project goes away, no one is any the worse for wear. But if you get pushback and the artist really wants to do it, then you have to seriously consider letting them have their way. So I contacted Rob's manager, Michael Lippman, who at one time had done a bang-up job as head of West Coast operations for Arista. We began the dialogue. Obviously, there were issues within the band regarding Rob's stepping out like this. I tried as hard as I could to reassure everyone, including Atlantic. Yes, we understood that Rob was in no way leaving Matchbox Twenty. This was a one-off event to honor a classic artist whom Rob greatly admired. We would do everything we could to make sure the situation worked for everyone. We wanted it to be a win-win. Finally, everybody agreed, and Rob did a sensational job with the vocal and in the memorably steamy video for the song.

With all this great material, we had to make sure the album hit with the force we knew it possessed. After all, Carlos had been away from the scene for so long, this was by no means automatic. We proceeded to set the album up, and we got some great opportunities. When Lauryn Hill was asked to perform on the 1999 Grammy Awards broadcast, she invited Carlos to join her as a featured guest, which provided valuable exposure. On the most obvious level, that was the performance Eric Clapton saw that convinced him he had to be part of the album. I reinforced the Grammy television exposure by arranging for Carlos to perform that year at my pre-Grammy party. Rob Thomas joined Carlos to perform "Smooth," and Wyclef and the Product G&B performed "Maria Maria" with him. I can still hear and visualize the roaring standing ovations both numbers received. It was still months before *Supernatural* would be released, but Santana emerging with those songs at this event, accompanied by those artists, sent out an unmistakable signal that the new Santana album was going to be very special. It was decidedly not going to be business as usual.

I can't say the album sold in huge numbers when it was first released in June. It entered the charts at number nineteen, which was certainly very respectable for a Santana album at that stage of his career, but not the game-changer we might have been fantasizing about. Richard Palmese, Arista's outstanding head of radio promotion, sprang into action and stayed hard on the case. Even stations that liked "Smooth" were initially resistant because Carlos was older than their perceived demographic, but Richard and his national staff, Ken Lane, Jim Elliot, and Tom Maffei, would not relent, going back over and over again each time another important station gave in and got positive results from its listeners. Having Rob Thomas singing on the track was enormously helpful in that regard as well. Matchbox Twenty was a franchise band for many Top 40 and modern-rock radio stations, so being able to mention Rob's name each time "Smooth" got played was a key asset. For his part, Carlos rolled up his sleeves and did everything he had promised to do. He visited radio stations and did every interview we asked him to do. He had built up a tremendous amount of goodwill over the years, and we all got the feeling that everybody would eventually get behind the record once they were convinced that they wouldn't pay a price for it with their audience. Everyone, it seemed, was waiting for a reason to hop on board, and, as the record built its momentum, Arista's crackerjack promotion team did everything it could to make sure they got all the information they needed to feel good about supporting it. Piece by piece, everything fell into place and a timeless classic was born.

As with Whitney's biggest successes, there came a point with *Supernatural* when it seemed that all we could do was stand there and watch it accelerate like a rocket heading for the stratosphere. Of course, it took an incredible amount of hard work to reach that point, but, as with anything, the more success you have with a project, the easier your job gets. No one needs to be convinced anymore. Your work becomes determining the best steps among the many attractive opportunities being dropped in your lap, opportunities that you would have killed for when you were initially trying to get the album moving. *Supernatural* reached number one in October and stayed there for twelve consecutive weeks. People simply couldn't get enough of Santana. For a time the album was steadily selling 250,000 copies a week, more than almost all of his albums since the early Seventies had sold in total. The Arista sales team, headed by Jordan Katz, kept reporting one killer statistic after another. Then Carlos became visible as a personality again, and his mystical explanations of the album's origins delighted fans. They remembered his indelible performance in the *Woodstock* film and associated him with the best values of that time. As with the Grateful Dead's comeback in the Eighties, *Supernatural* made people feel as if some of the idealism of the Sixties had been magically preserved and released into a contemporary world that was much in need of it.

I really couldn't have been happier myself. Closing out the twentieth century while enjoying unprecedented success with one of my most important early signings from decades back seemed like a dream. We all know that, in part, music is a business, but an artist like Carlos reminds you how important a role music plays in people's lives. He was so grateful for his success that it just made me and everyone else at Arista want to work harder in his behalf. So many artists take for granted what record companies do for them, as if their talent alone were a guarantee that they would reach an audience. Carlos, on the other hand, was so appreciative of everything we did that it just made us want to do more. *Supernatural* provided one of those rare moments when the artist, the record company, and the fans all seemed to be sharing in the same transporting experience. It was just wonderful.

Surreal as it seems, *Supernatural* has sold more than 15 million copies in the United States, and more than 27 million copies worldwide. At the 2000 Grammys it swept up ten awards, including Album of the Year and, for "Smooth," Record of the Year and Song of the Year. As the album's co-producer, I received two of those Grammys: Album of the Year and Best Rock Album. Carlos could not have been more gracious, generously crediting my contributions, and when we shared the stage to accept the Album of the Year award, it was a moment I will always remember.

After a success like *Supernatural*, people inevitably ask, "How do you follow that up?" The answer is simple: In 99 percent of cases, you don't. In part that's because, except in the rarest instances, success on that scale comes just once in a career. Also, you can't plan a phenomenon. Beginning with the influential, very successful records he made early in his career after I signed him to Columbia, Santana has proven himself to be a groundbreaking artist for more than four decades.

The year of *Supernatural*'s release, 1999, also marked the twenty-fifth anniversary of Arista Records, and everyone knew we had to plan something truly extraordinary to mark this milestone. Throughout the years, I would find different ways to celebrate what we were build-ing. After Arista's first year, I took over New York's City Center for two shows, a matinee and an evening performance, to showcase our already impressive artist roster and signal that a major new record label had entered the scene. For our third anniversary in 1977, red-hot Studio 54 hosted a lavish party that *People* described in great detail, crediting our growing and unique stable of artists. These parties and concerts became a tradition, and I was thinking about how to top the fifteenth-anniversary "That's What Friends Are For" fund-raising con-cert at Radio City Music Hall that CBS televised as a national special. This was a quarter century of music to mark and recognize. I'd started Arista from scratch with a handful of artists and high aspirations, and just look where we were. The planning for our twenty-fifth-anniversary show began in late 1999, and we decided to have our biggest event ever, at the Shrine Auditorium in Los Angeles, with the date set for April 10, 2000. The show was going to be filmed for later broadcast as a televi-sion special on NBC.

The big night arrived, and to me, it all went by like a fast-moving series of scenes from my life, every single moment a highlight. President Clinton sent a letter of congratulations that was printed in the show's program, and Dick Clark was there to present film clips from my ca-reer. It's hard to convey the waves of emotion I was feeling during the show as I tried to take everything in. I was both a spectator and a par-ticipant. Where do I even start? In terms of Arista history, the concert went from a powerhouse-hits medley by Barry Manilow, starting with "Mandy," to the newer artists Arista had just broken like LFO, with their smash "Summer Girls." Alan Jackson and Brooks and Dunn came from Nashville. Sarah McLachlan accompanied Patti Smith on piano on "Because the Night," and Barry did the same for Dionne Warwick on "I'll Never Love This Way Again." Annie Lennox did a stunning solo version of "Why." And Whitney that night was beyond description. She was going through a rough time then but did she ever rise to the occasion! She came out looking gorgeous in a dress that showed off her slim but newly curvy figure, and instantly took control of the stage with up-tempo hits. Then, before starting "I Believe in You and Me," she pointed to me in the audience and said, "This one's for you," and for

"My Love Is Your Love" she was joined onstage by an all-star girl group: Monica, Deborah Cox, Faith Evans, Angie Stone. Everyone delivered that night: Santana, Kenny G, Puffy, and for the finale, Dionne and many of the other artists brought everyone to their feet with "That's What Friends Are For." By that time, I was pretty wiped out. So much of what I'd dreamed of achieving at Arista Records was right up there on the stage of the Shrine. It was, of course, a profoundly emotional night for me, not only because of the role I'd played in the music and in all those musical lives, but also because throughout the entire night I knew that this was a kind of ending, and that life-defining changes and challenges were coming up very soon.

Instant Major

On Thursday, October 28, 1999, I went to Lutèce, one of my favorite New York restaurants, for a dinner meeting with Strauss Zelnick, the president and CEO of the Bertelsmann Music Group (BMG), and Michael Dornemann, BMG's chairman. While I always functioned with a great deal of autonomy, I reported to Zelnick and Zelnick reported to Dornemann on the BMG organizational chart. They had scheduled the dinner, and I assumed we would be discussing future plans for Arista and, perhaps, my contract, which would be ending in the middle of the following year. I thought the dinner also might be something of a victory lap for us. We knew that the very next day, Santana's *Supernatural* would dramatically take over the number-one spot on the pop charts, and that the momentum behind this unprecedented album was not letting up. We were a few months into a fiscal year in which Arista would post more than half a billion dollars in sales and the highest profits in its history. In 2000, we would be celebrating Arista's twenty-fifth anniversary with a major two-hour prime-time special on NBC. The days ahead looked promising indeed.

Unfortunately, I could not have been more wrong about the purpose of the dinner. Not long after we sat down, Dornemann said, "You know that Bertelsmann has a retirement age of sixty, and although you've been treated differently, we would like you to give up running Arista and become chairman of worldwide A&R for BMG and all its labels. L.A. Reid will be the new president of Arista." I went numb. I could not have been more shocked. I was sixty-seven at the time, and believed that I was at the very height of all my powers, a conviction that my current track record and all the recent P&L numbers fully supported. I can't claim that I knew how massive *Supernatural* was going to be, but it was evident even at that point that it would be an absolute triumph, the totally unexpected reigniting of a major artist's career under my guidance. We were just coming off Whitney Houston's multiplatinum comeback album, *My Love Is Your Love.* These two albums were not just released under my administration: I was each album's producer and I had personally chosen every hit song that propelled both these albums to giant worldwide sales.

I had been blindsided and I sat there completely stunned. For a few seconds it was almost as if I couldn't really understand the words they were saying. When I realized what they were proposing, I unequivocally told them I loved what I do, and what they were suggesting for me was absolutely out of the question. There really was nothing further to hash out, and it was just too painful to try to make cocktail small talk. I got up and walked out of the restaurant. They had shocked looks on their faces, but waves of emotion were running through me. I was hurt, confused, and angry. I went home and immediately contacted my personal attorney, the well-known Allen Grubman; Charles Goldstuck, my exemplary executive vice president at Arista; my son Fred; and Michael Stein, my longtime business manager. Fred and Charles came over to my apartment immediately, and the following morning we assembled the larger meeting. I needed to collect myself, and put together a plan. What would be the most appropriate strategy? It was hard to focus my thinking so soon after learning this mind-boggling news. Should I fight to stay at Arista? Was that the best way to go in the face of this blatant insult? Should I consider moving to another company? What about raising money and starting my own label? What would be the best direction? I would need to focus on all those options with the people who could offer me the best advice and cared about me the most, and then make a decision. In just one moment, my life had been turned upside down.

I realize that to many people the kind of offer that Zelnick and Dornemann made to me might have been a dream come true at age sixty-seven. It was a prestigious title, it would have carried a formidable salary, and it would have involved only as much hard work as I was interested in investing in it. Someone looking for the opportunity to sail luxuriously into retirement couldn't have written a finer ticket. But I was not that person. Just as many years earlier, when I was being groomed to move up the corporate ranks at CBS, I had no desire whatsoever to leave the front line of running a label, working closely with artists to bring their music to the public. I had absolutely no interest in giving up Arista. And I was at the very zenith of my success. Each week, as my battle with BMG raged on, Santana's *Supernatural* became startlingly bigger and bigger and bigger. The public loved having Carlos back. At every level the industry was exhilarated that a veteran classic artist was generating more wattage than the hottest young acts around. That reflected on me, and the more people learned that I was being asked to step aside just as all this was going on, the more bewildered and outraged they became.

And learn about it they did. As huge a business as it was at the time, the music industry is also like a small village. Virtually the day after my aborted dinner at Lutèce, rumors began flying about what had happened. Eventually it turned into a battle in the press, with reporters hot on the trail of one of the juiciest music business stories in years. Zelnick and Dornemann went on the attack, trying to portray me as someone who refused to name a successor because I couldn't imagine anyone being able to take my place. We refuted those charges. Charles Goldstuck was clearly my anointed successor, backed up by a tremendously able team of executives who were the industry's best: Tom Corson, Richard Palmese, Julie Swidler, Peter Edge, and Keith Naftaly, to name a few. In all of the coverage, I was deeply moved by the avalanche of support I was spontaneously getting from artists I had worked with, and from so many others whom I knew only casually. The industry as a whole rose up in my defense. If I could be moved aside while leading my company to the most successful year in its history, who was safe? The business was going through a period of wanting to skew younger. I was fine with that. Nurturing young talent, both in artists and executives, had been my hallmark. But did that mean that having a lengthy track record of success right up to the present moment meant nothing? Many people identified with my position, imagined it happening to them, and personally felt the unfairness of it all.

Completely unsolicited, artists and executives issued statements and made comments on my behalf in the press. "If Clive leaves, I leave," Aretha Franklin told the *Los Angeles Times*. "There are only a few record executives on the face of the Earth who love music the way this man does." In that same story, Patti Smith declared, "Clive Davis built this label out of the clay of his soul. There is nobody like him in the music business. He's like Robert Duvall in *Apocalypse Now*. I mean, he loves the smell of vinyl in the morning. Without Clive, there's no place for me on Arista Records." Carlos Santana's lawyer, John Branca, wrote to Zelnick, Dornemann, and their boss, Thomas Middelhoff, the CEO of Bertelsmann, stating that if I left Arista, "Carlos would certainly have to reconsider his relationship" with the label. Carly Simon said that my leaving Arista would be like "taking Manhattan out of New York." Kenny G, by this time one of the industry's all-time best-selling album artists, sent me a copy of a letter he wrote to Zelnick, which reads, in part, "By forcing a successor that I don't believe is capable of running this company with the same creative focus, energy and brilliance of a Clive Davis, it feels to me like you are also disrespecting me and all the hard work that I have put into my career at Arista Records." Tommy Mottola, who ran Sony Music, said, "When I first started out, I could only hope to come close to achieving some of Clive's success. His work in this industry is unrivaled. Everybody in this business looks up to him." Doug Morris at Universal Music said, "Clive is incredible. You can't replace a Clive."

That degree of outspoken, unqualified support from artists, friends, and competitors was powerfully touching. I was further bolstered by the announcement from the National Academy of Recording Arts and Sciences that I would receive the Trustees' Lifetime Achievement Award at the 2000 Grammy Awards ceremony. Around the same time, the Rock and Roll Hall of Fame announced that I would be inducted in 2000 in the nonperformer category. The timing of all this couldn't have been more dramatic or surreal. What could Zelnick and Dornemann possibly have been thinking?

As I planned my next career move, I found myself devoting a good deal of time to speculating about how things had come to this pass with BMG. Arista had become one of the music industry's most illustrious success stories. It's true that I operated with a great deal of autonomy, but I had considerable respect for the relationship Arista had developed with Bertelsmann over two decades. Without question, huge cultural differences existed between the highly traditional European corporate culture of Bertelsmann, which was based in Germany, and the independent style of the U.S. music business. Maintaining your individuality in the corporate world, a character trait I so admired in Goddard Lieberson when I started at Columbia, was not an ideal fit within the family culture of Bertelsmann. The corporation was always seen as more important than the individual there, and, even if I was not being held to the mandatory retirement age of sixty (a European concept if there ever was one), my exemption from it may have been a problem. Mark Woessner, who had been the enormously successful CEO of Bertelsmann for fifteen years, was turning sixty and was being given no choice this very year but to leave that position. The long-standing, very successful culture at Bertelsmann made it totally unlikely that, regardless of the quality of my performance, the board would block a plan hatched by Zelnick and Dornemann to move me out of a day-to-day role at Arista.

The plan to install L.A. Reid as the head of Arista and move me upstairs had clearly been developing for some time. Zelnick had approached L.A. about moving to New York from Atlanta, and was now in the process of negotiating a deal to purchase for a substantial sum the share of LaFace Records that BMG didn't already own. In addition, Zelnick arranged for L.A. to enroll in an eight-week executive training course at Harvard Business School to prepare him for his new role. That I had been L.A.'s mentor, had played a decisive role in his career when I hired him and Babyface to produce songs for Whitney Houston, making possible their first number-one pop hit, and had bankrolled their label, LaFace Records, as a joint venture with Arista, only made the entire situation sadder and more hurtful. It all felt like a betrayal.

I thought Strauss Zelnick's personal ambition must have been an important part of the equation. He was forty-three and had a job and title that anyone would envy. But in the music business, ambition takes a variety of forms. You can be an extremely successful executive, but if artists perceive you as a "suit," there is a certain acceptance and stature that you can never attain. For many executives that isn't a problem at all. Their talent lies in business and they're happy making their impact in that world. But show business and being around artists is very seductive, and I assumed that Zelnick must have fallen prey to its lure. He would arrange social meetings with Arista artists like Carly Simon and Kenny G, which was his right, but it was a breach of courtesy that he never informed me that they were occurring. And L.A., who would now owe his position to Zelnick and who had strong artist relationships, could provide entrée to the more exciting world that Zelnick wanted to be part of. Finally, with L.A.'s background primarily in the area of R&B, Zelnick might potentially be able to get more involved with some of the label's pop artists and have that much greater participation and visibility.

All of this had clearly been part of a master plan for some time. There was never a hint of it from Zelnick. He and I had breakfast about every eight weeks. His praise of me to me was lavish and constant. There were never any run-ins or confrontations. Everything was polite and cordial. And when Whitney's *My Love Is Your Love* broke worldwide in 1998 and 1999 and Carlos's *Supernatural* exploded, his tributes to my "genius" were delivered with deep sincerity, almost awe. In retrospect, it's staggering that this same person was long plotting what he knew would be a seismic change and was well prepared to do media battle if fallout occurred.

As for Dornemann, he had been an efficiency expert and was definitely not a music man. It was well known within the industry that when you met with Dornemann you were there to listen. You would hear his lengthy and elaborate views about this issue and that subject. He always knew best. He had spoken with me several times about helping him get publicity and media attention. If I were out of the picture, he could have a higher profile and a greater visible role. Also, Zelnick and Dornemann probably sold my removal from Arista to the Bertelsmann board as a streamlining and cost-cutting move. I was never just a salaried employee. I had a phantom equity interest in Arista, and as we heated up, it was becoming very valuable—to the tune of approximately $120 million by the year 2000. Yes, I was highly compensated, but the company I led was on fire and its overall net worth was soaring.

The phantom equity interest also importantly reflected my mind-set that, after I had sold my stock in Arista to Bertelsmann, in 1979, I was a partner in the corporation, not just an employee. This issue came up dramatically a few times during my dealings with Dornemann over the years. On the one hand, at the Bertelsmann corporate meetings held every two years in Gütersloh, emphasis was always wisely placed on internal growth. Why pay a multiple of earnings to acquire market share or greater growth if in fact you can do it on your own? It made perfect sense. So when I felt that it was time for the company to consider a country division in Nashville, I didn't look to see if a company was for sale. I believed I could build one from scratch. With middle-of-the-road music from the likes of Barry Manilow, Neil Diamond, and Barbra Streisand an increasingly unlikely bet on Top 40 radio, my instinct told me that great songs would never go out of style and that country music would be the format to benefit. All I needed was a head of a brand-new industry division to be called Arista Nashville, a two- or three-person A&R staff, a national promotion team of about five, and a small marketing and administrative staff of about six in total. The investment was small, the stakes were large, and the potential was huge. I would volunteer to carve out sufficient time from my workload to create this new opportunity that would be widely heralded. With much enthusiasm I went to Dornemann's office to share these plans, and I was met by a blank stare. "Clive, you can't do this until you put together a detailed five-year plan," he said. "And then I have to get the approval of Joe Galante." (Galante was the head of RCA Nashville, which was also part of BMG.) Now, Dornemann was totally within his technical rights in requesting budgets and P&Ls, but the larger picture was abundantly clear, though not to him. He was expressionless and noncommittal. And, despite my admiration and respect for Joe Galante, why would he welcome a competitor to his turf, his fiefdom? It took the wind out of me. You want a partner who intuitively gets the big picture and who is on your wavelength. You want thanks and gratitude for looking at the future and attacking it imaginatively and prudently. All I could say was, "Michael, your first reaction is to treat me like an employee, not a partner." He replied, "Well, you are an employee. You're not a partner." I blanched, kept silent, and walked out of his office.

Within a week, Dornemann did call me and approved Arista Nash-ville in principle, but I was still reeling from our partner/employee exchange. From the beginning, Monti Lüftner, the pioneering head of BMG, and Reinhard Mohn, the brilliant prime architect of Ber-telsmann itself, had always treated me specially and made me feel like a partner. I waited a few months, and when it was time to renew my contract, I asked for the signing to take place at Bertelsmann's offices in New York. We met in the conference room with our attorneys present, and Mark Woessner, the head of Bertelsmann, happened to be in New York and in attendance with Dornemann. Right before I was to person-ally sign, I looked up and, without explaining any of the background or referring to anything that had happened, I said, "Mark, before I sign I have one question for you. To you and to Bertelsmann, am I your partner or your employee?" He looked me in the eye and said, "Clive, to everyone at Bertelsmann you are our partner." I just nodded, didn't look at Dornemann, and signed the contract.

The other time there was a stark difference of opinion between Dornemann and me was about how the start-up costs for Arista's joint ventures were being charged. To my amazement, the start-up costs were coming out of my phantom equity interest. Here I was financing what would be the tremendously successful joint ventures of LaFace and Bad Boy Records, and the inevitable first- and second-year start-up losses were being charged to me. Naturally, I complained vehemently to Dornemann that while Bertelsmann was encouraging healthy, home-grown diversification, I was being penalized for accomplishing just that, rather than incentivized for it. His reply was that the contract allowed the company to do this, and a contract is a contract. I protested that it was not only patently unfair to me but it was not in the interest of Bertelsmann to deincentivize me. I was diversifying for the corporation in the most beneficial way, building assets worth hundreds of millions of dollars.

My complaint fell on deaf ears. Dornemann was immovable. I was disconsolate. I asked for a meeting with Mark Woessner in Germany to settle the matter. Woessner agreed to the meeting but asked that I come alone, without Allen Grubman. So I flew to Gütersloh. When I got to Woessner's office, Dornemann was there. It was awkward because

I was loaded for bear, ready to make my case, and Mark wasn't ready to hear it, although he couldn't have been more cordial and hospitable. He took us to his house, where his wife and chef had prepared a lovely lunch. I had to suspend my mission and somehow keep my feelings at bay, which I managed to do. Two hours later, when the three of us got back to his office, Woessner looked at me and said, "Okay, Clive, tell me what's upsetting you." I spewed everything out, but I called on my legal training and did so calmly and succinctly. I ended by saying, "Yes, a contract is a contract, but when the result is not in the best interest of either party, it's incumbent on you to take cognizance of that and do what's fair." Woessner didn't ask for a rebuttal. He just looked at us both and said, "I agree with you. We should and must incentivize you, not penalize you. I will fix everything." The meeting was over. Without saying a word, Dornemann and I walked out. There was one car waiting to take us both to the airport. At first we were silent as we rode. I knew Dornemann had to be smarting and I didn't want to seem discourteous or self-congratulatory. Finally he said to me, "I should mention that I put in a good word for you with Mark before our meeting." I didn't say anything. I knew his statement made no sense but I saw no point in refuting it. We just reverted to small talk until we arrived at our plane.

As 1999 drew to a close, I could feel my negotiating position with Bertelsmann getting stronger and stronger. The more people learned about how it all was going down, the more they sympathized with me. I'm not accustomed to being an underdog, but in this situation people empathized with a self-made creative person facing down careerist corporate executives. I was still running Arista, so I had to be extremely careful about what I said to the media; nonetheless, the situation was turning into a public relations disaster for BMG, and Zelnick and Dornemann's bosses began to take notice.

Perhaps it was the strong European culture of Bertelsmann, but I'm certain that everyone there simply assumed that I would take the position being offered to me. That's what Bertelsmann executives traditionally did on reaching retirement age. Of course, I had no intention of doing that, and while I was fighting to find a way to stay at Arista, I was fielding calls from other major labels to see if I might be interested in making a move. When BMG heard about that, I was immediately assured that Zelnick and Dornemann's plan was not at all designed to make me leave, and, while the essence of their proposal could not change, I was asked to let them know what I would need to stay with the company. In the meantime, Charles Goldstuck was encouraging me to raise money and launch a brand-new label. We had been working together only a year and a half, but we had a deep bond. We had become close friends and trusted each other implicitly. After my climactic dinner with Zelnick and Dornemann, both Charles and I had drafted counterproposals that would enable me to remain at Arista while bringing L.A. Reid on in a greater role. They were rejected out of hand. However, both Strauss and L.A. met with Charles and offered him everything under the sun to convince him to stay at Arista and work as L.A.'s number-two man, which would have provided important stability during a transition that was going to be rocky in the best of circumstances. Charles's answer was that if I were forced out of Arista, he would have to leave as well. It was a bracing display of loyalty. I finally told Charles to explore the idea of financing a new label, and I would keep my focus on trying to get Arista back. Thomas Middelhoff, the young Bertelsmann executive slated to replace Woessner when Woessner retired at sixty, owed his meteoric rise in the company to Woessner, so he couldn't possibly overrule what had been decided. But more and more, he was contacting me and asking me to hold on. As he met with more of his young American mogul counterparts who were poised to make their mark for the new generation, he kept hearing what a mistake BMG was making.

Bertelsmann, as it happened, had more than its troubles with me to worry about. Zelnick's other "Clive problem," as the media dubbed it, was that at the same time he was tangling with me, he had begun to alienate Clive Calder, head of the Zomba Group, which was distributed by BMG and was the home to Britney Spears and the Backstreet Boys, two of the hottest, youngest, and best-selling artists in the business. Calder had attempted to poach 'N Sync, the successful boy band signed to RCA, a BMG-owned label, for his own Jive label, and Zelnick filed a lawsuit against Zomba for making an improper contract offer within the BMG family. Calder, whose deal with BMG was set to end in 2000, immediately began meeting with other labels. The Zomba Group accounted for a third of BMG's market share, so if Calder left, BMG's bottom line would take an enormous hit. When a court threw out BMG's attempt to prevent Zomba from releasing a new 'N Sync album, Zelnick quickly agreed to a deal, and in exchange for a one-year extension of its distribution agreement with Zomba, 'N Sync was permitted to sign with Calder, which was an incredible coup for him. Word was that one of the reasons 'N Sync was determined to go with Calder was that Zelnick had treated the group dismissively at a meeting. All this was only the beginning of troubles with Calder.

Given this backdrop of very public problems, the company's reputation was suffering and it was being hurt. Other labels were beginning to lure artists by pointing to how out of control things seemed to be, and the public perception of the company had definitely been damaged. When *Supernatural* was nominated for ten Grammys in January 2000, with me personally nominated for two, the dubious wisdom of BMG's actions were underlined once again.

The world was gripped by millennial fever as the end of 1999 approached, and I was seriously contemplating my future. Actually, the time seemed right for change. It was becoming clearer to me that time was running out for Middelhoff to intervene, and I would have to relinquish Arista when my contract ended in June 2000. That was quite an emotional loss, there's no denying it. I definitely went through the stages of grief, but gradually the idea of new possibilities seemed enticing. Charles Goldstuck began to make headway with me about what a new label might look like. He asked me what I felt I would need to be fully satisfied about creating a new entity, and I said two words: *instant major*. I had no interest in starting a boutique label of any kind, and, after all this time, I didn't want to start from scratch. I wanted to come out of the gate with sufficient financing for a complete top-flight executive staff and enough important signings to make immediate impact. Those two words, *instant major*, generated a thorough, one-hundred-page business plan from Charles, so we now had something concrete to think about and work on. I might have still been hoping for a miracle with Arista, but having this exciting alternative in place definitely made me feel better, more energized, and more optimistic. The twenty-first century started to look very hopeful.

The holiday season rolled around, and I planned to travel to Hong Kong and Thailand, and then to Maui with my children and their families for the millennium celebration. Charles and his wife, Karin, had planned to go to the Caribbean, but we were still working on our plan, and it proved impossible to do that over the long distance. So I invited them to join me in Maui so he and I could continue to define what this potential new company should look like. They came, and Charles and I spent hours on the veranda of the beach house I had rented, working on our plan. We were getting faxes from the various people Charles had hired to formulate parts of the plan, and the wind was blowing pages all over the beach, and he and I would have to chase them down. It was fun and, somehow, an appropriate way to mark such a significant passage in time. The number that we came up with for the type of company I wanted to run was $150 million, a very formidable amount of money, roughly three times what any major-label start-up had previously cost. Charles was confident that he could raise that amount, so after he got back to New York, he began scheduling meetings.

As part of a deal to get him out of his contract with Arista, Charles agreed to stay on until August to help with the transition of the company to L.A. Reid, if that plan came to pass. I was leaving at the end of June. We were still working extremely hard at Arista, motivated by professional pride, strong financial incentives, a dedication to the devoted executive staff we had brought in, and a genuine desire to see the company excel through the time of our departure. Among the companies Charles first approached about our new label was Bertelsmann, but Zelnick did not show any interest. So Charles pursued other potential investors.

Then came the Grammys in February 2000, and Santana's *Supernatural* proved triumphant. That week kept building into a groundswell of music industry support, and it was increasingly difficult for Zelnick to explain the rationality of his decision. The taping in April of our twenty-fifth-anniversary special at the Shrine Auditorium and its prime-time airing in May on NBC shone another spotlight on the label's unique success since its inception. Other than Motown, how many labels begun in the past fifty years could command this sort of national attention?

By this point, Thomas Middelhoff had had enough. Charles and I assumed he must have instructed Zelnick that he had to do whatever he could to make a deal with me. Middelhoff understood the hit that BMG would undoubtedly take in industry and public perception if I were to leave, and he was determined to avoid it. From the outset, at out-of-the-way restaurants in New York, I had secret dinner meetings with Middelhoff in which he expressed astonishment at the needless destructive battles with me and Clive Calder. He assured me that he was going to do whatever he could to keep me within the company. Meanwhile, Calder and I were spending hours together, often in my apartment and always outside the public view, and he attended several of my strategy sessions. While we ran rival labels within BMG and were technically competitors, we always got along extremely well, and the difficulties we were having brought us even closer. I introduced him to Charles Goldstuck, who, like Calder, was born in South Africa, and the two of them connected as well. Calder not only provided astute advice, but he was also interested for his own reasons in learning as much as he could about the ways of Bertelsmann. He would soon make a move that would rock the company to its core, and that would have important implications for Charles and me.

With Middelhoff in the background, Zelnick came back to the table, and as the negotiations with Bertelsmann proceeded I was in little mood to compromise on any of the essential points of the new company I envisioned. Both Charles and I agreed that, despite everything that had happened, staying within Bertelsmann might be the best way to go. My mutually beneficial relationship there dated back two decades, and in eighteen months Charles had attained significant stature and was well respected. I might have occasionally bristled against some corporate limitations of Bertelsmann, but I also had great respect for the firm and all that it had accomplished. This scrape with Zelnick and Dornemann aside, I'd been treated well and fairly there. Charles and I understood the company intimately in all its worldwide aspects. This would shorten the learning curve that would inevitably accompany starting anew somewhere else. Leaving Arista behind would be sad, to put it mildly, but as the new plan took shape I began to feel real enthusiasm.

Of course, staying at Bertelsmann introduced additional complexities that had to be negotiated. I wanted to have an artist roster in place, and proposed that I could select five platinum artists and five up-and-coming artists from Arista to come to the new label. Those artists, needless to say, would have to agree to move, and I couldn't offer them terms that exceeded those in their existing Arista contracts. Arista, however, could sweeten those contracts as much as it wanted in order to keep those artists on the label. The same was true of the executive staff. I could approach anyone on staff at Arista about coming with us, but they would have to do so exactly on the terms of their Arista agreements. Again, Arista could offer whatever it liked to retain its executive team. Without question, one of the things in my career of which I'm most proud was that every Arista executive I approached came with us. I might be demanding, and no doubt everyone who has worked for me has his or her favorite "Clive story." But when given the choice of staying with the established label or coming with us to a start-up, every single key member of the Arista executive team chose to make the risky move of joining the new company. It was a ringing vote of confidence and a demonstration of loyalty that moves me to the core to this day. If we managed to pull this deal off, Charles and I would have the best of both worlds. We would be making a fresh start with a completely new label with $150 million in financing, a strong ten-artist roster, including the young Alicia Keys, and the unbelievable comfort level of working with the same absolutely first-rate executive team that we had built together and on whom we knew we could completely rely. Finally, I would have 50 percent ownership of the new company, with Charles getting a percentage of my half.

The negotiations with BMG began in earnest in the spring of 2000, and by mid-August we were able to sign the deal. We got everything we asked for, except that BMG understandably stipulated that we could not approach Whitney Houston, Carlos Santana, or Kenny G, and that Dido, who I had personally signed after being alerted by Hosh Gureli and Peter Edge to her exceptional songwriting ability, had just exploded with her debut album, *No Angel,* in 1999 (ultimately selling in excess of 21 million copies worldwide), couldn't be approached either. By the time of the signing we still had not come up with a name for the new label. I wanted something personal and had thought about Davis Records, but somehow I never got fully comfortable with that idea. I finally decided on J Records. My middle name is Jay, and Jay is the middle name of every male offspring in my family. Like Arista, J has a personal significance for me, but it also was not so specific that it would exclude, alienate, or confuse anyone. So on August 15, 2000, J Records was born.

While the J Records offices were being prepared at the prime location of 745 Fifth Avenue, between Fifty-seventh and Fifty-eighth Streets, we set up shop in a string of suites at the Waldorf-Astoria Hotel on Park Avenue, just a few blocks from my apartment. Since my apartment is two full floors, we also held many meetings with the J team there, and some executives more or less worked out of there. The key players in the new executive lineup, all of whom came with me from Arista, were Charles Goldstuck, president and chief operating officer; Richard Palmese, senior vice president of promotion; Tom Corson, senior vice president of worldwide marketing; Julie Swidler, senior vice president of business and legal affairs; Peter Edge and Keith Naftaly, senior vice presidents of A&R; Hosh Gureli, vice president of A&R; and Alan Newham, senior vice president of finance and administration. In addition, we continued our tradition of retaining the very valuable expertise of executive recruiter Warren Wasp, and Ron Gillyard became senior vice president, urban music; Scott Seviour, vice president, artist development; Ken Wilson, senior vice president, urban promotion; Lois Najarian, vice president, publicity; and Rani Hancock joined us as head of A&R administration. This team, without a doubt, defined this formidable new instant major.

We did whatever we needed to do to get things moving fast. Charles additionally worked out of a special area in a small restaurant at the Peninsula Hotel. Palmese liked to work out of a little restaurant at the Hilton Hotel because, in the days before cell phones became ubiquitous, there was an extensive phone bank there that he could use. He could make his calls, have his meetings, and if he found a potential hire he would walk them over to the Waldorf to meet with me. It was a wild and woolly time, but so much fun and so fulfilling. Everyone was determined to make J a success, so, as hard as we were working, it didn't feel like work.

As we were establishing J, things around us began to happen fast. In November 2000, just about a year since our fateful dinner at Lutèce, Strauss Zelnick and Michael Dornemann were both asked to resign their positions at BMG. Strange as it might seem, I didn't take any personal pleasure in their departure. By that point I was 100 percent committed to J and looking ahead to what I hoped would be a fantastic new beginning. But there is no question in my mind that their handling of the situations with me and Clive Calder was part of their undoing. Miscalculating my reaction to being asked to move to a corporate position at a career high point? What possible sense did that make? And then, in order to keep me and save face, giving me $150 million to start a new label filled with all the best executives from my old one? To anyone looking in from the outside, anyone who did not understand what had caused that situation, it just looked absurd. I would have been perfectly happy to stay at Arista doing what I loved and enjoying some of the biggest successes of my life.

As for Clive Calder, he renewed Zomba's distribution arrangement with BMG, but his contract contained a "put" option. Whenever he wanted to, he could "put" on the table the 80 percent of his company and the 75 percent of his publishing that Bertelsmann didn't own, and Bertelsmann would have to purchase it by multiples of sales and profits that, in the way the numbers worked out in this particular case, vastly overvalued the company. By 2001, with Britney Spears, the Backstreet Boys, 'N Sync, and R. Kelly firing on all cylinders, it was estimated that Zomba was earning $300 million in profits from $1 billion in sales. With numbers like those, Bertelsmann was contractually obligated to buy Zomba and pay Calder $2.7 billion, a truly shocking figure. Calder cashed his check and moved to the Cayman Islands, and Bertlesmann understandably was left reeling. The company then demanded to know if any other executives had such a clause in their contract. I did.

When Bertelsmann learned that, they came to Charles and me and explained that we needed to work out another arrangement. The company simply couldn't sustain the risk of another payout like the one it made to Calder. So Bertelsmann offered to purchase from us the 50 percent of J that it didn't already own, but the payout would be distributed over a five-year period. Charles and I decided to bet on ourselves and accepted a profit-sharing arrangement that would reward us handsomely, but only if J did extremely well, as we were confident it would. J launched with a number-one single, broke one new artist after another, and attracted major established artists. Bertelsmann subsequently put me in charge of the RCA Music Group, which greatly expanded our potential profit base. In 2003, when Arista under the new administration was in red ink, the RCA Music Group had turned itself around and earned very substantial profits. In January 2004, L.A. Reid and Arista parted company. In 2009, during an interview with Charlie Rose, he was asked about accepting the presidency of Arista as part of an arrangement to move me out. To his great credit and as a measure of his quality as a person, L.A. replied, "Who's foolish enough to think he can fill Clive's shoes? I thought it was growth. I thought it was some kind of accelerated career move. But as it turns out, it was a foolish guy stepping into the shoes of an icon, and it was difficult. . . . I really regret doing it because it hurt Clive, and I have so much respect for Clive." Let me voice my own respect for L.A. Reid here. His subsequent strong career success at Def Jam, his new position as the head of Epic Records, and his visible tastemaking as a judge on *The X Factor* have continued his important influence in shaping contemporary music. He is definitely one of the leaders of today's music industry.

J did so well in its first three years that Rolf Schmidt-Holtz of BMG kept coming back to us to take over other parts of its music business. First it was the RCA Music Group. Then, in early 2004, I was put in charge of BMG North America, which, along with the Zomba Group, included, extraordinarily enough, Arista Records. So the company I had founded thirty years earlier was now back under my direction. After everything I'd been through, I can't say that wasn't emotional and satisfying, but by this time our business was going gangbusters, and we were having a ball. The relationship with our corporate parent was a strong one, and Ira Sallen, BMG's senior vice president of global human resources, was always attentive and very helpful. We were working from early in the morning until late at night, and on the weekends Charles and I would be on the phone for hours at a time. We both cared deeply about what we were building. There was no need to gloat, and we didn't. The present and the future shone bright and we had little reason to look back.

Alicia

Emerging from the struggle over Arista Records with a new label funded with historic new financing and driven by an energizing sense of possibility was all to the good. But as we actually started to release records, we knew there couldn't be any sense of a letdown. In fact, it was important to demonstrate that J was more than a lucrative incentive for me to remain at BMG and help heal a public relations debacle for the company. We needed to bolt out of the gate in full stride, and we did. Our first release was by O-Town, a boy band assembled by the manager Lou Pearlman, who had brought the world the Backstreet Boys and 'N Sync, for the TV reality show *Making the Band,* which aired on ABC. (The show would later move to MTV, and Pearlman would later move to jail for financial shenanigans, but at this point he was a very successful figure in the music industry.) O-Town clearly was not a credibility signing, but, like the Bay City Rollers when Arista was launching, the band was timely and commercial. The signing of the band to J aired on the show, which was excellent visibility for the label, and the group's second single, the ballad "All or Nothing," rose to number three. The group's debut album, simply titled *O-Town,* also broke into the Top 5 and went platinum, so J demonstrated its promotion and marketing strength and hit-making prowess right off the bat.

Still, the album that made 2001 a defining year for J and established the label's reputation for quality was Alicia Keys's landmark debut, *Songs in A Minor.* We had signed Alicia when I was still at Arista. She was an artist I believed in 100 percent from the first time I heard her, but there were enough bumps on the road to getting her album released that when it finally came out and did so well it somehow seemed both miraculous and inevitable. Alicia obviously was a very special talent. She was the product of a biracial marriage, and her parents broke up when she was two. She and her mother lived in the Hell's Kitchen neighborhood of Manhattan, and her mother had her take classical piano lessons beginning when she was seven years old. Alicia, quite simply, was one of those young women who was certain that she would be an artist, and from the very beginning she took every aspect of her training seriously.

She signed to Columbia Records after graduating from the Professional Performing Arts School, a distinguished public school in Manhattan. She was accepted at Columbia University, but after a few weeks there decided to pursue her musical career without any distractions. Even though she was still in her teens when she got her recording contract, Alicia had a very strong sense of self as an artist and songwriter. As sometimes will happen in the music business, the team that had been overseeing Alicia's development at Columbia Records was let go while she was still working on her first album, and she found herself adrift at the label. Worse than adrift, she felt that she was completely misunderstood. She was being asked to collaborate with other songwriters and to record outside material. This deeply infuriated her. And while I've certainly encouraged some performers to do exactly those things, I've never done it with someone outside the pop realm. As a result of the label's misconception of her, Alicia lost faith in Columbia's ability to understand her talent and bring it to the marketplace in a way that she felt would be true to herself. She felt totally abandoned and, consequently, began to look for alternatives.

The Arista A&R man Peter Edge, who is now CEO of RCA Records, had been following Alicia from the very start. He was at Warner Bros. when she first began looking for a record deal, and he didn't sign Alicia there only because he planned to leave the label and he didn't want to orphan her. Ironically, that's exactly what happened at Columbia. Because Alicia and her manager, Jeff Robinson, knew and liked Peter, they contacted him when she began to have trouble at Columbia. They knew their mission was to get out of their contract, and they asked Peter to set up a meeting with me. Peter, in turn, brought her to my attention. I first watched a video of a brief television performance she had done and listened to some recordings she had made for Columbia. I was extremely impressed, and readily agreed to an audition. Peter and Jeff brought her by, and she sat at the piano and performed songs that would later appear on *Songs in A Minor,* along with some other material. I remember this as one of those transcendent moments. Listening to her in a small space playing songs that meant everything to her was simply overwhelming. The songs were powerful, intimate, and personal; her singing was strong and distinctive; and her playing was brilliantly evocative. She sounded both absolutely of the moment and yet deeply rooted in the most nurturing traditions of soul music. And she was young and startlingly beautiful. Alicia was still a teenager, but she was the complete package: a totally compelling major talent with absolute star power.

She was so good that when she was done, I just had to laugh to myself. Could this really be happening? Was this a genuine possibility? Yet I kept my cool and asked her about the creative vision she had for herself. I was later to learn that she was very struck by that question; evidently, no one at her record label had ever asked her that before. She proceeded to convey a very clear picture of what she wanted for herself, and it all made perfect sense to me: She said that she didn't want to record outside material and she didn't want to collaborate with outside professional songwriters. She passionately felt that the music was coming from within herself. We had a lengthy conversation, and finally I just said, "Look, I think you're phenomenal, and I absolutely would love to sign you to Arista. But I feel as if this entire meeting is just a terrible tease, because there's no way in the world Columbia is going to let you out of your contract. They'd have to be crazy." Jeff assured me that the matter of the contract would be taken care of and that Alicia would be free to sign with Arista. I leaned back, crossed my fingers, and hoped for the best.

Sure enough, Alicia and Jeff pulled off the miracle. Yes, it ended up costing us about half a million dollars but we were able to sign Alicia to Arista, and she set out to complete work on her album. As that work progressed it became very evident that she would meet all the extraordinary expectations we had for her. Of course, the drama then deepened. The corporation was asking me to leave Arista, yet it was creating a new label for me with unprecedented backing, financing and staffing.

Simultaneously, a new administration came into Arista and Alicia was still signed to the label. I made it absolutely clear that I wanted her to come with me to J. She was my major priority. But I also knew that L.A. Reid understood how talented she was and would make a strong direct appeal to her and Jeff Robinson to stay with Arista. Charles Goldstuck and I negotiated the right for Alicia to come to J, but like all artists signed to Arista, she would have to make her own decision about which label to be on. We couldn't offer her more money than Arista did, so we just had to rely on the support we had shown her when she was still at Columbia and hope that the solid bond we had formed would carry the day. There is no doubt that a huge additional factor was that the entire key Arista team that she had come to know and trust, most especially Peter Edge, was coming to J. Ironically, staying with us was more like staying with Arista than remaining on Arista would have been. It was a harrowing time waiting for her decision, and finally she made it: She would come to J. Whatever the reasons, I couldn't have been happier. I wanted Alicia to be the image of the absolute best that J Records represented.

When *Songs in A Minor* was completed, I knew we had the goods for her to be exactly that. Now it was the challenge of making sure that the album made as large a commercial impact as its quality warranted. We chose "Fallin' " as the first single, but our promotion staff warned that it might fall through the cracks. R&B stations might think it was too slow in tempo; pop stations might think it was too urban. If every problem conceals an opportunity, this one suggested that if we managed to win all the stations over that were at least considering playing the track, we would have a major hit on our hands. We just had to find a way to make that happen.

As it turned out, Alicia was an excellent ambassador for herself and her music. She has an incredible work ethic and was more than willing to do whatever interviews, personal appearances, and performances were necessary to help her album get a hearing. So we put her to work. Richard Palmese assembled a half dozen or so of the most important independent promotion men in the country, and I had them over to my Park Avenue apartment to hear Alicia play some songs from the album on my piano. Her performance was spectacular, and they all felt the spellbinding power of what her music could do. I also had the entire J marketing and promotion staff come to my weekend home in Pound Ridge to hear Alicia on the piano, and that performance was similarly riveting. For a while, every time I was invited to speak at an industry event, I brought Alicia along to perform and she always delivered big-time. In February, a few months before the album's release, I had her perform at my pre-Grammy party. Given the select and powerful audience, it's an incredible place to showcase and create a buzz, but, admittedly, I put her in a tough spot. She had to immediately follow Gladys Knight performing her signature song, "Midnight Train to Georgia." You have to remember that at this point, if anyone knew who Alicia was, it was only in terms of advance word of mouth or hearing a song or two. Following a legend like Gladys Knight singing a song that everyone knows and loves in front of an A-list crowd would be intimidating even for a seasoned performer, let alone someone just starting out. I explained to Alicia that I wanted to show an all-time performer doing one of her classics and then introduce her, a brand-new artist, as she was about to embark on her career. I assured her that I would introduce her by saying that we'd just seen one of the undeniable greats perform, and now I'd like to bring out someone who I believed would achieve greatness herself. Alicia brought a pragmatic confidence to the challenge. She was as direct and honest as could be. "I know this is a moment I'll never forget," she said. "I'm just going to have to do the absolute best I can." Characteristically, she brought the house down.

Each of those appearances was significant, but I needed to find a strategy that would really take advantage of all the inroads that had been made and that would create a critical mass of awareness of Alicia. Once people heard Alicia, I knew they would love her. It was time to think big. A few weeks before *Songs in A Minor* was set to be released, I did something I had never done before: I decided to write directly to Oprah Winfrey about Alicia. It would be a dramatic departure for Oprah to book an essentially unknown artist on her enormously successful and influential show, but that was exactly the point of my letter. Here is what I wrote, in part:

Dear Oprah: I've never written you about one of my artists but there's always a first time and this is that time. My newest discovery, Alicia Keys, is so special, so unique and clearly an 'all timer' that I felt I really must personally bring her to your attention. 99% of the time your program understandably showcases established music stars who have recognizable names and identities. I know you too are into discovery and perhaps once or twice a year, you might identify the next Aretha or Whitney or Lauryn Hill. Alicia Keys is such an artist. She writes all her own material; she's a great vocalist and musician; and she's a breathtaking beauty of twenty years old. One look at the enclosed video and you'll see why the Los Angeles Times, Rolling Stone, Vibe, *etc., are all heralding Alicia as music's great new star. I would personally like to ask you for Alicia to do your show. I think it would be a special moment that we'd all look back on historically.*

Whether or not she agreed to do it, I felt that Oprah would at least take my recommendation seriously. Sure enough, the executive producer of her show called me after receiving my letter, and we discussed what might be possible. During that conversation I suggested that she might want to consider doing a show on the young female neo-soul artists arriving on the scene who combined a hip contemporary attitude with a deep respect for the soul music tradition. Alicia would be part of the show, but I also brought up India.Arie and Jill Scott, neither of whom I worked with but both of whom I genuinely admired. Those three guests, along with Yolanda Adams and Mary Mary, would eventually all be on the show about neo-soul. But first I was asked some questions about Alicia's prowess as a live performer, a subject I was able to discuss with honest conviction on the basis of my own extensive experience with her. I reaffirmed that every time I put Alicia on a stage, she blew the audience away. I was then told that Oprah was going to be holding a major dinner for her key advertisers in Chicago the very next night, and she would love it if Alicia could join her and perform "Fallin'," the song that she would perform on Oprah's show the following week. That was yet another invaluable opportunity to spread the word, and we leaped at it. Alicia traveled to Chicago, aced the performance as I knew she would, and Oprah was completely won over.

Songs in A Minor sold 236,000 copies the week it came out in June 2001, and it debuted at number one. "Fallin' " had been released earlier as a single, but it, on the other hand, hadn't been making much of a commercial impact. Radio hadn't fully committed to it yet. Alicia's performance on *Oprah* changed that immediately. On the broadcast, Oprah, now familiar with the song, could be seen singing along as Alicia played "Fallin'," and suddenly the floodgates opened. The song eventually went to number one, and the album ended up selling more than 6 million copies in the United States and an equal number around the world. The album's second single, "A Woman's Worth," also entered the Top 10. A third single, a cover of Prince's "How Come You Don't Call Me," didn't become a major radio hit, but it boldly staked Alicia's claim to an exalted artistic lineage. In fact, just three years later, when Prince was voted into the Rock and Roll Hall of Fame, Alicia was the artist who made the speech inducting him.

The time seemed right for an artist of Alicia's extraordinary gifts, and J was very much the beneficiary of the stature she immediately assumed. Alicia performed "Fallin' " at the MTV Video Music Awards show in September 2001, which marked the twentieth anniversary of the channel's launch. The show was held at the Metropolitan Opera House at Lincoln Center in Manhattan, which, however ironic a setting, added luster to the event. I was sitting in a box above the orchestra, and when Alicia was announced as winner of the Best New Artist category, the entire audience rose, slowly turned toward my box, and enthusiastically applauded. Frankly, I had to keep my emotions in check; I was receiving a standing ovation at the Metropolitan Opera House, and I hadn't even had to sing! More seriously, it was a stirring acknowledgment of how I had come back after leaving Arista and how I had presented an artist of Alicia's singular talent. She had indeed become the standard-bearer for J, and it is indelibly stamped in my memory as one of the proudest moments of my life.

Just a few days after that, the September 11 attacks occurred, and the intelligence, seriousness, and emotional depth of *Songs in A Minor* made it one of the rare works of art that somehow seemed suited to that intensely painful moment. It was a source of both courage and solace. At the Grammys in 2002, Alicia won five awards, including Song of the Year for "Fallin' " and Best New Artist. She had fully established herself as one of the first major talents to emerge in the new century.

Alicia's second album, *The Diary of Alicia Keys,* made an even more dramatic debut at the number-one spot in December 2003, selling more than 600,000 copies in its first week and launching three Top 10 singles: "You Don't Know My Name," "If I Ain't Got You," and "Diary." Amid the rollout of the singles from *Diary,* Alicia also hit number one with "My Boo," a duet with Usher that appeared on his 2004 album, *Confessions.* At the 2004 Grammys, Alicia distinguished herself again, earning awards in the categories of Best R&B Album, Best Female R&B Vocal Performance ("If I Ain't Got You"), and Best R&B Song ("You Don't Know My Name"). In addition, "My Boo" earned a Grammy for Best R&B Performance by a Duo or Group with Vocal. *Diary* ended up selling more than 4 million copies in the United States, and about the same amount overseas. Alicia then taped a 2005 appearance on *MTV Unplugged* that was released as a live album later that year. Once again, she entered the charts at number one and impressively achieved platinum sales for a live album.

In 2007 the album *As I Am* continued Alicia's artistic and commercial momentum, again debuting at number one and this time selling nearly 750,000 copies in its first week, the most she has ever sold out of the box. "No One," the album's first single, won Grammys for Best R&B Song and Best R&B Vocal Performance. *As I Am* has sold more than 3 million copies in the States and close to 5 million worldwide. Alicia's most recent album, *The Element of Freedom,* came out in 2009, delivered platinum sales, and earned a Grammy for Best Female R&B Vocal Performance for "Superwoman." I know that these are a lot of facts and statistics but I want them to speak for how dramatically a promising and then successful new artist can emerge into the special category of an all-timer. And I would like to add that, apart from her own album, Alicia collaborated with Jay-Z on "Empire State of Mind," which in 2011 was nominated for Record of the Year and won Grammys for Best Rap Song and Best Rap/Sung Collaboration. Even more impactful is that the song has joined Sinatra's "New York, New

York," written by Kander and Ebb, and Billy Joel's "New York State of Mind" as classic anthems of love for New York City. Indeed, Alicia is a sufficiently iconic figure that even Bob Dylan famously name-checked her in his song "Thunder on the Mountain," on his 2006 album *Modern Times:* "I was thinkin' 'bout Alicia Keys, couldn't keep from crying / When she was born in Hell's Kitchen, I was living down the line / I'm wondering where in the world Alicia Keys could be." As Alicia herself acknowledged, making an appearance in a Dylan song is quite a memorable tribute.

I'd like to highlight here Alicia's evolution as a young woman, apart from all the awards that attest to her worldwide commercial ascendancy and her peers' deep respect and admiration. Alicia is truly a young renaissance woman seriously committed to the arts, to theater, to giving back. Her charity, Keep a Child Alive, is an active and important force in helping afflicted people in Africa. In no way is this an artist's token foundation effort. The charity has raised millions of dollars to provide medicine to families struggling with HIV and AIDS. It is doing a world of good, and Alicia has been hands-on, the unmistakable leader of the effort. Her heart and soul are as pure and as large as her talent.

Alicia and I continue to be close, warm friends. I was deeply struck by the bond we established early on, when we would listen to music as she was putting together *Songs in A Minor*. We communicated so honestly and so well that the difference in our ages not only didn't seem to matter, it didn't seem to exist. I've also had a strong and lengthy professional and personal relationship with her husband, the producer Swizz Beatz. Swizz also is actively involved in giving back to the community, and he has served as producer-in-residence at the Clive Davis Institute of Recorded Music, which I established at NYU in 2003. When I'm socially with Alicia and Swizz any generational differences between us melt away. Just last year I was having dinner with a group of friends and I kept getting calls from the people who work with Swizz, saying that he would be DJing that night at a club called Espace on Forty-second Street near the Hudson River. Alicia was going to be there, too, and they would love to see me. It was late, but after dinner I went there with my party of six and we had the best time with Swizz and Alicia, and also with Puffy and Pharrell, who were there with them. It was a long, fun night, more like a get-together with friends than an industry event. There is a very personal warmth that has characterized our relationship, whether I've had lunch at their home with just the two of them and their wonderful young son, Egypt, or a private birthday dinner of mine for friends and family.

Unfortunately, I was traveling out of the country when Alicia played at Joe's Pub in New York in 2011 to mark the tenth anniversary of the release of *Songs in A Minor,* so I couldn't be there. She wrote me a note that really moved me. I had showcased Alicia at Joe's Pub when the album first came out, and she clearly remembered that. It was a night that was deeply meaningful for both of us, and she wrote lovingly about it: "I did Joe's Pub on Tuesday night as a surprise show and it was such an amazing return to one of the most special moments in my life. So I just wanted to thank you for loving me and believing in me and putting so much into getting the world to listen to me. I am forever grateful."

Flash forward to April 2012, when I got a call from Alicia to pick a date to hear selections from her new album, *Girl on Fire,* which would come out in late November. So I met her on April 27 at the studio and, over a casual sushi lunch, we sat there, just the two of us in the control room, and I heard about six or seven of her new songs. I was knocked out. She just keeps on growing. Yes, she works at being current, and yes, the tracks are state of the art, but Alicia's music is timeless. I literally got goose bumps. More than thirteen years had passed, and I silently watched her listening intently and basking in the new musical birth as she shared it with me. This is what it's all about for me, why I continue working when many of my peers have sought retirement. I love music, I love classic contemporary music, and I love being there on the spot as new music is created. And I can't do better than hearing the new music of Alicia Keys, sitting right next to her with giant speakers right above us playing it loud, really loud, as our heads bop up and down together in unison.

The J Records Years

Beyond the wonder of Alicia Keys, as J began to release records, we presented a range of artists and styles that once again sought to reflect the breadth of what had been accomplished at Columbia and Arista. I wanted J to be competitive across the board, and we made that point in dramatic fashion in the label's first three years. Among the artists who came with us to J were Deborah Cox and LFO, both of whom had been platinum artists on Arista. They didn't match those numbers at J, but they sold credibly and their presence on the label demonstrated its range. The neo-soul singer Angie Stone also came to J from Arista, and she attained a gold record with her first album on the new label, *Mahogany Soul,* in 2001. The A&R man Peter Edge, who helped bring Alicia Keys to Arista, also brought Angie to my attention, and we had great hopes for her. She had co-written with D'Angelo, and her powerful voice and deep emotional connection to traditional soul music made her a critics' darling. Somehow, unfortunately, she and we were never able to come up with the defining hit that would truly cause her career to soar. Angie came to believe that she had been eclipsed by Alicia Keys, and in a sense that's true, though it was definitely not a reflection of any formal or informal policy at J. It's easy for an artist to say, "Oh, they've got a new favorite now," but history has shown that there's always room for another success. When we had Dionne, there was room for Aretha, and when we had Dionne and Aretha, there was room for Whitney and later Toni Braxton. We promoted Angie as strongly as we could, but after a couple of albums without major breakthrough cuts, she had plateaued as a gold-level artist. That's certainly more than respectable, and reflected Angie's real talent and sizable following. But the truth is Alicia looked to be an all-timer. She was the subject of tremendous interest in the media and the industry, and she was also writing and recording big hit singles. It would have been both foolish and grossly negligent not to support her as energetically as we did, but nothing was at the expense of the very gifted Angie. We did make one more album with Angie (*Stone Love,* 2004), after which she was to sign with Stax.

One of J's first major new signings was the rapper Busta Rhymes, with whom the label's executive staff and I had an initial meeting in the screening room of my apartment. I got a kick out of having the meeting there. Busta was instantly charismatic, witty, intense, intelligent, and clearly emotional about the potential of his future work. He was enjoying this grassroots meeting, and I knew the importance of this dialogue. With Bad Boy and LaFace, hip-hop had obviously been an important part of Arista's roster, and I was looking for Busta to establish J's standing in that genre. He was a respected star who had been having hits since 1996, and although his sales had leveled off at platinum, we both strongly believed that he could reach a bigger audience. There's lots of humor in Busta's songs and persona, but his music is undeniably raw. The team that had made the Notorious B.I.G., who had gone to high school with Busta and whose music was equally gritty, was still in place, and we believed that J could bring Busta to the sales heights that he aspired to achieve. Busta, in turn, wanted a fresh beginning and he liked the fact that J was a start-up. He knew that he was our first direct rap signing, and we turned that into a positive, assuring him that we would focus on him with tremendous energy precisely for that reason.

We signed Busta in 2001, and *Genesis*, his first album for J, came out in November of that year. *Genesis* opens with a recording of a scripted phone conversation between Busta and me in which I assure him that he's got "a ridiculous album" that is "hot to death." I then offer him the following words of advice as we take that album to the world: "Keep it gutter. Keep it grimy." It was warm, affectionate, and funny, and it announced to Busta's fans and the media that he had a new label that was fully behind him. *Genesis* was filled with notable guests and star producers, and it included the hit song "Pass the Courvoisier, Part II," which featured Puffy and Pharrell and which went to number eleven on the album chart. In 2002 Busta and Puffy opened my pre-Grammy gala with the song, and they had everyone on their feet within seconds. Eventually the album did go platinum and rose to number four on the pop chart, a very strong showing and a real achievement in keeping momentum going for Busta's career as his veteran status became clearer. But the album didn't materially exceed the sales of Busta's previous releases, so he ended up disappointed. He followed that album up a year later with *It Ain't Safe No More,* which included the Top 5 hit "I Know What You Want," which featured Mariah Carey. However, that album sold fewer copies than *Genesis,* rising only to the level of gold sales.

While our personal relationship never grew acrimonious, Busta ended up feeling that J didn't have enough experience and expertise at working hip-hop records. We, on the other hand, didn't think that was the reason Busta's albums didn't soar higher. I know that Ron Gillyard, who headed our black music division, worked around the clock on Busta's behalf. We put extra concentration on the depth and reach of the street teams we employed to make sure we were competitive and our promotion team put his records forward to radio with real fervor. The reality is that the hip-hop audience is notoriously fickle, always on the alert for the hottest new sound and new star, and that makes it difficult for long-established artists like Busta, notwithstanding that his talent was raging as stong as ever. Artists, of course, never want to believe truths regarding the impact of the passage of time. Another issue for Busta was that we had given him a label imprint called Flipmode, and he had a posse of artists that he wanted to sign. But we just didn't feel that Busta was identifying artists with the kind of potential that, for example, Puffy's signings at Bad Boy had demonstrated. For the most part, Busta couldn't make deals with us for artists he believed in very deeply, and that definitely upset him.

Personally, I always liked Busta a great deal. He was magnetic as a presence, very smart and funny. I wish we could have done more together. He was a prestigious signing, a talented artist with creative muscle. And he did deliver on our immediate goal of demonstrating that J could handle a rap artist of his stature. Going platinum to me is always major, and it was especially important in the label's early years.

Without question the biggest pop-rock act that J broke was Maroon 5. The group came to us through a deal we had made with a very talented A&R man named James Diener, who left Columbia Records to come work with us. He had a dual responsibility, doing A&R for J and running his own label called Octone. He had signed Maroon 5 to Octone, and the nature of our deal was that Octone would start working the band's debut album, *Songs About Jane,* and if some momentum built and the release would benefit from J's promotional power we would step in and help and the album would become an Octone/J release. Maroon 5 had a previous incarnation under the name Kara's Flowers and had put out an album on Reprise in 1997. Now, five years later, the band had freshened its lineup and its sound, and, despite having been rejected by just about every major label, *Songs About Jane* proved to be a powerful album that eventually became a huge hit, selling more than 4 million copies and spinning off four Top 40 hits, including "This Love" and "She Will Be Loved," each of which entered the Top 5. The album also earned Maroon 5 a Best New Artist Grammy in 2005.

Songs About Jane did a slow build, and part of the reason is that Diener and Octone's head of promotion, Ben Berkman, strongly believed that the group should be marketed as a modern-rock band. While we did get some initial modern-rock radio support, I always felt that the jig would be up when we got to release "This Love" and "She Will Be Loved" as singles. They were quintessential pop songs and they were at the core of the group's strength. Diener and Berkman are both very bright, and I had intense conversations with them on this and other subjects. They insisted that if we broke Maroon 5 as a pop group, they would never have any credibility as a rock band again, to which my reply was, "Well, suppose they don't?" Ultimately, to me the band had far greater potential in the pop genre than in rock. What's better, selling millions of albums as a pop artist or struggling to establish yourself in a genre to which your music is not really suited? Eventually, Diener and Berkman relented, and when we all worked together to push the band over the top, we got excellent results. John Mayer, who had attended the Berklee College of Music with Maroon 5's guitarist James Valentine, was extremely supportive of the band, bringing them out on the road with him and constantly talking them up in interviews. The band also had a great time playing my pre-Grammy party in 2005. The singer, Adam Levine, was agog that sitting at a table right in front of the stage were Puffy, Jay-Z, Missy Elliott, and Magic Johnson, the "coolest people," in his words, "ever at a Maroon 5 show."

Unfortunately, as the group began working on its follow-up to *Songs About Jane,* Octone had the right to set the financial terms for the future, and they made some demands on J that just didn't make economic sense for us to meet. We crunched the numbers and projected that J was likely to earn somewhere between $20 and $25 million if the next three Maroon 5 albums were successful, while Octone would have to pay us $38 million if it moved to another label. As had been the case with Busta Rhymes and the Flipmode Squad, we didn't see much commercial potential in the other Octone acts. It was very tough and painful to lose a band that we not only liked but had worked so hard to build, yet it would have been irresponsible to spend as much as it would have taken to keep the Octone label and its artists with us, so we took the huge buyout money. As it turned out, Maroon 5 were a little cold for a long stretch, before the benchmark single "Moves Like Jagger," with Christina Aguilera, and Adam Levine's role as a coach on *The Voice* restored the group to prominence. Adam has emerged as a genuine star, and Maroon 5 are once again enjoying top-of-the-chart success.

Gavin DeGraw was another artist who came to J through James Diener, this time in his role as an A&R man at J. James had Gavin come to my office to audition for me and other executives. Atlantic already had expressed interest in Gavin, which lent a certain degree of urgency to our decision. The fact that other labels are sniffing around should never be the determinant of a signing—when that happens you can really get into trouble by overspending because you're caught up in an insiderish competitive game rather than staying focused on your own realistic estimation of what an artist might really be worth—but interest on the part of other labels is important information to have because it lets you know that if you do want to sign the artist, you have to act quickly because you're not the only horse in the race. Gavin later mentioned in an interview that when he sat down at the piano to play at the audition he was "singing and shivering" because "Clive was just sort of the name that you hear, like Moses." He was playing an upright piano that faced the wall, which had to be unsettling for him, but there was nothing I could do about it. Some J executives sat behind him, but part of evaluating his performance was watching his face and his gestures as he sang, so I sat right next to the piano where I could see him. I wasn't going to learn anything by staring at the back of his head.

When he played and sang, Gavin didn't sound nervous at all. He did five songs and I was really impressed. He had a great voice, strong songwriting ability, and he was good-looking and charismatic. This was a time when a new generation of singer-songwriters—John Mayer, Jack Johnson, and Jason Mraz, among them—were breaking through, and Gavin seemed poised to join their ranks. Once again, however, as Gavin began working on his debut album, *Chariot,* it became clear that while we perceived him as a pop artist, he viewed himself as a rock artist. The tracks he was working on in the studio and playing for us sounded like arena rock. I told him he had to scale it down, and we finally got the elements righted. The album got off to a decent start when it came out in 2003, but it really took off when one of its songs, "I Don't Wanna Be," was adopted as the theme song of the teen-drama TV series *One Tree Hill.* That level of exposure triggered the hit single that lifted the album to platinum status, making it another of J's new-artist success stories. Gavin was slow in taking full advantage of that momentum, unfortunately. His next album didn't appear until 2008, and though he followed that one up quickly with another in 2009, he's yet to really fulfill his potential.

Along with Alicia Keys, Jamie Foxx also made a major commercial impact on J. Jamie was far better known as an actor, but he never lost his dream of a career in music, and he began doing cameos on rap songs and looking for a record contract. It has always been meaningful to Jamie that I signed him before his massive breakout playing the role of Ray Charles in *Ray,* for which he won an Academy Award for Best Actor. He had come to see me in my Beverly Hills Hotel bungalow and asked to sing a song or two at my pre-Grammy party that year. He just stood up and started singing. I was taken not only with his voice and his presence but also his innate musicality. He wasn't just dabbling in another vocation; he was immersed in music and a charismatic natural. I gave him a spot on our Grammy show, where he was to earn a standing ovation, and signed him to a recording contract. *Unpredictable,* his first release for J in 2005, went double platinum, and he followed that up with the platinum-selling *Intuition* in 2008 and *Best Night of My Life* in 2010. He's been an outstanding performing regular at my Grammy party ever since and, though it's little known, he's one of only four artists (Frank Sinatra, Bing Crosby, and Barbra Streisand being the others) who have won an Oscar in an acting category and scored a number-one album.

Then there were two well-established major artists who came to sign with us and made a considerable impact during the years at J. The first was Luther Vandross. Obviously, I didn't discover Luther—he was one of the most admired soul singers on the music scene before I'd ever met him. But our history went back a long way, beginning with his helping to guide Aretha Franklin to commercial prominence in the Eighties with *Jump to It* and *Get it Right,* as well as his production work for Dionne Warwick. When I signed Luther to J, he was ready for a change. He felt that his career had peaked and even dipped a bit in recent years. He had spent fifteen years with Epic Records, where he had established himself as a platinum-level artist, and his 1989 *Best of Luther Vandross* collection had sold more than 3 million copies. Then, in 1998, he released an album titled *I Know* on Virgin Records that fell well short of platinum sales. He was frustrated and, like his idols Aretha and Dionne in earlier times, he felt that he had fallen out of step with contemporary music—or, perhaps more accurately in his view, that it had fallen out of step with him. The elegance, melodic sophistication, and sonic smoothness that Luther prided himself on as a singer, songwriter, and producer had yielded to tougher, more rhythmic tracks influenced by hip-hop. While Luther was too proud to admit that he wondered if there was a place for him on the contemporary R&B scene, I know that he was very concerned about that.

Before he came to J, Luther and I privately met for dinner at the Four Seasons restaurant in New York, just the two of us, to talk about his career and to see if we could collaborate successfully. Luther was primarily concerned about a label having respect for his artistry. He wanted to work with someone who understood the depth of his talent and, while he recognized the need for a more contemporary sound, he didn't want to be pushed to try anything that would feel inappropriate or contrived. He wanted a younger audience without pandering to it. For my part I wanted to make sure that Luther was open to recording outside material. The whole point of his coming to J would be for him to have hits and revitalize his career. His voice was still impeccable, indeed spectacular, and I felt confident that we could help him rise again, but I feared that my hands might be tied if I were limited only to songs that he wrote himself. As artists tend to be when they feel that success has pulled away from them, Luther assured me that he would be open to quality songs that I found. We had a deal.

Signing Luther was a real jewel in our crown. Just about this time, I was asked to give the keynote address at a *Billboard* convention in New York, and I brought out the then unknown Alicia Keys at the beginning of my presentation to demonstrate the quality of new young artists J would be presenting to the world. And, at the end, I called Luther onto the stage and we announced his signing to J. There were more than seven hundred people in the room, many of whom worked in radio, so it was an ideal opportunity for both artists and for J. I then had a private dinner for Luther at my apartment with executives from J that was both a celebration of his coming to the label and a creative meeting with the staff to begin planning for his debut album with us. I played three songs for Luther that night, including "Take You Out," written by Warryn Campbell, Harold Lilly, and John Smith. Luther loved it, and it became the leadoff track on *Luther Vandross,* his first album for J, in 2001. Luther co-wrote five of the songs on the album, and he covered two Burt Bacharach songs, including the classic "Any Day Now," which received a Grammy nomination. Tom Corson led a spectacular marketing campaign, and *Luther Vandross* became a Top 10 pop album and magically restored Luther to platinum-sales status.

Luther had just completed vocals on his 2003 follow-up album, *Dance with My Father,* when, tragically, he suffered a devastating stroke. He was never to fully recover. Luther suffered from diabetes and hypertension for many years, and he was always battling his weight, which fluctuated wildly. He would talk about that struggle whenever we met for dinner, and, for the most part, he managed to keep his weight under control in those last years that I knew him. We were all crushed at J when we heard the news of Luther's stroke. The title track of his new album, which he co-wrote with Richard Marx, was the kind of song that comes along once in a lifetime. The sentiment of it was extremely powerful. When he first played it for me in my office he said, "This is my career song. This is my Song of the Year Grammy." It was a one-listen record. I knew instantly what he meant. The lyric just pulverizes you and the melodic hook seduces you. I sat there and didn't say a word. Luther knew he had totally captured me, and I knew that with that track leading the way, *Dance with My Father* would become one of the most successful albums of Luther's career. Luther and I spoke on the phone every day for weeks, planning the campaign ahead. We knew we had a winner, and both of us were as pumped up as we could be.

The album came out two months after Luther's stroke and went straight to number one, the first time he'd had a number-one pop album. I went to visit him in rehab, held his hand, and told him one exciting piece of news after another about the album and its lead single's reception. There is no question that he visibly perked up, and even the doctors were impressed with his reactions. I talked right into his ear and said, "Luther, we've got to go to the Grammys together. You've got five nominations, and we have to be there in person when you win." He smiled broadly. He was so proud of this album. He played it constantly during his recovery efforts. Unfortunately, it became clear that he would not be able to attend the ceremony. He won in four categories, including Best R&B Album and, as he predicted, Song of the Year for "Dance with My Father." The album sold more than 2 million copies. Heartbreakingly, Luther videotaped a statement for the Grammy broadcast in which he assured the audience, "When I say good-bye it's never for long, because I believe in the power of love." He sang that signature line, and his voice still had its affecting resonance. We all had to fight back tears as we pulled hard for his recovery.

But Luther just couldn't get his health back, and he died from a heart attack on July 1, 2005, just over two years after his stroke. After his death, in Luther's honor I assembled an album titled *So Amazing:*

An All-Star Tribute to Luther Vandross that featured performances of songs associated with him by Aretha Franklin, Mary J. Blige, Usher, Beyoncé, Stevie Wonder, Alicia Keys, Elton John, Céline Dion, Wyclef John, Babyface, Patti LaBelle, John Legend, Angie Stone, Jamie Foxx, and Fantasia. That album, too, got five Grammy nominations, Stevie Wonder and Beyoncé winning for their version of the title track and Aretha for her rendition of the Bacharach-David classic "A House Is Not a Home." It's impossible to express how much I would have loved to continue working with Luther. He was only fifty-four when he died, and it was thrilling that he was making music that ranked among the very best of his storied career. Reviving legendary careers and extending career longevity mean the world to me, and I know that Luther and I were just beginning what would have been an even longer and more successful run. He was a master, a singer's singer. And he was a friend whom I miss dearly to this day.

Rod Stewart and the
Great American Songbook

Along with Luther Vandross, the other classic art-
ist who was restored to superstar status during his years on J was Rod
Stewart. For a record company to increase its market share, it usually
requires the discovery of a major new artist. But it's a real plus if you
can sign an artist who is a star but is no longer a significant album-
seller. Over the years Arista had greatly benefited from the second life
that Dionne Warwick, Aretha Franklin, Carly Simon, and especially
Carlos Santana enjoyed. These were timeless, classic artists who had
gone through a fallow period, but had not peaked. With the right
material they could once again rule the airwaves and headline shows.
I see that in the world of film. For example, what major above-the-title
movie star could still come back? Are the looks still there? Is the acting
talent still way above the pack? Julia Roberts could be an example of
this. She hasn't been in a hit film in several years, but her star potential
is still there. I'd bet she could come back. I'd also bet that with the right
role, Michael Douglas could once again enjoy his star power. It was in
this frame of mind that I eagerly approached an opportunity with Rod
Stewart.

Interestingly, Rod was the lead singer of the Jeff Beck Group on
Epic, a label I oversaw when I was head of the CBS record division
back in the Sixties, but we never met then. Rod, of course, is a member
of the Rock and Roll Hall of Fame, and thoroughly earned his reputation as one of the greatest singers in the history of rock 'n' roll with
Jeff Beck, Faces, and as a solo artist. When he and his manager, Arnold
Stiefel, first approached me about working together, however, his sales
had fallen off, and even his long-standing popularity as a live act was

diminishing. But the truism is apt: When the going gets tough, the tough . . .

Initially, I heard that Rod was working on an album of Tin Pan Alley standards through Richard Perry, with whom I'd worked and been friends for decades, ever since I'd brought him in to produce Barbra Streisand's 1971 *Stoney End* while I was at Columbia. Richard explained that Rod was looking for a change in musical direction. He had grown up with these songs, his parents had loved them, and he came very naturally to the material. It made perfect sense to me. Rod is obviously a world-class singer, and the prospect of hearing him in this new context intrigued me. His deal with Warner Bros. was over, and he was certain that they would have no interest in his doing a project like this, so he was available. I told Richard that I'd like to hear what they had come up with in the studio, so he sent me the tracks he and Rod had been working on. I simultaneously began conversations—and what would turn out to be a great friendship—with Rod's manager, Arnold Stiefel.

I listened carefully to everything Richard sent me, and I had very clear ideas about it. By this point in my life and career I believed that I knew exactly how a collection of material like this needed to work, how classic songs should be recorded in order for them to make their maximum commercial impact. Success in the marketplace can never be taken for granted, but if you're even going to have a chance, certain elements have to be in place. I appraised how other artists in Rod's position had approached these songs, and the most significant problem that undermined them is that often they did not take the best-known songs or the best examples of the genre. They chose a few obscure personal favorites, or even some original material, and they were completely unaware of how such decisions fatally diluted the power of the concept. In one sense, they began thinking like critics rather than artists. They somehow thought the best-known songs would be too obvious, that people would be tired of hearing them. Rather they should have thought, These are the best and most-loved songs of this kind. Why not bring my own gift to them? The artists didn't realize—and this is a point I have to make over and over again to artists when they're doing a concept album—that they were co-starring with the songs. Often they would simply attempt to use the song as a vehicle for their voice, but people don't buy music like this to judge the nature of the artist's voice. They know they like the singer already. But in a concept album, there's a definite equal co-starring. I would testify that 50 percent of the success of a concept album is the nature of the material. The consumer unquestionably likes the artist, but what triggers the purchase is that he or she can get all these classic songs on one album from this artist. With all due respect to Rod Stewart's extraordinary talent and achievements, I would not have been interested in discussing an album of original material with him at this stage of his career. Such an album would most likely have sold 200,000 to 300,000 copies. At the same time I believed that, properly done, an album of all-time standards by Rod Stewart could be a very significant success. In one case, you're thinking about the possibility of millions of sales, and in the other, 200,000 to 300,000. It's the same singer. What's the difference? The concept, choosing exactly the right material and exactly the right arrangements.

That said, there's no doubt that the concept couldn't work without an artist who is distinctive and who can interpret the material exceptionally well, but some of the biggest artists in the world have done concept albums and fallen flat because they haven't realized that they're co-starring with the songs. I have been relentless over the years on this subject. Consequently, I was pretty definite in my comments to Rod, Richard, and Arnold. There could be no filler material on the album, no unlikely "surprise" choices. Every song had to be incredibly well known and a supreme example of the essence of the Great American Songbook, which is the thematic framework we chose for the project. The album had to play straight through with no weak spots. The listening experience had to be consistently great. I didn't want the arrangements to be soporific, meaning I didn't want the collection to be slow-tempo. Shudder to say, and critics pounce on this, but to really explode in sales, this particular album also had to sound great in trendy clothing boutiques and enlivening as background music at dinner parties all over the world. It had to make people feel good and want to move, and unconsciously get people to stop their conversations, start listening, and sing along, which is not easy to do. I very specifically told Richard, "I love what you've done with 'You Go to My Head' and 'They Can't Take

That Away from Me.' But then other influences came in—like jazz, blues, and slow ballads that brought everything to a halt. The tempo changed, and the mood was affected. On an album like this everything has got to move." I came up with this phrase, which became something like the motto of Rod's *Great American Songbook* project: "Could Fred and Ginger dance to it?" That's all I wanted to know. I was so focused on that phrase. It means that you just move along, that there's a glow and a flow. So I said, "Look, I will definitely keep those two songs, but regrettably you have to scrap everything else you've done and start from scratch." That was what I needed in order to make the deal. It wasn't easy for them to hear because what they had done had its own creative validity, but with Arnold Stiefel's help at all times, Richard and Rod bought it. So we had a deal. Rod told *Billboard*, "J is where I wanted to be, and for me, it's a dream come true working with Clive. I'm over the moon about the whole thing." At our meeting I was convinced that Rod genuinely loved this music, and that recording an album like this wasn't something that was foisted on him or a move he was making out of any desperation. He was open to different types of arrangements, and he recognized that some direction was needed, not necessarily in the vocals but in the overall approach to the album. He had paid for the sessions with Richard himself, a strong indication of his commitment since, as Arnold wryly noted, Rod is famously tight-fisted.

Rod described meeting me this way: "He kept saying, 'I want this to sound like Fred and Ginger, Fred and Ginger, Fred and Ginger. We were all sitting in his bungalow at the Beverly Hills Hotel one morning at eleven a.m. while he bludgeoned us over and over with Fred and Ginger. Then he got up and started dancing around the room." That's absolutely true, by the way. Because of my inadequate ability to talk in musical terms, I was trying to physically and visually convey to them the feel I was looking for. "So then I got up and started dancing," Rod continued, "and so did Richard Perry and Arnold Stiefel. Four grown men dancing around the hotel suite like Fred and Ginger. Before noon. It was the funniest fucking picture. He drives me insane, but he's a genius, that guy."

That's how the odyssey of Rod Stewart's *Great American Songbook* project began. I knew that, as far as critics were concerned, we were not inventing the wheel. I was doing it because I felt that there was a void and that this was a way to bring back both the brilliance of Rod Stewart and this incredible catalog of classic songs that I had loved since I began going to musicals as a teenager. Uncharacteristically, I spent a great deal of time in the studio on this project, often until the early hours of the morning. I felt that musically we had to use the best musicians as soloists—the likes of Dave Koz and Michael Brecker, on tenor saxophone, and Arturo Sandoval, on trumpet and flugelhorn. Their parts had to be outstanding, and, along with the producers, I communicated with each of the soloists separately. You needed to have that melodic feel, that forward motion. You had to be able to dance to it, to sing and swing and sway to it.

Richard of course stayed on the project. Sometimes it was tough because he and Rod had their own preexisting idea of what the album should be. But when we were in synch, it was terrific. We brought the feel of "You Go to My Head" and "They Can't Take That Away from Me" to "The Very Thought of You," "The Nearness of You," and "We'll Be Together Again." Those were the tracks that Richard ended up producing. We did bring in the great Phil Ramone to co-produce, and to fill out the album we selected "It Had to Be You," "That Old Feeling," "These Foolish Things (Remind Me of You)," "Moonglow," "I'll Be Seeing You," "Every Time We Say Goodbye," "For All We Know," and "That's All." I would go down to the studio with Phil to work with the musicians he chose. Phil was his usual wonderful self and helped put everything together. (He would later capture Rod's vocals in separate studio sessions.) We would set the tempo and create guide vocals, which were sung by the very talented Rob Mathes. I became obsessed with getting everything exactly right with these cuts. Keith Naftaly from J's A&R department often came with me to the studio to help communicate with Phil and the musicians. I had a firm idea of what was needed, and on this album I was working along with two great masters, Richard and Phil, who were also two great friends, and they put up with me. Arnold Stiefel always saw the larger picture and was indispensable in keeping the perspective clear. Rod said, "Clive was totally involved here. He was in the studio until three or four in the morning with the band, working to get the tracks right. I can't imagine any head of a record company doing that."

The album, *It Had to Be You: The Great American Songbook,* came out in 2002. To launch it we took over the big stage of the St. Regis Hotel in Century City in Los Angeles and invited select media and key members of the industry. I played almost all of the album and then Rod took the stage and sang four songs from it. It was a big, successful night. We created a buzz that intimated that this album could be the sleeper of the year. I have to give much-deserved credit to Tom Corson and Scott Seviour for their imaginative marketing plan, because this was not an album that would be able to benefit from radio airplay, which was essentially nonexistent. To help compensate for that, Tom and Scott made sure that the album reached every tastemaker. Every key clothing boutique was given this album six weeks before the release date to play while people were shopping, and they were amazed at its impact. The album became the scintillating soundtrack for innumerable dinner parties, the darling of hostesses everywhere. I remember playing it on a boat, introducing it to the eleven other friends who were there sharing it with me. It just made the evening. At that point I knew that we had something that could become a phenomenon.

And then the time came when we had to decide whether we would invest in a major television campaign to help spread the word. Would this be extravagant, as the total investment would be at least half a million dollars, or, since there would be no meaningful radio play, would it be a necessary ingredient in breaking this concept album wide open? We went for it. Instead of the usual music video, we taped a performance by Rod in a theater, filled to capacity with his fans. We had his musicians onstage with him as he captured the melodic choruses of all these great standards. This was all edited into a two-minute television ad that could be cut to ninety seconds or sixty seconds or thirty seconds, as necessary. Consumers would mail-order the album after seeing the ad. If the response was encouraging enough when we went on the air, we could extend the period of advertising beyond one month, to six or even eight weeks. It all worked. The response was very strong and we dramatically developed word-of-mouth support for the album, emphasizing the idea that you could get all these great songs on one album, inimitably delivered by Rod Stewart. Sales exploded to well over 3 million copies in the United States, and the album was nominated for a Grammy.

In like manner sales exploded in many countries outside the United States. People who hadn't bought albums in years bought it. It became a must-purchase. The album became the most successful rock-era standards project since Linda Ronstadt went into the studio with Nelson Riddle to record *What's New* (1982) and its two follow-ups. It was *huge*, and took the industry by storm. Inevitably, we made it the first album in a series.

It Had to Be You reflected a different strategy from what we had done with Santana and *Supernatural*, which was all original material, but the principle of taking an established artist and dramatically reviving his career in this startling manner again demonstrated what can be done with imagination, verve, and new ideas. You can meaningfully extend a career if you're working with an original, and Rod Stewart's an original. In emphasizing the songs earlier, I certainly didn't mean to diminish the importance of Rod's singing. That unmistakable voice: You know it's Rod Stewart the instant you hear it. You don't wonder for a second. And, for all the grit in his voice, his singing is very intimate and he makes you want to listen to him more. So yes, we were picking great repertoire. Yes, this was a concept album, relying heavily on the material. But we never could have done it without that voice, loved by millions of people around the world.

The combination of Rod Stewart and those songs caused word of mouth to spread rapidly. His voice unified the songs and animated the concept. Everybody went out and bought the album. It was playing everywhere. Along with the adult crowd, there was a whole new generation unaware of the Great American Songbook. Needless to say, I did not invent the phrase, but I did suggest using it for this project, and it materially helped popularize it. This was a great opportunity to show how long great songs could last and how long a career can last pairing them together. So we went on to volumes II, III, IV, and V. We certainly had plenty of great songs to choose from. On the first volume we didn't even get around to Rodgers and Hart. We hadn't done Irving

Berlin or Duke Ellington or Frank Loesser. We never even tackled a Johnny Mercer lyric until volume five, so finding great material was not a problem.

For Volume II, *As Time Goes By*, we kept that same production team, Richard Perry and Phil Ramone, but we introduced a couple of duet partners, Cher for "Bewitched, Bothered & Bewildered" and Queen Latifah on the title track, to enliven the concept. To help me with the musicians in the studio I brought in Steve Ferrera from our A&R department. Rob Mathes, a terrific musician, producer, and arranger, would continue to take my roughly given musical direction and sing guide vocals so we could all hear what the song was ultimately going to sound like. He was an irreplaceable help in so many ways.

When *As Time Goes By* came out in 2003, it repeated the success of the first volume, selling more than 2 million copies and rising to number two on the charts. It was great for J, and it was great for Rod's career. With this sales success, infusion of media coverage, and a whole new audience, he was selling out arenas everywhere in the world. He was still the ultimate rock 'n' roller, but he could incorporate three or four of these songs into his live act to great effect. He would do it in a grand fashion, wearing a tuxedo on a beautiful stage with formally clad band members. On Volume III, titled *Stardust*, in 2004, Richard Perry stayed on and Steve Tyrell joined as co-producer, and we just proceeded in our usual fashion. Steve was especially helpful in coming up with classy duet ideas, and brought more first-rate partners into the project. So "Blue Moon" featured Eric Clapton; Stevie Wonder appeared on "What a Wonderful World"; "Manhattan" became a duet with Bette Midler; and Dolly Parton sang with Rod on "Baby, It's Cold Outside." While the first two volumes had been nominated and lost, *Stardust* finally won the Grammy for Best Traditional Pop Vocal Album.

Volume IV of the project, *Thanks for the Memory*, came in 2005, again with Steve Tyrell co-producing and Steve Ferrera providing A&R assistance and working to help translate my ideas in the studio. By the time you get to the fourth volume of a conceptual series, you have to work harder to make it distinctive, so we pushed the boundaries a bit both in terms of repertoire and duet partners. We brought in Diana Ross on "I've Got a Crush on You"; the trumpeter Chris Botti is featured on "I Wish You Love"; Chaka Khan joined Rod on "You Send Me"; Elton John sang with him on "Makin' Whoopee"; Dave Koz did a solo turn on "Nevertheless (I'm Still in Love with You)"; and George Benson appeared on "Let's Fall in Love."

At that point we really thought we had completed the *Great American Songbook* project with Rod. In fact, in 2007 we released all four volumes together as a boxed set titled *The Complete American Songbook*, and it racked up triple-platinum sales. It was at this point that we believed we should do something different, and, drawing on Rod's roots, we came up with a concept album of rock classics. The wonderful Bob Seger song provided the title track for *Still the Same: Great Rock Classics of Our Time*, which came out in 2006. The album included songs by the likes of David Gates of Bread ("Everything I Own"), Cat Stevens ("Father and Son"), Bob Dylan ("If Not for You"), the Eagles ("The Best of My Love"), and Van Morrison ("Crazy Love")—all great titles, with John Shanks producing. We did get some airplay on the album, which entered the charts at number one and nearly went platinum, selling around 800,000 copies, a very respectable number for a veteran artist.

After that, Rod and I disagreed on the next best step for him, and he worked on an album of soul covers titled *Soulbook* that J released in 2009. Then Rod, Arnold Stiefel, Richard Perry, and I responded to continuing consumer demand and decided to bring the *Great American Songbook* project full circle with one additional volume. We released *Fly Me to the Moon* in 2010. While it didn't have the commercial impact of the earlier volumes, it certainly sold more than a million copies worldwide. All in all, the project succeeded beyond all possible expectations. Cumulatively, worldwide sales exceeded 18 million copies! It gave Rod's career a whole new dimension, showcased some seventy-five undisputedly classic songs, and became the most commercial pop franchise of the decade.

Rod and I might have had a few disagreements along the way, but we both really cherished what we accomplished together. It was a career highlight to work with him in such a sustained, successful way. He has one of the most identifiable voices in rock and pop history, and his happy-go-lucky image was an additional big reason for the success of the project. He combines high style and the common touch in a way that really communicates to people, and that worked perfectly to bring the Great American Songbook across to a vast new audience. It's always moving to see how warmly Rod is greeted when he takes the stage. For many people, his music provided their own personal soundtrack, the musical backdrop to so many signal events in their lives. He also has such a distinctive look. You could never hear or see him and think it's anyone else. You always know it's Rod Stewart.

The years that we worked together, Rod was always very family-conscious, very involved in his kids' lives, very parental in his care, concern, and love. He is fanatical in his devotion to soccer, and very loyal to his friends, many of whom are the friends he grew up with. We both aspire to the good life, so whenever we get together, we compare notes on restaurants, hotels, boats, and the like. It sounds a little highfalutin, but we both come from backgrounds that didn't offer a lot of those things, and we genuinely enjoy them. There has also always been a strong mutual respect between us. He shares both the gift and the attitude of Aretha. They study the material before they come to the studio, and neither has much patience for doing more than a few takes. I'm fortunate in that I have a strong relationship with each, so I might have had a little more success in getting them to take another turn at bat. But while he hates to sing the same song over and over, Rod can knock out three or four songs in one session. He exudes a casual air, but he takes his work very seriously and is certainly aware that he's among those few artists that have made history. He very much wants to stand the test of time. Obviously, as an executive you want to discover new artists, but when you look around and see how few are able to sustain a truly lifetime career, there's tremendous satisfaction in extending the careers of the ones who can.

With the Great American Songbook, we were definitely on a mission to call significant attention to this extraordinary body of work and bring it to a vast new audience. What might seem at first to be just a commercially clever idea really became much more than that in a creatively satisfying way. Those irreplaceable melodies, those literate, tongue-in-cheek, sophisticated, and timeless lyrics were going to be listened to again by millions of people all over the world. It's a great example of how, if you trigger it right, you can really go against all the trends. And then all of a sudden one of the great original Hall of Famers is topping the charts again with songs that will live forever. Rod Stewart's *Great American Songbook* project was a true and unique phenomenon.

Rock at the Dawn of the Twenty-first Century

When I took charge of the RCA Music Group in November 2002, I was able to come in contact with some of the most important rock artists on the scene during a period in which rock music was increasingly having difficulty making a commercial impact. While many people primarily associate me with the pop and diva superstars I've worked with, I initially earned my reputation by signing artists who would go on to become major rock stars. Indeed, my induction into the Rock and Roll Hall of Fame in 2000 reflects that.

I'd love to share a brief story that pertains to one of the great rock artists that slipped away from me, though I had the opportunity to sign him: John Mellencamp. As it happens, the night before *Rolling Stone*'s founder and editor, Jann Wenner, was inducted into the Hall of Fame in 2004, he threw a party at Elaine's to celebrate. I've been a strong supporter and a good friend of Jann's since he started the magazine in 1967, and I helped it in every way I could. By completely fortuitous coincidence, that night I shared a table with Bruce Springsteen, Jackson Browne, Don Henley, and John Mellencamp, just the five of us. It was an evening of amazing revelations, and a couple of anecdotes, in particular, stick in my mind.

I was chatting with Jackson Browne, and I mentioned that I knew we had met, but I also thought I might have auditioned him when he was starting out, though I couldn't quite remember. Jackson laughed and said, "I'll tell you exactly what happened." He reminded me that David Geffen, who was his ardently devoted manager at the time, brought him to my office for an audition. Jackson recalled how warmly I had greeted him, which he very much appreciated as a young artist just beginning his career. But just as Jackson started playing his song "Doctor My Eyes" on the acoustic guitar he had brought, my assistant came in and told me that Goddard Lieberson needed to speak with me right away. He had one urgent background question on an important deal before he signed the final approval memorandum. Goddard was my boss and had given me my appointment as president of Columbia Records, so I couldn't exactly ask him to wait. I apologized profusely to Jackson and David, assured them that I would be back momentarily, and left the office to go next door to see Goddard. I couldn't have been more than a minute, but Jackson explained that as soon as I left, David acted enraged and insulted that I would interrupt his artist. He told Jackson that he wouldn't stand for it, and that he would excuse himself and Jackson when I returned, and just say that they would schedule a new audition on my next trip to Los Angeles. Jackson told us that he was chagrined. He knew who Goddard was and completely understood why I had to speak to him. He wasn't offended at all. But David was adamant. I had been appropriately apologetic about the brief interruption, but David was calling the shots. Needless to say, the Los Angeles audition never happened. Ultimately, I don't really think I lost the opportunity to sign Jackson because of that incident. David founded Asylum Records with his partner Elliot Roberts and he very much wanted Jackson to be its inaugural artist, so things undoubtedly would have worked out that way even if I had been able to hear Jackson and make an offer. Regardless, I've always loved Jackson's work and very much liked him as a person. But it was astonishing to be filled in on that story, reminded that I never did audition Jackson, and to encounter, once again, the astuteness and keen sense of competition that distinguished the ever-brilliant David Geffen at all times.

At that point everyone at the table was riveted, and since we were talking about auditions, I said to Mellencamp, "John, I've got to admit to you that whenever I'm asked in an interview who's the biggest artist I could have signed that I passed on, I always say it's you. I remember your audition very well. Your very clever cigar-smoking manager, Tony DeFries, brought me into the studio, and you played a few songs on acoustic guitar. But to me at the time you sounded too much influenced by Bruce, and since I was involved in signing Bruce when I was at Columbia, I passed. And now without question you've emerged as one of the great original American rock artists of all time!"

It was a funny conversation to have with John while Bruce was sitting right next to me. I was hoping that John would take it in the right spirit. The table went quiet. Everyone was still listening intently, and, in fact, John took it completely in stride. "Listen, I've got to tell you that you were right," he said, reassuring me after all these years. "I was basically in a cover band at the time, and suddenly Tony DeFries turns up and said if I left the group to be a solo artist, he would get me a record deal in short order. He was the hotshot manager of David Bowie, so I figured, 'Great!' He then told me he would be setting up an audition with you, but that I had to write some original songs—in a few weeks! Bruce was the hugest influence on me, and that's what those songs ended up sounding like. So, I'm here to tell you that it was absolutely no accident that you felt the way you did. When I auditioned for you, I was nowhere near finding my own voice as a songwriter."

Now for the ones who didn't get away, but who came to me when I headed RCA, beginning with the Dave Matthews Band, who were already massively successful by the time I took over the label. The group's first two albums, *Under the Table and Dreaming* (1994) and *Crash* (1996), had sold more than 13 million copies combined; *Before These Crowded Streets* (1998) and *Everyday* (2001) had each sold more than 3 million copies, and *Busted Stuff*, which came out a few months before I came on board, would eventually go double platinum. Beyond that, the band was one of the biggest concert draws in the world, one of the few groups that had come up in the Nineties that could rival Sixties legends like the Rolling Stones and Eighties icons like U2 on the stadium circuit. Over the years the group had built an extremely loyal and devoted audience through intensive touring, and while their following was often compared with that of the Grateful Dead, Dave Matthews's fans significantly differed in that they bought the band's albums in impressive numbers. As far as their business practices were concerned, the band and its manager, Coran Capshaw, famously ran a tight ship and functioned very efficiently and effectively as a team. They did not seek input from outside, and, as with most rock bands who live or die on the strength of their own songwriting and performance skills, I was perfectly content to let them carry on as they'd done so successfully without my participation.

Interestingly, the Dave Matthews Band had accomplished all that it did without any significant radio play; it was pretty much nonexistent as far as Top 40 radio was concerned, and for as many albums as they sold, the band never got the support of rock radio in a way that seemed commensurate. Consequently, in the back of my mind, I always wondered how big they could have become with more radio-friendly songs. I also got the impression from Bill Burrs and his rock promotion team that Dave and the band believed that they were coming up with songs to which radio would respond, and wondered why they weren't getting more exposure in that medium. They were wrong about their songs—whatever their otherwise strong virtues, they were not the sort of material that radio programmers would respond to—but their complaints suggested that they wanted radio play, which left open the possibility that at some point I might be able to help them. They had attempted to make an album with the producer Steve Lillywhite, a hit-maker who had worked extensively with U2, which they ultimately decided not to release, though it was widely bootlegged online. Dave also had co-written all the songs on *Everyday* with Glen Ballard, who produced the album and who is perhaps best known for co-writing and producing Alanis Morissette's blockbuster debut, *Jagged Little Pill*. Clearly, Dave and the band were seeking a route to the next level of success, though with mixed results.

As all this was going on, the band's contract with RCA was due to expire, and re-signing them became a major mission for me, Charles Goldstuck, and Ashley Newton, the label group's executive vice president of A&R. Along with its commercial prowess, the Dave Matthews Band had become symbolic of progressive-minded rock 'n' roll that could still reach millions of people. It was essential that we keep them on the label. It was a tough negotiation, but a fair one, and Dave ended up staying with RCA. For their 2005 album, *Stand Up,* the band was interested in exploring a funkier sound. The A&R man Bruce Flohr, who, along with his fellow A&R executive Peter Robinson, deserves the kudos for originally bringing the band to RCA, introduced Dave to the producer and songwriter Mark Batson, who had worked with the likes of India.Arie, Eminem, and Anthony Hamilton. Batson ended up producing *Stand Up,* and he and Dave co-wrote all but one of the album's songs together. When that album was near completion, I remember Bruce playing it for me and saying, "Isn't this great? There's going to be one radio smash after another." Personally, I thought that "American Baby," which would become the band's only Top 20 hit to date, was a really good cut, but Bruce was talking about six or seven cuts, and I just didn't hear it that way. Some of them had the glimmerings of possibility for radio, but they needed additional work. I remember saying, "Bruce, I appreciate your playing this for me, but it's so late in the process. I have to ask you personally, are you going to ask the group to do more work to develop some of these cuts? With further development, there could be strong potential here. But as it is, I don't think much will happen with this album, at least as far as radio is concerned." Bruce assured me that, yes, they were going to do further work on the album. But I tend to think he was just being polite, and had played the album for me as a courtesy. In any event, nothing meaningful was done to the tracks, and, beyond "American Baby," nothing much happened on radio for the album, which eventually did have the momentum to go platinum, but sold fewer than any other of the band's albums.

In 2007, when the band was getting ready to work on its next studio album, *Big Whiskey & the GrooGrux King* (2009), I called Dave and asked to meet him one-on-one in my office. He agreed. Dave is laid-back to the point of seeming casual, but nothing in conversation gets by him. I saw no point in not speaking as directly as possible. When he came in, I simply said, "I completely respect your independence, and I also respect what you've achieved so far both in record sales and in live concerts. But I see a noticeably declining album sales history, and it's my job to at least talk about it with you. You haven't yet seen any decline as a live act, and you haven't lost any of your stature, but you're not selling albums the way you used to. There's so much more potential for you and the band. Would you consider working with a stronger producer?"

I was surprised and pleased by his response. He said, "Your timing couldn't be better. In the past I might have resisted a suggestion like this. I know you're pretty hands-on, and I appreciate that you've always let us do what we want. But now I'm open to considering any ideas you might have. Who do you have in mind for us to work with?" I mentioned a few names, and one of them was Rob Cavallo, who had produced Green Day. Rob eventually met with Dave and ended up producing *Big Whiskey*. Dave and the band wrote some tracks and submitted them to Rob and me for our input, and that process was moving along nicely until my corporate role changed and I was no longer in charge of the RCA Music Group. In any event, *Big Whiskey & the GrooGrux King* went platinum and earned two Grammy nominations, including one for Album of the Year. The Dave Matthews Band continues to be a dominant force on the concert stage, and their most recent album, *Away from the World*, released just last fall, debuted at number one on *Billboard*'s album chart. The group took their time in recording the album, and it paid off with strong reviews and sales. The Dave Matthews Band is still delivering quality music and riding high.

The Foo Fighters were another major rock group on RCA when I arrived. The band initially arose out of the ashes of Nirvana, when, after Kurt Cobain's death, the band's drummer, Dave Grohl, stepped into the front man's role as singer, guitarist, and songwriter of a new "group"—in fact, Grohl essentially recorded the first album on his own, and only later turned the Foo Fighters into a band. The Foos' first two albums, which both went platinum, were released on Capitol. But then Gary Gersh, who had signed the Foo Fighters to the label and whom Grohl had known since Gersh signed Nirvana to Geffen Records, was fired from his position as president of Capitol. Grohl's contract had a "key man" clause that allowed him to leave Capitol if Gersh did, so he went searching for a new label. Bruce Flohr, instrumental in signing Dave Matthews, also nabbed the Foo Fighters for RCA, a terrific coup. Eventually, I re-signed the group to RCA when its contract came up for renewal.

I always held the Foo Fighters in extremely high regard, and got along very well with Dave and the other very able members of the group. There are plenty of ways to relate to artists—you may recall, for example, my tic-tac-toe engagement with Jerry Garcia at the Rainbow

Room. With the Foo Fighters it was Ping-Pong. I visited them in the studio one day, and there was a Ping-Pong table available for anyone in need of distraction, as musicians often are when they're recording. As it happens—and as is not widely known—I'm a good Ping-Pong player, and the band and I really got into it. Some musicians get excited about the legendary artists you've discovered or with whom you've worked; others bond with you because you shock them with your Ping-Pong skills. The Foo Fighters and I have remained good friends since that day. Along with their astute manager, John Silva, they're regular attendees of my pre-Grammy party and opened the show one year, dedicating "Best of You," their only Top 20 hit, to me. I was also a guest at Dave's wedding to Jordyn Blum, whose father I knew from my days at CBS. Dave even initially considered calling the Foo Fighters' *Greatest Hits* album *An Embarrassment of Riches* because he was struck by that expression when I used it to describe the band's 2005 double album, *In Your Honor,* when he first played it for me. As with the Dave Matthews Band, the Foo Fighters had complete creative control over their music. They would play each album for me and Ashley Newton after it was completed, and then we would come up with a plan to bring it to the marketplace with as much energy as we could muster. They were always great to work with and be around.

The Foo Fighters have emerged as major worldwide artists, capable of filling large venues not only in the United States but throughout Europe, Australia, and the Far East. The worldwide sales of each of their albums consistently go double platinum, and the band thrives in the rock world and dominates rock radio from the moment its albums are released. Their videos also have been very distinctive, always distinguished by twists of humor and personality, a rarity in the typically very earnest rock world. Dave, of course, has grown into a charismatic, outspoken front man and personality himself—a musician who deeply believes in and understands rock 'n' roll, but doesn't take himself too seriously. He's extremely bright and articulate, and very funny, an ideal interview subject, so the media loves him.

Within and beyond the music industry, the Foo Fighters have come to be seen as rock 'n' roll standard-bearers, as evidenced by the band's twenty-five Grammy nominations and eleven Grammy awards. I realize that in some critical quarters, the Foo Fighters may not be granted as high a place in the pantheon of rock bands as I would accord them, but I know that they will eventually be in the Rock and Roll Hall of Fame, and very deservedly so.

A significant RCA band that has not yet made the commercial impact that the Dave Matthews Band and the Foo Fighters have is the Strokes. Still, the band, who came to the label through the A&R man Steve Ralbovsky, was important for prestige and credibility. The group hails from New York, and its garage-rock sound recalls that city's downtown tradition, all the way back through punk to the Velvet Underground. That alone made the band the essence of critics' darlings. That the father of the lead singer, Julian Casablancas, was the founder of the Elite modeling agency ensured that the band's shows were packed with gorgeous young women, though the group members' scruffy good looks, don't-give-a-fuck fashion sense, and insouciant manner hardly hurt in that regard as well. As it happens, the Strokes' guitarist Albert Hammond, Jr., is the son and namesake of an artist with whom I had a noteworthy Top 5 hit in 1972, "It Never Rains in Southern California." Beyond their talent, which is considerable, and the freshness of their sound, the Strokes were plugged in in ways that guaranteed massive media attention. And they got it. The band released a three-song EP in early 2001 on the independent label Rough Trade, and the heated critical response, beginning in Britain and quickly jumping across the pond, incited a bidding war, which RCA managed to win.

When I was given responsibility for the label, the Strokes' 2001 debut album, the wryly titled *Is This It,* had already established them as a media sensation. It racked up platinum sales and ranked high on many of the year's critical Top 10 lists. It also proved extremely influential, triggering a garage-rock revival on both sides of the Atlantic. It remains one of the most important albums of the new century, and *Rolling Stone* ranked it among the five hundred best albums of all time. The band's three subsequent albums, over which they had complete creative control, have neither sold as well as *Is This It* nor equaled its significance. True to form, though, the Strokes remain international stars, touring and playing festivals around the world, and their album releases are events that reinforce their premier status in the rock community.

Another RCA band from the States that got its start through an enthusiastic response in the U.K. is Kings of Leon, who, like the Strokes, were brought to the label by Steve Ralbovsky. The original notion was that the band would be built around the singer, Caleb Followill and his brother Nathan, a drummer. Instead, they recruited their brother Jared on bass and their cousin Matthew Followill on guitar, and with their co-writer, Angelo Petraglia, made a five-song EP, *Holy Roller Novocaine* (2003), that made the group stars in the U.K. Later that year, the group released its debut album, *Youth & Young Manhood,* which did not break through in the United States but sold 750,000 copies around the world. The Followill brothers formed Kings of Leon in Nashville, but they're originally from Oklahoma. Their father is a Pentecostal preacher, a fact that very much informs their songwriting and that deeply intrigued overseas audiences, particularly in the U.K. and Australia.

That the band sold so well internationally convinced us that their commercial prospects were great, but our promotion staff were continually frustrated because we couldn't seem to find the right song to help the band catch fire on radio at home. Then, after the release of the band's second album, *Aha Shake Heartbreak,* in 2005, Volkswagen used "Molly's Chambers," a song that had appeared on both *Holy Roller Novocaine* and *Youth & Young Manhood,* in a television ad for its Jetta model. The song got a huge response and radio was begging for a single. Our promotion staff, led by the indefatigable Richard Palmese and his very talented and colorful rock promotion head, Bill Burrs, was champing at the bit, certain that we had finally found the song that would put Kings of Leon over the top in America. Unfortunately, the band felt that the song was old news, and refused to release it as a single. This is where you really need to have the courage of your convictions. It's one thing to speak in general terms about a band having complete creative control; it's quite another to know that you have a major opportunity to make a real commercial breakthrough, and to have the band flat-out refuse to go along. If you believe in the band, you have no choice but to rely on your faith that another, hopefully even better opportunity will present itself. Winning at the expense of losing the band's trust is never an effective long-term strategy.

Fortunately, that opportunity came along in 2008 with the release of *Only by the Night* and its breakthrough singles "Sex on Fire" and "Use Somebody." The band had not yet widely broken in the United States, and so to herald them I chose them for the "best new artist" spot to open my pre-Grammy party in 2009. They were about to explode. The album spanned two Grammy cycles, earning nominations for Best Rock Album and Best Rock Song ("Sex on Fire") and winning for Record of the Year ("Use Somebody"), Best Rock Song ("Use Somebody"), and twice in separate years for Best Rock Vocal Performance by a Duo or Group ("Sex on Fire," "Use Somebody"). Basically, when I started with the RCA Music Group, Kings of Leon were just about to release a debut EP, and I left just after their multiplatinum, Grammy-winning breakthrough. We had a great ride with them and their smart and seasoned managers, Jack Rovner, Ken Levitan, and Andy Mendelsohn. And even though the band is currently going through substance abuse problems and is on hiatus, I have every hope that they will return to the heights they previously achieved.

Clearly, RCA had a very solid foundation in rock when I arrived, but I did want us to make some new signings to make it even stronger. That opportunity came along when, with great fanfare, Velvet Revolver formed in 2003. It was usually categorized as a modern supergroup, featuring the guitarist Slash, the bassist Duff McKagan, and the drummer Matt Sorum of Guns N' Roses, plus the lead singer Scott Weiland of Stone Temple Pilots. The guitarist Dave Kushner, formerly of Wasted Youth, rounded out the lineup. Even with the deafeningly loud advance buzz about the band, it was by no means a sure thing. The members' history of drug problems was notorious; Weiland was even arrested and imprisoned as the band was working on its debut album. When he was released, the time he could spend with the band in the studio was limited because he had to live in a halfway house.

Nonetheless, interest in the band ran feverishly high, and RCA was competing against at least three other major labels. Apart from the health and stability of the group, my other concern was whether Velvet Revolver was just a patched-together group of former superstars or an actual band. In that sense, bands are like sports teams. You can have as many stars as you want, but unless they set their egos aside and perform as a unit, they're not going to win. In order to make sure that was the case, RCA's head of A&R, Ashley Newton, and I went to hear the band audition for us at Weiland's studio in the Toluca Lake section of Los Angeles. They played five songs in a small room with a pool table in it, and Ashley and I just sat there and listened. The band was on fire, completely riveting, and even in that small setting, Weiland was a captivating and galvanizing front man. The star power was absolutely there, but this was no by-the-numbers star turn. They played as if their lives depended on every note. Ashley and I were both sold: We had to sign this band. Unfortunately, I also thought I might have to be hospitalized by the time they were done. It might sound as if I'm joking, but I'm not. We were very close to and staring straight into their amps, and they blasted those songs at maximum volume. My ears rang and my head throbbed for days. I maintained a professional demeanor afterward as we told the band how impressed we were, but I was genuinely afraid that I had done some irreversible damage. Luckily, that proved not to be the case.

The assault on my senses aside, the entire situation was very seductive. The band members were obviously pleased that I had flown to Los Angeles to see them, and I knew that with all the media attention and label competition, if we signed Velvet Revolver it would be big news for RCA. However, the nature of the past drug problems still concerned me. The band members were all charismatic, but in any situation like that you wonder, Are they the masters of their fate? You know you're taking a risk. There was also the possibility that their egos would clash and split the band apart. I found myself wondering how long the whole thing would be able to last. It's like meeting people who have a history of serious problems and trying to gauge, Are they permanently cured? You almost have to be something of a fatalist and take a leap of faith.

I discussed all this with Ashley Newton and we both knew that as long as the group was stimulated musically, they would be hot together.

We just had to cross our fingers as to how long that would last. And in their own way each member of the band was hungry. For all the buzz, plenty of people had dismissed them as being drugged out and washed up. They desperately wanted to prove those people wrong. They all obviously believed that Velvet Revolver could be the perfect means of satisfying their desire to be back on top. So we signed them in August 2003. I was very flattered when Slash later explained in interviews that even though we may not have offered as much money as other labels, meeting me and knowing my track record of success made him feel that RCA was the best label for the band. I was optimistic. They were already pretty far along in their recording process, so the album was essentially completed by October, but we didn't release it until June 2004 due to continuing delays caused by Scott's legal problems. We launched it with a party on the roof of the Hotel Gansevoort in the Meatpacking District in New York, and it was a star-studded event. All the band members and their wives and girlfriends were there, and I specifically remember Sean Penn participating in the festivities. The album, aptly titled *Contraband,* entered the charts at number one, sold more than a quarter of a million copies in its first week, and eventually went double platinum. Velvet Revolver got three Grammy nominations, and won in the category of Best Hard Rock Performance for "Slither." They were back on top.

Unfortunately, as the band began working on the follow-up to *Contraband,* the demons that everyone knew had been lurking in the shadows began to impose themselves. They started to work with the celebrated producer Rick Rubin, but things didn't go smoothly and eventually they brought in Brendan O'Brien. At one point Scott came to believe that the other members were interested in re-forming Guns N' Roses, and that issue needed to be resolved. The entire process took so long that by the time the band's second album, *Libertad,* came out in July 2007, much of the momentum driving the group's career had dissipated. The album peaked at number five and eventually went gold, but it was certainly a less stellar showing than that of the debut. Then, while the group was on tour, Scott's drug problems resurfaced and he eventually left the band, which caused the group to go on hiatus.

Ironically, given his fears about Guns N' Roses, Scott since has rejoined Stone Temple Pilots.

Perhaps it was predictable that Velvet Revolver would not survive for long, but it certainly made a big impact with its first album and solidified RCA's eminent standing in the rock genre. Slash was always the band member I was closest to, and our relationship continues. He's been extremely gracious about playing my pre-Grammy party, performing with musicians ranging from Lou Reed to Fergie, along with opening the party one year with a blazing performance by Velvet Revolver. He is, needless to say, a masterful player and a pleasure to work with, and I remain grateful that he did not forever damage my hearing.

Even though she's not a rock artist, I should mention that probably the most successful act on RCA when I arrived was Christina Aguilera. She was signed to the label while still a teenager by Ron Fair, who was senior vice president of A&R. Ron had her do a live audition in his office, and with the strength of Christina's voice, I can only imagine how powerful an experience it was to hear her in that intimate context. Her debut album, *Christina Aguilera,* released in 1999, sold 8 million copies in the United States and more than that in the rest of the world, making her an instant superstar. She also won the Best New Artist Grammy. To follow up her debut, she did an album in Spanish titled *Mi Reflejo,* which sold 3 million copies worldwide. Following a Christmas album, her next one, *Stripped,* came out just before I arrived at RCA, and the first single from it, "Dirrty," barely cracked the Top 50, which definitely caused some concern, given her previous run of hits. She had changed her image and was far more sexually provocative, which not all of her fans responded to. Fortunately, the next single, "Beautiful," written by the very successful composer Linda Perry, went to number two, and it became the commercial cornerstone of her album, which went on to be certified four times platinum. The song also earned Christina a Grammy for Best Female Pop Vocal Performance. Ironically, Christina was competing in that category against Kelly Clarkson, whose entry, "Miss Independent," Christina had co-written with Rhett Lawrence and Matt Morris. It had been intended for *Stripped,* though she never finished recording it. I was gathering material for Kelly's debut album, and Christina did not realize that Rhett Lawrence had offered us the song for Kelly. Meanwhile, I was under the impression that he had cleared it with her. Initially, Christina was upset, but eventually the situation sorted itself out.

Next, Christina wanted to release a double album, which is always a tough call for a record company. Even for a proven seller like Christina, it's asking a lot of fans to expect them to pay that kind of money, particularly in an environment in which sales across the board are shrinking. However, while I might have fought such a decision more strenuously with another artist or under other circumstances, I felt that Christina had earned the right to a project like this. She had put up big numbers in the past, was a hard worker, and definitely had her own opinions. What point would there have been in trying to stop her? As always, I made the commercial obstacles involved with releasing a double album clear to her, but it was her decision finally and I deferred to what she felt was best. She has the top manager in the business, Irving Azoff, and together they have guided the major decisions in her career. I always understood that *Back to Basics* was a very personal project for Christina. One disc was a collaboration with DJ Premier, the other with Linda Perry, with Christina co-writing virtually all of the album's twenty-two songs. The album was definitely entertaining as well as a creative leap, but without the kind of definitive single that would drive sales, *Back to Basics* stalled, though it did debut at number one and eventually went platinum. Perhaps the conclusion of the *Rolling Stone* review of the album expressed it best: "At one disc, this would have been nothing short of masterful." Of course, Christina is another artist with strong international appeal, so worldwide sales of the album were about 5 million.

Since then Christina has fought to maintain her commercial standing, which will invariably rise and fall depending on the strength of the hits on her albums. Like Maroon 5, her career got a strong positive jolt from her duet with Adam Levine on the huge number-one single "Moves Like Jagger," which was a massive hit around the world. Her role as a judge on *The Voice* has also renewed her visibility, and nicely positions her for success approaching the scale she has previously enjoyed. With the right material I believe Christina could once again rise to those heights. She certainly has a valuable platform on *The Voice*. That a singer with her talent and track record would require a television show to reinforce her stature speaks to the state of the music industry these days, and leads us to our next subject.

American Idol and Kelly Clarkson

*A*merican *Idol* has suffered a ratings downturn lately, but its problems in many ways stem from its phenomenal success. From 2005 through 2011 it was the most watched television series in the United States, making it one of the most successful shows in television history. That spectacular level of success is almost impossible to sustain even under the best of circumstances. Now, however, *Idol* is competing against a raft of other reality talent shows that have risen up in its wake. One thing can't be questioned: During a decade in which the music industry seemed increasingly to fragment and contract, *American Idol* provided a tremendously exciting environment in which a mass audience could intensely engage with music and emotionally relate to the singers the show presented. No doubt, the format has its limitations: An artist as unique and individual as Alicia Keys is not going to be discovered on a show like *American Idol*. And it is not a show for specialists. Artists who excel in only one genre like rock will have a harder time than more versatile pop singers. After all, the show originated in Britain as *Pop Idol*. And the performance aspect of the show encourages a style of bravura singing that will draw a standing ovation and elicit an immediate emotional reaction from the television audience. Singers whose offbeat approaches are more indirectly insinuating and who work their magic over time will not win against someone whose voice can shake the rafters. The show is not about subtlety.

I get people's objections to *American Idol* in the same way that I understand that most rock critics are never going to support artists who don't write their own material, regardless of how talented they might be as singers. But from the moment the show was introduced in the

United States in 2002, I believed that it had great potential, and that's why I agreed to appear on it regularly for years as a mentor, judge, and guest. I knew Simon Fuller, who created and produced the show through his company 19 Entertainment, because he managed Annie Lennox, and we always had a good relationship. In addition, I knew Simon Cowell well because he had worked very successfully in A&R in Arista's London office. We spoke often as the show was being brought to the States. I knew that both of those men know how to win, so the prospects for the show looked very promising to me. Both Simons were clear-eyed, intelligent, determined, and ambitious. They generated big ideas, but those ideas were grounded firmly in their own experience and in a reliable sense of what they knew could be possible. That combination of pragmatism and vision is what I always look for in executives. Either virtue can make for a successful career, but both in combination is what creates people who can change the game. Simon Cowell and Simon Fuller are those kinds of people. BMG had the right to distribute music by *Idol* winners in the States as a result of a deal that Fuller had made in Britain for 19 Entertainment. According to the terms of the deal, BMG was required to release albums by the winner and the runner-up, and in addition could make deals with any of the other contestants it was interested in. That arrangement seemed like a real opportunity to me, so I was happy, indeed eager, to oversee all aspects of the production and release of those albums in the United States.

From today's vantage point, this simply sounds like common sense. Who wouldn't want to be as involved as possible with one of the most successful shows in television history? However, back then there was no guarantee that *American Idol* would be successful at all. In fact, the situation was quite the opposite. No one, and I mean no one, thought *American Idol* was going to be that big a deal when it was announced. The show auditioned every music industry–related person to be potential judges, and the three people they chose were not exactly high-profile figures who would attract attention and drive ratings. Talented and charismatic as he is, Simon Cowell was an A&R man in the U.K. and completely unknown in this country. Randy Jackson was a musician, producer, and A&R man in the States and was also unknown to the general public. Paula Abdul had been a star, but her big hits had come years earlier. The co-hosts were also two unknowns: Ryan Seacrest and Brian Dunkleman. Fox began airing *Idol* in June as a summer replacement show, clearly a spin-off from the U.K. You do that when you're hedging your bets, waiting to see if the show manages to catch on, because viewership is down across the board at that time of year and the consequences for failure are relatively small.

Beyond that, talent competitions were considered cheesy. *Star Search,* the most recent show of that type, did nicely but did not signal that a revolution was in the offing when it aired from 1983 through 1995, though, tellingly, it was revived after the tidal wave of success of *American Idol.* It was essentially unthinkable that any important artist would emerge from a talent show. Yet, for a variety of reasons, I took the show very seriously from the beginning and wanted to get strongly behind it. From my own experience listening to *Major Bowes Amateur Hour* on the radio when I was a kid, I knew that if *American Idol* were done properly, audiences would really respond to it. People like to feel an emotional investment in a performer, and talent shows can materially build that connection—and a large potential following.

I never doubted the power of television. During my years at Columbia I saw firsthand the undeniable impact a weekly show could have on sales and careers with the likes of Mitch Miller, Andy Williams, Jim Nabors, and Johnny Cash. I took full advantage of outlets like *The Merv Griffin Show* to bring artists like Dionne Warwick and Whitney Houston before the public. Television is a rare medium that provides both intimacy and vast scale—millions of people feel as if they are experiencing performers very personally. Simon Cowell was unquestionably a believer and a pioneer here. We would often exult about the future of talent competitions as the elimination contest advanced and people formed a connection to specific performers. *American Idol* was capable of providing that type of powerful experience week after week. It would also have an effect well beyond the broadcasts themselves, as watercooler talk the next day would call attention to the show's performers, even from people who hadn't watched. Obviously, YouTube and other Internet sites would only maximize that impact even further when they came into existence.

Finally, I was happy that the show would grant a status to professional songwriters that they had not enjoyed in the post-Dylan world of self-contained artists who wrote their own material. I grew up in the world of Tin Pan Alley and the great Broadway songwriters who composed the standards that singers of succeeding generations would perform. That each week contestants would be asked to sing great songs of the past was very meaningful to me. Eventually, it seemed that every season someone performed songs that Whitney, for example, had made famous, which inevitably provoked a discussion among the judges, contestants, and viewers about the merits of Whitney's original performance and how the aspiring singer's version compared. The show restored respect for songwriters and singers like nothing else had done in many years.

I should say that, certainly in its early days, very few people were thinking in these terms about the show. I was concerned about a certain amount of personal image fallout, particularly in terms of my rock credentials. Many rock bands would not permit their songs to be used on the show. I had to make a call in order to try to get permission for a U2 song to be used, and the band's manager, Paul McGuinness, made it clear that it was only because I had personally made the request that the band granted permission for the song's use. These days, of course, everyone realizes the promotional power of *Idol* and all the shows like it, and U2 has actually performed on the show. Believe me, it was not like that in the beginning.

From the outset, in making albums with the singers from the show, I wanted to find the best songs possible in order to make the most credible records that I could. I had first-rate A&R men like Keith Naftaly, Steve Ferrara, and Larry Jackson working with me, and we searched for songs as if we were trying to find material for Whitney Houston. It was not an easy process at the time. Once an artist has a track record of selling millions of albums, songwriters line up to offer you their best songs. Since we were working with singers whose only reputation came from winning a talent contest, we had a much harder time. 19 Entertainment had locked down the show's contestants in contracts that guaranteed the company sizable percentages of all their activities, so in the early years they thought of whatever albums the contestants might make as little more than souvenirs that fans might purchase. That approach never even crossed my mind. It was essential to me that the albums be credible and that they contain songs that were potential hits. I felt that I was putting my reputation on the line. On the other hand, 19 wanted to get something recorded as quickly as possible and to get the singers out on the road as part of the "American Idol" tour. The company had a team of songwriters ready to provide material for the contestants so that 19 could participate even in the songwriting royalties. My team and I had something like ten weeks to find songs for the contestants on our own, which is a breakneck schedule. I know that Simon Fuller was shocked that I threw myself into the process of finding hit songs as seriously as I did. His team of managers would strongly favor the tour-and-merchandising prospects well ahead of making the album, and it repeatedly became a bone of contention between his company and us. But Simon is bright and shrewd, and he adapted quickly and was ultimately supportive. When platinum album followed platinum album he was profuse in his praise and his gratitude for validating the ultimate prize of his talent show. This had never happened on this scale before. The recording contract became invaluable and the nature of the competition became much more intense.

Just about all of the complexities of working with *American Idol* came into play with its first winner, Kelly Clarkson. Kelly obviously is very talented and has a big, powerful voice. I can't honestly say one way or the other whether I would have signed her if she had not been connected to the show. I did believe, however, that we could make very credible albums with her, and that was clearly established with her debut, *Thankful*, which came out in April 2003. Needless to say, it was extremely important to me that *Thankful* get a fair hearing, and that led to my first run-in with 19 Entertainment. As part of her deal with 19, Kelly had filmed a romantic comedy titled *From Justin to Kelly*, which co-starred another *Idol* contestant, Justin Guarini, who was the runner-up to Kelly in the show's first year. The plan was for the film to open shortly after the first season of *Idol* ended, and a few months before *Thankful* came out. The movie was screened in advance for me, and I was stunned by how bad it was. (This was not simply my own opinion, by the way; the movie has since been "honored" by the Golden Raspberry Awards, which annually note the worst in film, as the "Worst Musical of Our First 25 Years.") I was also terrified. *Thankful* was going to be the first album released by an *American Idol* winner, and this film was going to make it extremely difficult for anyone to take Kelly seriously, as if her association with a talent show wasn't enough of a problem in that regard. If the album was going to have any chance at all, the film's release had to be postponed until after the album came out. I couldn't take my concerns to Simon Fuller, because his brother Kim had written the film and, needless to say, 19 Entertainment had produced it. Personally, I was indebted to Simon for involving me in *American Idol,* so it was a conflict for me, too. But the film was just another easy way to cash in, consistent with the assumption that with all the *Idol* winners you just had to make your money while you can. So I became intent on doing whatever I could to delay its release.

I began by calling Kelly's lawyer, John Frankenheimer, whom I knew well, and telling him exactly this: "My God, John, we've got to get this film postponed. This is going to be really damaging to Kelly's career." I was concerned that there was lots of excitement about the film within the *Idol* camp; everyone involved was sure that it was going to be big. John told me to hold on for a week. Kelly was going to see the movie herself, and he would speak to her about it afterward. Once she had seen it, John called me and said, "Kelly doesn't think it's as bad as you do." At that point I was stymied. I was hoping Kelly would stand up and say that she wanted it postponed so that her album release would not be hurt by it. I suppose she thought she had no choice but to let the film come out as planned, given that she was managed by Simon and 19 Entertainment. I had to try a new approach.

I called a major television executive at 20th Century Fox, the company that was distributing the film. Again I explained the situation. Yes, the studio had the film, but it also had a vested interest in the TV show having credibility and in Kelly's album doing well. The more highly regarded the show and the bigger the star that Kelly became, the better the movie would do. Meanwhile, if the film tanked and the album tanked, it wouldn't do anyone any good. I essentially pleaded with Fox to postpone the release of the film and let the album have time to make its impact in the marketplace. My argument carried the day. *Thankful* was released in April 2003, and *From Justin to Kelly* opened in June. To this very minute few people have known that I helped delay the film's opening. I never discussed it with Simon, and I never discussed it with Kelly. Obviously, I had my label's interest in the album doing well, but I was primarily thinking about the show and Kelly's career as well. If the first album coming out of the show did not make a very substantial impact, *Idol* would have been seen as just another talent show and Kelly could have quickly vanished from the public eye, particularly if the movie were to reinforce a perception of the show as lightweight. As it is, the film came and went, grossing only $5 million in the United States, less than half of its budget, but *Thankful* established Kelly as a star and *American Idol* came to be seen as a major launching pad. Yet it was always within my consciousness that for Kelly to emerge as a real recording star we would have to diversify her credits and establish her identity independent of the show. When I met with the respected director Richard Curtis to obtain the rights to the soundtrack for his film *Love Actually,* starring Hugh Grant, he was at first reluctant to include a song by an *American Idol* contestant. I persuaded him that Kelly was a major future star, and then played him her recording of "The Trouble with Love Is." He liked it a lot, and agreed to use the song. It played over the credits sequence and was the lead cut on the soundtrack album, which also included songs by the likes of Joni Mitchell, Norah Jones, and Dido—not bad company for the winner of a talent contest.

We were on such tight deadlines with the *Idol* winners that we rarely had time to even speak with them about the material we were gathering for them to record for their first albums. Kelly won *Idol* with "A Moment Like This," a big, emotional ballad of the sort that became synonymous with the show. That song was released as a double–A side single, along with "Before Your Love," another massive ballad, written by Desmond Child and Cathy Dennis. The single was released before the album and went to number one. Given the power of Kelly's voice, however, Steve Ferrara, Keith Naftaly, and I felt that we could and must move her away from *American Idol* and its emphasis on melisma into more of a pop-rock direction. If it worked, such a move would provide her with an identity separate from the show, which would be vital for her in the long term. The track we picked to toughen up her sound was the appropriately titled "Miss Independence," co-written by Rhett

Lawrence, Matt Morris, and Christina Aguilera. At Keith Naftaly's suggestion, the title was changed to "Miss Independent." As previously mentioned, I didn't realize that Rhett had offered the song to us for Kelly without clearing it with Christina, and though Christina had decided not to use the song, she was distinctly miffed. (The problem was exacerbated when "Miss Independent" was nominated for a Grammy in the category of Best Female Pop Vocal Performance, only to lose to Christina's "Beautiful.") Eventually, everything was resolved between Christina and Kelly, but it was really bumpy for a while. *Thankful* became a number-one album and sold well over 2 million copies. In addition, the album got very respectable reviews and, overall, its performance lent major credibility to the *American Idol* franchise.

As Kelly was beginning to work on her second album, a song came in for her to do for the soundtrack of the 2004 film *Princess Diaries 2: Royal Engagement,* which Whitney Houston had co-produced. The song was "Breakaway," written by Avril Lavigne, Bridget Benenate, and Matthew Gerrard. At first Kelly didn't like it and didn't want to record it, but eventually she relented, and the song became a Top 10 hit for her. As we were gathering material for the album, however, I met with the songwriter-producer Max Martin, who had some songs he had written with his partner Luke Gottwald, better known as Dr. Luke, that he wanted to play for me. He told me that because of his extensive work with the likes of Britney Spears and the Backstreet Boys, he had somewhat gotten a reputation for softer pop artists, and he wanted these songs to be done by rock artists because he was tired of being typecast. The songs were "Since U Been Gone" and "Behind These Hazel Eyes." I heard them, and told him I really loved them both. Then I told him that I wanted them for Kelly Clarkson. He instantly lost his cool. "Are you crazy?" he said. "Didn't I tell you that I wanted these songs to go to rock artists? That I didn't want to be typecast? Now you want to give them to an *American Idol* winner!"

The fact is that I wanted Kelly to have those songs for the very reason that he had written them. Both songs had a sharp rock edge but were still capable of being pop hits. They would push Kelly in a promising direction for her, while maintaining and even growing her audience. I had a long relationship with Max dating back to Ace of Base, so

I was able to calm him down and try to reason with him. "You don't understand," I said. "Kelly's got a great voice, she's got real potential, and she likes edge. Look, you'll produce it. You'll get the right performance. If you don't get the right performance, I'll understand if you don't want to let the songs be used. But you've really got to give this a shot. I believe so firmly that this will be great for her. And for you." We spent a long time discussing it, and finally, based totally on my relationship with him, he said yes.

Max and Luke are very strong, hands-on producers in the studio. They are intent on getting the perfect vocal performance, and are relentless in that pursuit. It was hard for Kelly, who had come from the high of winning *American Idol* and then having a double-platinum debut album. You're young, everybody recognizes you everywhere you go. It's heady, and all that attention affects all *Idol* winners. But then suddenly you're in an entirely different world of making records in a studio, and you have to take direction. Kelly didn't like it. Max and Luke were merciless in pursuit of getting the right performance for their song. Kelly got her back up, and, from her perspective, she had a horrible experience in the studio. She'd never work with them again, she said. Then, after all the work was done, I listened to the performances. They were terrific. I could not have been more thrilled. This was a whole new direction for Kelly, so far away from "A Moment Like This," which defined her first year's experience. Obviously, "Miss Independent" was different as well, but this was really a strong rock-pop departure, and showed real depth and creativity. Everyone loved the end result, and I could just feel the momentum building.

Right around this time RCA was having an international convention in New York that I would be addressing. All the label heads from around the world would be there to establish our priorities for the coming year. I knew that with "Since U Been Gone" and "Behind These Hazel Eyes" we could make Kelly huge across the globe, not just for an audience that knew her from *American Idol*. I saw the whole picture in front of me of what could happen. I played the songs, and I said to the group gathered there, "I know you're setting your priority list for your own countries. I am telling you to forget that Kelly Clarkson is an *American Idol* winner. That is very narrowing, and it is no longer relevant in her case. You don't need the show to break these songs. I urge you to believe that both Kelly and these records are breakable in your country. She can be your next big pop artist. I have no doubt about it." I preached the Kelly gospel, played those two cuts, and the response was fantastic. On the basis of those two songs Kelly had been prioritized for massive worldwide success.

In the meantime, before any of this transpired, Kelly had requested a meeting with me, which was scheduled for the day after the international meeting. I was eager to tell her the incredible news about the response I got to her songs. We met in my office. Tom Ennis, an especially nice guy who had worked for me at Arista for many years and now worked for 19 Entertainment, Steve Ferrera, and I were there with Kelly. To this point I had never really spent much personal time with her, so I was looking forward to hearing what she had to say and to seeing how she would react to the news of the great response to her songs at the meeting the day before. Kelly began the meeting by saying, "I want to be direct and to the point. I hate 'Since U Been Gone,' and I hate 'Behind These Hazel Eyes.' I didn't like working with Max Martin and Dr. Luke, and I don't like the end product. I really want both songs off my album."

I sat there, shocked. It took a minute or so for me to absorb what she'd said, and when I responded I carefully watched my words. I said, "Believe me, Kelly, the last thing I want is for us to have a difference of opinion about your album, but this is a very touchy issue, and let me tell you why. I had to use a lot of personal leverage and persuasiveness to get those songs for you. We're dealing with one of the world's top producing teams, and you may not realize it, but there is still a taint connected with *American Idol*. You definitely don't have to work with Max and Luke again if the chemistry wasn't right for you. That's fine. And it might be a different thing if we hadn't already done these tracks and you were insisting that you didn't want to record them. I would respect that, even if I might try to convince you otherwise. But you have already recorded these songs, and they're sensational. I played them yesterday at our international convention, and the response was amazing. I've got the whole world excited for your album, and you are going to be the top international priority. Why? Because of 'Since U Been Gone' and 'Behind These Hazel Eyes.' I beg of you to understand the bigger picture here. Your first two singles must have tempo, must have drive, and must have edge. Consequently, I can't take them off the album. I just can't."

It was a very tough conversation, and it didn't get any easier when Kelly burst into hysterical sobbing. We all just sat there as she cried for several minutes. No one knew what to say. Then she left to go to the ladies' room. When she came back the tension in the room was thick. Finally, I said, "I don't know what to say. I feel terrible. Your career is really just beginning and I don't expect you to understand this, but I want you so much to love this record. What you're asking me to do is impossible. I've committed to all our executives all over the world. The stakes are just too high. 'Since U Been Gone' is going to be the first single, and it's going to be a game-changer for you." Kelly didn't say another word. She just looked at me with red, puffy eyes and a swollen face, and got up to leave. I truly felt awful. I've had differences of opinion with artists and my share of tough meetings, but I really had never been in a situation like that before.

Of course, the rest is history. "Breakaway," which became the title track, was released a few months before the album came out on November 30, 2004, but "Since U Been Gone" was the single that announced the album's release, and it exploded. It went to number two in the United States and, indeed, proved to be a hit around the world. "Behind These Hazel Eyes" followed it, and it, too, became a Top 10 hit in the States and an international smash. The third single, "Because of You," which Kelly wrote with David Hodges and Ben Moody, performed similarly well. In subsequent interviews Kelly said that she had to fight to get "Because of You" on the album, but that simply wasn't the case. I have no idea where she heard that, perhaps from someone intentionally trying to create trouble. Both Steve Ferrara and I loved the song and the record from the first listen and felt that it delivered on the promise that Kelly could indeed write hits. It is well known that we trumpeted it to everyone in promotion. Because of its tempo, I did say it should be the album's third or fourth single, but there was never any question that not only would it be included on the album, but that it would break out from the album as a single release. It's truly a shame that Kelly and I didn't have more direct contact to put the kibosh on such false information. That happens occasionally, and it's always damaging when there's little personal contact. The *Breakaway* album won a Grammy for Best Pop Vocal Album, and sold well over 6 million copies in the United States alone and nearly that many overseas. That's worldwide sales of almost 12 million! In addition, "Since U Been Gone" won a Grammy for Best Female Pop Vocal Performance.

The *Breakaway* album completely transformed Kelly's career and made her an international superstar, the number-one pop performer in the world. At no point, however, was there ever any personal acknowledgment from her that I had been right about "Since U Been Gone" and "Behind These Hazel Eyes," which are still the top signature songs of her career. At least Simon Fuller understood what I had done, and he was extremely grateful. He, Charles Goldstuck, and I had dinner together and he told me, "There is no *American Idol* that I ever want to do without you. It's unbelievable what you've done here." He knew how much the worldwide success of *Breakaway* had validated the *Idol* franchise. He was deeply respectful and appreciative of that, and I became a fixture on the show for several years. Despite her failure to personally acknowledge what I had done on her behalf, Kelly certainly carried her own weight on the project. Whether she liked them or not, her performances on those two giant hits and throughout the album as a whole were extraordinary. In promoting the album, she was extremely hardworking and totally professional. She traveled all over the world, worked her ass off, and her ever-growing audience became very devoted to her.

For her next album, Kelly decided that she wanted to move in a new direction from *Breakaway* and, as she thought of it, exercise a firmer grip on her career. She left 19, though she still was financially bound to the company, and got a new manager, Jeff Kwatinetz of the Firm. She also decided that she wanted to co-write all the material on the album. Historically, it's always worried me when I've heard pop singers say that, but I was open-minded about it in this case. Kelly had co-written "Because of You" on *Breakaway,* as well as "Walk Away," which nearly cracked the Top 10 and had done well around the world. Kwatinetz kept calling me to say that the new album was taking shape beautifully, that Kelly was "writing hit after hit," and that he heard five or six number ones on it. I told him I couldn't wait to hear it.

I eventually got a copy of the tracks she had recorded and listened to them by myself in my bungalow at the Beverly Hills Hotel. The only song I heard with anything like the potential to follow up the break-through of the *Breakaway* album was one called "Never Again." Even that song didn't sound like a number-one hit to me, but it was at least capable of making a strong showing on the charts, perhaps entering the Top 10. That was not true of anything else I heard on the album. I called Jeff and told him, "I've always said that I get paid a lot of money to worry, and now I'm worried. We don't have the hits here that you said we have." I explained that I was heading back to New York with the album and wanted to play it for Richard Palmese; Peter Gray, Richard's crackerjack head of national promotion; and Steve Ferrara to get their opinions, and I would get back to him right after that. When I played the album for Richard, Peter, and Steve, they agreed with me. The only song with any significant chart potential was "Never Again."

I then met with Kwatinetz and explained our views about the album. He simply said, "You're absolutely wrong, Clive. You're all wrong." He responded that the album, which would be titled *My December,* was deeply personal for Kelly, and it was important that it be released as it was. The album, it turns out, was about Kelly's breakup with David Hodges, who had previously co-written with her, and to my ears the songs were predominantly dreary. I told Jeff, who, after all, had only recently become Kelly's manager, "You know, I do have standing here far beyond just being head of the company." I explained all the work I'd personally done from the beginning to establish Kelly, the invaluable hit songs I had given her, the extensive effort that had been involved in distinguishing her from *American Idol,* the heavy investment the label had made in her career, and how extremely successful we had been. "I really don't want to hear a thing about the past," he told me. "You need to understand that what she has come up with for this album is magic. In fact, I am in the process of scheduling a worldwide arena tour for her to headline."

My response was very simple. "You are out of your mind," I said. "Your tour plan is suicidal. Let me do my job. We should all be on the same team." I know some of that sounds harsh, but I was not irascible. I was not intemperate. I calmly went on. "Look," I told him. "Our contract gives me the right to approve the material and not release this album if I don't want to. I'm not doing that. I'm also not going to hold up the release. But, I'm begging you, let me test these songs. We do market research all the time. We'll get a valuable pulse and an objective, independent point of view. It won't be me against you, or me against her. We'll get some time-tested, important information." Jeff finally said, "Okay, do your testing." (Record labels have for years paid to have records tested by independent market-research firms, not unlike what movie companies do when they test a film. A few hundred people are very selectively chosen as an ideal demographic sample. The record is played for them twice and the artist is identified. From the listeners' answers and reactions you can get a strong, and what I've found to be reliable, indication of how a record will perform.) So we did market research on seven or eight of the album's songs, which Jeff selected. My initial reaction was confirmed. "Never Again" came back as the album's only possible hit single. Nothing else remotely surfaced. I sent the information to Jeff and awaited his reply.

He called me and said that he had discussed the marketing results with Kelly. "She really doesn't care," he said. "She doesn't believe in testing. It's important for her as an artist to have the album come out as it is." I asked to meet with her personally, one-on-one. I flew to Los Angeles and the two of us met at my bungalow for a couple of hours. This time I was very direct. "I've got to give you my honest reaction," I said. "First of all, as far as I'm concerned, this has nothing to do with whether or not you wrote these songs or didn't write them. More than eighty percent of the artists I work with write their own material. I don't submit outside songs to Alicia Keys. I don't submit outside songs to the Foo Fighters. If you were Patti Smith we wouldn't ever be having this conversation. But we've got so much at stake here, and it's my job to put up cautionary flags when I see trouble ahead. You're following up a giant worldwide album, and your entire arena tour will be in instant jeopardy if you don't come out of the gate with big hits." I brought up the example of Pink and how a few years beforehand her album sales fell precipitously when she thought she was a rock artist and delivered an album without her usual quotient of pop hits. Pop artists must have a continuity of hit records, or their audience drastically falls away.

She said, "I understand what you're saying, but I don't care if I make any money. I don't need that much money to live." I really didn't know what to say to her when she told me that money wasn't important to her. I do, however, know what I wanted to say: "Well, money may not be important to you, but your lawyers are demanding a ten-million-dollar guarantee for this album, based on the performance of the *Breakaway* album, especially, ironically enough, 'Since U Been Gone' and 'Behind These Hazel Eyes.' Please explain to them how you don't care about money."

Of course, I didn't bring any of that up. It's never good to talk about money with artists. Still, it seemed hypocritical for her representatives to be making huge economic demands based on the performance of an album and songs that she had vigorously resisted while she was simultaneously insisting that she didn't care about money at all. As it happens, I have no choice but to care about money, and situations like this really test you. As I've noted, the *Breakaway* album sold nearly 12 million copies worldwide. It would have sold about 20 percent of that if I had agreed to take off the songs that Kelly told me point-blank to my face that she hated and wanted removed. Somehow, when artists and their representatives talk to you about how personally important an album is to them, they rarely complete that thought by adding, "In fact, it's so important that I'll do it for a much smaller guarantee." Their representatives don't allow it and it never happens. It's always "It's personally important to me" from the artist and "She'd like ten million dollars for it" from her lawyer.

I want to add here that I made it abundantly clear to Kelly in our conversation the difference between *My December* and Bruce Springsteen's *Nebraska* album. I explained that Bruce, whom I had helped sign to Columbia in the first place, had made five albums before he made *Nebraska*. In effect, he was saying, "Time out. This is not a regular commercial release. I have to do *Nebraska* as a bleak meditation on the vanishing American Dream as the Reagan era dawns." If Kelly were similarly to have said, "Time out. This is an album devoted to the environment or to my appreciation of the influences that shaped me," she of course could have done that. But *My December* is not that. *My December* is a pure pop album about breaking up with your boyfriend. We're not dealing with "The answer is blowing in the wind." There's a big difference. One is an art album, filled with poetry and meaning; the other is a pop album that still needs pop hits. All of this was stated very straightforwardly by each of us. No one was shouting. In diplomatic terms I suppose you could say our meeting was candid. I also assured her that, while it was my responsibility to warn her of what I believed the pitfalls of her decision might be, I would release the album as it was, even though I was not obligated to, and we would promote it as hard as we could. It certainly wouldn't do me any good to have one of my major artists fail. I should also say, though I didn't mention it to her, that I was not going to pay $10 million or any significant sum at all for it. As a responsible executive, I couldn't possibly do that.

In trying to minimize any downside commercial damage, I suggested that we release "Never Again" as a single to see how it performed before committing to releasing the entire album. That idea was also rejected. Then we were all taken aback when Kelly and Kwatinetz launched what amounted to a media campaign pitting her against the label and, more specifically, me. She and Kwatinetz spoke to the press, insinuating that I did not want Kelly to write her own songs because she was a woman. (I wonder how they would explain that to Alicia Keys, Patti Smith, Sarah McLachlan, and Annie Lennox.) The rock press, of course, ate all this up. It became a David-and-Goliath battle between an all-powerful music mogul and a solitary young woman fighting bravely for the right to self-expression.

More personally, Kelly explained to a reporter that she told me, "I get you don't like the album. You're eighty—you're not supposed to like my album." And there I was, a mere seventy-four at the time! I had also never said I didn't like the album; I was focused on how it would perform commercially and its impact on Kelly's career. Simon Cowell leaped to my defense. "Clive Davis at eighty is better than ninety-nine percent of the people in the music business in their twenties, thirties, and forties," he said. Once I realized that Kelly would not pull back or agree to any safeguards, "Never Again" was released as a single in April 2007. We worked it hard and it peaked at number eight. None of the other three singles released from the album cracked the Top 100. *My December* began with strong momentum from the huge *Breakaway* album, and it debuted at number two and eventually was certified platinum, but it was a tremendous drop from *Breakaway*'s six-times-platinum sales in the United States. Kelly's arena tour had to be totally scrapped. She fired Kwatinetz and hired Narvel Blackstock, who is Reba McEntire's husband, to be her manager, and she posted the following statement on her website:

> *There has been quite a bit of controversy surrounding the release of* My December, *much of which has focused on a supposed feud with my record label, in particular, Clive Davis. I want to set the record straight on this by saying that I want my band, my advisors, those close to me and my record label to be one big, tightly knit family. Like any family we will disagree and argue sometimes but, in the end, it's respect and admiration that will keep us together. A lot has been made in the press about my relationship with Clive. Much of this has been blown way out of proportion and taken out of context. Contrary to recent characterizations in the press, I am well aware that Clive is one of the great record men of all time. He has been a key advisor and has been an important force in my success to date. He has also given me respect by releasing my album when he was not obligated to do so. I really regret how this has turned out and I apologize to those whom I have done disservice. I would never intentionally hurt anyone. I love music, and I love the people I am blessed to work with. I am happy that my team is behind me and I look forward to the future.*

With the air cleared, I did work on Kelly's 2009 album, *All I Ever Wanted*. One track I brought in was "My Life Would Suck Without You," written and produced by, lo and behold, Max Martin and Dr. Luke. Narvel Blackstock thought the song might be too explicit, so I had to assure him that "suck" had by now entered the language as a slang term acceptable even on mainstream television. Max and Luke, meanwhile, called in Claude Kelly to rework some of the lyrics to make the song less sexually explicit. I also arranged for Kelly to write with Ryan Tedder after I had worked with him when he co-wrote "Bleeding Love," the monster hit that launched Leona Lewis's debut album, which I co-produced. This linkup with Tedder led to controversy when Kelly came to feel that "Already Gone," which Tedder had written for the original demo, was too similar to "Halo," a single that he had co-written with and for Beyoncé. But even before that problem another issue arose. When Peter Ganbarg, who was helping do A&R for the album, brought me a second demo of "Already Gone" after Tedder did some additional co-writing with Kelly on the song, I was struck by how the lyrics had gone in a much different direction from when I first heard Tedder's original version. The lyrics were now much more bitter, and to me they were damaging the potential impact of the song. Peter was with me when I called Ryan to find out what had happened. He explained that the lyrics Kelly had written were indeed affecting the song that way, and he agreed it was to the song's detriment. I asked him to please go back to the original version and try to restore as much of that bittersweet, as opposed to bitter, feel as possible. He called me the very next day and told me he would be able to do that.

As for the relationship between "Already Gone" and "Halo," Ryan and Kelly had written their song first, but Beyoncé's single came out earlier. As a result, Kelly was incensed and tried to have "Already Gone" pulled off her album, but it was physically too late in the production process for that to be able to happen. She then repeatedly bad-mouthed the song in the press, despite its ironic emergence as a very big hit single for her. Her subsequent 2011 release, *Stronger,* has achieved considerable success triggered by the very powerful hit single "What Doesn't Kill You (Stronger)" and the album has been certified platinum.

It's clear that Kelly Clarkson has a decidedly independent streak, to say the least, and often speaks in public before she realizes the implications of what she's saying. She even made an enthusiastic statement in support of Ron Paul in a tweet during the 2011 Republican primary campaign without comprehending how that would infuriate many of her fans. Those fans, however, are also drawn to her shoot-from-the-hip style. She's definitely outspoken and has built a very loyal following that loves her for it. Indeed, on the strength of her entire body of work, Kelly is now fully established as a bona fide star. With the right future material she can once again enjoy the major level of success she attained with *Breakaway*.

More on the *Idol* Franchise

However complicated some issues got with Kelly Clarkson, our success with her definitely helped establish *American Idol* as a powerhouse franchise. Both casual music fans and industry insiders began to view the show as a potential launching pad for talent who could not only compete effectively against one another on a show, but who could go on to successful careers.

In the show's second season, Ruben Studdard edged out Clay Aiken as the winner, and as singers and people they could not have been more different. Independent of the show, I probably would have hesitated to sign either of them. They were both competent singers, but neither had that indefinable star quality I always look for in new artists. They definitely had talent, but somehow their charisma really derived from the TV show, not from themselves. Still, the close competition between them generated intense interest in the show that season. They each established a large fan base that was eager to hear more music from them, and I was confident that we could make credible albums with each of them.

Now that the show was established, it was an entirely different experience to meet the contestants. Typically, when you meet an artist who is just starting out, they might be known to their local fans or to a relatively small audience they built online or through performing live. In this case it was as if the *Idol* contestants were already stars, even before they had made a record. If you went out with them in public, people would call out to them by their first names as if they knew them personally—"Hey, Ruben!" "Hey, Clay!" It was a brand-new phenomenon, and, as it did with Kelly, it complicated the contestants' relationship with the record company, with producers and songwriters, and with me. However gifted you might be, singing on television and winning a talent contest is a very different experience from making an album that radio will want to play and that people will want to buy. The normal insecurity that accompanies anyone who is just about to sign their first record deal was complicated by the contestants' sense that, not to put too fine a point on it, they were idols already. People were kowtowing to them at the same time that, underneath it all, they understood that there was still plenty for them to learn. It certainly made for some interesting times.

I met Ruben and Clay together, along with the two other finalists that year, at my bungalow at the Beverly Hills Hotel. To speak in somewhat stereotypical terms, Ruben was like a big, huggable soul man. Clay, too, was much like the character he portrayed on the show, a very likable nerd who was shedding his awkwardness as styling and the confidence of his appeal to audiences actually started to shape who he was. He became a hero of the socially awkward. I told Ruben and Clay that I was going to be looking for material for them because they were rehearsing for the "American Idol" summer tour of one-nighters. In each case, a single would be released before their album came out. For Clay it was "This Is the Night," which was, in effect, the finale song of the show. ("Bridge over Troubled Water" was the other song for the double–A side single.) Ruben's song was "Flying Without Wings," which had been a hit in the U.K. for the Irish boy band Westlife, but was unknown in the States. Both songs exploded, "This Is the Night" particularly so. It went to number one and held Ruben's "Flying Without Wings" at number two.

With respect to Ruben, I knew that the pop, Broadway, and country material he was being asked to sing during the *Idol* sessions was not at all reflective of who he was. He definitely had a more urban sensibility. We would have to find a balance of material that represented how the *American Idol* audience had come to know him combined with songs that reflected what he really loved and the artist he wanted to be. Clay was the only one at the meeting who really spoke up with a definite point of view. He wanted to make sure that there was no off-color language in any of his material or any sexual innuendo. He didn't care what it took to have a hit. He did not want material that did not speak for his values or that made him feel uncomfortable in any way.

Now, this was 2003 and we had not yet arrived at the point where Cee-Lo Green could enjoy a massive hit with a song called "Fuck You." Still, even mainstream artists were pushing the boundaries of what could be said in pop songs at that time, and, while I understood that the *American Idol* audience was not exactly cutting-edge, one way of providing an artist with an identity separate from the show was to roughen the edges of their songs, as our experience with Kelly Clarkson proved. Clay made it clear that that could never be the strategy with him, which raised the bar of difficulty in that regard. Still, he had a large, rabid following that had already begun to dub themselves "Clay-mates" and "Claymaniacs," and they would provide a very solid base.

Steve Ferrara and I got twelve strong songs in for Clay, written by the likes of Desmond Child, Kara DioGuardi, Rick Nowels, and Jimmy Harry. Beyond the conversation we'd had in Los Angeles, we had no time for additional discussions about the type of material to choose. I invited Clay to my weekend home in Pound Ridge to hear the songs we'd selected and to get his feedback. We went into my office in the main house and listened together to one song after another. It went as smoothly as could be. Clay had not been the most expressive or open person in the world, but he made it very clear that he liked all the songs. He said he was very apprehensive in approaching listening to the material, but honestly felt we really had done a good job. I would have preferred that he call the album *Clay Aiken,* in part to take as full advantage as possible of his *American Idol* visibility. Clay balked at that. He chose the title *Measure of a Man* from a track on the album that had been co-written by Cathy Dennis, and we went along with him. The album entered the charts at number one, selling an amazing 613,000 copies in its first week, and was eventually certified double platinum.

I do believe that Clay could have made an even stronger showing if we had not been hamstrung in terms of the type of material he would be willing to record. He quoted me in *Time* as saying that I wanted him to put "some balls" on his album, and while I don't specifically recall putting it quite that way, it's close enough. I often sent him back to the studio to rerecord his vocals in the effort to get something that was

honest, strong, and deep, not mechanical. As so many of the *Idol* singers have done, when I pushed Clay to try something with a bit more
edge, he pointed out that 12 million people had voted for him on *Idol*
for doing just what he wanted to do, just for being who he was. Fair
enough. But selling an album is not a popularity contest. There's a big
difference between motivating someone to vote for you in a talent show
and inspiring them to open up their wallets and buy your album. "This
Is the Night" is a very strong song, but it was a souvenir of the show,
and he had to get beyond that for the album. When you're aspiring to
become a career recording artist, the stakes automatically become different. Clay could no longer depend upon material like that. People
want to see if you can stretch and evolve. They definitely want to know
if you have some edge. I explained to him that you can't be paralyzed
by what the *Idol* audience expects of you. You're now competing against
many other artists in a much different context, and if you allow the
television audience to program your music, you will not be on the radio
and you won't be on MTV. And then where are you? You have to stay
ahead of the curve.

Clay, for his part, made it very clear that that was not how he viewed
himself. Though eventually he would come out as being gay, Clay grew
up in the South and was raised a Southern Baptist, a faith to which he
has returned. I believe he saw himself as having something like a mandate from America not to do suggestive songs. I could tell this was real
on his part, his honest conviction. In his geek-to-chic transformation
he very much viewed himself as the underdog who had triumphed.
That was fine and, I thought, accurate. But you can't pigeonhole yourself to do only sweet songs or love songs or uplifting songs. I didn't
need really suggestive songs, but I did need songs with edge. Clay didn't
at all realize how fickle the public can be and that making the transition from *American Idol* to recording artist was not merely an option
that happened to be put on the table, it was essential to his commercial
survival. Given all the issues in play working with Clay, it was decided
that his next project, scheduled for 2004, would be a holiday album. It
was as safe a choice as could be and the one that made the most sense.
Obviously, that type of song would not bruise anyone's sensibility or
raise controversial issues. Indeed, Clay's album nuzzled close to the

contemporary-Christian audience, a following that Clay encouraged without ultimately wanting to be limited by that niche category. Titled *Merry Christmas with Love,* the album went platinum and was the best-selling holiday album of that year and the next. More than merely a placeholder, the album sustained the aura of success surrounding Clay, which is precisely what it was meant to do.

But to use a biblical reference that Clay would likely recognize, the writing was on the wall. The more Clay toured and gave interviews expounding on his views, the less likely it was that he would ever be perceived as a Top 40 artist again. Despite still being in his twenties, he had become an adult-contemporary artist, and our best bet would be to treat him as such. It's not a category that triggers explosive sales, but whatever we were going to get from him we would get on that basis. Top 40 radio was not even a consideration at this point.

The album *A Thousand Different Ways* came out in 2006 and was co-produced by Jaymes Foster, who is David Foster's sister. (Two years later she would give birth to Clay's son, Parker Foster Aiken.) I've always loved the song "Without You," which was written by Pete Ham and Tom Evans of Badfinger and which Harry Nilsson helped make famous. I recommended it to Clay for the album, which included ten covers among its fourteen tracks. It did get some airplay and became a Top 40 adult-contemporary hit. The album sold more than 200,000 copies in its first week and was eventually certified gold. Clay was still successful but attrition had clearly set in, and by the time Clay began working on his 2008 album *On My Way Here* it was evident that he personally was not at all interested in any further guidance. Clay wanted to oversee the album on his own, and he brought in the producer Kipper, who had worked closely with Sting, with Jaymes Foster serving as executive producer. The album, his last for RCA, sold fewer than 200,000 copies, and his next album, *Tried and True,* a 2010 release on Decca, sold fewer than half of that. Of course, Clay has stayed active as a recording artist; he released an album on Verve in 2012 titled *Steadfast,* but by this time his audience had almost entirely disappeared. He has done some television work, and he performed in the Broadway production of *Monty Python's Spamalot.* He is active in causes that are important to him, like antibullying, AIDS relief, gay rights, and various children's issues. Like many performers who enjoy huge early success before they're knowledgeable enough or emotionally ready for it, Clay still seems to be searching for what he truly wants to do.

With Ruben, as I mentioned, we started out trying to strike a balance on his debut album, giving the pop-oriented *Idol* audience some measure of what he had done on the show and finding other songs that Ruben personally felt were closer to who he was. Ruben did have an urban sensibility and we wanted to reflect that. So on his 2003 album, *Soulful,* we addressed the *Idol* audience with "Flying Without Wings" and covers of the standards "For All We Know," the Bee Gees' "How Can You Mend a Broken Heart," and "Superstar," co-written by Leon Russell and Bonnie Bramlett and best known in versions by the Carpenters and Luther Vandross. Luther, the ultimate romantic R&B crooner, was the obvious model for Ruben. Unlike Clay, who could be somewhat unemotional at times, Ruben did generate electricity. Audiences loved him, and "Ru-BEN" became his fans' battle cry. Still, although he was professional, competent, and very likable, he was not a superstar or an artist with Luther's extraordinary gifts. But because he did have talent and the *American Idol* platform, we were able to interest writers and producers in the urban community to come on board for his album. Ruben was always excited when I told him that Larry Jackson, the A&R man who tirelessly worked with me on his project, and I were trying to attract the likes of Missy Elliott or R. Kelly to work with him. We ultimately couldn't deliver them, but we did uncover a very strong song composed by Harvey Mason and Damon Thomas with three other writers, called "Sorry 2004." That song became a big Top 10 pop hit for Ruben and a number-two R&B hit. "Superstar" also went to number two on the R&B chart. So the *Soulful* album successfully went close to double platinum, and we succeeded in establishing a real base for Ruben.

Similarly to Clay, we took Ruben out of the radio sweepstakes with his second album, a Gospel collection called *I Need an Angel* that came out in 2004. The title song was written by R. Kelly, and the album went gold, but Ruben was now following a trajectory similar to Clay Aiken's, with declining sales. We then made a renewed serious commitment to Ruben for his third album, *The Return,* which came out in 2006. We took him in a strong contemporary R&B direction and recruited top-name producers like Ne-Yo, Stargate, the Underdogs, Scott Storch, and, once again, Harvey Mason and Damon Thomas. But notwithstanding the fact that there was one semisuccessful single on the album called "Change Me," it failed to deliver meaningful sales. It's as if fans were gripped by Ruben as an emerging talent, but once he had arrived his gift just wasn't strong enough to compel his audience to stay with him. When that kind of decline occurs, disgruntlement typically follows, and unfortunately that was the case with Ruben. As an *Idol* winner, Ruben brought a certain set of expectations with him. How can you be a household name and not continue to sell albums? We tried to make the most of his *American Idol* stature while also separating him from it so that he could have a shot at an ongoing career. Ultimately, we did have success with Ruben, though not lasting success. Like Clay, Ruben has continued to record without making measurable impact, and has also tried his hand at acting. Clay and Ruben have even successfully toured together, a fresh way to take advantage of the enormous notoriety they earned through *Idol.*

Occasionally, you come across an artist whom you not only respect but personally like, and that was the case for me with Fantasia, the *American Idol* winner in the show's third season. She was very different from most of the contestants in that her edges were still very apparent while not at all detracting from her charm. In fact, they contributed to it. You knew she was soulful—you could hear it and feel it and see it. The only question was how well she would fit into a pop show, and she ended up doing a terrific job. She is an example of an *Idol* artist whom I would have definitely signed, totally independent of the show. You really believed Fantasia when she sang, and there's probably no higher compliment you can give a young performer than that. At the end of that season it came down to Fantasia and Diana DeGarmo, and they each recorded a version of the coronation song "I Believe," a new song co-written by a previous *Idol* finalist, Tamyra Gray. Fantasia's version went to number one and ended up being the best-selling single of 2004. Diana DeGarmo does have genuine talent, but I confess that

I was personally rooting for Fantasia to win. I loved her grit. There was simply nothing manufactured about her.

As the show was coming down to the finals, I was asked to choose songs for the contestants. The songs were supposed to be relevant to my own career, so I chose "The Greatest Love of All" for Fantasia. She did a beautiful job with it, and came out the winner. Interestingly, Jennifer Hudson was also a contestant on the show during this season, and she was eliminated surprisingly early. That gave rise to accusations of racism, since Ruben had won the year before and it was said that fans didn't want to see the contest come down to a vote between Fantasia and Jennifer, two African-American artists. The week after Jennifer left the show, Fantasia dedicated her performance of Gloria Estefan's "Get on Your Feet" to her. In her autobiography, *Life Is Not a Fairy Tale,* Fantasia recalled meeting me just before the top-three competition and my saying, "I want you to go out there and sing like you ain't never sang before!" To which she replied, "Yes, sir!"

After Fantasia won, I invited her to my office so I could get a better understanding of her and what type of material would work best for her. I played a few songs for her, and she enthusiastically responded. "Clive, you are gangsta!" she said. So, as with Ruben, we were in the position of making an album that would meet the expectations of fans who had seen Fantasia on *American Idol* and that would also help establish her as an urban artist. Her debut album, *Free Yourself,* came out in November 2004, cracked *Billboard*'s Top 10, and had major sales just shy of 2 million copies. Missy Elliott and Rodney Jerkins co-wrote songs for it, including the title track, and Jermaine Dupri and Soulshock & Karlin were among the producers. Very impressively, Fantasia received three Grammy nominations for the album, all in R&B categories. At my Grammy party in 2005, she performed the Gershwins' "Summertime" as a duet with Chaka Khan to a truly tumultuous response.

With Fantasia, however, we ran into another set of vexing problems that would be common with *Idol* contestants. It's important, particularly for urban artists, to visit radio stations, get to know radio programmers, do interviews with DJs, and perform at the stations' charity events. It's demanding and time-consuming, but essential. When you come up normally as a recording artist, as, for example, Usher and Alicia Keys did, you automatically learn that, and astute managers and record company executives will reinforce it. With Fantasia and the other *Idol* winners generally, when those requests came along they always had something else they had to do related to *Idol*. It wasn't really the artists' fault. In Fantasia's case her management purely and simply was not at all sympathetic to how important it was to court urban radio. They just saw it as a niche promotional activity for which she wasn't getting paid, so their impulse was to blow it off. It made for tremendous tension in trying to arrange for Fantasia to do those highly significant tasks, and it hurt her in radio's eyes. It seemed to them as if she didn't care.

Despite those problems, there's no question that *Free Yourself* had very successfully established Fantasia, though, perhaps inevitably, the sales decline that has affected so many of the *Idol* contestants set in with the next album, *Fantasia,* which came out in 2006. The album did go gold and she received two Grammy nominations. There still was some momentum behind her, and with no other distractions I believe that Fantasia's recording career would have taken root just like Kelly Clarkson's and Carrie Underwood's have. But Fantasia's life has taken some unfortunate turns, causing her a great deal of pain and public drama and making her a tabloid regular and a reality-show star. On the more positive side, she did a wonderful job assuming the lead role in *The Color Purple* on Broadway. She stopped the show a few times with her emotive singing, and all I could feel was pain that her tremendous potential was being sidetracked by the obstacles in her way. Fantasia played herself in a very strong performance in a Lifetime biopic based on her autobiography, and she definitely remains a legitimate artist. Like Mary J. Blige, she makes no effort to conceal her hard times and the impact those experiences have had on her. Through her music, she makes people feel the honesty of who she is, and she enables her audience to know that they're listening to her highly personal rendition of her deeply personal truths.

Carrie Underwood, who won the fourth season of *American Idol,* is probably the most successful artist that the show has produced. Kelly Clarkson might have been bigger internationally, but, for the most part,

Carrie has sustained the magnitude of her success in the United States, and she's quite distinctive in that regard. In her heart Carrie always wanted to be a country singer, which makes her *Idol* success, in which she was required to sing all kinds of material, even more impressive. The night I was a guest judge on the show and had to pick the songs for contestants to sing, I chose Roy Orbison's "Crying" for her. It's a classic song that straddles country and pop, and it needs not only a big voice but one that can bring out all the song's emotion. Roy Orbison had done a brilliant job with it, needless to say, as did k.d. lang in her captivating rendition. Meanwhile, Carrie picked "Making Love out of Nothing at All," a Jim Steinman song that I had once found for Air Supply. I told Carrie that I thought country pop was her forte, but she intuitively moved in a straight country direction.

When it was time to make an album with her, no one had demonstrated that *Idol* could have an impact in the world of pure country, so it made sense to consider how pop music might be part of what she did. She had built a base of millions of fans by winning on *Idol,* and it seemed like a commercial risk to forget that and make her debut album pure country, as both Carrie and 19 Entertainment would have liked. Finally, we decided to divide the album so that Joe Galante's Arista Nashville division would come up with at least half of it, with an eye to country radio and its requirements for all-important radio singles. I was given the other half to come up with songs that would bridge the album to the tastes of the *American Idol* audience that was waiting there to be tapped. So there was a hybrid approach, a balance, as we had attempted with the urban audience for Ruben Studdard and Fantasia. As it turned out, the country songs for Carrie's debut album, *Some Hearts,* proved to be very special. "Before He Cheats," "Jesus, Take the Wheel," and "Wasted" all became number-one country songs. The album included the *Idol* finale song, "Inside Your Heaven," which Desmond Child produced and which was a number-one pop hit. But from the beginning, Carrie made it clear that even though she had won *Idol* with that song and she liked it, she had not chosen it and she thought of herself as a country girl.

Some Hearts was an enormous success and went on to sell more than 7 million copies. It made Carrie a country superstar. Along with winning a Grammy for Best Female Country Vocal Performance for "Jesus, Take the Wheel" (she won that category again the following year with "Before He Cheats"), she also won for Best New Artist, only the second time a country artist had won that category and the first time an *American Idol* winner had even been nominated in it. Personally, I would have liked Carrie on subsequent albums to show her versatility and for her pop side to be more represented. I foresaw a return to what Shania Twain and Faith Hill had been able to accomplish, as demonstrated by what Taylor Swift has subsequently been able to do. At that time, however, Arista Nashville understandably did not want to dilute who Carrie had become with shots at crossover hits, but there's no question that she still has that crossover potential, where she can be both a country artist and a pop artist at the same time. I paid tribute to her and to the success of *Some Hearts* on *American Idol* in 2007, when I was asked to present her with the award certifying six-times-platinum sales for the album.

The ride that Carrie has been enjoying has truly been extraordinary. Her second album, *Carnival Ride,* came out in 2007 and was a complete country effort with no attempt to have pop overtly represented on it. Despite that, it went to number one on the pop charts, selling more than half a million copies in its first week and eventually going triple platinum. It also made history by becoming the first album ever by a female solo country artist to have five number-one country singles. She won another Best Female Country Vocal Grammy for "Last Name," her third in a row. Her third album, *Play On,* came out in November 2009, and had three number-one country singles: "Cowboy Casanova," "Temporary Home," and "Undo It." It's been certified double platinum. Of some concern is that her 2012 album, *Blown Away,* has sales below the commercial standard that Carrie has set for herself. Without a doubt, though, *Blown Away,* which has already achieved platinum sales, will be among the biggest albums of the year. Carrie's career has soared high, and I know it will continue its extraordinary arc. Carrie is singing better than ever. She's much more comfortable in her own skin and she's totally left her *American Idol* roots behind her. She's now firmly established as one of the queens of country music.

To me Chris Daughtry was the true bright spot of the fifth season of *American Idol*. Taylor Hicks and Katharine McPhee were the winner and the runner-up, respectively, but neither signaled that they would become major recording artists. *Rolling Stone* said it best when the magazine was handicapping the *Idol* race in April 2006 and picked Taylor Hicks to come in fourth, behind Katharine McPhee, Daughtry, and Kellie Pickler. The magazine called Chris "the best male singer in the competition and the only contestant who already seems like a pro." By the time I got to be on the judges' panel and had the chance to select songs for the finalists, Daughtry had already been eliminated. That's too bad, because he would have had dibs on Springsteen's "Dancing in the Dark," but since he was out of the running, the song went to Taylor, who was not quite up to the challenge. But Taylor was a good-looking guy and an engaging personality and he won the competition. There was a lot of surprise when Chris was eliminated, and a good deal of valid chatter online and elsewhere wondering if I would sign him. He was invited to audition to be the lead singer for Fuel, an offer that he appreciated but declined.

I had always felt during the competition that Chris was very talented, and I wanted to meet with him to see what his vision was for himself at this point. It would be the first time that anyone who had finished fourth would get signed. By this time we had four seasons of *American Idol* under our belt, but he was different from the other artists from the show with whom I had worked. There was a genuine rock overtone with him, but the reality was that he would have to have pop hits. Both his singing and his persona made it clear that there was no question that he qualified in the rock category. Yet he would not have a successful album if he were dependent only on rock material that did not cross over. My instinct was that he would be able to walk that line successfully.

This is what Daughtry told *Billboard:* "They basically have the option to sign you. That's their choice; you're not obligated to anything coming off the show, especially if you don't win. I was just very fortunate that Clive wanted to work with me, and I thought 19 [Entertainment] did a great job with us on the show. So I decided to stay with them. But my arm wasn't twisted to do anything I didn't want to. I'm glad I didn't win simply because I was able to form a band and come out as a band, not just Chris Daughtry. All I ever wanted to be was part of a successful rock band." And that's exactly how Chris presented himself to me when we met, that he would be the leader of a rock band called Daughtry.

Nevertheless, if you look at the cover of the first album, it's Chris front and center with the other band members behind him and out of focus, so it's not as though he suddenly receded into becoming just another member of the band. We brought in Howard Benson to produce the album, for which Chris wrote or co-wrote most of the songs, though Pete Ganbarg and I did solicit some songs for him and we suggested some collaborations. For the most part, though, we considered the process as nurturing Chris as a writer and artist, as well as shaping a debut album. Chris recorded the album with session musicians, while pulling his band together.

When I auditioned Chris and he articulated his vision of wanting to be in a rock band and said that he could write, I asked him to play some of the songs he'd written to see if they would hold up. He played "Home," and although he played a few others as well I basically heard that song and said, "You got it." It was obvious to me that "Home," which has since become a staple on *American Idol,* was a strong song and really showed that he had talent as a writer and that this could work. So he did write virtually all of his debut album, though we did submit "Feels Like Tonight," written by Max Martin, Dr. Luke, and Shep Solomon, and "What About Now," by Ben Moody, David Hodges, and Josh Hartzler.

Chris's fans from *American Idol* created a strong groundswell of support for him, and the band's 2006 debut album, *Daughtry,* entered the charts at number two and sold more than 300,000 copies in its first week. The album had a long life and eventually sold more than 4 million copies, while also receiving four Grammy nominations. It got play on both rock and pop radio and launched two Top 10 singles, "It's Not Over" and "Home." In promoting Daughtry, we deftly moved between the rock and pop audiences and, as a result, the album was consistently on the radio for well over two years.

Because the first album had been recorded with studio musicians,

Chris wanted the follow-up to be more of a collaborative band effort, so this time he co-wrote with band members as well as with outside writers like Chad Kroeger from Nickelback and Ben Moody and David Hodges. The album, also produced by Howard Benson, was recorded with the band actively participating in the arrangements. Titled *Leave This Town,* it came out in July 2009 and sold 270,000 copies in its first week, nearly as many as the debut. Although it eventually achieved very respectable platinum sales, it proved not to have the *Daughtry* album's hits or legs. The band's 2011 album, *Break the Spell,* went gold. It's a tough environment for rock bands in this day and age, but Daughtry are hanging in and still have a good following. I believe that Chris is one of the truly legitimate artists to have come out of *American Idol* and, thus far, he's the last contestant launched by the show to sell nearly 5 million copies.

I never got to work with Jennifer Hudson after she was an *Idol* contestant during season three, primarily because I couldn't take on both her and Fantasia at the same time. Was I impressed with her voice when I heard her on the show? Absolutely. Was I surprised that she was eliminated after she had gotten to the top seven? Without question. But since Fantasia had won, Jennifer just never came up for consideration because the material that Larry Jackson and I would be looking for would be so similar for each artist. It just would have been too tricky to navigate, finding the right songs and producers for two leading R&B female contestants from the same *Idol* season. So I focused on making Fantasia's album and Jennifer fell off my radar for a while.

In the meantime, Jennifer had tested for the coveted role of Effie White in the very-long-awaited film of the musical *Dreamgirls,* a role based loosely on Florence Ballard of the Supremes, who was marginalized when Berry Gordy decided to focus the spotlight on Diana Ross. Jennifer got back on my radar because Nicole David at the William Morris Agency sent me a copy of the full-blown screen-test audition that Jennifer had done. I knew she had been cast for the film, but I obviously had not previously seen her audition tape, and I was truly knocked out by it. Her raw honesty was searing. Her voice was powerful and so real. And could she soar! Those high notes were effortlessly delivered, and as a listener I sat there spellbound. I'm really indebted to Nicole. We had become good friends since she worked with Whitney Houston on all her film projects, and she was now also working with Alicia Keys. After watching the tape I just knew that Jennifer would be a household name once the film came out. Her film performance certainly proved to be one of the most vivid, meteoric, star-is-born moments in recent movie memory. She won every conceivable Best Supporting Actress award, including the Oscar in 2007.

Her debut album, *Jennifer Hudson,* came out in September 2008, and it dramatically entered the charts at number two, selling 217,000 copies in its first week. Stargate, Missy Elliott, Timbaland, and the Underdogs all produced strong tracks for it, but it's really difficult these days to find material for an artist with a voice as big as Jennifer's. R&B radio has been relegating big-voiced, ballad-singing artists to urban adult, which is a small fraction of the audience of urban mainstream. That's the challenge. How do you get mainstream recognition and accessibility for a singer like Jennifer? We wanted to mine the type of material that Jennifer had done for *Dreamgirls,* classic songs like "And I Am Telling You I'm Not Going," which we did include on the album. However, if she did only that type of song, we would be pitching her to a much smaller radio audience. Jennifer is the ultimate pro—an incredible vocal talent who came to every session totally prepared to sing whatever material Larry Jackson and I had chosen for her. We had strong success with "Spotlight," produced by Stargate and Ne-Yo, which became a number-one R&B single that crossed over to register as a Top 40 pop hit. And "If This Isn't Love" was a Top 10 R&B single.

Of course, far overwhelming the release of Jennifer's debut album were the shocking murders of her mother, brother, and nephew by the estranged husband of her older sister Julia. It completely shattered Jennifer, the sort of unspeakable personal tragedy that is nearly impossible to recover from. I went to Chicago for the funeral. It was heartbreaking to feel the pain throughout the church. Only their fervent religious faith could sustain her devastated family. Other than making sure Jennifer knew that I was available for anything she might need, I left her alone for a while to heal as best she could. Her first public appearance after the killings was in January 2009 when she sang the national anthem at the Super Bowl in Tampa. Her album had received four Grammy nominations, so she attended the Grammys in Los Angeles that February and won in the category of Best R&B Album. I was in touch with Jennifer right after New Year's and kept her informed about the album's success. She always instantly replied to my e-mails, and I knew she was grateful for both the good news and for the distraction. I was in constant communication with her dedicated manager, Damien Smith. Both Damien and I felt it would be a good tonic for Jennifer to perform at my pre-Grammy gala and for her to feel the love and support of her musical family. As you can imagine, Jennifer's appearance there was profoundly emotional and touched the heart of everyone in the ballroom.

Jennifer's second album, *I Remember Me,* which Larry Jackson and I again co-produced, also went gold. It features three tracks written or co-written by Alicia Keys, one by R. Kelly, and one by Diane Warren. Jennifer co-wrote the title track with Ryan Tedder, and the song expresses her desire to find herself again after the horrific tragedy that she endured. As part of that process, she has lost a substantial amount of weight and become the spokeswoman for Weight Watchers. She looks fantastic and exudes a positive attitude that inspires everyone who comes in contact with her. She is now a mother, and the joy she derives from her young son, David Jr., is indescribable.

We now are preparing to record Jennifer's third album. She has just finished shooting three films, all of which will be released this year. Jennifer is now focused solely on music and has never sounded better. In the CBS television special saluting Whitney last November, Jennifer performed a medley of Whitney's classic dance songs, and she brought down the house. She's projecting youth and vivacity. Yes, Jennifer faces challenges in today's contemporary R&B radio world, but she is simply so talented that I have no doubt that she has big albums in her future to go along with her major career in film and knockout touring performances.

Leona Lewis, finally, is an artist who didn't come to me through *American Idol* but through Simon Cowell in his role as a producer of *The X Factor,* which launched in the U.K. in 2004 and came to the States in 2011. Leona won the show during its third season in 2006. Simon and I had, of course, been in regular contact about *American Idol*, but one day he called me and said, "I've never approached you about any previous winner of *X Factor*, but we have a long relationship and I would love to work with you on the current winner, Leona Lewis. Please take the A&R lead on her album, and I'll stay involved. I think we can make a great album with her." He sent me all the reels of the shows that Leona had appeared on, and he sent her over to the States so that I could audition her. Once I heard Leona, it was a no-brainer. She clearly was a major talent. So Simon and I got to work on her album, and Steve Ferrara, Larry Jackson, and Sonny Takhar all participated in finding material. As with all the female *American Idol* winners, my primary concern was that we keep Leona's image and sound contemporary and avoid making her too much of a ballad singer. Because she was unknown in the United States, I organized a songwriters' conference at the Beverly Hilton Hotel in Los Angeles to introduce her. It was right around Grammy time in 2007, so everybody was in L.A., and the songwriting elite showed up so that they could hear Leona, get a sense of her, and see if they could come up with great songs for her debut album, which would be called *Spirit*. One of the writers at that summit was Ryan Tedder, and he said, "Clive may have used an old-fashioned technique, but . . . just about every hit she had from the *Spirit* album came from the people in that room."

Ryan was very impressed with Leona's singing, and he submitted the song "Bleeding Love," which he had co-written with Jesse McCartney for Jesse's forthcoming album. McCartney's label, Hollywood Records, had passed on the song, and Ryan was incensed. He was convinced that it was going to be a giant hit, and so he rearranged it for Leona, confident that she would nail it. He was right on all counts. The song is spectacular, Leona killed it, and it became a number-one hit around the world. Andrea Martin and J. R. Rotem were also at the songwriters' summit, and they submitted "Better in Time," which also became a big worldwide hit. Both those singles were not only hits, but they were the kind of songs that help create the image of an artist and make you want to hear more from them. They were the absolute definition of the type of singles that drive album sales. Leona was nominated for three

Grammys, and performed in 2010 at my pre-Grammy party. The album was just shy of double platinum in the United States and was a monster hit album elsewhere, selling more than 8 million copies around the world. Leona had certainly made her mark.

When it came to the follow-up album to *Spirit,* unfortunately, the signals among the various people working with her on it got somewhat crossed. Indeed, the album got off to an awkward start when several of its unfinished songs were leaked and posted on the Internet. The perpetrator, the aptly named DJ Stolen, had hacked the computer system of her U.K. record label, and ended up serving jail time for his thievery. Beyond that, Leona, who had two co-writing credits on *Spirit,* was being encouraged to write by her management, and once word of that got out to the songwriting community, it was difficult to get the best material from potential collaborators. Justin Timberlake, Ryan Tedder, and Max Martin did participate in the album, but Leona ended up co-writing nine of the album's thirteen songs. As usual in the case of pop artists, this unexpected turn was ill-advised. I certainly raised my warning flag. It really didn't turn into a battle, but to me the focus of the album, which came out in 2009 and was titled *Echo,* was off. While the songs Leona wound up with were fine, there was no single with the force of "Bleeding Love" to define and propel the project. Consequently, while *Echo* sold something like 2.5 million copies worldwide, it didn't even go gold in the United States. That international number is nothing to scoff at, and Leona can still headline arenas outside the States as she prepares for her third album. But there's little doubt that *Echo* didn't capitalize on the momentum that *Spirit* had built.

In the last few years, the world of reality talent shows has become much more competitive. They still are prominent in the ratings but their audience size and share have been steadily declining. And the winners of *American Idol* or *The X Factor* or *The Voice* just don't sell albums anywhere near what they used to. In the case of *Idol,* I don't think the competition has produced a genuine star since Carrie Underwood or Chris Daughtry. I do have to add that Simon Fuller, eager not to rock the boat and get into management battles with his contest winners, has ceded too much of the recording process and creative decisions to those winners. There was an awful lot written in the press about the writing talent of the new winners, with most of the articles expounding on their vision for themselves as recording artists. Of course it is important and indeed necessary to know what artists envision for themselves, but a convincing case can be made for questioning how much autonomy should be allotted to a career that's barely been born. No one wins a talent contest because of material they've written. At the beginning of their careers, brand-new pop artists very much need hits to be launched, and history has shown that wise professional advice and expert guidance don't hurt one bit.

Accepting Change and
Moving Forward

Shortly after I learned in 1999 that a plan had been hatched to separate me from Arista Records, a friend recommended the book *Who Moved My Cheese? An Amazing Way to Deal with Change in Your Work and in Your Life* by Spencer Johnson, M.D. As the best self-help books do, it provides a clear, concise, comprehensible way of thinking about problems that you're experiencing and suggests smart, incisive ways of addressing them. It proved immensely helpful to me. The book is a fable in which two mice and two "little people" discover that their source of cheese, which had been reassuringly reliable for a long time, had disappeared. Each of the characters responds to this loss in a different way, from anger and bitterness to acceptance and a determination to forge ahead and locate new supplies of cheese. The book's moral is not that change is good or bad; it might be either, with all the consequent emotions. But, regardless of how permanent any specific circumstance might feel, change is inevitable. Understanding that, preparing for it, and moving forward confidently is therefore an essential life strategy.

I found *Who Moved My Cheese?* valuable back then as I moved through something like the stages of grief, first grappling with the loss of Arista and then forging ahead to launch a dynamic, unprecedented new venture, J Records. And, in the way life unfolds, I found myself thinking about the book again in April 2008 when I met with Rolf Schmidt-Holtz, who was running all of Sony BMG Music Entertainment at the time. At that meeting I was informed that there was going to be a major reorganization. My right-hand man and chief operating officer, Charles Goldstuck, was being let go. I was being asked to assume the new position of chief creative officer for Sony Music Entertainment, and taking my current position as the head of BMG North America would be Barry Weiss, who had been president and CEO of the Zomba label group, succeeding Clive Calder, with whom he had worked closely over the years. The positive news was that in my new job I would be free to work with artists across the entire Sony BMG conglomerate. The bad news was that I would no longer be overseeing the operations of the RCA Music Group and, worse still, my working relationship with Charles, which had been the most satisfying of my life, would be over. We were as close as family. Charles is extremely able and eminently trustworthy, simply a terrific person. We had worked shoulder to shoulder to establish J and then to take over the RCA Music Group and BMG North America, a run of success that was more than a worthy follow-up to even my best years at Columbia and Arista. As far as his professional life went, I had no question that Charles would be fine. Indeed, he has gone on to take over as CEO of TouchTunes Interactive Networks, the world's largest manufacturer and distributor of pay-for-play digital jukeboxes, a business that he has dramatically and very successfully expanded. But both Charles and I felt that our work together, first at Arista and then at BMG, had just reached a point where we could really address not only our own business, but some of the larger issues that had come to vex the music industry in the twenty-first century. With Charles's fascination with the digital world, my creative track record, and our combined business savvy, we believed that we were ideally placed to help define the future of the music business. Then the cheese got moved.

So what happened? To answer that we have to look back to 2004, when the Sony BMG merger took place. The thinking at the time, and the thinking that still persists among the few major labels left standing, is that you have to merge in order to build muscle and market share. Charles and I had nothing to do with the planning of the merger. We had proven at the end of our time with Arista and during our years with J and the RCA and BMG groups that you didn't have to be huge to be successful. You just had to be deft and good, and make your impact with consistency. At BMG, at least as Charles and I experienced it in the North American context of the business, we were very much a culture shaped by the goal of best maximizing our business. We created and moved in an entrepreneurial, artist-development-oriented culture. And bear in mind, as we did indeed maximize our business, we personally did exceptionally well financially, and our parent company did even better. Everybody had the same objective, and everybody won.

With the merger, things necessarily changed. Because of its size and scale, Sony was really in the driver's seat. Andy Lack, who had made his reputation at CBS News and NBC News, was made the CEO of Sony BMG, and Howard Stringer, the well-known, well-respected chairman and CEO of Sony, a true renaissance man, was overseeing the entire worldwide operation. As the companies began to come together, we heard that eyebrows were being raised because of how much money it looked like Charles and I were earning. If you'll recall, after Bertelsmann paid Clive Calder $2.7 billion, a brilliant Calder–Allen Grubman special, I was asked to restructure my deal so that I wouldn't be able to ask for a similar, immediate onetime payout on anything like that scale. Grubman had also been, and still was, my lawyer, so he, Charles, and I structured a new deal in which BMG purchased the 50 percent of J that it didn't already own as part of a profit-sharing arrangement spread out over five years. As I was put in charge of more labels, those profits substantially grew, as did my compensation. We were on fire and earning more profits than they ever thought we would. When Andy Lack saw what I was being paid, he was reportedly shocked. To give you a sense of what kind of numbers we're talking about, in the three years from 2004 through 2006, I was paid more than $80 million. In the next two years, 2007 and 2008, I was paid just shy of $30 million.

Along with his salary, Charles was being paid a percentage of what I was getting, so, seen in isolation, his numbers looked wildly out of scale for his position. When the figures were looked at, I was most likely the highest-paid individual in all of Sony. How can that be? they must have thought. What everybody must have forgotten was that we had made our buyout deal at Bertelsmann's request, and essentially over five years we were being paid for our 50 percent ownership of J Records. The Sony BMG merger took place after our deal had been struck, so Sony had no role in it, and perhaps no one on the BMG side ever adequately explained it to them. What clearly could have been capitalized over that five-year period and not affected the bottom line was instead treated like ordinary expenses and charged to operating income each year.

To complicate matters further, in 2006 Rolf Schmidt-Holtz had offered Charles the position of COO of all of Sony BMG, but Charles had turned it down. One reason was that he would have had to relinquish his portion of our profit-sharing arrangement, so in financial terms, as prominent as the position was, it would have come at a significant cost to him. In addition, he believed that because of the competitive tension that already existed between certain Sony and BMG music executives as they jockeyed for power and position in the future corporate world order, he would never have been accepted in the COO role by the reigning Columbia and Epic music executives and his job would have been a constant battle. Finally, Charles knew that he and I were having just too much fun together. We'd made our move with J in 2000 and from there we'd gone from peak to peak. The position he was being offered might have been bigger corporately than what he had with me but he told me that it would be thankless.

Charles came to believe that Rolf never forgave him for turning the COO position down. How can someone refuse the number-two corporate role? The fact is that Charles was ready to run his own show, and Rolf was not prepared to leave music. He had come to see Charles as a potential threat. On the one hand, for years Rolf had often relied on Charles's perspective as issue after issue arose within BMG and then within the merged companies, and our long run of success had put unimpeachable substance behind Charles's views. However, by restructuring my position and getting rid of Charles, Rolf would be able to show how much he could save in costs. After all, I was seventy-six, and we shouldn't forget that in the Bertelsmann culture you had to leave the company when you were sixty. And Charles was now being perceived by Rolf as his competitor. In one quick stroke he could cut those costs and eliminate his potential rival.

It's ironic, but an indicator of how the cheese can move, that Rolf was such a champion of Charles every year beginning in 2000, and now in 2008 he came to my office to tell me he had to fire Charles because Charles wanted his job. Charles was stunned at Rolf's turning on him now. He knew that he had turned down the COO position, but betrayal? He felt that he had never betrayed Rolf with Howard Stringer or with anyone else. Since there's no way I would ever have agreed to Charles's termination, there was no doubt that it had to be done without me. So, the cheese was indeed being moved. What was I to do? Sony, and Rolf, were urging me to stay and offering me the title of Chief Creative Officer. I would have the expanded horizon of both Columbia and Epic in addition to the RCA Music Group to serve creatively and produce their artists. On a day-to-day basis, my circumstances would be made more than comfortable. I would get the most beautiful office, with a staff, on the top floor of Sony's great office building with breathtaking views of Manhattan and full access to Sony's world-class kitchen. It was a situation that not only could work but in which I could thrive. The temptation to launch a new venture again with Charles was definitely there but it really was impractical. I knew that Charles would land on his feet, and of course he has.

Consequently, I decided to stay at Sony, work within the structure I knew, and discover new cheese. It was not hard to find. I was still involved in projects with Whitney Houston, Carlos Santana, Jennifer Hudson, Leona Lewis, Rod Stewart, and Barry Manilow, and I was being offered Harry Connick, Jr., on Columbia. Now, frankly, if the hits were to stop, the fun would stop. You get a public report card from radio every Tuesday and from SoundScan every Wednesday. Failure is not a lot of fun. The love of music is very special but I have to admit that winning is part of the thrill. Whether you're an artist or an executive, there is the competitive factor: Everyone wants to have a number-one record, a gold or platinum album. That's true of new artists but especially true of established ones. The veterans have tasted success and they keenly want to taste it again. I don't care who the artist is and how many records he or she has sold before, that artist is hungry to still be on top. No one becomes immune to it. There is no elder statesman who does not want renewed success. There is no passive artist. Yes, there is the basic need on the true artist's part to create, but if there's no public, no breakthrough, no sales, the frustration and sharp disappointment are always there. That's why when Santana hit with *Supernatural* when he was fifty-two, he and it were genuinely acclaimed all over the world.

It made patently clear how long a career can last. I got tremendous personal pleasure when I reunited with Barry Manilow and his *Greatest Hits of the Fifties* album entered the charts at number one after his long absence from ruling the roost. So, in this period, continuing working with Santana, Manilow, and, of course, Rod Stewart's *Great American Songbook, Volume V,* kept my blood racing.

But it's the new records, reaching for new hits, that really tests you. I still never take anything for granted, and every weekend I still take home the new hits from every format and keep listening to make sure my ears are fresh and that I'm not going over the hill. In this business you have to keep proving yourself. They don't play your records because you discovered Joplin. And so, of course, I worry and prepare thoroughly to this very day. When "Bleeding Love" by Leona Lewis became the best-selling downloaded single of 2008 I breathed a sigh of relief. I celebrated her three Grammy nominations for 2009 with her at my pre-Grammy party, where she also performed. And despite not getting together officially to celebrate the terrific career Kelly Clarkson is now once again enjoying, I felt great that my ears were still working when "My Life Would Suck Without You" and "Already Gone" became big hits for her 2009 *All I Ever Wanted* album.

So I was busy. There was Jennifer Hudson and her successful debut album, which included "Spotlight." There were album presentations with Whitney in London, New York, and Los Angeles to launch the *I Look to You* album in 2009. Now, was it the same for me as running a label? No. I missed my wonderful team and all the action that I knew so well. Our Rolls-Royce was no more. But you don't look back. I really do count my blessings that at my age I'm still doing what I love. It's not always easy. Barry Weiss in his new position was always cordial and deferential but not readily forthcoming with new projects. All the artists and albums that came my way I had to truly earn from my past work with the artist or because Simon Cowell raised his hand that he wanted and needed me. But I didn't have to emerge from another's shadow, and it must have been tough for Barry to find his own space. He was careful to make sure that when I finished a project, all the necessary support was there as was the full opportunity for me to spearhead the marketing and promotion campaign. Barry left Sony in 2011 and since then he's sent me several warm and thoughtful e-mails to make sure I know of his continuing high regard and deep respect.

In 2011, the great record man Doug Morris was given the responsibility of running Sony Music Entertainment worldwide. He's been extremely welcoming, encouraging, and supportive from the start. We assembled a Whitney Houston greatest hits package this past fall. It includes a new version of "I Look to You" that I personally blended from a previously unheard Whitney vocal of the song and the powerful emotional rendition that R. Kelly delivered at her funeral service. In addition, with Doug's enthusiastic encouragement, I will once again be working with the great Aretha Franklin in 2013. She recently wrote me a letter declaring that she had left Arista in tears when we couldn't reach an agreement years ago. We're an unbeatable team, she said, and, in her words: "Gable and Lombard, Antony and Cleopatra, Clive and Aretha." Whatever the amusing hyperbole, who am I to disagree with the queen!

So it's been a wonderfully full life. I unexpectedly found both the passion of music and my career in the record business totally exhilarating—and, despite a few painful moments, fascinating and just plain fun. I've chronicled that fulfilling journey here because that's the main subject of this book. However, if that focus leaves you, the reader, with the impression that I had little or no life outside of work, let me correct that notion right now. First, I love my family, and since I don't believe in being a loving stranger, I make every effort to spend time with them. Each week I have dinner in New York with three of my kids, Fred, Lauren, and Doug—along with Fred's two sons, Austin and Charles, Fred's wife, Rona, and Lauren's husband, Julius, and their son, Matthew, and daughter, Hayley. That meal usually follows my custom from childhood of having Chinese food on Sunday, except during the summer, when some are in East Hampton and we do our best to schedule a weeknight in its place. My son Mitchell, his wife, Clare, and their son, Harper, and daughter, Sloane, live in Los Angeles, so when I'm there, which is about six times a year, we share at least one or two meals together on each visit.

In addition, I plan two vacations a year with the entire family, including, of course, my cousin Jo, who is an indispensable part of each of our lives. The big one occurs in the summer for ten days. I try to charter a boat to favored places like the Amalfi coast or the French Riviera or the Greek islands or, as we did this past summer, Spain. Having lost my parents when I was young, I know the enduring pain I still carry with me of missing them during my adult life. I try to instill in my offspring the love of family, knowing that in times of sickness or adversity, it's family members who feel the responsibility to be inconvenienced and to be there providing whatever you need. It's not that really good friends don't respond, but it takes the very special friend who feels that same responsibility—or is it guilt?—to go out of their way to care for you when it's difficult to spare the time.

I'm happy to say that I've built special friendships with about twenty people who have become like family to me over the years. My Pound Ridge home is where I spend every weekend when I'm in New York, and it's become a haven to me all year 'round. I listen to the records I bring home each week to study; I relax in a countrylike setting; and I watch a movie in a wonderful theater which comfortably seats about forty people. I love a good film and whether it's a new one like *Midnight in Paris* or classics that I want to revisit like *All About Eve* or *Network,* that's where I am every Saturday night from 6:30 to 9:00 before going out to dinner. I share these weekends with my friends. There are always at least two up there for the weekend, often four, and every Memorial Day weekend it's now a tradition for all nine of the bedrooms in the two houses on the property to be filled, along with several rooms in nearby inns. We gather on Friday night at one of the excellent restaurants in the area, and brunch on Saturday and Sunday, and dinner on Saturday, are catered for up to forty of us. Sunday night starts with a barbecue and ends in the theater with—of all things—Pound Ridge Idol! The competition is really serious in the warmest of atmospheres in which everyone is enthusiastically cheered on. It might sound hokey but it's stood the test of time, and each year everyone looks forward to this final night of what is always an unforgettable weekend. Finally, there is also a tradition of vacationing with these close friends during the summer. Whether it's a house in St. Tropez for one group or a boat cruising the Mediterranean with another, I do fill my annual five weeks of vacation with family members and family friends with the bonding that truly makes life a joy.

And so I come to the question: What about a relationship? Janet and I married in 1966 and, except for navigating tough issues like when my first wife, Helen, was to have her time with Fred and Lauren when they were young, all went well. I had just discovered music and its power over me, and my career thereafter took us to places and heights I never would have dreamed of. We had luxury and comfort neither of us ever expected. Then when I was fired from Columbia and a very tough two years ensued, Janet was ever loyal. In 1970 our son Mitchell was born, and in 1972 Douglas was born. We were at all times a family unit of six, as Fred and Lauren always lived with us. They were not half siblings; the four of them were brothers and sister through and through. We loved the period when Arista was born, and the rest of the Seventies were all wonderful. We had great friends and our life seemed complete.

But things eventually did change and we found ourselves arguing with each other more and more, sometimes about small, petty things but more often about Fred, Lauren, and Helen. Very distressingly, Janet and I gradually grew apart. I don't believe it was the fault of either of us. I believe we're both good people. But as too often happens in modern life, after a while I knew I was no longer in love. How I anguished over that! I never pictured myself twice divorced. I held on, felt real pain, and finally went to consult the psychiatrist Mitchell was seeing to help him figure out the complexity of dyslexia and its impact on his adolescence. Janet and I had been seeing the doctor along with Mitchell for over a year. We also took turns seeing him separately. At one of my solo meetings I confessed to the doctor that I didn't think the marriage was going to make it and that I felt terrible about it. I asked what the impact on Mitchell would be if I moved out. The psychiatrist sternly advised me that these were very sensitive and formative years for Mitchell and that my absence in the household could be and would be damaging. His advice was to stick it out for at least two years, and that's what I did. I would never do anything to hurt my son. Let me make it clear that at that point there was absolutely no one else in my life, nothing pulling me away. Janet and I thoroughly discussed the situation and we both agreed to stick it out. There was no hostility but it was really no picnic for either of us. Only then did intimacy between us stop even though we remained sleeping in the same bed. Relaxing, it wasn't!

And so it remained for the next two years. There was tension, but we remained a family and thankfully Mitchell grew stronger and more secure, and I knew I was doing the right thing. But there inevitably was emotional impact and fallout. It was still the era of Studio 54, which retained its uniquely seductive and sensual power. I had not had sex in several months when I was openly approached by a young man of about twenty-five who happened to be a huge music fan, which had led in previous months to many late-night conversations. A rapport had been built, and on this night, after imbibing enough alcohol, I was open to responding to his sexual overtures, my first such encounter with a male. Beyond my night journey back in the Seventies with Lou Reed, I had never been to a gay club or a gay bar, and all my sexual activity had very satisfactorily been with women. Was I nervous? Absolutely. Did the heavens open up? No. But it was satisfying.

During that encounter I found myself thinking back to a long conversation I once had in London with the singer-songwriter Harry Nilsson on the subject of homosexuality. Harry and I had become friends over the years, sharing a love of music and confiding in each other. As only Harry could so charmingly, he had waxed on, puzzled about why he always feared having sex with a man. He knew that he was straight to the core. He knew that he loved and was overwhelmingly attracted to women. But he wanted to face what he thought was an unnatural fear on his part. He vowed that at some point in his life he would muster up the courage to "do it." The worst that could happen, he thought, is that he would like it enough to repeat it if there was no woman around and he was horny.

I wondered for a time if that was true of me. I had to do considerable soul-searching and self-analysis. I didn't feel as if I had found, or was even searching for, my true self. I had not been at all repressed or confused during either of my marriages. I hadn't fantasized about men. I had never experimented during my adolescence or between my first and second marriages. I was not at all interested in anonymous sex. But sex with a male didn't repulse me, and it provided welcome relief.

I could be interested, however, only if there were sparks, if a real emotional connection took place. I didn't need a notch on my belt. I didn't need a conquest. I didn't need to prove to myself that I was still attractive. It was relationships that interested me.

And that's what happened after Janet and I separated in 1985. I entered into two successive sexual friendships with women, each for more than a year. Both women lived in Los Angeles, and the male with whom I had broken the ice at Studio 54 had moved there as well. So when I was in L.A. I saw him as well as each of the women I was involved with. I enjoyed my time with all of them and honestly felt I had no strong sexual preference. Naturally, all of this preoccupied me. I was now living a bisexual life, enjoying sex with two women and a man, each of whose company made me feel good. I was not looking for a lifestyle change. I had no inclination whatsoever for any club or bar life. I always enjoyed female company, the look of an attractive woman, the feminine perspective on things. But as a single male my friendships did broaden. There were married couples, gay couples, and single men and women, both straight and gay. A mixed group, based on my background and inclinations, was more comfortable for me.

I was working through the complexity of my personal life. Everything stayed outside the public glare as I tried to figure out my new bisexuality. To my intense disappointment when I did try to probe all this in conversation with others, it turned out that no one really believed in bisexuality. Heterosexuals and homosexuals alike didn't credit one word of any explanation I offered. In their eyes it was as simple as could be: If at any time, for any reason, you had sex with a man, you were gay. That's all there was to it. The fact that you liked sex with women as well didn't matter. As has been said: "You're either gay, straight, or lying."

Well, I knew that to be a lie. I knew what was true for me, and I knew what was true for many others I'd come to observe over the years. So I tried to custom-craft a life for myself that felt good amid all this genuine unrest. Basically, I'm totally relationship-oriented. My two marriages had failed but neither failed for sexual reasons. I don't regret either marriage and I have two wonderful children from each who are as fully a part of me as are my grandchildren.

In 1990 I entered into a monogamous relationship with a man. He was a doctor—I obviously couldn't escape the profession all Jews put on a pedestal—who had kept his preferences to himself and away from his family and the partners in his medical practice. He had three best friends—all straight women—so we had a very diverse group of close friends with whom we shared our life for the next thirteen years. We had separate apartments in the same building. Eventually, each of us had personal discussions with our respective families. Everyone was totally supportive, except that my son Mitchell had a tough adjustment period. What was my life like before I married his mother? Is that what broke up the marriage? I had been such a strong role model for him that he was really shaken and repeatedly asked me those questions. I assured him that I was exactly the same person he knew. I was only asking his acceptance of my bisexuality. After one very trying year, the issue became totally resolved between us.

Thereafter, what most defined my attitude toward my personal life was my strong feeling that I didn't want to be typecast. That was a primary reason why I've never gone public. I could certainly see the benefits to others from David Geffen and other prominent people revealing their homosexuality, but to me, admitting you're bisexual is to invite derision from all sides with no one ultimately benefiting. I'd privately experienced that to a great extent, and the notion of facing it in the public sphere seemed both daunting and pointless. Maybe that's an excuse for not being more courageous, but that's what I genuinely felt.

My relationship with the doctor ended in 2004. He longed to live outside of New York and subsequently did receive a terrific career opportunity, at least tripling his income. We remain bonded and close friends. After a year I met another special man and we have been in a strong monogamous relationship for the last seven years. Do I feel I could have been similarly attracted to a woman? The answer is yes. I know bisexuality really exists and I also know that society is moving forward ever so slowly on these issues. There's definitely been progress on the acceptance of same-sex marriage, but resistance is still very strong. Still, I know the future is absolutely clear. There will come a time when very few will care about other people's sexual preference—or preferences. I don't think that's wishful thinking. I just know that bias against gays and lesbians will diminish with each passing year.

And what about the misunderstood bisexual? Well, as I write this—on the very day, in fact, during the second week of August 2012—an article in *New York* magazine coincidentally has appeared declaring, "It was only last August that an academic study finally suggested that men who claimed attraction to both genders might not be hedging their bets or fooling themselves. Bisexuals might even outnumber gays and lesbians combined." I hope with all my heart that the issue of sexual preference and the prejudicial attitudes concerning it recede into the past and become matters of purely historical interest to all generations to come.

Finally, what is patently clear is that openness in all areas of life is an important component of happiness and success. Professionally, I've tried to remain open to all varieties of greatness and to not limit myself with too narrow a definition of what kind of music to make. Working with Barry Manilow or Gil Scott-Heron, Whitney Houston or Patti Smith, Bruce Springsteen or Alicia Keys—each of those artists had a remarkable contribution to make, and it was very fulfilling to help them realize their vision. Similarly, I've loved working with both artists and executives, helping to create timeless music and making business decisions about how best to get that music to the public. The worlds of art and business are not as separate as they might seem, and moving in both allows a three-dimensional view of the creative life that brings greater understanding and greater satisfaction. It also allows for more opportunities for collaboration, one of the greatest pleasures of my working life. Hiring the best people makes you better, and enlivens every aspect of all your tasks.

Much has changed in the music business over the past decade, most notably the challenges that digital culture has brought about. Beyond wanting to make sure that my labels' releases took advantage of the highest-quality technology available, I had never paid much attention to the various means through which music reached the public. I always believed it was most important to concentrate on the quality of the music itself. Beyond technology, a seismic shift took place when consumers, particularly young consumers, came to believe that all music should be free. It is now a life-or-death struggle for the music industry to educate the public that artists and other copyright holders need to be compensated for their work and investment in the creation of music. Progress is being made in that regard. The sizable and steady declines in sales have been arrested. I believe the industry is back on its way to growth.

I am confident about the future of the music business because I have no doubts about the value of what we are selling. Has music become a vestigial love, a nostalgic thing of the past? Far from it. Music means as much to people as it ever has. That makes me optimistic. But the digital era has raised another concern. As electronic dance music grows increasingly popular, artists have grown more faceless. Audiences seem to have lost interest in artists and what they have to say. In such a world where will the next Dylan and Springsteen, the next Patti Smith and Alicia Keys, come from?

I can't pretend that I have all the answers to these questions, but I believe that such innovative artists will come again. When I see unique artists like Adele and Mumford & Sons have so much success, I know that it's possible for the industry to attain great heights again, both artistically and commercially. Things might never be the same, but when do things ever remain the same? Music still plays an absolutely essential role in people's lives, and as long as that's true, a vital industry will exist to make sure that audiences discover the artists who can satisfy their souls.

On a more personal front, the tradition of my annual pre-Grammy party continues. This event has already become an institution, but it has taken on even more significance as the music industry has plateaued and fewer and fewer events aspire to bring the best of the music world together and pay tribute to the art form that has meant so much to all of us. When I left my position as head of BMG North America, I was fully prepared to underwrite any shortfall not covered by the party's sponsors, when Neil Portnow, the forward-thinking chairman of the National Association of Recording Arts and Sciences (NARAS), the organization that oversees the Grammys, contacted me and offered that NARAS officially make the party a Grammy-week event and that NARAS co-host with me. The party is still going strong—more exclusive, more unique, and more festive than ever.

And, now, coming all the way full circle, I'm about to realize another of my life's dreams: producing a Broadway musical. As I write this I'm about to close a deal to stage with Roger Berlind, Scott Landis, and the Jimmy Nederlander organization a revival of *My Fair Lady*, which is a fantasy come true for a variety of reasons. A Lerner and Loewe masterpiece, it is not only quite possibly the greatest musical of all time, but is a show that represented a pinnacle for Columbia Records and for my early mentor Goddard Lieberson. He was the man who taught me how to be true to myself within a corporate structure, a lesson I'm still living decades later. The *My Fair Lady* project, then, represents a nod to the beginning of a journey into the heart of music that has brought me more thrills and enriched my life beyond anything I ever could have imagined.

As important as love and work are, however, they're still not everything. It's essential to give something back and help the larger world beyond your family, friends, and colleagues. I thought long and hard about the best and most meaningful way I could help others. I've always been involved with philanthropic organizations, but in recent years I've had the good fortune and deeply satisfying pleasure to substantially increase both my contributions and my participation. At the top of my list is the Clive Davis Institute of Recorded Music, which I established in 2003 at the Tisch School of the Arts at my undergraduate alma mater, New York University. I'll never forget the hardship of my youth, and without the beneficence of others providing scholarships to NYU and Harvard, God knows where I'd be. At first I established scholarships for others at Riverdale Country Day School, which almost all of my offspring attended, as well as at NYU and Harvard. Music and education have been the two most important gifts of my life, and giving young people today the kind of opportunities that I had is deeply fulfilling. So when I was personally selected and invited by the Grammy Museum in Los Angeles to do so, I worked with the museum to establish the Clive Davis Theater there. It's a beautiful performance space that also hosts interviews, panel discussions, and educational events that, once again, encourage a deep appreciation of music and the people who create it.

I'm the last person to ever downplay the importance of hard work, but, when it comes right down to it, being lucky never hurts, either. How grateful I am to be living in a time when hypertension, the disease that killed both of my parents so young, can be controlled by taking two or three pills a day. Just living is a blessing, let alone all the good fortune that has come to me. As the journey goes on, I couldn't desire anything more than the time and good health to be able to travel the world with family and friends, studying other cultures and history so that the full picture of life becomes ever clearer, and continuing to enjoy doing the work I love so much. I think often of that day in June 1967 at the Monterey Pop Festival—the pulsating excitement of Janis Joplin's performance, the sense of possibility in the air, the exhilaration of realizing what a life pursuing your biggest dreams might be like—when a door opened to what the rest of my life would be. That so much came from the events of that one day has been an incredible gift, and the passion I felt then is with me still.

Dedication and Acknowledgments

I dedicate this book in loving memory to my parents, Flo and Joe, my sister, Seena, and my aunt, Jeanette. I also dedicate it with love to my immediate family: my children, Fred, Lauren, Mitchell, and Douglas; their spouses, Rona, Julius, and Clare; my grandchildren, Austin, Charles, Matthew, Hayley, Harper, and Sloane; and my cousin, Jo. Within our family, we have never become loving strangers. In addition, I dedicate this book to each of my dear friends who have become family, traveling the world with me, sharing the vicissitudes and joys of life as we grow ever younger together.

And, lastly, I dedicate this book a) to all my colleagues who have shared my professional journey with me. Whether it's been Columbia or Arista or J, what a magical ride it's been! I couldn't conceivably have done it without each and every one of you who has been in the trenches with me, loved the music, and fought the fights to make sure that the songs were heard and savored over and over again. And b) the artists, the writers, and the producers whose genius is responsible for much of the contents of this book.

I would like to make a very special acknowledgement to Anthony DeCurtis, who has been a tower of strength as my collaborator and partner in the writing of this book, and to Mitchell Cohen, who has provided both Anthony and myself with extensive material, research, and insight, significantly helping to make all this possible.

This book could not have been written without the invaluable assistance or input from the following:

Dick Asher

Mariela Bradford

Stanley Buchthal

Sean Cassidy

Paula Chaltas

Nicole David

Barbara Davis

Francesca Rose DeCurtis

Steve Ferrara

Elliot Goldman

Charles Goldstuck

Allen Grubman

Margot Harley

Arthur Indursky

Larry Jackson

Jonathan Karp

Laurie Kratochvil

Ken Levy

Roy Lott

Sandra Luk

Rose Marino

Alexandra MacDowell

DeShawn McCoy

AnneMarie Morrissey

Robert Morvillo

Keith Naftaly

Susan Novak

Richard Palmese

Michael Palumbo

Neil Portnow

Greg Schriefer

Jo Schuman

Jackie Seow

Eric Simonoff

Michael Stein

Randy Sturges

Tom Tierney

John Vilanova

Lois Walden

Jann Wenner

Glenn Whitehead

Mindy Whitehead

Don Zakarin

Index

Photo Credits

Springsteen, 1974, © Peter Cunningham; with Carlos Santana, 2000, Jeff Vespa/WireImage; with Whitney Houston, 2006, Clive Davis Personal Collection; with Aretha Franklin, 1981, Roger Ressmeyer/Corbis; with Alicia Keys, 2007, Ron Galella, Ltd./WireImage; with Sean "Puffy" Combs, 2002, Clive Davis Personal Collection; with Barry Manilow, 1995, Clive Davis Personal Collection.

CLIVE DAVIS is currently the Chief Creative Officer, Sony Music Entertainment. He is hard at work on albums by Aretha Franklin, Jennifer Hudson, and Carlos Santana, and is the album producer of the new Whitney Houston "Best Of" album. He has won six Grammy Awards, including the Trustees Lifetime Achievement Award, and is an inductee into the Rock and Roll Hall of Fame. He has received humanitarian honors from such organizations as the American Cancer Society, the American Foundation for AIDS Research, The T.J. Martell Foundation for Leukemia, Cancer and AIDS Research, and the Anti-Defamation League. In 2002, the Clive Davis Institute of Recorded Music was created at his undergraduate alma mater, New York University's Tisch School of the Arts. He is the father of three sons and a daughter.

Anthony DeCurtis is a contributing editor at *Rolling Stone,* where his work has appeared for more than thirty years. He is the author of *In Other Words: Artists Talk About Life and Work* and coeditor of *The Rolling Stone Illustrated History of Rock & Roll.* His essay accompanying the Eric Clapton box set *Crossroads* won a Grammy in the Best Album Notes category. He holds a PhD in American literature from Indiana University, and he teaches in the writing program at the University of Pennsylvania.